Tropical ZION

AMERICAN ENCOUNTERS/GLOBAL INTERACTIONS
A series edited by Gilbert M. Joseph and Emily S. Rosenberg

This series aims to stimulate critical perspectives and fresh interpretive frameworks for scholarship on the history of the imposing
global presence of the United States. Its primary concerns include
the deployment and contestation of power, the construction and
deconstruction of cultural and political borders, the fluid meanings of intercultural encounters, and the complex interplay between
the global and the local. American Encounters seeks to strengthen
dialogue and collaboration between historians of U.S. international
relations and area studies specialists.

The series encourages scholarship based on multiarchival historical research. At the same time, it supports a recognition of the rep-
resentational character of all stories about the past and promotes
critical inquiry into issues of subjectivity and narrative. In the
process, American Encounters strives to understand the context in
which meanings related to nations, cultures, and political economy
are continually produced, challenged, and reshaped.

Tropical ZION

General Trujillo, FDR, and the Jews of Sosúa / / / / / / / / / /

Allen Wells

Duke University Press
Durham and London
2009

To all who escaped persecution

and came to Sosúa

Only because of

the hopeless is hope

given to us.

WALTER BENJAMIN

Contents

Abbreviations

AGN	Archivo General de la Nación
AJC	American Jewish Committee
AMJ	Archivo del Museo Judío, Sosúa
APSR	*American Political Science Review*
ARA	American Relief Administration
BL	Butler Library
CILCA	Cooperativa Industrial Lechera, C. por A.
CU	Columbia University
DORSA	Dominican Republic Settlement Association
DP	DORSA Papers
DPS	Displaced Persons
FRUS	*Foreign Relations of the United States*
GANADERA	Cooperativa Industrial Ganadera Sosúa C. por A.
IGC	Intergovernmental Committee on Political Refugees
JDC OR JOINT	American Jewish Joint Distribution Committee
KOMZET	Committee for the Settlement of Jewish Workers on the Land
LBI	Leo Baeck Institute
LL	Lehman Library
NA	National Archives
OAS	Organization of American States
OZET	Society for the Settlement of Jewish Toilers on the Land
PACPR	President's Advisory Committee on Political Refugees
SERE	Servicio de Emigración para los Refugiados Españoles
SWP	Sumner Welles Papers
USHMMLA	United States Holocaust Memorial Museum Library and Archives

Prologue

People spat and hissed at us on the streets of Vienna. Other people
can call Trujillo a murderer, but he saved our lives.
HEINRICH HAUSER

"Dr. Trone asked me if I was afraid of hard work. He chose me because I was young and strong," my father remembered. Solomon
Trone, a recruitment agent for the Dominican Republic Settlement
Association (DORSA), interviewed twenty-two-year-old Heinrich
Wasservogel at the Hotel Neues Schloss, Zurich, in the summer of
1940. DORSA's recruiter was looking for pioneers for a new agricultural settlement in Sosúa on the north coast. For the last six months,
Heini had worked at a number of labor camps run by Swiss provincial
authorities. He had never heard of the Dominican Republic, knew no
Spanish, and had no experience as a farmer, but like many refugees
stranded in "countries of transit" along Germany's borders, he had
few appealing options.[1]

The Central European refugees who came to the Dominican Republic in the early 1940s could not have imagined that they would
become, in a few short years, successful dairy farmers. Generalizing
about their collective experience is difficult. Although they had much
in common—language, customs, faith, exposure to discrimination,
minimal experience on the land, and the anguish and uncertainty of
leaving family behind—personal histories varied and so, too, did the
situations they encountered and the choices they made while in flight.
They were fortunate to benefit from the timely assistance of complete strangers, Gentiles as well as Jews, and generous relief agencies.
Eighty-seven-year-old Elie Topf might have spoken for all his peers

when he told me, "I will tell you my story, but you won't believe it. I was a hundred times lucky."[2]

In truth, Topf, Wasservogel, and others who reached Sosúa made their own luck, overcoming adversity and thinking on their feet when opportunity knocked or danger appeared. Whether they used their last francs to pay off smugglers to spirit them across borders, presented forged papers, bribed diplomats to purchase visas, eluded capture by authorities intent on deporting them back to Nazi-occupied territory, worked unlawfully in countries of transit, or bartered for cigarettes, chocolate, or a piece of bread, they lived by their wits and did what was necessary to survive. No wonder this time of flight is vividly etched in their memories more than six decades later.

Tracing Wasservogel's journey to the Dominican Republic opens the door a crack into this little-known chapter in the history of the Holocaust. Most of those who came to Sosúa identified with what he went through before he left his native Austria, what transpired after he escaped, and why he was so grateful that an island nation he had never heard of offered him sanctuary and a fresh start after virtually every other country had turned its back on him.

FLIGHT

Born in Vienna's largely Jewish Second District in 1918, Wasservogel as a teenager first joined a Zionist youth organization before gravitating to a Socialist youth group. He was not particularly religious, though he sang in his synagogue's choir for seven years. Instead, he thought of himself as an Austrian of Jewish origin. His father, Albert, was the proverbial struggling artist, earning modest commissions for portraits and restorations of Old Masters. When his commissions faltered, Albert took a job as a salesman, only to be let go during the depths of the Depression. His mother, Victoria, a Serbian-born Sephardi, was a hausfrau occupied with raising five children in their tiny apartment.

Heinrich and his brother Rudolf decided to leave Austria soon after the Anschluss, Germany's annexation of the country on March 11, 1938, in part because he had a terrifying encounter with "brown shirts, members of the Nazi youth." After a political demonstration near City Hall in downtown Vienna on the eve of the annexation, where he and his fellow Socialists and a rival group of Fascists hurled insults at each other, he recalled: "I was walking home and they [the Nazi supporters] followed me. I started to run and they were chasing. I tried to hide in an alcove, the entrance to an apartment building, but the building was locked and they found me there. There were about five or six of them and they beat me with metal rods and sticks and called me all kinds of things, 'dirty Jew,' 'Socialist,' and a lot of things worse than that.

They hit me so hard that my neck and back were bleeding from the blows. I was protecting my head and looked back when one of them recognized me from when we were both classmates in school. Then he said something and they stopped beating me and let me go."

On the heels of that narrow escape, Wasservogel learned he had been fired from his job as a typesetter's apprentice, a position he had held for four years. His predicament was not unusual; friends were losing their jobs because they were Jewish. He subsequently had to endure the humiliation of standing in line to collect food for his family at a local charity. These incidents forced him to come to terms with his Jewishness while raising questions about his identity as an Austrian.

He was not alone in considering flight. Discriminatory measures implemented by the Nazis in Germany now were imported to Austria. Citizenship was revoked, property seized arbitrarily, businesses "Aryanized." Jews were dismissed summarily from places of employment, their newspapers and synagogues were closed down, and more than a thousand people were arrested on suspicion of violating racial purity laws. New identity cards were issued, and Jews were required to register their property.[3] This far-ranging assault turned Austria's Jews "systematically into a community of beggars" and gave greater urgency to finding places of refuge.[4] But the imposition of an emigration tax that seized anywhere from 60 to 100 percent of their assets turned would-be refugees into paupers overnight.[5]

Within six months, Wasservogel and fifty thousand other Jews had left their homeland; over the next two years, two-thirds of Austrian Jewry emigrated, many of them young males like Heini and Rudi.[6] Most spilled over into the neighboring countries of Czechoslovakia and Switzerland, while some sought sanctuary in the Netherlands, France, Belgium, Great Britain, or Scandinavia. Indeed, the Wasservogel brothers initially fled to Czechoslovakia but were caught and, lacking papers, were sent back to Vienna. Smaller numbers of Jewish emigrants, including their parents, relocated to Hungary, Yugoslavia, and Italy, even though these authoritarian states had demonstrated solidarity with National Socialism. Many waited in these countries of transit, often under difficult conditions, hoping for something better to materialize.[7]

Later that summer, the two brothers set out by train to Austria's northwest border with Switzerland and Germany, never to see their parents and twin brothers again. Their father, who left Vienna for Budapest in 1939, overstayed his six-month visa, was detained, and then was sent to a succession of labor camps before moving in late 1944 to a safe house in Budapest established by the Swedish diplomat Raoul Wallenberg. Ultimately, he was a casualty of shrapnel from an Allied bombing raid in early 1945. Their mother and twin brothers perished in a concentration camp in Serbia in 1942.

A rumor quietly circulating in Vienna had it that the best way to make it across the Swiss border was to pose as a tourist and tell border guards, if asked, that you had been invited to visit real or imagined relatives.[8] Years later, Heini recounted how he and Rudi escaped with four others on foot across the Swiss border. "We dressed as tourists, carrying our belongings in rucksacks on our backs. I brought along my father's lute and my brother, Rudi, wore a Tyrolean hat. . . . We were all very nervous. There was a guardhouse and a barricade across the road. It was early evening, dark and rainy. The [Austrian] border guards knew we were Jews, not really tourists. We gave them all our money, every last penny. What did we care? We were running for our lives."[9]

Their fear was palpable as the guards crowded them into the back of a truck and then drove along back roads before coming to a clearing in the woods. After ordering the travelers off the truck, the guards motioned to a narrow trail ahead. If they kept to the path, they were told, eventually they would reach the Swiss border. "We started walking and . . . it was raining very hard. We walked for hours on mountain paths and came to a place in the woods where there were two marker stones. It was about two or three o'clock in the morning and we were . . . wet and exhausted. The stones had letters engraved on them that we did not recognize. We later learned that they had been carved with centuries-old initials that we would not have understood. We decided to go in a certain direction, and that was fortunate, because that turned out to be Switzerland, not Germany. We were so lucky."[10] The Wasservogels were two of the six thousand who crossed the Swiss frontier in the months immediately following the Anschluss.

Quickly apprehended and arrested by the Swiss Alien Police and taken to a nearby jail, where they spent the night, the shivering refugees were met there in the morning by a local representative of a Jewish relief agency. The police released them to his custody, and he led them on foot to the northern city of Schaffhausen near the German border. Two days later, they were moved to a refugee camp near the mountain village of Buchberg—one of fifteen camps established by Jewish agencies in northeastern Switzerland.[11] There, Heini performed a variety of tasks, including cooking for the sixty refugees at the camp. Although not permitted to work for wages, he hired himself out occasionally to local farmers, cutting and turning hay in exchange for bread, bacon, and apple cider.

After March 1940, Heini and others were moved to labor camps run by provincial authorities, where they laid roadbeds, dug drainage systems, built barracks, cleared land, cut trees, and hauled stones from quarries. Until he left for the Dominican Republic in September 1940, he rotated from one camp to another every few months.[12] In his mind, the skills he acquired and the work ethic he demonstrated in the camps explain why he (and not others) was selected for Sosúa.

His recollection of the time spent in Switzerland was similar to those of others who have left memoirs.[13] Astounded by the country's natural beauty, grateful for the skills learned and friends made, and appreciative that he was not turned back, in retrospect, he knew he was fortunate. At the same time, he carried bitter memories of the treatment he and his peers received and of the anti-Semitism he encountered. With economic conditions deteriorating and food rationing the order of the day, there was little incentive to treat the internees well. What modest funds the Swiss government appropriated for the refugees were deposited in an emigration fund. Although some camp supervisors were humane and individual acts of kindness have been documented, the newcomers, by and large, were made to feel unwanted. Every effort was made to quarantine them from the general population and dissuade them from putting down roots. The threat of expulsion hung like a cloud over the internees.[14]

Faced with such inhospitality, the refugees were consumed with the idea of leaving for somewhere, anywhere. Heini recalled, "Everyone in the camp was trying to immigrate to different places, America, all over. You needed a sponsor in those days, connections. One man went to New Zealand and . . . everyone was jealous."[15]

Conditions in the camps did little to lessen feelings of displacement. Hygiene varied considerably, and most people slept on straw in barracks. Authorities forcibly separated married couples and families; men were sent to the make-work camps while women and the elderly were kept under supervision in private homes, where they sewed, mended, and knitted for those in the camps. Frequently, children were segregated from their parents and taken to foster homes, where they were brought up outside their faith. Even siblings were separated and dispatched to different foster homes. Male workers were shuttled from camp to camp, undermining solidarity. Heini Wasservogel's experience—three camps in six months—was not unusual.[16]

Many emigrants who had been professionals, merchants, and intellectuals had difficulty adapting to the uncertainty and the mandatory regimen of manual labor and became despondent. Heini related a chilling incident: "One night, several of us walked into the village, and I decided to go back earlier than the others for some reason, I can't remember why. . . . When I got back to the cabin and opened the door, there was a boy hanging there from the rafter, a suicide. I ran all the way back to the village, which was a long way. There was no moon, and you couldn't see your hand in front of your face. I remember it to be the darkest night I ever experienced. I was so scared. I don't forget those things."[17] That suicide was one of two he recalled, and in both cases he believed the victims, who came from families of means, had difficulty coping with "our primitive state."

Those who were more optimistic and threw themselves into their work were better positioned to cope with the rigors of camp life. Felix Bauer, who worked alongside Wasservogel in the Dipoltsau labor camp and later accompanied him to the Dominican Republic, thought the hard labor "felt so good. Most of us were in the best condition of [our] youth. [His friend] Walter enjoyed climbing on a sheer wall and hacking rocks from it with a pickax. Heini and I became experts in smashing them to small chunks and rolling them in wheelbarrows to the place where others constructed the roadbed."[18] A classically trained musician and a graphic artist, Bauer took it upon himself to organize small-scale theater productions and a music appreciation course in the camps "to make people do something and keep them busy." In addition, crash courses were given in shoe repair and tailoring to provide internees with skills that might prove useful in the future.[19]

In Heini's case, his father's lute opened doors. He recalled how nature lovers came to Buchberg on the weekends for day hikes and stopped by the camp to hear his group of friends play and sing Austrian lieder. Unfortunately, though, such conviviality was unusual. The relief agencies discouraged the internees from conversing with their hosts. Local priests, Heini was warned, had spoken out from their pulpits against the rising tide of immigrants entering the country.[20]

His timing, however, had been fortunate. Just weeks after he crossed the frontier, Swiss authorities, under pressure from Berlin for harboring enemies of the Reich, took measures to restrict future immigration.[21] "To protect Switzerland from the immense influx of Viennese Jews," the chief of police, Heinrich Rothmund, announced that henceforth Austrians were required to obtain visas. Fearful of what journalist Alfred Häsler called "the dread of inundation," on August 19, 1938, authorities closed the borders to those without proper documentation. A federal official invoked a melodramatic analogy that struck a chord with proponents of the government's restrictive policy, comparing his tiny nation to "a lifeboat in a great sea disaster, with only very limited space and even more limited provisions."[22]

To mollify relief agencies, Rothmund gave assurances that those already in

Switzerland would be permitted to stay. Border police were instructed, however, to return those entering illicitly to German border guards.[23] More than 24,000 were turned back, and the Swiss Foreign Service denied 14,000 additional requests for entry permits.[24]

To differentiate Jewish emigrants from others, Berlin agreed, at Rothmund's insistence, to stamp their passports with a large red *J*.[25] This edict would have far-reaching consequences: now other countries refused to accept Jews seeking to leave Germany.[26]

Such restrictions were disquieting to some Swiss, because "the right of asylum" for political and religious reasons had long been an article of faith. The nation had enjoyed a reputation as a haven for the persecuted ever since the Reformation, when Protestants fleeing Catholic repression found shelter in certain provinces.[27] Indeed, some sympathetic officials not only looked the other way but actually defied the new regulations and lent a helping hand to those crossing the frontier.

Denied a work permit, unable to reside permanently in Switzerland or secure a visa from the United States or elsewhere because of restrictive quotas, grateful to be alive but uncertain if he would see his family again, fearful of deportation, Heinrich Wasservogel said goodbye to his brother—who stayed on and married a Swiss woman—and accepted Dr. Trone's "offer."[28]

Accompanied by a Swiss police escort and representatives of a well-endowed philanthropy, the American Jewish Joint Distribution Committee (the JDC or Joint), Wasservogel, Bauer, and sixteen others were taken by train to Geneva and then bused to Barcelona in late August 1940. From there they took another train to Lisbon, where they finally embarked on a Greek steamer, the ss *Nea Hellas*, headed for New York.

The refugees had no clue what a logistical nightmare it was for JDC officials to get that first Swiss contingent out of Lisbon. While they rested up for their transatlantic crossing and experienced some semblance of normality while reconnoitering the Portuguese capital, their scheduled departure was repeatedly delayed. The JDC's Joseph Schwartz wondered whether he would ever be able to get them out of Europe: "In view of the present uncertainties . . . many doubts exist as to whether the *Nea Hellas* will be able to leave Lisbon. . . . [If not] it will be a major catastrophe here because as it is, there are hardly enough shipping facilities for the people who are waiting to go to New York and other points on the American continent. . . . Should they have to wait for accommodations . . . I am afraid it will be a matter of months, with all that this will mean in increased unrest and greatly increased expenditures for relief. In view of the state of our present budget, I hesitate to even think about these things."[29] Six days later, Schwartz cabled DORSA officials in New York with distressing news. Their U.S. transit visas had expired while the ship still languished in port. He begged U.S. consular officials in Lisbon to extend their visas. After protracted negotiations, the extensions were granted, and a relieved Schwartz cabled that the first Swiss group was set to depart for Ellis Island on September 4, 1940.[30]

They stayed at Ellis Island for a week, awaiting the arrival of the New York and Porto Rico Line's ss *Coamo*, which would take them to their final destination. Unbeknownst to Wasservogel, their arrival in New York attracted the attention of the press. Eager to garner favorable publicity and build momentum for the colonization project, DORSA had alerted the *New York Times*. A reporter met with the refugees and wrote up a human interest story that tugged at readers' heartstrings. "18 Refugees Sail for Sosúa Colony" focused on the youngest refugee, two-year-old Monica Maas. Monica's mother was already in the Dominican Republic, anxiously awaiting her daughter's arrival. The photographer also captured for posterity the fair-skinned, earnest-looking, well-dressed group of pioneers aboard the ss *Coamo*.[31]

On September 27, 1940, the fortunate 18 reached Ciudad Trujillo, and a week later were welcomed at Sosúa. The newcomers were no longer unwanted, stateless exiles; they were about to become farmers in the tropics.

"HE WAS *THE ONLY ONE*"

Like others who arrived in the Dominican Republic during what scholars now call the panic emigration, Wasservogel was eager to talk about Sosúa when interviewed in 1999. In his prime an ox of a man, he was by this time eighty-one, blind, frail, and infirm, living out his "golden years" in retirement in southern Florida. Even though his eyesight and body had betrayed him in recent years, he relished the opportunity to discuss his past—his flight from Austria, the two years in Switzerland, the subsequent, painful loss of much of his family in the Holocaust, and his resolve to reinvent himself from typesetter to farmer and cabinetmaker in the tropics. "I was never afraid of hard work," he related, wagging his finger in the air for added emphasis; and then, lowering his voice, he added, "I am a survivor." Pride in his accomplishments in the face of adversity was leavened with other emotions: the relief he shared with other Sosuaners about their safe passage, the anguish over his inability to get loved ones out, and the utter incomprehension of why he was spared when so many were not.

Reflecting fifty years later on his seven-year sojourn in the tropics, he sounded grateful for the opportunity. Without prompting, he lavished praise on the Dominican dictator, General Rafael Trujillo. "No one wanted us," he recalled. "He was *the only one* who took us in," his resonant voice punctuating those three small words for added emphasis.[32]

Wasservogel was not alone in expressing gratitude. Martin Katz, one of only a handful of the original pioneers still remaining in Sosúa, recently told a journalist that he did not know why Trujillo did what he did, but "the important thing is that he did. He saved my life."[33] While most refugees professed to be apolitical, they were well aware of Trujillo's brutality. Years later, Judith Kibel recalled, "He was a bad man who killed many, many people. . . . But to the Jews he opened his country."[34] It is one of history's small ironies that a man so feared and despised by many of his fellow Dominicans—and by neighboring Haitians—was admired by these immigrants.

Indeed, Trujillo had stunned the world in the summer of 1938 when his representatives announced that his nation was prepared to accept up to one hundred thousand Central Europeans. Why did a ruthless dictator admit these cast-offs fleeing fascism when few nations would accept them? What did these exiles have to offer him, and why did President Franklin Delano Roosevelt and State Department officials give their public blessing to the enterprise? Why, moreover, did the Joint Distribution Committee invest several million dollars in this modest colonization effort at a time when so many European Jews were in dire need of rescue and resettlement?

Tropical Zion speaks to the settlers' experience, a despot's racist efforts to remake his own society, the high cost of Washington's complicity with a brutal dictatorship in its backyard, and the reasons why a gritty, unconventional experiment saved lives and, given its small size and the numerous obstacles arrayed against it, flourished to the extent that it did. Within a decade, Jewish professionals from Berlin and Vienna, who had never set foot on a farm in the old country, had become successful pioneers. Their employee-owned dairy cooperative was producing one hundred thousand pounds of butter, a million pounds of cheese, and one-and-a-half million gallons of milk a year, and its prize-winning dairy products were marketed throughout the country.

Yet Sosúa failed to live up to Trujillo's lofty expectations, and at one time or another, the colonization project also confounded the Roosevelt administration, resettlement experts, Western diplomats, and philanthropists. For one thing, only 757 refugees made it to Sosúa, a fraction of Trujillo's initial offer.[35] That small number was a source of frustration for everyone concerned.

What is striking about the Sosúa episode is how securely these stateless exiles were tethered, without their knowledge or consent, to larger geopolitical concerns at a moment of world crisis—to Washington's anemic immigration policy, to Machiavellian diplomatic currents swirling around the refugee question, to the Dominican Republic's determination to assert itself as a power-broker in the Caribbean, to the wartime U.S. "Fortress America" strategy to cordon off the hemisphere from Axis aggression, to real and imagined fears of Nazi espionage and fifth column threats, and to fissures within the American Jewish community. As the colony repeatedly became a flashpoint for a number of heated debates, Sosuaners became pawns on *realpolitik* chessboards in Washington, Berlin, Ciudad Trujillo, New York, and London.

Sosúa's numbers pale in comparison to the nearly one hundred thousand Jews who escaped Hitler and reached Latin America.[36] But if the Sosuaners were a drop in the bucket, the initiative's timing, and its unique ability to capture the imagination of statesmen, relief organizations, and the general public on three continents suggests that the hopes and aspirations of many were riding on this diminutive experiment in social engineering.

Since the colony's fate was intimately bound by contingencies not of its own making, it is to this broader canvas that we now turn. We begin with General Trujillo himself, who from the outset cast an imposing shadow over the colony.

THE GENERAL, THE PRESIDENT, AND THE PHILANTHROPY

Trujillo had wasted little time in acquiring a well-deserved reputation for brutality during the first decade of his thirty-one-year dictatorship (1930–61).[37] His ruthless mistreatment of both the political opposition and Haitians living in the Dominican Republic compares with the most heinous Latin American dictatorships. The most egregious example was his army's unprovoked massacre of fifteen thousand unarmed Haitians during a ten-day rampage in October 1937.[38] The aftershocks of this tragedy continue to scar relations between these neighbors.

International public opinion condemned the massacre, and the dictator, reliant on U.S. military and economic assistance, quickly sought to defuse the crisis and restore his image abroad. He announced that he would not stand for reelection as president in 1938.[39] Although he continued as chief of the armed forces and ciphers occupied the presidency for the next four years, relinquishing de jure power was viewed favorably by his patrons in Washington. Welcoming German and Austrian Jews must be understood in this same light: as part and parcel of the dictator's efforts to re-establish good relations with Washington.

Roosevelt and his advisers knew full well who was responsible for the killing spree, a gruesome operation despicably labeled *El Corte* (the cutting down) because Dominican troops used machetes and clubs to murder their defenseless victims. A confidential U.S. intelligence report filed two months afterward laid the blame squarely on Trujillo's doorstep: "It is difficult to conceive that under a dictatorship such as exists in Santo Domingo a systematic massacre of the extent and duration of this one could have been carried out without his orders or against his will."[40]

Though it publicly condemned the massacre, the Roosevelt administration was reluctant to meddle in Dominican affairs. Building on the policies of his predecessor, Herbert Hoover, FDR had proclaimed that the United States would be a "Good Neighbor" in the Americas; and military intervention, a recurrent feature of U.S.–Latin American relations since 1898, was inconsistent with the principles of hemispheric cooperation.[41] Hoover had not stood in the way of the 1930 coup that brought Trujillo to power; nor did his successor encourage Trujillo to step down after horrific news reports first surfaced about the massacre.[42]

Instead, the State Department worked to lessen tensions between the Dominican Republic and Haiti. Undersecretary of State Sumner Welles, who was no friend of the dictator, sounded remarkably restrained when he recalled a conversation with Andrés Pastoriza, the chief of the Dominican legation in Washington, shortly after he learned of the massacre: "Our whole attitude was one of friendly concern in seeing that steps be taken sufficiently and promptly to prevent the controversy's assuming serious proportions."[43] Secretary of State Cordell Hull, although shaky on regional geography, was even less inclined to berate Trujillo publicly: "I have long considered President Trujillo as one of the biggest men in Central and most of South America . . . and being a big man, I feel we can only look to him to avoid friction with another country and to find ways to clear up such misunderstandings as exist between his country and Haiti."[44] Preoccupied with events in Europe and a looming Nazi threat in the backyard, Hull and Welles eschewed punitive action against Trujillo and focused their attention on a diplomatic solution.

This response was emblematic of Roosevelt's predilection for "nonintervention." When, at an Inter-American Peace Conference in Buenos Aires in 1936, Roosevelt underscored the need to improve policy coordination, economic relations, and cultural understanding, he earned the admiration of Latin American statesmen. Lessening barriers to trade through reciprocal tariff reduction was of particular importance to Hull, who concluded bilateral trade agreements with ten Latin American states.[45]

Liberalizing trade and renouncing the deployment of military forces, how-ever, did not mean autonomy for client states. If the new Pan American spirit fostered by the administration entailed recurrent trade talks and official vis-its by heads of state, it came with only a thin veneer of what one student of U.S.–Latin American relations has termed surface respect.[46] Diplomàtic jaw-boning, dangling carrots of military and economic assistance, and delaying recognition to recalcitrant regimes were tactics the State Department em-ployed to guarantee support for its initiatives.

Nonintervention, such as it was, often had unintended consequences. As U.S. forces withdrew from former protectorates, they left behind military lead-ers and armies they had trained and equipped, which ruled with impunity, no longer fearing intervention. In practice, Pan Americanism meant that Wash-ington was less likely to criticize authoritarian regimes. By 1939, all but five countries were ruled by military strongmen, and all enjoyed U.S. backing.[47]

With atrocities such as the massacre, Washington's muted response did not go unnoticed. Critics like journalist Carleton Beals reminded readers that something was amiss when an American president criticized totalitarian re-gimes in Europe yet showed unflinching support for the "Dictator Trujillo, in the Dominican Republic, [who] was butchering 12,000 peaceable Haitians— men, women, children and babes."[48] By feigning impartiality and upholding the twin principles of national sovereignty and nonintervention, the admin-istration left itself wide open to charges of hypocrisy.

Despite Washington's kid glove treatment, Trujillo, coveting U.S. aid, was anxious to mend fences. To placate the Roosevelt administration, the general sent representatives to Évian, France in July 1938, to an international con-ference on refugees from Nazism, proposed by FDR to deflect criticism of restrictive U.S. immigration policies. Thirty-two nations sent representatives, but only the Dominican Republic agreed to open its doors to those fleeing Nazism.

The dictator was not just making amends for murdering Haitians. He wanted to "whiten the Dominican race." Obsessed with stemming the tide of Hai-tian migration across his nation's western border, he welcomed Jewish refu-gees fleeing Nazi Aryanism—ironically themselves the object of scorn and derision in Europe because of their "racial" characteristics. After El Corte, Trujillo sought to seal off the ill-defined frontier with Haiti, encourage white immigration, foster intermarriage with Europeans, and establish agricultural colonies in underutilized parts of the country. At roughly the same time it welcomed Central Europeans, and for similar reasons, the Dominican Re-public admitted several thousand Spanish republican expatriates living in

France who had been driven into exile by General Francisco Franco after the Spanish Civil War.

Although "improving the race" through European immigration had been a desideratum for decades, and political leaders throughout Latin America actively promoted miscegenation to erase "blackness and indianness," the Dominican case was exceptional because the dictatorship went to extremes to recast racial categories to suit its ideological ends.[49] At a time when the country's population was predominantly mulatto, the 1935 census patently denied their existence. Astoundingly, the two out of three Dominicans of mixed black and white ancestry were labeled mestizos, even though it was common knowledge that the indigenous had been eliminated from the island centuries before.[50]

Race had been a persistent preoccupation of elites well before Trujillo, but it was under his rule that it became a pliable and effective tool to foment nationalism, cultural homogeneity, and a new Dominican identity. Although popular perceptions of ethnic and racial identity differed from official discourse, regime propaganda shaped how Dominicans of all social classes perceived themselves and their neighbors.[51]

During Trujillo's reign, the nation's Hispanic heritage (white, Catholic, and colonial) was celebrated while its "Africanness" was denied. While Mexico celebrated *mestizaje* and Brazil proclaimed racial harmony, Trujillo sought, in the historian Robin Derby's words, "to police the purity of the race" by stemming the tide of Haitian-Dominican miscegenation and contriving preposterous racial categories.[52] Although we know a great deal about Trujillo's regime, historians only now are beginning to understand the dictatorship's ideological underpinnings, its emphasis on "whitening" the race, and the measures it took to promote conformity.[53]

Recognizing the dictator's racial motives, a pragmatic JDC nevertheless embraced Trujillo's offer, hopeful that successful colonization in the Caribbean would persuade other Latin American states to open their doors. They knew they had exactly the right leaders to oversee this venture. Both James Rosenberg, a prominent New York corporate bankruptcy attorney, and Joseph Rosen, an eminent Russian agronomist, were fervent believers in colonization who boldly predicted that Jews would prosper in the tropics.

These administrators were not just incurable romantics. They had hands-on experience moving more than 150,000 Russian Jews from towns and cities in the Pale of Settlement in western Russia to the Crimean steppes. From 1924 to 1938, Rosenberg and Rosen, with the assistance of the Soviet state, which made available nearly two million acres of land, were the architects of a novel social experiment that transformed citified Jews into farmers. The JDC spun off a subsidiary, the Agro-Joint Corporation, to manage the multimillion-dollar collaboration between a capitalist philanthropy and a communist state. As the attorney raised funds in New York, the agronomist directed 250 cooperatives, preaching the gospel of crop rotation and high-yield seed varieties and bringing American-made tractors and water-drilling equipment to the Crimea.

It is interesting that these disciples of Jewish agrarianism were, like Trujillo, enamored of scientific racism, reasoning that thousands of years of living in cities had contaminated the Jewish gene pool. Toiling on the land, whether in the Crimea, Palestine, or the Caribbean, they contended, would cleanse the soul and regenerate the "Jewish race."

After the Crimean project was shut down by an increasingly xenophobic Josef Stalin in 1938, the Joint turned to the fundraiser and the colonization expert and asked them to direct the Sosúa initiative. Given the Agro-Joint's superb track record, it was not surprising that diplomats and relief agencies were bullish on Sosúa. After Évian, Sosúa was one of a slew of sites under consideration for possible resettlement. FDR liked to think big, and his aides were scouring the globe for large swaths of territory where hundreds of thousands of refugees could be relocated. But colonization experts, scholars, and politicians were still undecided on whether it was feasible or desirable to let Europeans settle in the tropics. These racially tinged debates, influenced by the pseudoscience of eugenics, had a long history; but at that conjuncture, when governments on both sides of the Atlantic were being pressured to revise their immigration policies, such "scientific" debates gave policymakers the political cover they needed to explain why their own colonial possessions or territories were unacceptable for resettlement. As potential sites fell by the wayside, Sosúa became, by default, one of the last best options.[54]

As Sosúa emerged as a plausible alternative, Trujillo, FDR, and DORSA became complicit partners, each demonstrating public support for the others. For more than two decades, this friendship never wavered, even as pressure mounted against the dictatorship from within and without.

For DORSA, the joint venture necessitated blind allegiance to Trujillo while papering over its differences with the Roosevelt administration regarding the quota system. DORSA administrators may have professed that they were apolitical, but their cheerleading for Trujillo and Roosevelt belied that claim. Rosenberg and his associates steered DORSA through turbulent, politically charged waters, and they seldom second-guessed themselves. To their way of thinking, loyalty to Ciudad Trujillo and Washington did not mean collusion, it meant survival. The association remained a steadfast supporter of the dictator until his assassination in May 1961, long after Washington had distanced itself from him.

Trujillo made sure of DORSA's fidelity in classic patron-client fashion, by personally donating a 26,000-acre tract along the north coast. The gift's symbolic value proved much greater than the property itself, which colonists soon learned had serious limitations. Since clients were expected to return favors by pledging loyalty, personal assistance, and service to the regime, lobbying policymakers in Washington quickly became a quid pro quo. In return, Trujillo signed a contract with DORSA that gave the refugees, who had been stripped of fundamental rights in their homeland, religious freedom and civil and legal rights. This bill of rights was no token gesture; it proved to be a persuasive fundraising tool for the philanthropy.

In such relationships, obedience and allegiance purchase favors, deference is expected, and transgressions are not taken lightly. If DORSA leaders had any misgivings, they were seldom apparent. Perhaps that is because it is not unusual in such vertical relationships for all parties to believe that they benefit disproportionately. DORSA considered lobbying the Roosevelt administration as simply the price of doing business with the dictator. But gift giving in patron-client relationships always reinforces the relationship's asymmetrical character.

For Washington, this partnership meant sustaining in power a reprehensible figure at a time when the United States was publicly critical of totalitarianism in Europe and reluctant to address the refugee problem forthrightly at home. Even though the dictator benefited the most from this uncommon alliance, he, too, was forced to accede to urgent requests from the administration and the philanthropy to give temporary asylum to prominent Jewish refugees. In reality, he never felt secure about the depth of Washington's support. He also had to fend off criticism from political opponents, who viewed Sosúa as little more than a publicity stunt. Indeed, Trujillo and FDR left themselves vulnerable to charges of bad faith when the promised one hundred thousand settlers never materialized.

The Sosúa initiative also sheds light on the rivalries within the U.S. foreign policy establishment. FDR deliberately provoked competition and jealousy among his advisers because he was convinced that infighting and personal and professional animosities inspired loyalty and fostered creative tensions that often led to imaginative solutions. Hull and Welles, in particular, were at odds on policy matters, and Sosúa was no exception. Welles's contempt for Trujillo diminished his enthusiasm for the small colony, which he dismissed as a Band-Aid on a gaping wound.

Despite Welles's reservations, Roosevelt understood that a successful Sosúa would deflect attention away from America's restrictive immigration policy.[55] Even though much has been written about FDR's refugee policies per se and the Good Neighbor policy in general, historians have yet to examine how Washington's geopolitical and domestic interests dovetailed, and how the administration's immigration policies and its overriding preoccupation with fighting fascism worked to strengthen relations with Latin American dictators like Anastasio Somoza (Nicaragua) and Fulgencio Batista (Cuba) for decades to come.[56]

By all rights, Trujillo should have had little room to maneuver with Washington, because his regime was a creature of U.S. policy. FDR's predecessors had turned the Caribbean into an "American lake." U.S.-Dominican relations fit this pattern to a tee. Considerable North American investment in the island's sugar industry during the late nineteenth and early twentieth centuries had led to ever greater involvement in the Dominican Republic's internal affairs. After the Dominican government defaulted on its debts to North American creditors in 1905, Washington assumed control of Dominican customs houses, garnishing their receipts; and when political instability precipitated a military occupation from 1916 to 1924, the Marines created a modern army meant to discourage unrest, which made it possible for an unimportant military officer like Trujillo to ascend to power in the first place. National sovereignty was further compromised by the Convention of 1924, an agreement that ensured that even after the Marines had departed, North American creditors continued to hold liens on customs receipts.[57]

Yet as the Sosúa episode makes clear, a subordinate position in an asymmetrical relationship does not mean that a shrewd leader cannot wring concessions to tighten his grip on power. Loyalty and deference became extremely effective weapons in Trujillo's diplomatic arsenal. Receiving Jewish refugees brought with it considerable residual benefits. When Washington pressured Latin American "republics" to clamp down on Nazi espionage activities in the summer of 1940 and curtail the numbers of refugees they took in, Trujillo complied, and welcomed North American training of his secret police. He then used those forces to crush domestic opposition. The dictator never invested a centavo in Sosúa; he believed the philanthropy was flush. Nor did he provide the essential infrastructure for a successful colony. But Sosúa restored his tarnished reputation abroad and helped bring about significant political victories at home that helped secure his hold on power for two more decades.

The Évian offer and the cooperation that ensued among the State Department, refugee organizations, and Dominican authorities smoothed the way for a revision of the 1924 Convention that had long rankled Dominican nationalists. The Trujillo-Hull Treaty, ratified in 1941, enabled the dictator to declare financial independence from the United States (although the treaty's fine print belied that claim). To sweeten the pot, the U.S. Export-Import Bank awarded the Dominican Republic two loans, and assistance from the U.S. Lend-Lease program, whereby the United States supplied war materiel to its Allies between 1941 and 1945, again bolstering Trujillo's armed forces. The Sosúan case, then, not only accentuates how FDR's emphasis on hemispheric solidarity and nonintervention dampened the prospects for democratic reform; it shows how loyalty and altruism bred longevity for crafty, purposeful tyrants within the "contact zones of the American empire."[58]

Less than two years after the massacre, Trujillo, trumpeted by regime panegyrists as The Benefactor, was not only back in Washington's good graces, he was touted as a humanitarian and faithful ally. Much has been made in the recent literature on U.S.–Latin American relations about the flexible character of hegemonic relationships and how weak client states can achieve limited successes when negotiating with the imperial state. Never a puppet on a string, Trujillo for three decades conducted relations with Washington that were characterized by constant negotiation, tactful redeployment, and measured resistance.[59]

Washington's attitude toward Trujillo and other dictators was never static, and Trujillo (and DORSA) often had to adjust to changes in U.S. policy. Periods of friction between Ciudad Trujillo and Washington, such as the short-lived tenure of Assistant Secretary of State Spruille Braden immediately after the Second World War, put the general on the defensive. But until his last years, Trujillo skillfully leveraged his assets in the U.S. foreign policy establishment, either waiting out the rough patches or articulating policies, be they antifascism during the war or anticommunism after, which he knew would play well. When that was not enough, he tapped his strategically placed retainers on the Hill, at the War (later Defense) Department, in the media, and in the private sector to outmaneuver his opponents.

COMPETING VISIONS

The Sosuan scheme also exposed the fault lines that rent American Judaism.[60] Even with Europe about to go up in flames, a plethora of decentralized American Jewish organizations repeatedly proved unable to set aside their differences and respond more aggressively to the needs of the refugees. Non-Zionists like the JDC never viewed Palestine as the only answer. They encouraged assimilation and dispersion; Jews, they insisted, must bloom where they were planted and prove themselves adaptable to all types of environments. Unlike Anti-Zionists, who vehemently opposed immigration to Palestine, Non-Zionists sought an elusive middle ground, opposing a Jewish state but not resettlement in Palestine per se. The Non-Zionist leadership of the American Jewish Committee (AJC) considered Palestine as *a* home for Jews, but not *the* Jewish state.[61]

Reluctant to pressure policymakers to liberalize quotas or participate in demonstrations or boycotts against the Third Reich, Non-Zionists were smeared by their rivals with the pejorative label of court Jews, medieval elders who placed greater emphasis on emulating their Christian sponsors than defending their community's interests. Although Non-Zionists contended that they had the best interests of American Jewry at heart, their reluctance to contest immigration policy earned them the enmity of many Jews who thought that persistent voices of protest were needed against Nazism. That is why the Sosúa experiment had tremendous symbolic importance for Non-Zionists, above and beyond its small numbers, and explains why the JDC was willing to invest as much as it did in Sosúa.[62]

Zionists, on the other hand, wanted FDR to pressure Great Britain to keep Palestine open for resettlement; any strategy that diverted attention away from that goal they viewed as a mistake. Although Zionists were far from monolithic—they disagreed on everything from tactics to ideology—they closed ranks on Sosúa's impracticality, calling it variously a boondoggle or a misguided attempt to save a few souls. It is understandable that Sosúa posed a threat to doctrinaire Zionists. It was not just a question of cornering competing resources, although that should not be underestimated. The project cut too close to home, raising the same vision of turning urban Jews from Central and Eastern Europe into farmers. Both Zionists and Non-Zionists wanted to turn these city dwellers into farmers, but the Non-Zionist vision of "bloom where you are planted" offered stiff competition to the Zionist obsession with a homeland as *the* home for Jews. Sosúa therefore was viewed in heretical terms, and every effort was made to discredit it.

The Zionist rhetorical assault on Sosúa did not go unanswered. Speaking to potential donors in October 1940, just months after the first refugees arrived in the colony, Rosen poignantly responded to DORSA's critics:[63]

You get the feeling of being so helpless before the magnitude of the problems confronting the world today. I consoled myself by remembering that years ago when I was young and handsome, I had to go through a fire and was badly burned. The doctors grafted tiny islets of skin on my face, and in time, these islets grew and became part of the whole skin, and I now stand before you today, still alive, though not quite handsome. In much the same way I tried to console myself with the thought that like the tiny islets of skin that were grafted on my face, so our settlement in Sosúa is but a tiny isle on the ocean of human misery, but it is these islets which may help bring light out of darkness, and civilization out of chaos. With this in mind, I tried to justify the saving of a few hundred people at the most—which is all it is as yet—in the face of hundreds of thousands now being destroyed throughout the world.

This touching rationalization, how he sought to "justify the saving of a few hundred" while "hundreds of thousands" remained at risk, mirrored the embattled character of Non-Zionism. Its inability to find common ground with its rivals and mount a concerted campaign to assist European Jewry did not win it contemporary admirers.

Historians have been equally unkind. It is revealing that most contemporary scholars have mimicked the Zionist critique of Sosúa; even Yehuda Bauer, who has written the most comprehensive histories of the JDC, bemoans the organization's "less than judicious" decision to invest "hundreds of thousands . . . into the fiasco that was the Sosúa venture."[64] The historian Henry Feingold demurs, contending that American Jewish leaders did not have the luxury of predicting the future, but did have the moral obligation to weigh all their options carefully when so many were in such desperate straits. Belittling Zionist obstructionism, he has concluded, "many more might have been rescued had there been more Sosúas"[65] (see figure 1).

Unfortunately, so much of the historiography on the rescue of the Jews centers on the fixing of blame. An enduring pitched battle considers (and reconsiders) the merits of who could or should have done more to save the lives of those who perished.[66] Without demeaning the relevance of that important question, this extended debate has so overshadowed the discourse about the international response to the Nazi regime that the fixing of culpability ultimately obscures as much as it reveals about the principals' motivations and responses. A careful examination of the documentary record indicates that the Joint, arguably with greater success than any other relief organization, worked tirelessly to rescue its European kindred.

The Joint's wealth and political clout made it a force to be reckoned with, but its influence was used to conciliate and accommodate. Sosúa was an important rhetorical weapon in its arsenal. Promotional literature for the project sought to persuade Latin American governments that Jews would flourish

FIGURE 1. View of Sosúa Bay, c. 1940. JDC ARCHIVES.

in the tropics while it helped to blunt the Zionist campaign to create a homeland. Not until devastating reports of the Holocaust reached American Jewish leaders after 1942 did the Joint set aside its differences with the other Jewish groups and reach a consensus on the need for a homeland.[67]

To Roosevelt, American Judaism's turf battles were a godsend. Such dissonance made it easier to resist responding more aggressively to the refugee crisis. The 1924 Reed-Johnson (or National Origins) Act permitted only 160,000 immigrants to enter the United States annually, 2 percent of each Caucasian nationality represented in the 1890 census.[68] But bureaucratic indifference, nativism, anti-Semitism, and concerns about low-wage immigrants displacing unskilled U.S. workers ensured that only 36 percent of the quota was filled between 1933 and 1945.[69]

The savvy Roosevelt, unwilling to buck public opinion that was dead-set against liberalizing the quotas, masterfully played Jewish organizations against each other. Certainly no one could have foreseen, or imagined, for that matter, what transpired in the gas chambers and concentration camps; and historians must be wary of criticizing politicians for not responding to events that had not yet occurred.[70] Nevertheless, the president was well aware by the time of Évian, and certainly after Kristallnacht in November 1938, that the treatment of Jews in Germany and Austria was unconscionable, that panic migration was spiraling out of control, and that urgent solutions were needed. The steps taken by the administration were reactive and ineffectual. Rhetorical indignation coupled with inaction was emblematic of Franklin Roosevelt's response to the refugee crisis.

Memoirs and celebratory tracts have been written about Sosúa, but many of them treat the colony as an island unto itself, cut off from Trujillo's police state and North American policy.[71] Just like the displaced and dispossessed fleeing fascism who relocated to such far-flung destinations as Shanghai's International Quarter or the Bolivian *altiplano*, Sosúa's pioneers met challenges head-on and proved remarkably resilient while building the island's most successful agricultural colony. Even though more than half the settlers took advantage of easier visa regulations and packed their bags for the United States after the war, the core that remained at the colony and put down roots on the island's north coast was a more cohesive and committed group.

It is not an altogether heroic saga, however. Sosúa was a contentious place, and its bifurcated character—part agricultural colony, part refugee camp—had a corrosive impact on morale that threatened to tear apart the fragile social fabric. Lacking an idealistic ethos, which Zionism had afforded pioneers in Palestine, the settlement was painfully short on trust and cooperation. Moreover, for all its commercial success, Sosúa met the same fate as other unplanned communities forged in the Diaspora during the panic emigration. As the bonds that were formed under duress frayed and the United States continued to beckon to the younger generations, the settlement ineluctably withered away.

Recovering the world that Topf, Wasservogel, Bauer, and other colonists made in the tropics occupies much of the second half of this study. But what distinguishes *Tropical Zion* is the narrative's intersecting threads: the colony's fitful evolution, U.S.-Dominican relations, Trujillo's multifaceted domestic agenda, and American Jewry's squabbles. These threads track the story from Europe to the United States to the Caribbean. They illustrate how exogenous forces affected the settlers and how, in turn, the colony and its founders prompted, in often surprising ways, diplomatic responses abroad.

A word about the book's title is in order. No one ever accused the Joint Distribution Committee of being staunch Zionists; nor were the great majority of refugees who found shelter from the Nazi storm fervent proponents of a homeland in Palestine. But at that hateful moment, when a Jewish state was little more than a pipe dream, this tiny agricultural settlement did represent a Zion in the tropics for Jews who yearned for places they could call and make their own.

To unravel the twisted skein that led to Sosúa, we turn next to the Évian Conference, which dashed hopes for so many but ultimately carried the seeds of a life-saving Dominican offer for refugees.

MAP 1. The Dominican Republic.

Part One / **THE REFUGEES' PLIGHT**

ONE

"Our Ethnic Problem"

> Efforts to intensify the cultivation of our lands are realized and,
> at the same time, indirectly, there is a favorable change toward
> ameliorating our ethnic problem, since these immigrating currents
> bring capable and desirable racial elements to our soil.
> RAFAEL TRUJILLO, 1940

More than two hundred delegates, journalists, and observers crowded into the Hôtel Royal in Évian-les-Bains, an idyllic spa town facing Lausanne across Lac Léman in southeastern France, for nine days in early July 1938. Roosevelt called the conference at Welles's behest to counter criticism of the restrictive U.S. quotas.[1] FDR's goals were modest enough: resettle political refugees still in greater Germany, assist with the most urgent cases spilling over into countries of transit, and create an international committee to pursue a long-term solution.[2]

State Department officials knew from the outset that getting the delegates to reach a consensus on these goals would not be easy. Finding a site for the conference proved challenging enough. Switzerland begged off as host to avoid embarrassing questions about its restrictive policies.[3] Many of the participating nations sent delegates reluctantly, out of respect for Roosevelt and, significantly, only after Washington assured them that they did not have to revise existing immigration laws and that relief funds would come from private sources.[4]

Even so, Great Britain needed additional prodding. Unwilling to repudiate its Arab allies, the Foreign Office refused to participate until Washington agreed that Palestine was off the agenda as a resettlement site. The British also instructed their delegation to make sure that

Jewish immigration to their colonies in the West Indies, British Honduras and British Guiana, was similarly excluded from consideration.[5]

Nor was France, heretofore the continent's most welcoming nation, enthused at the prospect of accepting more refugees. In the run-up to the conference, the French government declared that it had reached the saturation point with more than 3.5 million foreigners and was shutting its borders to permanent immigration. Just a week before the delegates assembled, a Foreign Ministry memorandum left little to the imagination when it asked rhetorically, "Is it in France's interest to appear as the refuge of all the misfits and . . . everyone Germany considers its natural enemy?"[6]

At the insistence of the British government, conference organizers conceded that only German and Austrian refugees were to be considered, ignoring five million Eastern European Jews.[7] It was the specter of that enormous number of refugees to the east that haunted the proceedings. Left unspoken was the fear that if Western nations agreed to accept Nazi Germany's discarded now, they risked opening themselves up to a much larger exodus in the future.[8]

Organizers never even acknowledged that Jews accounted for more than 90 percent of the refugees. Instead, the exiles were blandly labeled "political" refugees, to appease the Germans.[9] But this semantic sleight of hand avoided admitting that Germany and Austria's Jews were bona fide victims of discrimination who were being driven out for ethnic and religious reasons.[10]

Some observers refused to ignore the Reich's role in precipitating the crisis and implored delegates to take action. Myron Taylor, who headed up the U.S. delegation, spoke for many when he warned of "catastrophic human suffering ahead which can only result in general unrest and in general international strain which will not be conducive to the permanent appeasement to which all peoples earnestly aspire."[11] The allusion to appeasement was not lost on those already convinced, months before Chamberlain's visit to Munich, that negotiating with Herr Hitler was not only pointless but dangerous. Shortly after the conference began, foreign correspondent William Shirer filed a prescient report: "I doubt if much will be done. The British, French, and Americans seem too anxious not to do anything to offend Hitler. It is an absurd situation. They want to appease the man who was responsible for their problem."[12]

Pundits were quick to point out that *Évian* spelled backwards was *naive*.[13] The conference proved to be a spectacular failure; the participants agreed only to the creation of an Intergovernmental Committee on Political Refugees (IGC).[14] Even this meager achievement was unpopular with delegates, who fretted that it would raise expectations that could not be met.[15] The IGC's mandate was to negotiate with the Reich to secure an orderly release of its refugees and to let those departing take a portion of their assets with them, and to reconnoiter sites for permanent resettlement.[16]

Delegate after delegate came to the podium to insist that their nation's record on immigration was unassailable and that the restrictions their government had imposed were meant only to make sure refugees did not become public charges or pose a threat to native employment.[17] Some diplomats were uncharacteristically blunt, however, about why they refused to pry their borders open. The Australian delegate admitted that his nation had no interest in importing Jews: "as we have no real racial problem we are not desirous of importing one by encouraging any scheme of large-scale foreign migration."[18]

To make matters worse, representatives of twenty-one American Jewish organizations attending the conference as observers proved incapable of setting aside their differences and agreeing on how best to assist their brethren. These agencies had raised upward of fifty million dollars for relief since 1933 and had been invited to attend the conference only because Western governments had no intention of absorbing relocation costs. Zionist and non-Zionist groups openly bickered with each other, some advocating increased immigration to Palestine while others called for resettlement in underpopulated countries. American Zionists were divided between moderates who counseled firm lobbying of Great Britain and hawks who demanded the immediate creation of a Jewish state in Palestine.[19] This squabbling sent precisely the wrong message to the delegates, who did not have to search far for reasons to avoid making a commitment. One Jewish publication lamented that Évian was a "spectacle of Jewish discord and disruption."[20]

Neither the European countries bordering Germany, the countries of the largely underpopulated British Commonwealth and Empire, nor the Latin American republics came forward to amend their restrictive policies.[21] Roosevelt was especially disappointed that Latin American nations were not more responsive. Religious intolerance and anti-Semitism were so interwoven with economic concerns that experts often could not determine what underlay Latin American reticence. To be sure, Latin American governments had little interest in Jewish entrepreneurs and professionals. Contending with low wages and unemployment during the Depression, these states had restricted immigration to farmers and workers with specialized skills, effectively denying entry to almost all German and Austrian Jews.[22]

Latin American delegates resented America's self-righteous posturing; the Argentine representative chided the U.S. delegation when he reminded participants that since 1935, his country had accepted almost as many Jewish immigrants, even though it was one-tenth the size.[23] Although Nazi doctrines of racial purity and anti-Semitism were spreading like wildfire throughout the region, one knowledgeable observer contended that it was fear of German economic reprisals that best explained Latin American caution.[24] In the months after Évian, a number of countries, including Argentina and Brazil, which up to that point had had some of the most liberal immigration laws in the hemisphere, actually tightened their regulations.[25]

The German press had a field day with the proceedings, charging the Western nations with hypocrisy because they professed sympathy but refused to open their doors. The Nazi mouthpiece *Völkischer Beobachter* ridiculed the nations in attendance: "They weep crocodile tears over the Jews, but nobody is willing to make a sacrifice for these 'unfortunates,' since everyone knows what the Jew means within a national community. Thus it is impossible not to recognize the fact that those states who themselves refuse to take any Jews merely justify the German Reich's defensive measures against the Jews, measures which are in any case not yet sufficiently far reaching."[26]

Nazi racial policy had been predicated on forcing its Jewish population to emigrate, and now Évian had offered proof that the West was unwilling to accept its rejects. If the Third Reich "could no longer expect to export, sell, or expel its Jews to an indifferent world that plainly did not want them," the historian Robert Wistrich has observed, with the benefit of hindsight, "then perhaps they would have to do something even more drastic."[27] That awful moment came on October 18, 1941, when Germany radically altered its prewar policies by sealing its borders and prohibiting Jews from leaving. But until then, the German state continued to pressure its Jewish population to emigrate. Sadly, *Völkischer Beobachter* had it right when it crowed that "making a sacrifice for these 'unfortunates'" would never be a priority for the West.

THE DILEMMA FOR AMERICAN JEWS

Even before the conference, the gathering storm over what to do about the refugees provoked considerable debate in the United States, where it was invariably refracted through the lens of immigration policy. Roosevelt's negotiating team at Évian, led by Taylor and two prominent American Jews, Paul Baerwald, the chair of the JDC, and Rabbi Stephen Wise, the president of the American Jewish Congress, knew that the U.S. Congress and the public were opposed to raising quotas. Even though this was a land of immigrants—more than thirty-seven million Americans were foreign-born on the eve of the Second World War—nativist hostility to immigration had simmered during the

1920s and was rekindled during the Great Depression.[28] New York Representative Samuel Dickstein made efforts to transfer all unused slots in the British quota to the German one, but the White House spurned them, along with his proposal to mortgage future German slots to admit desperate refugees to the United States immediately.[29]

Indeed, this could not have been a worse moment to raise the issue. Unemployment rates were spiking upward during "Roosevelt's Recession" of 1937–38. Robert R. Reynolds of North Carolina, the Senate's Military Affairs Committee chair and a contributor to the anti-Semitic periodical *The Cross and the Flag*, captured the prevailing sentiment: "These aliens are constantly competing with our own American citizens for employment . . . the United States is the only one [nation] which has failed to protect its employment opportunities for its citizens. . . . They deserve first consideration and aid." [30]

Anti-Semitism only added fuel to the fire. Roosevelt was especially sensitive to charges that his administration had too great a Jewish presence. "Jew Deal" and "President Rosenfeld" were epithets invoked regularly by bigots such as Father Charles E. Coughlin, whose Sunday afternoon radio program boasted a nationwide audience of thirty to forty million. The priest filled football stadiums with loyalists eager to hear him spew invective about how Jewish financiers in cahoots with either international communism or the Bank of England had tampered with the money supply, dragged the United States into the First World War, and precipitated the Depression. The priest had the audacity to claim that *Kristallnacht* was justified by historic wrongs committed by Jews against Christians. Moreover, he serialized *The Protocols of the Elders of Zion* and published transcripts of Joseph Goebbels's short-wave broadcasts in his weekly *Social Justice*.[31]

Coughlin was not alone. William Dudley Pelley, a white supremacist, established a fanatical Silver Legion committed to the creation of a global Aryan Federation, and the German-American Bund filled New York City's Madison Square Garden with 22,000 supporters at a rally in 1939 that called on the faithful to "Stop Jewish Domination of Christian America!"[32]

Meanwhile, isolationists, America Firsters, and pacifists condemned American Jews and Roosevelt for warmongering and the president specifically for daring to summon the Évian conference.[33] Public opinion did not lag far behind. Even though Americans overwhelmingly condemned Nazi mistreatment of Jews, two-thirds of those polled by *Fortune* magazine in July 1938 thought the quotas should not be relaxed.[34]

Faced with such a mandate, some American Jewish groups were reluctant publicly to advocate liberalizing quotas. Moreover, State Department officials actually pressured Jewish leaders to tread lightly, warning that if the "issue of revision [of quotas] came up" on Capitol Hill, the "temper of Congress" was such that the laws would be tightened, not relaxed.[35] Instead, the Jewish leaders counseled silence or acceptance of restrictions so as not to prompt an anti-Semitic backlash or indirectly support those who had the political clout to make matters worse for the refugees. An AJC spokesperson articulated the dilemma: "While [the] humanitarian accomplishments in bringing . . . victims of persecution to the United States and finding work for them cannot be highly enough praised, this is helping to intensify the Jewish problem here. Giving work to Jewish refugees while so many Americans are out of work has naturally made bad feelings. As heartless as it may seem, future efforts should be directed toward sending Jewish refugees to other countries instead of bringing them here."[36] That as late as 1938, a prominent Jewish advocacy group was so reluctant to pressure the administration as to take this position illustrates just how anxious leaders were about anti-Semitism and how pessimistic about the chances of revising immigration policy.

Even Zionists were reluctant to rock the boat.[37] Indeed, a majority of Jews polled in 1937 were opposed to admitting the refugees.[38] That is why a number of key Jewish organizations preferred private lobbying the State Department rather than public posturing, and actively discouraged their membership from joining boycotts against the Third Reich.[39]

In truth, the Jewish leadership was reluctant to criticize Roosevelt publicly at all, let alone on something this controversial.[40] The president's compassion for ordinary Americans struck a resonant chord with Jews, earning him more than 90 percent of their vote in 1936. More to the point, Jews made up more than 15 percent of the Roosevelt administration's top hires, though they constituted only 3 percent of the population. But if the New Deal had converted Jews from political "outsiders to insiders," their ambiguous identity as Jews and Americans inhibited their ability to exercise power.[41]

In retrospect, the way Jewish leaders tolerated Roosevelt's inaction says a lot about the membership's status as assimilated Americans. Acceptance in society and access to power mandated that Jewish leaders conform to the roles and mores of their reference group, U.S. citizens. As such, they were loyal to a fault. According to the historian Jerold Auerbach, there was more than a hint of irony in FDR's methods, because in reality he gave American Jews very little: "By giving them nothing as Jews, he was confirming their status as Americans. Recognition as Americans was what American Jews craved more than anything else; it was all Roosevelt ever gave them, but it was more than enough."[42]

With Jewish organizations divided and diffident and the administration and Western nations unwilling to revise immigration policies, the Évian conference organizers were left clutching at straws. Small wonder that the Dominican Republic's unexpected offer to accept German and Austrian Jewish refugees on the third day of the proceedings electrified the attendees.

This generous offer was not open ended, and it was never meant to open the floodgates to indiscriminate immigration. The Dominican ambassador to France, the dictator's brother, Virgilio Trujillo, who presented the offer at Évian, emphasized that his nation wanted farmers, not businessmen. These "poor modern nomads" might be a good fit for his country's colonization program, he told a stunned audience.[43]

> The Dominican government, which for many years has been encouraging and promoting the development of agriculture by appropriate measures and which gives ample immigration facilities to agriculturalists who wish to settle in the country as colonists, would be prepared to make its contribution by granting specially advantageous concessions to Austrian and German exiles, agriculturalists with an unimpeachable record who satisfy the conditions laid down by the Dominican legislation on immigration. For colonization purposes my government has at its disposal large areas of fertile, well-irrigated land, excellent roads and a police force which preserves absolute order and guarantees the peace of the country. The Department of Agriculture could give colonists, in addition to land, seed and the technical advice which they need.

It was to be a controlled experiment under the watchful eye of a dictatorship, which, as political opponents could attest only too well, was prepared to preserve "absolute order." Officials surely realized that few of the refugees had the requisite agricultural background. Still, they intended to select only those "dedicated to manual, productive labor" who wanted to make the Dominican Republic their permanent home rather than a temporary stopover. The objective was to establish self-contained agricultural settlements.

Conditional though it was, the offer was more than a case of international grandstanding; it was tied to a series of domestic initiatives vitally important to Trujillo and was a significant component of his strategy to improve relations with Washington. The general believed it would not only heal the rift caused by the massacre, but would enable his government to secure needed military and economic assistance.

The international community did not quibble about the qualifiers. Labeled a pariah for an act of unconscionable brutality, Trujillo now was hailed as a humanitarian. So gratified was he by this response that he fired off a second salvo a month later at the IGC's maiden meeting in London, stunning diplomats, the media, and refugee organizations when he informed the committee that the Dominican Republic, a nation of a little more than one-and-a-half million inhabitants, was prepared to accept up to one hundred thousand Central European refugees.[44] Even as colonization experts questioned whether the small island nation could absorb anywhere near that figure, Western nations, desperate for solutions and grateful for initiatives that made no demands on them, rushed to praise the dictator.

The opportunistic Trujillo reveled in his new reputation. Throughout the summer and fall of 1938, he opened negotiations with the IGC, the State Department, and Jewish refugee organizations to transform his tantalizing proposal into a reality, and explored similar colonization ventures with such strange bedfellows as the Third Reich and Spanish republican exile organizations.

If his proposal caught foreign observers by surprise, colonization schemes had been on his mind for quite some time. Samuel Guy Inman, a colonization expert and a member of the High Commission on Refugees, reported during a 1935 visit to the island, "President Trujillo was very much interested in colonization and . . . the government is ready to give some of the best land to these colonies." Subsequently, Secretary of Agriculture César Tolentino met with Jewish representatives from Cuba to discuss the prospects for German Jewish immigration. Though he expressed reservations about "a foreign element with so well-defined racial and psychological characteristics," Tolentino concluded that the advantages outweighed the disadvantages.[45] Trujillo again entertained proposals to admit "young, healthy Jewish farmers" in 1936 and 1937 when the American Jewish Congress and the Jewish World Congress sent emissaries to meet with him.[46] Several months later, he agreed in principle at a meeting with American Jews to admit thousands of Jewish refugees.[47]

Cordial relations between Dominicans and Jews dating back to the early nineteenth century may have made officials amenable to Jewish immigration. Impoverished governments borrowed monies from a handful of Sephardic Jewish merchants from the Dutch West Indies, and intermarriage with Dominican elites resulted. Interfaith marriages were acceptable to native elites because Jews were perceived to be white. Several Jews went on to join the Dominican Foreign Service, and one became a cabinet minister in the 1880s before he ran afoul of a new president and was shot.[48] In 1882 Dominican president Gregorio Luperón encouraged the immigration of Russian Jews, but the plan failed to get off the ground.[49]

Yet as late as the mid-1930s, the Jewish community numbered no more than a few hundred, with most living in the capital. The historian Bernardo Vega has argued that the exploratory discussions between Jewish leaders and the Dominican government suggest that the inception of the Sosúa initiative was not a byproduct of the massacre.[50] The decision to admit Jews, however, gathered sufficient momentum only after the international firestorm ignited by El Corte, and after Roosevelt gave Trujillo a gift-wrapped opportunity to redeem himself at Évian.

Trujillo had more on his mind than rescuing Jews. Colonization, immigration, and the "Dominicanization" of the nation's ill-defined border with Haiti were complementary strategies designed to foster self-sufficiency in agriculture, entice white immigrants, and bolster the population base along the western frontier in the hope of creating a buffer against future Haitian migration.

RACE, COLONIZATION, AND IMMIGRATION

Trujillo created a number of colonies during his first two terms in office. Land grants were doled out to military officers and soldiers. Makeshift penal colonies, composed of convicts and vagrants from urban areas working off their sentences, were established to populate the frontier. In this way, Trujillo could proclaim that the very same army that had massacred "the enemy" was now an engine of economic growth. Even though some of the new farming colonies, like Sosúa, were not located near the contested border, all were part of the dictator's Dominicanization program—a euphemism for "de-Haitianizing" the border, augmenting food production, and improving the race. The intention, which was never fully realized, was to provide the colonists with schools, medical clinics, churches, land, credit, technical support, and infrastructure. According to the historian Frank Moya Pons, Dominicanization was a "crusade of national vindication," dedicated to regaining control of a region the nation had gradually relinquished to Haitian emigrés over the past century.[51]

A recent reassessment of the state's motivations for El Corte contends that it was as much about curbing a recalcitrant Dominican frontier population (which had more in common with its Haitian neighbors than it did with Dominican elites) as it was about subduing Haitians living in the Dominican Republic. According to this revisionist interpretation, the massacre sought to destroy a fluid, bilingual, and bicultural border zone where ethnic Haitians and Dominicans had lived and worked together for decades in relative tranquility, and to rebuild that region with Dominican and foreign colonists.[52]

The Trujillo regime's anti-Haitianism had its origins in elite fears of unchecked Haitian migration.[53] Attracted initially by employment opportunities in the sugar sector, Haitian (and West Indian) blacks had migrated in increasing numbers during the 1910s and 1920s to the southeastern end of the island for seasonal work on U.S. sugar company plantations. The recurrent antiblack rhetoric always had its limits; the Dominican state sometimes encouraged these migratory flows when sugar companies petitioned authorities for additional workers for their harvests and when large-scale public works projects required cheap manual labor. Despite high Dominican unemployment, the influx of foreign workers kept the wage scale depressed and bolstered foreign exchange earnings. Yet elites were ambivalent about these migratory movements. As a result, immigration regulations were tightened and periodic efforts were made to promote white immigration and expunge blackness from Dominican national identity through intermarriage.[54]

One curious response by Dominican intellectuals was to extol the benefits of the nation's short-lived indigenous past. Hitherto unknown indigenous leaders of the colonial period who had resisted Spanish colonization were lionized in fiction and in the press, while a self-consciously romanticized nationalist myth was constructed that promoted Indians as defenders of sovereignty against external threats by Haitian invasions and Spanish conquerors.[55]

Trujillo's ideologues took this racist discourse to vulgar extremes that would have been simply unimaginable just a decade earlier. The state's 1935 census incongruously identified more than two-thirds of the population as mestizos; officials marked passports and national identification cards of all nonwhites as *indios*, to avoid any allusion to an African heritage; and official publications depicted the archetype of the Dominican campesino, *el cibaeño*, as a light-skinned Hispanic peasant.[56]

Intellectuals also gave Dominicans object lessons in racial preference. In *Over*, a well-received novel by Ramón Marrero Aristy, the young protagonist, Daniel, courts a woman whose father and mother are mulatto and white, respectively. Daniel is taken with her because "she wasn't white, nor would I have wanted that. She was a radiant Indian, the color of cinnamon." She was, in the words of the literary critic Doris Sommer, "a perfect balance in which black and white were transmuted . . . into Indian."[57]

Trujillo also linked the nation's Hispanic and Catholic roots with aggressive efforts to "pacify" the frontier. The Catholic Church dispatched Jesuits to the new colonies to quell the growing popularity of Haitian vodou and to renew spiritual commitment to Catholicism. Schools were charged with promoting the Spanish language and Dominican culture and glorifying the general, while a new frontier mission of San Ignacio de Loyola organized patriotic celebrations of the Day of the Benefactor (Trujillo's birthday) and other national and religious holidays.[58]

Although the working classes never shared the elite's obsession with their nation's "Africanization," the cumulative effect of years of anti-Haitian propaganda could not help but have an impact on how everyday Dominicans perceived themselves and their neighbors. Moya Pons contends that if one asks Dominicans today what their race or color is, "they will most probably answer that they are *indios*. By that Dominicans do not mean that they are direct descendants of the aboriginal tribes that inhabited the island when Columbus arrived in 1492, but that they have a distinct color which is not black nor white, but which *resembles* that of the Indians."[59]

The Dominican government was not alone in promoting *mestizaje* (the racial mixing of whites and Indians)—it was a recurring theme throughout Latin America during this period—but it was anomalous in fabricating and imposing fictitious racial and ethnic categories that had little bearing on the nation's historical evolution and the composition of its population.[60]

After the events of October 1937, officials embarked on a concerted propaganda campaign to rationalize Dominican aggression against its neighbors in the most chauvinistic terms. Marrero Aristy lamented that Dominican inhabitants along the frontier were succumbing to Haitian superstitions and customs "that could place in jeopardy the purity of our Spanish customs and our Catholic religion."[61] Regime ideologue Joaquín Balaguer mocked Haitian mores, accusing Haitians of incest and other "barbaric practices, contrary to the Christian institution of the family, that are not unusual among the Haitian lower classes and constitute proof of their tremendous moral deformation."[62] Acting on these prejudices, the regime selectively enforced laws outlawing participation in vodou ceremonies.[63]

El Corte itself was portrayed as a defensive measure, meant to stem the tide of Haitian penetration, which was deemed an insidious attack on national sovereignty. Apologists compared the migrations to nineteenth-century Haitian military invasions and occupations of the fatherland. A steady drumbeat of state propaganda warned of "Ethiopianization," while the dictator who had ordered the repression was lauded in the servile press as the "savior of the nation."

The massacre was downplayed as a minor border incident that unfortunately had spiraled out of control when Dominican peasants—not the army— retaliated against Haitian cattle and goat rustlers. Machetes, bayonets, and clubs were used on the unarmed Haitians, giving rise to theories that Trujillo

FIGURE 2
General Rafael
Trujillo, 1936.

FROM *PRESIDENT
TRUJILLO: HIS WORK
AND THE DOMINICAN
REPUBLIC*, BY LAWRENCE
DE BESAULT. WASHING-
TON PUBLISHING
COMPANY, 1936.

"sought to simulate a popular conflict" or, according to the historian Richard
Turits, "at least to maintain some measure of plausible deniability of the state's
perpetration of this genocide."[64] Balaguer scrupulously avoided addressing
the roles of the military and the government, seeking instead to rationalize
the actions of local peasants, who actually never took part in the atrocities.
"The events of 1937, which enemies of the Dominican government have tried
to paint abroad as an unjust massacre of enormous numbers of Haitian masses,
were an outburst from the very soul of our campesinos, out of resentment and
protest against four centuries of depredations that have occurred in the northern provinces of our nation by bands of Haitian marauders."[65]

These official responses were meant solely for foreign consumption. Despite detailed coverage in the international press, state control of the national
media was so complete that for many Dominicans it was as if El Corte never occurred. No official account was ever published in the Dominican Republic.[66]

In addition to whitewashing the recent past, Trujillo had pragmatic reasons for viewing the massacre in "defensive" terms. He believed that the

sparsely populated border could prove to be an excellent staging ground for an invasion by his enemies scattered across the Americas. Securing the frontier therefore was, in his mind, essential to his survival.

There is also reason to believe that Trujillo viewed improving the race in more than just ideological terms. Racist indoctrination had been a part of his cadet training by the U.S. Marines at the Haina Military Academy during the U.S. occupation.[67] After he came to power, he made a point of disavowing his mulatto background. Although a grandparent on each side was Haitian, the general had his shills rewrite his family tree as "pure French" and "pure Spanish." This genealogical revision recalled the common practice during the colonial period of *limpieza de sangre* (blood purity), in which elites concocted family trees to hide Jewish or Moorish ancestors. A rubber-stamp Congress certified the whiteness of his ancestry. The general also lightened his complexion with pancake makeup, and official photographs and paintings were routinely touched up and lightened (see figure 2, above).[68]

Efforts to entice European immigrants to the island were an integral part of the strategy to Dominicanize the border. Speaking at an international conference just a month before Évian, Reynaldo Váldez, director of immigration, declared that attracting white farmers was an urgent necessity. State agronomist Enrique Curiel argued that by leavening the mix in the newly created colonies, Dominican peasants, who were "by nature indifferent," indolent, and captive to their traditional ways, would be more likely to adopt new techniques if they worked alongside industrious Europeans.[69]

Only a week before the massacre, Trujillo's director of statistics, Vicente Tolentino Rojas, produced a study on the country's receptivity to immigration.[70] Consistent with the optimistic message that the Dominican Republic later presented to the IGC, Tolentino Rojas contended that the country could absorb twenty-five thousand immigrants a year for the next twenty years. He blamed the nation's failure at racial improvement on climate, illness, and inadequate diet, and concluded, "the racial improvement of our population . . . is a matter that I urge us to undertake. By not confronting this problem, the country will soon be, in the best of cases, *mulato*."[71]

In a no-holds-barred assessment published six months after the offer, *La Opinión* insisted that the solution to the nation's Haitian problem was European immigration.

> We have at the west another nationality that has double the Dominican population with less territory, and with desires, never restrained, to send to our land their excess population which is a danger to our social and

ethnic condition, since it is a nationality of a different origin, of a distinct race and distinct customs. . . . It is only natural that in order to avoid this invasion, we look for a natural weapon, that cannot be realized without a great increase of the Dominican population which will assure in perpetuity the predominance of the white element in the island and the "status quo" of the frontier. . . . If the policy of intensification of immigration continues, and the frontier is held in check and moved back, it is certain that one of the more important problems of our national life will be resolved.[72]

The U.S. consul in Ciudad Trujillo read more into this article, believing it had all the earmarks of a "preparatory pep talk for the populace" to pave the way for the government's admission of "large numbers of white immigrants, namely Jews."[73]

In certain respects, Trujillo's colonization program resembled his predecessors' policies, especially those of Horacio Vásquez (1924–30), who tried unsuccessfully to coax peasants to populate the interior.[74] Trujillo was, however, much more aggressive than Vásquez in encouraging both Dominicans and Europeans to colonize the border zone. During the Depression, prices on exports like sugar, coffee, and tobacco declined, resulting in less foreign exchange and less cash to import foodstuffs. As a result, Trujillo made agricultural self-sufficiency a high priority, not only to populate the interior but to promote economic sovereignty, prevent vagrancy, and redress growing rural-to-urban migration, which overtaxed the resources of the nation's two largest cities, Ciudad Trujillo and Santiago.[75] Recent rural migrants, the un- and underemployed, and vagrants were "encouraged" to join agricultural colonies by the carrot and, if necessary, by the stick.[76]

In the fall of 1938, Trujillo concluded negotiations with the Servicio de Emigración para los Refugiados Españoles (SERE) to bring in several thousand Spanish republicans then living in exile in France. SERE paid all transportation costs and deposited one hundred dollars with the Dominican government for each immigrant, while the government agreed to provide land, housing, and seeds.[77] Spanish exiles were placed in the new colonies, even though most were professionals and city dwellers. When asked why Trujillo had welcomed such a mélange of anarchists, socialists, and communists, one Spanish émigré cracked, "we are white and we can breed."[78]

Apparently Trujillo mistakenly believed (or was led to believe) that SERE was better funded than it was, and lost his enthusiasm soon after subsidies dried up. Not surprisingly, most of the Spaniards took the first opportunity to leave the colonies and move to Ciudad Trujillo, or to leave the country for more ideologically compatible destinations, such as Mexico. By 1947, fewer than one hundred of the original Spanish settlers remained in the colonies.[79]

At the same time, Trujillo and a German official explored the possibility of bringing in forty thousand German (non-Jewish) farmers to populate the frontier.[80] That Trujillo even discussed such an undertaking raised eyebrows among policymakers in Washington, who were concerned about Nazi inroads in the Caribbean. But the move only underscored Trujillo's commitment to creating colonies with Europeans, whether they were German émigrés, Jewish refugees, or Spanish leftists.[81]

Trujillo appeared to cozy up to Nazi officials at different moments throughout the late 1930s. Given the noticeable similarities between the two dictatorships, this led some contemporaries to speculate that he was interested in closer relations with the Reich. The two regimes shared several attributes, including authoritarian rule, a single political party, excessive scapegoating of minority groups, racism, extreme nationalism, and megalomania. But as Vega points out, Trujillo never created a corporate state and had no imperialistic designs. Unlike Hitler, Franco, or Mussolini, the self-styled Benefactor was motivated by personal enrichment. By 1961, in one estimate, the net worth of the Trujillo family holdings had reached $500 million, and the president, his extended family, and his cronies monopolized three-quarters of the nation's industry and owned almost one-tenth of its land.[82]

Still, Trujillo was savvy enough to know his limitations. Although impressed by what European fascist leaders had accomplished, he was acutely aware of his nation's client status in a U.S. sphere of influence, and he understood how Washington perceived possible ties with the Nazi regime.

TRUE NORTH

Trujillo never let ideology stand in the way of self-interest; he did what he had to do with whomever, be it Jewish refugees, U.S. State Department officials, philanthropists, Nazi diplomats, Spanish anarchists, or Haitian politicians, as long as he benefited from the exchange and if it reinforced his ability to remain in power.[83] It was axiomatic that Washington's support was critical to his survival, and he was determined to maintain favorable relations with the Roosevelt administration. As a British minister stationed in Haiti observed, "Trujillo had a great deal of admiration for the Nazis, but he was aware that the North Americans would not tolerate favorable relations with Hitler . . . from an island so strategically placed in relation to the Panama Canal. Although Trujillo had little love lost for the Americans, he sufficiently feared the consequences of such a move that he never took the risk."[84]

This is not to imply that U.S.-Dominican relations were ever tranquil. But as Robert McClintock, a U.S. diplomat, put it in 1938, no matter how protracted the negotiations, inevitably "the compass of Trujillo's ship has returned, in spite of erratic variations, unerringly to this point [friendlier relations with Washington] as the true north by which he would be guided."[85]

Trujillo realized that his image had suffered as a result of El Corte. A sympathetic U.S. chargé d'affaires in Ciudad Trujillo, Eugene M. Hinkle, thought the international response "furnished him a bitter lesson and has given him a stigma in the United States press and abroad. He will have a difficult time to live this down, attempting as he is to recover the prestige the incident has cost him abroad."[86] Hinkle wanted to believe (and to persuade his superiors) that the incident had chastened Trujillo. His opponents, however, in exile or on the island, did not have that luxury. Trujillo may have been more aware of international public opinion and "relatively" more selective in his repression, but as a 1945 State Department report made clear, it did not inhibit the torture, murder, and imprisonment of dozens of suspected dissidents.[87]

To ensure his niche in Washington, Trujillo decided that it was best to terminate all contacts with German authorities, ban Nazi propaganda, and, with great fanfare, rename boulevards in Ciudad Trujillo after George Washington (later renamed Marine Corps Boulevard) and Cordell Hull. By the time Germany invaded Poland in September 1939, relations between the Third Reich and the Dominican Republic had cooled, and Trujillo had signed a military pact with the Roosevelt administration permitting the U.S. Navy to patrol Dominican waters.[88]

Trujillo knew he had an inveterate enemy in Sumner Welles, the State Department's resident expert on Latin American affairs. As early as 1934, Welles was convinced that the island presented "more cause for worry than any country in Latin America."[89] He knew the Dominican Republic and its history well, having spent two years there as special commissioner in the early 1920s. During that time, he negotiated a gradual withdrawal of U.S. troops, oversaw the transition to civilian rule, and researched what would become a two-volume history of the island nation. *Naboth's Vineyard* promoted democratization and pleaded for greater cooperation between Latin America and the United States based on equality and mutual respect, elements conspicuously absent from bilateral relations in the past.[90] Only by stimulating commercial ties, providing educational opportunities for Latin American youth, and offering technical assistance, Welles argued, would the United States achieve its long-term objectives. Conversely, "military occupation, military intervention, or armed supervision of elections" were, in his mind, self-defeating. The U.S. police action in the Dominican Republic was a case in point.[91]

Welles had insisted on a gradual pull-out to give the North American–trained Dominican military enough time to complete the transition from U.S. to Dominican control. Democracy depended on the "absolute impartiality" of this newly trained military. Marine officers would stay on in an advisory capacity after the occupation, ostensibly to ensure the professionalism of the National Police and to reinforce its nonpolitical character. Although well intentioned, Welles's notion of an apolitical army was naïve. Trujillo became the chief beneficiary of the U.S. withdrawal, earning a string of promotions during the early 1920s that placed him in a position of leadership.[92]

While Trujillo ascended the ranks, Welles and civilian politicians tried to plant the seeds of democracy. Welles was a strong supporter of Vásquez; even the Dominican president's self-serving decision to extend his term by two years in 1928 and charges of widespread corruption and mismanagement in his administration could not shake Welles's faith in the man.[93] By 1929, Vásquez was faltering; corruption was rife, the budget out of control, and foreign debts unpaid. When he asked for assistance, Welles assembled a blue-ribbon team of bankers, civil servants, and business leaders. A budget bureau was established, which "uncovered a trail of corruption leading to . . . army chief, Rafael Trujillo."[94] Warned of the impending investigation, Trujillo launched a coup in 1930, deposing Welles's protégé.

Welles was discouraged by the coup and also unhappy that the administration of Herbert Hoover did not withhold recognition of Trujillo. Hoover's unwillingness to insist on elections in the Dominican Republic and elsewhere, Welles believed, had contributed to a rash of seven coups and "revolutions" throughout Latin America. Welles told FDR, then a presidential candidate in the making, that only free elections would ensure regional stability and that diplomatic recognition should be withheld until a nation's electorate had spoken. Intervention should be a last resort.[95]

Welles did what he could to destabilize the new regime.[96] Openly aiding and abetting political exiles, he leaked their inflammatory broadsides to columnists such as Drew Pearson, who wrote a series of scathing articles about the dictatorship.[97]

While disavowing the Monroe Doctrine's hegemonic implications, Welles nevertheless juggled two competing desires: to discourage support for dictatorships and to uphold the principle of nonintervention.[98] Melding Progressive Era reformism and a healthy dose of paternalism, Welles believed that the United States should extend a "friendly hand" to promote stability, democratic governance, and fiscal probity. An interamerican system, predicated on low tariffs, reciprocal trade agreements, judiciously placed loans, cultural exchange, and military assistance, would foster trust.[99] Welles surrounded himself with Harvard-educated career diplomats who were intensely loyal to him, had firsthand experience in the region, and shared their mentor's distaste for the meddling that had characterized past U.S. administrations.[100]

During the Roosevelt years, however, the State Department did not speak with one voice. A second group, led by Secretary of State Hull and Assistant Secretary Breckinridge Long, thought about U.S.–Latin American relations pragmatically. They not only viewed the region within a larger international framework, but assumed that Latin American states tacitly expected Washington to set the parameters for hemispheric policy. For Hull, this meant liberalizing trade and removing tariff barriers and exchange controls implemented during previous administrations.[101] On his watch the State Department negotiated a bevy of bilateral trade agreements with Latin American states. Unlike previous North American diplomats, who were often arrogant and patronizing, the humble and folksy Hull appeared to be the very embodiment of the Good Neighbor.[102]

Hull had a preference for strong rulers, especially when they proved loyal. In his mind, working with the Trujillos of the world was far preferable to chronic instability, anti-U.S. rhetoric, or revolution. This was as true in Europe (Mussolini) as it was in Asia (Chiang Kai-shek) or Latin America. As the Second World War approached and as security concerns moved to the fore, Hull expected Latin American leaders to follow the U.S. example and sever ties with the Axis, no questions asked. For this reason, Hull approached bilateral relations more instrumentally than Welles, and had fewer reservations about doing business with dictators.

FDR encouraged the sniping and bureaucratic bloodletting in the State Department, often assigning two advisers with diametrically opposing views to work on the same matter. He did this partly because he thought the State Department was inefficient, filled with politically appointed deadwood, and prone to leaks.[103] Moreover, the president apparently "enjoyed" the personal rivalries, believing that they reinforced loyalty while fostering creative solutions.[104]

Among department officers, personal and professional animosities became enmeshed, straining relations and often clouding policy formulation. The patrician Welles had attended Groton, the same New England prep school as Roosevelt, and shared FDR's sense of noblesse oblige. His personal friendship with the president was an ongoing source of friction with Hull, who believed that Welles traded on that friendship and was disloyal to the State Department. FDR did little to discourage Hull's suspicions, consulting with Welles on substantive matters, more often than not leaving the secretary of state out of the loop. One student of the department's labyrinthine inner workings thought Welles's ties to Eleanor Roosevelt, who had an abiding concern for the refugees, was another source of friction between Welles and Hull, especially when she personally asked Welles to intercede and overrule obstructionist consuls in Europe.[105]

Complicating matters, the secretary of state tried to hide his wife's Jewish ancestry and overcompensated for it by abstaining as much as possible from refugee matters.[106] The diplomatic historian Irwin Gellman is convinced "that this Jewish connection made him [Hull] vulnerable to attacks from anti-Semites, who would argue that his wife had forced him to support Jewish causes, and therefore that he had succumbed to un-American influences." Hull's presidential aspirations also shaped his measured response to the refugee crisis; they help explain why he was quick to delegate the matter to subordinates.[107]

Hull and Welles were very much an odd couple: Welles, the quintessential Foreign Service lifer with years of experience negotiating with Latin American leaders, and Hull, a political appointee with no prior experience in foreign affairs, who, after his nomination was confirmed, faced a steep learning curve.[108] After 1938, moreover, Hull required extended medical leaves to obtain treatment for diabetes and tuberculosis. His failing health led to uncertainty in the department and strengthened Welles's position with his colleagues and the president.[109] As Welles grew in stature, he became a threat not just to Hull but to Trujillo.

Such competing views and contrasting personalities represented both a challenge and an opportunity for the Dominican dictator. On the one hand, it was sometimes difficult to discern which State Department camp had the upper hand at any given moment on policy matters; on the other hand, Trujillo knew where he stood with each group and mapped strategy accordingly.

Until the massacre, Hull's approach had checked Welles's influence. If he now lost the secretary of state's patronage, Trujillo reasoned, the results might be catastrophic. Trujillo therefore read a great deal into Hull's response to El Corte. Just four days after reports of the massacre reached Washington, Hull informed Pastoriza, the Dominican legation chief, with uncharacteristic candor that he was personally disappointed in the general because he had gone to great lengths to assist Trujillo in matters of interest to the Dominican

Republic, including a recent increase in the island's sugar quota. "Imagine my disappointment," Hull told Pastoriza, "to have this matter flare up at this critical stage in world affairs."[110]

Hull also dangled the carrot of cooperating "to the very limit" on the Convention of 1924, which was particularly galling to Dominican officials because the bondholders controlled the customs houses. Violating the island's sovereignty was not the only reason they objected; the agreement also acted as a brake on the nation's export sector. Article 4 limited the Dominican state's ability to modify import duties, and that, in turn, tied the hands of negotiators willing to offer possible concessions in reciprocal treaties.[111] But Hull now let it be known if the "interests of the bondholders were respected . . . the United States would welcome the opportunity of relinquishing the obligations which it assumed under the terms of the Convention of 1924."[112] Hull, the genteel Southerner, was, with unusual frankness, linking the agreement's abrogation to the political fallout from the massacre. For someone as astute as Trujillo, this made reading tea leaves unnecessary.[113]

To combat his critics in Washington and elicit a dialogue with policymakers about the agreement, Trujillo enlisted lobbyist Joseph Davies, a key Democratic Party operative and close friend of FDR. As Davies courted Hull and congressional leaders, however, Trujillo inexplicably undercut his own lobbyist when he gave a series of incendiary speeches in the spring of 1938, threatening to unilaterally abrogate the agreement if the United States did not renegotiate in good faith. Drawing a parallel to his vicious handling of the Haitian border problem, he asserted that previous politicians had lacked the "courage" to tackle that dispute. By the same token, he warned that if negotiations with Washington on the agreement stalled, he would again take matters into his own hands. This may have played well domestically with nationalists, but it did not reassure jittery bondholders in New York or the irate State Department, which abruptly broke off negotiations.[114]

A year later, a more conciliatory Trujillo asked Roosevelt to reconsider. The Dominican Republic, he reminded FDR, had an "immaculate record" of repaying its debts, and the arrangement was "vexing and anachronistic" and could "hardly be reconciled with the new continental spirit." If a Dominican could be appointed general receiver of Dominican customs, it would lessen the perception that the nation did not control its own fiscal affairs. Momentarily putting off Trujillo, FDR responded that the idea was a good point of departure but a more general revision of the agreement was needed.[115]

Roosevelt's advisers disagreed on the wisdom of rescinding the agreement. Hull, Treasury Secretary Henry Morgenthau, and Interior Secretary Harold

Ickes all counseled FDR to settle debt issues with the Dominican Republic and other Latin American republics and to write new Export-Import Bank loans to draw these nations more tightly into the U.S. defensive orbit. Hull, in particular, contended that the agreement was anachronistic, a vestige of U.S. interventionism inconsistent with Pan Americanism and free trade.

Welles and the bondholders demurred, demanding ironclad guarantees of repayment. Welles was convinced that Trujillo was circumventing the agreement by increasing tariffs on rice, sugar, and wheat. The tariffs discouraged imports and diminished customs duties significantly.[116] The bondholders pointed out that the dictator had increased the country's debt during the 1930s, flouting a key provision of the agreement.

As the negotiations continued, Sosúa became a key component of Trujillo's strategy to repair the damage done by El Corte and wring concessions from Washington. With the benefit of hindsight, Turits has portrayed Trujillo's efforts to attract foreign immigrants to colonize the countryside as " limited measures and often superficial gestures" cynically designed to curry favor abroad. Yet if Trujillo's plans for large-scale foreign colonization ultimately were frustrated, they were inhibited by external forces beyond his control and by his subsequent disillusionment with the type of desperate immigrants his wartime schemes attracted. While Turits is correct that the numbers attracted were modest and that foreign colonies were relatively unsuccessful in comparison to the size and number of colonies the regime created with landless Dominican peasants after the Second World War, it does not follow that the regime's rationale for the Évian offer was merely a cynical ploy to bolster its international image. Sosúa was small, but it soon became a very public part of a complex calculus designed to achieve a number of interrelated goals. It was a gift that continued to pay the Benefactor handsome political dividends for the next two decades.

For the moment, though, Trujillo was buoyed by the U.S. response to his offer. It did not take Hull and Roosevelt long to forgive and forget.[117] Not surprisingly, Undersecretary Welles was not as impressed with the offer. All too familiar with the general's modus operandi, Welles initially downplayed Sosúa and instead pushed Angola as a much more desirable site for large-scale colonization.[118]

As word got out about Trujillo's offer, however, Dominican consulates throughout Europe were besieged by refugees. To cope with the flood of requests, and to ensure that the country received the type of colonists it wanted and not those with little interest in farming, Dominican authorities first had to revise the nation's open-ended immigration code.

Soon after Évian, Trujillo asked Hull to send a technical team to the island to help draft a new code that would facilitate "white" immigration while keeping out undesirables. The United States, which had the most restrictive immigration policies of any American republic, dispatched two Labor Department officials and a visa expert from the State Department to Ciudad Trujillo in the summer of 1938. Trujillo turned to the United States for assistance because U.S. policy was steeped in the purported science of eugenics. Eugenics explored "the social uses to which knowledge of heredity could be put in order to achieve the goal of 'better breeding.'"[119]

Eugenicists like Charles Benedict Davenport and Harry Laughlin of the Eugenics Record Office at the Carnegie Institution in Washington had played key roles in the passage of the National Origins Act, which limited immigration through a system of quotas based on national origin. "To set up certain standards and limitations in numbers, race, and individual quality, and, thus, establish a selective basis for admission of would-be immigrants," Laughlin contended, governments should pursue a policy of preventive eugenics to improve the nation's health by cleansing it of factors deemed damaging.[120] Code phrases such as "ethnic homogeneity," "desirable genetic endowment," and "the proper demographic mixture of high-quality immigrants" peppered subsequent immigration codes, belying their racist motivations.[121] Although some scientists (and social scientists) questioned the underlying assumptions of race theory, restrictive immigration legislation and the racialized and nativist politics behind those policies ensured that academic criticism of eugenics was muted, at best, during the interwar period.[122]

In Latin America during the 1930s, where military regimes and conservative ideologies proliferated, "constructive miscegenation" was regarded as a desideratum, since scientific racism held that white genes eventually would triumph over "weaker," darker ones.[123] Military rulers adopted tougher immigration laws to keep out undesirable elements while still permitting admission of "preferred races" of "eugenically valuable stock" believed to be more capable of assimilation. One way to ensure that specific needs were met was to write occupational restrictions into the regulations.[124]

The pseudoscientific theories in vogue at the time had worked to demean the reputation of Jews throughout the hemisphere. But to Dominican leaders, Jewish immigrants with little or no experience in farming were preferable to Haitian peasants; thus, in this unusual case, Central European Jews actually benefited from current theories of scientific racism. This is why Trujillo approached Hull several months before Évian to ask for help in rewriting its immigration law.

For nearly six months, Albert Reitzel and Leigh Nittleton from the Department of Labor and Julian Harrington from the State Department worked with a special Dominican commission charged with rewriting the immigration code. The technical mission understood its mandate; in an October 1938 memo, Harrington noted, "The primary purpose of the projected law . . . in addition to providing a scientific system of control of the entry of all aliens . . . was to facilitate 'neo-white' immigration and at the same time effectively curb the immigration of 'blacks.'"[125]

If Haitian migration was what had spurred the Dominican desire to revise the immigration code, new concerns in the fall of 1938 prompted the commission to alter its original directive. As Consul Edward Anderson recounted, in the wake of Kristallnacht came fears that the island would be "overrun with Jews, who being predominantly tradesmen and shopkeepers would disrupt the national economy." New racial laws in Germany and Italy had triggered an exodus of refugees and driven up visa applications, swamping Dominican consulates in Europe and the United States. The commission was concerned that these refugees would become public charges or generate unwanted competition for local merchants and businesses.[126]

Since existing law stipulated that white settlement was free and unlimited, the Dominican consulates in Europe had issued visas for between 150 and 160 Jewish families in the months leading up to the Évian conference. Foreign Minister Arturo Despradel told an American visitor interested in promoting refugee resettlement, "for some unknown reason, these people did not scatter throughout the Republic, or devote themselves immediately to some trade, business or agriculture, but they remained in or about Ciudad Trujillo . . . without producing anything, and causing strong popular resentment." Within months, however, Viennese bakeries, photography studios, and other small shops and businesses had sprung up. Although, Anderson said, "there is no Jewish problem in this country and up to the present time there has been no religious or racial prejudice . . . the situation was considered serious enough by the powers-that-be" that regulations had to be adjusted to cope with an anticipated increase in applications after Trujillo's immigration offer.[127]

Before the code could be rewritten, the Foreign Ministry took steps to curb the indiscriminate flow of Jewish immigrants. It instructed its European consuls in the fall of 1938 that future visas would be issued only with prior authorization and that consuls were "not to issue visas to refugees holding passports . . . [who] had no citizenship or nationality." Applicants without citizenship or nationality were predominantly German or Austrian Jews, since German authorities had issued them special passports which stipulated that the bearers were not German citizens or nationals. That measure was adopted to avoid having to take back refugees if they were deported from the countries to which they migrated. The Foreign Ministry edict also shut down Jewish immigration for asylum purposes; only twenty out of two thousand visa applications were approved in the first four months after Évian. Consistent with its pronouncements at the conference, the state was solely interested in refugees committed to "productive" (that is, agricultural) occupations.[128]

The technical mission drafted a series of new regulations, which, in the words of the secretary of the interior, would encourage "large scale immigration of acceptable, healthy, vigorous, hardworking, intelligent, well-mannered individuals of the *white race* who want to stay here permanently and are interested in agriculture, industry, or the arts" (emphasis added).[129] The Interior Ministry's 1939 annual report called these new laws "indispensable" to the national interest and boasted that they "took into account the nation's racial, economic and political needs."[130]

The centerpiece of the new legislation, Law 95, approved on April 14, 1939 by the Dominican Congress, provided for "different fees for those of a different race, place of origin, nationality or aptitude for providing and fulfilling the needs of the Republic." Several of its articles tightened entrance requirements for and improved oversight of seasonal migrants (that is, Haitians and other nonwhites from other Caribbean islands) working in the sugar industry. The law also addressed the flood of applications (the director of immigration estimated six thousand from Germany alone) from refugees "who leave their countries of origin with no resources and are driven out in a veritable exodus by the weight of racial laws that annul their rights as citizens."[131]

Article 9b of the new code addressed the concern about Jewish immigrants becoming public charges by requiring members of the "Semitic race" to pay a five-hundred-dollar residency fee. The new law's intent, the Interior Ministry's annual report concluded, was to select "assimilatable ethnic elements, adaptable to agriculture, without diluting the nation's racial stock."[132] Consul Anderson thought the new law would have the desired effect of deterring Jews from coming to the island and then applying for visas to the United States.[133] Dominican officials were pleased that the new fees yielded twenty thousand dollars in revenues, which then were applied to the indemnity it owed the Haitian government for the massacre.[134]

For eighteen months after the code was rewritten, Trujillo tried to make the most of the positive press he received. Although his objectives were quite transparent, the U.S. government initially was ambivalent about the Dominican offer. While harboring hopes that it would encourage other nations to step forward and take in refugees, FDR pressed his aides to come up with more viable solutions as soon as possible. To understand how the Dominican Republic became the Roosevelt administration's last best option, we must become familiar with the pressures brought to bear on the White House on the eve of the Second World War.

Think Big

> We have been working, up to now, on too small a scale, and we
> have failed to apply modern engineering to our task. We know
> already that there are many comparatively vacant spaces on the
> earth's surface where from the point of view of climate and natural
> resources European settlers can live permanently.
>
> FDR, 1939

FDR had hoped that Évian would make the refugees an international humanitarian concern. Instead, procrastination ensued,
and events soon forced the president's hand. Less than three months
after the conference, Hitler's incursions into the Sudetenland and the
subsequent Munich agreement sent 20,000 more Jews into exile. That
was just the tip of the iceberg, relief agencies warned, because Czechoslovakia's 350,000 Jews were poised to follow, if and when what was
left of the Czech state fell into German hands.[1]

Then, on November 7, 1938, a 17-year-old Polish Jew living in
Paris, Herschel Grynszpan, shot the third secretary of the German
embassy. The diplomat's death two days later touched off Kristallnacht, a pogrom that left 91 German Jews dead, more than 7,000 Jewish businesses looted, and 267 synagogues burned.[2] Thirty thousand
male Jews were arrested and sent to concentration camps, including
several men who eventually came to Sosúa.[3] Less than a month later,
German authorities "Aryanized" all remaining Jewish property, forced
Jewish organizations to disband, and required Jews to deposit all their
securities, jewels, and art in designated banks.[4]

The Reich Central Office for Jewish Emigration was established to
encourage emigration of Jews "by every possible means." As Gestapo

raids and arrests continued, droves of Jews headed for countries of transit. Almost half of the total Jewish emigration from Germany and Austria took place over the next twelve months.[5] Neighboring countries sent some refugees back, but that was a trickle compared to the numbers pouring in without proper documentation.

Roosevelt criticized the persecution, and extended the visitors' visas of more than 12,000 German Jewish refugees already in the United States for another six months. FDR and his advisers faced not only the immediate problem of what to do with the 200,000 to 300,000 refugees harbored temporarily in countries of transit but the potentially catastrophic problem of how to cope with the millions in Eastern Europe if and when war broke out. He had few good options. Americans shared the president's outrage over Kristallnacht but still opposed liberalizing the quotas. Even so, the administration never contemplated a policy change, because the numbers were so daunting. Moreover, Roosevelt's advisers believed that congressional opposition to increasing the quotas would only delay more comprehensive solutions.[6]

The British were increasingly uncooperative. Under pressure from Arab allies to curtail Jewish immigration to Palestine, where the Jewish population had grown from 60,000 to 416,000 since the end of World War I, they issued a White Paper on May 17, 1939, which announced that separate Jewish and Arab states in Palestine were impractical; that within ten years, Britain intended to relinquish its mandate over Palestine to the Arabs; and that over the next five years, Britain would reduce the flow of refugees to Palestine to 75,000. After 1944, further Jewish emigration "would be subject to Arab consent"—a euphemism for an end to the Zionist experiment.[7] This announcement also took Palestine off the table as an option for refugees in the short run. Perhaps the only silver lining was that it actually united quarreling Zionists and Non-Zionists, who vowed to work more closely to keep Palestine open as a viable destination.[8]

According to one estimate, as of May 1939, more than four hundred thousand Jewish refugees had left Germany, Austria, and the Sudetenland. As table 1 indicates, that number was about equally divided in destination between sites of temporary refuge and permanent settlement.

The panic emigration forced refugees to use whatever means they could to make their escape. Forged papers, bribes, and blackmail reached epidemic proportions.[9] Some people bribed German peasants to sign certificates attesting to their qualifications as farmers so they would qualify for visas. Opportunistic Latin American consuls in cahoots with shady middlemen gouged refugees "for documents that usually turned out to be invalid."[10] Brazil

TABLE 1 *Estimates of Jewish Refugees from Germany, Austria, and the Sudetenland to Countries of Immigration and Refuge, May 1939*

Countries of Immigration	Number of Persons	Countries of Refuge	Numbers of Persons
USA	63,000	United Kingdom	40,000
Palestine	55,000	France	30,000
Argentina	25,000	Poland	25,000
Brazil	13,000	Czechoslovakia	25,000
Bolivia	7,000	Netherlands	22,000
Chile	6,000	Belgium	20,000
Uruguay	5,000	Switzerland	11,000
Ecuador	1,000	Italy	5,000
Colombia	1,000	Denmark, Norway	3,000
Cuba	500	Sweden	2,000
Union of South Africa	5,500	Other European countries	9,000
Australia and New Zealand	4,500	Far East	15,000
Other overseas countries	7,500		
Total	194,000	Total	207,000

Source: Vernant, *The Refugee in the Postwar World*, 60

permitted entry to those who owned real estate, which led to a thriving trade in land titles. Since some Latin American countries were more willing to take in Catholics, baptism certificates sold briskly.[11]

In addition to this thriving black market in documentation, the illegal shipment of refugees to Palestine and other clandestine sites enabled shipping companies to turn a healthy profit. Contemporaries compared the human trafficking, often under appalling conditions, to the Atlantic slave trade. "Errant vessels," as they came to be called, were shunted from port to port, in search of a nation that would waive its regulations.[12]

One of the most tragic examples was the harrowing odyssey of the ss *St. Louis*. This ship left Europe for Havana in May 1939, despite having received IGC notification that the Cuban government had nullified the landing permits of the 937 refugees (most of them Jews) on board. The Hamburg-Amerika Steamship Line was under intense pressure from the Gestapo, which wanted to provoke an anti-Semitic backlash in Cuba and throughout the Western Hemisphere.

Intimately involved in discussions with Cuban authorities was the JDC's James Rosenberg, who soon would be negotiating with Trujillo about the Sosúa initative. When Cuban officials ratcheted up their financial demands for admitting the passengers, Rosenberg agreed to half a million dollars, against the advice of his colleagues, who thought such a ransom would encourage similar gambits. But the Cubans changed their minds and refused the ship anyway, perhaps spurred by xenophobic street demonstrations in Havana instigated by the Cuban Nazi Party, and pressure from the State Department, which feared that these passengers would later reach the United States and set a precedent.[13]

For about a week the *St. Louis* drifted between the Florida Keys and Havana. Unwilling to take in the passengers, Roosevelt dispatched the Coast Guard to make sure that none swam ashore.[14] Newspaper reports that Trujillo was willing to admit the refugees proved incorrect. The JDC and other relief agencies finally "persuaded" England, France, Holland, and Belgium, at a cost of five hundred thousand dollars, to accept the wanderers.[15]

After that debacle, a hypocritical administration had the temerity to pressure Latin American governments to admit "involuntary emigrants," but was rebuffed by every one.[16] Most Latin American republics had closed their borders by early 1939; in May and June alone, Chile, Cuba, Argentina, Mexico, and Costa Rica barred entry to Jewish refugees.[17]

If governments were reluctant to think creatively, refugee organizations, the groups most likely to press for a timely solution, wrestled with the stark implications of subsidizing ever larger numbers of immigrants. The Joint's leadership struggled with the question of whether to cooperate with the Nazis. Rosenberg worried that if the Joint and German authorities participated in any scheme to evict Jews from Germany, the Polish and Romanian governments soon would follow suit and expel their minorities. In an internal memo, Rosenberg callously played devil's advocate: " there is a notion that American Jewry can meet all sorts of emergencies . . . [but] after all we are in a world war and there are times when you have to sacrifice some of your troops. And these unfortunates are some of our troops."[18] Others echoed Rosenberg's tough talk, but the Joint ultimately disregarded his advice. Such posturing, meant only for internal consumption, illustrated the lesser-of-two-evils choice relief agencies faced.[19]

Staring down the Americans and the British was Hitler, who, even as he excoriated the Jews, sought to shift the responsibility for resettlement to the West. "The world has sufficient space for settlements, but we must once and for all rid ourselves of the opinion that the Jewish race was created by God only for the purpose of being . . . a parasite and feeding on the body and productive work of other nations."[20] Tension escalated after Hitler delivered a frighteningly prophetic address to the Reichstag on the sixth anniversary of his coming to power, January 30, 1939. He reminded Germans that he had promised to "settle the Jewish problem" once and for all before he came to power. Then he added, "Today I will once more be a prophet: if the international Jewish financiers in and outside Europe should succeed in plunging the nations once more into a world war, then the result will not be the bolshevization of the earth, and thus the victory of Jewry, but the annihilation of the Jewish race in Europe."[21]

In the face of such threats, FDR needed alternatives. Treasury Secretary Morgenthau floated an ambitious plan to offer loans to Latin American governments in return for taking in refugees and urged Roosevelt to fill the German quota for the next five years immediately, thereby letting in 135,000 without delay. They were to be housed in former Civilian Conservation Corps and Army camps with a government-run corporation administering the specially designed communities. But Morgenthau's price tag for the loans and the costs of interning the refugees came to half a million dollars, and that estimate was enough to quash the imaginative idea.[22]

Roosevelt also weighed various schemes the Nazis had proposed to the IGC. Negotiations centered on which and how many assets refugees would be permitted to take with them when they left. The president coaxed George Rublee, a corporate lawyer with considerable experience in international affairs, out of retirement to serve as the IGC's director. Rublee wrote Cordell Hull in November 1938 that the situation in Germany was getting progressively worse: "new laws and decrees are going into effect each week which render the position of the involuntary emigrant more difficult. . . . New places of settlement have not been opened up . . . the only constructive indication I have received is that some of the governments of the countries of settlement might be willing to reconsider the situation should I be successful in persuading the German Government to permit the involuntary emigrants to leave with a substantial amount of property."[23] No country would accept these involuntary emigrants without money, but the German government wanted to make it as difficult as possible for those leaving to take their wealth with them. German negotiators also insisted that any agreement on emigration had to be linked to an increase in exports to offset the overvaluation of the Reichsmark and the growing impact of an international boycott of German goods.

In late 1938 Rublee and German officials hammered out a tentative, complex compromise, which would have forced German Jews to relinquish most of their assets. The monies then were to be put into a trust fund, and an out-side agency, composed of representatives of "international Jewry," would purchase goods from the Nazis. The profits realized from these transactions could then be used for resettlement. Sumner Welles admitted to Roosevelt that this plan was "better than we had hoped for."[24]

But to some American Jewish leaders, the scheme smacked of extortion. Rabbi Stephen Wise believed that the Germans had duped Rublee, conclud-ing that "he is so bent upon doing something for the refugees that he may be misled . . . into doing things that would mean the beginning of an epoch of extortion and blackmail against Jews everywhere."[25]

Roosevelt initially agreed with Wise, dismissing the plan as "asking the world to pay a ransom for the release of hostages in Germany and barter hu-man misery for increased exports." Negotiations dragged on between the IGC and the Germans until February 1939, when Rublee, who doubted that his own government or Great Britain was really serious about reaching an agree-ment, resigned in exasperation.[26] Still, Roosevelt was reluctant to walk away from the bargaining table. He urged Wise and Paul Baerwald to create a clear-inghouse to coordinate the work of the many relief agencies and to continue negotiating with German authorities. The Coordinating Foundation was cre-ated on April 15, 1939, with the JDC contributing a million dollars.[27]

Some Jewish groups viewed the foundation's negotiations with the Nazis as a betrayal of their boycott and noisily refused to participate. Even Rosenberg was not optimistic; he told a group of Jewish leaders, "I have no faith what-ever that the Foundation will . . . accomplish anything . . . because it cannot do anything because the governments of (the countries of) emigration and immigration make it impossible."[28] But the Joint was unwilling to alienate Roosevelt. Baerwald met with German leaders in early June 1939 to salvage the negotiations, but the talks went nowhere.[29]

Even before these discouraging events, Roosevelt had begun to think along more imaginative lines.[30] He had met with aides in November 1938 and asked Welles to forward him any information on potential sites for Jewish coloniza-tion anywhere in the world. Then he brought in Isaiah Bowman, president of Johns Hopkins University and also a geographer and noted colonization expert, to advise him on resettlement.

Bowman's approach was rational, orderly, and scientific: "The whole enter-prise ought to be conceived not as an emergency measure for a population in flight but as a broad scientific undertaking, humanitarian in purpose, orderly in its functioning, hopeful in its outlook, and essentially serving the self-interest of those who receive populations." Bowman viewed the refugees as aspiring entrepreneurs, who, if provided with sufficient capitalization, would galvanize production in the tropics.[31]

Unfortunately, Bowman also was an inveterate anti-Semite. At Hopkins, he had overruled a unanimous vote from the History Department and refused to award tenure to a Jewish historian, informing the faculty that there were "already too many Jews at Hopkins." In 1942 Bowman implemented a Jewish quota in the faculty because, as he told his dean, "We're becoming a practically Jewish organization." It is unclear whether Roosevelt was aware of Bowman's anti-Semitism when he appointed him, but it is more than ironic that a man of such strong prejudice became FDR's chief adviser on Jewish resettlement.[32]

Roosevelt asked Bowman to think globally. He was to look into possible sites in Venezuela or Colombia that might sustain anywhere from fifty thousand to one hundred thousand settlers. Bowman replied that "Northern South America offers no place for colonization, on a large scale," but suggested that other sites in South America might. FDR pushed him about a possible large site in Costa Rica, which Bowman initially had identified as promising, but Bowman had a change of heart, citing "political difficulties which a large foreign immigrant group would create if planted in this small Latin American country."[33]

Undeterred, FDR asked Bowman for a more systematic study, including the possible purchase of a homeland or protectorate for the Jewish people, enough land to meet the needs of five million refugees. Morgenthau was asked to prepare a list of the thousand richest Jews in the United States to finance what was termed the Roosevelt Plan. Along these lines, presidential adviser Bernard Baruch had proposed a refugee commonwealth in Africa—a United States of Africa, which he envisaged as a British protectorate stretching across a swath of British, French, Belgian, and Portuguese colonies.[34] But Bowman was cool to Baruch's ambitious idea; refugees, he believed, should be distributed in small groups at multiple locations rather than at one site. Instead, his lieutenants at Johns Hopkins issued 93 reports that assessed potential sites for resettlement on five continents.[35]

Roosevelt also received advice from the President's Advisory Committee on Political Refugees (PACPR), an interfaith task force he had created just before Évian. Composed of Catholic, Protestant, and Jewish leaders, including Wise and Baerwald, and the former League of Nations High Commissioner for Refugees, James McDonald, the task force served as a broker between the administration, the IGC, and private relief agencies. Emblematic of FDR's handling of the refugee crisis, the PACPR was rarely consulted; and it received its funding from interfaith organizations, not government sources.

But Roosevelt did agree to a PACPR request in the fall of 1938 to prod the IGC to pursue Trujillo's offer. Over the next two years, the IGC and the PACPR also investigated sites in British Guiana, the Philippines, Colombia, Venezuela, Mexico, and several states in Africa.[36] The problem was that each site posed its own idiosyncratic challenges. The PACPR secretary, George Warren, told Hull that colonization was best pursued through quiet negotiations on a case-by-case basis so that "involuntary emigrants" would "prove to be assets instead of liabilities to the countries admitting them."[37]

Whether it was even advisable to pursue large-scale immigration to warmer climes, however, was an unsettled question in the experts' minds. Scholars disagreed on whether white settlers could prosper in the tropics.

DEBATING THE MERITS OF TROPICAL COLONIZATION

Were European refugees capable of "tropical pioneering?" For more than a century, geographers, anthropologists, biologists, and colonization experts had been debating the finer points of "acclimatization," or anthropoclimatology, the study of the relationship between climate and humans. Scholars agreed that races, like animal species, were distinctive and best suited to certain regions and that climate acted as a control on migration, settlement, and "the habitability of regions."[38] But some groups were believed to stand a better chance of prospering than others. Those with "darker" complexions from Mediterranean Europe were considered more adaptable than fairer-skinned northern Europeans, while female settlers and children were thought to have greater problems adjusting than males. Lower fertility rates among white women, physicians believed, needed to be offset by periodic infusions of new pioneers if colonization was to succeed.

It is interesting that the Jewish "race" was thought to be the most malleable. One early proponent of acclimatization pointed to "Jews as a paradigmatic case, having scattered across the face of the earth, they had undergone physiological changes that suited them to the new climates within which they found themselves."[39] As late as 1939, an anthropologist contended that Jews, whether Ashkenazic, Sephardic, or Oriental, were chameleonlike; wherever they settled, they assumed "to a considerable extent, but not completely, the racial character of the Gentile population of that area."[40]

While scientists agreed that advances in hygiene and medical science made it possible for the white race to make the best of inhospitable environments, opinion differed on just how adaptable they were. "Quinine, kerosene and mosquito netting have accomplished wonders," Andrew Balfour, director of the London School of Hygiene and Tropical Medicine, admitted, but "so far as the [white] race is concerned . . . the hot and humid tropics are not suited to white colonization and never will be . . . even if they were rendered as free from disease as England."[41]

Balfour belonged to a school of thought that compared whites in the tropics to "a wilting plant that has been carried beyond its natural habitat."[42] Harvard climatologist Robert De Courcy Ward preferred the metaphor of settlers fighting a drawn-out but ultimately futile campaign against their tropical opponent. Medical breakthroughs in the treatment of yellow fever, hookworm, malaria, and dysentery and proper attention to sanitation may have cut mortality rates and lessened the incidence of disease, but "it is absurd to say that a reduced death rate, directly due to the careful avoidance of every possible exposure, is an evidence that such exposure can be endured." Even those who did not succumb to disease "become wrecks of their former selves and are unable to carry on." Caucasians could not reproduce over successive generations "their kind without physical, mental and moral degeneration." Like Balfour, Ward concluded that tropical colonization was "impossible."[43]

The Yale geographer Ellsworth Huntington was of like mind: "tropical inertia" afflicted settlers. "Man appears to be handicapped by a definite lowering not only of his physical energy, but of his mental activity and moral vigor" and, as a result, resistance to disease was diminished.[44] Whites were believed to be especially susceptible to nervous system disorders, such as insomnia, irritability, chronic fatigue, and nervous exhaustion, or neurasthenia. The latter ailment lessened energy levels, lowered vitality, diminished the capacity to fight off disease, and led to depression, a medical authority opined.[45]

The tropics also were thought to bring out temperate man's most lascivious and debased urges. As Ward related, "Life in the tropics, away from home associations and traditions and standards, is extremely likely to lead to the excessive use of intoxicating liquor, to lowered moral tone, to sexual indulgence, to a distaste for and avoidance of reasonable physical exercise; to any incorrect and poorly-balanced diet."[46] Physicians counseled settlers to eat lightly, drink in moderation, and keep out of the sun as much as possible. To repair the degeneration caused by exposure to such an alien environment, it was recommended that settlers take an extended vacation to temperate regions or higher elevations every two years.[47]

Other experts countered that colonization was inevitable because the white race was inherently "aggressive and migratory"; and though some loss of life was to be expected, Caucasians could survive in the tropics, but "only as a master race." Manual labor was best left to the natives.[48] Moreover, pioneers should choose their destinations wisely, since tropical colonies were not all the same; established, well-administered colonies enjoyed a better track record of containing diseases than newer colonies.[49]

According to advocates of tropical pioneering like the Joint's Joseph Rosen, the key to success was for settlers to remain active. A bias against manual labor, he contended, was a self-fulfilling prophecy. If settlers did not perform "at least the major part of the necessary work themselves, the whole enterprise would be fraught with dangers; an economy based on the exploitation of local colored labor is bound, sooner or later, to lead to serious complications." If colonists altered their working habits and diet and took special sanitary precautions, they had "a reasonable chance of adaptation to the climatic conditions."[50] Critics, of course, countered that self-serving colonization experts like Rosen simply ignored the "scientific" research.[51]

Refugees carried additional baggage that inhibited their adaptation to new surroundings. Whereas immigrants generally came with capital, farming experience, and the option of returning home, refugees seldom brought money with them, had little or no experience on the land, and were reliant on the generosity of relief agencies. They also bore the scars of being permanently uprooted from their homeland. Relief organizations, furthermore, did not have the luxury of identifying prospective pioneers with the requisite skills and motivation.[52] An expert on refugee resettlement, Desmond Holdridge, published a report for the PACPR titled "Can Refugee Colonies Succeed in South America?" which warned that if European settlers were sent to the countryside they would eventually slip away to urban areas and offer "strong competition to the very people who constitute the greater portion of the ruling classes of South America."[53]

The debate swirling around tropical pioneering was not just an academic exercise. It played itself out as various sites came under consideration by politicians looking for a solution to the refugee problem. Invariably, scientific (and pseudoscientific) findings ran headlong into the political realities of the moment.

THE POLITICS OF RESETTLEMENT

Given the paucity of options and the pressures brought to bear by international public opinion, Western governments had to weigh the risks when considering specific sites. One place that drew considerable attention was the French colony of Madagascar. The German and Polish governments originally proposed this island in the Indian Ocean southeast of Africa as a possible site. Anxious to appease Hitler, the French and the British took up the matter. Indeed, the notion of using Madagascar as a dumping ground for forlorn refugees became synonymous with Western nations' deflecting attention away from their own possessions.

A year before Évian, the French Colonial Office approached Rosen and the JDC to gauge their interest in settling Jews on the island. The Joint gave Rosen twelve thousand dollars to form a committee to study the matter, but that is as far as the idea went; he never visited the island. The British colonial secretary asked the French foreign minister to reconsider the island in April 1938 because "no one wants these wretched hunted people, and Madagascar seems to me a chance."[54] It was revived again as a possible option after Kristallnacht, when France announced at the December 1938 IGC meeting that it was prepared to move ten thousand of its non-German refugees to Madagascar and New Caledonia and to absorb a similar number of German refugees who "had crossed the frontier illegally and were now lodged in various jails." But the offer was only on the condition that "other participating governments" did the same. No nation stepped forward to match the French offer.[55]

Still, there was pressure to respond in some meaningful way after Kristallnacht. Prime Minister Neville Chamberlain, speaking before the House of Commons on November 21, 1938, stopped short of a substantive commitment but agreed to sponsor an investigation into resettlement in British Guiana and Tanganyika.[56] In February 1939, the PACPR asked Rosen to serve on an Anglo-American commission to consider a ten-thousand-square-mile tract for colonization in British Guiana.[57] The British Guiana Survey Commission's eventual report, which raised all the predictable concerns about unfavorable climate and health risks, inferior soils, and lack of infrastructure, recommended a pilot program because "immediate large scale settlement is neither possible nor advisable under present conditions in British Guiana."[58] Asked to weigh in after the commission released its findings, Bowman threw cold water on the idea and advised that money would be better spent elsewhere.[59]

Cynics were quick to point out that the commission's report was released, coincidentally, on the same day as the White Paper to deflect attention from the curtailment of immigration to Palestine. Despite some misgivings, in the spring of 1939 the PACPR and IGC recommended the establishment of an experimental settlement of five hundred pioneers in British Guiana. Relief agencies agreed to raise three million dollars. The British Foreign Office was delighted to announce even this meager news. Yet by summer, the foreign secretary, Lord Winterton, was backpedaling on the plan, and when war broke out in September 1939, the British, concerned about German nationals infiltrating their colonies, quickly killed the project.[60]

Not all potential sites were located in the tropics. In late 1939, FDR's aides considered an Alaskan resettlement plan. Surveys indicated that the territory could support at least 12 million immigrants. Proponents argued that properly financed immigration would combat a number of problems affecting Alaskan development: a transient working population, absentee ownership, and winter idleness. Furthermore, the Army and Navy believed that a larger population in Alaska would bolster national defense. Jewish leaders, however, were reluctant to embrace the idea. Wise wrote the U.S. Supreme Court Chief Justice Felix Frankfurter, "It makes a wrong and hurtful impression to have it appear that Jews are taking over some part of the country for settlement."[61]

A proposed Alaskan Colonization Act would have settled ten thousand refugees a year over a five-year period, but Roosevelt, fearful of a political backlash, insisted that this colony would not be solely for Jewish refugees.[62] Public opposition to the bill was, as expected, vocal, as opponents argued that the Alaskan territory was a backdoor entrance into the continental forty-eight states. Neither Welles nor Hull thought much of the idea. Seeing the handwriting on the wall, FDR lost whatever initial enthusiasm he had had, and the bill died quietly in subcommittee.[63]

Large-scale resettlement plans in general also were unpopular with Jewish leaders. Suspicious of any proposal that deflected attention from Palestine, Zionists like Morris Rose, president of the New Zionist Organization of America, voiced their opposition to FDR: "A particularly distressing sign of the times is the manner in which projects have been recently formulated with a view to corral the Jewish people in reservations . . . the Jews are no longer treated as a people to be saved, but as a group of pariahs to be sent where ever they can best serve other people's interests. . . . While the obstacles are too great for any of these projects to materialize to any appreciable extent, the very fact that they are looked upon without horror and are even seriously discussed by decent-minded men and nations indicates to what terrific depth of degradation the Jew has fallen in the eyes of the world."[64]

The president, however, remained taken with these schemes; the grander the vision, the greater his interest.[65] He had even secretly corresponded with Mussolini in late 1938, probing the dictator about resettling refugees in the southern part of Italian-occupied Ethiopia.[66] Historians, critical of FDR's vacillating position during the refugee crisis, have condemned his support for massive resettlement plans as so much political expedience. Feingold contends that FDR's passion for an initiative increased in direct proportion to the distance the projected havens were from the Western Hemisphere."[67]

Even though progress proved elusive, FDR could not be dissuaded from thinking ambitiously. In December 1939 he asked Welles to tell Paul Van Zeeland, the head of the Coordinating Foundation, that it should think big, because something was needed to "stimulate the imagination of potential contributors." Such schemes, in Roosevelt's view, had to "appeal to the idealism of the contributing public." He envisioned "one or two large-scale settlements, measured in terms of a million square miles and millions in population, where the refugees might found a coordinated, self-sustaining civilization—some people on individual farms, others nearby in small villages, still others devoting themselves to public works, still others in small manufacturing communities, all contributing to a huge, rounded-out project planned on an enormous scale."[68]

With doors closing all over the world and with the British digging in their heels in Palestine, the only possibility was a Jewish homeland. Influenced by Bowman, Welles became a strong proponent of a plan to resettle Jewish refugees in the Portuguese colony of Angola.[69] Both Welles and Roosevelt asked Myron Taylor to discuss the idea with the Portuguese prime minister. Portugal would receive a tidy sum in compensation, an amount that dwarfed what it "has ever gotten out of Angola."[70] But the prime minister refused even to consider the proposal.

Why did Welles prefer Angola over the Dominican Republic? He believed it offered the prospect of a permanent homeland for all of Europe's Jews. In a painfully frank letter to Taylor, he admitted that despite all the efforts at Évian to limit the scope of the problem to those lodged in countries of transit, "the fact must be faced that there exists in Central and Eastern Europe a racial and religious group of some seven million persons for whom the economic and social future is exceedingly dark." In a particularly pessimistic passage, Welles admitted the enormity of the challenge: "While the Intergovernmental Committee has wisely treated the German refugee problem as being one of involuntary emigration regardless of race, creed or political belief, it must be frankly recognized that the larger Eastern European problem is basically a Jewish problem. Acute as the German problem is, it is, I fear, only a precursor of what may be expected if the larger problem is not met before it reaches an acute stage, and indications are rapidly increasing that such a stage may be reached in the near future. The increasing seriousness of the problem may shortly make the political difficulties in finding a solution appear trivial in comparison."[71] An orderly yearly emigration from Europe of 160,000 "young persons of employable and marriageable age" was needed. The only lasting solution was a Jewish homeland "capable of absorbing substantially unlimited Jewish immigration."[72]

The Dominican Republic also was distasteful to Welles because it meant working with Trujillo. But as locations for resettlement were proposed and scuttled in dizzying fashion, Trujillo's offer, which initially had been received coolly and had been thought of as nothing more than a stopgap measure, garnered more attention.

While FDR and his advisors struggled to find a solution with international governments, the PACPR, working through the Refugee Economic Corporation, a U.S.-based relief agency, sent Alfred Houston, an attorney, to the Dominican Republic to explore the prospects for colonization.[73] Carrying a letter of introduction from Welles and a memorandum, "Plan for the Settlement of Political Refugees in Santo Domingo," Houston met with Trujillo, President Jacinto Peynado, and Foreign Minister Arturo Despradel.[74] Despradel told Houston that his government wanted immigrants who devoted themselves to agriculture and was happy to accept either Jews or Christians, but "will not accept, under any circumstances, men of black or yellow races."[75]

Houston's memorandum stipulated that the government should make suitable lands available for purchase by a settlement association. Once an understanding had been reached, the PACPR would contract with scientific experts to conduct preliminary surveys of possible sites. Funding for the undertaking would come from abroad, and the immigrants would acquire Dominican citizenship.[76]

When Houston informed Trujillo that he was having a difficult time arranging an appointment with Peynado, Trujillo suggested they walk over to the president's office together. Houston handed Peynado the memorandum, but Trujillo interrupted before Peynado had had a chance to read it and informed him that he had read the proposal and discussed it fully with Houston, and "was entirely in accord with the plan." To which the puppet president was said to have succinctly replied: "That is the opinion of our country."[77]

Chargé d'Affaires Eugene Hinkle reported to Welles about Houston's trip, noting that the initiative suited Trujillo's needs to a tee. "The Dominicans consider themselves lucky to be able to get much desired white immigrants and to have somebody else do the financing." Hinkle felt certain Trujillo was likely to use this "humanitarian" gesture to extract some quid pro quo from

Washington. "The Dominicans will undoubtedly be out for their pound of flesh and it will most likely require considerable maneuvering to keep this down to a reasonable amount."[78]

Houston also seemed certain that Trujillo would demand his "pound of flesh,"[79] but nevertheless filed an optimistic report with the PACPR about the prospects for success. He also briefed Hull, who thought Trujillo's offer of one hundred thousand immigrants unrealistic, but was intrigued enough to write Rublee that "an opportunity for the settlement of large numbers apparently does exist."[80]

The PACPR asked Bowman to assemble a team of specialists to investigate properties on the island. Accompanied by Houston in April 1939, three Department of Agriculture specialists in crops, soils, and forests and a tropical public health expert from Puerto Rico spent six weeks exploring a dozen sites.[81] It is interesting that half the properties were owned by Trujillo. While some were clearly unsuitable, others, the team believed, could sustain up to 28,500 immigrant families. The specialists recommended a modest pilot project with additional settlers to be added as feasible.[82] Trujillo was reportedly miffed by the team's measured assessment.[83]

Clearly, this was not the quick fix sought by refugee advocates and FDR; but given the circumstances, the report was interpreted as a green light to move ahead. Robert Pell compared the scheme to a laboratory experiment, "perhaps the only test tube which we have in this hemisphere at this time for studying the ways and means of arriving at the right way of life and relieving the frightful pressure resulting from a sick Europe. Like any scientific experiment, it must be approached with great care. Each move must be carefully weighed in the laboratory."[84]

The next step for this test tube was to find a private agency that would start the settlement project in motion—secure financing, hash out the contractual details with authorities, select a site, choose the settlers. The agency the IGC and the PACPR chose to work with was an old hand at colonization projects. To understand why they selected the Joint Distribution Committee and what motivated its administrators, it is necessary to follow the circuitous route that led the philanthropy to the Dominican Republic. The JDC's past struggles and accomplishments would shape its expectations for Sosúa, and will help explain why these Good Samaritans were willing to do Trujillo's and Roosevelt's bidding.

There were, however, tremendous demands on JDC resources, and taking on another project was by no means a given. By 1938 and 1939, getting Jews out of Europe had become an all-consuming affair. Executive Director Joseph

Hyman later recalled that his office was inundated with requests, "all desperate, all talking about the same dire consequences."[85] Moreover, justifiable concerns were expressed about the feasibility and cost-effectiveness of initiating a small settlement in the tropics while chaos and anarchy ruled in Europe and war was imminent. After contentious discussions, the JDC's Executive Committee agreed to move forward. One of the reasons board members assented was the conclusion that they had precisely the right vehicle to manage the project.

THREE

Jewish Farmers

> The city Jew, nervous, impatient, fidgety, restless and eager. Little
> by little he learns to adjust himself to the even disposition of the
> animal, learns something of the value of slow, steady, deliberate,
> patient work. He can't hurry his ox, his crops, the sunshine, spring-
> time. He becomes a part of the deep current of Nature. Thank God.
> JAMES ROSENBERG, 1927

Years later, Rosenberg recalled Myron Taylor urging Paul Baerwald, "Here is this one little country which is willing to open its
doors to the refugees. You have to do something!" That is how Sosúa
was "wished on Rosen and me."[1] Taylor went to the Joint because of
its proven track record in resettlement, and Baerwald knew exactly
where to turn; the sixty-four-year-old Rosenberg and the fifty-one-
year-old Joseph Rosen each had fourteen years of experience with
colonization in the Soviet Union.

From 1924 to 1938, Rosenberg and Rosen participated in an unprecedented experiment to move upwards of 150,000 Jews, who had
never set foot on a farm, from the cities and towns of western Russia
to the rolling plains of the northern Crimea and the southern Ukraine.
The Soviet government set aside nearly two million acres of land, and
the JDC invested the extraordinary sum of seventeen million dollars
in this unique collaborative project.[2]

Rosenberg and Rosen persevered despite opposition at home
and abroad. Two dissimilar individuals hailing from very different
worlds—one, an idealistic New York corporate lawyer with his head
in the clouds, the other, a pragmatic Russian agronomist with his feet
firmly planted in the fertile soil of socialist agrarianism—forged an

unlikely partnership that made it possible for persecuted Jews in Russia and later in the Dominican Republic to build new lives for themselves and their families on the land.

COLONIZATION AS PANACEA

James Rosenberg was the grandson of a German rabbi who had immigrated to Pittsburgh after 1848. As a youngster, he moved with his family to New York City, where his parents enrolled him in classes at the Society for Ethical Culture, an offshoot of Temple Emanu-El in midtown Manhattan. This progressive organization had been founded in 1876 by Dr. Felix Adler to promote the advancement of social justice.

Rabbi Adler called on Jews to shed "the narrow spirit of exclusion" and to follow Immanuel Kant's "categorical imperative" to treat human beings as an end and not as a means. In Sunday morning meetings where no prayers were said or religious services performed, Adler attempted to arouse "the conscience of the wealthy, the advantaged, the educated classes." There Rosenberg and the four hundred other Ethical Culture members learned the value of "the universal pursuit of individual moral perfection" by serving the common good. Adler's motto, "Not by the Creed but by the Deed," melded longstanding traditions of Jewish self-help and humanitarianism with Progressive Era reform. Secular German Jews, uncomfortable with the practices of Judaism and intent on assimilating American values, educated themselves about urban problems, such as immigration, public health, sweatshops, and tenement housing, by listening to Sunday morning lectures by reformers like Eugene V. Debs, Samuel Gompers, Booker T. Washington, and W. E. B. Du Bois.[3] The society's leadership helped found the National Association for the Advancement of Colored People and the American Civil Liberties Union. As S. S. Schweber, a historian of science, has noted, "The Ethical Culture movement became a way station to complete assimilation for many of the moneyed, European-born, first-generation American Reform Jews who joined it."[4]

Ethical Culture classes emphasized working for a better world and developing an aesthetic appreciation for the environment. They had the desired effect on the precocious Rosenberg. Taking its cue from Kant, Adler's curriculum was rooted in the "intellectual mastery of nature, the glorification of life in art and with its consecration in morality."[5] These principles resonated with Rosenberg, who developed a lifelong passion for art and conservation— before the label "conservationist" became fashionable. He later described his feelings about organized religion in a couplet: "Let others go to synagogues or churches, / I worship God beneath his pines and birches."[6]

Rosenberg continued his education at a private New England boarding school and then went on to Columbia University, where he earned his bachelor's degree in 1895. As a result of reforms that chose "entering classes on the basis of individual merit and future promise and not on family prominence or religion," he was admitted to Columbia's law school, one of the best in the nation.[7] But when he graduated three years later, his prospects for employment were by no means assured. First he put up a shingle with law school friend (and soon-to-be brother-in-law) Joseph Proskauer on January 1, 1900 in New York City. After some early struggles, the two eventually went their separate ways in 1902 and built successful practices, with Rosenberg making a name and a fortune for himself in the field of corporate bankruptcy law.[8] Within a few years he had moved uptown from Manhattan's Lower East Side to a West End Avenue brownstone, the quintessential example of the successful German Jewish American.

Assimilation had its limits, however. After graduation, Rosenberg and Proskauer were invited to become charter members of a Columbia University literary society established by their beloved English professor, George Woodbury. But when they applied for membership to an affiliated social club, they learned that their faith had prompted objections from some of its members. Even though they were later extended invitations to join the Columbia University Club, they demurred, in Rosenberg's words, so as "not to raise an anti-Semitic issue."[9]

This episode forced Rosenberg to come to grips with his own identity. The path he had followed—attending a Waspish boarding school in New England and college and law school at Columbia—all drove home just how uninviting the world he aspired to was. Discrimination in late-nineteenth- and early-twentieth-century America was often social in character, outside of the state's jurisdiction. Professional organizations, social clubs, hotels, and private schools were sites where nouveau riche Jews like Rosenberg encountered anti-Semitism.[10] He later wrote about his experiences at Columbia: "I saw the Jewish boys at college making friendships with their Christian classmates, but somewhere, as in a gray mist, an invisible and impenetrable wall existed. We were on one side of it; they were on the other." He and his Jewish colleagues felt excluded at every turn—fraternities, the college rowing team, and eventually the legal profession.[11]

Rosenberg wrestled with anti-Semitism in a revealing essay written in 1915, "The Gentile's Attitude toward the Jew as a Jew Sees It." "He locks his house against us. He bars us from his clubs. He refuses our children his schools. He keeps us from the places where he and his women-folk gather."

At the same time, Rosenberg had noticed how Gentiles were relying with ever greater frequency on Jewish bankers, lawyers, and physicians. "Let him suffer deeply in his purse, health, reputation, let him stand in great peril, and his most intimate doors are thrown open and he calls aloud for us." In his corporate practice, he had heard Christians badmouth Jews repeatedly, yet he had earned his clients' trust and respect. He concluded that Jews had to win over Christians one at a time. The young lawyer with a passion for painting eloquently captured his feelings by drawing an artistic analogy: "If I were a Rubens or a Rembrandt, I could almost paint my picture of the Gentile's picture of the Jew; a great canvas; in the background, countless dark, sorrowful Jewish faces, with the persecution of generations written on them and sinister shadows blotting them out, in the foreground, a Jew, one that has fought forward from the shadows; one who as an individual, as one man, facing the world, has proved himself worthy of trust and confidence, esteem, friendship and affection."[12] The American dream had afforded him the opportunity "that out of the unhappy host of Jews in the shadow any one of us may emerge."[13]

If certain social settings presented barriers to entry, this did not stop Rosenberg from meshing well with prominent German Jewish banking families like the Warburgs and the Schiffs, who personified philanthropy during the first decades of the twentieth century (see figure 3). Second-generation New York Jews embraced charitable work with enthusiasm, partly for its own sake but also because it fostered communal and ethnic ties, no matter the social class. It also connected Jews to nonsectarian traditions of philanthropy in mainstream America, which tied beneficence to free enterprise. Philanthropy was something that bourgeois Jews shared with all Americans. Implicitly, it held out the promise of social acceptance for the upwardly mobile.[14] Rosenberg's ongoing commitment to philanthropic work ultimately would define who he was as an American and a Jew.[15]

New York German American Jews, many of whom were well educated and prosperous, were sometimes referred to as uptown Jews because a significant number had moved to comfortable brownstones on Manhattan's West Side.[16] Proponents of Reform Judaism, they considered Judaism a religion with a universal message and defined Jews as a religious community rather than a nation. Members of this social elite were sophisticated and urbane, patrons of the arts, and justifiably proud of their philanthropy and their German heritage. They believed that it was incumbent upon immigrants to accommodate themselves to the customs of their adopted homeland. Their patriotism was unquestioned. It is revealing that they often referred to themselves as "Americans of Jewish origin" rather than American Jews.[17] All the while, they

FIGURE 3
DORSA's James
Rosenberg
(left) and State
Department
liaison Robert
Pell (right). JDC
ARCHIVES.

struggled to reconcile their identity as Jews with their hard-won "American-ness." In all these respects, the American Jewish community resembled its coreligionists in western Europe. Such dual loyalties, however, made them very anxious about the waves of Eastern European Jews coming to the United States at the turn of the century.

From 1880 to 1920, American Jewry's composition changed radically. From 250,000 predominantly German-born Jews in the late nineteenth century, the Jewish community expanded to more than 4 million by 1925, of whom five-sixths were of Eastern European origin. Prompted by poverty, competition, social dislocation, economic discrimination, and repression, Eastern Euro-pean Jews fled westward in droves.[18] Many of these working-class immigrants were rabid Zionists, some were leftist radicals, and others were staunch sup-porters of trade unionism. More than a few were devout Orthodox Jews who believed that Reform Judaism was a sham and its practitioners less than au-thentic Jews. Zionists, in particular, gravitated toward Conservative Judaism, which was committed to the revival of the Hebrew language and the Jews' survival as a distinct group. The propensity of these new arrivals to cling to their Yiddish heritage—in all its cultural forms, including theater, journalism, and literature—baffled uptown patrons like Rosenberg, who felt that clinging to the past obstructed the new arrivals' path to acculturation.[19]

The leaders of the Jewish establishment expressed ambivalence about these newcomers. Fearful that the seemingly endless waves of the great unwashed would overwhelm their philanthropic resources, initially they were in the uncomfortable position of occasionally siding with nativists who advocated immigration restrictions. Yet even as they expressed that concern and treated the recent arrivals as social inferiors, they showered them with charity, educational opportunities, and other assistance.[20]

Uptown Jews were also concerned that Zionist appeals to Jewish nationalism among their newly arrived brethren would trigger new waves of discrimination. Their stewardship of refugee relief was designed to "prevent the Jewish masses from becoming floating centers of anti-Semitic infection."[21]

The German American Jewish leadership founded the American Jewish Committee in 1906 to defend Jewish interests on immigration, anti-Semitism, and other issues important to the community at home and abroad. The JDC was established eight years later when philanthropists joined forces with mutual aid societies, the Jewish labor movement, and Orthodox Jews to assist European Jews dislocated by the First World War. The Joint administered funds that had been raised by affiliated organizations and then distributed those monies through its overseas relief network.[22]

As the AJC and the Joint grew in stature, their leadership began to overlap. By 1931, twenty-seven of the JDC's forty-two directors served on the AJC's Executive Committee and seventeen of the AJC's leadership sat on the Joint's counterpart.[23] Rosenberg was a case in point; he was a fixture on the JDC board and regularly served in some capacity with the AJC. Despite this interlocking relationship, the Joint distanced itself from political activism. Others might squabble about Palestine or immigration, but the Joint's mission, as leaders reminded would-be donors and activists alike, was to provide relief for the less fortunate. Recent immigrants could be excused if they found these distinctions less than clear-cut. They certainly resented the advice freely given by their sponsors on "how to dress, speak, pray and vote."[24]

Joint leaders like Rosenberg and Rosen viewed Zionists as impractical dreamers and refused to see Palestine as a panacea for what ailed their community. Initially opposed to the creation of a Jewish state in Palestine, Rosenberg gradually came to view it as one among many destinations that deserved American Jewish support. But he stubbornly opposed efforts to bring about a rapprochement between Zionists and Non-Zionists.

A perfect illustration of his reluctance to compromise was an angry exchange with Wise in 1936, soon after the rabbi announced the formation of the World Jewish Congress. In a pamphlet accompanying the announcement, Wise derided the JDC's reconstruction efforts as "palliative," asserting that its leadership acted arbitrarily and did not "hold themselves accountable to any form of public opinion." Implicitly indicting the Joint for not embracing a Jewish homeland, Wise chided, "Not having a vision of the future, they always prefer the immediate task—the task of the day—leaving final solutions untouched, and as a matter of fact, often resent proposals that involve long-term programs that might lead to permanent results."[25] In a tersely written reply, Rosenberg fumed, "I have no confidence in your cause; it has already created conflict and resentment instead of cooperation; it is breeding further anti-Semitism . . . it contains a grave menace to Jewish life." Invoking the names of philanthropists like Baron de Hirsch and Baron de Rothschild, who had invested their time, energy, and fortunes into colonization projects, the defensive Rosenberg ended his ten-page missive by asking the rabbi, "Is there not at least one single Jewish constructive effort of the last quarter of the century deserving something better than scorn or condescension?"[26]

Rosenberg and a prominent backer of the Crimean initiative, Sears, Roebuck and Company magnate Julius Rosenwald, believed that Jews had a right to live in the countries of their birth. Rosenwald's rationale was not unlike that of many of the donors who supported Russian colonization. "I am not opposed to Zionism. I have been willing to help any efforts made in Palestine for years and have done so, but I have never been a believer in subsidizing immigration to the extent of moving people in masses from one country to another and trying to establish them with funds."[27] In other words, the Russian Jewish problem was best addressed there, rather than in Palestine or the United States.[28] Rosenwald viewed his donation to Crimean colonization in business terms—"in the spirit of speculation"—as a constructive opportunity to relieve the suffering of Russian Jews.[29]

While the Joint funded resettlement in Palestine, it also zealously defended its commitments to refugees elsewhere. Wishing to present itself as nonpartisan, it accepted the aims of the 1917 Balfour Declaration and viewed Palestine as a site of religious and cultural significance for the Jewish people. Yet it carved out a middle ground between nationalistic Zionists and Anti-Zionists, who opposed immigration to Palestine at any price. Along with the

AJC, the Joint worked to forestall the creation of Jewish mass organizations that bolstered Zionist influence.[30]

This is not to imply that Non-Zionist leaders did not care deeply for their flock; indeed, they viewed themselves as advocates. Political and cultural brokers had their feet in both worlds, and their wealth bought them a certain measure of acceptance in the political establishment yet still made it possible to maintain ties with their "less fortunate" brethren.

In the 1930s, Non-Zionist leaders would be ridiculed as court Jews when they refrained from pressuring Washington policymakers to liberalize quotas, for example, or were reluctant to join other Jewish organizations in public demonstrations against Nazi policies.[31] The ability to operate in both worlds presented challenges and ultimately carried risks. As Auerbach has indicated, ambivalence and contradiction were their defining characteristics: "If the Court Jew needed his community, he also needed to escape from it. . . . So in speech, dress and manners he emulated his Christian protectors, to whom he, in turn, was subservient . . . he was creative yet constrained, defenseless yet arrogant, successful yet apprehensive, privileged yet eager for the trappings of privilege to conceal his own uneasy status."[32]

Entree to political power may have validated the American identity of optimistic Jewish leaders like Rosenberg, but Zionists threatened to destroy the deference that court Jews had come to expect. Zionist political tactics made the German American elite uncomfortable; that some Zionist spokespersons were prominent religious leaders, like Rabbi Wise, only compounded the problem.[33]

Such deep-seated divisions proved especially damaging when the refugee crisis intensified. The AJC's and JDC's apparent stranglehold over the disbursement of philanthropic funds infuriated Zionist leaders, and the distribution of charitable funds for resettlement and reconstruction in Palestine, Russia, and later in the Dominican Republic became a major flashpoint between the rival camps.[34]

Philanthropy also gave these patricians the opportunity to engage in social engineering as they imposed their vision of progress on recent émigrés.[35] Uptown Jews like Felix Warburg and Rosenberg, who were wedded to an urban way of life, paternalistically counseled immigrants to leave the city and their politically objectionable ideas behind and either move to smaller towns and cities to pursue their trades in a less congested environment or take up farming. Here assimilationists took their cue from European Jewish leaders, who had encouraged coreligionists to leave towns and ghettoes and move to rural areas throughout the nineteenth century.[36] The Jewish Colonization

Association, headquartered in Paris and backed by a ten-million-dollar gift from the Baron de Hirsch Foundation, subsidized colonization in the southern Ukraine in the 1890s. Similar efforts were undertaken outside Europe: five thousand families (thirty-one thousand persons) were resettled on more than three hundred thousand acres of the Argentine Pampas in the 1920s. Baron de Hirsch insisted that it was "quite possible to reawaken in the race this capacity and love" for the land.[37]

New York's uptown Jews set up similar self-help programs to retrain Jews, sending them away from the teeming cities along the Eastern Seaboard. In 1909, German Jewish Americans founded the Jewish Agricultural Society and placed more than fifteen thousand Eastern European immigrants on farms in small communities in New Jersey, Texas, and South Dakota.[38] The Hirsch Foundation also established an experimental agricultural school in 1891 at one its colonies in Woodbine, New Jersey, to train the children of immigrants as farmers. Two key Joint operatives in Russia, Joseph Rosen and Boris Bogen, first served as administrators at Woodbine's Baron de Hirsch Agricultural School.[39]

Despite the widespread perception that Jews did not have the aptitude to be farmers, these leaders took heart from William Kirsch's book *The Jew and the Land* (1920), which proclaimed colonization as a cure for the woes of urban living. Kirsch called for federal and state aid for vocational training and farm tenancy "internships," where young settlers could be socialized to a life on the land. Successful colonization, Kirsch contended, countered the anti-Semitic charge that Jews were parasites who lived off the toil of others. As one proponent quipped, "the sower of oats is as good as the sewer of coats."[40]

Ironically, both Zionist and Non-Zionist proponents of colonization, although their motivations and goals were often at odds, implicitly accepted this notion of Jewish parasitism. What these social engineers failed to take into account was that anti-Semitism followed Jews from urban centers to rural districts.[41]

The actual colonization experiments in the American heartland were fraught with difficulties, and most either withered away or failed outright. Only the agricultural colonies in southern New Jersey partly overcame the obstacles, but at a tremendous financial cost. After years of cost overruns, inefficiencies, and feuds, sponsors closed down the Woodbine school and gradually weaned the colonists off subsidies.[42] Rosen was the school's last superintendent, so he had ample opportunity to reflect on the lessons learned from the failure of Jewish agrarianism in southern New Jersey. Although he faced different challenges in his future colonization work, each of the problems that bedeviled the New Jersey colonies resurfaced in the Crimea and the Dominican Republic.

No matter how many setbacks they encountered, Rosen and Rosenberg remained committed to Jewish agrarianism. Rosenberg, in particular, was convinced of the spiritually regenerative powers of nature. An avid trout fisherman, he spent summers at his thousand-acre camp, Shanty Brook, in the Adirondacks.[43] A related passion was painting. He also studied lithography under the master New York printmaker George Miller. Many of Rosenberg's prints and paintings were impressionistic landscapes that conveyed the environment's healing powers. As he later wrote, "I have never encountered anti-Semitic sunshine, storms, trees, brooks, forests, mountains."[44]

In contrast, his lithographs and paintings of urban scenes, influenced by German Expressionism, were often dark and foreboding, and critiqued modernity. For example, *Dies Irae* (Days of Wrath), hurriedly made in Miller's print shop on the afternoon of October 28, 1929, in response to the stock market crash, captures the panic that gripped Wall Street that day, replete with tilting skyscrapers, ominous storm clouds on the horizon, and anxiety-stricken New Yorkers.[45] (It subsequently appeared on the front page of the *New York Times Magazine* on January 12, 1930.) In a similar vein, his powerful 1944 exhibition, titled "Ironism," included paintings with titles like "Steel, Smoke and Steam," "Ingot Farm," "The Master Race Pays a Visit," and "Tranquil Evening at Dachau," and decried how technology had been transformed from people's servant to their master.[46]

Rosenberg's experience with colonization only confirmed his faith in nature's transformative effects. In 1926 he toured the Crimean settlements, and later published a travel narrative called *On the Steppes*, which publicized the redeeming qualities of a life on the land. Visibly moved by what he saw, he sought to convince others that this enterprise would succeed. "Today, these [Russian] Jews feel a hope. They feel that hope through colonization, and it is their only hope. . . . If we fail these Jews, it will be a collapse of dreadful significance."[47] The citified attorney had found his calling, and he dedicated a generous portion of his life to proving that Jews, if given the chance, could thrive in rural settings.[48]

Rosenberg reasoned that thousands of years of living in cities had contaminated the Jewish gene pool. He, like the Dominican leadership he would soon work with, believed in the principles of scientific racism. He wrote to a friend, "I wish I had time to dwell on the eugenic aspects of the work. I wish you could see the young Jewish boys . . . galloping over the Steppes. . . . That's a better sight than seeing the boys at a cabaret or bending over a machine or trying to eke out a living selling a few needles."[49]

If Rosenberg was a romantic idealist, Rosen was an energetic pragmatist. The agronomist believed that the Crimean program was an "unusual opportunity"; it brought together a supportive government, plentiful land, a modicum of cultural change for the settlers, and funds from abroad needed to guarantee success.

Born in Moscow in 1876 and raised in Tula, one hundred miles to the south, Rosen attended Moscow University. A Menshevik at seventeen, his revolutionary activities got him in trouble with Tsarist authorities, and he was sentenced to five years' exile in Siberia. After six months, however, Rosen managed to escape and flee to Germany, where he studied chemistry and philosophy at the University of Heidelberg.

In 1903, Rosen arrived in the United States, virtually penniless. He worked on farms as a day laborer for two years in Iowa, Kansas, and Nebraska before enrolling as a graduate student at Michigan Agricultural College in East Lansing. While in graduate school, he wrote a number of articles on U.S. agriculture, which brought him to the attention of Ukrainian agronomists. After receiving his master's degree in agriculture in 1908, Rosen was hired by Ukrainian officials to head a bureau in Minneapolis to study U.S. agricultural methods that might be profitably adapted back home.

A year after graduating, Rosen sent his alma mater a pound of pedigreed winter rye. The hybrid seed was planted experimentally by the college and soon attracted national attention because of its high yield—more than twice that of regular varieties—and because it prospered in soils of limited fertility.[50] Rosen's Rye would soon make its mark on a Soviet state desperate to feed its war-exhausted population. Rosen himself stayed in Minneapolis until 1914, when he received his doctorate in agricultural chemistry at the University of Minnesota. During that time he wrote 13 comprehensive studies on U.S. farming, totaling 1,300 pages. In 1921 he returned to Russia with a handful of American "specialists in tractor farming" to assist famine victims.[51]

Rosen saw eye-to-eye with Rosenberg about the polluting character of the city. "I have seen hundreds of young boys walking the streets in the cities and towns, with no future before them; a dreadful process of degradation. These young men [the settlers] have something to look forward to. They have no time to loaf; they are making plans for the building of houses, for planting wheat and oats and barley."[52] Eugenics also crept into his thinking when he noted, "life in the fields will make the Jews into taller, bigger, stronger men."[53]

FIGURE 4
Sosúa's first director,
Dr. Joseph Rosen.
YIVO ARCHIVES.

His reports emphasized farming's salutary effects, "the eugenic value of having a large number of coreligionists get out into God's sunshine once more to earn their bread by the sweat of their brow."[54]

Like his colleague, Rosen believed in cooperative farming, not Zionism, but for practical rather than ideological reasons. He estimated the cost of "rehabilitating" urban Jews from the Pale of Settlement to the Crimea at one-tenth the cost of resettling them in Palestine.[55] As late as 1938, he had his doubts about the viability of a Palestinian homeland. "If it were possible to eliminate political difficulties, Palestine would naturally have to receive first consideration. . . . But nobody has yet suggested a real way of eliminating these difficulties in a way satisfactory to all parties concerned and we are confronted with a situation, not a theory. Besides, Palestine could never be expected to become a peaceful country, being, as it is, in a pivotal position in the center of interest of the three great religions."[56]

All who came into contact with Rosen praised his ingenuity, character, and commitment (see figure 4, above). Even though he often found himself caught between the demands of the settlers, the dogmatic strictures of Soviet authorities, and the advice of his American Jewish donors, he maintained the trust and admiration of everyone.[57] Rosen developed an international reputation as a colonization expert and frequently served as a consultant to governments and philanthropies alike.

Rosen believed that the Crimean experiment would serve as an influential model for other nations. He also turned out to be an excellent fundraiser. When he came to the United States to speak to potential donors, he instinctively knew how to reach his target audience—successful American Jewish professionals who might feel a twinge of guilt because they had assimilated so successfully. He told an audience of Jewish business leaders, "Since the Diaspora, for twenty centuries we Jews have been pushed from pillar to post. We have never been given a decent chance to settle on the soil. . . . The accusation is always leveled against us that we are exploiters and profiteers, lawyers, bankers, etc. It has remained for Russia . . . to give Jews the first opportunity in modern history—indeed the first opportunity in two thousand years—to prove that the accusation leveled against us is a lie."[58]

The Crimean project was fraught with symbolism for true believers like Rosenberg and Rosen. It was a golden opportunity to prove to critics once and for all that Jews were more than moneylenders and merchants, that they could succeed if they were just given the opportunity. But many critics in the Soviet Union and in the United States entertained serious reservations about this "bizarre hybrid of Park Avenue charity and Marxist agriculture."[59]

THE AGRO-JOINT IN REVOLUTIONARY RUSSIA

Since its inception, the Joint had dedicated itself to rescue, relief, and reconstruction efforts. By the Second World War, the philanthropy was operating in more than fifty countries; in the interwar period, its relief expenditures amounted to nearly one hundred million dollars. Acting out of equal parts *noblesse oblige* and pragmatism, the JDC did its best to steer clear of political controversy at home and abroad. Although emergency relief remained its central mission, Joint executives showed that when circumstances permitted, they were open to transforming disaster relief into reconstructive projects.[60]

In July 1924, the JDC created the American Jewish Agricultural Corporation (Agro-Joint) to assist the Soviet government in moving Jewish city dwellers to the countryside. A natural outgrowth of the Joint's earlier relief work, the Agro-Joint would spend millions—staffing soup kitchens, establishing credit unions and cooperatives, and running special child care trains—to attend to the five million refugees set adrift by the First World War and the Russian Revolution.[61]

Russian Jews were especially vulnerable at this time. After the Bolshevik victory, Jewish petty capitalists and Zionists became frequent targets of ideological harassment, synagogues and religious schools were expropriated and closed, and the Hebrew language was denounced as a counterrevolutionary tool.[62] In the Ukraine, where more than 1.5 million Jews lived (out of a total of 2.6 million across the Soviet Union), an autonomous counterrevolution raged, and Jews were persecuted by nationalists, irregular military forces, Red and White armies, and anarchist peasant bands.[63] By one estimate, pogroms and additional deaths from disease and starvation claimed the lives of some two hundred thousand Jews, produced three hundred thousand orphans, and drove half a million refugees into newly created Poland, Rumania, the Baltic countries, and overseas. The Joint rushed emergency relief assistance to assist them.[64]

In 1921 the JDC again responded to crisis in the Soviet Union when, along with other private agencies, it answered the call of Herbert Hoover and the American Relief Administration (ARA) to combat a famine estimated to have killed more than five million people, arguably the worst in European history. From 1921 to 1923, more than fifty million dollars was raised for Russian relief from government and private contributions. The Joint alone provided more than eight million dollars in a remarkable humanitarian effort.[65] Rosen earned the sobriquet of "the famine angel of Russia" for his efforts. He was fortunate to survive the experience; on a trip through the affected districts, he came down with typhus and nearly died.[66]

After the famine abated and as the ARA began closing down its operations, pragmatic Soviet leaders, desperate to keep the flow of U.S. hard currency and technology coming in, agreed to work with the Joint.[67] In 1922, the philanthropy appropriated one hundred thousand dollars toward a pilot program for colonization. The Joint named Rosen to head up the program.[68]

The successful famine relief effort was not the only reason JDC leaders opted to work with Soviet officials to resettle Jews in colonies in southern Ukraine and northern Crimea. Domestic factors in the United States also played into their decision. Joint leaders were disheartened by the nativist hostility that had motivated calls for new restrictive immigration legislation and the racist and anti-Semitic rationale behind them.[69]

Prominent politicians stoked xenophobic fears. First the 1921 Emergency Immigration Restriction Act, or Johnson Act, established the principle of a quota, assigning to each sending nation an upper limit of 3 percent of the number of its nationals resident in the United States in 1910. Three years later, Congress passed the National Origins Act, which reduced the quota to 2 percent but now based the figure on the 1890 census. The bill was directed at Russian and other Eastern European Jews, Slavs, and Italians, who were thought to be particularly resistant to assimilation.[70] The quotas had their intended effect. Whereas before the First World War, one hundred thousand Eastern European immigrants a year came to the United States, the National Origins Act now fixed the quota at a combined 9,443 annually. Russia's quota alone fell from more than 24,000 to 2,712.[71]

A cautious JDC decided not to fight the bill openly because public debate would exacerbate anti-Semitism without appreciably altering the law. Since Eastern European Jews were the legislation's principal targets and were certain to feel its impact, JDC leaders reasoned that it made more sense to invest in the economic improvement of Jewish communities in Russia and Poland.

Still, the leadership was leery of breaking ground with Bolsheviks. The postwar Red Scare had linked Jews with communists in the minds of many Americans. To persuade the doubters, advocates sought approval from the State Department.[72] This was a significant step, setting a precedent for future initiatives. As Rosenberg put it, "We must not and cannot let our desire to help suffering cause us to lose our moorings. Our rule must be 'When in doubt, ask the State Department.'"[73] Once policymakers gave their blessing, the philanthropy moved into action, all the while, in its promotional literature, emphasizing the apolitical character of its collaborations.

New York–based philanthropists and Soviet leaders shared a common interest in transforming urban Jews into farmers. Soviet officials believed that Jewish petty capitalists, the great majority of whom had been relegated to commercial pursuits by the Tsarist regime, were anathema to the building of communism, and that Jewish predominance in such trades as tailoring, shoemaking, and moneylending fueled anti-Semitism.[74] At the same time, authorities believed that transforming Jews into farmers would solve the "Jewish question" by literally and figuratively giving the Jews a stake in the land while encouraging solidarity with the revolution's goals and diminishing attachment to their faith. In addition to addressing the Jewish question, foreign investment was critical to rebuilding the nation after the devastation wrought by the war, the revolution, the counterrevolution, and the famine that followed one after another in deadly succession.[75]

An estimated two million Jews living in the cities and towns of the Pale of Settlement in Ukraine and Belorussia had been, along with other petty capitalists, stigmatized by the Soviet state as *lishentsy* (declassed or disen-franchised). Stripped of their right to vote, denied food rations and access to hospitals and schools, unable to occupy administrative posts, excluded from political life, labor unions, and clubs, and discouraged from participating po-litically in the new regime, Jewish "archcapitalists" were now "encouraged" to redeem themselves by leaving their towns and cities and embracing the life of the peasantry.[76]

Rosen, as director of Agro-Joint's operations in Russia, cabled his superi-ors in New York in March 1926, painting the plight of the lishentsy in omi-nous tones. "Situation in small towns desperate . . . this is not a temporary crisis . . . but a permanent situation facing Russian Jewry . . . it is adaptation or extermination."[77] Overcrowding and malnutrition in the Pale were breed-ing grounds for disease; he estimated that 70 percent of Jewish children had some form of tuberculosis.[78]

The Agro-Joint chairman Rosenberg (he served in that capacity from the organization's inception until 1942) informed board members that hospitals were instructed by authorities to treat workers and peasants first, before lish-entsy. He added that once these townspeople opted for a new life in the coun-try, authorities viewed them in a much better light.[79] The JDC later boasted that thanks to its intervention, the percentage of lishentsy was reduced from 70 to 5 percent in little more than a decade.[80]

Rosen's expertise and dedication impressed the Soviets. He preached the gospel of crop rotation to the Jewish farmers and donated American seed corn and rye, innovations that increased food production without increasing the acreage sown.[81] When the pilot program for two colonies in the Ukraine proved successful, the Soviet state and the Agro-Joint joined forces "to rehabilitate and productivize" urban Jews by replicating it with several more settlements.[82]

In the northern Crimean steppes, authorities set aside 1.3 million acres for development. Arid and windy, the steppes presented formidable challenges. The region was thinly populated and the acreage under cultivation limited, but fertile soil, a warm climate, and a strategic location on the Black Sea close to markets made the region enticing to the colonizers.[83]

In Ukraine, the Soviet state provided half a million acres, and Jewish settlers were given allotments averaging forty-five acres.[84] In the more arid Crimea, the plots were increased to seventy acres. In both regions, the settle-ments were organized into cooperatives (precursors to collective farms), and settlers were offered several incentives: exemptions from the draft and taxa-tion for three years, tracts of timber, and reduced rates for transporting their crops to market.[85]

The Joint contributed seven million dollars during the first four years, while the Agro-Joint provided training, seed cultivation stations, housing, livestock, and tractors and other farm machinery. American Keystone water-drilling equipment was imported to sink the necessary artesian wells for irrigation.[86] Rosen imported eighty-six John Deere tractors, the first farm machinery Russia had seen since the war.[87] Rosen's tractor squads, which the Agro-Joint rented out to settlers, roamed the countryside; in 1923, they plowed one hundred thousand acres, 70 percent of which were in non-Jewish villages. The Soviet authorities were impressed by the Agro-Joint's altruism, the new technology, and the advances in agronomy that Rosen introduced.[88]

Rosen hired Jews who had recently graduated from Soviet agricultural schools to act as extension agents. He proudly reported that his entire staff, with the exception of one American tractor mechanic, was native-born. By 1926, 50,000 Jewish families were growing everything from winter wheat to fruit on more than 180,000 acres across the steppes, the properties managed by either Agro-Joint or Soviet authorities.[89] Modern technologies, the Agro-Joint's boosters claimed, more than compensated for the Jewish farmers' lack of experience.[90]

Rosen stressed the new settlements' cooperative character, something he would seek to emulate, with notably less success, in the Dominican Republic. "It would be utterly impossible," Rosen reported, "for the individual farmer with his small means to succeed on the land in the Ukraine or Crimea, where it takes a team of five horses to pull a plow and where modern machinery must be used to make farming profitable." The colonies featured cooperative ownership of farm implements and machinery, and in typical socialist fashion, settlers shared in the proceeds of the crops based on the amount of labor contributed. Colonists also maintained their own private garden plots.[91]

While Rosenberg raised funds in New York and Europe, Rosen managed operations on the ground, with the help and under the watchful eye of two Soviet bureaucracies, the KOMZET (Committee for the Settlement of Jewish Workers on the Land) and its chief propaganda arm, OZET (Society for the Settlement of Jewish Toilers on the Land).[92]

Unfortunately, the colonization program soon became enmeshed in policy debates about the Soviet Union's ethnic nationalities.[93] Some officials noted that all minority groups had been treated unfairly by the tsars. Now that discrimination was to be a relic of the past, Bolshevik leaders insisted that each nationality must find its place in the new order. A few even argued for an autonomous Jewish republic in the Crimea, an idea the Agro-Joint leadership greeted with marked ambivalence.

During the first years of the Crimean project, Joseph Stalin straddled the political fence, pitting ethnic nationalities against each other. But as his power grew in the late 1920s, he sought to quash regionalism and divisive ethnic nationalisms. The "Jewish question" was just one of many ethnic problems to be resolved.[94]

Recognizing how volatile the topic of ethnic autonomy was, Agro-Joint leaders kept mum while other groups called for a Jewish republic in the Crimea. As it was, the topic met a fierce backlash from indigenous Tatars, who viewed the land allotments as an "outright provocation" and who were especially wary of Moscow's efforts to throttle their autonomy.[95]

Stalin moved in March 1928 to deflect criticism of the Crimean settlements. He gave KOMZET the authority to develop a new colonization zone in Siberia along the Manchurian border "for the purpose of the dense settlement of free lands by working Jews." Birobidzhan, a mere five thousand miles east of Moscow, was a fourteen-thousand-square-mile tract about the size of Massachusetts and Connecticut. It posed serious challenges for would-be colonists. A severe climate, ubiquitous swamps, swarms of flies and mosquitoes, a densely forested landscape, and the absence of sufficient infrastructure all made it much less attractive than the Crimea.[96]

Proclaimed a Jewish Autonomous Republic nevertheless in 1934, Birobidzhan was poorly funded and organized. Jewish autonomy was nowhere to be seen, as Jews and non-Jews alike were "recruited" for the colony. Despite the romance associated with creating a homeland for Jews in the Far East, away from populated settlements, Birobidzhan seriously undercut the Crimean initiative and confused both American and Russian Jews about the Soviet state's intentions.[97]

The Agro-Joint expressed no interest whatsoever in a separate Jewish republic, downplayed the importance of religious worship, and emphasized the imperative of fostering Jewish integration into Soviet life. Rosen, whose sympathies were with the moderate Mensheviks, found it hard to make sense of the shifting political landscape during the revolution's tumultuous first two decades. Although he accurately predicted Leon Trotsky's demise, he underestimated Stalin's staying power. He sympathized with the revolution's collectivist ends even as he was critical of its means. It is easy in hindsight to criticize him for his naïveté about Stalin's ruthless reforms, yet few contemporary observers predicted the nature and the severity of the changes implemented during the Five Year Plan.[98]

There were, furthermore, accomplishments that appeared to justify Agro-Joint's cooperation. Despite the ominous political developments, Rosen was able to restore voting rights for Jewish artisans and petty traders—approximately 50 percent of the declassed lishentsy. Moreover, the small dollops of credit the Agro-Joint made available were indispensable to many.[99]

Rosen had to walk a perilous line. Even though the Agro-Joint worked closely with Soviet officials, he himself, responsible for raising crucial funds in the United States, often had to overstate the case for the autonomous character of his activities and to downplay the difficulties of working with apparatchiks.[100] A devout belief in the benefits of reconstruction persuaded Rosen and JDC leaders like Felix Warburg to overlook the regime's persecution of rabbis and its efforts to eliminate religious worship.[101] Rosen also avoided telling donors about the friction between colonists and their "non-Jewish neighbors near the settlement tracts," who thought the Soviet state was favoring Jewish farmers.[102]

In the United States, Rosenberg battled Zionists who vehemently criticized the undertaking and discouraged potential donors. Zionists were quick to point out that the Soviets had closed Jewish schools, proscribed worship, and arrested hundreds of rabbis, Hebrew teachers, and Zionist leaders.[103] It was immoral, said the Zionist Organization of America, for Jews to collaborate with a state that openly practiced anti-Semitism.[104]

To deflect Zionist criticism, the Joint decided to fund the Crimean project through individual donations from a smaller group of well-heeled patrons, rather than through its general appeal.[105] Rabbi Wise was outraged that Julius Rosenwald had given an initial one million dollars to the Agro-Joint. The contribution was "an affront to the Jewish people. It is a continuance of the attitude . . . of deciding for world Jewry by the power of one's money what ought to be done. The Rosenwald contribution . . . is proof to me of the utter breakdown of the Jewish nation. Millions, including a very large sum from Warburg [philanthropist Edward, son of Felix], are poured into Russia. Palestine gets investigations."[106]

Facing mounting criticism, Rosenberg used a variety of novel promotional strategies to market the colonization program on the radio and in Jewish and mainstream newspapers. He sent artists to the settlements who, on their return, exhibited their work; and he even commissioned a silent film about Felix Warburg's trip to the colonies in 1927, *Back to the Soil: A Story of Jewish Hope, Struggle and Achievement*, which painted the colonists in heroic terms.[107] His clever appropriation of modern methods of mass communication would be replicated in the Dominican venture.

For fourteen years, the Agro-Joint worked tirelessly in Russia with Jewish farmers to create a secular Zion. Even in the depths of the Depression, fundraisers in New York managed to keep the project alive. But the combination of hard times and Rosenwald's untimely death in January 1932 (and the subsequent legal wrangling over his estate) meant that expectations and financial commitments had to be scaled back.[108] By the mid-1930s, furthermore, worsening conditions for Jews in Germany increasingly occupied the Joint's attention and resources. Rosen fought a rearguard battle with Soviet bureaucrats who, for ideological reasons, resented working with foreign capitalists. And the colonies' prosperity made them inviting targets for non-Jewish neighbors, who, on occasion stole or destroyed farm implements, squatted illegally on pastureland, and, in a few cases, attacked settlers.

Additional forces undercut the settlements. The tumultuous Great Transformation that recast Soviet society during the late 1920s and early 1930s, the collectivization and industrialization impulse at the heart of Stalin's bold Five Year Plan, his purges of 1936–38, his decision to eliminate KOMZET, and an American backlash against Soviet collectivization all took their toll. Hardliners were quick to brand the Agro-Joint colonies as dens of materialist inequity.[109]

Collectivization, which was supposed to be introduced gradually, was given new urgency during the Depression, and had severe consequences for the Russian peasantry.[110] But the Agro-Joint's role as broker between the colonists and the state cushioned its shock and "profoundly improved the position and treatment of the colonies." Indeed, the Soviets offered Agro-Joint 750,000 acres of prime farmland in the midst of collectivization. As conditions in other peasant communities materially worsened, the Agro-Joint's insistence on diversifying production and its provision of credit and tractor teams to the Jewish colonies sheltered its settlements.[111]

When the state's motives became clear, many Jewish settlers left the farms for the factories; some even were forcibly removed from their lands by the regime because they were labeled *kulaks*, or prosperous farmers.[112] As more jobs became available in the industrial sector, more than 350,000 Jews nationwide found employment in manufacturing by 1932. Many settlers' children moved to take advantage of educational and economic opportunities in urban areas.[113]

By the early 1930s, the settlements were shadows of their former selves, and the Agro-Joint Board began to think seriously of pulling out.[114] Rosenberg and the board now rationalized that they had never envisioned Agro-Joint as a permanent fixture in the Crimean countryside. It was supposed to be there long enough to provide the infrastructure and training that settlers needed to sustain themselves. Some Soviet leaders opposed the Agro-Joint withdrawal, arguing that the regime had even more need for U.S. capital and farm machinery than it had had a decade earlier.[115]

What clinched the Agro-Joint's withdrawal was the Stalinist purges of the mid-1930s. Hundreds of Russian Agro-Joint staff members were harassed and eventually eliminated by Stalin's police during the Great Purge of 1937–38, and the Jewish leadership of KOMZET and OZET met a similar fate.[116] As a representative of a U.S. philanthropy working in Russia, Rosen's work had always required absolute circumspection; but in the teeth of the repression, contact with capitalist countries was tantamount to treason. Although he and his senior staff were spared, many of his Russian subordinates were not. Rosen was horrified by the severity of the repression.[117] He did all he could to petition Soviet security agencies to release his staff, but by the end of his stay, his frustration was palpable: "I would feel like a dog should I let them go down under Stalin's tyranny and myself escape because I happen to be an American citizen."[118]

It was the Crimean experiment's ties to American capitalists that sealed the fate of Rosen's Russian staff. An increasingly xenophobic Soviet regime finally ordered the Agro-Joint to leave in January 1938. Rosen left Russia for the last time in July. All that remained were twenty-five thousand Jewish farm families, who had been subsumed into Soviet collectives. They continued to be economically viable up to the outbreak of the Second World War.[119]

Sadly, Jewish collective farms in the Ukraine were almost entirely annihilated when Nazi armies invaded in 1941. The *Einsatzgruppen*, professional killing squads, were deployed to make the Soviet Union "Jew-free." Some inhabitants of Jewish farms in the Crimea were evacuated to the east; others were left to their own devices and, more often than not, were deported to the gas chambers or killed by the German army or its local accomplices, many of them neighboring Tatars and Ukrainians.[120]

The two leaders of the effort were devastated by the termination of their enterprise. A disconsolate Rosenberg called the episode an "utter, complete, black tragedy."[121] Rosen apparently had kept Rosenberg in the dark about the political machinations for fear that they would hurt fundraising. Rosen later reported that life in Russia was still "very difficult, the standard of living is still very low; there is still a great deal of misery and suffering." In retrospect, he was honest about the Agro-Joint's work. "Nor has our own path . . . been strewn with roses. We have had our full share of troubles, disappointments, heartbreaks, and heartaches, from without and within. . . . [The revolution] was neither made by the Jews, nor for the Jews, nor against the Jews. Our people in Russia were simply caught between the millstones of history and were confronted by a dilemma—either to be crushed and turned into historical dust, or to extricate themselves by a determined effort of readjustment . . . to the changed conditions, no matter how painful and torturous this process should prove to be."[122]

With more than a hint of self-justification, Rosen concluded, "Russian Jewry was unable to save itself without outside help."[123] That proved to be an overstatement; while the Ukrainian settlements were never repopulated, Jewish farmers did move back to their Crimean lands after the war. Employees who survived both the purges and the Nazi repression took positions in Soviet economic ministries and also returned to the Crimea.[124]

While Joint administrators were no doubt naïve about their hosts' motives, they could not have imagined the problems they encountered when they began their cooperative venture. Living in a pre-Hitlerian world where the dream of a Palestinian homeland was seen as a partial answer at best, these paternalistic social engineers believed that Jews should be given the opportunity to pursue a better life in their country of origin. Many Russian Jews were grateful for what the Agro-Joint provided.

What lessons did Rosenberg and Rosen take away from more than a decade of colonization work in the Soviet Union? Despite their disappointment, their willingness to throw themselves into the Sosúa project such a short time later indicates that they never lost faith that urban Jews could be transformed into successful farmers. When Rosen returned to New York, the first question he asked Rosenberg was, "What is our next program?"[125]

Still, they must have been startled when Paul Baerwald presented them with the opportunity to try again in the New World. Perhaps they imagined that after Stalin's machinations, working with a dictator of a small tropical island would be child's play. There were no ideological differences to speak of, and the site was significantly closer to home. The scale and layers of bureaucracy involved in the Crimean project were so large that neither man could forge the kind of personal ties with Stalin that they might with Trujillo. On the other hand, they were buoyed by the knowledge that the Agro-Joint had extricated itself in good financial shape; eight hundred thousand dollars would be a sizeable nest egg for the Dominican project and other colonization schemes in the Americas. Moreover, hard-won lessons from the Soviet Union about moving Jews from the cities to the countryside seemed readily transferable to the tropics.

Reflecting on his experience in the Crimea, Rosen concluded that Jewish refugees faced special challenges in making the transition from city to countryside. In 1938 he told a national conference on Jewish welfare that to settle Jews on isolated farms or in small, atomized groups was a project doomed to failure. (This is particularly revealing because, as we shall see, the Sosúa enclave would contradict that basic premise.) He went on to tell his audience that what would be suitable for peasant immigrants was "thoroughly unsuitable for Jews." Dependent on external funding from absentee philanthropies, Jewish settlers "will almost invariably drift apart, sliding in the direction of least resistance and turning to more familiar occupations of peddling, petty trading, etc., thereby supplying fuel for anti-Semitic propaganda which is ever ready to flare up. With peasant immigrants of other nationalities, settlement in a new country is mainly a process of acclimatization; with Jews it must be a double process of acclimatization and physico-psychological retraining." He knew that there was an abundance of young Jewish men and women in Europe who would be willing to undergo "hardships and privations" abroad; the task would be to organize "these young pioneers into disciplined labor front units" that could do the advance work necessary before large numbers of settlers arrived in the new colonies.[126]

Less than two years after leaving Russia, Rosen was traipsing around the Dominican backcountry inspecting sites for a new colonization effort. The frantic months leading up to and immediately after the signing of the January 30, 1940 contract between DORSA and the Dominican government that led to the creation of the Sosúa colony were a critical juncture for the settlement's future. Rosen and Rosenberg each learned very quickly what authorities wanted out of this arrangement.

Part Two / **CONVERGING INTERESTS**

FOUR

"The Eyes of the World Are on the Dominican Republic"

> I am deeply interested to cooperate in a practical way with the humanitarian plans of President Roosevelt. I hope the immigration of European refugees to the Dominican Republic will stimulate the progress of our country and will intensify the development of our national resources as well as our industrial capabilities.
>
> TRUJILLO TO ROSENBERG, 1939

Trujillo visited the United States for the first time in July 1939 as a guest of the U.S. military. An official visit to the U.S. capital, certain to bolster his image back home, had long been a priority, but the State Department had repeatedly rebuffed his requests. He could not understand why he had kept getting the cold shoulder; after all, regional strongmen like Fulgencio Batista and Anastasio Somoza had not had a problem securing permission for their state visits. He also was miffed that Haiti and Cuba had obtained loans from the Export-Import Bank while Dominican negotiations on the 1924 Convention continued to languish.[1]

Since the general was technically not a head of state but commander of the armed forces, Sumner Welles insisted that Trujillo's trip was not officially sanctioned. But his stay in the nation's capital had all the trappings of a state visit. His commanding officers during the occupation, Marine Commandant James Breckenridge and Colonel Thomas Watson, now literally and figuratively rolled out the red carpet. Trujillo purchased a lavish 225-foot yacht for the occasion to "better . . . awe the Americans," and he was accompanied wherever he went by "a retinue of bodyguards, army officers, and aides."[2] He had informal meetings with FDR and Hull about the debt negotiations and continental defense, receptions hosted by Breckinridge and Army chief of staff George Marshall, visits to the Tomb of the Unknown Soldier and Quantico Marine Base, a reception at the Pan American Union, and dinners with members of Congress.

Trujillo went on to New York, where he received a full-dress parade and twenty-one-gun salute at West Point, a second barrage at the New York World's Fair during a ceremony at the Dominican Pavilion, and a dinner hosted by one of his lobbyists, Representative Hamilton Fish, at which he was the guest of honor. Despite the visit's martial flavor, the general did not dress for the part as he normally would at home. Instead, he opted for business suits, to appear more statesmanlike.

Trujillo met criticism in New York. His visit sparked opposition from Mayor Fiorello La Guardia, who refused to have his picture taken with the dictator; and the journalist Heywood Broun, writing in the *New York World-Telegram*, who not only criticized the administration for supporting regional strong-men, but saw through Trujillo's offer. "The murdered men and women at our doorsteps were Negroes of Haiti. The persecuted folk of Germany are Jewish. And it seems that such things can be overlooked by certain statesmen."[3] In the Dominican Republic the visit was, of course, played up as a diplomatic triumph by the general's imagemakers.[4]

If his brief "unofficial" meetings with the secretary of state and the president made little substantive progress, the political climate was clearly propitious for a change. Negotiations between Dominican and U.S. officials on a host of economic and military matters proceeded apace as opposition from Welles melted away and Sosúa occupied center stage.

PLANNING THE SETTLEMENT

Andrés Pastoriza and JDC representative Arthur Lamport corresponded throughout the summer and fall of 1939 to formulate a blueprint for the new colony. Lamport, a New York investment banker and philanthropist, hired consultants to investigate the island's economic potential and to collect statistical information on a wide range of topics, including cash crops, industrial activities, and imports.[5]

Pastoriza and Lamport agreed that it was essential to grow the settlement gradually. The colony would start small, with five hundred pioneers, preferably young families between the ages of eighteen and thirty-five. The settlement would include a small number of "elders" and technical specialists. A

training center for adolescents would be established outside the capital to prepare trainees and ease them into their new surroundings. Lamport surmised
that two hundred thousand dollars was needed for start-up costs. Following
the advice of the survey team, the principals agreed on a fifty-thousand-acre
tract to begin with; more properties would be added as needed. The government promised to help secure a property title, while the Joint would create an
autonomous corporation, the Dominican Republic Settlement Association,
to manage the settlement.[6]

One stumbling block was the five-hundred-dollar residence permit fee that
the recently revised immigration legislation required of "Semitic" peoples.
Lamport asked and the government agreed to waive the fee for the pioneers.
Pastoriza insisted that "neither the Corporation nor its employees are to engage in any political activity whatsoever in the Dominican Republic" and that
DORSA guarantee that the immigrants not become public charges.[7] He also
made it clear that the settlement would not be permitted to cultivate crops
restricted by export or import quotas (that is, sugar) without authorization.
To discourage settlers from leaving at the first opportunity, Pastoriza wrote
a sweetener into the contract: naturalization laws would be relaxed to make
colonists eligible for citizenship after two years' residency. Authorities also
consented to full civil rights and complete religious freedom.

While Pastoriza and Lamport brainstormed, events in Europe preoccupied the president, State Department officials, the PACPR, and the IGC.
At the IGC's meeting on July 19 and 20, Secretary Sir Herbert Emerson reported that 150,000 refugees from greater Germany were currently in countries of transit and that approximately 60,000 of them were either wholly or
partly dependent on charity from refugee organizations. The JDC and other
relief agencies, which had accepted responsibility for the maintenance of refugees with the expectation that they would emigrate in a short time, were now
in a bind. They faced financial commitments of so great a magnitude that it
was impossible to see how they could continue to meet their obligations.[8]

The Joint had allocated twenty million dollars for overseas needs in 1939,
eleven million of which was earmarked for repatriation and refugee aid, effectively doubling the previous year's outlay.[9] The demands were so high that the
organization was forced to take out bridge loans to maintain liquidity. As one
European country after another fell under Nazi control, the organization's
prior distinctions between refugee aid, emigration funds, and emergency relief blurred. War, unemployment, and capital flight meant that relief agencies
were stretched dangerously thin.[10]

Costs were spiraling out of control for countries of transit as well. Great Britain had accepted more than forty thousand refugees since the Anschluss, half of whom, the foreign secretary, Lord Winterton, insisted, "must eventually be re-emigrated." At the IGC's July meeting, Lord Winterton floated the idea of Western governments' putting up matching funds, even though such a gesture went against the Évian mandate that funds come from private agencies. Increasingly concerned with the numbers of refugees languishing in England and the thousands of illegals pouring into Palestine, Winterton threatened to withdraw his government's support for the IGC if Washington and other Western nations did not ante up for refugee relief. The United States refused to take the bait, nor did other nations.[11]

FDR realized that something had to be done "to dramatize the needs of the refugees and the urgency of a comprehensive settlement." He called for a special meeting of the IGC in Washington in mid-October. James McDonald of the PACPR warned Welles that unless the president was prepared to "throw something substantial into the common pot, the chances for the success of the [October] conference were slight, and that the final result might be worse than if the Conference had not been held." McDonald pleaded with Welles for a comprehensive solution that would include substantial public outlays to ease the burden on overcommitted private agencies. Better to cancel the meeting than to raise the refugees' expectations and squander goodwill. Otherwise, the upcoming meeting would become another Évian. While a major commitment was not in the offing, Welles and McDonald conversed about obtaining seed money from the Export-Import Bank or other government agencies to get the Dominican colonization scheme off the ground.[12]

Such conversations about federal start-up funds for resettlement dovetailed with ongoing discussions in the administration about the U.S. foreign assistance program. For some time, exporters and bank officers, hurt by the Depression, had been pressuring the State Department to liberalize its lending policies. The 1938 Mexican nationalization of Standard Oil's Mexican holdings also led policymakers to rethink how U.S. companies were perceived in the region and how loans might be used as a tool to ensure a more hospitable climate for U.S. business interests.

The most significant factor was that the international context of trade relations was changing rapidly, and the administration was reexamining its traditional reluctance to extend credits abroad. Growing German economic penetration of Latin America, predicated on trade agreements, barter exchange, and subsidies for Latin American products, had made a strong impression in Washington. FDR had warned a group of senators that the Ger-

man threat was predicated on dominating world trade and building an economic fence around the United States. Trade trends were worrisome: in 1935
German exports to Latin America doubled, and a year later the Reich surpassed the United States as Brazil's chief trading partner. By 1938, Germany
imported 10.5 percent of all Latin American exports and provided 17.1 percent
of the region's imports, up from 9 and 7.3 percent, respectively, in 1932. A
growing trade rivalry, officials reasoned, would have significant implications
for U.S. security.[13]

Since U.S. investment in Latin America topped five billion dollars and a
third of U.S. manufactured goods were shipped to the region, a great deal
was at stake. Although German barter arrangements invariably came with
strings attached, Latin American nations, hurt by the Depression-era collapse
of commodity prices, the closing of Western European and North American
markets to Latin American exports, and escalating tariff walls, were in dire
straights.

Roosevelt pushed through a series of Export-Import Bank loans for public works programs.[14] In 1939, funds flowed to Brazil, Nicaragua, Paraguay,
Argentina, Chile, and Colombia. Then in June of that year, Roosevelt asked
Congress to appropriate an additional five hundred million dollars. Congress,
which had just set the bank's ceiling at one hundred million dollars, did not
give the president everything he wanted, but doubled the ceiling in March
1940.[15]

The Export-Import Bank became an indispensable tool in the State Department's arsenal to ensure hemispheric cooperation against Axis aggression—
what staffers would come to call Fortress America.[16] With the logjam on intergovernmental loans broken, the State Department was now "alert to the
possibility of trade openings for American goods, either in fitting out settlers
or in taking advantage of new opportunities that will be created after settlements get underway and are productive." Welles told McDonald the Dominican Republic could ensure the settlement's success if new trade openings
with the United States were linked explicitly to the colonization program.
"Such a development would fortunately supply the means of guaranteeing
the stability of settlement operations in the Republic which we have been
seeking, as America would then have a continuing stake in the Dominican
Republic."[17]

There was, however, one qualifier: funding from the bank or other congressional sources had to be "convincingly non-sectarian in character." Projects that benefited just one particular group were considered discriminatory
and would not pass legal muster. The refugee organization selecting the

immigrants should seek out "Protestant, Catholic and other refugees with no church connections at this time."[18]

Germany's invasion of Poland on September 1, 1939, left all sides momentarily unsure how to proceed. But Great Britain did not take long to announce that because of security concerns, German emigrants would not be permitted to enter its colonies. Since this declaration eliminated British Guiana and other parts of the Commonwealth and the Empire from consideration as potential resettlement sites, Sosúa's stock rose.[19]

The PACPR initiated conversations with the JDC about the Dominican initiative. Throughout September PACPR members corresponded with a State Department liaison, Robert Pell; members of the coordinating foundation; and the JDC to gauge their respective interest. Aware of the pressures now being brought to bear on the administration, the PACPR secretary, George Warren, urged the JDC to act on Trujillo's offer because the State Department "would probably be disappointed if we stalled."[20]

The JDC's Executive Committee agreed that the Agro-Joint should, after securing the State Department's blessing, appropriate two hundred thousand dollars of its Crimean nest egg to establish a corporation to manage the colony.[21] Rosenberg and Trujillo then met for the first time in September 1939 at the Plaza Hotel in New York City. Later that month, at a meeting held in Rosenberg's New York home, Joint Executive Committee members and Rosen met to review Lamport's and Pastoriza's preliminary report. Lamport related that Trujillo was keenly interested in improving trade with the United States and viewed the colony as a means to that end. An Export-Import Bank loan would be considered a good faith gesture.[22]

Just as he had with the Crimean venture, Rosenberg refused to move forward without Washington's blessing. By the first week of October, Rosenberg had received written letters of support from the State Department, the IGC, and the PACPR. Rosenberg and Pastoriza then finalized the contract's language and made plans for Rosen's upcoming visit to the island in mid-December to select a site.

While Rosenberg drew up DORSA's incorporation in New York State, the Dominican Foreign Ministry moved ahead with plans for the "intensification of our relations with the USA." The war promised to diminish, and in some respects paralyze, exports to England, France, and Germany, a Foreign Ministry memo stated. These nations "purchased most of our Dominican products" and, given the uncertainties that war presented, it was essential to create new markets. "The U.S. can buy Dominican coffee, cacao and sugar, which we have been sending to France, England and Germany and other European countries." Since the island already had an unfavorable balance of trade with America, "every possible effort [must] be made to increase commerce with the United States."[23]

With Sosúa about to become a reality, Roosevelt and his advisers now believed that they had something worth presenting at the October 17 IGC meeting in Washington. The president would open the meeting with a statement, later distributed to the press, which praised the "generous attitude" of the Dominican government and expressed the hope that this would be "a forerunner of many similar projects in other nations." The initiative was presented as a quick fix to get refugees out of countries of transit, not a long-term solution.

But Roosevelt's statement envisioned millions of refugees displaced by the war and called for engineering and economic surveys of potential sites to prepare for that eventuality. Even though he reminded the delegates that the United States had "been built in great measure by people whose dreams in other lands had been thwarted" and then invoked the words engraved on the Statue of Liberty—"to build new refuges for the tired, for the poor, for the huddled masses yearning to be free"—he refused to tinker with his government's quotas.[24] As McDonald had feared, Roosevelt offered only platitudes and few practical solutions for either the short or the long term.

The British and French delegates evinced little interest in Roosevelt's ideas about a vast, long-term resettlement effort. From their perspective, winning the war was the best solution to the refugee problem. Committee members did confirm one overarching principle, first articulated at Évian, that would have far-reaching implications for Sosúa. The IGC should not facilitate the departure of refugees from Germany and German-occupied territories. To do so would only play into the hands of the Reich, which was determined to rid itself of Jewish nationals. That principle would materially limit the numbers and type of refugees DORSA recruitment agents could draw on in the future as they searched for the right "human material."[25]

Two days later and a full fifteen months after Évian, the Dominican government issued a formal proposal to accept German and Austrian refugees. Trujillo invited the not-quite-incorporated DORSA leadership to come to the island in late January 1940 to formalize an agreement. Subsequently, Rosenberg hosted a luncheon in the general's honor at the Hotel Carleton in Washington, where the dictator was feted by an array of prominent Washington insiders, including PACPR and IGC members.[26] Also present were Paul Van Zeeland, the head of the Coordinating Foundation, and both Assistant Secretary Adolf Berle Jr. and Robert Pell from the State Department.

Trujillo presented Rosenberg with a letter that must have been music to the ears of Jewish philanthropists and Roosevelt's advisers. Emphasizing how his offer was consistent with the principles of the Good Neighbor, he declared that his government was "keenly desirous of making this undertaking a milestone in the difficult refugee problems which confront the world, and will take all appropriate steps to see to it than there shall be no discrimination against such settlers but that they shall be given an honorable, just and equal opportunity so that they may pursue their occupations and life free of molestation and persecution."[27] The formal text of the offer was read aloud at the luncheon and distributed to the press the same day.[28] To allay State Department concerns, Pastoriza emphasized that both "Jewish and non-Jewish" settlers were to be included in the first group of five hundred families. DORSA was to be financially responsible for the settlers' transportation and their welfare in their new home. It was to select the colonists, but subject to the government's approval.[29]

Pastoriza linked his government's offer to Roosevelt's call two days earlier to seek out "vacant spaces on the earth's surface" for European settlers. He cautioned that his government would not be hasty in implementing this colonization project, even though there were "apt to be early and pressing appeals from unfortunate refugees for the further opening of our doors; appeals to which we shall not wish to be deaf, but which we can meet only in due time."[30]

Welles was invited to the dinner but, given his feelings for Trujillo, did not attend. He did offer Rosenberg encouragement in a letter: "You know of my deep and abiding interest in the work which you and your associates are doing, and I feel as you do that this first project in the Dominican Republic may prove to be only a forerunner of similar projects of outstanding importance and usefulness."[31] He also worked behind the scenes, asking the president to make a public show of support for the initiative. Rosenberg deserved the administration's backing, said Welles, because "he is one of the few figures who has emerged in this work who not only wishes to get things done but sees that they are done."[32]

Roosevelt offered his congratulations in writing in December, calling the Dominican initiative "a turning point"; and then he met with Rosenberg in person at the White House in early January, just a day before the attorney left for the Dominican Republic to sign the contract.[33]

Media response to the project was, by and large, positive. *The Nation*, which had been highly critical of Trujillo's actions during and after the massacre, published an article titled "Mercy and Statesmanship." Although the magazine found it ironic that refugees were leaving one dictatorship for another, it noted that such an occurrence was not unusual. Refugees, after all, could not afford to be choosy.[34]

Rosenberg proved a superb publicist, as puff pieces about the agreement appeared throughout the fall and winter of 1939–40. DORSA sent cables to the *New York Times*, the Associated Press, the United Press, the *Washington Post*, and various Jewish newspapers. Dominican panegyrists did the same at home, extolling Trujillo's humanitarianism in the national press.[35]

But there were dissenting voices, especially in the American Jewish community. Wise blasted the enterprise as a mirage, demeaning the Joint for its "ceaseless persistence."[36] The Zionist press compared Sosúa to Birobidzhan, predicting it would end up just like its predecessor—an endless sieve for well-intentioned but naïve Jewish philanthropists. The *American Jewish Chronicle* erroneously chastised the Joint for investing in the Birobidzhan experiment and for breaking bread with Trujillo when the earlier experience with Stalin had failed so ignominiously. "With so many refugees seeking a landing place, the danger is great that this latest castle-in-the-air may attract even greater sympathy than the Russian project and cause even more grievous disappointment and heartache." The newspaper was especially dubious about the contract's guarantees of political and religious freedom: "And who will enforce this guarantee should it ever please the government, in the light of its past practices, to repudiate it? Why invest human lives and wealth in a country where the entire population is practically devoid of rights? A ruler who exiles political opponents can hardly be trusted not to exile alien immigrants, once they have enriched his treasury."[37]

An editorial in the Jewish newspaper *The Day* blasted the contract as an act of "international cowardice" and fumed at its nondenominational veneer. "As if in the face of the terrific anti-Semitic destruction of Jews of Europe, we can deny the character of the refugee problem." The editorial pointedly asked "what goyim" did DORSA "want to care for. Or will they strain to find a few goyim in order to prove the colonization plan is not purely a Jewish affair? Whom are they trying to please?"[38]

Dominican exile leaders also dismissed the contract as a publicity stunt. Persio Franco reminded Pell that the Trujillo regime was the "most dictatorial in the history of Latin America" and raised concerns about the contract's legitimacy. "Is it not to be expected that when this regime is ended whatever it has done without the consent of the people will be undone?"[39]

One critic, who evidently knew something about recent Dominican history and anti-Semitism, wrote Rosenberg that "history has again and again shown that once the welcome wears off there is merely a new Jewish problem, and in this case there will be a new and complicated racial problem." Why move Jews from "where the doctrine of Aryan superiority is rampant" to a place where racism against blacks was ubiquitous. The letter concluded by reminding Rosenberg of the Haitian massacre and the economic reasons for that tragedy, and cautioned that Jewish colonization might spark a similar backlash and trigger "the jealous resistance of the inhabitants."[40]

Even the PACPR had reservations about the project's scope and the general's intentions. Warren wrote the State Department that Trujillo lacked a "far-sighted view of the degree to which these refugees might contribute to the economic development of the country." Trujillo's principal rationale was not humanitarian but "to augment the white population of the island." Warren also raised concerns about the discrepancy between the original promise to take in one hundred thousand refugees and the current decision to introduce only five hundred families. How many would eventually settle there, he wondered.[41]

Despite the carping, organizers pushed ahead. The rest of the fall was taken up with DORSA's incorporation, Rosen's visit to the island, and preparations for the formal contract signing in late January. Rosenberg and Rosen were named president and vice president of the new association, and an ecumenical board was put together, including representatives from the American Friends Service Committee and the National Council of Catholic Men.[42]

Rosenberg later admitted to Lamport that drawing up DORSA's incorporation papers, fine-tuning the contract, attending the endless round of meetings with State Department officials and Trujillo's lieutenants, and communicating with the media were taking their toll. "I have never worked so hard as I have the last few months," the sixty-six-year-old Rosenberg said.[43]

THE GIFT AND THE SIGNING

When Rosen and his assistant Frederic Perlestein arrived in December 1939, they visited a number of sites that first had been examined by the Department of Agriculture team. Unfortunately, while touring the countryside, Rosen came down with malaria. He must have thought this was déjà vu; he had nearly died from typhus at the start of his Crimean odyssey. His health never recovered from the malaria's lingering effects, however, and he would have to turn over the day-to-day administration of the new colony to subordinates in 1941. His subsequent absence would be a setback for the settlement during its critical first years.

Rosen selected the Sosúa site, ten kilometers east of Puerto Plata on the north coast. A few days later, he and Rosenberg learned that Trujillo intended to donate those lands to DORSA. Trujillo had purchased the property just a year earlier for fifty thousand dollars from the United Fruit Company, which sold it to him in appreciation for the protection afforded when he was head of the army.[44] Did the dictator make such a grand gesture only after learning of Rosen's interest? Or did Trujillo insist on Sosúa? Did Rosen feel obliged to select one of the dictator's properties?

Although answers to these questions were not forthcoming, the gift had to raise eyebrows in New York and at the Department of Agriculture. Why did Rosen select Sosúa when he knew full well that the department's team had serious reservations about the 26,000 acre property? If we can believe a promotional brochure DORSA published in early 1940, Rosen was swept away by the site's picturesque setting on the Caribbean. But Sosúa's recent history and the experts' lackluster assessment should have raised questions in Rosen's mind about the site's viability.

Before the United Fruit Company acquired it, the property, which was named for a very modest river that flowed through the site to the bay, had never been developed commercially. Only a small garrison had been stationed there. By 1916, United Fruit had given up on cultivating bananas at Sosúa because of its poor soil, scattered rock outcrops, and lack of water.[45] At that point the company hired a caretaker, who raised a few head of cattle on the site. For the next two decades, the property, approximately eight miles wide along the coast and seven miles wide inland, remained substantially unimproved. When Trujillo purchased it in June 1938, it was with the intention of turning Sosúa into a cattle ranch, but he did little to improve it in the year he owned it.[46] There was a large house on the premises, an office, a milking barn, a number of usable buildings, some twenty houses—most of them in disrepair—running water, electricity, miles of wire fencing, and the remains of an old pier on the beach.[47]

The survey team's report noted that the site was surrounded by local landowners and that "it would be difficult to increase materially the size of the property if such was needed in the event of colonization." Although the north coast region generally received adequate rainfall, it was susceptible to periodic droughts. The shortage of water, erratic rainfall, shallow topsoil, boggy areas, and rocky terrain led the team to conclude that coffee, cacao, or sugar could not be cultivated profitably at Sosúa. Conventional farming would be difficult, to say the least: "a horseback ride over the tract failed to reveal any sizeable area of plowable lands." The report concluded, "the property, primarily, is suited to pasture" and was not for "general settlement purposes."[48] Although a fifty-thousand-gallon reservoir lay on a hillside, the water originated in a polluted stream and, as a later report noted, carried "all the pollution to be expected from a tropical river used as a laundry and as a bath for man and beast." As a result, settlers were advised to boil all drinking water. Since much of the land was calcareous limestone, the soil was very porous. That meant that even wells were susceptible to surface pollution.[49]

The team's public health specialist warned that although malaria was ubiquitous throughout the country, its incidence was higher along the coast. He advised that other sites at higher elevations would be "more favorable to white settlers from the standpoint of pleasant temperatures [and] freedom from mosquito pests, than some of the low lying areas."[50]

As if the written report had not been damning enough, Rosen met personally with the team before his trip to review their findings. But apparently his physical inspection of the site was enough to ease whatever concerns he may have had.[51] A year later, Rosen would write that Sosúa "offered the possibilities for developing within the shortest period of time."[52] While it was true that time was of the essence and some housing and infrastructure already was in place, the same could be said of other sites under consideration as well.[53]

Rosen violated one of the most important precepts of agricultural colonization. Especially in tropical settings, a diversity of soil types and lands is essential. Lands suitable for just one agricultural activity, such as livestock, were problematic; experts encouraged diversification and self-sufficiency to mitigate the need to purchase basic staples.[54] Therefore, what moved this expert agronomist, someone with years of experience in colonization—admittedly in temperate lands—to question what specialists in tropical agriculture had recommended? Why not defer to the experts? It is especially puzzling because Rosen's Crimean colonists had struggled with arid climate, insufficient water, and poor soils. Why choose a problematic site like Sosúa, a place where it would be well nigh impossible to practice the kind of communal farming he so ardently believed in, when several other sites were well thought of by the team?

If Rosen felt obligated to select a property Trujillo had owned, there were certainly several others on the list that the team considered more suitable. In an address to donors in New York City two weeks after the contract signing, Rosenberg, reluctant to go into detail, claimed that the impetus came from Rosen and Rosen alone, but did acknowledge that other sites were more fertile.[55]

Leon Falk, a Pittsburgh industrialist who succeeded Rosen as the colony's director in 1941, offered a plausible explanation several years later. Rosen conceived of Sosúa as a point of departure, a training site where settlers could come for a short period to acclimate themselves before moving on to other locations more conducive to communal farming practices. Falk and Maurice Hexter, who replaced Rosenberg as chief operating officer in 1943, both contended that Rosen was fully aware of Sosúa's limitations. Falk told a meeting of the boards of Agro-Joint and DORSA in 1946, "As far as agriculture was concerned, he [Rosen] planned to move into other parts of San Domingo where there were better lands—where for instance, the Dominican government was opening up irrigation projects."[56] Hexter said as much when he reported to the Agro-Joint Board a few years later that the "Sosúa area was not intended to be the site of the settlement but essentially an orientation and training ground, an intention which factors beyond our control made it impossible to realize."[57]

In any case, DORSA administrators were surprised to learn of Trujillo's unexpected gift just days before the signing. In his letter of January 20, 1940 to DORSA announcing his intentions, Trujillo more than generously estimated the property's value at one hundred thousand dollars, double what he had paid to United Fruit a year before.[58]

The dictator's donation should be seen as the symbolic origin of what would become an instrumental friendship. Implicit was the expectation that other gifts would be forthcoming by both parties. Marcel Mauss, an anthropologist of symbols, writing about precapitalist societies, views gift exchange as a social compact, part of a larger ritual process. Each step in the ritual carries social and moral significance. Mauss's insights are applicable to the clientelistic ties Trujillo forged with subordinates throughout his tenure in power. The exchange is both utilitarian and ideological; there is an obligation not only to give presents but to gratefully receive the gift so as not to insult the giver; and then, of course, to repay it. The fascinating part of this dialectical relationship is that both parties may come to believe that they have benefited disproportionately.[59] DORSA officials, grateful that Trujillo welcomed their refugees when no else did, would prove loyal to a fault; and the general's specific requests for personal services, including lobbying the Roosevelt administration, were, in their minds, a small price to pay.

The exchange was not just manifested publicly; Rosenberg sent thoughtful personal gifts to the general from the outset, including some of his own artwork, and a paddle tennis set for Trujillo's young son, Ramfis.[60] Such reciprocal gift giving, both personal and public, sealed a friendship between the two that endured for the next two decades.

Such institutionalized gift giving was consistent with the dictator's modus operandi. At official ceremonies Trujillo dispensed all manner of gifts—everything from artificial limbs for the disabled to bicycles for children and food for workers. According to the historian Robin Derby, such offerings recast the general's authority in familial terms while creating ties of dependency with constituents.[61]

Although aware of the symbolic value of the donation, some JDC board members expressed reservations about DORSA's accepting the gift. To mitigate the appearance of impropriety, they (through Rosenberg) insisted that Trujillo accept one hundred shares of DORSA stock, a figure equal to the property's value. Rosenberg recalled that Trujillo initially refused the shares but finally acceded after Rosenberg informed him that it was important to the settlers not to feel that they were getting something for nothing, and that they were expected to repay DORSA "all our investment."[62] DORSA later cemented its ties officially by naming the general to the organization's Board of Directors. As another gesture of goodwill, Rosenberg sent Ramfis a token share of stock.[63]

While Rosen was shown around the island, Rosenberg worked tirelessly on preparations for the contract signing in Ciudad Trujillo on January 30, 1940. Both DORSA and Dominican authorities understood the public relations value of such a visit. Rosenberg invited (and coordinated the arrival of) representatives of the State Department, the PACPR, the IGC, and the Coordinating Foundation, each of which would give the enterprise its official blessing. Before leaving for the Dominican Republic on January 11, he also crated up a dozen paintings, some from his valuable private collection and some of his own work, to give to the dictator as a token of his appreciation.[64]

In the capital, the general's lieutenants made preparations for the event; no expense was spared. The regime held many ceremonies; they were equal parts public ritual and spectacle. Banquets and receptions were lavishly appointed. Such ostentatious public events were designed, according to Derby, to help Trujillo legitimate his rule and impose a new moral order. Civic parades, local and national pageants, mass baptisms, unveilings of new monuments and public works projects occurred with such regularity throughout the Trujillato that they became part of the normal course of events. Historian José R. Cordero Michel estimates that each year four hundred masses were offered for the dictator's continued good health, and the state bureaucracy organized three hundred spiritual retreats, twenty-five hundred political conferences, and more than eight hundred meetings, parades, and demonstrations across the length and breadth of the country. An estimated three-and-a-half million Dominicans attended these state functions annually.[65]

Such ritual was invariably packaged as a generous gift from *El Benefactor* to the Dominican people. The dictatorship's clientelism lay in the insistence on mutual obligations and the selected use of coercion.[66] As Derby explains, these lavish celebrations were more than patronage, since they were not directed to any one individual. "It was certainly a throwback to a seigniorial mode of authority, one based on a normative system in which the state was obliged to assist and protect its citizenry, in compensation for their lack of representation."[67] The state's ritual expenditures indebted the people to their ruler, and were carefully designed to accentuate patriotism and unity. Nationalism was a potent theme that publicists stressed in speeches and slogans, but it was not the only one. Hammered home at virtually every function were the themes of peace, order, progress, secure borders, and the well-being of the Dominican family.[68]

Social classes that previously had been excluded from participation in civil society were now intentionally invited to participate in the ceremonies. Through their involvement, they lent their consent for and loyalty to the regime. The result was a staged "choreography of consent" that confirmed the dictator's power. Trujillo's "theater state" engendered the direct or indirect participation of all social classes and was an important tool employed to monopolize public discourse and promote the dictator's national agenda.[69] Even events closed to the public, like the DORSA signing, were shared with the general population through extensive media coverage. This enabled the masses to become consumers, if not voyeurs, of affairs of state.

More than one hundred dignitaries were invited to the National Palace for the signing, including the diplomatic corps, the archbishop of Ciudad Trujillo, the cabinet, congressional leaders, the chief justice of the Supreme Court, members of high society, wealthy Americans living in the capital, and other foreign VIPs.

Messages sent especially for the occasion congratulating the dictator on his humanitarianism were read from a long list of statesmen, including Taylor, Winterton, Van Zeeland, McDonald, and Hull, while homage was paid in person by the figurehead president of the republic, Jesús María Troncoso de la Concha; Pell; Stephen Morris, head of the IGC; Harold Linder, representing the Coordinating Foundation; and Rosenberg.[70]

Trujillo's generosity was extolled in a succession of tributes, none more hyperbolic than that delivered by Pell. Calling the contract historic, he told those assembled, "the eyes of the world are on the Dominican Republic," and declared that this agricultural experiment represented the first scientific effort to bring order to a world in chaos. He applauded Trujillo by invoking the sacred (for Dominicans) symbol of Christopher Columbus, who "discovered" the island in 1492. In what would give new meaning to the concept of rewriting history, Pell stated that Trujillo embodied the explorer's commitment to those "without hope and the oppressed."

Not only did this represent a serious mischaracterization of a ruler who, a little more than two years earlier, had ordered the massacre of fifteen thousand unarmed Haitians, but it imputed humanitarian motives to Columbus that even his most generous chroniclers had never ascribed. Although Pell might be excused for taking liberties on an occasion like this, what such exaggeration really accentuated was just how far Trujillo had come in the State Department's estimation since October 1937.

Speeches by Stephen Morris of the IGC and other guests contained similar platitudes. Rosenberg, by all accounts a superb speaker, rose to the occasion, reminding those present of Trujillo's efforts to rebuild the capital in 1930 from the devastating San Zenón hurricane, which had cost the lives of twenty thousand residents and caused an estimated twenty million dollars in property damage. Now, *El Benefactor* was intent on reconstructing "the tortured lives of those destroyed by the hurricanes of war and persecution."

The evening's most revealing remarks, however, came from an unlikely source. Never considered an eloquent speaker, Trujillo himself eschewed the clichés and came to the point, explaining why this social experiment was critical to his nation's future. "Efforts to intensify the cultivation of our lands are realized and, at the same time, indirectly, there is a favorable change toward ameliorating our ethnic problem, since these immigrating currents bring capable and desirable racial elements to our soil." His willingness to broach the racial issue at that moment suggests that he was speaking primarily to his domestic constituents rather than the distinguished invited guests from abroad.

Yet his decision to forego the diplomatic niceties and invoke "our ethnic problem" in this setting must have struck some of the invited dignitaries as ironic at best. The IGC's Morris and JDC officials like Rosenberg and Linder were working to save Jewish refugees fleeing from a madman who had condemned an entire race of people. Now American Jewish philanthropists and those in the international community most empathetic to the refugees' plight were making common cause with a megalomaniac who viewed these refugees as an answer to his nation's racial dilemma.

The gift of Sosúa and the very public, ritualized contract signing ensured that all of the key players, from that moment on—the Dominican state, Washington, the international refugee organizations, and DORSA—had thrown their lot in together. It would set in motion reciprocal linkages guaranteeing that each partner would come to the aid of any other as circumstances warranted.

The public celebration and symbolic gift giving did not subside with the signing. A week later, the regime's largesse continued when Rosenberg was awarded an honorary degree for "services to oppressed refugees without regard to race and religion" from the Universidad de Santo Domingo Law School—only the fifth such degree conferred in the university's four-hundred-year history.[71]

Rosenberg's acceptance speech represents a fascinating melding of the converging interests that had led to the new colony's creation.[72] His close friend McDonald, the former League of Nations High Commissioner of Refugees, had resigned his post in 1935, frustrated by the League's impotence in the face of Nazi persecution of its minorities. Now Rosenberg began his speech by lamenting that the League's World Court was powerless to settle disputes among sovereign states and that the court's incapacity to act decisively had contributed to the war. "Today when more than half the world is at war, the World Court is helpless. . . . Men, women, children are driven into exile; robbed, bombed, reduced to slavery, wantonly murdered. God is denied. . . . Treaties are scraps of paper." The Nazi repression of the Jews represented a threat not just to one oppressed minority but to the principles of international law. It was gratifying to see that heroic figures like the general were responding to a world in chaos. Preaching to the choir, Rosenberg paid tribute to Trujillo, certain that the Évian offer ultimately would be regarded as "a voice of humanity in today's wilderness of man's inhumanity to man."[73]

He then compared the *Generalíssimo*, as he affectionately called him, to Simón Bolívar, the architect of South American independence and the statesman most commonly associated with the principles of Pan Americanism. Bolívar had called a congress of the newly independent Latin American nations in 1826 to promote interamerican solidarity, to counter the threat posed by European powers intent on retaking their former colonies. Now, with the insidious specter of Nazi imperialism hanging over the Americas, it was time, Rosenberg believed, for statesmen to send a similar message to the Reich. Rosenberg reminded his audience that Bolívar, too, had been a great believer in the benefits of European and North American immigration to Latin America.

FIGURE 5 "Your nation's hospitality is a symbol of the supreme law of the Good Neighbor."
JDC ARCHIVES.

Rosenberg assured his audience that eugenic principles would be applied to the selection of pioneers for the new colony (see figure 5, above). "We shall see to it that the settlers shall be fine, sturdy material and we shall make it our business to bring to your shores men and women whom you will welcome." DORSA's managers, he emphasized, were veterans in colonization. Seeking to dispel the notion that Jews were incapable of adapting to farming, he spoke of the Agro-Joint's efforts in the Crimea and their support for ongoing colonization projects in Palestine, boasting that "over four hundred thousand Jewish tillers of the soil have created vast new riches for their countries by modern, scientific farming." Here Rosenberg shrewdly sought to allay fears that the new settlers were wolves in sheep's clothing; that they would desert the colony as soon as possible, find their way to Ciudad Trujillo or Santiago, and thereby pose a threat to the island's commercial sector.

Rosenberg also explained how this new undertaking was consistent with the principles of the Good Neighbor. He lauded FDR and Hull for their statesmanship, their commitment to nonintervention, bilateralism, and mutual reciprocity. He concluded his address with a rhetorical flourish: "Your nation's hospitality is a symbol of the supreme law of the Good Neighbor. . . .

I have traveled widely. Never—and I measure my words—never in all my life has such hospitality been showered on me; and in that I take great heart and courage. It is for hapless exiles that I am here as spokesman and pleader; and so I know that in opening your doors and your hearts to me you have done so for them."[74]

To be sure, Rosenberg knew how to sell this initiative, but he was also personally taken with Trujillo. A letter to his wife, Bessie, five days before the signing offers an indication of his first impressions.[75] Treated like "visiting royalty," Rosenberg was given the use of a luxurious home with a swimming pool and a staff of attendants, including a chauffeur, an armed bodyguard, a butler, and a French chef. "But these are trifles," Rosenberg allowed. "The big fact is that this *Generalíssimo* is a dynamo. Absolute ruler. Determined to make this a success. Likes me immensely. . . . Most expressive face that I ever saw. Mind like lightning." These rapid-fire characterizations were similar to those of other contemporaries, who invariably commented on Trujillo's personal magnetism and forceful personality.[76] More to the point, Rosenberg confided to his wife, in a series of staccato phrases suitable for a telegram, that Trujillo was "obsessed with the idea of more whites. Wants Jews. Not guessing. I know. Wants us. Has the vision to see he needs us."[77]

Rosenberg also acknowledged Trujillo's flair for the dramatic. On January 18, two days after he arrived in Ciudad Trujillo, he and Rosen met with Trujillo, and Rosen purportedly spoke of his interest in Sosúa. The next day, Rosen and Rosenberg traveled across the island so that Rosenberg could see the property. His first impressions were uniformly positive. "Sosúa thrilled us," he later recalled, and the magnificent waterfront and beach were "of surpassing loveliness."[78] Yet he was startled by Trujillo's response just one day later. "And what a sense of drama. Offered it [the Sosúa property] in a letter delivered to me on the estate 250 miles from here when I was there—letter sent by motorcycle policeman to be handed to me . . . his mind is a first-rate businessman's mind. . . . So you see it's an amazing experience."[79] That Trujillo presented the tract to DORSA at such an opportune moment, in such an uncommon manner, and in such a beautiful setting overlooking the Caribbean, is testimony to the general's uncanny ability to ensnare potential allies.

If the dictator's publicists knew how to spin the good news in the capital, Rosenberg, an old hand at fundraising from the Crimean project, understood how to build on the media response that the signing had generated back home. His carefully prepared press releases were sent to prominent newspapers up and down the Eastern Seaboard. The *New York Times* and the *Herald Tribune* featured the story on the front page, and the *Tribune* carried Rosenberg's speech at the signing almost verbatim.[80] Lowell Thomas was just as generous on his January 30, 1940, NBC broadcast: "Today in the old city of Santo Domingo now called Ciudad Trujillo, a ceremony was enacted—a ceremony bearing upon a pitiful problem now so much obscured by the thunder of war, the problem of the refugees from Nazi Germany. Today, General Trujillo, the strong man of the Dominican Republic, presided at the signing of a contract to settle five hundred refugee families on farm lands of the great West Indian island. . . . These five hundred families are just a beginning. The plan is to settle one hundred thousand refugees in Santo Domingo."[81]

Basking in the limelight, and perhaps carried away by his newfound international reputation, Trujillo decreed in April that henceforth all government agencies date all published materials from the regime's inception in 1930 with the moniker, "Era of Trujillo."[82] An upbeat Eugene Hinkle wrote Cordell Hull that Trujillo, although still ruthless on occasion, was showing evidence of maturing as a leader. He pinpointed the massacre as a turning point in the general's evolution; coupled with his recent trips abroad, there were indications that "the ruthless caudillo is being merged with the benevolent statesman."[83]

Yet just two weeks before the signing, the general's brutal methods again were in plain sight. Several officers and thirty soldiers and civilians were arrested and killed (some while detained in prison) for allegedly plotting to kill the dictator's brother, Héctor, the army chief of staff.[84] The exiled leader Franco vehemently protested to the State Department, "It is as if this (latest) massacre was the salute which Trujillo deemed . . . convenient" to send to the assembled dignitaries as they made arrangements for the arrival "of 100,000 European immigrants."[85]

After returning home, Rosenberg urged Trujillo to continue to publicize the initiative aggressively in the States, because keeping the story alive would help DORSA raise funds. He asked Trujillo to have his lieutenants highlight the Dominican Congress's imminent rubber stamping of the contract. To accentuate its newsworthiness, he wrote Trujillo, the press release emanating from Ciudad Trujillo should be concise and written in the form of a cablegram. Rosenberg provided sample text, suggested outlets for the release (the Associated Press, the United Press, the *Washington Post*, the *New York Times*), and even recommended what time of day the message should arrive. "They should not go too early on the 20th [the day the congress ratified the contract], because if they do, the stories might be carried in a few afternoon papers here in the United States, and if that is done, then the next morning the morning papers will not carry the story." He even offered Rosen's services to help get the cablegrams out.[86]

Rosenberg capitalized on the manufactured publicity to kick-start the fund-raising. He had written Taylor that DORSA had two hundred thousand dollars in the Agro-Joint account but needed an additional three hundred thousand to get the colony up and running.[87] He invited a number of potential donors to an open meeting at the Town Hall Club in New York City on February 15. Pell, as he had been in Ciudad Trujillo, was there to show the flag.

Tailoring the message to his corporate audience, Rosenberg related that DORSA's goal was to make the still-to-be-selected pioneers self-sustaining as soon as possible. He employed the same reasoning that had worked so well with Trujillo. DORSA, he insisted, would not be a handout for the misbegotten. "We are determined to make this a self-sustaining, sound economic project, and expect the settlers in due time to repay all our investment. . . . We have not for a moment forgotten that in such an undertaking humanitarianism crumbles to bits without a solid agricultural and economic foundation."[88] He then invoked the names of legendary entrepreneurs and philanthropists, Felix Warburg, Julius Rosenwald, and John D. Rockefeller, all of whom had contributed to Crimean colonization.

Like all successful salesmen, Rosenberg embellished as needed, informing his audience, "In the Sosúa region, there are hundreds of thousands of additional acres, largely Government owned, of fertile, undeveloped land with room for many thousands of settlers."[89] It was critical, he concluded, that this experiment succeed. "In Europe, there is only death or something worse. In the Dominican Republic there is asylum and hope." Jews, objects of rejection and humiliation elsewhere, would be welcomed to this tropical island. Why? "They need us. They want us. They tell us so. Vast rich undeveloped acreage awaits the toiler's hand. . . . The Dominican Republic is a model of future immigration projects. Today they hesitate to accept large-scale immigration. It is for us to wipe away those doubts by proving that those victims of oppression, torn and tortured by insensate hate and persecution, will become rich assets to the Dominican Republic."[90]

The Town Hall Club fundraiser and subsequent arm twisting in New York and Palm Beach, Florida exceeded even Rosenberg's expectations. By March, DORSA had five hundred thousand dollars in its coffers and had opened offices on Broadway in New York and on the Malecón in Ciudad Trujillo.[91]

There were, however, other important matters that required Rosenberg's attention. He left New York immediately after the fundraiser and went to Washington to lobby administration officials on behalf of the Dominican government. The savvy attorney, who had plenty of experience defending shrewd corporate clients and more than a decade's worth of negotiations with a Soviet tyrant, was about to go to work for the dictator; and nothing ever came from the general without strings attached. If paternalism defined working relationships and political patronage was the mortar and bricks of the Dominican state, Rosenberg and Rosen were about to receive an object lesson in how Trujillo's dictatorial mansion was constructed.

FIVE

One Good Turn

> Here we expect to give new hope to the oppressed. If we are to live,
> if civilization is to endure, this era of hatred and oppression must
> end. . . . Tonight, when Europe's lights dim, concealing millions of
> people trembling with fear about the engines of war, Sosúa's set-
> tlers sleep in peace.
>
> JAMES ROSENBERG, 1941

Trujillo called in his chits soon after the signing. He needed assistance getting negotiations moving with Washington on two
key matters: ending the customs receivership and increasing the sugar
quota. Trujillo's representatives approached Rosenberg while he was in
Ciudad Trujillo and asked him to lobby the administration. He wasted
no time contacting key figures at the State and Treasury Departments
and had good and bad news to relay to the dictator via Pastoriza.

He could do little to help with the "sugar problem." Dominican
sugar interests had been buoyed recently by negotiations before the
London Sugar Council, a clearing house for sugar sales destined largely
for the European market. Until recently, much of that market had
been closed to exports because of protectionist measures by major
countries, which privileged their colonial sugar producers. But now
prices were high, and the Dominican market share had grown over
the last two years.[1] Trujillo turned his sights on the U.S. market. Even
though he did not yet have a personal stake in the sugar industry—he
would not drive U.S. companies from the island and take personal
control until after World War II—sugar exports were taxed, and the
funds went directly to state coffers, bypassing the receivership's controls. Throughout the 1930s and early 1940s, sugar exports generated

more than half of the nation's export earnings, enabling Trujillo to invest in an extensive public works program of bridges, highways, and docks that was popular with all social classes. By 1938, sugar exports were generating nearly two million dollars in revenues.[2]

But the U.S. Sugar Act of 1934 reserved only 4 percent of the U.S. market for foreign sources, except Cuba and the Philippines. When in 1937 their share of the U.S. quota increased from three thousand to thirty-two thousand tons, Dominican officials were bullish on the commodity's future. But that increase came about only because Philippine sugar producers had not met their target and the unused portion of their quota was reallocated to other countries. Dominican producers could not predict from year to year whether the Philippines or Cuba would fill their allocations. What Trujillo wanted was a larger and more predictable market share. In 1938, Pastoriza asked the State Department for a fivefold increase in the quota to 150,000 tons a year, but the department rejected that fanciful request out of hand.[3]

The real obstacle was the powerful sugar lobby, Rosenberg asserted. There were "powerful interests concerning firstly the production and manufacture in this country, and secondly those of the American possessions and Cuba." Even if he agreed to speak to all the senators and representatives favorably disposed toward Trujillo, and even if they spoke on the floor of Congress in favor of increasing the quota, "all of this is like barking at the moon."[4] An increase in the quota would have to come at the expense of other domestic and foreign sugar producers. Since Western U.S. beet sugar growers had tremendous clout in Congress, an increase would put sugar cane exporters at a disadvantage. Unfortunately, the very same U.S. sugar companies that dominated Dominican production would not "be sincerely interested in obtaining a raise in our quota at the expense of the Cuban and Puerto Rican quota, where these companies have great interests with which they benefit much more."[5]

The sugar quota, Rosenberg informed Pastoriza, was dominated by "invisible forces which are difficult, not to say impossible, to overcome. Even the State Department is powerless in this manner." He suggested that the Dominicans hire a consultant and gave Pastoriza the name of a lawyer who was well recommended, even though he did not know him personally. If the consultant thought it was in the Dominican government's interest to press the issue, Rosenberg would contact "his friends" at the major media outlets to see if they would advocate an increase in the quota.[6]

Given Rosenberg's pessimistic assessment, Trujillo decided to move in a different direction. Preoccupied with the prospect of wartime shortages, the

British agreed to purchase four hundred thousand tons from the Dominican Republic for nine cents a pound. That amount represented the entire annual sugar crop. A year later the British extended the agreement at triple the price. Although the war brought with it disruptions in transatlantic shipping, and the Dominican Republic in 1942 mustered just under half the sugar the British wanted, the higher prices translated into larger profits for sugar producers and increased revenues for the national treasury.[7]

It is interesting that Rosenberg's information gathering about the "sugar problem" was not a secret. In an article that otherwise praised the Sosúa initiative, *The Nation*'s correspondent alluded to Trujillo's apparent quid pro quo for admitting Jews. "Trujillo naturally resents American control of Dominican customs, and so of its finances. He also resents special preferences granted to Cuban sugar. A group of influential Americans, like those sponsoring the Settlement Association, will have an interest in promoting Dominican rights and Dominican prosperity in Washington."[8] Linking DORSA, the Joint, and the State Department so explicitly to such influence peddling may have created some discomfort in New York and Washington, but it did little to deter a grateful Rosenberg from assisting the general.

Fortunately, Rosenberg had better news to report about the Convention of 1924. He had met with "several important friends at the Department of State" and had communicated the Dominican rationale for eliminating the customs receivership. He reiterated Trujillo's talking points, that the agreement was anachronistic and was inconsistent with the Good Neighbor's noninterventionist spirit. Since 50 percent of all customs revenues went directly to service the debt and the government was prohibited from taking out any new loans or raising tariffs without U.S. consent, the receivership effectively put the Dominican economy in a vise. The country was on firm economic footing and politically stable, and with regular payments made on the debt, bondholders could rest assured that the government was not going to end up insolvent.[9]

It became apparent to Rosenberg that the Roosevelt administration was anxious to move on this matter, because the 1940 presidential elections were on the horizon and no one could predict if a Republican administration would be similarly inclined. If Trujillo was willing to compromise, he felt certain that a deal was within reach. Perhaps the Dominican government could get 75 percent of what it wanted now, but "the remaining 25 percent would be easier to obtain in not a distant future, because by that time the impressions of that shock would have passed and the final stroke would then be easier to accomplish." Rosenberg recommended that Trujillo hire a capable, well-connected attorney; and he knew just the man, a close personal friend of President Roosevelt, George Rublee, the former IGC chairman. "He has the absolute confidence of the President," Rosenberg told Pastoriza, and "he is very much interested in the Dominican refugee project." Pastoriza decided to contact Robert Pell and get a second opinion. Pell not only gave Rublee a glowing recommendation but promised to introduce him to Pastoriza.[10]

Trujillo went so far as to ask Rosenberg to represent the Dominican state in the negotiations, but Rosenberg demurred, concerned about the appearance of a conflict of interest with his job as DORSA chairman and the possibility that "it would impair the refugee project." Of course, he informed Pastoriza, he would be happy to help Rublee behind the scenes.[11]

Rosenberg worked his contacts, speaking with Pell and Berle at the State Department and taking Morgenthau to dinner. The secretary of the treasury was pleased to learn of the signing and Trujillo's gift of Sosúa. This was providential, because Morgenthau long had been an advocate of renegotiating the Convention and, perhaps more than any member of the cabinet, he empathized with the refugees' plight.

At that moment, national security concerns took precedence over the bondholders' fiduciary rights. Even before the outbreak of war, Washington's chief foreign policy objective vis-à-vis Latin America was to strengthen its hemispheric defenses. Nazi propaganda in the region, German economic overtures to cash-strapped Latin American nations, and the presence of eighty German ships in Latin American ports were all genuine causes for concern.[12]

In addition, a string of right-wing coup attempts in Argentina (1939), Uruguay (1940), Colombia (1941), and Bolivia (1941) had raised concerns of possible Nazi machinations. As Hull recollected, "The threat was no mere conjuring by an excited fancy; our diplomatic representatives in Latin America had given us literally hundreds of concrete instances. . . . To me the danger to the Western Hemisphere was real and imminent."[13]

In Roosevelt's mind, national security was an outmoded concept; the United States now had to think in terms of hemispheric defense. Although policymakers did not believe that the Reich would militarily invade Latin America—a transatlantic attack was unlikely, given the limited range of aircraft—they were convinced that it might well seize power through more insidious, indirect means. Their best defense against the Axis, Pentagon planners believed, was to establish a more visible U.S. military presence in the Caribbean. To promote cooperation with Latin American militaries and to familiarize themselves with the Caribbean basin, military missions were formalized with their allies. Five hundred thousand dollars was appropriated for the missions in 1940. By 1941, every Latin American state had U.S. military advisers, and more than one hundred military personnel were assigned to Latin American duty.[14] In addition, in October 1940 the chiefs of staff of Latin American militaries were invited to tour U.S. military installations. In return, Latin American nations were expected to provide the United States with naval and air base rights, fortify their intelligence operations, maintain surveillance over suspected German agents, and exchange information with Washington.[15]

So often a backwater of U.S. diplomacy, Latin America suddenly had palpable geopolitical significance. Washington also negotiated what one diplomat aptly characterized as a series of "political loans" as a metaphorical down payment on a multidimensional strategy to improve relations with governments in the region.[16] Just five months after the signing of the Sosúa contract, Trujillo was pleased to learn that the Export-Import Bank had approved a two-million-dollar loan to dredge the port of San Pedro de Macorís and to obtain refrigeration equipment for a Trujillo-owned slaughterhouse that would supply meat to the Canal Zone and Puerto Rico. The loans were approved even though diplomats and bank officials had misgivings about the propriety of funding projects that amounted to a windfall for Trujillo's businesses.[17]

In addition to "political loans" and expanded military missions, the administration sought to improve cultural ties. In 1940 the Office for Coordination of Commercial and Cultural Relations between the American Republics (later renamed the Office of the Coordinator of Inter-American Affairs) was established to counter German influence and improve interamerican solidarity. Its director, Nelson Rockefeller, focused on propaganda—magazines, shortwave radio broadcasts, motion pictures—and social and economic assistance to win the hearts and minds of Latin Americans. Although initially budgeted at $3.5 million, the office's expenditures mushroomed to more than ten times that amount by 1942. Programs were funded to control disease, improve water supplies, and build roads and public works.[18]

This new policy initiative represented a natural extension of the Good Neighbor policy, which had sought ways to defuse tensions between the United States and its neighbors. In the preceding decade, the administration had ended a two-decade-long occupation of Haiti; had lifted the despised Platt Amendment in Cuba, which had given the United States the authority to intervene in that country's internal affairs; and had refused to intervene when President Lázaro Cárdenas of Mexico nationalized U.S. oil companies in 1938.[19] Roosevelt had been reluctant to retaliate against the Mexican president because he feared that repudiating the nationalization decree would weaken Cárdenas and thereby hasten to power, on America's doorstep, a rightist government that was more amenable to Berlin.[20]

Roosevelt's refusal to consider reprisals in Mexico made a strong impression on Trujillo. He watched with interest how everyday Mexicans responded to the decree. Huge demonstrations were held in Mexico City to congratulate Cárdenas for this declaration of economic independence, while Mexicans lined up to empty their pockets to raise funds to help indemnify Standard Oil. Since nationalism was such an important pillar of his regime, Trujillo realized that there was political capital to be earned if the receivership was eliminated.[21] Heeding Rosenberg's advice, he hired Rublee and mounted a concerted campaign to reach an accord.[22]

Morgenthau, Hull, and Ickes did not need much persuading. They believed that Latin American debt default was of little consequence, especially when measured against hemispheric unity. Hull drove home the point, calling the receivership the Good Neighbor policy's "last sore thumb."[23] American diplomats emphasized the urgency during a regional conference held in Havana in July 1940, where Germany's victories in western Europe raised alarming prospects of the Nazis' securing a beachhead in French and Dutch possessions in the Caribbean.[24]

Not surprisingly, Trujillo's chief opposition in the State Department was still Sumner Welles, who sided with the bondholders. He knew that the dictator, while crying poverty for his nation, was pocketing millions of dollars in government revenues and placing them in personal accounts in U.S. banks.[25] Morgenthau announced, nevertheless, that the administration would begin direct negotiations with Latin American nations to set a "pattern for cleaning up Latin American finances."[26] He and Roosevelt were convinced that the best way to ward off Nazi influence was to extend capital and credit. Outmoded arrangements like the receivership had to go.[27]

Trujillo responded by giving the administration what it wanted. Diplomatic relations were severed with the Reich and "to ensure the continental defense," Washington was informed that U.S. planes and ships could use "as often as they desire . . . [the country's] harbors, bays and territorial waters."[28] The U.S. minister to the Dominican Republic Robert Scotten reported that Trujillo "even went so far as to emphasize that should it be necessary the Dominicans were willing to spill their blood in this cause."[29] Few other Latin American countries were that forthcoming. Washington and Ciudad Trujillo agreed on the parameters of a military assistance pact during the spring and summer of 1940.[30]

Trujillo did not just strengthen his military capabilities. He gave new meaning to the term *war profiteering*. The legation estimated that wartime price controls netted Trujillo family–run businesses $2.5 million a year. U.S. demand also spurred Trujillo's nascent industrialization program, enabling him to diversify his and his cronies' business holdings to include hotels, agricultural processing plants, textiles, airlines, and shipping companies. By war's end, Trujillo had obtained or was in the process of acquiring monopolies in sugar refining, salt, cigarettes, and meat processing.[31]

The deliberations on military and economic assistance took place simultaneously with the receivership negotiations. In mid-August 1940, Welles sent a team of negotiators to Ciudad Trujillo, a clear signal that the administration was ready to reach an agreement. The two sides quickly came to terms.[32] For the first time since 1905, customs were to be managed by Dominicans, although the customs receiver was to be jointly appointed by the bondholders' representatives and Dominican authorities. Debt servicing would now come from general government revenues rather than customs receipts, giving the Dominican government greater flexibility in managing its income. This was all highly favorable to Trujillo; but the fine print said that all the funds collected were to be deposited in the National City Bank of New York's branch office in Ciudad Trujillo, and bank officials, representing the bondholders, then would divide the funds between the Dominican government and U.S. creditors.[33]

The agreement was named the Trujillo-Hull Treaty. In late August, Trujillo had the Dominican Congress declare him Ambassador Extraordinary on a Special Mission so that he could personally sign the accord in Washington (even though he was battling a painful outbreak of anthrax on his neck).[34] On September 24, 1940, Trujillo and Hull signed the treaty in Hull's office. A delighted Rosenberg congratulated the dictator on his "splendid accomplishment."[35]

Less than a month later, Trujillo appeared before a joint session of the Dominican Congress boasting that he had reclaimed the nation's sovereignty. Seventy thousand people participated in a government-organized "March of Victory" on October 20 as one hundred Dominican business leaders waved U.S. flags and both the Dominican and U.S. national anthems were performed. September 24 was declared a national holiday, the pen Trujillo used to ink the treaty was deemed a national treasure, and a bronze tablet commemorating the event was placed at the Baluarte Gate in the capital, the symbolic altar of the Fatherland.[36]

"The Restorer of the Financial Independence of the Republic" seized the moment to press ahead with his agenda.[37] On the same day that he declared victory before the Dominican Congress, Pastoriza asked for another three million dollars in Export-Import Bank loans to build roads and hotels. A showcase hotel would be built on the Malecón, the seawall in Ciudad Trujillo, with these monies. Bank officials vehemently denied that the loan had anything to do with the treaty. In reality, the loan and the Trujillo-Hull Treaty had everything to do with Fortress America. As diplomatic historian Eric Roorda has noted, the slew of agreements constituted "a new kind of Good Neighbor Policy" for Washington and Ciudad Trujillo: "This version cut through the long-standing moral tension between nonintervention and approval of dictatorships, a tension that had nurtured State Department opposition to ties with Trujillo, and instead fully embraced his regime for the sake of national defense."[38]

But were other factors at work? A *New York Times* report on the loan explicitly linked the deliberations to Sosúa. Subtitled "Economic Gains Laid in Part to Country's Policy toward European Refugees," the story praised Trujillo for his open-door refugee policy: "Of all the nations of the world the Dominican Republic has imposed the fewest restrictions on refugees desiring to enter the country." The *Times* accepted the administration's rationale that the new loans had nothing to do with the Hull-Trujillo Treaty but speculated that the agreement was "due at least in part to the Dominican policy on European refugees."[39]

Only one obstacle remained: the treaty's passage by the U.S. Senate. Leaving nothing to chance, Trujillo's lobbyists in the United States worked overtime churning out propaganda throughout the fall of 1940. Publicists used the first anniversary of the signing to remind Americans of Trujillo's generosity. Trujillo went to the well again, asking Rosenberg to stage an elaborate celebration in the Dominican Republic to garner favorable press coverage.

THE SELLING OF SOSÚA

In November, before Rosenberg's visit to Ciudad Trujillo to celebrate the colony's first anniversary, Baerwald warned him to beware of falling into Trujillo's clutches and compromising DORSA's objectives. Rosenberg should understand, Baerwald cautioned, that the dictator was using DORSA to stage an elaborate anniversary celebration just to get the treaty ratified. "They [the Dominican government] are encouraging you in that publicity *for a purpose.* Foreign bondholders will have a hearing in a 'closed' session next week before the Senate Committee. . . . The Administration, of course, is anxious to get the treaty passed—the proceedings of a 'closed' session do not always remain secret. There are other voices against S. D. [Santo Domingo]; they should not be, but there are always unfriendly purposeful people around."[40] Baerwald's message to Rosenberg was unmistakable: Sosúa could become a casualty of political horse trading between Washington and Ciudad Trujillo. It was best to avoid entangling alliances. By doing the general's bidding, DORSA risked incurring the wrath of powerful interests, of the regime's opponents at home and in the United States who might use their influence, either intentionally or not, to impair the colony.

But Rosenberg paid no attention and plunged headlong into preparations. He persuaded Paramount News to produce a newsreel for the festivities. Paramount's promotional editor, W. P. Montague, thought highly enough of the story that he planned to distribute it to viewers in Latin America, England, Europe, and Canada. Montague wished to accentuate Trujillo's leadership and asked Rosenberg for assistance in obtaining pictures of the dictator. "The first scene," he storyboarded, "to be made here in New York, would include if it could possibly be arranged, some scenes of General Trujillo, Mrs. Trujillo and other officials of the enterprise, discussing the subject over a map showing the land that has been donated by His Excellency to the project. We would combine this with scenes of the next group of refugees arriving in New York being met by officials of the Association and being bid good-bye on their departure for Santo Domingo."[41] Montague envisioned the second part of the newsreel to be filmed on location in Sosúa, focusing on how the first 250 pioneers were adjusting to their new life in the tropics.

In addition, Rosenberg and the Dominican government whipped up detailed press releases to publicize the anniversary festivities. Given prominent mention were two additional ballyhooed "donations" from *El Benefactor*. Trujillo had announced days before the celebration that he was donating a fifty-thousand-acre tract adjacent to Sosúa and three hundred acres in the mountains near Jarabacoa, several hours away from the settlement, where settlers could come for rest, relaxation, and a break from the heat and humidity. The promise of an adjacent tract was especially significant to DORSA officials. If there was any hope for expansion for the colony, more (and better) land was needed.[42]

Rosenberg praised the gifts as "an act of historic generosity." Unfortunately, Trujillo never made good on the additional property; the colony would have to make do with what it had. The mountain retreat did materialize, however. DORSA built a few cabins in Jarabacoa, and a number of settlers who contracted malaria and other ailments would eventually use them to convalesce.[43]

Press releases announced that dignitaries from the State Department, the IGC, the Coordinating Foundation, and the PACPR were set to attend the anniversary celebration. The Dominican government asked the IGC to host its next meeting in Ciudad Trujillo at the same time. The IGC, which had pitifully little to show for its efforts to repatriate refugees, leaped at the chance to show its support for Sosúa. Delegates came to Ciudad Trujillo from the United States, Great Britain, France, Switzerland, the Netherlands, Belgium, Colombia, Costa Rica, Cuba, Ecuador, Mexico, Haiti, and Peru.[44]

Politics, however, ensured that little was accomplished in Ciudad Trujillo. Pell sought to derail a French initiative proposing that the United States take in sixty thousand refugees a year from unoccupied France over a three-year period. He had no authority to discuss, let alone negotiate, "the substance of the refugee problem, and . . . there was no intention on anyone's part . . . of holding a working session of the IGC." Instead, the IGC meeting was to be much pomp and little substance. A welcoming dinner and reception was convened on January 30 by President Troncoso; DORSA hosted a dinner at its Ciudad Trujillo offices the following night; and then all the guests traveled across the island to Sosúa to visit the settlement from February 1 to 3.[45] Rosenberg had to adjust matters on the fly when he learned in late December that Trujillo needed emergency medical treatment in New York and would not be in attendance. If anything, the first anniversary ceremonies attracted more press coverage than the original contract signing.[46]

Released several weeks after the festivities, Paramount's four-minute newsreel, "War Refugee Solution," was icing on the cake for Trujillo and DORSA. It conveyed how the Dominican government and the settlement association sought to represent Sosúa to the North American public.[47] At the outset, narrator Gilbert Martyn invokes Pell's test tube metaphor, describing how nations from around the world have sent delegates to attend the IGC meeting to witness the Sosúa experiment. The dateline Trujillo City is followed by shots of a bustling downtown filled with paved macadam, new automobiles, and modern storefronts, while the voice-over reminds viewers that this island nation has a rich history and first "welcomed" Christopher Columbus. Although Trujillo does not appear in person, his formidable presence is conveyed as the camera pans to a huge portrait of the ruler (sans military garb) on a wall overlooking Troncoso as he welcomes the delegates attending the opening reception. The irony of the dictator's painting peering over the shoulder of his marionette president would not have been lost on Dominican viewers and exiles, who were thoroughly familiar with Trujillo's penchant for oversight and surveillance. Next the newsreel introduces Rosenberg, shown bantering with Pell, serving as confirmation that the U.S. government is firmly behind this new venture.

After this upbeat introduction, the scene shifts to Europe, the background music turns somber, and the images show bedraggled refugees with their young children in tow, boarding trains, carrying what is left of their belongings. The shots of exhausted families awaiting transport at train stations are deeply moving, while Martyn voices phrases like "bleeding Europe," "desperate to get out," and "trainloads of unwanted people, who seek some place of living rest." Almost in the next breath, he announces that this is a nonsectarian undertaking; Jews, Protestants, and Catholics alike are fleeing Europe. The message has unmistakable echoes of Évian: this is not only a Jewish problem; all of Europe is at risk in confronting the Nazi menace.

The film's third segment follows the refugees by boat to the Dominican Republic. A small group of happy, better-dressed refugees is shown disembarking at Ellis Island in transit to the Caribbean, with the potent symbol of Lady Liberty looming in the background. Next, a map of the island with the settlement's location prominently displayed situates the colony for the viewer. This portion is filled with images of young, earnest colonists settling in at Sosúa. Several beaming men and women introduce themselves in halting English, explaining where in Europe they hail from and what their previous occupations were. Later, a Belgian civil engineer is shown digging in the fields alongside a Bohemian lawyer. Sosúa is presented as a collective enterprise where city folk from all walks of life collaborate to build a better future. Since the newsreel was intended for foreign consumption, Dominicans are conspicuously absent.

The narrator runs through a litany of talking points that DORSA and Dominican publicists already had mentioned in their printed materials, informing the audience that the settlement is the projected home for "one hundred thousand of Europe's homeless," that Trujillo has generously provided the initial twenty-six thousand acres, and that an additional fifty-thousand-acre bequest is on the way. Quick shots of rows of tomatoes, corn, and bananas under cultivation appear alongside images of hardworking white Europeans beating back brush with machetes, working together to cut down a tree with a double saw, and hoeing the soil. A powerful image of a settler's hands coursing through the loose soil is followed in staccato rhythm by frames of a young man atop a John Deere tractor and a settler employing modern road-paving equipment, all to illustrate how this cohort of Caucasian farmers is taking advantage of the best that technology has to offer to tame the tropics. As these images scroll by, the narrator reminds viewers that the settlers are handpicked for their physical fitness and character.

Positive results are already apparent. New Yorkers, we learn, already have sampled Sosúa's delicious cheese—proudly displayed in woven baskets—while we view scenes of contented settlers milking cows and working in the cheese factory. Colonists, after an initial break-in period, are settled into brand-spanking-new four-room bungalows and given a deed to ten acres of land. But homesteading is not a gift, Martyn informs us. DORSA's advances will be repaid in time by the fruits of the colonists' due diligence. The segment concludes with the settlers frolicking with their young children on Sosúa's gorgeous beach. Rosenberg's imprimatur on the production is obvious: the progressive colonization project has transformed citified Jewish civil engineers and attorneys into modern, productive farmers. Sosúa is a shining example of the spiritual regeneration of a broken, oppressed people.

A short epilogue concludes the newsreel by lauding this humanitarian experiment. The film returns to the capital, where Columbus's statue stands with arm outstretched in the old section of the city. "Columbus's free, new world reaches out democracy's helping hand," the narrator intones. *Liberty* and *democracy* were two words that few observers would have associated with the Trujillo regime.

Although cloying from start to finish, "War Refugee Solution" served its purpose. It helped DORSA's fundraising efforts and celebrated Trujillo's improved reputation abroad. The film was distributed throughout the hemisphere as part of the propaganda efforts of the Office of Inter-American Affairs to convince Latin Americans of the benefits to be gained from opening their doors to the refugees.[48]

A late February release of the newsreel came too late to be of much use to Trujillo in his campaign to win support for the Trujillo-Hull Treaty in the U.S. Congress. But he would not need it. Congress, preoccupied with the Lend-Lease Bill, quickly ratified the treaty with only one dissenting vote on February 14, 1941. The despised customs receivership came to an end six months later.[49]

The receivership ended because, from the administration's perspective, it had outlived its usefulness. The bondholders were furious, but the news was greeted with euphoria in the Dominican Republic. It was perhaps the single most important foreign policy triumph of Trujillo's 31-year reign, and it paid huge domestic dividends. Since Trujillo had seized power in 1930 illegally and had wiped out opposition in the first six years of his rule, the dictatorship, although secure, never enjoyed an aura of legitimacy, especially among elites. The massacre—the dictatorship's other major "accomplishment"—although terribly successful for political and ideological reasons, was something that officials were reluctant to celebrate publicly. Here was a momentous victory that carried with it enormous prestige at home and abroad.

It is important not to overstate Rosenberg's role in bringing the two sides together to the negotiating table. Serendipitous timing, a fortuitous international context, and the particular balance of competing interests in the Roosevelt administration all worked to shed old animosities and bring this matter to a successful conclusion. Trujillo retained an army of lawyers, journalists, public relations consultants, members of Congress, and boosters in the U.S. military; Rublee and Rosenberg were just two of many who peddled influence. But Rosenberg was well connected and highly regarded by key players at State and Treasury. His identification with Sosúa represented one of the few successes the administration could point to in its feeble efforts to assist the refugees, even if there was precious little to show for Sosúa at that moment. In sum, Rosenberg's presence as a facilitator, although not indispensable, certainly improved the climate for negotiations.

Trujillo probably would have negotiated a settlement with or without Rosenberg. The administration was determined to get a deal done. Rosenberg's inability to tell Trujillo more than what he probably already knew about the sugar quota was less a reflection of Rosenberg's lack of influence and more an indication of the Dominican Republic's weak position in the sugar market.

Nor did this setback deter Trujillo from asking Rosenberg for assistance again. New York's Guaranty Trust Bank initially had balked at serving as fiscal agent for the Dominican Republic's external debt. Rosenberg asked his law partner, George Kennan Hourwich, to smooth things over with the bankers. A pleased Trujillo responded, "I wish to reiterate [to] my good friend Mr. Rosenberg my appreciation for the good services which you have rendered me," concluding his note with "Your most affectionate friend."[50]

That Rosenberg undertook the lobbying at all, and did so willingly, had important ramifications for the evolving relationship between DORSA and the Dominican state. Over the next year, Trujillo asked Rosenberg for a number of personal favors; among them, to serve as a "social reference" for his wife's lease of a fashionable New York townhouse. Rosenberg also secured a three-month card for Trujillo and his personal secretary, Paino Pichardo, entitling them to full privileges at New York's posh Lotos Club, where Rosenberg was an "esteemed" member. Rosenberg considered himself on good enough terms with the Trujillo family that he wrote the dictator's daughter a get well card during her stay at a New York City sanitarium in the spring of 1941.[51]

There would be ample opportunity for all sides to work together over the next two decades; each, in turn, would be asked to do favors for the others. Indeed, the next to ask would be the Roosevelt administration. Just as the first 250 colonists were settling in, the State Department and the PACPR asked both DORSA and Trujillo to take in additional refugees who had no interest in farming. These immigrants were far from the hardy, youthful stock that Rosenberg had promised and that the general desired.

SIX

Lives in the Balance

> There is definitely an unfriendly attitude toward the settlement
> project in certain high Government quarters, based on the fear
> that German immigrants will be traitors. I am not giving you this
> as gossip, but as reliable, firsthand information. There is the same
> fear from Dominican army circles that German spies will be let
> in. The basis for all these fears is that people have been brought in
> directly from Germany. It seems pathetic to think that the poor
> oppressed Jews of Germany should now be looked upon with
> suspicion.
>
> ROSENBERG TO ROSEN, 1940

"As soon as we have received the complete dossiers, we will forward them to you," DORSA's secretary, Becky Reyher, informed Alfred Wagg, its liaison at the State Department, in February 1941. As she had done countless times before, Reyher began the painstaking process of petitioning the State Department for transit visas, this time for the Breslau family, several of whom wanted to leave Marseilles and one who was stranded on the northern coast of Africa. Since the summer of 1940, the only way to reach the Dominican Republic was via Ellis Island in New York; thus the need for U.S. transit visas. Such a stop-over and the vetting process that went with it enabled State Department officials to track European immigrants and, in theory, keep Nazi spies out of Latin America.

Each dossier had to provide an airtight case that the applicant did not represent a threat to national security, or Wagg's colleagues in the Visa Division and the Department of Justice would not approve it. Pertinent supporting materials for the Breslaus, Reyher had learned, were en route from the JDC's European headquarters to DORSA's New York office, because Maria Breslau had been a longtime employee of the philanthropy. The Joint's secretary in New York, Moses Leavitt, was particularly anxious that Becky move heaven and earth to expedite these requests. He reassured the cash-strapped DORSA office that the JDC would pay for its employees' maintenance as long as they stayed in the Dominican Republic. Leavitt knew how insistent Rosenberg was that the Joint pay for its own, especially since the Breslaus, if they were like the majority of its employees and relatives who came to the island nation, would never set foot in Sosúa.[1]

As soon as Wagg, who had replaced Pell as DORSA's contact, received Reyher's note, he set in motion the cumbersome task of referring the request to Avra Warren, the chief of the Visa Division, and to a civil servant in the solicitor general's office at Justice, who both reviewed the applications.[2] Warren sent the standard bureaucratic reply to Reyher: the "cases were not yet complete," but "appropriate notifications" would be sent to U.S. consulates in Europe once DORSA had vouched for these applicants by submitting approved Dominican visas obtained from the Foreign Ministry in Ciudad Trujillo.[3]

That procedure had its own serpentine path. First, Reyher submitted dossiers to the secretary of the interior and the police, who scrutinized the files and then sent them to the Foreign Ministry, which instructed its consular agents in Europe to provide the immigrants with the proper documentation. Meanwhile, the U.S. Legation in Ciudad Trujillo double-checked the immigrants' status and alerted the Visa Division of what was forthcoming. Once the Visa Division and Justice had reviewed the dossiers and had not found anything suspicious, Warren notified his consular agents abroad, who then issued the prized transit visas.

In other words, to bring a refugee to Sosúa, Reyher had to obtain a Dominican visa and a U.S. transit visa, and that required the interventions of two Dominican ministries, their U.S. counterparts at State and Justice (and later an interdepartmental review board), and supporting documentation from the IGC (Wagg), DORSA (Reyher), and in some cases, the PACPR (George Warren). Then it was a question of waiting—and the wait could seem like an eternity for those concerned—for berths on a ship willing to risk the perilous trip across the Atlantic.[4]

The documentary record is silent on whether these requests were ever approved and whether the Breslaus actually made it to the Dominican Republic. If they did, they might have lived out the war in the capital on JDC largesse, biding time until they could begin anew in the United States. Or they could have lived at El Batey, Sosúa's administrative hub and town center. At one point, more than three hundred "nonsettlers," as they were called, inhabited El Batey, easily surpassing the number of homesteaders, even though very few ever had any intention of becoming farmers. By the end of 1941, Sosúa was equal parts agricultural colony and refugee camp, and it stayed that way until after the war—a combustible combination that had a pernicious effect on morale. No wonder Maurice Hexter later came to the conclusion that it had been a mistake "to herd the sheep and the goats together at Sosúa."[5]

That the overworked staff had to spend so much time and effort getting these nonsettlers out of Europe, which diverted them from the principal goal of getting the colony up and running, may have irritated DORSA officials, but it infuriated Dominican authorities. The last thing officials wanted were transients with no interest in farming who viewed their island as nothing more than a stepping stone to the United States. More than any other factor, having to accept a sizable number of nonsettlers soured Trujillo on Sosúa.

Yet DORSA was besieged by requests, and the general, under pressure from Washington and the association, reluctantly agreed to admit the nonsettlers. In addition to their patrons at the JDC, Rosenberg and Reyher heard from the likes of Albert Einstein, Cornelius Vanderbilt Jr., powerful members of Congress, PACPR members, and scores of anxious relatives living in the United States who were anxious to get their family members to safety. If political influence did not suffice, there were rumors—some on good authority—that Dominican visas could be purchased for a certain price. What the petitioners had in common was that they knew someone who needed to get out of Europe in the worst way.

The Breslau case, as unremarkable as it appears, actually speaks to a number of serious challenges that DORSA faced during the colony's chaotic first years. Even as the first 37 settlers arrived on May 8, 1940, the Dominican and U.S. governments were backing away from their ringing endorsements of Sosúa as security concerns trumped all other matters (see figure 6). After so much optimism and goodwill four months before at the signing, the war threw a wrench into the plan. Only 252 colonists had reached Sosúa by the end of 1940.

Many factors impinged on settling the colony: the vicissitudes of Atlantic shipping during wartime, State Department fears of Nazi infiltration into the Americas, and Washington's subsequent refusal to take any Jewish refugees from German-occupied territory, this last because of the widely shared perception that settlers with family back in Europe made tempting marks for Nazi blackmail. There was the cumbersome requirement that each applicant first had to be checked in Washington and then in Ciudad Trujillo, and the

FIGURE 6 First pioneers arrive at Sosúa, May 1940. JDC ARCHIVES.

Dominican government's outspoken frustration with the slow pace of build-ing the settlement and the type of immigrants brought to the country. Taken together, these factors placed the colony in jeopardy from the outset.

Also slowing efforts to bring in settlers were the unanticipated high cost of extracting refugees from Europe and DORSA's burgeoning financial problems. Rosenberg's mantra to Rosen during the first eighteen months was twofold: "go slow" to keep within an eviscerating budget and be careful whom you ac-cept, lest the wrong kind of immigrants enter the colony and DORSA's skittish sponsors withdraw their support altogether. It soon became obvious that the original projection of one hundred thousand refugees would never come to pass. The end result was a far cry from initial projections.

Rosenberg, who perhaps naïvely thought he was building a farming colony in the tropics, was surprised to learn that in addition to seeking out the right type of settlers in Europe, his association had been ceded de facto authority by the Dominican Foreign Ministry to determine which immigrants—set-tlers and nonsettlers alike—were to receive visas, a direct result of the govern-ments' fear of Nazi saboteurs in the Caribbean. It must have been astonishing to some observers, who knew how difficult it had been for the Dominican state to secure its financial independence from the "Colossus of the North," to witness Trujillo hand over his nation's sovereign right to admit immigrants to a New York–based colonization association and the U.S. State Department.

The life-and-death responsibility of deciding whom to admit weighed heavily on Rosenberg and Rosen. Compromises were inevitable; those chosen were often far from the hardy "human material" they had promised authorities. The complicated process of selecting pioneers from refugee camps produced uneven results. Recruiters did not have carte blanche to choose whomever they desired. Since DORSA did not begin recruitment in earnest until after the contract was signed, staffers were limited to a small subset of refugees drawn from countries of transit. Reflecting on this years later, Rosenberg admitted, "we could not have any assurance of getting good settlers because we couldn't get any people out of Germany (where there were trained *chalutzim* [pioneers]), because we were beggars and not choosers, and we had to take the material that we could get."[6] Therefore only a handful of the refugees had any experience whatsoever as farmers. Desperate to leave Europe, they often told DORSA agents what they thought they wanted to hear—that they were willing to make the necessary sacrifices to adapt to a new way of life. As Hexter later recalled, recruiters "let their hearts run away with their heads."[7]

To make matters worse, the Dominican government's predilection for young adult males, who, in theory, would intermarry with Dominican women, led to a crippling demographic imbalance at Sosúa that was never corrected. Males outnumbered females by nearly two to one from the outset. In this case, Dominican desire for single men dovetailed with the absence of women in European refugee camps, since fifteen thousand young Jewish women already had left for England to become domestic servants. Young women also were less likely to leave Germany and Austria in the first place because they could still find jobs in the Jewish sector, or they had to care for their elderly parents and relatives, or their parents were reluctant to let them emigrate alone.[8]

DORSA's decision to accede to the Dominican government's request and give priority to young, unmarried males failed to bring about the desired unions. What it did foster was serious morale problems. Only nine male settlers married Dominicans in the first six years (and only seven of those stayed on), creating a large pool of eligible, potentially mobile bachelors who, in general, were less committed to the enterprise. Many young males saw little future on the farm, gravitated to the El Batey refugee camp, and became some of the first *Amerika-Fahrer*s (America Leavers) after 1945. Sosúa never fulfilled Trujillo's "racial" aspirations.

But it was the external dynamic—a succession of lightning-quick German victories throughout western Europe during the last six weeks of spring 1940; the resulting dislocation for emigrants in countries of transit as ports closed and the number of transatlantic ships declined precipitously; and Roosevelt's concerns about a fifth column threat, or internal traitors—that put a crimp in DORSA's plans and forced it, like the dictatorship, to toe Washington's line. Although Hitler did not close the door entirely to Jewish emigration until mid-October 1941, the successive Nazi military triumphs and Washington's refusal to take in refugees from the occupied territories meant that DORSA remained a beggar. Neither Rosenberg nor Trujillo seriously questioned the administration's policies, even if they squabbled on occasion about aspects of those policies and occasionally achieved limited success asking for exceptions. For Rosenberg, who, realistically, had little recourse but to follow State Department directives, maintaining good relations at least gave DORSA the chance to achieve some of its goals, although even that would be a struggle.

Certainly the colony did not meet Trujillo's expectations either, but loyalty was its own reward, assuring him continued U.S. support. His rule went unchallenged, always his first priority. But what had been a *ménage à trois* with some measure of give and take now gave way to Trujillo and DORSA's uncritical acceptance of Roosevelt's Fortress America.

Acquiescence came at a high price for the colony. The optimism administration officials had expressed publicly for the Sosuán test tube before January 1940 dissolved with the German army's advance through western Europe. Until 1945, Sosúa, in the minds of most policymakers, represented an annoyance at best and a security risk at worst.

No part of the Sosúa story illustrates the fickle role of contingency better than the obstacles that the U.S. government and, to a lesser extent, the Dominican state placed in DORSA's path during its first years of existence.

A SCALED-BACK SOSÚA

Just back from an inspection tour of the colony in June 1943, Hexter complained that something needed to be done about the "nonsettler cancer" eating away at the colony. Frankly, he told Reyher, he could not understand for the life of him how so much extra baggage had wound up in an agricultural settlement in the first place. In a confidential memo remarkably absent of any hint of defensiveness, Reyher confided how Sosúa came to be both agricultural colony and refugee camp.

> From the beginning the State Department evidenced that DORSA's immigration policies were subject to their approval. They asked for and received DORSA's detailed reports and cooperation and assurance that no immigration matter would be taken up with the Dominican Government before

clearance with them. . . . The history of immigration to the Dominican Republic as far as DORSA is concerned, would warrant the belief that the Dominican authorities, in all cases, as indicated to us by Minister Pastoriza and others, was always considered by that government in relation to whatever the wishes of the United States government might be, and that in consulting our own government as to their views, we were not only doing so as an American organization operating in a foreign country, but because we knew that unless we got our answer direct from the American authorities, the same answer would be given to us in a more indirect way by the Dominican offices.[9]

These trenchant observations were part of a detailed twenty-eight-page typescript sent to Hexter. From the outset, Reyher related, DORSA's efforts to get refugees out of Europe were "subject to their [the State Department's] approval." Her office's deliberations with the Dominican government gave every indication that Washington and Ciudad Trujillo were on the same page and that the latter invariably moved in lock-step with U.S. policy.

U.S. concerns about Nazi infiltration into the Americas were voiced just as the first group of refugees was to leave the Continent. That contingent of 37, which sailed from Genoa on the Italian liner *Conti Blancamano* in May 1940, was to have been the precursor of a group of two hundred prospective settlers already identified for DORSA by Jewish relief organizations in Germany and Austria. As early as April 1940, Pell had warned Rosenberg about taking refugees directly from Germany; when he learned of DORSA's plans to bring more from German-occupied territory he could not hide his disappointment. "I placed myself on record with Jimmy Rosenberg as doubting the advisability of bringing the settlers for the Dominican project from Germany. Of course, one is aware of the human tragedy involved, and the terrible suffering which those remaining in Germany have to endure. At the same time we as a Government are committed to a policy . . . which is to relieve the stress in the Allied countries and the countries of refuge first."[10]

Rosenberg had to assure U.S. officials that DORSA would not take any additional settlers from the occupied territories. He had been led to believe that the Visa Division would make an exception for those two hundred already awaiting transit visas, and even had instructed the recruiter Solomon Trone and his wife, then in Switzerland, to go to Germany to "examine and vouch for each person." But before they could do so, the State Department changed its mind and refused to authorize the transit visas.[11] Just as the *New York Times* heralded the first settlers' impending arrival in a feature article titled

"35 Refugees Sail for Dominican Port," hailing it a "unique experiment in the resettlement of European refugees," the highly charged political climate in Washington threatened to call the entire initiative into question.[12]

The reason was that refugees escaping Nazism had become synonymous with the fifth column threat in Washington.[13] German advances in the spring of 1940 persuaded Roosevelt and his advisers of the need to ensure "more effective control over aliens."[14] The swift capitulation of Western Europe was attributed partly to a well-planned infiltration by a cadre of Nazi agents, disguised as professors, journalists, diplomats, tourists, and refugees, in the months before the invasion. *New York Times* reporter Otto D. Tolischus commented on the myriad ways the fifth column stalked its prey: "They take charge of previously organized resident armies, which, often in disguise or in the uniforms of the enemy's own forces, seize strategic points, reinforce parachute troops, organize espionage and sabotage behind the enemy's lines and throw confusion into the enemy army and population through false orders and reports."[15] Sensationalistic media reports that purportedly documented how German-born residents dressed in inconspicuous disguises, ambushed Dutch troops, or assisted German parachutists had a profound effect on international public opinion.

Even though historians later offered correctives about the nature and extent of the Nazi fifth column's role in these conquests, the perception at the time among the Allied military establishment, the press, and the public on both sides of the Atlantic was that such furtive activities were vital to the Nazi war effort. Unsubstantiated rumors and erroneous reports, some surreptitiously placed by British intelligence, which sought to sway U.S. public opinion, fueled suspicions that the Reich would use nefarious tactics to achieve world domination.[16]

If enemies were feared to be living among the general population, it was perhaps understandable why refugees became such handy scapegoats. Each time a refugee in the United States was rumored to be a spy, whether the rumor was later corroborated or not, it lent credence to the restrictionist argument that excluding all refugees was a matter of national security. With questionable logic, officials also contended that closing the borders was justified because it warded off anti-Semitism at home. Targets of discrimination in their homelands and in the United States, Jewish refugees thus were victimized by a curious rationale that gained greater resonance as it merged with fifth column paranoia.[17]

In this foreboding climate, Roosevelt transferred the Immigration and Naturalization Service from the Labor Department to Justice to guard better against Nazi sabotage and espionage, while pointedly warning Americans in a fireside chat, "we know of new methods of attack, the Trojan horse, the fifth column that betrays a nation unprepared for treachery."[18] The speech, which came hard on the heels of Charles A. Lindbergh's radio broadcast that charged the administration with fomenting "a defense hysteria," gave FDR the opportunity he had been waiting for to lash out against his isolationist critics.[19] In May 1940, FDR warned Congress of Germans leapfrogging from North African bases to Brazil and then sending ground troops up the Isthmus through Central America to Mexico. It would be no time before a Luftwaffe airbase in Tampico, Mexico, could strike at the American heartland in a few hours.[20] With more than 250,000 German-born residents in the United States, isolationist sentiment fed xenophobia and provoked a "mania for security against imagined threats from 'radicals' and foreigners."[21] An obedient American public took the threat seriously. In just one day in May 1940, the FBI received more than 2,900 reports of suspected sabotage.[22]

By June, Congress had passed the Smith Act, which required aliens to register and be fingerprinted and gave the government the power to deport current or past members of fascist and communist organizations.[23] Roosevelt defended the need to watch refugees, invoking an alleged Nazi threat to shoot family members of German Jewish refugees unless the latter consented to work for the Reich as spies. Throughout the summer, State Department memoranda went out to consular agents in Europe urging them to reject or suspend any application for a visa "about which there was any doubt."[24]

The new regulations had the desired effect. Only 21,000 refugees were admitted from Axis-controlled nations for the duration of the war, a paltry 10 percent of the mandated quotas. If the new restrictive policies had not gone into effect and the quotas had been met, an additional 190,000 persons might have made it to safely to the United States.[25]

Officials considered Latin America an especially inviting target for Nazi infiltration. Just as Hitler had conquered western Europe, he could build support for fascism in the Southern Cone and then march north to the U.S. border. The journalist George Britt devoted an entire chapter of his book *The Fifth Column is Here* to the threat from the south. It began, "From Patagonia, bleak windblown southernmost tip of South America, northward across the equator and the isthmus all the way to the Texas and California border, armies without uniforms are on the march today. These Fifth Column armies, at least 5,000,000 in actual strength and consecrated to dictatorship, are bent not only on seizing and consolidating the territory underfoot, whatever ground they may occupy, but they hold also the long view of conquest across the Rio Grande—economic conquest, political sterilization and, if necessary, military attack."[26]

With the benefit of hindsight, it is clear that the U.S. response to subversion in Latin America was well out of proportion to the threat. As the historians Leslie Rout Jr. and John Bratzel contend, German military intelligence networks (*Abwehr*), even in Southern Cone nations where substantial numbers of German nationals lived, were "hastily built and poorly developed." Antiquated transatlantic communications equipment and inadequate training of agents stymied Axis efforts to infiltrate Brazil, Argentina, Chile, and Mexico. The Reich made only token efforts in smaller countries like the Dominican Republic.[27]

War Department officials stationed in Ciudad Trujillo remained nonetheless vigilant, and suspicious of the tiny refugee population. A rumor circulated that Dr. Adolf Meyer, an acquaintance of the dictator, had formed a spy ring in the Dominican Republic and Cuba that was in contact with the German military.[28] Seeking to discredit Trujillo, the exile opposition labeled the dictator a Nazi sympathizer. Juan Jimenes Gruillón informed State Department officials that Germans were sending agents disguised as Jewish refugees to the island.[29]

Captain John Butler, the U.S. naval attaché in Ciudad Trujillo, painted the immigrants with a broad brush. Even though evidence linking refugees to espionage was circumstantial at best, Butler felt confident in generalizing from examples elsewhere in Latin America: "the dangerous fact that the German government has made use of the refugee exodus to admit spies and agents into the Western Hemisphere" justified a ban on granting visas to "those persons whose intimate relatives continue to reside in Germany." While Butler admitted that DORSA officials had "given this office excellent cooperation," he regarded the refugees as "a doubtful class, to be kept under vigilance and subjected to control," concluding "it [was] unwise for this Republic to permit further immigration during the war."[30]

Such paranoia explains why DORSA's first contingent would be the first and last group to come directly from German-occupied territory, although a few fortunate émigrés did make it to third-party countries on their own with valid Dominican visas and eventually did obtain transit visas. Rosenberg told Rosen to inform Trujillo that DORSA was taking the threat seriously. Concerns about the first group's origins had placed the project at risk: "I can tell you that there is definitely an unfriendly attitude toward the settlement project in certain high Government quarters, based on the fear that German immigrants will be traitors."[31]

Years later, DORSA officials lamented that although they had supporters in the State Department's European Division, the Latin American Division was not too familiar with the colonization project, and this proved detrimental whenever security concerns were raised. Perhaps the gravest threat was the ascension of Breckenridge Long to assistant secretary of state in June 1940, a promotion that coincided with a new "get tough" policy on all requests for visas.

Rosenberg tried his best at damage control. He insisted that Rosen send a file on each of the refugees in the initial "German" cohort so that he "could prove to people in our Government, beyond a shadow of a doubt that none of this handful of immigrants is by any possibility traitors or Fifth Columns."[32] Meanwhile his "splendid watchdog," Reyher, checked and rechecked each dossier for possible subversives.[33] He dismissed out of hand the possibility that Jews were Nazi agents. In a letter to Pell he declared, "experience in this war demonstrates that danger comes not from the persecuted Jews, but from the so-called German businessmen, tourists, professors, students, etc."[34]

Such assurances failed to assuage officials, however. Long made it clear in an internal memorandum in June 1940 that delay and obfuscation henceforth would be the department's modus operandi when it came to dispensing visas. "We can delay and effectively stop for a temporary period of indefinite length the number of immigrants into the United States. We could do this by simply advising our consuls to put every obstacle in the way and to require additional evidence and to resort to various administrative advices which would postpone and postpone and postpone the granting of the visas."[35]

Although this policy change was kept in house, it did not take long for Rosenberg to get the message. He decided to take up the matter directly with Roosevelt, but an exchange of letters accomplished little. The president, although supportive, was evasive.[36] A month later, at a DORSA board meeting, Rosenberg stated the obvious: "Fear is a fact, but those fears, wise and unwise, exist, and, therefore, much as we would like to bring the right kind of splendid material from Germany, where its young people are being persecuted, we must not at this time open the doors of the Dominican Republic in any way, excepting as Mr. Pell and the State Department approve."[37]

The State Department informed DORSA that it would now be necessary to obtain signed pledges from prospective settlers that it was their intention to remain in Sosúa permanently. These pledges would become part of the dossier that Reyher compiled on each settler for the Visa Division. Satisfactory qualifications were synonymous, Reyher related, with "refugees from unoccupied territory, prepared to settle permanently on the land."[38]

Indeed, DORSA's New York office received a scare in early August that made it rethink its strident objections to the hysteria sweeping Washington. Lee Lane, a German, came to the office asking to see Rosenberg. Since Rosenberg was busy, Lane spoke with Reyher about the possibility of bringing in a nonsettler interested in setting up a small business in Ciudad Trujillo. He averred how much he hated Hitler, what wonderful work DORSA was undertaking, and how he had money to invest. He showed Reyher letters of recommendation from the U.S. embassy in Berlin and bankers in New York. Reyher was immediately suspicious and alerted Rosen, who subsequently learned through his contacts that Lane was connected to Hermann Goering and was in the business of liquidating Jewish estates in Germany. The incident brought home the saliency of the threat to DORSA officials, who quickly alerted the State Department about Lane.[39]

In the interim, Dominican authorities also had grown concerned. On June 14, 1940, the government informed the U.S. legation that it was suspending previously issued visas of prospective European immigrants and prohibiting future immigration from the Continent, except for those already under contract. Eleven days later, the secretary of the interior issued a directive to foreigners that political activities of any kind would not be tolerated, and that those arrested for taking part in such activities would be sent to detention camps.[40]

Several factors appear to have influenced the government's thinking. Trujillo wanted to reach closure on the Convention agreement in the spring and summer of 1940 and knew that Washington would be more amenable if he fell in line with U.S. strategic interests just as negotiations were set to resume. Hinkle was pleased to report that the Dominican government's action "has undoubtedly been hastened by the reports from abroad that Nazi influence was increasing in this country and that there were Nazi sympathizers among the refugees. In a few refugee cases there are indeed suspects."[41]

Other factors also probably played a part in the determination to follow Washington's lead. Even before the contract signing, the Foreign Ministry and its consulates abroad had been inundated by requests for visas. As conditions worsened in Europe that spring, the numbers of requests mushroomed. The Washington legation was besieged by pleas for help from relatives of refugees stranded in Europe.[42] Opportunistic Dominican consuls in the United States and Europe preyed on those relatives, and on the refugees. Reliable reports furnished by DORSA to the Dominican government indicated that certain unscrupulous officials were reaping a windfall selling visas to whoever could pay. Reyher reported, "it was obvious from the evidence sent and given to us that there was large scale racketeering in Dominican visas." She recalled one incident where "eighty[-]odd Dominican visa holders" reached Ciudad Trujillo aboard the French liner ss *Cuba*, "many of whom had visas apparently bootlegged and they were not honored by the Dominicans."[43]

DORSA remained preoccupied with what Rosenberg perceived as a "dangerous traffic in visas in New York." He wrote Rosen in early July that Dominican visas were selling for between $250 and $300; although the visas surfaced in New York from Dominican consulates, he was sure they originated on the island and that "some subordinate in the Dominican Republic must be approving this without knowledge of Troncoso."[44] It would not be difficult to imagine how the forged visas could fall into the hands of Nazi agents. "Somebody buys a visa in New York; the visa is for somebody who is now in Germany; the visa gets into the hands of that person in Germany. If that person in Germany is a Nazi, that person will be able, with the help of the Nazi Government, to find transportation, maybe via Yokohama and through the Panama Canal, and when that person shows up on the dock at Ciudad Trujillo, there the person is with the proper papers."[45]

He urged Rosen to speak to Troncoso about the racketeering. At first Rosen begged off out of fear that he would "stir up a hornet's nest," but later relented. Rosenberg was relieved to learn "that Chief [Trujillo] and President [Troncoso] will take immediate steps to eliminate abuses."[46]

What better way for authorities to nip such corruption in the bud, relieve themselves of the endless number of visa requests, and demonstrate support for Washington's policies than to clamp down on dissidents on the island and prohibit all subsequent European immigration, except for those expressly approved by DORSA for its colony. On July 6, 1940, Pastoriza told Rosenberg that he had received a cable from his superiors that "no person, agency or organization is authorized to seek visas for entrance into the Dominican Republic, excepting the Association."[47]

Racketeering was symptomatic of a much more serious problem, one that threatened to undermine DORSA's credibility in Ciudad Trujillo and Washington. What drove the market for visas was not the handful of pioneers DORSA had sent to Sosúa or even those they planned to send over the course of the next year. The word was out in Europe and the United States that it was possible—for a tidy sum—to secure a visa for immigrants who wanted to wait out the war on the island and—again for a price—DORSA would place those fortunate visa holders either at the colony or in the capital. As nonsettlers began to arrive that spring, Dominican officials vented their displeasure to DORSA and the State Department, complaining that letting such immigrants in went against the spirit of the agreement and defied the recently revised immigration code.

Was DORSA really serious about this colony? authorities wondered. Most perplexing was that the Roosevelt administration had initially encouraged the decision to bring in nonsettlers. Why was Washington pressuring Trujillo and Rosenberg to accept individuals totally unfit for farming? The nonsettler problem and all its permutations threatened to drive a wedge between the Dominican and North American governments and DORSA.

UNSETTLING NONSETTLERS

From the outset, the selection process was ruefully politicized. Rosenberg was under pressure from influential Jewish philanthropists, "including the Rosenwalds and other large donors to Jewish charities, [who] urged us to make an exception of their relatives who might find haven in the Dominican Republic until such time as they could enter the United States," Reyher related.[48] Lessing Rosenwald, the son of Julius, a major benefactor of the Crimean project, had followed in his father's footsteps and donated the princely sum of $125,000 to DORSA.[49] Such requests could not be easily ignored.

The association had to walk a fine line. On the one hand, it was searching actively for funds to build the settlement; on the other hand, what signal did it send that preferential treatment was to be given to nonsettlers "merely because their relatives have money?"[50]

Compounding the problem was that some of Rosenberg's colleagues at the JDC viewed DORSA as a means to get their European employees like Maria Breslau out of harm's way. Rosenberg was not thrilled about the prospects of seeking visas for former Joint employees who did not want to farm. In addition, he was frustrated by the mixed signals the JDC was sending. After initially encouraging him to accept this assignment and providing start-up funds, the philanthropy now was withholding monies at a time when DORSA desperately needed them. Priority was given to the catastrophe unfolding in Europe. In the first six months of 1940, the philanthropy expended nearly $4.5 million for relief and emigration aid, and by year's end the figure had increased to $6.3 million. In addition, the JDC was supporting an estimated 110,000 refugees who had found asylum throughout Latin America.[51] Although Rosenberg knew better than anyone how acute the philanthropy's financial predicament was, he fretted that his project was being set up for failure.

A testy Rosenberg refused to ask for visas for the philanthropy's employees until JDC executives assured DORSA in writing that they would not become public charges.[52] After the Joint agreed, about one hundred transit visas were secured for its employees "through DORSA sponsorship" and a "special procedure was established for the handling of the visas" by Pell. As Reyher recalled, the same arrangement for Dominican visas "was made known to the Dominican authorities and approved by them." Other European relief agencies added some of their own employees to the JDC lists.[53]

Nor were the Dominican officials immune to pressure to take in nonsettlers. In most cases Pastoriza sent a polite rejection, informing the anxious relatives about the limits on "semitic" immigration under the new immigration law.[54] Some of the relatives, however, refused to take no for an answer. Thomas Vradelis wrote Pastoriza seventeen times about a Dr. Michaelides.[55] In certain cases, special pleading paid dividends, as Pastoriza intervened and asked Rosenberg to make exceptions. He received a request from Representative Sol Bloom for visas for the Zamosciansku family in Poland, whose relatives lived in his home district in Pennsylvania. Since Bloom was on the House Committee on Foreign Affairs, it is not surprising that Pastoriza took a more active interest in this case.

Cornelius Vanderbilt Jr. asked Pastoriza to secure a visa for a twenty-six-year-old Romanian cartoonist stuck in Genoa, Saul Steinberg, whose caricatures had appeared in *Harper's Bazaar* and *Life*. Vanderbilt assured Pastoriza that if a visa could be obtained, "his financial needs there [on the island] would be amply insured by friends in this country [the United States]." Pastoriza asked Rosenberg to "see if it can be arranged that Mr. Steinberg is permitted to reside in the Dominican Republic" and told Vanderbilt the good news that he would be "informing him [Rosenberg] of my interest in obtaining a favorable consideration."[56]

For every exception, however, Rosenberg and Pastoriza turned down dozens of requests. The case of a Mrs. Eugene Klein, whose married daughter and son-in-law were in Prague, then under German occupation, was not atypical. Rosenberg's response to Pastoriza was unenthusiastic: "no money at present to make a deposit to assure against these people becoming public charges." Even though "these are evidently charming, educated and cultured people," they offered little. "The married daughter is an actress. Neither she nor her husband have been trained to be farmers on the soil. Moreover, with the condition of shipping and transportation as it is, I don't see how we can get them out of Prague into Italy, nor, if we did, how we can get them from Italy to the Dominican Republic."[57] Apparently Mrs. Klein did not have the wherewithal to sustain her daughter and son-in-law, and DORSA would not issue the visas.

From the Roosevelt administration, DORSA received mixed messages about nonsettlers from different constituencies. The State Department warned that accepting nonsettlers entailed significant risk by sending the wrong message about the settlement's intentions. It just gave ammunition to restrictionists who felt that the colony might prove to be a security risk. But Reyher noted, "the pressure to help . . . the nonsettlers, however, was so great not only for people of means who could adequately support their relatives there, but also for distinguished refugees and scientists on whose behalf Thomas Mann, [Albert] Einstein and others were pressing us to secure asylum, that Mr. Rosenberg and Dr. Rosen explained the situation to Dominican authorities and secured their approval."[58]

The PACPR also pressed Rosenberg to accept nonsettlers. This committee, which had been a midwife to DORSA's birth and had acted as a go between and backer with the State Department, was now busily screening requests from prominent writers, artists, and scientists on behalf of prominent refugees. Five days before the DORSA contract was signed, George Warren was already thinking about the colony's accepting a "temporary asylum group," practically all of whom would eventually come to the United States.[59]

Moreover, the PACPR was insistent that the settlement be nonsectarian, largely because it hoped to secure contributions from Christian relief agencies in the United States and because the administration had conceived of the PACPR as an ecumenical advisory body dedicated to the welfare of all political refugees. Warren sought applications for the colony from Catholic and Protestant refugee agencies in Utrecht and Geneva. Not everyone thus recruited would be suitable for the colony, but "it ought to be possible to work out the process of providing temporary asylum on an orderly honest basis with the Dominican authorities and with profit to them."[60] It is difficult to read that last, pregnant phrase without imagining the political and private gain that accrued to authorities who were asked to make exceptions.

Warren knew that Rosen was in basic agreement with this two-track, settlers and temporary asylum group policy but first had to work out the details and then present them to Dominican officials. Lack of planning and mistakes in the selection process by Spanish refugee organizations had prompted a backlash from Dominican authorities, who cancelled plans for admitting additional Spanish republicans. Warren did not want history to repeat itself with the Dutch and Swiss refugees. Warren promised to meet with Rosen when he next came to New York "to talk about the various plans for selecting the immigrants who are to be recommended to the Dominican government for admission."[61]

By the end of March, Warren, Rosen, and presumably Rosenberg had drawn up a blueprint for the selection of refugees. Five categories of immigrants were prioritized, with only the first three groups destined for the Sosúa settlement. Highest priority was given to "young, physically strong and mentally sound single men and women and married couples." Next, adolescent trainees were to be identified and brought to a camp, designed along the lines of the Civilian Conservation Corps. The strongest and most adaptable trainees would graduate to become full-fledged settlers. A third group was to round out the colony, composed of those specializing in manufacturing or other commercial pursuits deemed essential.[62]

The last two categories reflected Warren's second track: those who would come for a temporary period to await admission elsewhere, and others unfit for the colony but who wanted to make the Dominican Republic their permanent home. If the first three categories were to be funded by and understood to be "within the competence of DORSA," applications and funding for the fourth and fifth groups were to be generated from other U.S. relief agencies. Rosenberg continued to insist that DORSA would not accept nonsettlers unless funds first were made available from other relief agencies.[63]

Warren sheepishly admitted that the Dominican government "has virtually turned over all responsibility for semitic immigration to DORSA . . . [and] presented us with monopoly control over all such immigration to the Dominican Republic. This decision has sent us a flood of applicants, steamship agents, and relatives in America who desire to send refugees to the Dominican Republic. The pressure is pretty heavy and we are under the necessity of organizing very quickly to meet it."[64] The "us" and "we" in Warren's statement document how intimately involved the PACPR was in bringing immigrants to the Dominican Republic.

In early April Warren met with Rosenberg to firm up procedures for temporary asylum cases. The National Refugee Service would make inquiries and financial arrangements with relatives "here who desire to send refugees for temporary stay in the Dominican Republic." An official would be sent to Ciudad Trujillo to supervise "their housing and the use of their time there." Nonsettlers would either have to be self-sustaining or receive assistance up front from relatives or friends in the United States, and would come only after the first group of settlers arrived in Sosúa. "We cannot afford to have the temporary asylum group interfere in any way with the development of the settlement." This initial determination to keep nonsettlers away from the settlement would soon be badly compromised, much to the consternation of Rosenberg, Warren, and Trujillo.[65]

Fortunately for Warren and the nonsettlers, there was a loophole in the DORSA contract that provided some room to maneuver for both DORSA and the Dominican authorities. Article 4, Section D contained a catch-all clause that stipulated, "The Association may furthermore recommend to the Republic for free admission all those who may be specialized in their professions, trades or occupations, experts, artisans and other persons acceptable to the Republic."[66] That open-ended clause, however, proved insufficient to win over a reluctant Trujillo.

What ultimately persuaded the dictator was a Rosen-Warren plan to guarantee funding for nonsettlers. Rosen explained that donors would be required to sign a legally binding "maintenance trust agreement," which held them financially responsible for their nonsettlers as long as they remained in the Dominican Republic. Relatives would first make deposits of $1,500 per individual and $2,500 per couple for temporary residents awaiting U.S. visas. Relatives of permanent residents—the fifth category—would establish annuities large enough to produce $30 a month for life. In return for a nominal charge, DORSA would distribute funds to the nonsettlers and assist with their "adjustment to life" on the island. A committee to evaluate all nonsettler cases was established. Serving on it were Reyher, Warren, a DORSA board member, and representatives of the International Migration Service and the National Refugee Service.[67]

Rosenberg understood the risk that nonsettlers presented. He counseled Rosen to move cautiously; a sizable nonsettler population in the capital might provoke an anti-Semitic backlash. First and foremost, authorities must be comfortable with the rate of immigration: "You and I must resist the pressure of proposed immigrants and must not let immigration of nonsettlers exceed such rate or pace as is heartily approved by the Government. I have never seen any undertaking successful when it started as a mastodon or a behemoth. That is not the way that crops grow or that human undertakings develop. . . . We must at every point know through your informal private talks with people highest in the Government what rate and pace of immigration they can feel safely and wisely be absorbed and accommodated. We must watch for any uprising of anti-Semitism, and if there is any in the press, I want to see it."[68]

Nonsettler immigration, Rosenberg preached to Rosen, should not jeopardize their fundamental mission—to build the new colony. If Rosen harbored reasonable doubts about particular immigrants, he should not accept them—the pressure be damned. "We have two great tasks. One is the farm settlement work. The other relates to the other immigrants. We want to be fair to these other immigrants, but we cannot let kindheartedness put rosy-colored glasses on it and cause us to lose our true vision."[69]

Warren was happy to report that relatively small contributions were on the way from Jewish donors like Louis Bamberger ($10,000) and Falk ($5,000), and $5,000 each from the Committee for Catholic Refugees and the American Committee for Christian Refugees. By late May, Warren reported that 160 visas had been secured for temporary asylum and more than $225,000 in guarantees had been deposited. By the time the first settlers arrived, the U.S. government had approved more than four times as many transit visas for nonsettlers as it had for the agricultural settlement.[70]

Rosenberg wrote to one of his superiors at the JDC, "the fact that the Dominican Government is ready to grant visas virtually on the say-so of the DORSA carries with it a moral responsibility."[71] Caught as it was between the demands of friends, colleagues, and donors on the one hand and its determination to marshal its resources to build the settlement on the other, DORSA had difficulty reconciling how it went about exercising that duty. Although Rosenberg's missives seemed cold and impersonal, he understood the daunting responsibility that such oversight carried with it. Lives were in the balance. Yet the more DORSA caved in to pressure and let in nonsettlers, the more questions about the settlement's future it had to answer. By June 1940, Dominican authorities were coming to the conclusion that they had been deceived about Sosúa. Although "some of the refugees were desirable," Foreign Minister Arturo Despradel informed the U.S. chargé, "the great majority were not."[72] As the spring turned to summer, both governments put DORSA officials increasingly on the defensive.[73]

Then suddenly, just months after the two-track plan, including the maintenance trust agreements, finally had been ironed out, Ciudad Trujillo did an about-face. As the usually dispassionate Reyher put it: "without any explanation or warning, just as abruptly as if a curtain were run down, the Dominican authorities notified us that this plan was not one that they wished continued, and that no further nonsettler visas would be granted. We had a great many candidates and a great many people who were in the process of having such arrangements made for them when we had to stop all such activity."[74]

The decision, announced on June 12, 1940, was so abrupt and unanticipated that it left hundreds of refugees in Europe in the lurch and refugee organizations in the United States and Europe scrambling. Rosen cryptically cabled DORSA's New York office that the suspension of nonsettler visas was "taken as precautionary method against Fifth Column infiltration possibilities on advice of allied sympathizers." Reyher believed that authorities had reached the conclusion that "refugees in the city [Ciudad Trujillo] constituted a possible danger and were henceforth against any but settler immigration." Indeed, she added, "there is reason to believe, from the correspondence, that the Dominicans were influenced in that decision by the United States government."[75]

Despite the Dominican government's change in policy, pressure to make exceptions continued. Those with political influence and money found ways to work around and through the system. For example, nonsettler maintenance trust agreements were drawn up for relatives of Herbert Lehman, the governor of New York.[76] The spigot remained open, if only a crack.

DORSA also had to employ creative methods to get around the ban. Apparently under pressure from the JDC official Arthur Lamport, Rosen came up with the idea of bringing elderly refugees with sufficient resources to Sosúa.[77] In an arrangement similar to the maintenance trust agreement, these senior citizens, with the assistance of affluent relatives in the United States, purchased property and built cottages in what would be called Garden City near El Batey. Authorities found this arrangement more palatable because the elderly residents were to live in the colony itself, not in the capital, and land was actually being purchased in the transaction. Relatives put up a thousand dollars for DORSA to construct each cottage. Since the wisdom of bringing in the elderly was questioned both inside and outside the colony, only six were built under this plan. A memo stipulated that this group was to receive "as little publicity as possible," lest any announcement send the wrong message about DORSA's intentions. The general principle was to be reaffirmed: "Sosúa is a pioneer project for young people and it is agreed that DORSA cannot afford to have the burden of allowing other people on its premises who may prove interfering or not generally personally acceptable and wholeheartedly in conformance with the rules and regulations of the community."[78]

Another group of nonsettlers deemed acceptable under certain conditions were "industrial" immigrants. These people, who were trained in manufacturing, had to come with "fluid capital" and to announce in a sworn affidavit their "intention to invest." Maintenance trust agreements were required for this group as well. Just as with the visas for the elderly there were few takers, because those who had the background and experience in a specific industry often could not leave Europe with sufficient capital to fulfill the requirements.[79]

The Garden City visas and the industrial category offered tangible proof of how the colony's initial goals had been compromised. By October 1940 a total of 208 nonsettler visas had been issued, and a year later the number reached 400—although a significant number of those were relatives of the settlers.[80]

PACPR's efforts to get intellectuals and artists out of Europe via the Dominican Republic or elsewhere met stiff opposition from restrictionists in the State Department. Despite special pleas by the First Lady, Roosevelt accepted Long's rationale about the perils of admitting refugees.[81] By June 1940, Avra Warren, who had headed the Visa Division since 1938, was on his way to Europe to inform consuls that they should drastically cut the number of refugees entering the United States. From mid-1940 to mid-1941 only four thousand refugees entered the United States, compared to forty thousand in the previous twelve months.[82] Warren, who in 1942 left the Visa Division for the Dominican Republic as U.S. minister, was Long's hatchet man, shamelessly boasting that he was responsible for reducing the number of visas issued. Long continued to paint the refugees with an incriminating and indiscriminant brush, explicitly tying them to the fifth column threat: "there has to be a sieve or screen somewhere through which can be filtered persons acceptable to the United States, thereby excluding persons who might be sent into the United States by interested governments in the guise of refugees."[83]

In the spring of 1941, DORSA renewed its efforts to persuade the State Department to reconsider its policy on nonsettlers still in Europe who had already been issued visas and had been waiting, in some cases, up to a year for transit visas. Avra Warren was very discouraging. DORSA, he wrote, "might not wish to become involved as sponsors for persons wishing to proceed to Santo Domingo merely for purposes of residence while awaiting visas for the United States. It would seem to be a more direct procedure for such persons to apply for immigration visas in European countries in the same manner as other refugees and to wait until they may come to the United States direct."[84] Warren's terse rejoinder was of a piece with evolving administration policy. In June 1941, the Russell Act effectively slammed the door on what had only been a trickle since the outbreak of war. Contending that Nazi agents had infiltrated the refugee ranks, the legislation prohibited consuls in Europe from issuing visas to applicants with "close relatives" in occupied Europe.[85] Few refugees did not have relatives who fit into that category. After the middle of June, consulates throughout Germany, Italy, and Nazi-occupied Europe closed down.

Immigration policy had its desired effect—at home and within the U.S. sphere of influence. From that point on, an Interdepartmental Advisory Committee in the State Department issued all visas, and it took six months or more to process each application.[86]

The nonsettler problem in all of its complexity continued to plague the Sosúa colony until after the war. It not only sent ambiguous signals to Dominican authorities and the U.S. government about the legitimacy of the colonization project, but it had serious consequences for the colony's day-to-day operations. In some respects, the ban did have its desired effect. Even as they quietly agreed to take in some "exceptions," DORSA administrators now could openly tell the overwhelming majority of applicants and their sponsors that their hands were tied and that only those who were serious about being farmers need apply. But two factors combined to moderate the force of that message: the limited pool DORSA had to draw from in the dwindling countries of transit, and the growing desperation of those awaiting exodus.

Unfortunately, in Rosenberg's words, DORSA remained a beggar, not a chooser, its choices circumscribed by the combination of Fortress America and German victories. What type of "human material" did DORSA really want, and what did it actually get? And how did conditions in Europe shape the choices recruiters made in 1940 and 1941? It is to these questions that we now turn.

SEVEN

Playing God

I know of course: it's simply luck / that I've survived so many friends. But last night in a dream / I heard those friends say of me: "Survival of the fittest" / And I hated myself.
BERTOLT BRECHT, "I THE SURVIVOR," 1942

In the spring of 1940, the JDC office in Amsterdam was a madhouse, and the man in charge, Kurt Bondy, had his hands full. On top of attending to the needs of thousands of Jewish refugees spread across northern Europe, now his superiors in New York had pressed him into making the initial selections for the new Dominican settlement. Applications were pouring in from relief committees throughout Europe, and Bondy and his staff were overwhelmed. They needed to be relieved of the responsibility for the colonists' selection soon, the JDC's European head, Morris Troper, informed Rosenberg.

Rosen's trusted confidant, the Latvian-born Solomon Trone, was rushed to Europe in mid-April to relieve Bondy.[1] Before departing, however, Trone received detailed instructions about the kind of colonists Rosen wanted. Drawing on his experience in Russia, Rosen wrote up a document, "Selection of Settlers for the Dominican Project," that explained who Trone should be looking for as he read applications, conducted interviews, and moved through the refugee camps in countries of transit. Of the first 150 to 200 choices, Rosen wrote, 80 percent should have some agricultural training, or at the very least be accustomed to manual labor. Ten percent should be handy with tools, and sprinkled among those must be half a dozen skilled mechanics. The rest could be service providers—"tailors, shoemakers, butchers, cooks, bakers, etc."

The first two hundred could arrive in one or several groups; Rosen did not have a preference, but if possible young men and women, "strong healthy people of good character," between the ages of twenty and thirty-five, "preferably young couples without children, or single people, members of larger families who are capable and anxious to do preliminary work with the intention of bringing over the other members of their families at a later date."[2] The emphasis on young couples, to be followed later by efforts to reunite families, certainly would have displeased authorities, but it made little difference because Trone found precious few couples in the camps.

Rosen's preference was groups of agricultural trainees from Germany or Austria "so as to have a nucleus of settlers who have known each other for some time and have learned to work together and live together." Even in the best of circumstances that would have been difficult, since less than 2 percent of German Jews (as against 29 percent of Germans) had worked on the land.[3] Rosen also warned Trone of refugee committees seeking to rid themselves of their problem cases.[4]

Rosen expected the settlers to perform three-quarters of the manual labor at the colony. He did not want the settlement to mirror the paternalistic landlord-peasant relations found throughout Latin America. Pioneers would work in the fields alongside Dominican campesinos, just as Jewish colonists had rolled up their sleeves near their Tatar counterparts in Russia. "Should the Jewish settlers become landowners employing Dominican peons the project would be a failure," Rosen wrote, adding, "I for one am not going to have anything to do with the project."[5]

The pioneers were required to complete an Application for Admission to the Dominican Republic (for Settlers Coming under the Auspices of the Dominican Republic Settlement Association), which asked (in Spanish, German, or English) whether they had prior manual training, whether they intended to apply to authorities at a later date for the admission of their relatives, and whether they were prepared to settle permanently and engage in agricultural or other manual work.[6] In a few straightforward clauses, the document laid out the philanthropy's and the government's expectations.

Unlike some people associated with the project, Rosen had little interest in a nonsectarian settlement. George Warren and Rosenberg had tried with limited success to raise funds from Christian sources, and there had been some cooperation with Catholic and Protestant relief agencies in Europe and the United States. But Rosen was dubious about the wisdom of recruiting non-Jews. If it should become absolutely necessary, for political or other reasons, to include such a group, he counseled Trone, "we would prefer not pure

Aryans, but mixed married couples, or couples of partly Jewish origin. These are a little simpler to integrate in our Jewish settlement. Should it become necessary to take in a few pure Aryans, you may do so, try to keep the numbers down, and give preference to people whose religious scruples are not too pronounced. To set up a Catholic group with a Catholic priest, especially one who would have missionary inclinations, would be a thing which we could accept as a matter of very extreme necessity, and I hope you will succeed in persuading your friends in a diplomatic way, that a project of this kind has great disadvantages."[7]

He was not just worried about the right mix of settlers. Since DORSA's funds came "from purely Jewish sources and with the present situation of our people," Rosen felt it morally irresponsible not to "use our limited resources for settlement of non-Jews who are, after all, in a comparatively better position than our own people, when it comes to emigration."[8] One wonders what DORSA's allies at the PACPR would have said if they had known of Rosen's feelings. Although DORSA's fundraising materials continued to emphasize the settlement's tolerant character, recruiters heeded Rosen's advice.[9] Only Jews needed to apply to Sosúa.

Armed with these instructions, Trone, who had been coaxed out of retirement by Rosen after having worked for General Electric's overseas division as a personnel director for more than twenty-five years, headed to the camps. He was encouraged by what he found in Switzerland. He praised the Jewish relief organizations and the Swiss government, which had created meaningful, albeit temporary, possibilities for emigrants. "There is a healthy atmosphere in these camps, useful work is carried on, such as forest clearing, road building, etc. The people engaged in this work do not have the feeling of being supported beggars . . . a certain community spirit has developed which helps all concerned."[10] Trone's blissful characterization of the Swiss camps, however, was framed by a longer, more pessimistic appraisal after his next stop, at refugee camps in Italy.

Trone was unprepared for what he witnessed when he toured the camps outside Genoa. Until August 1939, Italy had been taking in up to seven hundred refugees a month. Even stateless transients could obtain six-month permits if they proved they had funds to sustain themselves. As a result, German and Austrian Jewish emigrants poured over the Italian border, legally or illegally, because there were few viable alternatives and it was still possible to book passage on ships sailing out of Italian ports.[11]

Relief workers were unable to keep up with the influx, and conditions in Italy were "much worse than we could have imagined in our wildest dreams,"

Trone reported. Compared to the relief committees in Switzerland, the Jewish organizations in Italy were destitute. Emigrants received only three lire a day (about fifteen cents), and because no one was allowed to work, "this is not enough to cover the most primitive needs." Their material condition was tough enough, Trone wrote Rosenberg, "the emigrants are undernourished, poorly clad, and have difficulty keeping clean." What was more troubling was their emotional and psychological response to their plight. "The worst is that these people have lost all feeling of responsibility and desire toward any goal. They can do nothing to change their situation. They have become objects of circumstances and powers which they can neither influence nor control. Only very strong people—inwardly strong—can maintain themselves. The majority of them break down. . . . It is a tragedy, the extent of which can hardly be imagined. Everyone wants to get away—where—it doesn't matter."

The refugees' dispirited condition was understandable. Some had already experienced concentration camps after the Kristallnacht roundups. Trone continued, "The fear of war here has created a psychosis which particularly depresses the German emigrants; they assume that they will be sent back to Germany and since they have experienced the concentration camps there, their spiritual condition is a sad one. . . . It is naturally not simple to find suitable materials for the Dominican settlement under these conditions."[12]

The recruiter added that "the most robust people want to go to Palestine." Even though it was next to impossible to get passage there, he was struck by how "many prefer to wait here with the hope that they will somehow be able to get to 'Eretz.'" Trone had lived in Palestine for five months, and he was aware of the symbolic freight it carried: "here one can clearly see of what importance a real idea can be for people and how it helps them even over the most difficult times." His perceptive comments about the power of an idea to unify the refugees must have resonated with Rosen, who, from his Crimean experience, understood the significance of imbuing pioneers with a unifying vision of a new life cultivated out of hard work and working on the land. It was Trone's hope that the Dominican Republic's "healthy surroundings," "material and political security," and "the participation in a common endeavor . . . if not carrying the thought of Zion . . . will nevertheless be strong enough to bring forth a well-founded, sound, Jewish community."

Despite his pessimistic assessment of the Italian camps, Trone told Rosenberg, "we are convinced that we can and will find sufficient good material." He selected 44 prospective colonists in addition to the 16 he already had identified on his quick swing through Switzerland. Trone also learned that refugee organizations in Berlin and Vienna had identified another 150 "ready to sail for San Domingo," and Prague's relief agencies were poised to send 24. The majority of those interviewed, however, were from the professional classes and had no background in farming. Trone also raised a red flag about the pool's imbalance, since the number of prospective male candidates vastly outnumbered the women.[13]

Rapidly changing circumstances conspired to disrupt recruitment. Italy refused to issue any more transit visas, and those that had been granted already were recalled and invalidated. In May 1940, the last remaining ports of embarkation were closed and anti-Jewish riots broke out, only adding to the unsettled climate.[14] Trone immediately went to Rome and appealed to authorities to make an exception for his group. He received assistance from the head of the Dominican legation and his counterpart in the U.S. embassy, who together managed to persuade authorities to revalidate the transit visas. Trone then tried to book passage for the forty-four refugees waiting in Italy on one steamer after another, only to learn that a ship's sailing had been postponed or delayed or, in the case of one U.S.-owned shipping company, only U.S. citizens would be accepted. When the German and Swiss borders with Italy were closed, Trone was cut off from prospective colonists who had been identified by Jewish relief organizations awaiting transport to Italy.

Weeks of delays turned into months as Italy's entrance into the war effectively ended direct steamship service to the Dominican Republic. Now ships leaving Europe had to be routed from Lisbon (and some Spanish ports) through New York, complicating matters further for DORSA because of how long it took to secure U.S. transit visas.

Only thirty-seven of the original forty-four who had been stranded in Genoa eventually secured those visas. Because they could no longer sail from Italy, DORSA had to find them transportation to Lisbon. It arranged to fly them to Barcelona at the astronomical cost of five hundred dollars per immigrant. After the refugees reached Spain, they continued by train to Lisbon and from there secured passage to the Dominican Republic.

Rosen wrote Trone that DORSA could not sustain such prohibitive costs. Combined with the interminable delays in ports like Genoa and Lisbon and the related costs of lodging and maintenance while in transit, they forced Rosen to order Trone to reduce the number of refugees selected.[15] Nevertheless, as table 2 illlustrates, Trone and other DORSA recruitment agents sought out potential pioneers wherever they could find them.

What did Trone tell refugees about the settlement and what they could expect to find in the Dominican Republic? Otto Papernik provides a detailed

TABLE 2

Location of Sosúa's First Selected
Colonists (Countries Granting Visas)

Country	Number
Switzerland	98
England	55
Germany	37
Italy	35
United States	7
Haiti	4
Cuba	2
Portugal	1
Dominican Republic[a]	13
Total	*252*

Source: Kerem, "Nuevos hallazgos," 697

[a] Selected from refugees already living in the Dominican Republic.

description of Trone's visit and speech to a group of refugees at a camp in Mousserolle, France.[16]

> One day the news spread that an American and his wife were coming to the camp to select some people for an agricultural settlement, sponsored by the Agro-Joint Committee, located in the Dominican Republic. Hardly anybody knew where this country was located. . . . When the couple arrived, they started to explain to us that at the Conference in Évian, France, where thirty-two countries were represented, nobody had given the European refugees permission to enter their country except one, Generalissimo Leonard Trujillo; the so called "dictator" offered his land for immigration and to start with 100,000. The American, a Mister Trone and his wife told us from the beginning that they had only fifty visas and that he was ordered to select people with professions and good health but not older people or people with children because there were no facilities at this new settlement, called "Sosúa," for those people. There was a small hospital, barracks would be used to sleep in and whoever was selected would have to consider himself a kind of pioneer. Naturally, everybody tried to be in this group but since we were 296 they could only take those they thought best fitted for the jobs.

Although Papernik understandably mistook the Latvian for an American, his detailed recollection of the recruiter's pitch is consistent with other accounts. Trone's retelling of Trujillo's offer made a strong impression on Papernik and others, who could have been excused from wondering if any nation in the world wanted them.

Trone surely realized that the refugees shaped their stories, their backgrounds, and even their appearance to fit what they believed the recruiter wanted. Hellie Goldman chuckled when she related that before her interview with Trone she removed her nail polish "so I looked like a peasant." She knew enough to project a serious demeanor during the interview; the taciturn recruiter had turned down friends of hers "because they made jokes."[17]

Not everyone was enamored with Trone's methods or his officious attitude. Even though Ernest Hofeller ultimately was selected, he bristled at the thought that one man was given the right to play god. Nor did he think Trone was particularly qualified for the job. "The idea of sending one single solitary person to Europe to select Jewish settlers seems, in retrospect, ludicrous. What counted at that point was to get people out of the European continent instead of selecting them at the rate of 30–40 persons per transport, in drips and drops. . . . What his criterion for choosing prospective farmers was is unknown. His experience was nil. He was born in Latvia . . . had a background in engineering. He might have been experienced in selecting people for industrial enterprises, but he certainly lacked any knowledge to evaluate the qualifications of Central European Jews to become farmers in a subtropical country."[18]

As Trone traveled through Western Europe, he realized the refugees were far different from Rosen's ideal prototype. Difficult choices had to be made, not just by DORSA recruiters but by the refugees themselves. Settler Jacob Sondheimer remembered, "It sometimes happened that valuable young people who had been chosen could not come because the representative did not want to take the parents and the young man did not want to leave without his parents."[19]

But Trone did show flexibility when circumstances permitted. When he interviewed Papernik and his fiancée, Irene, he chose Papernik right away because Papernik was a cabinetmaker. Trone initially refused to take Irene because she was underage and needed parental consent. But Papernik refused to go without her, and since his skills were so highly prized, Trone reconsidered.[20] Trone knew how high the stakes were. Reflecting on his time scouring the refugee camps, he lamented, "We have seen and lived with the refugees there, and one of the hardest tasks we were up against was to select—we being the judges—who will have homes, who will have sunshine, who will have a chance to live."[21]

Although each country of transit presented its own special problems, the acquisition of time-sensitive transit visas that permitted refugees to move from one country to the next, the frequent need to extend visas because of transportation delays, and the seemingly endless paperwork all were constants for the Trones and their colleagues at JDC offices in Paris and Lisbon. European travel was a labyrinth; in addition to transit visas, agents scrambled to secure technical documents, including exit and entrance permits, residence permits, food cards, and berths on ships for the prospective colonists.

DORSA also was frustrated by countries that, for political expediency, took the rhetorical high ground, pledging to grant transit visas, but often dragged their feet. The Vichy government played a particularly duplicitous game, demanding that the United States do more to persuade other states in the Western Hemisphere to open their doors to the more than three hundred thousand refugees in France, while, in response to pressure from the Nazis, refusing to issue exit visas. Indeed, the armistice that Marshall Petain signed with the Nazis in June 1940 specified that refugees were to be taken back to Germany, and the Gestapo was dispatched to the French camps to compile lists for future deportation. An annoyed Cordell Hull berated Vichy officials, charging that DORSA already had selected a number of refugees but these immigrants were still awaiting the requisite paperwork to leave.[22]

Yet even while he expressed indignation, Hull, concerned about Nazi infiltration at home, instructed his consuls to require that those immigrants first obtain exit permits from the Vichy government before contacting one of them. Despite strenuous lobbying by Eleanor Roosevelt and others, the State Department refused to alter this policy. Ultimately, precious few permits were granted in France, as the Americans, the Germans, and Vichy played what Henry Morgenthau later called the "refugee run-around."[23]

Once the prospective colonists had been selected, a Jewish relief agency provided them with tickets, information about visas, and transportation to Lisbon. DORSA reimbursed the agency for its costs and posted a one-hundred-dollar bond for each immigrant, as required by the shipping company. (The fee was refunded when the settlers reached New York.)[24] In the Portuguese capital they awaited passage along with approximately twelve thousand other immigrants.[25]

Lisbon was a step closer to freedom, and most refugees had positive memories of their time there. Felix Bauer remembered that the city was clean and that "for the first time there was an aura of peace." He even recalled having time to attend the 1940 World's Fair, "with pretty girls in national costumes, proud to be photographed."[26] Hellie Goldman recalled seeing her first movie in color, *The Wizard of Oz*, as well as going to the theater and sitting down to a steak dinner. Otto Papernik remembered spending twelve glorious days there, fresh from a French internment camp, and it was the small things that left a large impression: "for the first time in many months or even years we saw all the street lights were lit and the whole city was bright like daylight." Later Otto and Irene went to a delicatessen, bought a can of pineapple rings in syrup, had the can opened right then and there, "and ate the whole contents on the street. It was a great satisfaction to have overcome all the bad times we had had."[27]

For all their tribulations, the Trones at least were spared the difficult task of selecting and shepherding refugees from England. There DORSA worked with the IGC's director Sir Herbert Emerson and three assistants; Solomon Adler-Rudel; Eric Guttmann, a refugee psychiatrist; and Rosenberg's daughter, Elizabeth, a psychiatrist who had a practice at a London mental hospital—none of whom had any colonization experience.[28] England's peripheral position made it an attractive target for recruitment efforts, since the State Department was much more sympathetic to requests for transit visas from refugees living in the British Isles than on the Continent.[29]

Besides choosing prospective settlers, DORSA's English recruiters were given an additional task when the U.S. Committee for the Care of European Children asked if Sosúa would take in adolescents from England. The committee, which was formed on June 20, 1940, and had the backing of Eleanor Roosevelt, primarily wanted to place refugee children in U.S. homes, and had asked the State Department to waive quota restrictions to permit the children to come to the States. At the same time, it approached DORSA about bringing children to its settlement.[30]

Robert Pell also lobbied DORSA to accept the British children. The association could not say no to Pell after all his efforts, so it asked for and received permission from Dominican authorities to take in the youngsters.[31] Indeed, Pastoriza and Lamport had envisioned just such a program to prepare teenagers for the rigors of rural life when they cobbled together a draft agreement a year earlier. Although the original plan had called for a training center just outside the capital, Rosen opted instead to create a "subtraining camp" at Sosúa. Reyher and the National Refugee Service searched for sponsors willing to put up funds for these trainees. The aims of the DORSA trainee program appeared to dovetail perfectly with the U.S. committee's request.

Rosen persuaded Dominican authorities to issue blank visas for 500 children and 500 trainees "selected among the German refugees who have lived for some time in England." DORSA's New York office contacted relatives in the

United States, asking them to sponsor the trainees. But DORSA was unable to raise enough funds to accept the full complement of children and trainees; instead, Emerson's committee sent a total of 200 trainees beginning in the fall of 1940. Reyher estimated that an additional $230,000 was needed to bring the rest. George Warren was working feverishly with the IGC, she told Pastoriza, to seek additional funding from charities and foreign governments to get these "homeless refugee" children to the Dominican Republic.[32]

The trainee program turned out to be a bureaucratic nightmare for the London committee, since the adolescents were "interned or scattered all over the country." Although he took solace that some youngsters eventually made it to Sosúa, Rosen fumed that "our efforts appear pathetically futile."[33]

Meanwhile, two glaring problems surfaced during the second half of 1940, as the selection process for adult colonists gained momentum and successive cohorts of prospective colonists began arriving in the Dominican Republic. Those chosen fell far short of Rosen's expectations, and DORSA's expenses regularly outpaced its fundraising.

By disposition an optimist, Rosen was increasingly disturbed with the quality of the pioneers selected by Emerson's committee, Bondy, and Trone. Bondy received withering criticism for choosing less-than-stellar candidates from camps outside Lisbon. An angry Rosen wrote Bondy's supervisor, "I really cannot understand what were his reasons for accepting these people. One of them is absolutely unfit to do any physical work. It is sufficient to take a look at him once to be convinced that a disfavor was done him by sending him to Santo Domingo. . . . The other people claim that they told Dr. Bondy that they do not intend to become settlers and want to come to Santo Domingo merely as a jumping place to the States. You may tell Dr. Bondy in my name that I would have never expected him to be so careless, to say the least, in loading up with misfits."[34]

Rosen and Reyher were just as disappointed with Emerson's committee. One of its members, Adler-Rudel, appeared to want to shift responsibility— he blamed the refugees' precarious mental state—and warned that the selection process was inherently problematic: "I must again point out to you that it is no easy job to make a satisfactory selection in times as strenuous as the present. There is great nervousness and tension amongst the refugees and they are prepared to go everywhere and to give every promise if they see the slightest chance to leave the country."[35] He assured Rosen that nothing was promised to the settlers and they were told repeatedly that life in the Dominican Republic "will not be easy, that the climate conditions are difficult and that they will have to work very hard."[36]

But Rosen did not suffer fools gladly and refused to let Adler-Rudel off the hook. He was livid about the choices made by the three-headed committee: "My impression is that most of the people have been selected by some kind-hearted ladies"; he added sarcastically, "it is, of course, possible that no suitable human material is available in England among the refugees but then it is better to discontinue taking immigrants from your country at least for the time being."[37] He also chided Emerson for sending three women to the island in the advanced stages of pregnancy, noting that such decisions were not in the interest of the settlement or the women.[38] A few months later little had changed, and Rosen again upbraided Emerson. "There is a need for women settlers, who are not occupied with the thoughts of high-heeled slippers and polished finger-nails, who are ready to come to this country and work and settle down and expect in the course to marry a settler."[39]

Apparently, some trainees selected by Emerson's committee had no intention of making it to Sosúa. Rosen wrote Rosenberg to watch for one particular group when it passed through Ellis Island on its way to the settlement, because some of the "youngsters of the English group" were "plotting to get to New York as stowaways," while others had "secretly written to the American consulate." He concluded, "in their hearts and minds a majority still hope sooner or later to have a chance to go to the States, which is identical with going to New York."[40]

A second and debilitating problem was the shortage of funds. Although DORSA had inherited start-up funds from the Agro-Joint's Crimean account and had supplemented those with Rosenberg's successful fundraising after the signing, the office was unprepared for the enormous cost of getting refugees out of Europe. "Go slow" became DORSA's unofficial slogan during its first year.

That was the message Rosenberg drummed into Rosen. "The vital thing . . . is to resist temptation and hold the settlement down to such small numbers that we do not run into a financial jam." Rosenberg knew he could not tap the JDC for additional funds: "the financial situation of the JDC . . . is such that you and I cannot count on money from the JDC, not even a cent . . . In all the many years of my JDC service, I have never seen the financial situation so serious as it is now." Harkening back to their past experience in Russia, Rosenberg added: "So hold back like the devil, dear Joseph, because it is not like the old days when I could feel a genuine sense of confidence in getting large monies. If, with only two hundred settlers at the very most, you can make a success and you can solve the most difficult problems, namely, the psychological ones—viz. handling the matter so that the settlers are content, and if they are in good health and able to work and things are right, then we will have our supreme test next winter. By then big money should come in from Van Zeeland, the Lessing Rosenwald group, so if you could show success with small numbers then big bucks will come from these guys . . . So I repeat, go slow."[41]

There were political costs to growing too quickly. It was better to build slowly rather than make mistakes and risk losing the support of Ciudad Trujillo or Washington. "It takes only a few mistaken actions on our part to cause the Dominican Government to lose confidence in our judgment, and if this should happen, the whole effort will be smashed to pieces," Rosenberg wrote. "Horrible as it is to say so, it is better to risk sacrificing a few people at the beginning than to jeopardize this great undertaking."[42]

The trainee initiative only exacerbated the financial pressure. Rosenberg asked Pell if Roosevelt would help fundraising efforts by publicly endorsing the program. Perhaps influenced by the First Lady, FDR consented, and a jubilant Rosenberg seized the moment to call a meeting of prospective donors at the Lawyer's Club in Manhattan, at which Roosevelt's letter of support was read aloud. All of the principals spoke at the fundraiser, including Pastoriza, Warren, Baerwald, and Wagg; and a glossy pamphlet titled *Concerning Refugee Settlement in the Dominican Republic* was published afterward. Yet even the president's blessing and a commitment from the JDC to underwrite the trainees' transportation expenses failed to solve DORSA's funding woes.[43]

Rosenberg's orders to Rosen to hold back and build a smaller colony certainly were not what Trujillo wanted to hear. Anxious to show meaningful results and build on the favorable publicity he had received, Trujillo wanted proof that the settlement was forging ahead. Rosenberg tried to reassure the dictator that building slowly had its own rewards: " I am so tremendously concerned to see to it that we get only the right kind of people."[44] But Trujillo remained impatient about the slow pace of arrivals.

Authorities did not hide their disappointment either, communicating their apprehension directly to the State Department. A well-placed informant weighed in that "the highest official circles" in the Dominican Republic had concluded that the settlement was not a "serious undertaking."[45] Reyher later complained that the criticism was unjustified, because officials knew full well how restrictive the State Department was about transit visas and still "they [Dominican officials] periodically seem to wonder, and even resent, that the Sosúa population increased so slowly."[46]

As the end of 1940 approached, only 250 settlers had arrived and DORSA's precarious balance sheet had not improved. Generating funding was proving more problematic as the same few big donors were besieged by all the major philanthropies. Rosenberg approached Baerwald and asked the JDC to step up and demonstrate its commitment. He wanted to announce at the colony's first anniversary celebration that he had "commitments for another $550,000 from the JDC." The way the request to Baerwald was couched suggests that he was feeling the heat from Dominican authorities: "If I have to go down there empty-handed so far as new commitments are concerned, it will be a tragic failure on our part. If we are obliged for lack of funds to stop taking settlers, even though it may cost $300 per settler for transportation, we are writing in large letters the word FAILURE on our own effort."[47]

Baerwald tried to calm Rosenberg. He was disappointed that Rosenberg had apparently led his Dominican colleagues on about how much the JDC could be expected to invest, and counseled restraint: "You have made or implied promises about bringing a lot of money with you when you go down [to the Dominican Republic in January]. I don't see where you will find it to the full extent you desire between now and January. You are dealing with money questions with people whose minds are occupied in many directions and whose help, nevertheless, you and we all do need." Baerwald's allusion to "people . . . occupied in many directions" no doubt referred to the large donors Rosenberg was so keen to approach. Unfortunately for DORSA, the JDC and others already were leaning heavily on these same benefactors to finance their relief efforts.

Rosenberg's persistent pleading, however, eventually wore Baerwald down. In mid-January 1941 the Joint agreed to come through during calendar year 1941 with a large enough appropriation to bring in one thousand more settlers. This was certainly excellent news, as it came on the eve of Rosenberg's trip to the island and he was sure it would do much to allay concerns among Dominican officials. Now it was up to DORSA to show that it could bring enough settlers to Sosúa to develop the colony. Once again, however, mitigating circumstances beyond its control frustrated the association's efforts.

"SOSÚA WAS CRAWLING WITH SPIES"

Reyher immediately shared the goods news with the State Department and requested assistance in securing transit visas for the prospective settlers. The State Department actually had just given DORSA special permission to bring over 150 refugees from Germany and 50 trainees from the Netherlands. Accepting refugees from Germany represented a significant departure from past policy; the ostensible reason was that many of these refugees were immediate relatives of Sosúa's first settlers. As part of its appropriation, the Joint agreed to provide maintenance for these relatives for one year, "hoping the settlers could then take such relatives to their own homesteads and maintain them." Other visas were earmarked for relatives of nonsettlers living in Ciudad Trujillo.[48]

DORSA administrators had argued that bringing these relatives out of the occupied territory was critical to the settlers' mental well-being and the colony's future. Wagg, who visited the colony during the first anniversary celebration, had listened to complaints of preoccupied settlers, who reminded the dignitaries present that DORSA had promised it would do all it could to get their loved ones out of harm's way. He was convinced that "settlers cannot have any feeling of permanence until they have some assurance that they can be united with their families. Bringing mothers and fathers, wives and husbands, brothers and sisters to Sosúa is a guaranty of stability; and it is strongly urged that the bars [against taking refugees from greater Germany] recommended by the IGC should be let down at least so that families may build their new homes together."[49]

Reyher wanted to be sure that the State Department's often prickly Visa Division would make good on its word. She alerted State Department officials that Trone was prepared to leave Lisbon and go to Germany to conduct interviews. Jewish relief committees in Germany and Austria were anxious to get their people out because conditions were awful inside Germany. The majority of those identified by the relief committees already had received special "protective" Dominican visas "to save them from deportation." These special visas were issued "with the stipulation that, before such people could leave for the Dominican Republic, further arrangements would have to be made to give them actual visas."[50]

What concerned Reyher was that over the last six months, the State Department had gone back and forth about these transit visas. First, because of security concerns, the original requests had been rejected. Then DORSA appeared to get a green light, but at a time when it had barely enough funds to move refugees out of Lisbon and England. Now that DORSA had received its subsidy for 1941 and was ready to act, Reyher asked Pell again in January 1941, "Can we secure U.S. transit visas for them? Have you any hope of getting a favorable answer?" Since Pell was on his way down to the Dominican capital with Rosenberg, she wondered, "Would it perhaps be useful for you to have this in mind so that when you get to Sosúa you can report that you have personally seen the settlers and believed that the settlers are so well known to our organization, that bringing their relatives over would probably be one of the most carefully checked groups we could have and then, would there be a hope for us to assure settlers that we could assist in bringing their relatives over?"[51]

A distraught Pell telephoned Reyher the very next day. An article had just appeared in the *Washington Times-Herald* that sent shock waves throughout the nation's capital. Unnamed sources claimed "Sosúa was crawling with [Nazi] spies." Washington was a city of "whispering comments" and, as a result, "we are practically back where we started in connection with our possibilities in Germany." He quickly disabused Reyher of the notion of sending Trone to Germany; "It would be inviting criticism to have Trone go to Germany after that article. . . . Nobody from Germany *at all* at this time." An exception might be made after the anniversary celebration, Pell mused, but he was not even hopeful about that.[52]

DORSA's shrinking goodwill at the State Department was made manifest by Pell's added comment that it would be a mistake to ask for any transit visas from an increasingly intransigent Visa Division while he and Wagg were away in the Dominican Republic. The only good news he could offer was that DORSA could, upon their return, proceed with those refugees awaiting transit visas in Lisbon or unoccupied France. In an aside, Pell admitted that his colleagues regarded him as "an agent of the Association" and, as a result, his views were "not taken with full consideration by the State Department."[53]

Pell's rise and sudden fall from grace became a cautionary tale for Rosenberg and his staff. DORSA's State Department liaison had earned his spurs as an aide to Myron Taylor in the Évian delegation, and a year later became an indispensable part of George Rublee's IGC negotiating team. In 1939, after negotiations broke down with the Nazis, Pell was promoted to assistant chief of the Division of European Affairs, and his desk became the clearinghouse for all refugee-related matters. The job was both demanding and exhausting, but more than that, it had become a minefield, given the tense atmosphere in the State Department. Pell performed heroically on the association's behalf, but the tide had turned decidedly against him.

Less than a year after his promotion, Pell, then 38, found himself out of step. He painted himself into a corner when he penned a feisty memo in late February 1940 urging aggressive action to spirit refugees out of Europe. Even though he was the department's representative to the IGC, Pell lashed out at the committee's feeble diplomacy, platitudes, and stonewalling: "These gentlemen . . . will make pretty speeches, or in most cases will not speak at all. . . . The hopes of the unfortunate refugees will be raised by the announcement that a meeting is to be held, and, as on previous occasions when the

Committee has assembled, will be dashed to even lower depths after the session. It would seem that the moment for oratory and exchange of compliments in relation to the refugee problem has passed. . . . The approximately 140,000 German refugees in countries of refuge have to be resettled."[54] In contrast, Pell praised the work of "Mr. Rosenberg's Dominican project," which was doing something constructive about the problem.

Pell received a strong rebuke from none other than the president, who, with uncharacteristic forcefulness, retorted, "I do not agree with the memorandum from the Division of European Affairs." Roosevelt continued to hope that the IGC could play a constructive role over the long term, and chided Pell for thinking only of the "immediate needs of a definite number of German, Spanish, Polish, Czecho-Slovak individuals and families" and for failing "to appreciate the enormous long-range view which will take into consideration new home seekers from France, Great Britain and even the United States."[55]

From that point on, Pell was branded an advocate for the refugees in general and DORSA specifically, and his position in the Department became increasingly untenable. Dispirited, he wrote to his division chief, Ray Atherton, "Those of us who had the responsibility in refugee matters in this Division were working more or less in a void. I have had very little indication of interest in the Department in this work; in fact, every indication that the work was to a large extent unpopular and disapproved. Mr. Morris [Stephen Morris, Pell's assistant] and I have had very largely to improvise in our dealings with outside organizations and persons and convey the impression that this Government still was interested in aiding refugees when there has been every indication inside the Department that the interest here has—with notable exceptions—waned."[56]

In March 1941 Pell asked to be relieved of his duties. He was reassigned to a position in the Office of Current Information, which must have felt like a demotion, because he soon took a leave of absence to serve as a liaison in the political office of Supreme Allied Headquarters. His successor, Wagg, also a friend and ally of DORSA, saw his temporary position at the refugee desk "redefined" and, despite special pleading from Pell, was unceremoniously fired in the winter of 1941. Pell and Wagg's dismissals were a bitter blow for DORSA, which lost two key advocates at a critical moment.[57]

Wagg did not do DORSA any favors when he took a parting shot at his former employers in a article titled "Washington's Stepchild: The Refugee," in the *New Republic* in March 1941. He did what career foreign service officers like Pell could not: publicly blast "Washington officialdom" for putting the refugee problem on the back burner as "something to be admired in principle and then dismissed as 'inopportune.'" He commended a small group of committed individuals, most notably DORSA administrators, who "have struggled against great odds in an atmosphere of opposition and suspicion and with a minimum of support from the official makers of our foreign policies. . . . The refugee effort has been at best a stepchild in Washington to be beaten and buffeted, and at worst a football for anti-Semitism and for petty bureaucrats."[58]

Calling on the administration to "fish or cut bait," Wagg praised the Sosúa initiative as an innovative model of how to cope with the refugee problem. He criticized the Reich for its "wickedly clever German strategy [which] has a double objective:" to rid itself of the Jews while making the hapless refugees appear to be saboteurs. This double objective was meant

> First, to dump scared, destitute human beings in great numbers across frontiers or the ocean. This taxes the already overburdened facilities of his opponents, creates chaos and, above all, stimulates dissension. Second, to arouse by this act, in the camp of Hitler's enemies, racial and religious hatreds, petty persecutions which rapidly grow into major persecutions, bribery and corruption. Hitler, through his agents, works both sides. Not only does he dump the refugees where their sudden arrival creates a maximum of confusion, but his agents, and their unsuspecting victims, begin to whisper immediately that the refugees are probably secret Nazi sympathizers, that they undoubtedly are working underground for Germany, that they have not forgotten their Fatherland, that in short they and not the real Nazi agents are the peril.[59]

Yes, the Nazis were to blame for this diabolical strategy, Wagg declared, but such propaganda "reaches high places in many governments including our own, places where the wish is father to the thought, and where the seeds of anti-Semitism and anti-liberalism are already sprouting." He ended his missive with a call to action: "This country *must* have a refugee policy. Today, it has next to none. 'Refugee' in Washington today means 'alien' to the bureaucrat, 'secret agent' to the military man. For the sake of all we mean when we talk about defending democracy, the refugee should be clothed with human dignity once more, and the problem of his resettlement regarded in true perspective as one of the fundamental problems of democracy—to be solved, not dodged."[60]

Wagg's swan song did not play well in the department. Both Pell's and Wagg's demise were inevitable, given the hardliners' impregnable position. Bringing refugees out of occupied territory was ruled out once and for all in the spring of 1941.

When German and Austrian relief committees learned of the latest reversal they were apoplectic. Rosen knew that the committees were extremely frustrated. "It is obvious that our friends in Germany do not understand the situation and suspect that we do not want to cooperate with them or help them. We could not write them frankly what the real situation is." Rosen was anxious to have Trone travel to Germany to speak with the relief organizations personally and set the record straight: "If you are in Germany and see them, you have to explain to them that the trouble is not with us, and not even the difficulties of getting transportation, but with the attitude of our own State Department, which makes it inadvisable and impossible to bring over people directly from Germany or German-occupied territory . . . we have been strongly advised by our friends in the Department to leave this matter well alone—otherwise we may endanger the entire settlement project. This is a sad situation, but for the time being we can do absolutely nothing about it."[61]

The stark reality that confronted German and Austrian Jews was a kind of double jeopardy. The State Department viewed them as potential enemy aliens, painting them with the same broad brush as those who had condemned them to annihilation. Meanwhile, DORSA's staff, ready to shepherd them out at a moment's notice, was powerless to do anything but sit and wait.[62]

The association's efforts in January 1941 to unify its settlers' families and bring refugees out of greater Germany had been stymied by a sensational, unsubstantiated newspaper story. Despite subsequent investigations by Dominican and U.S. intelligence officials, the allegations of espionage at Sosúa were never corroborated. The U.S. Legation in Ciudad Trujillo suspected twenty-four refugees in the Dominican Republic, but only two were arrested and deported to U.S. detention camps, and neither was from Sosúa.[63] For the journalist John Gunther, who visited the island in 1941, the overheated rhetoric coming out of Washington was much ado about nothing: "There is virtually no Fifth Column problem, because no local Fascist party could exist and Germans are almost unknown."[64]

This would not be the last time that harmful suspicions and stories would scuttle DORSA's efforts to save lives. A more elaborate rumor circulated a year later, for example, that refugees at Sosúa were signaling ships out in the bay every night. The frequency of these scares was enough to make DORSA staffers suspicious. The usually circumspect Reyher mused, "As time has gone on, I have begun to wonder whether the charges, scares, articles, etc., are of wholly a sporadic nature."[65]

As news of massive deportations of Jews to Poland spread in the winter of 1941, Sosúa's settlers became increasingly apprehensive about their loved ones back home. An exasperated Rosenberg went over Breckinridge Long's head and pleaded to Sumner Welles,

> Since last May we have not applied for Dominican visas for settlers or their relatives residing in German-occupied territories. This was because we were advised by Mr. Pell that such applications would not be in accord with current State Department policies. Germany has intensified persecutions, especially of Jews, and has recently announced large-scale deportations to Poland to take place by April 1. Many of the settlers in the Dominican Republic have relatives in Germany or German-occupied territories—parents, brothers, sisters; also a number of fiancées. Because of the April 1 deadline the settlers in the Dominican Republic have made piteous and urgent appeals to us to secure Dominican visas for their relatives. We believe we are in a position immediately to obtain from the Dominican government visas for these relatives or fiancées. We believe that possession of such visas may well mean the difference between life and death. Hence the future of the entire settlement project may be at stake in this matter.[66]

This is about as pointed a letter as the loyal-to-a-fault Rosenberg ever penned to the administration he deeply admired. The extreme language he uses suggests how much pressure he was under at that moment and how desperate DORSA was to secure the release of the settlers' relatives. Rosenberg concluded by asking Welles for guidance and noted that with Pell's pending transfer and Wagg's termination, "at this point there is no one in the State Department whom we are in a position to consult. Hence this urgent letter to you."[67]

Welles directed Rosenberg to meet with Long and Avra Warren, not exactly what Rosenberg wanted to hear. He was informed that a career foreign service officer, a Long appointee, henceforth would serve as DORSA's contact in the State Department. The hardliners, perhaps at Welles's prompting, appeared to offer Rosenberg some hope, giving DORSA the green light to secure 181 Dominican visas for relatives and intendeds, "hoping that this will at least prevent their deportation from their homes and thereby give them a chance for rescue." Reyher cabled Trone with the hopeful news, adding that she would assemble dossiers on the loved ones so that the association could apply for transit visas. Rosenberg reported to Avra Warren that the news "had a most beneficial effect at Sosúa."[68]

Yet it was one thing to have visas issued and quite another to get the refugees out of the occupied territories. Despite Rosenberg's entreaties and Welles's intervention, Avra Warren, in quintessential bureaucratic fashion, then deflated Reyher by insisting that she had to provide concrete evidence in each case to the appropriate consular official in Europe that transportation arrangements had been made for the refugee in question.[69] Given the difficulties inherent in getting refugees out of Europe and the vagaries of Atlantic shipping, that was no simple task in early 1941.

Back at Sosúa, anxious settlers pressed administrators to move heaven and earth to get their family members out. Indeed, each time DORSA succeeded in bringing a few relatives to the settlement, it inevitably raised the hopes of others desperate for the same result. Nothing created more resentment at Sosúa than the widely shared perception that DORSA was not doing enough to rescue family members. Few had any idea how difficult it was to get refugees out of Europe at that time. Understandably, fewer still could think rationally about the matter. The settler Heinrich Wasservogel recalled quite emotionally, nearly sixty years after the fact, how he had pleaded, to no avail, with DORSA officials in New York to get his mother and twin brothers out of Yugoslavia. Rosenberg's reply sought to encourage him and to convey that the association was doing all that it could under the circumstances. "Thank you for writing to me about your mother and twin brothers, whom you wish to have join you in Sosúa. I quite understand your desire to be reunited with your family, and Mr. Falk, Mr. Schweitzer [both DORSA administrators] and I are doing everything to make this possible." Rosenberg asked Wasservogel to look to the future and not dwell on the past, ending his letter on a constructive note. "It gives me great pleasure to know that you are happy in Sosúa and will soon have your own homestead."[70]

Unfortunately, Wasservogel, like many of his peers, was never reunited with his family.[71] He and other Sosuaners, just like Bertolt Brecht in this chapter's epigraph, had been spared from a likely death, but carried the weighty psychological burden of wondering why they had been saved while other family members and friends had not. The failure to reunite families cast a pall over the settlement during the war years, even though, in retrospect, most colonists came to appreciate that DORSA was doing the best it could under impossible circumstances.

DORSA officials, however, knew where to place the blame. An increasingly dour Rosen fixated on "the growing influence in our own State Department of the exclusionist group which has been and still is antagonistic to our project and is ever ready to place all kinds of obstacles in our way." He captured the hardliner's "us versus them" mindset regarding the Sosúa settlement: an "expanding hypnotic scare of the Fifth Column Phantom, particularly in relation to the Dominican Republic, with its strategic position," had effectively brought about a "moratorium on growth."[72]

That the settlement's first year coincided with the vicissitudes of war, along with hefty doses of paranoia and disappointment from U.S. and Dominican bureaucrats, left staffers less than sanguine about the colony's future. Rosenberg's characteristic idealism and optimism, so evident during the contract signing, had given way to sober realism just eighteen months later. By June 1941, the stress of trying to save lives had gotten to the indomitable sixty-six-year-old, and he had to be hospitalized. That fall his doctors urged him to lighten his workload; to give up his "speech-making activities and cease your travel about the country."[73] He wrote to his daughter Elizabeth in June 1941 reflecting on the difficult hand his fledgling association had been dealt. "This work has been surrounded with multitudinous difficulties so great that if I had foreseen them, I would, perhaps not have undertaken this tremendously difficult effort. We have had also the endless difficulties on the part of the Government of the United States with regulations, you understand, we *must* and wish to comply with to the letter, and which shift and change. Their enforcement is in the hands of people not all of whom, by any means, are in sympathy with this or any other refugee effort. . . . Lastly, we have not had the financial support on which we counted."[74]

It would be too generous to describe what DORSA went through in its first year and a half as growing pains. Although publicly Rosenberg and Rosen extolled the virtues of the settlement as they went about raising funds in New York and elsewhere, privately they and their patrons realized that the colony that eventually was established would be but a shell of its imagined self.

Afterward, Rosenberg and his aides could take solace in the knowledge that DORSA had saved more than just the refugees who had reached Sosúa. He boasted that the association had saved four thousand Jews all told during the course of the war by providing many in Europe with Dominican visas, which protected them from Hitler's death camps. Maurice Hexter later claimed as many as ten thousand saved.[75] Although the existing documentation does not permit a reconstruction of the precise number who owed their lives to what Rosenberg called his "Dominican insurance policies," and although exaggeration was standard operating procedure for DORSA's tireless fundraisers, Sosúa's impact clearly went far beyond those housed at the settlement. As Herbert Agar, a JDC historian, put it with just a tad of justification: "it is not given to many to save even 4,000 lives."[76]

In June 1940, however, organizers concentrated their efforts on the difficult task of building a settlement from scratch on the north coast. While DORSA's staff wrestled with officious bureaucrats and would-be donors, those refugees fortunate enough to make it to the Dominican Republic tried to adapt to their new surroundings. Like DORSA's founders, they were heartened by their beautiful first impression of Sosúa Bay.

Part Three / **GROWING PAINS**

EIGHT

First Impressions

> They could walk under a blue sky, inhale a different and quiet air,
> watch a sunset containing colors of which they had never even
> dreamed, and feel the joy of being secure and be able to start life
> anew.
>
> JOSEF DAVID EICHEN, SETTLER

Felix Bauer had fond memories of his trip across the Atlantic in early September 1940 with the first group of eighteen German and Austrian refugees from Switzerland destined for Sosúa. After an arduous bus trip from a camp in Dipoltsau to Perpignan in southern France, followed by a grueling trek over the Pyrenees to Barcelona, then by train from Madrid to Lisbon, the voyage aboard the Greek ocean liner *Nea Hellas* felt like paradise to Bauer. He was appalled by what he had witnessed in war-torn Spain during the summer of 1940: "bombed out houses, some city blocks completely in rubble" in Barcelona, suffocating heat that "compared easily with Dante's inferno" in Madrid, shortages of food and water, and beggars at every turn. In comparison, the passage across the Atlantic, despite bouts of seasickness, was leisurely and filled with anticipation about how this new chapter of his life would unfold. He was not only well fed but treated with respect aboard ship. What Bauer found especially gratifying, and at the same time ironic, was that the waiters dressed and acted the part when serving those not too nauseous to dine: "It was an unbelievable feeling for us, who had escaped the degradation of Hitler and being of the second rate category of refugees, to be served by waiters with white gloves."[1]

Bauer's sober response suggests the psychological transformation that those fleeing oppression underwent on their journey to freedom. That process of renewal, begun in earnest as soon as he stepped aboard the ship, of "becoming human again," as one refugee headed for Bolivia phrased it during the same panic migration, must have been at once discomforting and liberating.[2] Bauer and the other refugees were literally in the same boat, and yet they were also in a liminal state. Natally alienated from rights or claims of birth by Nazi bureaucrats, they were now, on the one hand, outsiders experiencing a secular excommunication from their past, and on the other, unwanted exiles looking for a new home where they would feel a modicum of acceptance.[3] Set adrift, they were moving toward a place they could not yet imagine. Disoriented, and sad about what had they had gone through, they were at the same time relieved, nervous, and hopeful about an uncertain future. No matter how they tried to remain positive, they harbored feelings of displacement and resentment and were understandably anxious about their enforced separation from family and friends.[4]

For some, banishment had come about in stages, in fits and starts. A number of those bound for Sosúa had been trapped in what had once been countries of transit, which subsequently came under German occupation after their arrival; there they had lived as transients in labor or internment camps. The trip across the Atlantic represented the next phase of that uprooting.

Arriving in New York harbor, Bauer, like others, was overcome by the sight of Lady Liberty, but then just as quickly disappointed when he was dispatched on a small launch to Ellis Island, where he waited for a week for a South Porto Rico Company steamer that would take his group to Ciudad Trujillo. Fifty years later he told an interviewer, "we knew that America doesn't want us, but we overcame [it]"[5] That ten-day stopover at Ellis Island, on the outside looking into America, made a powerful impression on the young immigrant. Manhattan's skyline was so temptingly close that some of his fellow travelers longed to cut short their trip right then and there (see figure 7).

Bauer slept in a bunk in a room with other men—the sole female and child in their group roomed elsewhere with other women. The visitors could walk or kick a soccer ball around an open-air yard surrounded by a high wire fence. "Everything was clean, and food, towels and soap were plentiful." Even new bedspreads, he remembered with a chuckle. Heinrich Wasservogel, who came with Bauer, recalled heaping bowls of bananas and citrus fruit, delicacies hard to obtain in Europe. Bauer's soon-to-be wife, Martha, was beside herself that butter was plentiful—she had been lucky to get even a pat a week in England, where she had fled after Kristallnacht—"and we had napkins every

FIGURE 7 George Warren greats the first Swiss group at New York Harbor. JDC ARCHIVES.

day and a fresh table cloth." She simply could not fathom why some were unhappy. They were even given chewing gum, but the novices did not know what to do with it. "So we tried to eat it," Bauer joked. "It was difficult and we were sorry for the poor Americans who had that kind of candy. After awhile we gave it to people who could appreciate the rubber, as we called it."[6]

Ellis Island was a veritable Tower of Babel, where Bauer met Jews wearing caftans, black hats, and sidelocks who spoke an unintelligible language and who had the temerity to ask for kosher food. And they got what they asked for! In their ample spare time, the refugees sketched a mural of sorts in pencil on the wall of their room, replete with caricatures of each of them; wrote letters to friends and family back home; and read newspapers like the German-language Jewish *Aufbau*, which boasted an international readership and included the latest news about the war and tidbits about friends and neighbors scattered around the world. They also played chess or cards and conversed with travelers bound for other destinations throughout Latin America. This first Swiss group also met with Rosenberg and George Warren, who came down from DORSA's nearby offices at 165 Broadway to greet them; they were the first contingent to make it out of Europe since the original settlers had arrived in early May. The media-savvy Rosenberg had the group pose for promotional photographs with the Statue of Liberty and Manhattan Harbor as a backdrop.[7]

Ellis Island had a very different meaning to refugees in transit than it did for those awaiting entry into the United States. It did not escape their attention that, despite its relatively pleasant accommodations, the island had been designed by authorities to keep them out of the country. The visitors were locked up every evening, and neither the bedrooms, bathrooms, nor dining hall had any windows. "The only windows were in the big hall, two stories high and barred with steel and wire, constantly visible to the guard on duty," Ernest Hofeller remarked. When they left their sleeping quarters for the great hall, where they dined, a guard with a counter ticked them off one by one to make sure that all were present and accounted for. Even the area where refugees could meet relatives was screened. No wonder the dour Hofeller compared the island to an "escape-proof prison."[8] To be treated like potential criminals at Ellis Island when their only offense was having fled from Hitler was disappointing to those who idealized the United States.

The usually perceptive Bauer provides little clue of his feelings as he left Ellis Island for the Dominican Republic, but we can imagine the ambivalence he and others shared about their predicament. Thankful about leaving Europe behind, uncertain about their future in the Caribbean, the émigrés were just a stone's throw from the glistening world they had heard so much about from relations and friends. Some even had the chance to hear firsthand about the *goldene medina* from relatives who came to visit them. New York City was at once new and exciting yet comparable to the bustling metropolitan centers of Central Europe. Culture, education, and economic opportunity awaited those fortunate enough to possess a prized visa. Realistically, why would they want to be anywhere else? Yet, like Moses gazing longingly at Canaan, they were denied entrance.

The historian C. Harvey Gardiner argues that the stopover at Ellis Island proved to be a "key formative experience" for those Sosúa-bound and that their stay there, as brief as it was, subsequently persuaded a number of them to make inquiries with U.S. consular officials soon after their arrival on the island about the possibility of emigrating to the States, a gesture that did not sit well with DORSA and Dominican officials.[9]

Still, in reading memoirs and speaking with former settlers about the trip from Europe to New York and then from New York on to their final destination, one is struck by their unflagging optimism (see figure 8). Even though memoirs and oral histories surely filter out much of the uncertainty felt at the time, the accounts suggest that the travelers made the most of their new lease on life. Papernik captured that joie de vivre in his description of a chance encounter with a Caribbean-bound church group aboard the *Algonquin*, the ship that transported his Luxemburg group from New York to the Dominican Republic. "On board we met . . . religious young people that were going to help build a church. When we heard them for the first time singing spiritual songs a cappella, we were very much impressed and liked it very much. Naturally we answered with singing our old German and Austrian lieder. As usual I was with my mandolin and we made an agreement with this group; they would sing one song and then we would sing one. They had heard our songs only in the movies and they did not want us to stop. We had a marvelous time with them."[10] During a three-day stopover in San Juan, Puerto Rico, Bauer was delighted to visit museums, attend orchestra rehearsals, and, as he put it, come "into contact with a Central American civilization" for the first time.[11]

A day later they finally arrived in what Bauer characterized as a drab Ciudad Trujillo, "a letdown after the vibrant life of San Juan." They stayed in the capital for only a few days; time enough to receive their identification cards (*cédulas*) and to obtain a fresh round of inoculations. Bauer was incredulous at the number of injections they had received since leaving Switzerland; each country, in turn, seemingly wanting to immunize the refugees from the microbes of the previous one. No country seemed to trust the other, he remarked. "Surely, by now, we must have had serum in our body instead of blood."[12]

Ruth and Ernie Schreiner, who came with the second Swiss group in late fall 1940, had difficulty coping with the withering heat in the capital. Ernie remembered that the hotel dispensed mosquito nets to each guest. Not everyone knew, however, what this netting was for and how to use it. "Poor Otto Wohlmuth," he recalled, "thought it was a sheet and was badly bitten up. He learned how to use that net fast!"[13]

The refugees were taken by car or bus across the island to Sosúa, where they were introduced to the DORSA staff and the first settlers. The sights and sounds of the trip were unforgettable to Elie Topf, who arrived in the winter of 1942. After spending the last two years in several dreadful French detention camps, admittedly anything might have looked good to Topf, but he was unprepared for how green and inviting the landscape was. What still stayed with him sixty-five years later, however, were the aromas wafting in the air whenever their hired car pulled off the road to take a break. "I could smell roasting coffee beans on the campesinos' open hearths, small boys coming up to you selling bags of *mani* (peanuts), and the smell of charcoal was everywhere."[14] Twenty-seven-year-old Judith Kibel's first impressions of the impoverished countryside were not quite as affirming, but not atypical: "As we were riding

FIGURE 8 Excited to leave Europe behind, grateful for a new opportunity in the tropics.
JDC ARCHIVES.

into Sosúa, I saw little houses where the floor was earth and the beds were hammocks. I said to my husband, 'here I will not live.'"[15]

Spirits improved when the refugees arrived at Sosúa. The journalist Freda Kirchwey, who traveled to Sosúa from Ciudad Trujillo along with the first pioneers in March 1940, wrote this evocative description of their first glance of the settlement: "As the road grew worse, the country became more and more beautiful. Green mountains and fertile valleys showed that rainfall was plentiful. . . . Then, suddenly, as we rounded a shoulder of a high ridge, the land fell off toward the sea, Sosúa lay below us. We first saw the beach, white and sleek, bending around the green-blue water of the bay. Then we saw hills and pastures reaching down to the shore, and a collection of red roofs. The two Austrian doctors, our fellow-passengers, looked for the first time at the land that was to be their home, perhaps for the rest of their lives."[16]

It was hard not to be taken in by the site's sheer beauty. The high ground just off to the side of El Batey, aptly named Bella Vista, afforded a magnificent view of Sosúa's half-moon bay. Not surprisingly, Bella Vista was chosen for

FIGURE 9 A dictator's gift, c. 1940. JDC ARCHIVES.

the settlement's first ten homesteads. The colony's location was deceptively beautiful, Rosen later told the New York press. "We still have to find a single person who visited the place and was not enchanted by its beauty. If people could live on beauty alone, we would not have to worry about the prospects for our settlers."[17] (See figure 9, above.)

The colonists quickly learned that much of the property was unsuitable for anything other than pasture. A shallow layer of topsoil, sandy soils in certain sections, dense, boulder-strewn hills in others, outcroppings of limestone and coral rock that inhibited plowing, sizable areas of swampland, and punishing episodes of drought all combined to diminish what was materially possible. Of the 26,000 hectares of land donated in Sosúa, only a small portion proved suitable for agriculture. A Brookings Institution report on the settlement's potential, based on a site visit by a team of colonization experts in late 1941 and early 1942, estimated only 160 hectares of arable land, and most of that was bunched together along the bluffs near the seacoast. Less than 2,000 hectares were fit for pasture.[18]

That dissonance between the settlement's attractiveness and its all-too-apparent limitations as a colonization site may have been apparent to DORSA managers, but neither Rosen nor Rosenberg ever admitted as much, publicly or privately, lest it send the wrong message to donors and settlers and insult their host, who had donated the land. A dearth of funds, the difficulties of getting refugees out of Europe, and a shortage of suitable colonists led Rosenberg to consistently soft pedal the need to seek out new lands. Ongoing disagreements about Sosúa's utility as a site would drive a wedge between Rosenberg and Leon Falk, leading the latter to abruptly resign his position less than a year after he had replaced Rosen.

Fortunately, such squabbling did not filter down to the émigrés themselves. A honeymoon effect suffused the settlement during its first year, and all concerned sought to make the best of what had been given them, imperfections notwithstanding. Bauer's and Papernik's salutary first impressions in particular are notable for their attention to detail, candor, and sense of humor. Although the next few chapters will place their observations in a broader context, what they initially felt and experienced is revealing: not only does it foreshadow challenges the settlers had to overcome, but it gives a sense of how urban Central Europeans absorbed their new surroundings.

BUILDING A SETTLEMENT

The first two families to arrive in Sosúa did not come directly from Europe. The Weinbergs and the Sichels already were living in Ciudad Trujillo when they were relocated to the opposite end of the island on March 16, 1940. Jakob Weinberg was an accountant and Max Sichel was a civil servant, but on their very first day they were put to work building a pen for twenty pigs and a boar. The merchant Marec Morsél joined them from the capital in early April. These three families and DORSA officials would serve as an unofficial welcoming committee for the first group from Europe.[19]

When the first group arrived at El Batey, it moved into barracks that had been hastily constructed by Spanish republican exiles and native laborers to accommodate the anticipated influx. DORSA could be thankful that it had something to work with when it assumed ownership. In addition to the dilapidated buildings, the colony inherited a tram track, which locals called *ferrocarril* (railroad), which knifed through the property. The fruit company had constructed it so that mule-driven wagons could haul bananas from field to pier. DORSA later built a road alongside it. Other structures still standing were the Casa Grande, which became the association's main office; workers' homes, barns, storage sheds, rural guard barracks, and a post office.[20]

TABLE 3 *Construction Work at Sosúa, June–December 1940*

Completed

3 Barracks without kitchen, 132 feet long each
2 Barracks with kitchen, 132 feet long, with a 45-foot annex
3 Matrimonial barracks
1 House for 4 couples
4 Company houses for staff and guests
1 House for the water pump
1 Cement schoolhouse for the Dominican school
11 Settler houses
1 Movable shed
1 Dormitory in La Gina (Charamico)
1 Garage for 5 cars
12 Houses for workers
1 Laundry

Under Construction

Central electrical plant and distribution grid
Office for technical work
5 Settler houses for Laguna Ferrocarril
2 Houses for employees in La Gina (Charamico)
2 Kitchens and dormitories for workers
1 Staff house

Source: "Report of the Meeting"

The expectation that large numbers of pioneers were on their way set off a mini construction boom. To cope with the expected onslaught, DORSA contracted out much of the new construction to a Dominican firm. Table 3 (above) documents this flurry of activity. In the first six months, more than thirty thousand dollars was spent on building materials, and labor costs climbed above twelve thousand dollars.[21]

In addition to structures listed as "Under Construction," by the end of 1940, ground was broken for a synagogue, a schoolhouse, a dairy barn, a small hotel, a bakery, a woodworking shop, three wells, and five "Garden City" houses for elderly nonsettlers. Although some colonists who demonstrated an aptitude for and interest in construction were put to work, Dominicans made up the bulk of the work crews. An optimistic February 1941 report from a visiting IGC team explained management's reasons for choosing this strategy: "It seemed unwise to divert the settlers even temporarily from learning tropical agricultural practices to doing construction work, besides being less efficient."[22]

Aside from native lumber, virtually everything needed to outfit the colonists came from the United States. Building supplies, electrical and plumbing equipment, and such farm implements and materiel as tractors, fencing, milk pails, insecticides, incubators, cement, and fertilizers were shipped to Sosúa. Even beds and mattresses, blankets, towels, lanterns, and mosquito netting had to be imported. In all, the colony imported more than $160,000 worth of equipment and supplies during the first year alone, for 250 settlers.[23] Dominican officials must have wondered when or if this enclave would ever spur the development of Dominican businesses and industries its advocates promised.

Housing was the critical need that had to be addressed right away. By mid-1941 there was a separate two-story building for unmarried women, four barracks-cum-dormitories for bachelors, and two for married couples (see figure 10). Novelist Lore Segal, whose uncle Paul Steiner lived in the barracks when he and his wife first came to Sosúa in 1940, painted this spartan picture of the accommodations: "The barracks had a long, narrow corridor, with washrooms at either end and rooms leading off of it, rather like the compartments in continental trains. Each room was furnished with an iron bedstead, a washstand, and two wooden chairs, and was separated from its neighbors by wooden partitions. Paul named their room the *Badekabine* for its resemblance to a swimming-pool cabana."[24]

The bachelors' dormitories had room for forty. Eventually, one of the barracks was transformed into a meeting room with a platform at each end and movable wooden benches, and was used for dances, plays, and group meetings. The "matrimonial" dormitories were subdivided into eight rooms, each large enough to hold two beds, a locker, and a small chair or two.[25] One of the original barracks was quickly converted into a dining area "where three meals a day were served, prepared and cooked by previously arrived ladies, mostly Germans and Austrians, so we got the food we were used to at home," Papernik remembered.[26] By the fall of 1940, meals were routinely prepared for eighty in the communal dining room. This type of regimen was all too familiar to those fresh from camps similarly organized by Jewish relief committees.[27]

From the outset, Dominicans gravitated toward the colony from neighboring villages to take advantage of employment opportunities. Rosenberg proudly reported at the anniversary celebration that the payroll surpassed a thousand dollars a week.[28] By 1942, a small community of local workers was established in the western portion of the colony called La Gina or Charamico (later Los Charamicos). The workers built homes there, ostensibly leasing

FIGURE 10 Barracks at El Batey. JDC ARCHIVES.

the land from DORSA, although few paid their nominal rents. DORSA provided electricity and water gratis. Charamico, which means place of little sticks, was a world apart, "physically and culturally different" from El Batey, and there was little interaction between the two communities, despite their proximity.[29]

ADAPTATION AND ACCOMMODATION

Despite the obvious cultural divide and communication problems, Dominicans and their new neighbors appeared to get along well, with the former teaching the latter much of what they needed to know about their new surroundings. Papernik was quick to note the warm welcome they received upon their arrival in Puerto Plata. "Even if we could not understand a word they were saying, . . . their friendliness and smiles meant a lot to us."[30] As the historian Kai Schoenhals notes, that type of welcome "was an overpowering event for these Jews who were used to being treated as outcasts in their countries of origin."[31] The settler Luis Hess was surprised by the absence of anti-Semitism. "The word *Jew* was not an insult here," he recalled; "Dominicans treated us as they did any other ethnic group."[32]

Bauer had nothing but praise for his neighbors, "a clever and gorgeous looking mixture of Spaniards, blacks and *indios*," who patiently instructed the new arrivals in the "do's and don'ts" of life in the tropics. "We learned from the natives that precious drinking water could be obtained from certain plants . . . [and] how to keep the water in earthenware to make it cooler." He was amazed by the craftsmanship of the Dominican carpenters, who combined "primitive tools" and native mahogany to create "exquisite showpieces."[33]

Sometimes, the lessons learned were hard won. Papernik tells of the first time he purchased "bananas."

> On the way to the beach we saw some native women sitting under trees, selling all kinds of fruits, some of them we had never seen. When I saw the size of those bananas, I bought the largest one and could not wait to take the first bite. When I did that piece in my mouth got bigger and bigger and I could not swallow. I had the feeling of having a piece of soap in my mouth then finally was told that I had bought a plantain. This fruit cannot be eaten raw. I was spitting for an hour but could not get that soapy taste out of my mouth. Later I found out that the woman who had sold me the plantain had tried to warn me, but I did not understand what she meant. In my eagerness to get the largest fruit I found out the hard way not to be too greedy.[34]

Papernik's moral—missed the larger point. He and his peers had much to learn from their fellow Dominicans if only they were open to it. Papernik recalled another encounter.

> I had paid 11 pesos for the horse and when it came to buy a saddle, I wanted a nice comfortable one and had to pay 35 pesos for a beautiful Mexican saddle. With that saddle I bought a bottle of leather oil to make it soft and also for protection, as I was told. Living or sleeping still at the bachelors' barracks, I made a gadget to hang the saddle on the wall. That evening I rubbed the oil on my beautiful saddle and hung it. . . . When I came [back] to the barracks [later in the evening] the light was already out and everybody was sleeping, I sneaked in, got undressed and went to bed, but not for long. I felt some movement on my bed and turned the lights on and to my surprise saw the whole bed from top to bottom completely covered with ants that fell from the saddle hanging over my bed. The saddle was also completely covered. . . . [I] threw the saddle out of the window into the grass. It took me hours to get rid of the ants in and on my bed, but I learned a lesson, never to use oil on anything that ants can get on.[35]

It is not surprising that the immigrants felt varying degrees of physical and psychological discomfort in their new surroundings. Students of immigration believe that there is a direct correlation between the degree of personal distress experienced and the cultural gulf between the immigrant's past and present worlds. It is hard to imagine a greater chasm than the one facing

Sosúa's colonists.[36] Virtually everything about their new neighbors was un-familiar, including their language, dress, foods, and customs. Many pioneers were reluctant to learn Spanish even though the administration strongly en-couraged it. In addition to providing night classes in Spanish at the settlement's elementary school, Escuela Cristóbal Colón, Hess, a former schoolteacher, published a regular column, "Spanish for Settlers" (*Spanisch für Siedler*) in the settlement's bilingual newsletter, *La Voz de Sosúa* (*The Voice of Sosúa*).[37]

Even a veneer of friendship and acceptance, however, could not conceal the enormous cultural divide between rural Dominicans and the Central Eu-ropean transplants. The settlers all too often looked at their neighbors conde-scendingly through the blinders of "civilization" and "barbarism." Words like *primitive* and *backward* crop up frequently in memoirs and interviews. As a re-sult, misunderstandings and generalizations inevitably surfaced. Papernik, for instance, was critical of his Dominican coworkers in the wood shop. A pater-nalistic attitude is evident in the Old World craftsman's recollections, even as he praises his colleagues about their apparent willingness to adapt to European norms of workmanship: "The workers turned out to be very intelligent but had very little education and worked in the most primitive way. With a lot of pa-tience and willingness from their side I was able to introduce them to a more sophisticated method. They accepted my advice. Every day I could detect that they had learned to do their work the better and easier way, even when we had to give up some of the primitive look of the furniture we made."[38]

Another Papernik anecdote illustrates how the pioneers impatiently came to terms with local work habits. "Every Saturday was payday. The first week I made the payroll for the workers and went to the office to get the money to pay the weekly salaries. The next Monday only one man, our foreman . . . showed up. When I asked him where all the others were, he did not know. He asked me whether I had paid them their full salaries. Upon hearing my 'yes,' he knew right away what had happened, that he had forgotten to explain that I should not pay the full salaries because that gave them too much money at one time and they made themselves a holiday. That was a good lesson and from that day on I paid one half on Saturday, the other half on Wednesday."[39]

Typically, refugees are treated as second-class citizens in their new sur-roundings, and their cultural values are held in low regard. Discrimination is a defining characteristic of their experience, and they internalize their feel-ings of inferiority. Clearly, however, this did not happen to the Sosuaners; the Dominicans thought highly of them. The settlers themselves, by con-trast, thought of their neighbors as less educated and less worldly than they. Inverting this fundamental premise had significant ramifications for the colony's future. For one thing, it erected physical and psychological barriers that made Sosúa a world apart from Dominican society.[40]

A perfect case in point was the marriage of Luis Hess, who became the first settler to wed a Dominican woman. Even though one of the experiment's stated objectives was miscegenation, an administrator was upset to learn of Hess's engagement. He admonished Hess for setting a bad precedent and tried to dissuade him from marrying. Didn't Hess realize that Luis and Ana Julia's offspring would have dark skin and nappy hair? Despite the upbraiding, the couple soon wed, and she was warmly accepted by fellow settlers, according to Hess. Ana Julia quickly learned to speak German by working alongside other settler seamstresses and later converted to Judaism.[41]

Settlers not only had to adapt to local custom; they had much to learn about social mores. Soon after he arrived, an uninhibited Papernik walked down to the beach wearing two red handkerchiefs as a surrogate bathing suit. A member of the rural guard promptly arrested him for indecent exposure, and scolded him for good measure: "This is a civilized country and not a jungle." A DORSA official intervened and secured his release, "explaining that this young man had just arrived and did not know the laws of the country."[42]

To assist settlers with their feelings of displacement, an orientation program was formulated to help them adjust to the new *ambiente*. Refugees were first given a number, determined by the order in which they arrived in Sosúa. However, the settlers came to be better known by the country in Europe where their group had originated. Hofeller, for instance, who came in the fall of 1940, was number 120, but was identified as a member of the second Swiss transport.[43] The "rookies" were taken to a warehouse and given bedding, mosquito netting, quinine pills for malaria, suitable work clothing, and shoes. Their orientation also included a tour of the settlement, a medical examination at the colony's clinic, and all of three days to get accustomed to their new surroundings.[44]

Rosen believed that from a technical standpoint, the training period was an "absolute necessity." Pioneers needed "to adjust their habits of sleeping, dressing, bathing, particularly eating and drinking." Altering dietary habits was especially vexing. In addition to letting them drink only boiled water, Rosen tried, often unsuccessfully, to get his charges to substitute rice and beans for the European staples of bread and meat.

Nothing required more of an adjustment than the debilitating climate, which was "fiercely hot" during the day. Bauer and his compatriots had problems acclimating to the intense heat and humidity. DORSA supervisor Solomon Arons allowed that many shied away from agricultural work in favor of milking cows or pig farming because they preferred working in the shade.[45] Road construction in Switzerland for "days and days at a stretch" did not leave them "feeling half as tired and worn out as here." Echoing tropical colonization experts, Arons wrote Reyher, "In den Tropen kann man nicht so arbeiten" (Man cannot work so hard in the tropics).[46]

During the early morning hours the air was exceedingly still. The settlers were so grateful for the sea breezes, wrote Bauer, that "blew exactly from 10 A.M. to 4 P.M." Bauer qualified this observation, because not all could take the "constant strong wind." He speculated that the persistent breeze might have contributed to an early suicide. If the heat did not get to them, the humidity and dampness certainly did. "It was not only the almost constant driving rain, but also the enormous humidity and soft ground which became a nuisance. Everything got moist and moldy. The road between our settlement and the center [El Batey] was elevated and always passable, but between our homes and the road there developed a remarkable shallow lake. The only way out was to grab the mane of a horse with one hand, holding the saddle in the other, and letting the horse swim to the road. Then we saddled it and went on."[47]

The boggy conditions were an excellent breeding ground for malaria, something that plainly worried the staff. Unfortunately, the richer the soil, the greater the potential for the *Anopheles* mosquito to breed. A Viennese doctor and his wife, Israel and Helen Klinger, who initially set up a small infirmary and attended to the community's medical needs, sought to defuse settler concerns by issuing a report contending that Europeans could prosper in the tropics. It allowed that "those who have adhered faithfully to rules and regulations of hygiene which were laid down at the very beginning (such as quinine prophylaxis, boiling water, etc.), have lived and thrived at Sosúa." Klinger, a former professor of bacteriology and hygiene at Hebrew University, and his wife, a biologist and nurse, had lived in Palestine for more than twenty years. They brought ample experience to bear on public health matters in tropical settings.[48]

To reduce the incidence of malaria, the Klingers—who Bauer half-joked were the only refugees working in their chosen fields—organized a detachment that was sent out to oil and drain stagnant pools, water holes, and livestock troughs on the property, prime breeding grounds for mosquito larvae. Bauer describes the teams' relatively successful efforts to root out the mosquitoes: "Malaria had been rampant. To the natives it was a sickness like having a cold, they had built up a resistance to it, we had not. . . . We tracked through the jungle to find all pools of water and poured kerosene on them when the young larvae needed to come up for air. The treatment was effective."[49]

Their energetic efforts did not stop some forty settlers from contracting "mild" cases of malaria during the first year.[50] The most afflicted were taken up to the mountain retreat in Jarabacoa, where they recuperated.[51] Arons reported as late as 1942 that almost all of the twenty-two settlers living in the La Bombita area of Sosúa had contracted malaria and "have continual relapses, have become debilitated, look yellow, emaciated and sick." DORSA had to hire Dominican laborers to compensate. The low-lying, boggy La Bombita site quickly acquired a well-deserved reputation as unhealthful. The settlers were instructed to keep everything near their homes meticulously clean and dry. Future homestead construction, Arons insisted, should be positioned on higher ground or at the very least where the sea breeze diminished the potential for infection. DORSA's claims to the contrary, it took years to root out malaria. Arons reported that tracts near Sabaneta along the Yasica River were scouted as potential sites for expansion to accommodate more homesteads. Despite finding rich soil, the area was written off as too malarial. As Arons related to Rosenberg, "It is a general maxim in the tropics, where there is real good soil, there is malaria."[52]

Potable water posed another public health challenge for organizers. Water came from the Sosúa River and two wells along the coast and had to be boiled, sometimes for extensive periods, because of a "high content of organic and mineral matter." Moreover, wells had to be bored to secure a sufficient supply for the colony's growing population.[53]

Most settlers did adapt to the weather and local conditions. Papernik was incredulous that when his group arrived, on a beastly hot day, the settlers who greeted them wore warm jackets and scarves. "They had come a few months earlier and we thought they wanted to show off, but when asked they said 'just wait, next year you will be doing the same, our blood is getting thinner and we really feel cold.' Well, the next year we did the same."[54]

Home and family were never far from the colonists' minds. Jakob Weinberg recalled the first Passover seder as a particularly sad occasion, when parallels were drawn between their own plight and that of their ancestors. But unlike the early Israelites who had to flee Egypt, Sosúa's settlers were preoccupied about relatives and friends left behind. They also gave heartfelt thanks to Trujillo for his generosity—the colonists' first of many expressions of gratitude for El Benefactor.[55]

Their unceremonious disconnection with their immediate past no doubt helped build some solidarity among the Sosuaners. No matter how difficult the transition was, they knew they were the fortunate few. Their shared language, cultural origins, religion, and determination to keep each other informed about events transpiring in Europe helped them construct a collective identity of sorts. Historian Leo Spitzer's eloquent description of a similar group of exiled German and Austrian Jews who fled Europe for Bolivia resonates well with the dynamics at work in Sosúa: "No matter what their background differences had been in Europe, the vast majority of refugees arrived in South America in dire straits, with few personal possessions and very little money. This in itself had a leveling effect, cutting across their previous class distinctions. . . . Despite differences in the details of their particular experiences, they were all 'in the same boat.' . . . the German language (which they spoke at home and among themselves) was their vehicle of inquiry, information, and unity, allowing them to communicate intimately and to express themselves with a degree of familiarity that most could never attain in the Spanish language of their surroundings." Spitzer documents how these refugees sought to recreate the bourgeois way of life that had been familiar in Europe. By "recreating a version of a way of life and of a cultural reality that they had previously known," the exiles drew on their past to build their future. [56]

The immigrants' memory of growing up in Vienna and Berlin cut both ways, however. The nostalgia romanticized their formative years, but their shared sense of persecution and rejection helped paper over the differences among them in their current surroundings. Their narratives cast them as both victims and survivors.[57] A leitmotif of correspondence (and later, interviews) was the hope that sometime soon the settlers would reconnect with their loved ones. That shared aspiration may have given them something about which to commiserate, but could prove to be a source of frustration and petty jealousies.

Voluntary migration, let alone involuntary exile, can induce trauma and trigger personal crises. Despite their generally optimistic outlook, Sosúa's inhabitants were understandably insecure. One psychological study of migration has singled out the initial period as a particularly vexing time for some immigrants, when "the predominant feelings are intense pain for what one has left behind or lost, fear of the unknown, deep-rooted loneliness, need and helplessness."[58] Lion Feuchtwanger, the most widely read German author to go into exile, who wrote about the emigrants' fragile emotional state, explains why refugees like Sosúa's first pioneers were such a contentious lot. "Most of them became egocentric, lost their judgment and sense of measure . . . [and] used their misery to justify every excess and caprice. Thrust from secure into uncertain living conditions, they became nervous, at once impudent and servile, quick to quarrel, demanding know-it-alls. They were like fruit that one has ripped too soon from the tree, not ripe, but dry and bitter."[59] The result, according to Feuchtwanger, was frequent "petty, ridiculous squabbles." Without knowing it, he added, "they saw their own image in someone else and cursed in the latter's pettiness their own inadequacies."[60]

Closer to home, an empathetic Rosen recognized that his colonists faced significant psychological challenges: "We must not lose sight of the fact that while naturally endowed collective and individual organisms have remarkable powers of regeneration, it is often easier to mend a broken body than a broken heart and broken spirit."[61]

Otto Papernik, although an inveterate optimist, conveyed the same picture when he recalled, with mixed emotions, his own wedding day in August 1941. A secular wedding, presided over by a justice of the peace at nearby Puerto Plata, was followed by a religious ceremony conducted by a Viennese rabbi at Sosúa. The Paperniks' entire Luxemburg group was present to celebrate the first wedding among them, along with DORSA officials and many of their new friends. Despite the festive occasion, both Otto and Irene's thoughts were elsewhere. "It was a very nice short [ceremony] darkened only by the thoughts that none of our family could be there with us. Especially Irene was very sad, thinking of her little sister, somewhere in a concentration camp and probably alone or not even alive anywhere. I was also very sad."[62]

Psychotherapists Leon and Rebeca Grinberg, who treated refugees with similar difficulties, explain why coming to terms with such a loss was so painful: "They carry away with them the anxiety of not having said their goodbyes, which makes them feel that they are crossing the frontier between the land of the dead and of the living. At the deepest level, all the loved ones they could not say goodbye to and whom they fear they will never see again become transformed into the dead, from whom they cannot achieve a satisfactory separation. And they feel that they, too, have become dead to others."[63] Since many refugees had family who could not get out when they did, and because others had suffered more, they somehow felt less legitimate in mourning the absence of family, home, and nation.[64]

Complicating matters was that unlike many exiles who believed that they would one day return to their homeland, Sosuaners wrestled with a raft of emotions during the war years and gradually, inexorably, as they came to learn more about the horrors of what was transpiring in Europe, had to come to the conclusion that that they would never return home. This dynamic process shaped how they confronted the new challenges placed before them.

Particularly vexing for DORSA administrators was how to promote solidarity among this embryonic group. Although most came from similar backgrounds, were driven out for the same basic reason, often shared comparable experiences before and during displacement, in some cases had even fled together, and agreed about the injustice of what had transpired, they often viewed their past and each other very differently. Seeing them come to Sosúa as refugees led others to perceive them as similar, but what is obvious from their narratives is that they did not think of themselves that way, especially when they first arrived. The difficult challenge for DORSA's management team was to forge a sense of community out of such individualistic elements.[65]

Constructing a rural settlement had temporal dimensions for many Sosuaners. There was the here and now, and then there was the future—after the war. Sosúa's enclave character and the residents' inability to integrate into Dominican society only reinforced the idea that it was a temporary haven and that the United States was their ultimate destination. Unlike many exiles, Sosúa's residents did not feel compelled to make a good faith effort to assimilate. They often viewed their new home as confining or a poor substitute for an idealized past. As the Grinbergs suggest about similar refugees, "rejection masks their guilt toward those they left behind and disguises the rancor and hatred toward the country which expelled them, which is projected onto the new country that has received them. Thus, instead of seeing the new country as their salvation, some exiles see it as the cause of all their troubles while idealizing their original country with never-ending nostalgia."[66]

Taken as a group, the Sosuaners were, in today's vernacular, high maintenance. Quick to direct open hostility to the staff, they often projected all responsibility for their uncertain predicament on DORSA. Some even came to believe that they were entitled to what was provided for them and deserved to be rewarded for their fortitude. Others felt unworthy and thought it humiliating to receive handouts. As the philosopher and exile Hannah Arendt has put it, "if we are saved we feel humiliated, and if we are helped we feel degraded." This discomfort stems, Arendt believes, from the striking contrast between the refugee's privileged background and current destitute predicament; "we are afraid of becoming part of that miserable lot of *schnorrers* [n'er-do-wells] whom we, many of us former philanthropists, remember too well."[67]

The émigrés' uneasy psychological adjustment dovetailed with their hasty initiation into the tools of their new trade. After orientation, each of the novices was given a taste of life on the land when they were taken to the tomato patch, where they were instructed on how to remove worms from the plants. "This worm-plucking," which lasted three weeks, Papernik recalled, "was supposed to be the first step for the future farmer."[68] Only 13 of the first 350 refugees had been farmers in Europe, although several more had received some modest agricultural training in the old country.[69] Wherever possible, DORSA management took advantage of the refugees' skills. For instance, several Polish workers who had experience curing hams did the same at the settlement. Similarly, "former French perfumers . . . raise flowers, with which they will be able eventually to produce a scent similar to that they made in France."[70]

For the great majority, enervating manual labor was the norm during the first year. Papernik soon decided he had had quite enough of worm-plucking, however. When administrators asked him to use his carpentry skills to make windows and doors for settlers, he let it be known that "under no circumstances [would he] go back to the tomato field, because I was selected and brought to Sosúa as a cabinetmaker and carpenter and that I had no intentions to become a farmer."[71] He was not alone in insisting that manual labor was not in his enlightened self-interest. It did not take long, according to Luis Hess, for some city slickers to develop an aversion to hard work. Judith Kibel, a musician with classical training in Vienna, was appalled that she had to scrub pots and wash dishes in the community kitchen in El Batey.[72] Hess joked that colonists quickly acquired enough rudimentary Spanish to learn the expression *mucho trabajo, poco dinero* (much work, little money), as the romance surrounding this new experiment quickly gave way to the reality of toiling beneath an unrelenting tropical sun.[73]

The rookies' hands-on training in the tomato patch foreshadowed future growing pains. Frederic Perlestein, Rosen's assistant, who had prior farming experience in the more temperate climes of Prussia but was learning on the job in the tropics, stubbornly refused to listen to his Dominican assistants or anyone else, for that matter, and insisted on having the settlers plant the tomatoes in April with the dry season upon them. The results, not surprisingly, were less than ideal. When the colonists eventually produced more eggplants, green peppers, and tomatoes than they could consume, the surplus had to be thrown away because of the vagaries of transport and the absence of local markets.[74] On one occasion, when inexperienced farmers proudly vacuum-packed their tomatoes in large cans and shipped them off to be marketed in the capital, the cans exploded in a Ciudad Trujillo warehouse, a casualty of the intense heat.[75] Moreover, Dominicans never developed a taste for some of the "European" vegetables that the colonists insisted on planting.

DORSA's team initially set up a three-stage program to develop the settlement. First, land was prepared for cultivation near El Batey, the settlers were trained, and then new tracts of land farther away from the center were canvassed, and, if considered worthy, developed. A surveying company from Lansing, Michigan, already engaged by a U.S. company on the island, made

FIGURE 11 Homesteads. JDC ARCHIVES.

an aerial survey to help map out the settlement.[76] Much of the first year was spent clearing land with tractors and "brush-breaker" plows, building and repairing roads, and constructing houses to permit settlers to move out of the barracks and onto homesteads as soon as possible. Ten miles of new roads had been built during the six months, one report said, "so that it is now possible to reach nearly all parts of the huge tract by motor instead of having to travel by horseback, as was the case when the land was acquired."[77]

Settlers moved into the first homesteads by December 1940 (see figure 11, above). At the same time, farm machinery was employed to prepare the soil for planting, and settlers built fences around half-acre subsistence gardens adjacent to their new homes. During the first 6 months of 1941, approximately 250 acres were readied for plantings of corn, yucca, papaya, bananas, cabbage, cucumbers, and sweet potatoes, among other crops. Cultivation was handled largely by native labor because the settlers lacked expertise. Some of these early experimental plantings failed to bear fruit. Neither coconut nor bananas prospered, their failure blamed alternatively on heavy, black clay soil, drought, and wayward cattle.[78]

Fortunately, Perlestein promoted dairy farming. Holstein and Guernsey cows were crossed with Creole cattle, thanks to a housewarming gift of seventy head from the *Generalíssimo*, which helped produce a hardier stock.[79] It soon became apparent to administrators and settlers alike that dairying would be the settlement's economic motor (see figure 12). Yet even though tending to

FIGURE 12 Colonists preferred working in the shade. JDC ARCHIVES.

livestock was less labor-intensive than agricultural pursuits and was a better fit than other products, Sosúa was by no means ideal for dairy farming. "Pasture lands suffer severely from the least drought," Arons noted, "because [the soil] has no moisture holding capacity." He informed Rosenberg that milk production dropped by 40 percent during the dry season.[80] Still, by the end of 1940, the colony boasted 538 head of cattle, including 164 milk cows, 100 pigs, and close to that number of horses, donkeys, and mules. By mid-1941 a dairy cooperative was established that produced first-rate cheese and butter, which proved to be the colony's lifeline.[81]

A strict gendered division of labor was enforced from the outset. While men worked in the fields, women prepared and cooked the food in the main kitchen (and in a special kosher kitchen for a smaller contingent of religious Jews) (see figure 13). They made beds in the bachelors' rooms and washed and ironed clothes. As with the planting, in all these domestic tasks, Dominican women assisted the female settlers, gradually assuming an increasing share

FIGURE 13 Preparing food for the communal kitchen. JDC ARCHIVES.

of the workload. The laundry detail, which grew to more than thirty women, received soiled clothes on Mondays and returned them cleaned and pressed by Saturday at no cost to the settlers.[82]

A typical workday during this early period would find the pioneers out in the fields from 6:30 until 11:30 in the morning. After cleaning up, they were served a hot meal. Then they went back to work at 2:30, worked another three hours, and ate dinner at 6:00. The evening hours were spent at the café or passing time reading magazines and playing chess.

While living in the dormitories at El Batey, the settlers initially also received an interim "maintenance" package, which covered food, clothing, lodging, medical attention, a nominal three-dollar-a-month stipend, agricultural training, and Spanish language instruction. If and when they moved onto their homesteads, they were given a nine-dollar-a-month credit at the DORSA store in lieu of the food and lodging received in the barracks. Children under ten merited an additional six-dollar stipend. The maintenance package was meant to last only one year, but settlers came to view it as an entitlement and successfully fought administrators tooth and nail to extend the allotment. Maintenance was interest-free for the first two years; after that, colonists were to be charged a nominal 3 percent a year on the outstanding principal.[83]

By the end of 1941, the colony could boast some notable accomplishments: 60 houses, 9 dormitories, 12 shops and warehouses, a small clinic, and a schoolhouse had been constructed; 100 acres were placed under cultivation, more than double that in seedlings; 415 acres of soil were cleared for planting, and another 3,000 prepared for use as pasture.[84]

Basic necessities were wanting early on, especially electricity, running water, and refrigeration.[85] Complaints also surfaced about the management team. Rosen, who had to rush back to the settlement because of persistent grievances about his inexperienced staff, wrote in October 1940 that the authoritarian Perlestein had "succeeded in creating an atmosphere branded by the settlers as a 'concentration camp.' The place was almost on the verge of a 'revolution' before I came out here; the most tragic point being that Perlestein was and is quite sure that everything is in perfect shape."[86]

Perlestein did have his advocates, but they surfaced only after he had been relieved of his duties and then only in comparison to a less demanding supervisor. Recruiter Trone, who visited Sosúa in 1941 after the easygoing David Schweitzer had replaced Perlestein, pined for the Prussian's "strong discipline," with which "everyone did work and things were accomplished." Trone, who had handpicked most of Sosúa's first settlers, preferred to place the onus on his charges, who, he felt, lacked autonomy and initiative.[87] Bauer implied that there was enough blame to go around; he castigated administrators for their lack of experience but also lit into his inexperienced, stubborn associates, who had to learn the hard way about farming. According to settler Josef Eichen, "Five men usually had seven different ideas" during those chaotic first months.[88]

The jury was out, as far as Rosen was concerned, as to whether this inchoate group of city folk could prosper. In late August 1940, he told a group of donors in New York that after observing this "average group of young men for four months," although it was far too early to tell for sure, there was reason for optimism. In response to the question, could the refugees earn their bread, the plainspoken Rosen said that with "proper scheduling of working hours" and good hygiene and sanitation, workers were becoming more productive. To highlight their progress, he compared the settlers to their Dominican counterparts. "In the beginning, work was extremely inefficient, you watch a person learning to use a machete; you see him lagging behind the natives; in about an hour he feels like sitting down. After a few days you notice that he is beginning to pick up. Inside of a month, he is keeping up with the natives . . . when he begins to use machinery the efficiency of his work is then above that of the natives."[89]

But could the colonists improve their standard of living enough to repay their debt to DORSA and create a better standard of living for themselves than that of the Dominican peasantry? Rosen could offer his donors only a qualified wait and see. Not until farming became more mechanized, not until large-scale cooperative enterprises were initiated to take advantage of economies of scale, and not until new products and crops were introduced would the colony truly prosper. To this end, DORSA had elicited the cooperation of the U.S. Department of Agriculture to bring in a number of experts to make economic surveys and write reports about what products were a good match.[90]

It might be argued that Rosen's report to donors was a cleverly thought-out ploy designed to elicit financial support for the next phase of the colony's development. Capital certainly was needed to develop the infrastructure required to remake the property into the modern, mechanized plantations that the director envisioned. These donors, however, were shrewd business leaders, whose hearts may have been in the right place but who had to choose from a number of worthy causes to support. They probably would have seen through an overly optimistic assessment. Rosen was all too aware of what he had to work with in Sosúa, of the settlers' inexperience and lack of interest in farming, and knew that it would be a monumental challenge even to approximate his earlier successes in the Crimea.

From its inception, the colony faced a multitude of challenges. In addition to the human dynamics, it was readily apparent to detached observers, self-interested refugees, and hardheaded staffers that the site's inadequacies; a transient, at times inflexible staff; tempestuous management-settler relations; and the colony's insular, almost clannish character combined to limit what was possible. As matters came to a head between management and settlers, DORSA management in New York and Sosúa would have to lick its wounds, acknowledge its missteps, respond to settler criticism, alter its idealistic vision, and set more realistic goals. Earning each other's trust would take time as Sosúa's growing pains proved to be a learning experience.

NINE

Flawed Vision

> The development of cooperative enterprises requires an educational effort, particularly with refugees coming from Germany. Their civic and cooperating instincts are in a surprisingly rudimentary state. In this respect, refugees from eastern European countries are much more promising human material.
>
> JOSEPH ROSEN, 1941

Rosen never doubted he could adapt his Crimean blueprint to Sosúa. After all, he had taken tens of thousands of urban Jews from *shtetls* in the Pale of Settlement who knew nothing about farming, provided them with the requisite training and modern machinery, and performed miracles. He was in for a rude awakening. What had worked so well in the Crimea failed miserably at Sosúa.

As he had in the Soviet Union, Rosen insisted that Sosuaners share mechanized farm implements and establish processing cooperatives to take advantage of economies of scale. After the orientation and training phase, homestead clusters were established, with each group carrying out its own work plan. The groups varied in size from three or four unmarried males to ten families. On average, each cluster was given thirty hectares per family (or unmarried male) to be held in common and two hectares for individual gardens.[1] Each group rotated tasks every two weeks: milking cows, attending to chicken coops, cultivating garden patches, and caring for the horses and pigs. Rosen envisioned these groups sharing in the proceeds based on the amount of labor contributed. Just as on the steppes, colonists maintained their own private plots for subsistence, and each group specialized in a "for-profit" collaborative enterprise.

TABLE 4 *Start-up Costs for Homesteads*

Item	Cost
House on one hectare of land	$800
One additional hectare of garden land	35
Furniture, fixtures, and garden tools	120
Small livestock	25
Horse or mule	45
One saddle	15
Two cows	45
Miscellaneous equipment	15
Credit per family at DORSA store	500
Total	*$1,600*

Source: "Homestead Plan for Sosúa Settlers," 1941, File 50a, DP, JDC
Archives

The homestead plan was predicated on the colonists' moving out of El Batey and onto their farms after six months of orientation, a goal not always realized. DORSA and an elected three-person Settlers Council (called the Rat, German for "council") jointly determined when an individual or family was deemed ready to move from the barracks to a homestead.[2] Heads of households initially received a house, either a horse or a mule, two cows, a few smaller farm animals, and farm implements and other equipment. Parents obtained additional subsidies depending on the ages of their children. DORSA never expected to recover the cost of transporting the refugees from Europe to the Caribbean or the maintenance allotment, but did expect settlers to repay the $1,600 cost of the homestead (see table 4, above).[3] Modest frame houses made from native pine with sheet-iron roofs were built, with some exceptions, by Dominican labor. The homes, which cost $740 to build, consisted of two rooms, a kitchen, a bathroom, and a full porch.[4]

Colonists also were provided with a five-hundred-dollar line of credit at the general store (El Colmado) for a special enterprise or project of their own design. As with the maintenance package, repayment terms were nominal—no interest for the first two years and a 3 percent rate thereafter. But reimbursement was expected; the association's mantra was "rehabilitation, not charity."[5]

DORSA also agreed to buy up any surplus the clusters produced; some of it would be consumed by the communal kitchens, with the remainder to be sold at El Colmado or marketed in the capital or in other urban centers.[6] Fulfilling that promise proved expensive, as settlers occasionally took advantage of it and produced ill-advised crops to secure quick cash. Some of these products were not readily absorbed by the kitchens; and since the temperate crops that settlers initially preferred to grow did not always appeal to Dominican palates, DORSA was hard pressed to market the surplus and often had to swallow the losses.[7]

Critical to Rosen's socialist agrarian vision was the ability to foster cooperation and teamwork among his Central European transplants. The sooner the homestead groups relied on each other rather than on DORSA's largesse the better, for management and settlers alike. Colonization demanded selflessness, hard work, and sacrifice, whether in temperate or tropical climes, Rosen preached. The key was to encourage self-sufficiency and autonomy as quickly as possible. Self-governance was an important component of the cooperative model; after three months in residence, every colonist was eligible to vote and stand for election to the Rat.[8]

Aware that Sosúa would never conjure up the weighty idealism of Palestine, Rosen nevertheless sought to inspire his charges even as he instructed them in the basics of farming. He used suitably revolutionary metaphors to energize his troops; they were not just farmers but "an advance guard" for "Jews that have been persecuted," and they labored not just for themselves and their families but for Jewish refugees everywhere. If Sosúa was successful, he reminded settlers and donors alike, "the doors of Latin America may perhaps be opened."[9]

He quickly was forced to revise his thinking about the colonists' capabilities. Although maintenance was supposed to be terminated after one year, Rosen soon realized that the pioneers were far from ready to be weaned from DORSA, so he made a verbal commitment to extend it indefinitely. He explained his reasoning to Rosenberg in the fall of 1940: "We may also have to take into consideration the partially unsatisfactory human material we have been getting which may prolong the period of their becoming self-supporting for another year or so. Frankly speaking, some of the settlers imposed on us . . . are rather potential permanent boarders than pioneer farmers."[10]

Rosen's determination to extend the maintenance haunted his successors, as the Rat used it repeatedly as a bargaining chip to wheedle concessions. But Rosen's generosity only reinforced the settlers' admiration for their director (see figure 14). What was most contagious was his passion for his work and his unshakable conviction that working on the land would transform and empower those who dared embrace this new way of life. It was obvious that the

FIGURE 14 Dr. Rosen addresses his charges. JDC ARCHIVES.

aged informants interviewed for this book still retained tremendous respect for the kindly Russian agronomist—whom they called the Menshevik—admiring his intelligence, experience, and humanity. Although he could be quite caustic in his assessments of the settlers in his correspondence with Rosenberg and his staff, he always personally returned the respect the colonists gave him and sympathized with how they had been uprooted. In short, Rosen was a beloved figure; indeed, today a street in Sosúa is named after him. (In retrospect, this is rather ironic, since he actually spent very little time there.) As is sometimes the case with leaders, his reputation actually improved after he left Sosúa for good in early 1942. Feisty homesteaders, who complained about everything and anything, invoked his name in hushed, reverent tones, especially when they nurtured a grievance with his successors.

Even though Rosen lacked experience in tropical colonization and uncritically appropriated a model that had been applied in an entirely different setting on a much more expansive scale, he moved quickly to implement that model. Perhaps he took for granted how much assistance the Agro-Joint had received from state apparatchiks in the Soviet Union, who had provided land, logistical support, an ideological rationale, and legitimacy—all of which was conspicuously lacking from their Dominican counterparts.

In reality, Trujillo treated the settlement as an anomaly. Unlike other state-supported colonies that incorporated foreign colonists, Sosúa received no government funding, nor was it listed in the Ministry of Agriculture's publications or factored in its statistical data.[11] This was somewhat surprising, since Sosúa was much more successful than other state-supported colonies. Including data on the settlement's productivity in reports would have embellished Trujillo's colonization program and lent credence to his often-stated goals to populate the countryside and make the nation self-sufficient in food production. Indeed, government officials rarely missed an opportunity to inflate the regime's accomplishments, so it is puzzling that they failed to include it in statistical surveys. The omission certainly indicates that authorities viewed and treated Sosúa as if it were distinctive.

This is not to suggest that the regime's public relations machine ignored the colony. While Trujillo's publicists lauded the general for his humanitarian role and irregularly published updates about the colony's progress, authorities treated Sosúa like a private enterprise, similar to the U.S. sugar companies operating on the southeastern end of the island. Although Rosen and his staff relished that autonomy, the state's hands-off approach insulated the settlement from its hosts, excused authorities from providing essential services, and left the colony entirely dependent on what funds Rosenberg and the philanthropy raised stateside.

Left to their own devices, Rosen and his skeletal staff sought to persuade the colonists that a gradual, slow-but-sure approach would give them the time they needed to implement their model. Yet from the start, a host of problems surfaced that called his vision into question. In retrospect, the cooperative model proved to be a spectacular failure; indeed, it subsequently drove a wedge between the pioneers and the administrators, fostering an adversarial relationship that was never really patched up.

Perhaps the colony's most unanticipated setback was Rosen's deteriorating health. Having contracted malaria while reconnoitering the countryside, he threw himself nonetheless into his responsibilities. He had to divide his time, however, between Sosúa and DORSA's offices in Ciudad Trujillo, and was never a consistent presence at the settlement. Since the association had been given the time-consuming task of securing visas and spiriting the refugees out of Europe, it was incumbent upon Rosen to remain in contact with Becky Reyher in New York, Solomon Trone and JDC officials in Europe, and Dominican and U.S. officials in their respective capitals, which would have been logistically impossible from Sosúa.

Eventually Rosen became so ill that he had to leave the island, in the summer of 1940, and return to New York, where he devoted himself to fundraising while trying to recover. In his absence he turned over day-to-day management of the settlement to Frederic Perlestein, whose haughty demeanor managed to alienate the colonists in a matter of months. Subsequent administrators during the war years performed even worse, and the best a weakened Rosen could manage was brief trips back to the colony throughout 1941 to hear complaints and offer counsel. Then, in the spring of 1942, he unexpectedly suffered a stroke and never really recovered. Although he continued to oversee the colony's management from the New York office, his absence on the ground was sorely missed.

All of these factors, combined with the dribs-and-drabs manner in which refugees arrived, help to explain why Rosen failed to impart his vision. Additional factors also contributed. Because so few families came to Sosúa initially, male colonists, who outnumbered females by about two to one, had to be grouped together under different schemes. Rosen tried to put one married couple in each cluster "so that there would be a woman to do the cooking and laundry for the other members of the group."[12] The heavily male-dominated groups were meant to serve as surrogate extended families.

Administrators later decided to compose the clusters by grouping settlers who knew each other best. In practical terms, this meant bringing together those who might have worked beside each other in camps in Europe or befriended each other in transit. In most cases, though, these ties were attenuated. Just because they broke bread together in the same internment camp or came to know one another aboard a transatlantic steamer, this did not mean that they got along, shared common interests, or contributed complementary skills and training.

Each cluster had its own leader, although it was unclear how these "first among equals" were selected or what responsibilities the leader's position entailed. Groups were named after their leader or leaders, the homestead's location, or in some cases by a combination of these methods (see table 5).

The tiny Leitner-Rosenberg cluster offers a good illustration of why cooperation and teamwork were lacking during this early phase. Only two pioneers in that cluster, according to Elie Topf, could be described as diligent workers. David Kahane, recently wed to Topf's sister Lisle at Sosúa, was motivated to be as productive as possible. He and Lisle had a newborn baby, his mother was living with them on the farm, and his future brother-in-law had just stepped off the boat to join the colony in the winter of 1942. But others apparently were much less motivated; either they were lazy or they had little incentive to do their share. Instead, they went off each day to El Batey, ostensibly to collect leftover scraps for the pigs, and spent the rest of the day there, schmoozing, playing cards, dining at the kitchen, and relaxing at the beach, according to Topf. Indeed, when Topf arrived, he immediately asked Kahane

TABLE 5 *Early Homestead Clusters*

Group Number[a]	Name	Number of Members
1–2	Laguna Higuera and Laguna Ferrocarril	22
3	Deutsch	1
4	Swiss Group	8
5	Kohn	2
6	Katz	8
7	Rosenzweig	2
8	Wohlmuth-Schlesinger	4
9	Baum-Scheer-Wolf	5
10	Moritz-Meier	2
11	Leitner-Rosenberg	3
12	Gerber-Wieselberg-Hauser	8
13	Sonnenschein	3
14	Atravesada-Kirstein-Czarlinsky	6
15	Gutter	4
17	Drucker	10
20	Luxembourg Group	10
21	Wehasely	3
Total		*103*

Source: "Change of Membership of Homestead Groups," 1941, File 47, DP, JDC Archives

[a] Groups 16, 18, and 19 were not included in this undated list, suggesting that they disintegrated before the list was compiled.

if he could pitch in and work for the cluster, but relations were so strained that he was actually discouraged from it. Better to find a job at El Batey with DORSA than to work with us and give the laggards an additional reason to shirk their responsibilities, Kahane grumbled.[13]

What was readily apparent was that although the groups varied in size and motivation, they were still very small—too small to forge a meaningful cooperative relationship. Why weren't larger groups cobbled together? Group size had to be restricted partly because of insufficient pasture and water and poor soil quality. Moreover, clusters could be created only when homes were ready for occupancy, settlers were prepared to occupy them, and lands had been cleared, fences put up, and roads built. After the initial burst of construction, problems getting equipment and supplies from the United States and funding shortfalls slowed the pace of opening up the new homesteads. Due to the lack

TABLE 6 *Homesteaders' Former Professions*

Profession	Number	Profession	Number
Agriculture	10	Metalworker	1
Attorney	3	Musician	1
Butcher	7	Photographer	1
Candlemaker	1	Plumber	5
Carpenter	1	Printer	4
Cattle dealer	2	Radio technician	1
Craftsperson	1	Saddler	1
Electrician	2	Shoemaker	1
Engineer	4	Student	3
Gardener	3	Tailor	1
Jeweler	1	Teacher	1
Leather manufacturer (tanner)	2	Textile worker	2
Mechanic	2	Upholsterer	1
Merchant (including clerk)	26	*Total*	88

Source: "Former Professions of Homesteaders," Undated, File 47, DP, JDC Archives

of arable land, groups had to be scattered throughout the settlement, creating logistical problems for overtaxed administrators.

This model also made it more difficult for dispersed homesteaders to become acquainted with peers from other groups. La Bombita, the site of one of the largest homestead groups, was six miles from El Batey, and that distance was sufficiently great that residents decided to open their own store and school.[14] To socially active Berliners and Viennese accustomed to the hustle and bustle of a cosmopolitan city and its cultural amenities, living in isolated settlements, even those only a fifteen-to-twenty-minute walk from El Batey, was less than satisfying. La Bombita must have felt like exile. Some colonists eventually traded in their more spacious homesteads to live in residential neighborhoods closer to schools, medical clinics, El Colmado, and their peers. Some settlers actually opted to live in El Batey and work their homesteads almost as if they were absentee landlords, hiring Dominicans to do the daily chores and checking in on their properties from time to time.

On-the-job training was the order of the day. Homesteaders' former professions indicate that few had practical experience in their new line of work (see table 6, above). Only ten had prior experience in agriculture, three in gardening, and two in cattle dealing; the great majority had been tradesmen, merchants, and artisans in Europe. In sum, there was ample reason why early

TABLE 7 *Age and Sex of Sosúa's First Settlers, ca. 1940–41*

Age	Men		Women	
	Unmarried	Married	Unmarried	Married
Under 15	6		2	
15–20	32		6	5
21–30	59	28	3	37
31–40	25	31	1	10
41–50	2	4	0	1
Total	*124*	*63*	*12*	*53*

Source: Kirsch, "The Golden Cage," 63

efforts to transform the refugees into successful farmers met with limited success. A shortage of women did not help matters, either.

SEND WOMEN

Gender imbalance undermined the collaborative zeitgeist. The disparity was apparent by the end of the first year, when unmarried men outnumbered single women by 10 to 1 (see table 7, above). Excluding boys under the age of 20 and girls under 15, there were 86 unmarried men and only 10 unmarried women. Although informal liaisons between male settlers and Dominican women were commonplace, marriages were exceptional. Only a handful of such marriages occurred, and none between female settlers and Dominican men.

Even though married couples and families were a minority, couples grumbled that bachelors received the same stipend as male heads of household while wives and children were entitled to a reduced maintenance allotment.[15] Managers addressed this problem by establishing a few satellite communal kitchens at the larger clusters, which were staffed by female colonists. In return for their labor, the women received full allotments. In the abstract the idea made sense, because it bolstered the allotments of married couples and, at the same time, relieved bachelors of some of their domestic chores. But the plan fell apart as "gradually all women withdrew and the cooking for the bachelors [was] done by natives." Sources do not speak to why women opted out of the satellite kitchens, but it is not difficult to imagine that family responsibilities and building up their own homesteads took precedence over preparing meals for neighbors.

FIGURE 15 Communal dining hall. JDC ARCHIVES.

The demise of the satellite kitchens meant that married homesteaders had to sustain their families on reduced allotments. The Rat complained to DORSA officials: "the married men are at a disadvantage, as a married man has to provide for two, or in some instances, three persons, out of his share, which is only as much as a bachelor receives."[16] The dissolution of the satellite kitchens also made the clusters less enticing to single men, who were left to fend for themselves or travel back to El Batey to eat at the communal kitchen (see figure 15, above).

Of much greater concern to DORSA and JDC officials was the paucity of eligible Jewish brides. Joseph Hyman, the JDC president, who visited the colony in the summer of 1941, realized that the imbalance undermined Rosen's model. Rather than encourage unions with Dominicans, the association looked elsewhere for Europeans. Hyman sent out a plea to Laura Margolis, who worked in the JDC office in Shanghai, where several thousand refugees had settled during the war. Hyman's discreet request to seek out young (under thirty), healthy women is worth quoting at length for what it has to say about the pernicious impact that the dearth of females had on morale.

> There is one matter on which a great deal of the spirit and morale of the colony obviously hinges—and that is the desirability of building up a healthy family life among the people there. Unfortunately, there are not enough women for the much larger number of men who are looking for help-mates in building up their new lives. When I was at Sosúa I attended two weddings and was present at the birth of the first child born in the colony. All of these affairs were occasions of great rejoicing. But I could see around me considerable numbers of men there who were about to get their own plot of five acres, their own house, cow, poultry, etc., who found it difficult to proceed to build up their own economy because there was no woman in the household. It is therefore one of the real needs to build up an economy to have marriageable young women brought to Sosúa.[17]

The initial $1,600 debt and the attendant start-up costs of building a homestead were daunting. How realistic was it for these bachelors to take on such an obligation without a partner? Heinrich Wasservogel, who worked in the Wohlmuth-Schlesinger group for twenty months before moving to El Batey, openly admitted that he shied away from settling down on a homestead for precisely these reasons. Instead, he apprenticed himself to Otto Papernik's carpentry shop. But Otto Wohlmuth, the group leader, married a Dominican woman and stayed put, even as his small group fell apart.

Rosen instructed Hyman that not just any women would do, and Hyman, in turn, relayed the director's preferences to Margolis: "Girls who are more interested in manicuring their nails or in cosmetics are hardly the kind who can adjust themselves to becoming the wives of farmers or settlers in Sosúa. There is a real opportunity for a new life—a healthy and successful existence. Not a rich one, not one that will have luxuries, but one where a man and wife working together and bringing up their own family can earn a decent livelihood by decent self-respecting toil."[18] He closed his letter by asking her to tactfully let the prospective recruits know that there would be an expectation after a time that they find settlers whom "they might become interested in or who might become interested in them, and with whom, as would be true in any similar case where people are brought close together, and, with whom, . . . they would be glad to share the common experience of life and work." Despite promising to "keep my eyes open for desirable young women for Sosúa," however, Margolis was unsuccessful in redirecting single female refugees from Shanghai to the Dominican Republic.[19]

The skewed gender dynamic remained a sensitive issue because the settlement population essentially stagnated throughout the war years, and the imbalance was never corrected. But there were other demoralizing problems that management had to rectify before the settlement was headed in the right direction.

BAD APPLES AND MANAGERIAL MISSTEPS

The colony's size and makeup may have been beyond DORSA's control, but the same could not be said for the failure to provide adequate training. Management was learning on the job and was, by any measure, woefully understaffed. Initially, the entire resident staff consisted of Perlestein, an agricultural specialist, a clerk, and two physicians. By August 1941, DORSA had added a livestock expert, an engineer (Rosen's son, Eugene), a purchasing agent, and an accountant to the mix, during a time when the settlement grew tenfold, from 37 to more than 350. The Brookings team criticized DORSA for not enlarging the staff at a significant moment in the colony's germination.[20]

Compounding the problem was poor communication between management and settlers. The DORSA Agricultural Department's first supervisor was a Spaniard who, unfortunately, could not speak German or English. He was eventually replaced by Douglas Blackwood, a "wiry and weather-beaten Virgin Islander" who headed the Animal Husbandry Department, and Edwin Anderson, who directed the Agricultural Department. Both came with ample experience working in the tropics but spoke English and Spanish, not German. Since few colonists were conversant in either English or Spanish initially, agricultural extension services amounted to an elaborate combination of hand signals and charades.[21]

When settlers lacked motivation and esprit de corps, abandoned their groups, and deserted the fields, accountability was difficult to enforce. "Once people found out that nothing would happen to them, they drifted off to look for some activity to their liking," Ernest Hofeller observed.[22] Blackwood allowed that the collectivist approach enabled those inclined to loaf to work as hard as the least productive farmer in their group. More than a few colonists came to the conclusion that they were not cut out for the rigors of life on the farm. If many made a good faith effort to adjust to their new occupations and were grateful to DORSA for rescuing them and providing security until they could get on their feet, it was all the more noticeable when, as one traveler reported, more than a few "bellyachers and malcontents among them cut such an ungraceful figure."[23] Hofeller, who never had the slightest interest in testing his aptitude for farming and latched onto a job with the administration, at least was honest enough to admit his shortcomings. One day his boss returned to find him overcome by the heat, "sitting motionless on a pile of lumber." His supervisor shouted at him: 'Hofeller, do something, even if it's wrong.'"[24]

Although the implacable Rosen seldom let his frustration show to the colonists, he thought his Central European charges were self-absorbed and "their civic and cooperating instincts are in a surprisingly rudimentary state," especially in comparison to the colonists he had worked with in the Crimea.[25] If he was willing to admit as much in public, it is not surprising that he was even more critical in private correspondence with Rosenberg. In one memorable letter, the Russian-born Rosen asked that the recruiter Trone be told to look for Russian, Latvian, and Lithuanian Jewish refugees to add to the mix. "I hope that a sprinkling of these Russian, etc., Jewish settlers may dilute the somewhat too concentrated smell of the German atmosphere here."[26] As far as he was concerned, German and Austrian Jews were living up to their reputation for arrogance, cupidity, and egotism, all of which was anathema to his collaborative vision.

Rosenberg politely yet firmly disagreed. The problem was not one of cultural predisposition. Countering Rosen's ethnic pigeonholing, he reminded his colleague of their travails in the Crimea. "It is not a difference in psychology, but of geography," he opined. "In our Russian work, we did not transplant single people thousands of miles from everything—of their upbringing and their past. We didn't take them to an entirely different climate, an entirely different government, an entirely different language, and an entirely different society. We didn't smash families to pieces. We didn't take young boys and girls away from their parents. When a family migrated from the ghetto in Odessa to the steppes of Russia, they soon found out that there was a community of the same kind in which they had lived all their lives, and with your skill in being able to build up communities, this change was no more than one from city to country."[27]

For Rosenberg, whose own family came from Germany, the issue was not insufficient idealism or materialism run amok but the catastrophic uprooting that had dealt these Central Europeans a severe blow. They had not yet come to terms with what had happened to them, nor did they yet have the ability to constitute new families. He drove home his point with an intriguing analogy that drew on his own experience spending summers at his Shady Brook camp in upstate New York.

> It was the kind of change I would take if I left my apartment in the city and decided to spend the rest of my life in the Adirondacks. That would be quite a change, I admit, but in the Adirondacks everybody would be speaking my language; they would be the kind of people with whom I was used to being with, a little different perhaps, but fundamentally, there would be no real difference. The Elizabethtown [New York] people would all say, "Fine. Glad to have you with us." Although the Elizabethtown people are mostly Christians, my background, mores and general mode of life are a great deal like theirs (excepting that I have a little more money). These young people, on the other hand, who have had to come to Sosúa have had to make a complete break with their past lives . . . and with all those catastrophic changes, and remembering the tragedy of their past seven years [since Hitler assumed power], I think there is not a difference in psychology, but a difference in what has happened to them.[28]

His poignant characterization of "the tragedy of their past seven years" underscored that it was a matter not simply of geographical uprooting but of psychological disruption. Indeed, Rosenberg's subsequent solution, to dispatch a social worker to Sosúa to help heal the refugees' bruised psyches, confirms that he believed this. The social worker would make sure they learned Spanish, might set up classes in dramatics, chorus, music, and crafts, and schedule outings to the movies in Puerto Plata periodically to break up the monotony of life on the farm.[29]

Trone had much less patience and empathy than Rosenberg. After his only visit, in 1941, he was critical of both management and settlers. The man who had handpicked many of these refugees was convinced that things had fallen apart when Rosen left the colony and returned to headquarters. Only Rosen enjoyed the colonists' respect. After he left, according to Trone, discipline and accountability went to hell in a hand basket. "People work as they please, fields neglected . . . agricultural instruction inadequate, leading to the breakdown of the group leader system."[30]

Settlers had a right to question the administration's directives, Trone asserted, because many of DORSA's own projects, which utilized trainees and refugees awaiting their own homesteads, had been started and forsaken in rapid succession. "The settler does not see directed work leading to results; half-grown crops on DORSA fields have repeatedly been abandoned; pig-sty started and abandoned; chicken farm started and abandoned; coffee plantation started and abandoned. The settler was told to plant tomatoes, potatoes, onions, etc. for the market—and now there are rumors . . . that these crops should be replaced by others more adapted to local soil and climate. General confusion prevails which leads to discouragement."[31] In reality, a rash of experimentation is not unusual during a colonization project's formative stages. Atherton Lee, a colonization expert who visited Sosúa as part of the Brookings team in 1941, thought this sorting-out process actually was a sign of strength, not weakness. Not only did it take missteps and trial and error to decide where a settlement's comparative advantage lay, but it signaled a healthy willingness on the part of management to take risks.

Experimentation did not inspire confidence among the rank and file, however, and when protests bubbled up, Trone wrote, the staff, fearful of a settler backlash, "hushes them up with goodness and jobs, giving in to their demands and, nevertheless, not satisfying them—for the settler, too, understands that the main wish of the administration is to make Sosúa appear rosy and not let the complaints seep out."[32] Those who groused were often offered cushy desk jobs. Too much was handed to the settlers on a silver platter. Jokes were circulating that Sosúa was a Potemkin village. "Those who work in the fields look like fools in the eyes of those who succeeded in getting jobs." As a result, Trone concluded, homestead group leaders had little legitimacy, and a few rotten apples were spoiling the rest.[33]

Trone knew full well that DORSA's executives had a low tolerance for negative publicity. Rosenberg and his New York staff needed to paint a positive picture for donors. It was one thing to be attacked by New York armchair Zionists with an axe to grind; it was quite another if word got out from internal sources that paradise was in turmoil and inmates were running the asylum. As a result, the staff did its best to mollify and coddle the settlers. If the colonists initially had little idea how much leverage this gave them, they proved a quick study when local administrators started backpedaling on their demands.

Rosen thought his recruiter hypercritical; but, in reality, Trone's pessimistic report was a direct byproduct of the frosty reception he received from the settlers, who reminded him that he had promised before they agreed to sign on that the association would do all it could to rescue their loved ones. They believed that management had reneged on something that, in their minds, was non-negotiable. Trone, in contrast, thought the settlers ungrateful for all the association had done for them.

Despite the ill will that swirled around his visit, Trone's diatribe was effectively corroborated by homestead group leaders, who offered their own indictment of both management and their peers. They reported that too many settlers looked on DORSA as a resource to be consciously milked, and these were the same ingrates "who have shunned systematically every bit of laborious work in the fields." By too readily acceding to these shirkers' demands and offering lazy good-for-nothings office jobs to pacify them, DORSA was raising suspicions about whether it was truly interested in creating a sustainable colony. The Rat cast itself as the one earnestly committed to the "development of a vitally enduring settlement."[34]

Rosen blamed himself and his successors for the "us versus them" state of affairs in a revealing letter to Reyher in February 1943. Even though collaboration had been at the core of his vision, "self-government and cooperation tendencies were definitely discouraged and made an object of ridicule" by his successors. Unfortunately, supervisors, instead of nipping avaricious tendencies in the bud, fostered them by standing aside and watching colonists enrich themselves at the expense of others. Rosen castigated himself "for having undertaken to start the work at an age when I could not have possibly expected to bring it to a more or less completed stage. Now somebody else will have to clear up the mess and make the best of it."[35]

A related problem for the cooperative model was the availability and attractiveness of inexpensive native labor. Dominicans were utilized by both administration and homesteaders for every task imaginable. Whatever success the settlement achieved was predicated on the Dominicans' sweat equity. Rosen's admonitions during the winter of 1940 that "we did not bring refugees here to add more landowners to exploit the peons," and that settlers should perform 75 percent of their own work were soon forgotten.[36] It is ironic that a settlement which was set apart from Dominican society forged a hierarchical set of labor relations so familiar to its inhabitants.

"WE ARE NOT 'GOOD NEIGHBORS'"

Overreliance on their neighbors undercut the pioneers' willingness to embrace Rosen's lemma that working on the land was its own reward. Try as they might to stop the use of native labor, administrators had little option but to employ Dominicans to tackle large infrastructural projects beyond the colonists' capabilities, to harness mushrooming operating costs, and to increase productivity. In June 1942, Dr. Max Isgur bluntly told Rosenberg, "the natives ridicule the settlers for the fact that they are not doing the work themselves . . .

the native attitude is that the settlers don't want to work. They have a dole attitude, a sense of entitlement."[37]

Isgur's caustic remarks blended three interrelated themes: the settlers' indolence, their sense of entitlement, and their propensity to hire Dominicans to maintain their homesteads. The three fed off each other. An elastic and inexpensive supply of labor, DORSA's relatively generous maintenance, and the sheer unattractiveness of working in the taxing heat and humidity combined to convince settlers and a reluctant administration that it was not only logical but necessary to hire native workers, especially for onerous tasks.

DORSA had foreseen the temptation. In its "Rules for the Establishment of the Settlement," which each refugee was required to sign before leaving Europe for Sosúa, it permitted settlers to "employ peons and other servants . . . only in the case of emergency or when the additional labor is needed during harvest times," and only with the express consent of the administration.[38]

Managers may have regularly complained, but it is not difficult to see why both settlers and administrators gravitated toward the use of local workers. Dominican labor was cost-effective; the prevailing wage was anywhere from 35 cents to $1.25 a day.[39] At any one time, upwards of several hundred Dominicans worked at Sosúa either part- or full-time.[40] Such minimal wage costs were within reach even for homesteaders on maintenance. This was not lost on DORSA's staff, which thought the allotments the root of all evil. As homesteaders increased the size of their cattle herds, however, and began to generate modest revenue streams from dairying, they had additional resources at their disposal to hire Dominicans. David Stern, who had worked with agricultural settlements in Palestine before signing on to direct Sosúa in 1944, was puzzled that homesteaders' wives did not work in the fields and had Dominican maids working in their homes. Fresh from a very different model, he must have wondered what kind of colonization project he had agreed to lead.

Some settlers apparently had no compunction about asking DORSA to lighten their load by hiring field laborers at the association's expense. The requests came so frequently and seemed so nonessential that administrators issued a directive to all departments that Dominican laborers should not be provided for homesteaders "except in extraordinary or emergency cases like grave illness where danger exists that the fields would be neglected to such an extent that it would endanger the subsistence. Also, in such cases, measures should be taken that instead of Dominican help, settler help should be [first] extended. In exceptional cases, where it is recognized that the settler could not do the work himself and he would be obliged to engage for a short period native work, for which he would be unable to pay himself, the DORSA may grant ultra short term credit repayable from the income of the next crop. In such cases, the settlers would have to prove that they paid the native help."[41] We can infer from the regulation that settlers took advantage of management's better nature by asking for assistance when it was unnecessary, and that they failed to document their expenses.

Even so, the colonists continued to ask for help clearing land, building fences, and attending to the livestock. To a settler's request that the association provide him with laborers, Solomon Arons retorted, "No philanthropic organization should or could provide you with peon labor."[42] Small wonder that prolonging the maintenance allotments became such an article of faith to the homesteaders.

The colonists also learned from the example set by the administration when it hired Dominican men for its major infrastructural projects, such as road building, laying water pipes, clearing pasture, and constructing barracks and homesteads. Native women were hired to perform domestic work in the kitchens, the laundry, and the medical clinic. It is interesting that officials often preferred to hire Dominicans over colonists "because familiarity with the settlers makes discipline difficult and the [European] employee does not like to work for someone he considers his equal."[43]

There were times when administrators, under pressure from the New York office to cut costs, took advantage of the situation and exploited the locals. Eugene Rosen was so upset with the staff's paternalistic attitude that it factored into his decision to leave the settlement in the summer of 1943. In his resignation letter, Rosen wrote that the administration's method of cutting corners by hiring temporary workers was patently unfair and counterproductive. "No attempt is made to educate the settlers to a more neighborly attitude towards the Dominicans. In the treatment of local labor the DORSA sets a horrible example in word and act. The policy is hire and fire, even when the slightest exercise of managerial skill would provide even more employment. The Dominicans are upset and resent DORSA and 'these Jews.'"[44] Temporary hires were a false economy, Rosen contended, "since transients can have no loyalty towards the company and no interest in doing their job right. We are not 'Good Neighbors,'" he concluded.[45]

Evaluating just how neighborly the refugees were would, in the best of scholarly worlds, require independent confirmation from DORSA's Dominican employees. It is not surprising that their voices are seldom heard in the association's records, in memoirs, newspapers, or even in the Dominican national archives, for that matter. Absent their vital perspective, we are left to infer how they were treated by sifting through the words and commentary of administrators, who at times lost patience with less-than-conscientious settlers and criticized them for their insensitivity toward their new neighbors.

From such incomplete and admittedly imperfect sources it is, nevertheless, possible to discern that either the administration's discriminatory attitude toward native workers filtered down to the settlers or the settlers already harbored similar perceptions. The refugees exhibited impatience with native workers and, at times, indifference to local customs. Some of this can be understood as a byproduct of miscommunication, given the settlers' uneven facility with their adopted language. But some colonists were arrogant, and believed *los muchachos*, as they referred to them, inferior. A distraught Mrs. Solomon Arons wrote Rosenberg, "There is one important and very sad thing, the racial problem. . . . Our settlers do not behave very civilly to the working population. They consider themselves a higher race. They consider the natives peons."[46]

Her husband had tried to address this discrimination by demanding that El Batey residents work alongside Dominicans in the kitchen and elsewhere. But Arons's forcing the issue only provoked an indignant and insensitive response, Mrs. Arons related: "In the kitchen there are some native labor and settler women doing the work, but they do not work together. The natives work on one porch and the settlers on another porch. A delegation of the Settlers' Council came to Mr. Arons with a request that they should not be able to do the same work."[47] Her husband was furious with the Rat's request, reminding the councilors, "You, of all people in the world, being thrown out of Germany and being treated like that, you should not act that way." When a Rat member replied that one could not compare the two situations because "we are of a higher culture than them," Arons fired back what could charitably be described as a very mixed message: "That is why you should behave decently to the people. . . . The natives feel the attitude and do not like it. The natives are a very proud race."[48]

Sosúa's prosperity could not have been achieved without local labor, but it came at a very high cost as far as DORSA's architects were concerned. Labor relations replicated local gender, class, and racial divisions, even though the settlers were, in the main, destitute and dependent on DORSA. Language barriers only exacerbated the social and cultural divide. We have seen how DORSA's Dominican employees lived in a discrete settlement on Sosúa's western end, segregated from the Europeans, a distance that only perpetuated misunderstanding. Meanwhile, as the clusters gradually came undone and individual homesteaders came to be *minifundistas*, or small property owners, the attenuated threads of solidarity loosened and gradually pulled apart.

UNDOING THE CLUSTERS

Leon Falk realized that he had to address the homestead clusters soon after he arrived to take over as director in 1941. His concerns about the Laguna groups, which he shared with the Rat, could have just as easily applied to the other clusters. "I found at least fourteen settlers are good, a few fair, and others entirely unsatisfactory—for example, Hugo Hirsch or others who could not prove to the visitor's satisfaction that they were doing their utmost in order to develop their homesteads."[49] Falk's assessment matched the Brookings report, which identified three types of settlers: some enthusiastic and motivated, "others not particularly enthusiastic but capable of getting along," and still others who evinced scant desire. Brookings pegged that disconcerting third group at about 15 to 20 percent of the colonists.[50] Many of these settlers eventually gravitated away from the clusters to El Batey. The Laguna cooperatives proved so dysfunctional that Falk decided it better to admit failure and "carry through a speedy separation," breaking them up into smaller groups.[51]

Less than a year later, Falk's successor, Arons, had to threaten another group to "get with it and buckle down" or he would forcibly remove them from their homestead. Another group was so at odds with each other that Arons asked the Rat to intervene, but after "dozens of conferences" he finally "pulled them off the homestead because they couldn't get along." DORSA assumed control, hiring Dominicans to milk the cows and keep up the farm until new refugees could be moved onto the homestead.[52]

Economies of scale could not overcome petty jealousies and infighting. Even though Martin Katz's group comprised a number of Germans like himself, he realized soon enough that the group dynamics left something to be desired and that his future did not lie on a homestead.[53] He took a position at the settlement's dairy cooperative, where he would work for twenty-nine years. Felix Bauer lasted two-and-a-half years on a homestead and then threw in the towel, moved to the center of town, and became an office manager in the health clinic and the art and music teacher at Escuela Cristóbal Colón.[54]

The clusters gradually fell apart during the course of the war years. On June 30, 1942, there were 83 settler "units" in homestead groups, of which 38 consisted of married couples, 44 were single men, and 1 a single woman. Including wives and children, 143 colonists lived on homesteads, or about one-third of the settlement. By the end of the war, however, 61 settlers had abandoned their groups after an average stay of just over 18 months. Two-thirds of those who left moved to El Batey, where many lived until they could obtain entry into the United States. Eight moved to Ciudad Trujillo, and 7 obtained employment in Sosúa as artisans. All except one cluster, the Leitner-Rosenberg group, experienced some attrition, and the larger groups—the Swiss and Luxemburg, the Drucker, the Gerber-Wieselberg-Hauser, and the Laguna cooperatives—were proportionally the biggest losers.[55]

Although management stubbornly persisted with the cooperative model until mid-1944, Rosen's collaborative vision foundered in a sea of individualism well before that. Absent was the idealistic mindset cultivated so assiduously in the Crimea and Palestine. In the latter, hardworking pioneers toiling on the kibbutzim were honored as patriots, heroic symbols of a new nation.[56] The message that Sosúa's pioneers internalized was very different. Performing manual labor was something to be avoided if at all possible.

More to the point, some of the refugees had come from relatively well-to-do bourgeois families and now faced the prospect of starting over with scaled-back economic horizons. For all concerned, Sosúa initially meant a lowered standard of living. This was perceived as both an economic setback and a social slight. Refugee experts Arieh Tartakower and Kurt Grossmann posit that German Jewish refugees felt the loss of social status acutely because "in Germany social station and titles are more prized than in any other country."[57] The adjustment to manual labor was considered socially degrading, especially for bourgeois women, who now had to perform domestic duties.[58]

The carping and the occasional malingering no doubt reflected the perception among a number of settlers that they could not prosper at Sosúa. As a result, the colony became, for more than a few, a holding pen, a place to bide their time until they could move to the United States. Unfortunately, that grousing manifested itself as a lack of trust in each other and in management. Sosúa's "problem children" were not that different from refugees who were fortunate enough to come to the United States during the war years. American social workers who treated German Jewish refugees having trouble adjusting found that those who had experienced deprivation and oppression demonstrated "an intense compensatory drive to make a place for themselves and get ahead, and this drive was accompanied by impatience with limitations and restrictions, and by aggressive behavior."[59] Sosúa's collection of clubhouse lawyers fit that description to a T.

In the face of such recriminations, Rosenberg continued to counsel patience to anyone who would listen. Growing pains were to be expected, he reminded DORSA stockholders in May 1943. "We could not pick and choose trained agriculturalists. The best manpower was being kidnapped for slave labor. All the experience of colonization shows that you cannot, within two or three years, pronounce such an effort successful. The experience in Palestine and elsewhere in colonization shows that it takes a considerably longer period of time—at least five years—before people can thoroughly readjust themselves in a new climate, new agriculture and totally new living conditions in a strange land."[60]

Perhaps because Rosenberg and his staff knew what they were working with and how much time it would take, they clung uneasily to Rosen's cooperative model even as they realized that adjustments were necessary. Sosúa was plainly an unhappy place during its first years, as lessons begged to be learned about the virtues of teamwork, sacrifice, and hard work. What to do with the bad apples became an animated topic of conversation among DORSA staffers. Efforts to ship the colony's problem children to Ciudad Trujillo prompted a dialogue with Dominican authorities. The resulting negotiations tell us a great deal about Trujillo's perceptions of the colony, what he was willing to tolerate, and what was not negotiable.

TEN

Containment

> I do not believe it is possible to freeze a colonization project.
> Colonists must have the feeling that they are engaged in a dynamic
> enterprise, and in addition, so far as it is possible, that they are the
> "avant garde." . . . Freezing the situation, even though justified by
> war, finance and other reasons, cannot help but give a body-blow
> to the situation.
> MAURICE HEXTER TO JAMES ROSENBERG, 1942

In the fall of 1942 DORSA sent forty-five "troublemakers" packing to
Ciudad Trujillo. The move outraged Dominican authorities, who
"objected to the unauthorized movement of European nationals."[1]
This was not the first time DORSA had shipped out discontented colonists to the capital; just six months earlier, Falk had relocated fifteen of
them. But the size of the second group and its arrival so quickly on the
heels of the first prompted a response. Trujillo had witnessed Spanish
republican exiles leaving colonies along the Haitian border and taking the path of least resistance. Officials were concerned that the Jewish settlers now would do likewise and either become public charges,
take jobs away from Dominicans, or compete successfully with local
businessmen. Moreover, why should DORSA be permitted to dump its
problem children in Dominican communities? No matter that four
out of five refugees residing in the capital were said to be "living off
the Joint."[2]

Authorities asked the newly appointed U.S. ambassador, Avra Warren—the very same diplomat who had been such a thorn in DORSA's
side when he headed the Visa Division in 1940 and 1941 to intervene. Warren informed the association that Trujillo believed the ex-

colonists posed a threat to the "commercial habits of the country," and was "determined to put an end to it."[3]

DORSA had debated the costs and benefits of exporting its misfits. Its leaders realized that troublesome former colonists unable to make it on their own outside the settlement were likely to draw attention, attract unfavorable publicity, and possibly engender anti-Semitism. As Falk put it, "it would be unwise for large numbers of idle refugees to become conspicuous in the cities of Santo Domingo." But their presence at the settlement was undermining morale.[4]

DORSA's contract stipulated that colonists could obtain citizenship after two years. But the Dominican government had delayed granting them that status because the colonists were largely German and Austrian, and Trujillo knew how the United States felt about giving Axis nationals freedom of movement during the war.[5] DORSA believed there was another reason why authorities were reluctant to give settlers citizenship: once they were citizens they were eligible to apply for passports, and this increased the likelihood that they would emigrate for good.[6]

A police order was issued to return the forty-five settlers to Sosúa. A few months earlier Rosenberg had asked DORSA's attorney, George Hourwich, if the association bore unlimited responsibility for settlers who "turn out unsatisfactory." Hourwich's legal opinion was that DORSA indeed was liable: "If they are misfits, if they go into business, etc., police are within their purview to investigate the circumstances surrounding the presence in the City [Ciudad Trujillo] of a large number of individuals originally admitted as settlers, who are now engaged in wholly different occupations." DORSA's responsibility abated once settlers could prove they were self-sustaining, Hourwich added.[7]

The government's decision angered Rosen. In a letter to Rosenberg he fulminated about Trujillo and other "benevolent" rulers. Hinting at anti-Semitism, he contrasted Trujillo's kid glove treatment of Spanish republicans with the dictator's response to DORSA: "Out of more than 2,000 Spanish refugees in the Dominican Republic, only a handful remained there and of these none on the farms. . . . Nobody makes a fuss about it. . . . But when a few Jewish refugees who have to undergo a terrific process of social readjustment, try to get out of the country or to change their occupation . . . we are all accused of being scoundrels and criminals. If we had any country of our own we would not have to look for the 'benevolent' attitude of the Trujillos."[8] That an inveterate territorialist like Rosen, who believed that Jews could flourish wherever they lived, was now touting the virtues of a Jewish homeland indicates just how upset he was with Trujillo for singling out Sosúa for special treatment. No doubt, decades of contending with arbitrary despots like Stalin and Trujillo had worn his patience thin.

Protracted negotiations between DORSA and the Dominican authorities led to a compromise. The police order was revoked, and this contingent was permitted to stay in the capital, but in "the future no settlers may move out of Sosúa without prior consent of the authorities."[9]

A weeding-out process was under way at Sosúa. Colonists who discovered they had little aptitude for farming were moved to El Batey, while others, if they proved sufficiently bothersome, had to be sent away. But after this confrontation with authorities, shipping them out in such large numbers would no longer be an option. In the future, settlers interested in relocating would be handled on a case-by-case basis.[10]

Trujillo also was reluctant to permit freedom of movement because of security concerns. Rumors resurfaced periodically that certain members of the tiny German and Austrian community on the island were Nazi saboteurs. Indeed, in 1942, Sosúa was singled out when officials claimed that German agents had infiltrated the settlement and were sending "shore-to-sea light signals, short-wave radio transmissions, and supplying enemy submarines with fuel and food." The FBI sent an agent to Sosúa to investigate the charges and found that although some residents harbored ideologies of various persuasions, "there is no indication that any activities inimical to the Allies are being carried on by refugees residing in the Sosúa colony."[11] Still, DORSA administrators felt compelled to allay Dominican concerns and decided to inventory settlers' cameras and radios.[12]

The FBI's conclusions are revealing. Not only did they absolve the colonists of any seditious activities, but they reinforced how isolated the settlement was. No Sosuaners, for instance, were members of the fledgling Free Austrian Movement, a group of 270 Austrians established in Ciudad Trujillo in February 1940. The organization had been created with the government's consent, partly as a mutual aid society, but it also maintained contact with other Free Austrian groups throughout Latin America.[13]

DORSA officials also harbored suspicions that Trujillo wanted to bottle up the settlement to head off competition with his own lucrative businesses. Seeking to expand domestic and foreign markets for its high-quality cheese, butter, and meats was a matter of economic consequence to the colony. Unfortunately, Trujillo enjoyed monopolies—what Maurice Hexter, who took over as director in 1943, called Racketera Trujillo—on the island's dairy and meat industries, and feared competition. The dictator was the nation's largest landowner and cattleman; his Hacienda Fundación, which was run by the army and which took advantage of convict labor, realized profits, by one estimate, of one hundred thousand dollars a year. His Sociedad Industrial de Carnes secured a generous loan from the U.S. Export-Import Bank to construct a new slaughterhouse; this enabled it to lock up the capital's fresh meat market and drive out competitors. Managed by Trujillo's brother-in-law, the meat monopoly earned an estimated half-million dollars annually. Similarly, all fresh dairy products had to be distributed through the Trujillo-run Central Lechera.[14] For the colony to sell milk and fresh meat was out of the question.

Even though the colony's line of processed meat and dairy products did not conflict directly with Trujillo's monopolies, David Stern told DORSA executives that the association still had to walk a fine line so as not to alienate the dictator. Stern had approached Jewish businessmen in Curaçao about purchasing kosher meat from the settlement. "They are producing very good sausages in Sosúa—better than in Ciudad Trujillo. Then it was question of competing with Trujillo's factory. I told them the buyers in Curaçao are Jews and we can produce kosher meat. . . . There are many thousands of Dutch Jewish families ready to take everything we can produce . . . [but] his Excellency has his institutions, his factories," he told colleagues. Even though Trujillo's plants did not produce kosher meat and concentrated on fresh rather than processed meat, DORSA managers were convinced they would be turned down if they sought export licenses.[15] Sosúa, of course, was not alone in having to contend with Trujillo's economic juggernaut. Entrepreneurs across the island had to move very cautiously when their businesses rubbed up against the holdings of the dictator, his extended family, and his business associates.

Aware of Trujillo's efforts to control the movement of both goods and individuals, DORSA took steps to ensure that its colonists stayed put. An elaborate "grounds registration system" was implemented to inhibit movement and collect information. Each resident was given an identification card, similar to the *cedula* that Dominicans had to carry with them. The office manager, William Bein, wrote Falk that the *ficha personal* "represents the central card showing the movements of every person in Sosúa. . . . On it are noted the changes of residence, occupation, departures from the grounds, sicknesses and other remarks of interest." The Settler Assignment Department also kept a daily work attendance card for each colonist. "Deviations from regular work attendance are noted daily on the *ficha personal*."[16] Travel outside the settlement also was monitored: "Persons desiring to leave the grounds apply for a travel paper . . . which has to be approved by the head of the department for which the person works, or the head of the Settler Assignment Department.

If approved, the travel paper is issued, stamped with the grounds registrar stamp and signed."[17]

If settlers left the colony without the written consent of management and were apprehended by police, they should not expect assistance from the administration, Bein warned. In addition, security guards and night watchmen were to write down the license plates of all cars passing through the settlement. The intent of this registration system was to verify the whereabouts of all residents. "Thus," Bein concluded, "the unaccounted absence of a person from Sosúa should be immediately visible."[18] Although DORSA's tracking system paled in comparison to the Dominican police state, it was clear that the association felt obliged to keep tabs on its colonists.

Trujillo's containment policy and DORSA's tracking system only reinforced the settlement's enclave character and undermined the colonists' integration into Dominican society. It also ensured that, except in unusual cases, misfits and troublemakers alike remained on site. DORSA's efforts to monitor settler movement were not its only way to display loyalty, however. The association and its settlers also demonstrated unconditional allegiance to the regime whenever asked to do so.

HEAR NO EVIL, SEE NO EVIL

Dominican officials regarded the association as an ally in their ongoing strategy to win over U.S. politicians, the media, and investors. They expected DORSA to portray the regime in a positive light; and Rosenberg and his staff never failed to disappoint, seldom missing an opportunity to publicly acknowledge their gratitude. DORSA promotional literature was filled with paeans to Trujillo's generosity. The offer, Trujillo's gift of Sosúa, and the clause granting the colonists freedom of worship were invoked repeatedly in press releases and in-house publications. Never was heard a discouraging word about Trujillo or his police state. Whenever that uncomfortable subject was brought up, settlement staff avoided the topic, proclaiming themselves apolitical. Perhaps that is why one informant who later moved to the capital told the historian C. Harvey Gardiner, "We kept our eyes closed. We saw no evil. We heard no evil."[19]

Still, DORSA leaders were disingenuous when they claimed to be apolitical. When Trujillo was attacked in the North American press, they often counteracted negative articles with platitudes that would do even the most obsequious of regime propagandists proud. The Settlers' Council, for instance, wrote an effusive letter to the editor of the *New York Times* extolling the dictator's

FIGURE 16 Taming the tropics. JDC ARCHIVES.

altruism in a response to an editorial that had characterized him as a ruthless tyrant. Hexter followed with his own response, noting that "Jews of the world consider Trujillo to be a great statesman. I am proud to call him my friend."[20] To the regime's exiled opposition, such lock-step allegiance was troubling.

A mutual admiration society developed between the association and the dictatorship as promotional pieces about the settlement were printed regularly in Dominican magazines and newspapers, as well as in a special English-language glossy publication, the *Dominican Republic*, which was given away free to the press, investors, and politicians by the embassy and consulates.[21] One memorable image that received wide play in both Dominican and DORSA publications captured a blond, strapping young homesteader, Heinrich Hurwicz, atop a tractor in an open field under cultivation. The magazine *Cosmopólita* published the photograph with an artfully worded caption that conveyed the Trujillista mantra of modernization, progress, and agricultural self-sufficiency: "The tractor cuts through the fertile soil, opening up furrows of well-being and progress. The refugee, far from the snows of Central Europe, puffs his chest out proudly under the tropical sun."[22] (See figure 16.)

Trujillo trotted out the Sosúa initiative whenever he thought it would promote his agenda abroad. For instance, his publicists periodically announced plans to bring refugee children out of Europe during the war years, even though the chances of getting them across the Atlantic were remote. The

FIGURE 17 "We have found a new home and share in the triumph of the Benefactor." JDC
ARCHIVES.

announcements usually coincided with other diplomatic initiatives or were
designed to offset negative press that the regime was experiencing at that
moment.[23]

The association also performed personal services for the general. Hexter
was asked to extricate Trujillo's daughter, Flor de Oro, from an undisclosed
"serious scrape in the States." Could Hexter get her out of the country as soon
as possible? "He was sending a private plane to Teterboro Airport [in New
Jersey]," Hexter later recalled. "Well, we owed him something. He had helped
the Sosúa settlers. . . . So I did what I could that night. I hustled her onto her
father's plane at Teterboro. When I saw Trujillo after the war he embraced me
and thrust a thick roll of one hundred bills at me 'for your splendid services.'
I thanked him and said I was glad to help the man who had helped so many
Jews. No other reward was necessary."[24]

The regime also staged lavish ceremonies on the anniversaries of the signing to remind Dominicans and foreigners of Trujillo's gesture. On the seventh
anniversary, for example, the settlers presented Trujillo with a handsome
photo album, which, in addition to documenting some of the colony's most
notable achievements, included a photograph of the smiling Benefactor on
the album's frontispiece, as if he were blessing its contents.

DORSA, furthermore, along with countless national and local groups and
organizations, was expected to demonstrate support for the regime at civic

FIGURE 18 Flowers for El Generalisimo. JDC ARCHIVES.

parades, on national holidays, and at pageants, patron saint festivals, and other staged ceremonies. These public displays were critical to the regime's legitimacy, enabling Trujillo and his architects, through constant repetition, to instill "the values of this new moral order." The contrived ceremonies were equal parts mass mobilization and impressive display of unity, as citizens of all social classes and organizations were expected to participate, exhibiting their love for their country and paying homage to the general. This endless succession of parties, dances, rallies, and beauty contests confirmed Trujillo's generosity to his subjects and his hold on power.[25] Trujillo's birthday, "San Rafael" Day, which was celebrated as a national holiday across the island, was given its due at the local elementary school, settler Luis Hess remembered. "Pictures of Trujillo were everywhere in the school."[26]

The association showed its support with gusto, helping to confer legitimacy on a ruthless dictatorship. One such occasion was the Dominican Party festivities, a civic parade on May 10, 1942. From 4:00 to 6:30 PM, thousands of people marched up the Calle del Conde in the capital past the official reviewing stand at the Ateneo Dominicano, where Trujillo and the diplomatic corps witnessed the procession. Each group carried its own distinctive banner; Sosúa's bore the following inscription: "We have found a new homeland. We are always grateful to share in the Benefactor's triumph."[27] In another parade, the men wore white suits and the women white dresses (see figure 18, above). The men carried a banner proclaiming "Dominican Republic Settlement Association. Colonia de Sosúa-Puerto Plata," while the women carried a bouquet of roses to honor the ruler.

The settlement also was involved in the yearlong centennial celebration of Dominican independence in 1944. Officials organized public relations junkets to Sosúa to show off the colony to foreign dignitaries visiting the island. On March 2, the Falks brought a reporter from *Harper's Bazaar*, and on the following day Flor de Oro arrived with the president of the Women's Clubs of America, members of the Pan American Union, and Twentieth-Century Fox Films. "We served them luncheon and showed them as much of Sosúa as we could during the few hours of their visit," Bein dutifully reported, and then in the same letter asked the New York office to mail pamphlets and brochures about the settlement to the visitors.[28]

Colonists sometimes showed their gratitude to Trujillo personally. Otto Papernik, the skilled Old World craftsman, carved a statue to the dictator out of one-hundred-year-old mahogany for the centennial. It depicted a large figure of a mother with her hands spread out in front of her, representing the Dominican motherland, next to two smaller shapes of a woman holding a baby and a man with a shovel slung over his shoulder. Intentionally or not, Papernik's rendering captured some of the regime's most resonant themes: nationalism, hard work, and patriarchy. After he finished it, delighted DORSA officials asked Papernik to set aside his usual carpentry work to carve two marble plaques with inscriptions, which would be mounted on an arch at the entrance of a new park at Sosúa to be dedicated in Trujillo's honor for the centennial. As a reward for his services, DORSA named Papernik its representative at the celebrations in the capital, asking him to take motion pictures that would be shown at the settlement's movie house.

Papernik's adventures in the capital are worth recounting in some detail because they indicate the great lengths that appreciative settlers went to demonstrate their support for *El Generalíssimo*. He was determined to get a good picture of Trujillo and his family, who were perched on a platform overlooking the massive parade route, but he was blocked by a soldier. Thinking on his feet, Papernik boldly swung into action.

> I was dressed in khaki pants and a khaki windbreaker, typical "Americano," and had my movie camera on a tripod. With that clothing and camera-outfit I just went to the officer and with my few words of English said "excuse me," pushed him slightly aside and went upstairs. I must have looked to him as a foreign photographer, because I was admitted to the room next

to the president's balcony. Leaning forward I caught the attention of the President and begged him to smile. He and few members of his family . . . gave me a real "cheese" smile and made me the happiest person around. I did not leave the platform without taking movie shots of the parade. . . . I showed [the film] in our movie house many times. To my great sorrow I lent it to somebody to show and never got it back, but at least I had the satisfaction of having President Trujillo smiling into my camera.[29]

The way Papernik proudly recounted the incident years later, after Trujillo was badly discredited in the eyes of most Dominicans, is suggestive of how some Sosuaners continued to feel about their patron.

Not all settlers were as proactive as Papernik; some had to be prodded. The colony was surprised one day when a military staff car arrived, bringing a high-ranking officer, who insisted on speaking to the veterinarian immediately. Apparently hundreds of Trujillo's calves were dying, and no one could ascertain why. A nervous Hans Rosenberg, who, like many settlers, had learned his occupation at Sosúa, was summoned; the officer explained the problem in some detail and asked Rosenberg to come with him as soon as possible to Trujillo's estate. Rosenberg was reluctant to go, informing the officer that he was not professionally trained.

Of course, "it was impossible to refuse a call from the Benefactor," Papernik related. "Hans Rosenberg was taken in a military vehicle to the farm in question and he saw immediately what was wrong. The animals were normally on pasture, but since they were all very valuable animals, they were kept in stables, and the reason they had died was that the roofs were too low and the heat caused dehydration. He immediately ordered the calves out of the stables, the sick ones to be killed, and the healthy ones put on pasture, this way saving a few hundred animals."[30]

Trujillo thanked Rosenberg personally and asked him if he had any special needs. Rosenberg demurred, replying that it was an honor just to serve the general. When Trujillo insisted, a plainly embarrassed Rosenberg, not quite sure what to ask for, requested and received a revolver. "He got the license for the gun . . . (he probably never fired a shot) but always carried it in his holster," Papernik recalled. Several weeks later, an appreciative Trujillo also sent the colony a prize bull, the settlement's first pure-bred animal.[31] Still, despite more than one invitation, Trujillo never visited the settlement even once.[32]

It is perhaps understandable that administrators and settlers were grateful to the general. He had, in a real sense, rescued them and, in some cases, their relatives from a likely death. No other nation had made the same kind of open-ended offer to take them in. At a time when anti-Semitism was endemic, when synagogues and torahs were desecrated across Europe, the Sosúa contract guaranteed them freedom of worship. Trujillo's pledge, moreover, was not just empty words. The colonists never experienced persecution or discrimination because of their religious beliefs, either from the regime or from their neighbors. They were left alone by a state which, through its containment policy, indirectly helped insulate them from any prejudice they might have encountered otherwise. Moreover, the repressive state apparatus applied very different standards to the colony than it did to the rest of society, given the settlement's symbolic importance as an exemplar of Trujillo's beneficence, its international reputation, DORSA's influence in Washington, and its relative autonomy. The settlers' privileged status and all they had been through under Nazism, in turn, dissuaded them from speaking out against the regime.

These settlers, however, should not be so easily excused for their unquestioning support for a brutal dictator. The refugees had experienced or witnessed persecution firsthand in Europe; they had refused to speak out in protest for fear they would be shipped off to concentration camps; they had lost most, if not all, of their material possessions and had been driven from their homeland by a tyrant who labeled them subhuman and members of a degraded race. Yet these settlers, living in Sosúa's protective shell, and their association not only conveniently chose to ignore the machinations of a reprehensible ruler whose innumerable cruelties had spawned a climate of fear, but also consented to be used by a regime notoriously effective at spinning propaganda to serve its own interests. Their willful ignorance of the dictatorship's seamier side was akin to that of uncomfortable guests at a dinner party when a family squabble flares up. Both settlers and management felt like guests in the Dominican Republic and, in their minds, it was impolite for guests to get involved in family disputes.

Presenting a favorable image of the colony and the Dominican regime was further complicated, however, when DORSA and Trujillo received a spate of bad publicity from an unexpected source.

THE BROOKINGS DEBACLE

DORSA was quick to blame settlers for their shortcomings, and vice versa, but what was apparent to colonists was that the administration itself was in flux and was failing to present a united front. Differing methods and styles of operation and open disagreements among upper-level management undermined DORSA's credibility and retarded the colony's progress.

By the time Rosen stepped down as director in 1941, DORSA's leaders had come to the conclusion that the job had become too onerous for any individual. Administrative duties henceforth would be shared between a director at Sosúa, who would handle everyday operations, and a president, who would assume many of Rosenberg's duties but who could also be a presence at the colony, attend to recruitment, oversee DORSA's offices and warehouses in Ciudad Trujillo and New York, and handle negotiations with the Dominican and U.S. governments.

There was another reason for the change. A weary and ailing Rosenberg, then 67 years old, had been ordered by his doctors to cut back on his workload. He decided to step down as president in October 1941 but retained his post as chairman of the board. He remained the face and voice of the organization in the United States and its chief fundraiser, while Falk, a wealthy Pittsburgh steel manufacturer who had served on DORSA's Executive Committee, was named president.

Even before assuming the presidency, Falk had made several fact-finding trips to the colony in 1940. During his visits he became convinced that a fresh perspective was needed. At his foundation's expense, Falk paid fifty thousand dollars to hire a team of experts from the Brookings Institution in Washington to make a scientific study of the prospects for refugee settlement in the Dominican Republic in general, and to offer specific recommendations to improve the colony.[33] The team was led by Professor Dana Munro of Princeton University, who had formerly served as minister in Haiti and chief of the Latin American Division in the State Department, and included economic, agricultural, and ecological experts.

The key questions posed by the Brookings team were: Was the Dominican Republic a suitable place for refugee settlement? What was the island's capacity to absorb immigrants? What would Sosúa's likely impact be?[34] Framed in this way, the report was guaranteed to provoke a response from the government, the JDC, and even DORSA itself, each of which was extremely sensitive to bad press, even if it was intended as constructive criticism. Zionist critics, furthermore, were bound to seize upon any weaknesses. Rosenberg worried that Falk could be handing DORSA's bitter rivals an unexpected present. He could not fathom Falk's motives; after all, hadn't the PACPR commissioned a similar survey in the spring of 1939 that asked many of the same questions?[35] Perhaps if the Brookings team emphasized the potential for future development at Sosúa and throughout the country, Rosenberg hoped against hope, the report would open the door for future immigration.[36]

If, however, the report concluded that the Dominican Republic did not contain sufficient lands and resources suitable for large-scale colonization, as Trujillo and Rosenberg maintained, what did that say about the entire initiative? The island's capacity to absorb immigrants was a similarly loaded question, especially at that moment. Just when Dominican and U.S. authorities were turning off the spigot of future immigration because of security concerns was not, in Rosenberg's mind, the best time to ask such a question.

Above all, what if the report slammed the settlement itself? What impact would that have on fundraising? Rosenberg fretted that the political fallout from such a report could be devastating. Years later he told Herbert Agar, then writing a history of the JDC, that he had asked Falk, "For God's sake, give me one promise. Before it is published, it will be submitted to me." After all, Rosenberg reasoned, the Joint had invested more than a million dollars in the colonization enterprise and therefore had the right to see the survey in advance of publication. Rosenberg also insisted that to protect the association, Falk share a draft with Trujillo.[37]

Falk did neither, presumably because his foundation had funded the survey and because he did not feel there was anything objectionable in the report.[38] Rosenberg never forgave Falk for that. After the report was released, he fumed, "it was not fair to take a thing in its infancy, less than two years after the first settlers got there, and ask for a public survey on such a subject."[39]

While Falk could be accused of naïveté and political insensitivity, he did have good reasons for hiring Munro's team. He agreed with Rosen's initial prognosis that Sosúa's limitations would never allow it to become more than a staging ground and orientation center. Additional sites for expansion were needed, and he wanted to know when, where, and how the settlement should expand. He had befriended Trujillo and knew that the Dominican state had identified areas across the island where state-sponsored irrigation projects were to be undertaken. In his mind, it was a mistake to think in terms of consolidating the existing settlement. With the report as ammunition, he planned to approach the general and enlist his assistance in securing additional properties—lands of higher caliber than Sosúa.[40]

Even though Falk misread how others would react to the study, the 410-page tome, *Refugee Settlement in the Dominican Republic*, published in 1942, presented a measured and balanced assessment of Sosúa. After spending several months on the island, the team concluded that the settlement had made an auspicious beginning but that challenges lay ahead, and they urged management to proceed cautiously and gradually. The settlement itself could not sustain further growth, the report concluded, but other tracts were available that should be investigated to provide homesteads for additional settlers.

Unfortunately, the consultants noted, Sosúa was turning out to be a pricey undertaking: the unit cost per male settler was $3,000, nearly double DORSA's projected cost ($1,600). Almost as if following a script written by Rosen and Rosenberg, the experts recommended that the association not grow Sosúa too fast too soon. Every refugee rescued from Europe was someone saved from death or squalor; but "unless it seems imperative to bring large numbers of people to the Republic simply to save them from persecution, it would clearly be better to establish a small colony on a sound basis than to take the chance of failure by over-rapid expansion."[41] Of course, Rosenberg had spent the better part of the last four years arguing the case that Sosúa was just such a haven for the oppressed, even while he insisted that his lieutenants build the colony slowly.

The Brookings prescription for Sosúa's ills was hardly earth-shattering; indeed, the evaluation was consistent with Rosenberg's own analysis. If it were not for the damaging fallout it engendered, Rosenberg, Rosen, and other DORSA staffers might even have embraced it. Arons thought there was much in the report that was on the mark and told Rosenberg that DORSA ignored the conclusions at its peril.[42]

Only one-third of the report dealt with the colony itself. The other two-thirds assessed the economic and social viability of the Dominican Republic as a site for future colonization and dealt with the island's capacity to absorb refugees. Whereas authorities had offered to take in one hundred thousand Central Europeans, Brookings said that at best the island could accommodate five thousand immigrants.[43] To make matters worse, although the team compiled a wealth of data on everything from climate and agricultural resources to industry, trade, and transportation, the report included some sweeping sociological generalizations, many of them unflattering. It said, for instance, that the campesino's diet had not changed since before the Conquest. It mentioned that vodou and other African rites were still practiced in the countryside, a statement guaranteed to raise hackles among the race-sensitive Dominican elite.

One stunning comment discussed the desirability of Sosúa and other immigrant settlements' segregating themselves from Dominican society. After noting the historical decline of the island's white population, the report warned, "Here is a rising tide of color that must inevitably engulf but the most carefully prepared and protected white settlement. In many of the communities 'negroidation' of the whites is complete, and, with but few exceptions, mis-cegenation and absorption is gradually coloring such white groups as still remain in the Caribbean area. Modern colonization continues to ignore this aspect of the settlement."[44] Then, as if to punctuate that point, the report went on to lament the shortage of female settlers at Sosúa, counseling DORSA to redress the imbalance as expeditiously as possible.

When Dominican authorities read the published report, they were livid. One of Trujillo's motivations had been to whiten the population, not segre-gate it. Even more disturbing was the report's contention that the Dominican Republic did not have the natural endowments and human resources to serve as a site for large-scale colonization. That contradicted more than a decade of government propaganda that had sold the island as an optimal destina-tion for European immigration. Trujillo responded aggressively, immediately hiring a New York journalist, Julius Moritzen, to write an article for North American audiences arguing that there were plenty of open spaces for im-migrants on the island.[45] Then the dictator formed a commission, headed by former president Troncoso, to respond more fully and deliberately to *Refugee Settlement*'s conclusions.

Trujillo's commission took Brookings to task for exaggerating the settlers' needs. The Dominican Republic was underpopulated, especially in com-parison to its Caribbean neighbors. Each head of household did not need thirty-five acres to sustain a family. That measure was better suited for "colo-nizing uninhabited places or to supplant the undesirable natives in uncivi-lized countries." The Dominican state, Trujillo's ministers asserted, had made a generous offer "inspired by the Christian desire to divide our bread and our home with the expatriated who, cast out by their European neighbors, in vain implored shelter in American countries more prosperous than ours."[46]

The problem, as far as authorities were concerned, was Brookings's inflated expectations, which anticipated that immigrants would be transformed into independent, self-sufficient landowners. What the magnanimous Dominican government had in mind was much more circumscribed. The refugees' own expectations were much more realistic than Brookings presumed, the com-mission asserted. "And the majority of these refugees did not come with the intention of being turned into well-to-do landowners." Instead "they came to the shores with only the clothes on their backs, like shipwrecked peoples who are grateful to be alive."[47]

The Dominican response, *La capacidad de la República Dominicana para absorber refugiados* (The Dominican Republic's Capacity to Absorb Refugees), reminded readers of the project's original racial rationale. Refuting Brookings's contention that vodou was still practiced in rural areas, *La capacidad* contended that such rites were a thing of the past since Trujillo's successful Dominicanization program along the Haitian frontier. Summarily rejecting Brookings's call for segregation, the document hammered home the point that from the outset, miscegenation between Europeans and Dominicans had been a desideratum of the state's colonization policy.

> European immigration, or more exactly, the immigration of men and women of Caucasian origin, of a culture similar to that of the nucleus around which the Dominican people has been formed and which, in spite of its ethnological adulterations, . . . is an immediate necessity of our national life . . . [because of] the successive surges of Haitians who come in warlike invasions or in pacific infiltration, and the persistent immigration of the Negroes of the Lesser Antilles; all these factors have created conditions which may end by alienating the Dominican people from its original Spanish sources, if care is not taken in time to modify it by introducing European immigration. And this procedure of adulteration cannot leave indifferent a people whose independence is dependent on the maintenance of barriers protecting them from the material and spiritual invasion of populations of pure African origin which surround them. [48]

La capacidad reiterated in no uncertain terms the racist motivation for admitting refugees. Although Spanish republican immigration had not panned out the way the general had desired and the Sosúa experiment was at best a work in progress and had not brought about the desired mixing of races, the authorities were far from discouraged about the prospect of bringing in white Europeans.

The commission's response, however, was, in a number of respects, disingenuous, especially when it contended that immigrants were free to go anywhere on the island after an initial training period at Sosúa. Claiming that it did not want immigrants who could not speak the language and who were not Catholics living in isolated colonies, the commission argued that the only way European immigration would succeed would be to integrate settlers into the fabric of society so that they "would not break the national unity."[49] As we have seen, the dictatorship did everything in its power to curtail the refugees' freedom of movement while discouraging them from pursuing livelihoods that threatened local interests.

One may wonder why publication of the commission's rejoinder to Brookings was delayed for three years and then appeared simultaneously in three languages (Spanish, English, and French), with great fanfare. The Brookings report may have been a public relations disaster for Trujillo, but it would not have any immediate effect on immigration as long as the United States remained vigilant for fifth column threats. Immigration had ceased to be a contentious issue, and it would remain that way until after the war. In 1942, moreover, U.S. relations with the dictator could not have been better. Trujillo's staunch defense of Washington's Fortress America policy assured him generous Lend-Lease military assistance, and his nemesis, Sumner Welles, was preoccupied with the European theater. There was no reason to engage in a public dispute with the Brookings consultants. Only when Trujillo's dictatorial methods drew renewed criticism from the State Department in 1945 and, the end of the war precipitated the relocation of large numbers of European displaced persons would the general think it useful to reassert his humanitarian credentials and reaffirm his interest in attracting Jewish immigrants. In that new context, the commission's findings would prove politically helpful.

Not surprisingly, the Zionist press had a field day with the Brookings study. *Congress Weekly* wrote Sosúa's epitaph in a piece titled "Failure of the Dominican Scheme."[50] The noted refugee expert Arieh Tartakower wrote an opinion essay dripping with sarcasm. Calling the colonization scheme "the end of another illusion," Tartakower had the nerve to accuse the Joint and DORSA of taking advantage of Hitler's tyranny to further their own agenda: "Hitler's catastrophe strengthened the wave of territorialistic plans among the Jews . . . for San Domingo is not the last territorialistic plan and not the last territorialistic failure. . . . The sooner we succeed in convincing all Jews and all other people of good will that there is only one manner in which to solve the Jewish problem [a homeland in Palestine] . . . and not squander money and energy elsewhere, the better it will be for ourselves and others."[51]

The timing could not have been worse for the philanthropy. Just as news was filtering back from Europe of the unfolding tragedy there, the Brookings study was once again tagging Sosúa as a boondoggle. The worse the news from Europe became, moreover, the more the pendulum of opinion in the Jewish community swung away from Non-Zionists like Rosenberg and the Joint and toward the Zionists.

From May 9 to 11, 1942, sixty-four American Jewish organizations set aside their differences and, in an unprecedented show of solidarity, met at the Biltmore Hotel in New York and passed a resolution calling for the creation of a Jewish state in Palestine and the abrogation of the British White Paper. Meanwhile, membership in American Zionist organizations was growing by leaps and bounds as entire synagogues were enlisted. Twelve state legislatures even passed pro-Zionist resolutions.

The movement picked up so much momentum that the U.S. and British governments decided that they had to defuse the call for a Jewish homeland. They called an Anglo-American Refugee Conference in Bermuda, which turned out to be an Évian déjà vu; noble proposals and heartfelt speeches ran rampant, but the two countries steadfastly refused to alter their immigration policies either at home or in the Middle East. Yet despite the policymakers' intransigence, the impetus to create a Jewish homeland in Palestine was palpable.[52]

The JDC and its allies were clearly on the defensive, and for many at the philanthropy, Sosúa had become a costly albatross. The settlement, as the Brookings report made abundantly clear, would never become prosperous and successful enough to serve as a model for the rest of Latin America; the Dominican Republic did not have the capacity to sustain large-scale immigration. The Non-Zionist JDC, which was plowing millions of dollars into the rescue of Jews from Europe, would have to make some hard choices in the years ahead; they did not have the luxury of supporting expensive resettlement projects like Sosúa. DORSA would have to figure out a way to extricate itself gracefully from the colony.

For the moment, Rosenberg opted to take the high road and not respond to the Brookings Report or the Zionists, so as not to draw attention to the report's unhappy findings.[53] Falk realized that his report had alienated Rosenberg and the DORSA board, and he submitted his resignation soon thereafter. Due to financial and human limitations, the board refused to follow the study's recommendation to seek out additional tracts of land to expand the settlement.[54]

After Falk's hasty exit and an interim period without a director, Hexter, with nine years of colonization experience in Palestine, assumed command of DORSA. He inherited a messy state of affairs. Four directors in four years—Perlestein, Schweitzer, Arons, and Falk—had tried unsuccessfully to fill Rosen's shoes at Sosúa. Rapid turnover had been a problem in itself, conveying a lack of direction to settlers and staff members alike.

A critical complication to these difficulties was that by 1942 the settlement was, for all intents and purposes, frozen. Except for relatives of settlers already there, only a handful of new refugees were being added. Facing budget constraints and a recalcitrant State Department unwilling to budge on visas, the Joint had little choice but to maintain the status quo.

TABLE 8
DORSA Expenditures in the Dominican Republic, 1943

Item	Cost ($)
Medical Expenses and Other Services	25,000
Settlers' Maintenance and Relief	72,000
Miscellaneous Expenses (Agriculture, Industrial Training, Technical Supervision, and Operating Expenses)	53,000
Administrative Expenses	43,000
Total	*193,000*

Source: "Statistical Information Regarding Refugees and Settlers in San Domingo," December 7, 1943, File 49, DP, JDC Archives

FREEZING THE SETTLEMENT

Before stepping down, Falk had warned Rosenberg that the State Department was digging in its heels over the visa issue. Reading between the lines, Falk believed that DORSA should, for the foreseeable future, expect to make do with what it had: "The present feeling [in Washington] is that the picture will be frozen as it stands at this moment, that is, no more American visas; also no more Dominican visas; refugees in other Western Hemisphere countries to remain where they are for the duration of the war and no more to come over."[55]

Falk's gloomy assessment was old news to Rosenberg, who had battled Warren's Visa Division to no avail throughout 1940 and 1941. But Falk's appraisal came at a significant moment for DORSA, a time when the JDC was reassessing its commitment. The colony was hemorrhaging money, and it was clear the settlers would not be able to stand on their own any time soon. The Agro-Joint's nest egg from the Crimea was a distant memory, and fundraising was difficult with so many more pressing needs in Europe. DORSA's operating costs topped forty thousand dollars a month by the end of 1942. When staffers submitted a budget for 1943 of three hundred thousand dollars, the Joint put its foot down and ordered cuts across the board.[56]

Even so, DORSA's operating expenses in 1943 still amounted to $193,000. Table 8 illustrates that 30 percent of the budget went to settler maintenance and refugee relief, while the costs of administration ate up more than one-fifth of the expenditures. The total represented an enormous outlay for 546 settlers, relatives, and refugees. The JDC not only provided funds for its former employees working at the settlement and in Ciudad Trujillo, it also laid out $1,500 a month to support 77 of the 92 relatives who had been brought over to join colonists already at Sosúa. Many of these relatives were aging parents of the young settlers who lived in El Batey, and could not effectively contribute to the colony's economic vitality.[57]

The sobering realization that Sosúa would remain at its present size until the end of the war had far-reaching effects on everything from fundraising to the acquisition of spare parts to the future of the homestead clusters. The war had curtailed imports from the United States of essential items like tires, tubes, and gasoline. Office manager Bein sent out a memo to all departments to restrict automobile and truck usage to a minimum to preserve tires and tubes. "In farming and construction," he wrote, "wherever possible we will have to use ox carts and all unnecessary trips with the cars will have to be cut in order to save tires."[58]

Fundraising became increasingly problematic. Rosenberg asked the American Friends Service Committee for a grant of $250,000 to supplement JDC funding for the rest of 1942, just as the decision was being reached to freeze the colony. Before responding to Rosenberg, the philanthropy's director, Clarence Pickett, turned to the JDC's director, Joseph Hyman, for a confidential assessment. Hyman was candid: although much had been accomplished, Sosúa would probably tread water for the foreseeable future.[59] Rosenberg's hands were effectively tied. He told Arons to inform the settlers: "In this world of total war . . . this means necessarily the strict limitation of the Sosúa work. You will explain to all why it has been impossible to send material from the U.S. to Sosúa. You will also explain why there must be the most stringent economical basis for the work from this time forward, looking forward toward having the settlers and other persons at Sosúa becoming self-supporting at the earliest possible moment."[60]

Hexter was upset about the determination to freeze the size of the colony. Pointing to failed colonization efforts in Cyprus and Turkey and a number of unsuccessful colonies in Palestine, Hexter warned Rosenberg about the deleterious impact that such a decision would have on settler morale: "Colonists must have the feeling that they are engaged in a dynamic enterprise, and in addition, so far as it is possible, that they are the 'avant garde.' "[61] He urged Rosenberg to reconsider, but that prospect seemed like a pipe dream until the war was over.

Dominican officials were also miffed at the reports that the colony would not expand, although its immigration policies were a major reason that the colony was unable to attract new blood. Manuel Peña Batlle, the Dominican secretary of the interior, inspected the settlement in August 1943 and demanded to know if DORSA was "freezing the project with a view towards gradual dissolution or whether it intended to revive activities as soon as world conditions would again permit so." Even though he was assured that the status quo would be maintained only for the duration of the war, he asked to see proof that DORSA was continuing to invest in the colony and worried aloud that homesteaders' expectations about their standard of living were unrealistically high for a small-scale operation like Sosúa.[62]

External factors thus continued to bedevil the settlement's expansion. When these exogenous constraints are coupled with the unraveling of Rosen's collective model, administrative turnover and mismanagement, and ongoing struggles between settlers and administrators, we can understand why observers questioned the colony's viability. What the doomsayers failed to account for, however, was the settlers' entrepreneurial drive. Through experimentation and trial and error, a small band of industrious colonists, with no relief in sight, willed themselves to prosperity and, in the process, belatedly discovered the benefits of collaboration.

ELEVEN

Trial and Error

[The CILCA dairy cooperative] actually captured the butter market of the Republic, over the competition of the "King" [Trujillo].
And the butter is superb. . . . You would be delighted to pay a dollar a pound here [New York] for the kind of butter that they have
produced down there. . . . It is clean, it has very little water in it, it
is very well processed.
JAMES ROSENBERG, 1946

What the turmoil camouflaged was an *ambiente* of fitful experimentation that suffused the settlement. Trial and error was its
modus operandi; the colony was a veritable hothouse of small-scale
entrepreneurial activity during the war years. All kinds of crops—
tropical and temperate—were cultivated, small-scale industries initiated, and processing cooperatives established. DORSA hired experts
in tropical agriculture and small industry who visited the settlement
and wrote up comprehensive reports, each recommending specialized
products guaranteed to flourish. Seemingly every new administrator
in New York and Sosúa had a pet theory about what product would
earn a niche in the American, Dominican, or circum-Caribbean mar-
ketplace.

Opportunity knocked, experts proclaimed, citing wartime scarcity
and the need for certain strategic goods in the United States. Everything from lemongrass and citronella grass oils to coconuts, from castor beans to coffee was planted during the first years, each crop an
ignominious failure. Sometimes the problem lay in the inability to locate accessible markets; other times it was the result of poor natural
endowments or the vicissitudes of transporting goods from a relatively

isolated area. Each new initiative turned, however, on insufficient capitalization and a misreading of the challenges and limitations of farming in the tropics.

Ironically, such risk taking and failures in due course saved the colony and forced the individualistic settlers to set aside the esoteric crops and their misgivings for each other and management to cooperate on the one activity in which Sosúa enjoyed a relative comparative advantage: dairy farming. A handful of the settlers, like Paul Cohnen and Arthur Kirchheimer, had been experienced dairymen in the old country; others knew something about making cheese, butter, and sausage. While familiarity played into the equation, it was the property's ecological constraints that best explain why Sosúa turned in that direction. Meager soil and water endowments were barely enough to sustain modest herds, but not to cultivate other crops. Only when diversification was consigned to the dustbin did Sosúa begin to hit its stride. Settlers developed their farms (*fincas*) gradually, renting out neighboring parcels as needed to accommodate their surplus herd. Since cattle ranching required only a modicum of labor, it was possible for those who preferred a more "cosmopolitan" way of life to move to El Batey and, with the assistance of a small staff of Dominicans, still attend to their fincas. Dairying had the added bonus that the milking could be done in the shade, a point that surfaced not infrequently in correspondence. Indeed, on some homesteads a curious division of labor appeared, in which Dominicans were hired to complete tasks in the tropical sun while settlers gravitated toward labor that could be undertaken in the shade.

By 1944, 6,300 out of a total 6,830 acres were devoted to pasture. Fortuitous breeding of imported Holsteins with native stock pushed up average daily milk production (per cow) to nearly twice the national average.[1] However, everything was a challenge at Sosúa. Solomon Arons complained that pasturage was susceptible to the least drought because it had "no moisture-holding capacity." As a result, milk production invariably dropped during the dry season.[2] Still, the settlement's output defied the experts, surpassing the most optimistic projections.[3] Just as Rosen had drawn up, the settlers, with DORSA's backing, formed three complementary cooperatives linked to dairying, which laid the foundation of what turned out to be a surprisingly successful, albeit, smaller colony.

The dairy-processing plant was the colony's linchpin. Walter Biller, Martin Katz, and a few colleagues founded the Cooperativa Industrial Lechera, C. por A. or CILCA, in 1941. The cooperative began modestly enough with the milk

FIGURE 19 First cheese press. JDC ARCHIVES.

collected early in the morning, brought back to El Batey, and taken to a small shack behind Biller's home, where it was pasteurized, Papernik remembered. "It started in the most primitive way, one man handled the crank turning the machine and a woman poured the milk into the container."[4] Biller, who had been a group leader of the Swiss group in La Bombita, initially hand-churned the butter in a spare room before relocating operations to a more central place.[5] (See figure 19.) He and a colleague began making cheddar cheese after having apprenticed for two months at the island's only cheese factory.[6]

Shares in CILCA were sold to the cash-strapped settlers; one hundred shares could be purchased for ten dollars each. No matter how many shares a farmer acquired, he or she was entitled to one vote at co-op meetings. Old-timers joked that in the early years the shares were as worthless as "toilet paper," but those savvy enough to reinvest and not cash out their dividends were rewarded for their foresight. Since many colonists lacked the wherewithal to invest, DORSA stepped forward and advanced funds to the cooperative and the dairy farmers.[7] In its first year of operation CILCA produced four hundred pounds of cheese, two hundred pounds of butter, and forty-two thousand liters of milk.[8] By late 1942, butter production had surpassed five hundred pounds per week.

Arons asked for funds to install a "cool" room to replace the inadequate household refrigerators. Anticipating that butter production would soon double, he wanted to divert a portion of the milk to cheese production. He begged the New York office, "A modern community without refrigeration, especially in this climate, is like living without any sunlight."[9] There is little question that CILCA would not have succeeded without DORSA's financial backing, and Rosenberg, Hexter, and others were quick to trumpet its shining story.[10] CILCA's modest product line quickly acquired a reputation for excellence nationwide, winning gold medals at agricultural fairs.[11]

By 1945 the cooperative, employing 15 people, collected milk twice daily from settlers. It was processing 100,000 pounds of butter, a million pounds of cheese, and 1.5 million gallons of milk a year, and its products were distributed and marketed throughout the rest of the country.[12] It also began to pursue foreign markets and had notable success cracking the market in Martinique.[13]

CILCA's collaborative model proved so successful that there was a rush to emulate it. On its heels came the establishment of the Cooperativa Industrial Ganadera Sosúa C. por A., or GANADERA, dedicated to meat, ham, bacon, and sausage production; and the general store, Cooperativa Colmado Sosúa C. por A, both of which were organized along the same lines as the dairy cooperative. El Colmado sold CILCA and GANADERA products and opened a branch store in Charamico, where it marketed its products to Dominicans. (Additional processing cooperatives would be established, but soon fell by the wayside.) A credit union was created to provide seed money for homesteaders, artisans, and small-scale manufacturers. Although GANADERA and El Colmado would not prove as successful as the dairy cooperative, they demonstrate that DORSA and the settlers collaborated when colonists saw the value of pooling resources and when economies of scale necessitated it.

Experimentation was not confined to the farm and the field; artisans and business-minded colonists opened up storefronts and small factories in and around El Batey during this effervescent time. About twenty-five different shops, businesses, and industries were operating by 1944. Seed capital came from an investment fund earmarked for small-scale enterprises that the philanthropist Arthur Lamport established. A carved turtle shell gift business, a haberdashery shop, a shoemaker, and a plumbing shop, just to name a few, all opened their doors.[14] More than a few women earned extra income by working in their homes.

DORSA also had several of its own enterprises, which complemented these private initiatives, such as a cabinet- and furniture-making shop that filled orders in the capital and a sawmill, which harvested trees from the Caoba section of Sosúa's property.[15] On a smaller scale, Blackwood's budding rooster operation netted $20–25 dollars a head and later was turned over to two settlers.[16]

Hans Goldman's story was typical of the colonists' entrepreneurial proclivities. After clearing land and planting tomatoes and carrots during orientation and then marking time at the dairy cooperative learning to make butter, Goldman decided that manual labor was not to his liking. Since motion pictures were all the rage, he and a friend decided to open up a "Cine Bar" (a combined movie theater, restaurant, and bar) in El Batey. It became one of the most popular places to socialize during the war years. The Cine Bar offered everything from coffee to lemonade, beer, whiskey, and Ida Dicker's Viennese pastries. Later, the menu expanded to include the cream cheese and anchovy spread liptauer and frankfurters. Saturday night dances featured American swing music on the gramophone and alternated between Han's place and Beno Stockmann's café.[17]

Hans was not the only industrious member of the Goldman family. His wife Hellie, who had gone to trade school in Vienna, where she learned to be a dressmaker, and then had practiced her craft as a refugee in Switzerland, opened up a seamstress shop with Lola Breinhoelter in the married family barracks. When Hellie arrived in Sosúa, she was surprised to learn that Dominican seamstresses charged as little as thirty cents a dress. But Hellie believed she could produce fancier dresses and soon found a settler who paid her eighty cents apiece for each dress. Although her husband originally frowned upon her working, he relented and even brought back fabric and a sewing machine from Puerto Plata. "Before we knew it, we had so much work, we couldn't keep up with the demand," Hellie remembered. At first she and Lola worked side by side in the stifling barracks, sewing everything from gowns to shorts for residents. The styles echoed Paris or Berlin, but the material was another matter, as silk gave way to breathable cotton. Jealousy and competition eventually led to a breakup of the partnership, and each woman established her own shop after she moved out of the barracks and into her own home. Each had her own patron who wanted special dresses made for the popular Saturday evening dances. Business took off, and eventually Hellie hired a Dominican assistant to help keep up with demand, as her small shop turned out six to seven dresses a week.[18]

Small wonder, with enterprising residents like the Goldmans, that the settlement's hub soon began to approximate a small urban center. A compendium

TABLE 9 *Professions and Professional Knowledge, 1945 (number of colonists, excluding homesteaders)*

Advertising 3	Fishing 1	Pharmacist 1
Art shop 2	Food business 5	Photography 1
Artist, painter 1	Fountain pens 1	Pig breeding 4
Attorney 1	Furrier 2	Plumber 1
Barber, hairdresser 4	Glassmaker 1	Printer 2
Blacksmith 1	Grocery 4	Saddler 3
Bookbinding 2	Hatmakers 3	Sailor 2
Brassieres, corsets 1	Horse dealer 1	Sausage maker 4
Butcher 7	Hotels, restaurants 4	Shirtmaker 3
Button maker 1	Ironing 3	Shoemaker 11
Canner, fruits and veg. 3	Jeweler, goldsmith 3	Social worker 1
Carpenter 16	Lathe work 3	Sports trainer 1
Carpet worker 1	Leatherwork 1	Statistician 1
Cement work 2	Livestock, cattle 6	Straw worker 3
Chauffeur 14	Locksmith 4	Sugar manufacturing 1
Cheese production 1	Masseur 1	Tailor, dressmaker 26
Chicken farms 3	Mechanic 22	Teacher 3
Cook 12	Metalworker 1	Textile technician 6
Cosmetics 3	Miller 1	Tinsmith 3
Cutter 1	Milliner 1	Typewriter mechanic 1
Doctor 4	Mosquito control 2	Upholsterer, decorator 3
Drink manufacturers 2	Movie operators 4	Waiter 4
Electrician 7	Nurse 15	Watchmaker 1
Farm implement technician 1	Painter 3	Wood expert 5

Technician (with diploma, including architect, 2 chemists, ceramics, engineer) 5

Technical employee (including surveyor) 6

Former commercial activity (Merchant, clerk, commercial employee, salesperson) 45

Source: "Professions and Professional Knowledge," undated list, File 47, DP, JDC Archives

This list blends professions the settlers practiced before arriving in Sosúa with skills they acquired through retraining at the settlement. Some individual settlers figure in more than one category. Not all on this list practiced these skills in El Batey.

of "Professions and Professional Knowledge" testified to the colonists' diverse range of talents (see table 9, above).

The settlement's waxing productivity by war's end—although not all of it took place in the fields—provided a sorely needed confirmation of Rosenberg's and Rosen's initial projections. The administration had reason to take pride in its core group of homesteaders, who had seized the initiative to move the settlement forward. Exhibiting patience, hard work, and impressive drive, the colonists had learned from hard knocks that they had to spearhead the colony's future.

According to Maurice Hexter, this burst of ingenuity and productivity was tied to the depressing news arriving daily about the atrocities in Europe. "These people now realize what I told them two years ago that if the JDC and Jimmy Rosenberg had not taken hold of DORSA at the time, most of them would be dead. They know that now; they are beginning to hear of their colleagues, in the same camps from which we took them, who are finished."[19] Absorbing this sobering reality not only gave the refugees the strength to persevere but led them to look to the past as a coping mechanism, as a means of coming to grips with their expulsion from their homelands. Leo Spitzer has documented how German and Austrian Jews refugees in Bolivia appropriated their past traditions and culture as a symbolic act of cultural defiance against a Nazi regime that had ostracized them. "When the future seemed darkest to them, as the news of Nazi military victories and Nazi atrocities against Jews enveloped them, they turned to the past as a way to gain some sustenance and stability in their present. In this respect, however, the creative communal reconstruction engendered by nostalgic memory showed their cultural resistance and cultural survival, a denial of success to Nazi efforts to disconnect and expel them from the Austro-German *Kulturkreis* in which they had played such an integral part."[20]

Sosúa's energy and vitality, then, cannot be measured only in rounds of cheese, links of sausage, or the size of herds, or even how colonists partially reined in their individualistic *mentalité* to join together to process, transport, and market their goods. Equally important was the rich and varied cultural life they cultivated in and around El Batey. As the colonists struggled to establish their businesses and fincas, they went about fashioning a social and cultural approximation of their urban past.

LITTLE VIENNA

It is a commonplace that immigrants seek to replicate their way of life in their new surroundings. Sosuaners were no exception; the colony's insularity aided efforts to reproduce an ersatz version of the cosmopolitan milieu that had been taken away from them. By any measure, they were successful in building a Little Vienna in the tropics. Operating in a German lingua franca that reinforced shared traditions, they sang and played their old lieder and wrote, directed, and performed in musicals, operettas, and plays. The small

FIGURE 20 Theater rehearsal in El Batey. JDC ARCHIVES.

Eastern European contingent, according to one student of the settlement, "tried to help awaken feelings of Jewish identity by staging plays in Yiddish," like S. An Ski's *The Dybbuk* and Sholem Aleichem's *Mazel-Tov* and *Tevya der Milchig*er. These plays and a musical, *Die Romainishe Khassena*, observers agreed, were high-quality performances that drew the entire community together (see figure 20, above).

All manner of eclectic talent was available to be tapped, even if it had little to do with agriculture. An invalid scholar gave lectures on Pasteur, the Dreyfus Case, and Theodore Herzl, while a stand-up comedian and entertainer from Vienna, Bruno Beran, wrote and staged a comic opera. Otto Papernik, who played the mandolin, and a friend who played accordion and piano mixed and matched some familiar opera arias to Beran's libretto and "because most performers knew those arias we had no problems rehearsing the show. It became the greatest success of all shows and everybody was singing the songs for months and years."[21]

Felix Bauer filled the role of self-appointed cultural czar, responsible for spicing up the colony's social calendar. He organized a small choir of "90 percent nonmusicians" and whipped them into shape, teaching them songs he had learned in a camp in Switzerland. The talented musician created an aerobics class that met two evenings a week, where members of both sexes met to practice calisthenics and gymnastics to rhythmic music he composed especially for the class. Apparently, Bauer's sports nights caught on, because four of his prize pupils traveled to Puerto Plata, where they performed gymnastic routines at a little movie theater. The local press dubbed them the Great European Olympic Team. "Not a word was true," Bauer deadpanned, "but the photographs looked good in the newspapers."[22]

When they were not showcasing their artistic and musical talents, the settlers joined together for friendly competition on the soccer pitch, the baseball field, and the basketball court.[23] By 1946, ninety-five residents had joined sports teams in basketball, baseball, men's and women's soccer, women's gymnastics, ping-pong, and badminton, competing against teams from Sosúa, Puerto Plata, Santiago, and Ciudad Trujillo.[24]

Settlers re-created their past but also adapted to their surroundings and embraced new challenges. Learning the rules of an American sport like basketball was easier said than done, however. Since no one knew how to play, DORSA sent for and received a rule book, "but since it was in English we had a hard time learning because very few understood or spoke English," Papernik recalled.[25] Colonists were quick to pick up, however, on the popular dance, the meringue. "Once you knew how to dance you just could not sit still because this rhythm got into your legs and system, and one couple tried to outdance the other." The dances were extremely popular because after a week of hard work, "everybody was looking forward to the Saturday evening entertainment without having to spend too much money anyway—[money] they did not have anyway."[26]

One local custom to which some colonists never adapted was the midday dinner. Making few concessions to the climate, Arons wrote, residents ate a very full main meal in the evening as they had in Europe. His description indicates a fusion of traditional culinary favorites with local produce. "The average meal is some fruit grown by settlers, soup, chicken, vegetables, mostly rice (grown by settlers) and peas, sweet potatoes, yucca or ordinary potatoes, dessert, tea or coffee."[27]

A favorite pastime on Sunday afternoons revolved around a sampling of familiar pastries (*Kaffee und Kuchen*), as neighbors got together for leisurely visits to each other's homes. Papernik, with his keen eye for detail, recounts how the tradition was revitalized in a very different setting. "Every Sunday a whole group of people used to ride [on horseback] to explore the surroundings and visit homesteads. We always tried to be at a certain settler's house, the Kohns, by four o'clock because we knew that his wife made the best cake and apple strudel and for a token pay, to help pay for the ingredients, we had a home-made afternoon snack."[28]

Sosuan ingenuity knew no bounds, but there were always lessons to be learned about the new environment. In the back of the Viennese coffeehouse, Papernik's carpentry shop built a bowling alley. "I had to make the pins and turn the bowling ball," he recalled. Unfortunately, the wood he used was "freshly cut and still green. That did not matter for the pins, but the balls, after a few days of use, became oval because the wood started to dry. Everybody cursed me for having to play with those oval bowling balls."[29]

The children of settlers and Dominican employees were taught by four teachers at Hess's Cristóbal Colón primary school. Dominican students were charged a nominal tuition, but that did not deter local applicants. The curriculum was monitored by the Secretary of Education, and students had to demonstrate proficiency by passing their exams before a government school inspector in Puerto Plata. Classes were taught in Spanish, but instruction in German, English, and Judaism added variety to the mandated curriculum. It is instructive that German lessons were phased out by the end of the war, proof that the colonists were becoming more familiar with the vernacular. The school observed all national and Jewish religious holidays. In addition, newly arriving colonists took night classes in Spanish there.[30]

By 1947 the colony boasted a library that held 1,500 books, a record collection, and magazine and newspaper subscriptions from the United States and the Dominican Republic. A biweekly, bilingual (German and Spanish) newsletter, the *Bulletin*, edited by Franz Drucker, covered local happenings and national and international news and events. For a time it switched to only German, a change that worried Becky Reyher in New York, who thought this decision was ill-advised. Later renamed *La Voz de Sosúa*, the paper reverted to both languages and undertook to help settlers improve their Spanish by including basic vocabulary alongside recipes for native cuisine, crossword puzzles, Jewish humor, German poetry, and children's stories.[31]

Even though DORSA always proclaimed Sosúa an ecumenical settlement and most of the colonists were secular Jews, regular services were held in the synagogue, and attendance was strong for the High Holidays of Rosh Hashanah and Yom Kippur and the communal Passover seder. Led initially by a young orthodox rabbi from Vienna, the weekly services drew fifty to sixty

FIGURE 21 Though a secular settlement, religious observance always had its place. JDC ARCHIVES.

people. A children's choir performed at the annual Purim and Hanukah festivities. The governor of Puerto Plata was invited to one performance, which blended Hebrew and Dominican songs. "The singing of our children moved him greatly and brought tears to his eyes," Bauer recalled.[32] (See figure 21.)

Nonreligious settlers, Arons wrote, worked on Saturdays, a matter that troubled the devout minority. In 1945 this group formed a new organization, the Association of Jewish Settlers, and published a mimeographed sheet patterned after *La Voz de Sosúa*, called *Kaulenu*, or Our Voice, promoting Jewish thought and culture. Although the religious group never attracted many followers, *Kaulenu*'s readers did take principled stands when DORSA policies offended them. They demanded that the association close its offices on Saturdays to observe the Sabbath.

Since livestock operations continued seven days a week, DORSA manager Walter Sondheimer was puzzled as to how to respond and asked William

Bein, then in the New York office, for advice. "Of course, we are for giving any Jew desirous of keeping the Sabbath rest ample opportunity to do so. This, as you know, has always been practiced in Sosúa," Sondheimer wrote. On the surface, the request seemed reasonable enough to the administration, but since Sosúa was predicated on Dominican labor, shutting down operations on Saturdays had a ripple effect. Sondheimer worried that the colony would not be able to attract enough local workers willing to give up their Sundays. "Native workers cannot be educated to work on Sunday when there are cockfights and other entertainments to be enjoyed, and on the other hand they want the pay for the sixth day of work." Eventually DORSA relented and closed its offices on Saturdays and Sundays, but the controversy reflected disagreement about the colony's identity as a Jewish settlement.[33]

Medical facilities were nothing short of remarkable. At first a doctor from Puerto Plata made regular visits to attend to patients, but by war's end, the clinic boasted a full-time staff consisting of two doctors and three nurses. They saw an average of 800 patients a month, half of whom were Dominicans working at the settlement or living nearby. Blood work and other laboratory tests were performed, and each settler was given a complete physical upon arrival. In addition, doctors logged on average 125 house calls a month. A 16-bed hospital included a quarantine room for infectious diseases and a maternity area.

Arons wrote a tongue-in-cheek memo about the rush to take advantage of Sosúa's state-of-the-art birthing facilities: "33 babies were born last year [1942] in Sosúa, half are boys; circumcision costs 25 cents. The women like to have babies here. They say this is the best place to have a baby. No other place will be so convenient and DORSA pays all the expenses. The babies do wonderfully well here. The climate is ideal for babies. Dr. Klinger says he furnishes birth control to those who ask for it or want it, but practically none want it. Dr. Klinger says, since so many of us are being killed or die of starvation [in Europe], it is a good thing to have more babies wherever possible at this time."[34] (See figure 22.) Martha Bauer, a registered nurse at the clinic, asked her husband to teach a calisthenics class for pregnant women. Business was so brisk at the clinic that she remembered putting in twelve- to fourteen-hour days. A Dominican doctor, she recalled, taught the Medical Department about tropical illnesses, and over time she became something of an expert on public health, as well as developing a strong respect for the local flora and fauna. She later joked that she never let her infant son "step on the ground. The first time he stepped on ground was in America."[35]

FIGURE 22 Baby boom. JDC ARCHIVES.

The minor baby boom sent Papernik's woodworking shop into high gear. "I started to make very primitive looking baby carriages. Because I had no rubber wheels I used v-belts that were discarded at the garage and . . . made those carriages into halfway decent looking strollers, without springs—the box just hanging in a frame made out of flat steel rods but painted in bright colors. It was not very easy to maneuver them but since we had nothing better available, they were just fine."[36]

The Medical Department inoculated school-age children against typhus, smallpox, influenza, diphtheria, and whooping cough. A range of dental services was available to colonists, staffed by a dentist trained at the University of Vienna and two nurses. The Medical Department also performed regular checks on sanitary conditions at the slaughterhouse, dairy cooperative, bakery, and bottle factory. Drinking water was inspected regularly.[37] Veterinary services, including artificial insemination of cattle, were provided by DORSA.[38]

As the war lingered on and the settlement stopped receiving refugees from Europe, the colony's frame of reference shifted from the old country to the United States, as American popular culture, in the form of books, magazines, movies, food, and cigarettes, flooded the colony. Radio was another godsend, Ernest Hofeller remembered. "By a meteorological fluke, the radio programs of the Armed Forces Network beamed to the U.S. troops in the Pacific were reflected to the Caribbean, so that we enjoyed perfect reception of American programs."[39] The settlement could also hear news directly from Germany on shortwave broadcasts. Hofeller recounted a tense moment in the barracks that demonstrates that the war was never far from anyone's mind. "A fellow named Guggenheim used to listen to [German shortwave broadcasts] at midnight. In the silence and the warm night air which seemed to carry sounds from far away, the transmission was audible through all rooms, even though he played it very softly. One night, a malaria-ridden Luxemburger became so enraged by the German propaganda, that he entered the room, ripped the radio out of its socket causing a short circuit, and smashed it."[40]

What the surge of entrepreneurialism, the success of the dairy industry, and the settlers' passionate embrace of a vibrant cultural life had proved to a significant minority was that it was possible to build a new life at Sosúa. For those traumatized by their exodus from Europe, the opportunity to build something tangible and to help each other cope with this new social milieu proved cathartic and invigorating.

Not everyone was willing to make that commitment, however. Some had already come to the conclusion that Sosúa would never provide the economic security they desired. They decided to bide their time and wait until the war was over and then emigrate to the United States. That sizable contingent, many of whom lived in El Batey, acted as a collective drag on the settlement's dynamic activities. In the meantime, the homesteaders, feeling the pinch of DORSA cutbacks, frustrated by two managers who lacked even the most basic interpersonal skills, and upset that so many resources were lavished on El Batey rather than on the colony's life blood—its dairy farms—lashed out at the administration, demanding greater autonomy. They called for DORSA to make up its mind once and for all whether it wanted Sosúa to be an agricultural settlement or a refugee colony.

A CANCER AT EL BATEY

The Batey cancer, as it came to be called, was part and parcel of an early decision imposed on management to accept nonsettlers and others deemed unsuitable for colonization. Although this was a well-intended policy designed to save as many lives as possible, the nonsettlers' presence had far-reaching consequences. Most had not been screened by recruiters and lacked the desire or the ability to adapt. Another group living in El Batey consisted of relatives of settlers, many of them elderly, who also were unfit to work in the fields. Despite DORSA's best efforts to rid the colony of some of the undesirables, management was saddled with a sizable group who made their unhappiness evident.

The dissension culminated in a near-mutiny by the homesteaders in late 1943 and early 1944. Furious that resources were being diverted to nonsettlers, the homesteaders insisted that DORSA address their needs. It might seem counterintuitive that this struggle unfolded at the same time that the dairying industry was taking off. Yet it was precisely the industry's first successes that ratcheted up animosity between management and colonists. The settlers' calls for greater freedom met resistance from the administration, which contended that its guidance and monetary support had enabled the settlement to turn the corner.

To understand how matters could have reached such a boiling point, it is necessary first to probe the wellsprings of the colonists' discontent. In addition to widespread dissatisfaction with Rosen's clusters, the homesteaders were frustrated with David Schweitzer's ineffectual eighteen-month tenure as director. By all accounts, the man who replaced Rosen avoided making decisions and delegated too much authority to his subordinates.[41]

Eugene Rosen painted a dire picture of Sosúa for Rosenberg. "How sad is the plight of your stepchild!" Inefficiencies were everywhere; "the bookkeeping is a mess," a "radical overhaul" was needed. "We are all to blame, New York as well as Sosúa." Foreshadowing his eventual resignation, he ended his missive on a disquieting note. "You probably know that Sosúa has never been just a job for me—I'm no idealist, but I did have the hope that I would be taking part in building something worthwhile and enduring—it's a hope which I am still loath to give up."[42]

Policies were continually being reversed in response to "squeaky wheels." It is interesting that Dr. Max Isgur believed that Rosen's periodic visits to the settlement after he had stepped down as director had an unsettling effect. "He tried to discuss situations with individual settlers . . . there was no other way he could get the facts. He asked them about what they felt concerning the administration. This gave the settlers the impression that the administration was under fire; it gave them the feeling that they had something over the administration . . . all the settlers know that some sort of shake-up is coming."[43]

Rosenberg took action in late June 1942, recalling Schweitzer and asking Rosen's brother-in-law, Solomon Arons, who had been a purchasing agent in the New York office and was then working under Schweitzer in Sosúa, to take over as administrative head. Bein, who, like Arons, had worked in the administrative offices, was made Arons's second in command.

Rosenberg told Arons to write a full and frank evaluation and to take a tougher line with shirkers. This was not the time for compromises. The settlement was frozen, fiscal resources were drying up, and the settlers needed to know that the time was coming when DORSA could no longer support them in the style to which they had become accustomed. No new homesteads were to be developed. A good administrator shared many of the same characteristics as a successful football coach, Rosenberg wrote to Arons. "Such a man has to train and instill a fighting spirit."[44] He urged Arons to inculcate discipline "for participation in community activities and real work, even if there are complaints," and challenged him to "go ahead vigorously, bravely, and courageously, and don't let fears that these people will yelp or criticize deter you from doing what you consider the wise and courageous thing."[45]

Arons did what Rosenberg asked of him, and it cost him his job. In an open letter to homesteaders, he gave the bad news first. Soon, "perhaps not in the very distant future," the settlers would have to go it alone. Maintenance had been extended well past the original period promised, and settlers could not expect DORSA to continue providing all the essential services indefinitely. Then he tried to appeal to their nobler instincts: "You, from among millions, have been given the unique opportunity to establish yourselves and to develop an existence with a good chance for a better life in the future. The DORSA gave you this opportunity. It is up to you from this point on and forward to build for yourself and family a life in accordance with your ambition, initiative and energy."[46]

Apparently lacking the finesse and requisite interpersonal skills to motivate his charges, Arons instead browbeat them. "I tell them that DORSA does not and cannot guarantee any living standards to anyone," he wrote Rosenberg. The tough-talking Arons berated colonists for their "refugee psychology," telling them, "I do not believe in appeasement as has been the practice before."[47]

Such patronizing treatment grated on the settlers, who, because of their newfound success, were feeling empowered. Even though Papernik worked in El Batey for DORSA, he criticized management for favoritism and inconsistency. He was puzzled that some settlers "did not have to ask twice" while others "had to . . . shout or even use threats to get what they were asking for."[48] Speaking for many of the colonists, he was convinced that the administration's methods were counterproductive: "The big problem with the Administration . . . was that for some strange reason they did not seem to understand our needs as settlers or professionals. They tried to make us feel that they were in charge and we had to obey. Most of us, already of mature age and with ideas, did not always agree with the Administration. We did not ask for anything unreasonable, but most of the time for a few more cows or materials needed on the farm, just to make life more secure and to make it possible to make a living."[49]

Arons and Bein alienated not only the settlers but also the staff. Eugene Rosen, the most popular face of management after his father returned to New York, had nothing but contempt for Arons, who he thought was too much of a bureaucrat, and for Bein, who was "clever, too clever, the most hated among settlers and minor employees . . . there is a streak of pettiness and almost meanness to him."[50]

By the summer of 1943 the settlement was roiling. The younger Rosen abruptly announced his resignation on July 24 after a nasty showdown with Bein and Arons. "Petty intrigue, suspicion, and distrust," Rosen wrote to Rosenberg in his resignation letter, had clinched his decision to leave. Echoing his father, he declared that even though "the human material was far from perfect let no critic convince you that it was hopeless." He then asked a number of rhetorical questions. They not only illustrate that he took the settlers' side, but also open a window on the underlying reasons for the colonists' unease.

> Why do administrative expenses in Sosúa take up such a high percentage of the total expenditures? Why are settlers given no voice in Sosúa's affairs? Why does the administration insist on keeping every detail of settler life under its control? Why do we constantly overpay on many purchases? Why does the administration discourage every instance of initiative and individual enterprise in the settlers? Why are non-productive jobs created to show settler employment? Why does the administration make every effort to make itself necessary forever, instead of trying to work itself out of its job? Why is the primary aim of the majority of the settlers, homesteaders included, to clear out of here as soon as possible, and why is nothing being done to counteract it?[51]

Central to Rosen's and the settlers' concerns was the administration's refusal to relinquish control and its unwillingness to cut waste. "We are no model for anybody," Rosen lamented. "A spirit of general antagonism prevails rather than cooperation," fostered by an administration that pitted "settler against settler, group against group, homesteaders against industrial settlers." Nothing could stand on its own except CILCA, Rosen continued. "Many of our 'flourishing' enterprises—bar, dance hall, woodworking, etc.—are built on air and could not be supported by our community if it were not for DORSA money jingling in the pockets of our non-productive population."[52]

The Rat met on August 3 and, in an unusual display of solidarity, approved a motion by a vote of 234 to 9 (with 19 abstentions) to send Rosenberg a letter decrying administrative instability and high-handedness. "With every change in management of the experts, hopes for a consolidation of the settlement went high, only to give way to bitter resentment afterwards." The Settlers' Council called on the New York office to send "independent" people to investigate and demanded greater oversight of the colony's own affairs.[53]

Adding fuel to the flames, a day later Arons wrote an infelicitous open letter to the settlers, blaming the letter on a small, unrepresentative "group that is creating hysteria and whipping people up . . . misguided malcontents and disappointed employees who have succeeded by insidious and organized propaganda and playing on the instincts and emotions of the people." He implored the troublemakers to cease and desist.[54]

Just as he had done when matters came to a head in the spring of 1942, Rosenberg relied on outside counsel to cope with the settlers' agitation. He asked Hexter to go to Sosúa and ease tensions and then persuaded him to assume DORSA's presidency, a position left vacant since the Brookings-Falk disaster. Hexter realized that he needed someone on the ground who could restore settler confidence in management. He asked David Stern, an agronomist who had worked under him in Palestine, to become the colony's director. The momentous decision to bring in a professional like Stern marked a turning point in the colony's development and did much to ease tensions.[55]

In the interim, Hexter spent fifteen days at Sosúa in November 1943 and came to the conclusion that the real obstacle to the settlement's evolution was El Batey. While he found the homesteaders "serious and energetic and [they] stand a fair chance of being self-sufficient" and their morale "better than expected," the situation in El Batey was alarming. "The Batey group are being too well cared for, they look forward only to leaving Sosúa and going to the United States as soon as possible." Residents there had an untoward sense of entitlement and few cooperative instincts. Living day-to-day on DORSA's penny, they used those funds to hire native labor to complete their tasks. Hexter concluded that El Batey needed to be quarantined from the rest of the settlement "so as not to infect" homesteaders.[56]

El Batey's population actually was growing as the clusters came undone, as settlers gravitated to the colony's cultural and commercial hub, and as some homesteaders, squeezed by management's efforts to control costs, decided to give up farming. The settlement had 487 settlers in the spring of 1943 (261 men, 158 women, and 68 children up to the age of 16). Of those, only 201 colonists lived on homesteads, however, and even that number was deceiving because it contained 42 relatives, many of them elderly, who contributed little to the economic success of those clusters. Only 55 were financially independent of DORSA, and many of those were artisans and small businessmen. Everyone else was either employed by the association or receiving maintenance.[57]

Robert Wishnick, a member of DORSA's board, was exaggerating just a trifle when he told Stern that more than half the settlers were "charity cases."[58] Furthermore, El Batey was costing DORSA plenty. Not counting the deficits incurred from various work relief projects, the association pumped $125,000 into El Batey and its sundry operations in 1945.[59] It is revealing that out of a total of 250 residents living in El Batey by the end of 1944, more than 130 were single men, many of them living out the war and waiting until they could go to America or elsewhere.[60]

El Batey's resident population also included a number who were unstable or mentally ill. They needed to be dealt with separately, Hexter informed Falk.[61] "The presence at Sosúa of a group living on the dole acts as a constant psychological deterrent to our homesteaders." It did not take long for Stern to arrive at the same conclusion: "The large bulk of the population in Sosúa is not colonizable through no fault of their own, and we are faced with the problem of sending a large proportion of them either for resettlement in the cities, trying gradually to remove them from Batey, or maintaining them for many years on relief, or until such time as many of them could filter out into Cuba or other places."[62]

It would be better for all concerned if the "fitter ones" were distributed throughout the island, Hexter believed. Knowing of Falk's close friendship with Trujillo, he asked him to intervene on DORSA's behalf to ship out "a few hundred people at most from the colony . . . many of these non-agriculturalists can be helpful developing business and industry in the cities." Hexter also wanted Falk to speak to Trujillo about the possibility of reworking the original contract provision that held DORSA fiscally responsible for the refugees once they left the colony. If Trujillo consented, then the association could propose a "drop dead date, say January 1, 1947, by which DORSA could suspend payments to settlers . . . [that date] would send a message to settlers that the dole will not go on forever."[63]

While Hexter was in the Dominican Republic, he met with Arturo Despradel, who now was secretary of the interior. They agreed that a small number of people from Sosúa could be moved out of the colony to the capital and other cities, but this had to be done "a few people at a time," with DORSA first locating work for them. Despradel wanted El Batey residents spread throughout the provinces, but the refugees, Hexter told him, were reluctant to leave Sosúa for small provincial towns.[64]

Falk did meet with Trujillo and told Hexter, "the President is . . . ready to be helpful in the transfer of certain of our Batey families to other parts of the country," and he would personally oversee their transfer to government-run colonies. He asked that DORSA send him a "list of candidates for transfer prepared . . . and handed to him directly."[65] That was not a viable solution, of course, because if El Batey residents had been up to the task of working on an agricultural settlement, DORSA already would have provided them with their own homestead.

Hexter concluded that despite Trujillo's good faith efforts, the colony would have to tackle the matter internally. He and Stern decided that the refugee camp needed to be cordoned off and given its own administration.[66] A social worker, William Baum, was sent to the colony in the spring of 1944 to manage a newly formed Batey administration. Baum oversaw all independent artisans, shopkeepers, and trainees. His assignment was to "change the attitude of mind of the 300 people living in Batey, from one of dependence and hostility to one of self-reliance and cooperation," a DORSA executive wrote JDC board members. The staff was given a clear directive to cut costs, pare Dominican workers from the payroll, and put refugees to work. Communal kitchen expenses were to be cut by 30 percent and wages for kitchen help by 50 percent. By the end of 1945, El Batey was costing DORSA 33 dollars a month per capita, a 25 percent cut in expenditures in a little over a year.[67]

In addition, Baum established a straw workshop and a shoe manufacturing plant as work relief programs to give El Batey residents the feeling of "self-support." Although the straw workshop was initially nicknamed the Workshop for the Blind, a pejorative tag for those on the dole, production of baskets and bagging increased to meet growing demand from local and U.S. markets. Native labor was employed to work alongside the settlers on the weaving looms.[68]

Management was torn by the straw shop's success. Administrators wanted to employ refugees living at El Batey, but the shop could hope to realize profits only by utilizing low-wage Dominican labor. At its busiest, the work center employed 100 El Batey residents and 150 Dominicans. Staffers questioned whether it was worth even having a profit in an industry where "it was necessary to employ so many natives." Hexter thought it better to give preference to El Batey residents even if it meant lower profits.[69]

Since it employed so many, the straw shop was a considerable financial drain, prompting a backlash from homesteaders and DORSA staffers in the general administration, who worked with the farmers. Bein mocked the program, calling it WPA prosperity. Stern, although pleased that Baum had been so successful, pointed out that "in many instances the Batey people are able to earn more with greater ease than homesteaders." Officials would continue to debate whether to subsidize the work relief program, but Hexter believed that it had served its purpose by mitigating discontent in El Batey and improving morale more generally throughout the settlement. He praised Baum for succeeding "in transforming a demoralized psychology into a desire on the part of Batey settlers to do something for themselves."[70]

The decision to create two separate administrations was a key structural change, but it was not until Stern arrived and homesteaders came to know and trust him that differences with the administration were patched up. Stern came to the same conclusion as his predecessors. Bemoaning the "dole mentality" that led to "settlers being called *schnorrers*," Stern sounded eerily reminiscent of Rosen.[71] Two weeks after he arrived he sounded an optimistic note: "Life here is beginning to respond to the vibrations of a period of transition. There are people here who understand the time of philanthropy is ending. There are people here wanting to create something and to be productive."[72]

The settlers were wary of lofty rhetoric, however. They had proved themselves tough negotiators, and they knew that DORSA wanted to pull the plug on the maintenance and slash the association's overhead. What they wanted were titles to their own land—what DORSA officials came to call parcelation— and more say in how the settlement was run.

It is one of Sosúa's most exquisite ironies that a grizzled old kibbutz hand would bring about the colony's privatization. How Stern gained the settlers' confidence and ushered in an era of peace and prosperity at precisely the time when more than half the colonists were abandoning Sosúa and packing their bags for America is one of Sosúa's most inspiring stories. But even the golden age that Stern oversaw had its challenges.

Part Four / **MIDDLE AGE**

The Man Who Saved Sosúa

> I did it precisely because I *am* a Zionist. The Talmud says there is
> salvation for him who saves one Jewish soul. The work in Palestine
> has moved forward and is now in capable hands. Here there was
> still a job to do, and I accepted the task. But I am the last director.
> The time will soon be here when the colony will stand on its own
> and be completely self-supporting. Then there will be no need of
> me or anyone else in my capacity.
>
> DAVID STERN, 1949

David Stern brought the settlers together soon after he was appointed executive director in 1945. He introduced them to his
wife and two daughters, and warned them, "I will go with you through
fire and water, but don't let me go through fire and you through water." His admonition was clear: if Sosúa was to survive, the Rat's trade
union mentality had to give way to meaningful cooperation. In return, he promised to be their advocate in New York.[1]

Stern thought Hexter's assessment was on target: Sosúa was at a
crossroads, and concerted action was needed if it was to survive. Colonists were demanding their own homesteads with free and clear title
to the land, while making it clear that Stern's predecessors had promised them DORSA's maintenance as their birthright. Stern's marching
orders, however, were to cut costs and remove the settlers from the
dole. After four years of acrimony, he knew that repairing the combustible relationship between the administration and the Rat would
not be easy.

Stern believed from the start that he could turn the colony around.
Problems could "be solved," he wrote his superiors, "by men with the

willingness to strike roots in this place and overcome all present difficulties for a secure, permanent existence. I am certain that, in spite of the different metamorphoses of this place during the past few years, there are such men here, and this is why I believe in the future of Sosúa."[2] Stern's abiding philosophy, hard won from more than a decade of colonization work in Palestine, was that success was a byproduct of colonists' taking ownership. He told a combined meeting of the DORSA and Agro-Joint boards, "We have to tell them: 'This is your plan, this is your colony; you have to administer it yourselves, and you have to be responsible for the results.'" It was just as important for the colony's long-term viability that DORSA recede from day-to-day operations, because "an administration cannot forever rule a place; if a place is ruled by an administration, and not by itself, it will not progress."[3]

It was critical to foster self-reliance among colonists who had been dependent too long on Mother DORSA. But first there were problems to be resolved. What should be done with that hothouse of discontent at El Batey? With the end of the war fast approaching and U.S. visa restrictions likely to be relaxed, pent-up demand to leave the island posed the headache of how to find replacements for departing colonists, some of whom had expertise essential to the settlement.

A dramatically altered postwar landscape posed challenges unimaginable just a few years before. The territorial impulse to encourage Jews to bloom where they were planted, trumpeted for decades by Non-Zionists, became a lost cause in a post-Holocaust world; it was replaced by an imperative, shared by Western governments and Jewish organizations alike, to create a homeland for the Jews. Henceforth, private and public funds were to be pooled to resettle displaced Jews from Europe and throughout the Diaspora to the Holy Land. The American Jewish Committee and the Joint, which had long resisted Zionism, resigned themselves to the inevitable and closed ranks with their longtime adversaries as prewar bickering gave way to postwar solidarity.

The JDC hierarchy did not take long to question openly why the organization should continue to fund Sosúa when the need was so great in Palestine. More than three million dollars had been invested in the colony up to that point, with little to show for it. The colony was not about to become self-sustaining anytime soon. The debates taking place about the colony's viability at the philanthropy's headquarters had settlers and DORSA's staff on edge.

Hiring Stern to lead Sosúa was by no means an easy task. It required a sales pitch from Hexter, who knew the settlement needed a strong leader, a *mensch*, someone with backbone, who suffered no fools and who also could make the case for the colony's needs in the philanthropy's contentious boardroom. Joint executives voiced reservations about Stern, since he was not one of their own. Born in Russia in 1889, he had moved as a youngster to Palestine in 1905, and his life's work had involved "building up" agricultural settlements. His Zionist credentials did not endear him to the more dogmatic Non-Zionists at the philanthropy.[4]

Hexter pleaded with his colleagues that the colony was adrift and Stern was the right man to take the helm. In an unusually honest mea culpa, Hexter acknowledged, "You and I know how, after Rosen's illness, Sosúa quickly floundered. . . . We have tried since Rosen's illness . . . to find someone to carry on. We failed." The JDC board relented and gave Stern a five-year contract at an annual salary of twelve thousand dollars.[5]

Hexter gave Stern a tremendous amount of latitude, because he did not have the time and energy to devote to the colony himself. DORSA was an add-on for Hexter, occupying a small part of his busy schedule. As executive vice president of the Federation of Jewish Philanthropies, he was busy raising funds for a bundle of worthy causes and guiding and directing allocations of almost a half a billion dollars in contributions. One of the pioneers in the field of social work, first as a practitioner with the Federation in Milwaukee and Cincinnati and then as a teacher and scholar at Harvard during the 1920s, Hexter was an experienced problem solver with excellent interpersonal skills and a keen sense of humor. He first became involved with the Joint after World War I, raising funds for relief and resettlement and traveling throughout Eastern Europe and Russia. In 1929, when the philanthropy asked him to administer the Jewish Agency's agricultural colonization program in Palestine, he came to know and appreciate Stern's work with colonists.[6]

Hexter was deeply moved by the dedicated, idealistic settlers he encountered in Palestine and, like Stern, he was a fervent advocate of colonization. "I was powerfully impressed [in Palestine] . . . by the caliber of the people. . . . I felt that something was happening there and that something could be done, obviously, that the Jewish spirit could live there much more readily than it could anywhere else," he recalled years later. Still, even though he collaborated with Zionists like Stern at the Joint, he never became a true believer: "I never paid the shekel. . . . that *meshugge* [crazy person] I had not become, but I had a deep interest in Palestine as a place . . . where Jewish life could be uniquely lived." He disagreed with "the hot-headed Zionists" who insisted that statehood was essential. His background in colonization work, fundraising abilities, and Non-Zionist sensibilities made him the perfect choice to guide DORSA after Rosenberg stepped down. But Hexter's time-consuming responsibilities with the Federation made it impossible for him to give himself fully to the settlement. It is instructive that his autobiography devotes less than two pages to his experience in the Dominican Republic, even though he would serve as chairman of DORSA's board for more than thirty years. He needed a strong leader in charge on the ground, someone who could size up problems and act on them, and Stern proved to be the right man for the job.[7]

Stern's approach to Sosúa's seemingly insurmountable array of obstacles was to dedicate himself with steely determination and boundless energy over the next five years to promoting his vision of a self-sustaining settlement. DORSA must facilitate its own extinction, he told settlers and staffers repeatedly, gradually divesting itself of its responsibilities as the colonists took charge. At some point, Stern believed, it would be in Sosúa's best interest to become an incorporated village, so that the community could negotiate directly with provincial authorities concerning rural and urban planning, streets, water, electricity, and antimalaria spraying.

Former administrators had talked the same talk, of course, but Stern, the man who homesteaders came to believe "saved Sosúa," succeeded where others had failed. This was because, unlike those who tried unsuccessfully to mediate disputes and placate rival homesteaders and El Batey residents, he consciously took sides. He and Hexter agreed that Sosúa would never have a future if it did not jettison its refugee camp and rededicate itself to its raison d'être.

Stern made it clear that Sosúa was to be a farming colony—case closed. In retrospect, this should not have been surprising to anyone familiar with his work in Palestine, but it was a jolt to a sizable portion of the settlement located in and around El Batey. As Jacob Sondheimer, manager of the general store and a DORSA employee, put it, "the present administration makes it quite clear that it is interested only in the establishment of homesteads, that is, in the settlers, and would like to see that everyone else leaves. In practice this means favoritism toward the homesteaders."[8]

By advocating for the homesteaders, Stern gained their loyalty but alienated the more numerous refugees living at El Batey. He judged correctly, however, that this would be a short-term problem with a viable exit strategy for those who did not share his vision, most of whom eventually would be heading north. His abrasive treatment of the America-Leavers, as those who left after the war were pejoratively called, his shrewd handling of the parceling of individual homesteads, and his calculated way of foisting increased responsibilities onto the settlers' shoulders eventually earned him the admiration of most Sosuaners, but not without a fair measure of criticism. Stern could be testy and bullheaded, admitted Elie Topf. "He called a spade a spade and used salty language to get his point across. But when he said something, you knew that was it." Finally, the settlers had a leader who was just as stubborn as they were.[9]

Stern worked hard to imbue the settlement's future, its youth, with idealism. When he arrived, he found forty adolescents drifting without a purpose. "They live without dreams and ideals. They know life from the negative side. Most of them will not take root here. I wanted to fan a spark of hope in them. I wanted to explain the love of earth, pioneering, the romanticism of the cow barn." Not all youngsters were persuaded by pep talks, however. Some dismissed Stern as a Zionist recruiter; others thought he was grooming workers for the homesteads. But some were taken by his passion for working on the land.[10]

Even America-Leavers like Otto Papernik and Heinrich Wasservogel came to appreciate Stern's mettle. It was not just his lifting of the shackles of dependency but his flexibility that explained his success, Papernik related. "It became a much healthier atmosphere because he approached each problem individually." Except for Rosen, no administrator commanded more respect among the colonists than this diminutive agronomist.[11]

Stern did not deserve all the credit. It was the remaining settlers (reinforced after the war by a small, entrepreneurial contingent of transplants from Shanghai) who met him more than halfway. Together they overcame the exodus for America and diminishing financial support from New York. By taking on all but the most essential services and by establishing cooperatives on the successful CILCA model, the colonists finally suffered the consequences of their own actions and weaned themselves from the administration.

CONSOLIDATION

Sosúa's turnaround began with the agronomist's decision to parcel out farms to homesteaders. When Stern told the homesteaders, "I will fight for you," they knew he meant it.[12] What was left unsaid, but was obvious to those paying close attention, was that if settlers were not willing to commit to the colony, Sosúa was better off without them. Stern needed a critical mass of committed homesteaders to make a go of it. It was a proven fact that colonization schemes were successful if 30 percent of the arrivals stayed, he told the settlers. That rule would be put to the test, because more than half the colonists left in the first five years after the war, and a steady stream continued to depart throughout the 1950s, further depleting the settlement.[13]

When Stern first arrived, he identified two key problems: Rosen's clusters and the repayment of settler debts to DORSA. Echoing former administrators, he wrote to Hexter, "You can't force 18 individuals with different mentalities and abilities to work communally. They are always fighting amongst themselves so that one must always mediate between one and the other, losing time and effort."[14]

In Palestine, Stern had gained a familiarity with both the kibbutz and moshav movements; the former was founded on communitarian principles, while the latter emphasized the collaborative purchasing of supplies and marketing of produce but individual (or family) land ownership. It was this latter model, with some judicious adjustments, that Stern implemented at Sosúa.

The moshav movement in Palestine developed in the 1920s and 1930s as a compromise between the rigorous, communally based kibbutzim and large agricultural colonies based on plantation monoculture and private property. Moshav leaders sought to combine the advantages of the self-sufficient family farm with communal solidarity and cooperation. This model, which excluded hired labor and eschewed dependence on any one product, was attractive to immigrants coming to Palestine from Germany and Austria in the 1930s. Families specialized in the production of certain goods or crops, but the community as a whole strove for self-sufficiency. Communally run processing cooperatives were established to take advantage of economies of scale. In this way, individual initiative and the accumulation of family wealth were balanced against community needs. A village general assembly functioned as a legislative body, which made sure that cooperation was not just a means to an economic end but an essential facet of communal life. Like most kibbutzim, the moshav was secular in its aims, "skeptical of religious truth and opposed to religious education."[15]

Stern realized that the moshav did not ideally fit the conditions at Sosúa, but believed that there were enough points of convergence to merit adapting this model to the colony. The emphasis on the family farm, production cooperatives, community self-governance, and secular values all were a good match. But the reliance on dairying undermined the settlement's self-sufficiency. Aware of the pernicious effects of monoculture, Stern initially encouraged the colonists to diversify.[16] *Pace* Rosen, he was concerned that the colony's reliance on Dominican labor undercut the settlers' attachment to the land and diminished their need to rely on each other. This forced most homesteaders to seek complementary business opportunities, finding employment with DORSA, taking on a job as an administrator for one of the cooperatives, or opening up a private business in Sosúa. They were so caught up in these ancillary activities that they became absentee owners, with "milking done by a Dominican muchacho," which kept them away from their farms.[17]

But the colonists had learned the hard way about the site's physical limitations. The first five years of trial and error had convinced administrators and settlers that dairying was their only viable option. Stern soon realized that Sosúa's best chance for success rested with production for the market, not self-sufficiency.[18] After consultations with settlers and staffers, he set aside his reservations and strove to maximize the dairy industry's potential. Even though that contradicted one of the moshav's fundamental principles, he was flexible enough not to put Sosúa into the straitjacket of an imported model.

Stern's solution was to break up the remaining clusters into thirty-hectare (seventy-five-acre) homesteads. In an arrangement similar to Rosen's homestead plan, each property contained two arable hectares so that crops could be cultivated for subsistence and for the market. The rest would be set aside for pasturage, with one large pasture for the main herd and smaller pastures for bulls and calves. Homesteaders received ten cows (with one additional cow for a settler's wife and two additional for each child), a horse, a mule, and a loan to purchase pigs.

DORSA also agreed to provide water and electricity for the homesteaders, and, for the time being, continued to manage the hospital, the elementary school, and sanitation. Stern insisted, however, that the settlers take over the slaughterhouse, the smokehouse, the general store, and other services. Stern worked up a two-part contract: an individual agreement with each homesteader covering mutual rights and obligations and a codicil with the Settlers' Council pertaining to matters of common interest. Coming to terms with the Rat, however, was made more difficult by years of bickering and mistrust.[19]

While the Rat applauded Stern's efforts to bring about parcelation or consolidation, the settlers proved to be savvy negotiators. The debt was an especially delicate matter; they were adamant that assurances had been given that they would not have to repay all of the initial cost of the houses. Laguna residents insisted that both Rosen and Falk had promised that they would not have to reimburse DORSA for the lands originally given to the clusters. But Falk, still on DORSA's board, vehemently denied that any special deal had been cut with Laguna's clusters. Stern recommended not caving in on this point. Handing over the properties was a prescription for disaster: "In this case we must be absolutely extremist," he told the board, "otherwise we will never finish with Sosúa." Until the homesteaders had a stake in their own properties, they had little incentive to improve their sites.

The value of the homesteads was another point of contention. DORSA's initial investment was six thousand dollars each, but postwar price increases for materials and labor had elevated their cost to ten thousand dollars per site. Stern compromised and fixed the debt for the first fifty-seven homesteaders at about four thousand dollars; later properties were assessed at six thousand dollars to reflect the higher costs. Two percent interest was charged, but DORSA agreed to forego even this nominal rate if settlers doubled up on the ten-dollar-a-month mortgage payments for the first five years.

The Settlers' Council, which was renamed the Homesteaders' Council to better reflect its enhanced clout, also asked what would happen if and when DORSA washed its hands of the colony. Would the settlers' land titles be subject to Dominican law? With DORSA no longer around to protect them, what would stop capricious authorities from seizing properties? The council reminded Stern that the original contract had promised them citizenship after two years, and they were still waiting for their papers. As foreign nationals, what rights did they possess under Dominican law?

Stern reported homesteader concerns to his superiors. Rosenberg thought the Agro-Joint should cosign the individual agreements in the event that DORSA went out of business; but other board members demurred, arguing that this would tie their hands unnecessarily. Bringing up this sensitive issue only hinted at the larger question swirling around the colony's uncertain future: how much longer was New York willing to commit to Sosúa?[20]

While the philanthropists deliberated, the settlers resisted Stern's entreaties to sign the agreements. Dragging their feet, some believed, might win them further concessions. Facing such stalling tactics, Stern counseled the board to be patient: "We don't intend to force them to sign any obligation, although it should be clear that no more money will be invested in Sosúa before the final contracts are signed. If they want to delay the execution of the consolidation plan we are prepared to wait with patience until they are ready. No more concession will be made to them nor any changes granted in the contract, nor any further reduction in the size of the debts."[21] Stern's patience paid off: by July 1, 1945, about half the settlers had come to terms, and by year's end most of the seventy-four had signed the agreements.

Stern, meanwhile, was everywhere at once, meeting regularly with the Rat about the consolidation, lobbying Dominican officials about opening up new domestic and foreign markets for the colony's products, listening to complaints from disgruntled El Batey residents, and writing up detailed reports to keep New York apprised.

In addition, he asked for and received from the board a one-time appropriation of seventy thousand dollars to complete the consolidation. Douglas Blackwood, the animal husbandry director, brought in five hundred additional Dominicans to clear new pasturage, put up barbed wire fences, run power lines, lay water pipes, and construct windmills on sites where it was not cost-effective to connect to the central water system. Breaking up the clusters and establishing individual homesteads was "hard to do on the fly," Stern related to Hexter, because it meant reallocating and establishing "pastures and land while settlers are occupying it and are obliged to derive their livelihood [from it]. . . . In order to establish the pastures, most of the settlers will have to stop using the pastures and milking for an interim period of three to six months."[22] The supplies and equipment for the redesign, moreover, had to be imported from the United States; and even though the material was tax-exempt, the pipes, barbed wire, and other materials got stuck in a bureaucratic logjam in transit. Stern asked Falk to enlist Trujillo to pressure the Foreign Economic Administration in Washington to move more expeditiously on releasing the materials.[23]

The spring and summer of 1945 brought a withering drought, which caused further delays. For Elie Topf, who had just been awarded a homestead, "the cows were starving and dying off. I had to put some on rented pastures just to survive. That first year was just one disaster after another." If his mother-in-law, who was preparing to leave the settlement for the United States, had not offered him a loan, he later recalled, he might not have survived.[24] DORSA staffer Walter Sondheimer offered a similarly bleak assessment. He wrote William Bein in New York that the combination of the lack of rain, inadequate labor for fencing off the new properties, and insufficient feed for the animals were wreaking havoc on the consolidation schedule. Reconfiguring properties and constructing new homes was taking much longer than planned. Still, Stern pushed ahead, and by the end of 1946, fifty-seven homestead sites had been completed with twelve more scheduled for the following year.[25]

If the settlers had reservations about working together in their clusters, they soon realized that they had to band together and pool their resources for the larger processing operations. CILCA's modest profits had offered proof of the benefits of collaboration. Indeed, a kind of cooperative frenzy came over the settlement as shares were sold and swapped for everything from the sausage factory to the hotel. Generally, each cooperative replicated CILCA's method of organization; shareholders came together at a yearly general meeting and elected a board of directors for the next year.

To meet growing postwar demand, CILCA ramped up production. A new factory with two cool rooms and modernized equipment capable of meeting national requirements for pasteurized milk products was opened, to great fanfare, on the cooperative's tenth anniversary, October 24, 1951. Half of the funds for the expansion came from shareholders, the rest from a DORSA loan. In just six years, CILCA's gross earnings skyrocketed from $57,000 to $275,000 (1951). In 1950 and again in 1951, the cooperative received the gold medal for its products by Puerto Plata's Provincial Fair; and a poll taken by the Ciudad Trujillo daily La Nación declared CILCA's butter the best on the island.[26]

CILCA assumed responsibility for maintaining the settlement's agricultural equipment and transport vehicles. Its trucks retrieved milk each day from the fincas and carried it to the processing plant. In 1946 the cooperative purchased a special refrigerated truck which, twice a month, took its products and those of the other cooperatives to the capital and other urban centers.[27] Early on, the cooperative decided not to get into the business of distributing its products, opting instead to work out exclusive agreements with regional wholesalers across the island. A former settler distributed CILCA products in the capital, while Dominican wholesalers did the same in Santiago and Puerto Plata.[28]

One cooperative that had an especially hard time getting off the ground was the GANADERA. Before Stern terminated DORSA's subsidy for the slaughterhouse and smokehouse in 1946, he lobbied officials to permit the cooperative to sell its products in the capital and for export. The sticking point was that Sosúa's slaughterhouse was an independent entity, free of government oversight; therefore it legally "could slaughter, produce and sell only within the boundaries of Sosúa." Stern proposed to establish a municipal slaughterhouse in Sosúa under Puerto Plata's jurisdiction. "This would give Sosúa the right to process, sell and export her products legally." After protracted negotiations with federal and provincial officials, the municipal slaughterhouse was approved. DORSA floated a long-term loan to the GANADERA to build a new facility to government specifications.[29] Shares initially were sold at twenty dollars each, and by the end of 1946, GANADERA was butchering seventeen thousand kilos of beef and pork monthly. Sales for the year amounted to fifty-two thousand dollars. Leo Goldstein, who had learned how to make sausages from his uncle, a butcher, in his native Luxembourg, operated the smokehouse and produced superb kosher salami and sausages. But a fire gutted the factory in 1947 and it had to be rebuilt from scratch. By 1949, the cooperative was back up and running, but the combination of growing pains and the fire meant that shareholders realized few dividends during its formative years.[30]

El Colmado, the general store, became a cooperative in 1945. DORSA, which had managed the store up to that point, turned over the building and its inventory to the settlers, and 160 colonists paid $20 a share to provide working capital. Despite declining numbers of residents, Colmado grosses increased from $80,000 in 1949 to $117,000 in 1951.

A settler credit union, the Caja de Préstamos y Ahorros, was established at the end of 1946 to provide short- and long-term loans to homesteaders and business owners. Individuals received up to three hundred dollars a year, with provisions made for larger loans to cooperatives and private businesses. The JDC provided some seed money for the bank, and by 1949 the Caja had made 130 loans to homesteaders, 21 to small businesses and artisans, and 15 to other cooperatives.[31]

A hotel and restaurant were consolidated into a cooperative in the hope of promoting Sosúa as a tourist destination. Shareholders believed that wealthy Dominicans would flock to the settlement's beach in the summer and during Easter Week, and that foreigners would come during the winter months. Soon vacationing Dominicans from Santiago and the capital were staying at the hotel's five cottages and enjoying the new concrete terrace dance floor, refreshment kiosk, and children's playground. Foreign tourists, however, were more difficult to attract because Sosúa was off the beaten path and officials did little to promote tourism abroad.

By 1949 DORSA had turned over the electrical plant, the medical service, sanitation, and some of the other services to the Rat, but continued to subsidize these operations because the colonists were not in a position to assume the costs of upkeep and maintenance.[32] Although DORSA was committed to scaling back its financial exposure, it continued to assist the settlement in other ways. Blackwood ran his own agricultural extension service of sorts, creating a thriving nursery with two thousand mahogany, three hundred orange, and five hundred avocado trees. He taught the settlers how to graft grapefruit, lemon, and mandarin orange trees. Blackwood also installed five incubators, each with a capacity of two hundred chicks, and soon Sosúa was marketing its eggs in Ciudad Trujillo.[33]

Settlers also learned from each other. When the Topfs were awarded a homestead, Elie, realizing that he was in need of a quick tutorial, asked one of the more successful farmers, Alfred Rosenzweig, if he could stop by his finca and learn how to care for cattle. "There was so much to learn," Topf recalled.

"How to milk cows, how to tell a good one from a bad one, and how to treat them when they got sick or what to do when they hurt themselves on the barbed wire." He proved a quick study and eventually built a herd of more than one hundred.

Topf's cattle were of such high quality that they attracted the attention of the dictator's brother Virgilio, who had made the original offer at Évian and was considered an excellent cattleman. Trujillo approached Topf about purchasing three of his best animals, a cow and two heifers. The deal fell through, however, when a nervous Topf, anxious about setting too high a price and incurring the wrath of a Trujillo, suggested a swap of his three animals for one of Virgilio's young bulls. Still, Topf was proud that the dictator's brother thought so well of his cattle.[34]

Other colonists emulated Topf's success. Stern was happy to report that on average, homesteaders owned twenty cows, three or four heifers, and ten calves. The smallest finca had ten cows and five calves, which, Stern acknowledged, "in these times constitute wealth."[35]

With these encouraging achievements, Stern believed that by the end of 1945 the colony had turned a corner: "The homesteaders . . . feel much stronger and more responsible than before. The cooperation between [them] and the General Administration is very close and the spirit of the majority . . . looks to be good. The initiative of the people will increase especially now when they feel the ground under their feet. Most of the people are disgusted by the maintenance and being governed by somebody."[36] By undoing Rosen's misbegotten clusters, offering homesteads on favorable terms to those ready to make a long-term commitment, facilitating the growth of processing cooperatives, and diverting monies away from Batey's refugee camp to his privatization plan, in five short years Stern had lain the foundation for a successful settlement.

Not everyone shared his optimism, however. El Batey residents understandably were not quite as taken with the wholesale changes. Never shy about speaking their minds, the refugees went over Stern's head and voiced their displeasure to New York. When word arrived soon after v-j Day that American visa regulations were to be eased, many opted to vote with their feet.

FRAYED NERVES

Stern's favoritism toward the homesteaders went well beyond building fences and settling debts. He also imposed economies that discriminated against El Batey residents, leading many of them to conclude that they had no future at Sosúa. High on his agenda was redirecting monies away from the unproductive refugee camp to his favored consolidation program and allied enterprises. When he took over, only one of four colonists lived on the land, and more than a fifth of the budget went to care for those living at El Batey.[37] If Sosúa was to move forward, Stern contended, both colonists and resources had to be redirected toward the homesteads. To accomplish this, "we had to re-organize or liquidate certain enterprises, established during the war, which economically cannot exist on post-war conditions."[38] Maintenance and make-work projects were the settlement's twin Achilles' heels, and they needed to be pared down if Sosúa was to become self-sustaining. Maintenance for El Batey residents was slashed from thirty-five thousand to ten thousand dollars in his first year alone.[39] Sosúa could no longer afford the luxury of unproductive enterprises.

Stern closed down the settlement laundry and the public kitchen and began to charge colonists seventeen dollars a month for full board at the association-owned restaurant. After five years of free board, needless to say, "this was not easily accepted by the people concerned." Now El Batey residents had to pay a dollar a month for a room and four to five dollars a month for houses. Such was the sense of entitlement that outraged residents wrote letters to New York protesting the new fees. Stern also closed DORSA's carpentry, mechanic, and blacksmith shops and gave three thousand dollars in start-up loans to artisans and entrepreneurs (some of them former DORSA employees) to establish their own businesses.[40]

Perhaps Stern's most controversial move was to shut down the straw shop. Although this work center never realized a profit despite taking advantage of low-wage native labor, "the goods produced were favorably accepted by the local and U.S.A. markets and orders were gradually coming in" until the end of the war. After V-E Day, however, orders had dried up.[41] Stern's prudent decision to close the shop proved very unpopular, however, as dozens of El Batey residents were now without work and had to be put back on relief.[42]

El Batey residents vented their displeasure to travelers, tourists, and staffers. Ira Morris, a writer who spoke fluent German, visited for two weeks in 1946 and came away convinced they had reason to feel aggrieved. In a letter to DORSA board member Robert Pilpel, he called El Batey unacceptable, "a living standard unsuited to Europeans even of the peasant and workman class." Many residents, including married ones, were "still living in rickety, marginal-nature barracks." Morris derided Stern's elimination of the straw shop, citing the action's harmful impact on those let go. "The unemployed receive maintenance payments so low it is quite impossible for them to do more than buy the bare food necessities." Everyone knew that Sosúa's annual budget was over a quarter of a million dollars a year, Morris noted, so why the need for "over-stringent economies inaugurated by the present director?" While Morris certainly exaggerated when he estimated that three-fourths of the homesteaders wanted to leave, his diatribe conveyed the depth of feeling against Stern among the nonsettlers. Few El Batey residents would have disagreed with Morris's characterization of Stern: "tactless, hard-boiled, insensitive to refugees . . . he has said time and again that he is 'not interested' in the townspeople of Batey though the majority of Sosuans live there."[43]

Stern thought he needed to respond to Morris's broadside and to the "gossips and agitators." "They are demoralizing the existing population, and part of them is spreading rumors and complaints against Sosúa and its administration not only in this country, but abroad, too. It is understandable that visitors and tourists in Sosúa are sometimes impressed by their complaints and rumors and might get the impression of a Sosúa in liquidation."[44]

The furor over Stern's reorganization plan occurred at the same time that approximately one hundred El Batey residents and an unanticipated number of homesteaders were beating a path to the U.S. consulate in Ciudad Trujillo. Word that President Harry Truman had issued a series of executive directives on immigration on December 22, 1945, hit the settlement like a lightning bolt.

AMERICA-LEAVERS

Even though existing limits on immigration were not altered, preferential treatment was to be given to displaced persons or people who, as a result of the war, had been forcibly removed from their homelands and who needed assistance until they could be resettled or repatriated. Of special interest to the settlers was an executive order stipulating that for the next year, two-thirds of the quotas for all nations were to be allotted to Germany, and German displaced persons (or DPs) could now emigrate without having a relative in the United States. This meant that Sosúa's German-born could immigrate to America with relative ease. In addition, Truman's directives permitted the use of corporate affidavits, which provided "blanket financial guarantees for groups of successful applicants." This facilitated emigration and was an "efficient alternative to the time-consuming work of preparing individual guarantees."[45]

But just who was a German was an ambiguous question. Austrian-born Sosuaners who had witnessed their country annexed to the Reich in March 1938 were now, according to Truman's new directive, no longer considered

Germans, because the new criterion was place of birth. Even though many Austrian Jews had registered before the war under the German quota, Washington now determined Austria to be an independent country, and the refugees' prior registrations were canceled.[46] Sorting out the legal technicalities of these changes to immigration procedures did little to soothe the nerves of anxious El Batey residents.

Officially, DORSA's policy was not to stand in the way of anyone wanting to leave the colony. Staffers were told not to "urge or stimulate anyone to stay or leave."[47] But it was clear that administrators in Sosúa and New York felt betrayed by the prospect of a mass exodus. They worried that the visa rush might snowball and draw in homesteaders. Papernik related that "the DORSA Administration took a dim view" of those choosing to leave. New York informed Stern that those homesteaders applying for immigration "had to give up their farms and move to the Batey while they were waiting for affidavits.... Those farms were to be given to settlers who intended to stay."[48] As a result, the decision to leave, Papernik recalled, was made easier by the stigma that management placed on those who chose to do so.

Stern, moreover, made few friends when he curtailed maintenance payments and designed a make-work program expressly for the America-Leavers. With much of the Dominican labor force occupied with building fences and other infrastructure associated with the consolidation plan, Stern needed workers to construct housing for the new homesteads. He asked Papernik to assemble two work details of twenty-five America-Leavers and give them an overnight education in rough construction.

"Unofficially that was to be a punishment for abandoning this noble undertaking and ingratitude toward the country that had given us a haven and security during the war," Papernik sneered. When Stern told him how much DORSA was prepared to pay the inexperienced work teams, Papernik retorted, "I told [him] that for those amounts we could not even expect them to come to the building site—much less to do some work." Sure enough, a dispute broke out about wages as five America-Leavers refused to participate, deriding Stern's initiative as "Hitler work." The rest of the work detail showed up, however, if only to pass the time while they waited for their visas and to save money for their move to the United States.[49] Stern told his superiors that after a bumpy start, attitudes improved, "most of them are glad to work and . . . only very few refuse to do construction work."[50]

Stern bore the brunt of the criticism of those preparing to leave, and it started to take its toll. "My nerves are sufficiently strong to struggle in an open fight with different people here in Sosúa, who are here only temporarily and whose only desire is to get from DORSA as much as possible," he wrote. "But sometimes it is difficult to avoid a knife stabbed in one's back."[51]

Homesteaders rallied to Stern's defense to counter the criticism coming from El Batey. They wrote to Hexter in May 1946 that although sensitivity had not been Stern's strong suit in dealing with the America-Leavers, he had in good faith tried to respond to their complaints, even though everyone knew he was better disposed to address colonization matters. The Rat reminded Hexter that several years earlier it had complained bitterly about Arons, who needed to be fired. Now it was time to stop airing Sosúa's "dirty linen," they concluded: "today we oppose such letters [from Batey residents] because we know that they want to harm not only the administration but also Sosúa, and we won't permit it that we should be hurt in our development and our building. We beg you to support Mr. Stern."[52]

If Stern could take some solace from knowing he had the homesteaders' backing, he also refused to paint all El Batey residents with the same brush. "Most of the people leaving for the United States . . . are trying to be loyal and to negotiate with me honestly even in matters of different opinion." Nevertheless, the sooner the America-Leavers left the better, as far as he was concerned.[53] He reported in early 1946 that "those awaiting their visas, their moral attitude . . . is that of 'I don't care.'" They not only had little interest in what happened to the settlement afterward, but they were likely to persuade others to join them.[54] The way the refugees justified leaving was to denigrate the administration, to convince others that the settlement would continue to sputter and had no real future, and to persuade themselves and their peers that America offered a better future.[55]

Leaving was a protracted affair; the paperwork took anywhere from one month to one year to be processed.[56] Security checks, medical examinations, and layers of bureaucracy created anxiety for the emigrants and headaches for management. Rumors circulated about why some people received their papers and others were delayed. Papernik captured the anxious moments well: "It was a constant coming and going to the capital and all kinds of stories were told, how a small affidavit was accepted and a larger one refused, and an x-ray plate showed a scar on it and the man was refused because they suspected lung problems."[57]

Even though America's allure was very strong, the decision to move there was not made without considerable soul searching. For those who had married, given birth to children, and watched them grow up at Sosúa, the settlement was their home. Some friends were choosing to stay while others wanted to go, making the decision that much more difficult.[58]

Otto and Irene Papernik really wrestled with the decision, and Otto was remarkably reflective about the choices facing individuals and families. He and his family did not choose to leave right after the war, as did so many of his neighbors in El Batey. He had his own cabinetmaking shop and, although he had little interest in farming, he had the talent and drive to prosper at Sosúa. The decision to leave in 1950 proved agonizing. "We, who thought that Sosúa would be our permanent residence, began to worry. We saw our doctors, nurses, barbers, and other professionals leave for the United States and reporting back of a completely different life there. Better sanitary conditions, larger incomes and best of all, regular schools for the children. . . . It was with great sadness when we finally made up our mind to leave Sosúa."[59] "Mixed feelings" marked their departure; "having to say 'good-by' to so many friends was one of the hardest things to do."[60]

Ultimately, going or staying came down to a personal decision. Topf, who had fallen in love with fellow colonist Susi Ehrlich at Sosúa soon after he arrived in 1942, told her that although he loved her very much, he needed to wait until his personal situation clarified before committing to marriage. "I didn't know where my people were. We had no news. It was agonizing. Maybe I would go back to Austria and try to make things better there, or go to America. I just didn't know," he recalled. After the war ended, however, he received the bittersweet news that although his mother had been gassed in Auschwitz and his father had died in Buchenwald, miraculously, his sister had survived by working at a munitions factory near Auschwitz. All his other siblings had survived the war as well; two were in England, one was in Switzerland, and Lisle and his brother-in-law David Kahane had their own homestead at Sosúa. When Stern offered him a homestead should he and Susi marry, it clinched their decision to stay. They were married in October 1945, and a year later moved onto their finca.[61]

Sometimes serendipity led to America. Hellie Goldman recalled that one day an affidavit unexpectedly arrived in the mail from her husband's brother in Bridgeport, Connecticut, sponsoring the Goldmans. "We went to the U.S. consul, who told us the affidavit was as good as gold."[62]

Those with families had to weigh whether the Dominican Republic was where they wanted to put down roots. An unidentified Sosuaner simply could not imagine a future for his family as Dominican nationals. "For a while we lived as in a golden cage. They [DORSA] took care of us . . . but soon our children grew older. . . . When they reached their teens, we knew it was now or never. We had to leave or face assimilation."[63]

As difficult as the decision was, the exodus of more than half of the settlement during the postwar years put Stern and his superiors in a quandary. For every America-Leaver who had added little to Sosúa and had lived out the war in anticipation of this day, there were others who had been contributors and whose talents would be sorely missed. Stern needed replacements right away if his vision was to become a reality. JDC leaders, however, were not prepared to meet him halfway.

"STANDSTILL IS RETROGRESSION"

Facing the prospect of losing a considerable number of colonists, Bein pleaded with Hexter in September 1945 to clarify the philanthropy's commitment to the colony. "We are daily asked [by homesteaders] as to what will be the future of Sosúa? Will those leaving Sosúa be replaced by newcomers? What is the policy of the DORSA concerning additional immigration to the Dominican Republic? Can such a small community exist on its own?"[64] Those questions were on the collective mind of the JDC, the Agro-Joint, and DORSA leaders as they met throughout the second half of 1945 and the winter and spring of 1946.

Walter Sondheimer, Sosúa's manager, and William Baum, the manager of El Batey, were called to New York to present a "state of the settlement" briefing at a joint meeting of the JDC and DORSA boards on October 16, 1945. Sondheimer spoke about the consolidation program and the homesteaders' unsettled frame of mind, while Baum discussed the America-Leavers and the general situation at El Batey.

Reminiscent of Hexter's admonition about the dangers of "freezing" a colonization project two years before, Sondheimer began by pleading with the boards to locate replacements for the America-Leavers as soon as possible. "At present Sosúa is static. Standstill is retrogression. As an . . . isolated community in a strange subtropical land the settlement is doomed to disintegration. Like all live communities, particularly during the pioneering stage, Sosúa must have a steady flow of prospective settlers through its structure, so that those properly suited for the community will truly settle there. Otherwise if no new immigrants come, even the homesteaders will leave in due course. . . . European immigrants of the proper type can be made self-supportive in Santo Domingo and in Sosúa. This has been learned, admittedly at considerable cost."[65] Then Sondheimer took a step back and reflected on DORSA's larger objectives. Those who worked for the association believed in its mission and were committed to keeping Sosúa alive "as a nucleus for eventual postwar colonization in the western hemisphere. We felt we had the possibility for World Jewry to eventually prove its ability to undertake group settlement in the American subtropics." Those lofty sentiments may have moved philanthropists before the war, but Sondheimer knew that the pragmatic men at the table were struggling with priorities and that Sosúa's significance paled in comparison to coping with the demands of postwar resettlement. Still, the Joint's indecision was causing "appreciable moral damage" and actually encouraging the settler exodus. Sosúa was reaching a critical moment, Sondheimer cautioned. Be decisive, he urged the boards, because if no clear signal was given, "the pressure of time and the stream of events will eventually dissolve whatever has been built up. You will have a natural liquidation."[66]

Baum's presentation largely focused on El Batey, but he, too, made a heartfelt plea "to fill up the gaps left by those leaving." Even a modest number of replacements, perhaps 250 to 300, would be sufficient; half to replace those leaving and the rest to give the settlement a fighting chance. He estimated that it would cost roughly an extra $250,000 to $300,000 to bring that number in and integrate them into the settlement. If the JDC could not commit to that, then the settlement should be shut down and an immigration office opened at Sosúa "to bring about an orderly liquidation."[67]

Paul Baerwald, the JDC's chairman, responded that investing that amount of money in Sosúa was difficult to imagine, given all the competing requests. Deliberations languished through the winter and spring of 1946. What brought matters to a head was Stern's extraordinary one-time, three-hundred-thousand-dollar request to establish twenty more homesteads for new arrivals from Europe and elsewhere; to resettle an additional forty "relative families," who would move in with their kin already established on homesteads; and to bring in fifty artisans to replace those heading north. On June 11, 1946, the boards met with Stern and Hexter in New York, ostensibly to consider whether the Joint and its two subsidiaries could meet Stern's special request.

The meeting took place at a pivotal moment. Everyone in attendance, from the Joint's board chairman, Edward Warburg, to DORSA warhorses Rosenberg and Hexter to Stern and his lieutenants, knew what was at stake. As if to accentuate that point, in an unusual step, a stenographer was present to record the deliberations, and the frank, unusually forthcoming exchanges later were bound and printed for posterity. The result is a revealing document that illustrates how divided the JDC and DORSA were at that moment about the colony's future and how the settlers once again had become pawns in a larger chess match, their prospects tied to a new international reality.[68]

An irritated Moses Leavitt, the JDC's secretary, cut to the chase soon after Stern formally submitted his request. In view of all the other urgent needs that the JDC was trying to address after the war, Leavitt thought Stern's three-hundred-thousand-dollar request "an extravagance." "In the year 1946, when we are keeping people on starvation diets in Europe, we are asked to think in terms of this sort of budget. I am not saying that all your . . . experimentation is not desirable, but I do say it is a tremendous luxury for us . . . and there is a real question in my mind as to whether the JDC has a right to indulge in that luxury. For a long time it has done so. One hundred thousand displaced Jews who had survived the Holocaust, many of them "half-starved, needing not only medical care but literally every type of assistance," were littered from Germany to Austria, from Italy to Shanghai, and they had to be resettled quickly, Leavitt recalled years later. A determination had been made to relocate many of the DPs to Palestine.[69]

Too much had been invested in Sosúa to walk away now, Stern countered. "Settlers say that if the settlement is frozen, they will leave. That will be not only a loss of money; it will mean a moral shock if we do not finish our work in Sosúa."

Leavitt shot back, "with all the good intentions on the part of Mr. Stern, I don't believe that it [Sosúa] would become a self-supporting community." Jewish communities, he lectured, required costly communal services, such as hospitals, schools, water supply, road repairs, and so on; expenses "that ordinarily are taken care of by a community" taxing itself. He added, "300 people living in Sosúa cannot tax themselves sufficiently to take care of those services. If we go into it, we have to think in terms of a steady annual grant. Our hope is that it will become less and less as the years go by and as those people become more and more established."

Joseph Hyman added that someone here or there might be interested in resettling in the Dominican Republic, but it was clear that worldwide Jews were speaking with one voice about Palestine. "That is what the Jewish people want—and, as long as they want it, we are bound to go along with their wishes and their desires." Hyman went on to pose a question, one that must have given Stern pause: "If the only justification is to prove to everybody concerned, including Latin American opinion, that Jews can settle successfully, that, of course, is a valid contention. However, I wonder if its validity is as important, in relation to the sum total of Jewish need all over the world, as it is to put the same effort to bear in sending people to Palestine today."

All present knew that Stern had divided loyalties; a Zionist, he had left work that he sincerely believed in to help a small number of struggling Jews halfway across the globe, and now his judgment was being questioned. Hyman and the Joint had resisted efforts to subsidize colonization in Palestine for decades. Who were they now to lecture Stern about the propriety of funding this tiny settlement? Still, Hyman would not let the matter drop. "I know this is a tough thing to say to you, Mr. Stern, as an old Zionist and a colonizer in Palestine. Some of us were never Zionists, but some of us have come increasingly to the conviction that this is the only thing we can do in terms of successful settlement. Is it the right thing for the JDC, in the light of all its present obligations, to put in more money to sustain this present colony?"

Hexter leaped to Stern's defense, asking board members to put themselves, for a moment, in the settlers' shoes. "I can't blame the settlers if they want to leave! What has a successful homesteader who has a hundred cattle got to look forward to? There he is, 225 kilometers from the capital city, with a lopsided biological pyramid there and with a system of education that is tertiary in the main city—and you can imagine what it is out in the province of Puerta Plata. . . . I wouldn't blame them for wanting to leave under those circumstances."

Hexter had identified three key factors weighing on America-Leavers' decisions to stay or go: the absence of quality education for their children, the settlement's future economic viability, and the question of whether clannish Jews would ever feel comfortable in a racially diverse society like the Dominican Republic. The only reason a settler might consider staying, Hexter continued, was if he saw the possibility of "more people coming, of more people becoming independent, of his children having a Jewish society in its best sense." Otherwise, Sosúa "will go the way of all those abortive attempts to start colonization in other parts of the world."

Hexter was obviously upset with the philanthropy's reluctance to see the Sosúa experiment through. Didn't they see that they were just spiting themselves? After all, "by taking away money from the Agro-Joint," he had written JDC board member Isaac Levy a year before, "they're taking away money from themselves. . . . The Agro Joint is their very own child." He never would have agreed to become DORSA's president if the JDC had not been committed to the enterprise. Now, two years after he had signed on, it appeared that the JDC wanted to cut its losses and move on.[70]

Levy objected to Hexter's insinuation that the JDC had a moral obligation to continue to support Sosúa. Hexter had a nerve to lecture the board; after all, it was the Joint that had "bailed out a nearly bankrupt DORSA" after the Brookings report was released and had continued to support it in the face of criticism. Levy reminded Hexter that the JDC had invested in four or five different surveys for Sosúa, "each one eventuating in something different. Different problems and difficulties were discovered." Now Stern was presenting them with a new consolidation plan. "We have had proposals in the past that we have supported, and they have been failures." The straw shop was a case in point, Levy reminded the boards. He closed his rebuttal by reminding Hexter and the others that the Joint had always said yes to Sosúa, "never no." But now, "we're being hit up with requests from all over, Poland, Palestine, etc., all desperate, all talking about the same dire consequences, urgent needs. We have to correlate this situation with other situations."

Next, Warburg weighed in, seeking to bring closure to the contentious debate. "I think that what is over the dam is over the dam." It was time to stop assigning blame, he counseled. The JDC had spent a pretty penny on Sosúa, and decisions had been made in the heat of the moment that had turned out poorly. "We are at a turning point at which a decision is required of the JDC. . . . First, it is hoped . . . it cannot be guaranteed by anybody . . . that, with the grant . . . that the colony might well become a self-sufficient colony. . . . Balancing that picture . . . the alternative is that if such funds are not available and if we go along constantly with patch-work grants—small sums here and there—the colony will start to disintegrate because of the lack of encouragement to the settlers, and the settlers will try to go elsewhere." Before the boards arrived at that decision, Warburg had questions of his own: "What is the penalty of liquidation? . . . What will be its psychological effect, its international effect? . . . Could [the settlers] find a place elsewhere?"

Sosúa's advocates argued that it would send a chilling message to the DPs in Europe to close down one of the few (relatively) successful examples of colonization still extant. Then Stern honestly answered Warburg's question about what would befall the settlers should Sosúa be liquidated. Yes, the homesteaders would be fine, if that was what was decided. They would take what they had earned and move on, and build new lives for themselves in the United States or elsewhere. The meeting ended with the boards' agreeing to give the matter some more thought before reaching a decision.

Meanwhile, the Joint also had to respond to an unusual request; and although they did not know it, the homesteaders were suddenly thrown a life preserver from an unexpected source. General Trujillo sent the Joint a proposal that forced it to reconsider pulling the plug on Sosúa. Trujillo wanted the Joint to bring in thousands of Jewish DPs right away, and wondered if the philanthropy would also consider investing in the Dominican Republic's economic future. To the old-timers at DORSA and the Joint, it must have seemed like Évian déjà vu. To the Sosuaners, it was another indication of how their lives were once again bound up in decisions made in distant capitals for reasons that had little to do with their settlement.

THIRTEEN

A *"Splendid President"*

> No matter how much Mr. Stern tells the Dominican Government
> that Jewish refugees coming to the Dominican Republic, not at our
> insistence, are not our charge, they will be a problem for the JDC
> and the matter will be on the doorstep of the JDC.
>
> JAMES ROSENBERG TO EDWARD WARBURG AND MAURICE
> HEXTER, 1946

Avra Warren was no friend to DORSA, but he was everything Trujillo ever could have wanted in an ambassador. He "presided over the closest Dominican-American relations in history" during his tenure in Ciudad Trujillo from 1942 to 1944.[1] To reward Trujillo for his unflinching support for the Allied war effort, diplomatic representation was elevated to embassy status in both capitals in 1943 during Warren's tenure.[2] The opening of ports for U.S. Navy refueling, the establishment of military missions, and steps taken to root out Nazi sympathizers made it easier for the ambassador to overlook the dictator's brutality.

Warren also took pleasure in Trujillista pomp and circumstance and made every effort to visibly demonstrate support at civic parades and patriotic celebrations. At the general's 1942 inauguration, Warren presented Trujillo with an honorary degree from the University of Pittsburgh, praising his humanitarianism and his accomplishments in education and finance. That honor had been arranged by DORSA's Leon Falk, who hailed from Pittsburgh and had ties to the university. It was DORSA's way of reciprocating for the honorary degree awarded to James Rosenberg by the Universidad de Santo Domingo Law School eighteen months earlier. Trujillo later returned the favor once again by having the university bestow an honorary degree on the U.S. ambassador.[3]

Warren and Trujillo formed an especially close bond. The ambassador even enrolled his son in the Dominican Military Academy at Haina. In the past, the War and State Departments had been at odds about whether and how the United States should demonstrate support for the dictator. But now the State Department's envoy had no compunction about aligning "his policies with the American military [and empowering] the military attachés on his staff." Not surprisingly, during Warren's two-year stay, the Dominican Republic received ample Lend-Lease materiel, including aircraft, tanks, and arms, making it possible for Trujillo to build the most potent military machine in the Caribbean.[4]

Warren's tenure as ambassador coincided with internal upheavals in the State Department that had ramifications for U.S.-Dominican relations, DORSA, and Sosúa. Cordell Hull's position as secretary of state had become increasingly problematic. As the diplomatic historian Irwin Gellman notes, "In public, Roosevelt continued to rely on Hull's great prestige, but in private the president still belittled him and single-handedly directed wartime policy."[5] Moreover, Hull chafed at Sumner Welles's privileged access to Roosevelt. The undersecretary's stature had eclipsed his own.

The more Roosevelt demeaned Hull and distanced him from the conduct of the war, the more he consulted Welles, and the more Hull suspected his subordinate of disloyalty. Then, in the summer of 1943, rumors of Welles's homosexuality surfaced, and Hull seized the moment to demand that the president remove his rival. FDR reluctantly agreed, and rather than accept a demotion, Welles resigned in August.[6] Even so, Welles's resignation did not give Hull any greater access to Roosevelt—Hull did not even have prior knowledge of the Allied invasion of Normandy—nor did it win him friends in the administration or at the State Department. His failing health and frequent leaves of absence only added to the perception that he was not paying adequate attention to the refugee problem.

Henry Morgenthau was furious particularly with the State Department's callous inattention to the plight of European Jewry. By 1943 the Nazis' heinous crimes were common knowledge, and the Secretary of the Treasury had his staff work up a no-holds-barred report of State Department ineptitude and inaction. On January 17, 1944, he presented "his indictment" to Roosevelt. Morgenthau argued that Hull's State Department was badly compromised and asked if Treasury could assume responsibility for handling the refugee crisis. Realizing that public opinion was now more sympathetic toward the

Jews and that his administration needed to take some action, Roosevelt instructed Morgenthau to form the War Refugee Board in January 1944. American Jewish organizations were relieved that the State Department was no longer an obstacle, and they jumped at the opportunity to work with the new board. The Joint generously stepped up and contributed fifteen million of the twenty million dollars authorized by the War Refugee Board during its seventeen-month existence. But the board's effort, although "commendable . . . was a prime example of too little, too late."[7]

Welles had been Trujillo's long-time nemesis. With Welles ousted, many of his supporters at the State Department, who shared his revulsion for the dictator's methods, were effectively neutralized. Perhaps even more significant was that the exiled Dominican political opposition had now lost a powerful advocate. Welles's fall from grace meant that Hull's more instrumentalist approach to U.S.–Latin American affairs, which only gave lip service to democratic reform, would hold sway at the State Department.

The new architect of policy was Nelson Rockefeller, who had just been appointed Assistant Secretary of State. Rockefeller and Warren, both Republicans, were committed to Hull's pragmatic approach. Rockefeller promoted Warren to head the American Republics Division. With Trujillo, Warren, and Rockefeller all on the same page, economic and military assistance flush, and domestic and exiled opponents on the defensive, the future seemed bright for the general. Matters were so well in hand that, for the moment, there was no need to call on Rosenberg and DORSA to lobby on his behalf in Washington.

That honeymoon proved fleeting, and it did not take long before DORSA was once again asked to smooth over tensions between Ciudad Trujillo and Washington. Warren's successor as ambassador, Ellis Briggs, arrived in June 1944 and immediately began to criticize the dictator. An acerbic New Englander, Briggs was infuriated by Trujillo's "colossal vanity" and greed and was appalled by the sycophants who surrounded the general.[8] The worst policy the United States could pursue with someone so "hard, competent, corrupt, ruthless and unbelievably vain" was appeasement, Briggs informed Hull. Briggs also saw through Trujillo's carefully constructed reputation for humanitarianism. Sosúa's administrators would have been chagrined to learn that Briggs believed the colony was "largely a failure."[9]

Briggs's account of Trujillista tyranny was eerily reminiscent of Welles's. Indeed, Trujillo erroneously thought the former undersecretary was behind Briggs's one-man offensive.[10] In a report written four weeks after he arrived in the Dominican capital, Briggs called the regime "most efficient," one in which more material progress had been made than any other in the nation's history;

but he was quick to add that "a shadow of fear covers the country" and "the most representative gesture of a Dominican citizen is looking over his shoulder to see whether he is being overheard." If one hallmark of the regime was the silencing of its enemies, another was its aggrandizing pursuit of wealth. Trujillo's regime was "an enterprise operated primarily for the personal enrichment of himself, his relatives and his satellites. His greed results in the impoverishment of the Dominican people, economically and morally." Of course, Briggs understood why Washington did not criticize past collaboration with Trujillo.

> I realize that during the period between Pearl Harbor and our invasion of North Africa—during which a German attack on the New World was a real possibility—the security of the Caribbean was a matter of supreme importance, overshadowing all other considerations. That however was two years ago. . . . The fact that Trujillo has declared himself to be "on our side" in this war, and that he is collaborating with us in certain international matters, should not blind us to the realities of his domestic administration nor to the implications within the important area of our general international relations, of our doing business with Trujillo on any except our own carefully considered terms. Those terms should be based on fair and honest dealings and on unwavering insistence upon reciprocal integrity in the dealings of the Dominican Government with us.[11]

In other words, with victory in Europe now imminent and Dominican military and political support for Fortress America no longer a matter of geopolitical necessity, it was high time that Washington demand more than loyalty from its clients.

Briggs went even further. The straight-shooting, if impolitic, diplomat urged U.S. companies to shun state functions and avoid even the appearance of support for Trujillo's upcoming re-election. Briggs also turned off the Lend-Lease spigot, a move that infuriated the dictator.[12]

Trujillo sought to put the ambassador in his place by going over his head and appealing to Briggs's superiors at State and to his old friends at the War Department. He asked Warren, and Warren agreed, to come down to Ciudad Trujillo and appear at a public function to demonstrate continuing support. Briggs was livid that he had not been informed about Warren's visit. Trujillo hosted a state dinner in honor of Warren's good friend, Rockefeller, in November 1944, at which the guest of honor was placed at the head table and the ambassador was shunted to a table out on the floor, a slight the sensitive Briggs characterized as an "insult to the president of the United States." The ambassador was left to twist in the wind when Rockefeller appointed Warren chief of the American Republics Division. The coup de grâce came after FDR's reelection to a fourth term in 1944, when Briggs, along with all the other chiefs of mission, tendered his pro forma resignation. His was the only one accepted. Briggs was convinced that Trujillo had asked Warren to fire him.[13] It seemed that Trujillo once again had weathered the storm.

Trujillo's end-run around Briggs brought him only temporary respite. Hull's tuberculosis had spread by October 1944, and a month later he submitted his resignation. Roosevelt's death the following April signaled that the administration's Good Neighbor policy was now open for reinterpretation.

Hull's resignation unnerved Trujillo; it would have been difficult to imagine a more supportive secretary of state. With the man who had called Trujillo a "splendid president" no longer in power, the antidictatorial camp in the State Department seized the initiative. Seven months after his resignation was accepted, Briggs rose from the ashes when Spruille Braden replaced Rockefeller as assistant secretary in the fall of 1945. Briggs had worked under Braden in Cuba, and they saw eye to eye on Trujillo. "Unlike his predecessor, Avra Warren," Braden later recalled, "who had been palsy walsy with . . . Trujillo, self-styled 'Benefactor' of Santo Domingo, Briggs treated the monster with chilly correctness and soon won his venomous hate by interfering with his schemes."[14] What must have given Trujillo additional pause was that both diplomats were well acquainted with the exiled opposition from their stay in Havana, and knew that his opponents were scheming to launch an invasion of their homeland to overthrow the dictator.[15]

Braden had just made a splash, appearing on the cover of *Time* magazine for his criticism of Argentine president Juan Perón's fascist leanings. His appointment by Truman suggested that policy toward dictatorships throughout the hemisphere in general, and toward Trujillo specifically, was about to undergo a sea change. Unlike Welles, whose disapproval of dictatorships always had been reined in by his pragmatic boss, Braden was given a free hand by the new secretary of state, James Byrnes, who told Truman in March 1946 that Trujillo was the "most merciless" tyrant "and we ought scrupulously [to] avoid even the appearance of giving him any support."[16]

Braden treated Trujillo coldly but correctly. In certain cases, he contended, U.S. nonintervention—a cornerstone of the Good Neighbor policy—actually inhibited free elections and promoted authoritarianism. Braden refused a Dominican request for additional arms, informing the Foreign Ministry that as far as he could surmise, "the only possible use to which [Trujillo] could put such arms was against his neighbor Haiti or against his own long-suffering and exploited people."[17] He then named Joseph McGurk to replace Briggs as ambassador; McGurk conformed to Braden's (and Briggs's) views of Trujillo. McGurk stayed only long enough to contract malaria and left the island in October 1945. He was not replaced for nearly a year. This served as notice from Braden that the Dominican Republic's relevance to policymakers had dipped precipitously.[18]

When Trujillo had the gall to propose renaming the border town where the 1937 massacre had begun "Franklin D. Roosevelt," Braden protested so vehemently that the general thought better of it and dropped the idea.[19] Then Braden sent a scathing aide-mémoire to Trujillo's Foreign Ministry, which explained why the U.S. would no longer pander to Trujillo. "The Government and people of the United States necessarily have a warmer friendship for and a greater desire to cooperate with those governments which rest upon periodically and freely expressed consent of the governed. This Government has over the past years observed the situation in the Dominican Republic and has been unable to perceive that democratic principles have been observed there in theory or in practice."[20] An insulted Trujillo pouted to a U.S. diplomat, "We are still your friends, even if we are your mistreated friends," and then called on his well-paid lobbyists to take his case straight to the White House.[21]

Even though Trujillo made certain that the aide-mémoire never became public knowledge, he decided, for the first time since he assumed power in 1930, to make concessions and give the domestic opposition the opportunity to form political parties for the 1947 presidential elections. Cynics suggested that Trujillo did this only to flush them out. Politicians, university students, and labor organizers took advantage of the opening throughout the summer of 1945, forming independent labor unions and holding anti-Trujillo demonstrations. The democratic renaissance proved short-lived, however, and several months after the opposition surfaced, the regime cracked down.[22]

Of greater concern to Trujillo than the weak domestic opposition, however, was the fear that an about-face in Washington would encourage the better-organized and -funded exiles. With dictatorships giving way to democratic governments in Venezuela, Guatemala, and Cuba, new civilian presidents throughout the region began to assist the exiles, who operated openly in Cuba and Venezuela and made common cause with dissidents from other Caribbean and Central American nations intent on overturning their own dictatorships.[23]

The Caribbean Legion, as this loose conglomeration of exiles, adventurers, gangsters, and mercenaries came to be called, staged a series of military actions against the Dominican Republic and Nicaragua over the next few years. Dominican exiles were the Caribbean Legion's most dynamic and consistent presence. Convinced that Trujillo's ironclad grip on the nation precluded a domestic uprising, the Legion committed itself to launching an armed invasion from abroad.[24]

Trujillo responded in kind by attempting to destabilize the regional democracies that gave the Legion cover. He funded an unsuccessful military uprising in Venezuela against Rómulo Betancourt's presidency in November 1946. At the same time, he conspired with rebellious elements in the Cuban military to overthrow President Ramón Grau San Martín, who Trujillo believed was aiding and abetting exiles in Cuba.[25] Trujillo also sought alternative sources of arms to bolster his own military, approaching Great Britain, Canada, Argentina, and Brazil for armaments that Braden refused to supply.[26]

Braden extended the U.S. cold shoulder to the economic sphere. Henceforth, aid would be forthcoming only if it benefited the Dominican people, not the regime.[27] Trujillo protested, reminding McGurk's successor, George Butler, at a meeting at the embassy that he had been a loyal ally during the war and was "deeply hurt" and confounded that "now he is treated like a Hitler or a Mussolini."[28] Butler, like McGurk and Briggs before him, adhered to a policy of strict neutrality concerning internal political matters, a 180-degree shift from Warren's tenure. By neither supporting nor opposing Trujillo, Butler implicitly gave a green light to Trujillo's opponents abroad, who moved ahead with plans to invade the island in 1947.

Trujillo acted just as he had in the past, wielding both the carrot and the stick. In addition to crushing domestic dissent and trying to undermine circum-Caribbean states that gave sanctuary to his enemies, he sought to refute critics by pushing ahead with initiatives to reaffirm his generosity. His well-oiled public relations machine not only reminded the foreign media that he had taken in Spanish and Jewish refugees in the past when no one else had, but that the Dominican Republic was now prepared to extend an *abrazo* to those displaced by the Second World War. In the fall of 1945, Trujillo's publicists went on a well-coordinated diplomatic offensive to revalidate his compassionate credentials.

GOING TO THE WELL AGAIN

"Dominican Republic Renews Refugee Bid," a full-page advertisement in the *New York Times* proclaimed on November 24, 1945. Publicists spruced up the language of the Évian offer: to "all persons endangered by racial, religious or political persecution" the Dominican Republic stood poised "to open its territory, through previous immigration agreements, to all those persons who find themselves in danger."[29] By putting in the clause "through previous immigration agreements," Trujillo and his lieutenants qualified just how open-ended his new proposal would be; but at that moment, what, if anything, came of the initiative was much less important than the gesture itself.

Next, Trujillo sent Andrés Pastoriza to the IGC's Fifth Plenary Session. The IGC, which had been so ineffective in aiding refugees before the war, was now charged with relocating and resettling displaced persons. Pastoriza announced that his nation was prepared to accept twenty-five thousand refugees.[30]

The public relations blitz continued a month later when Pastoriza amplified the invitation before the United Nations, stipulating that his nation wanted "eventually to accommodate 100,000 immigrants." Selecting that outlandish but all-too-familiar figure, of course, was meant to remind the international community that this was not the first time Trujillo had made such a generous pledge. Sensitive to the momentum building for a Jewish state, Pastoriza allowed that his nation had "no intention of interfering with the aspirations of the Zionists." But just in case a Jewish homeland did not become a reality, the Dominican Republic was ready to step into the breach.[31]

That same week, the New York Times also published a letter to the editor from Symon Gould, praising Trujillo's "unconditional invitation." Gould pointed out that the Dominican Republic was the only member of the United Nations to make a concrete offer "to any part of those Jews who managed to survive the Holocaust in Europe and who are slowly deteriorating and dying owing to delays engendered by committee hearings and the international dalliance." Évian's echo was unmistakable: if twenty million of the more than one hundred million dollars that was being raised to relocate European Jews was diverted to the Dominican Republic, Gould concluded, twenty thousand refugees could be resettled there immediately.[32]

Trujillo then released his government's response to the long-forgotten Brookings report, which had concluded that the Dominican Republic was not an ideal site for immigration. It may be recalled that even though Trujillo had immediately formed a commission to respond to the Brookings criticisms, he had not released its findings at the time. But now, to make his offer more credible, he needed to set the record straight about his nation's capacity to absorb immigrants. He had the rebuttal translated from Spanish to English and French and then published simultaneously in all three languages.

The move caught DORSA unawares. The Brookings debate did not conjure up fond memories. Trujillo, however, thought the positive spin generated by publishing the rebuttal would more than compensate for the risk of dredging up the original criticisms about the country's limitations. After all, his principal goal was to deflect condemnation of his dictatorial methods; all these activities were just promotional strategies to remind the media and U.S. officials that he had been and still was a benevolent statesman who deserved their thanks.[33]

Trujillo had additional ulterior motives in promoting this new immigration scheme. At the same time that he announced this initiative, he created the Comité Dominicano Pro Inmigración Hebrea (The Dominican Committee in Favor of Jewish Immigration). A prominent Jewish businessman from Ciudad Trujillo, Haím López-Penha, chaired the committee. In addition to promoting immigration, the committee's mandate was to encourage American Jewish investment. Unlike the Évian offer, the regime now was interested in encouraging Jewish companies and philanthropies to invest in commerce and key infrastructural projects, such as hydroelectric power, transportation, and communications. Authorities also were anxious to promote investment in the export of fruits and vegetables and the construction of processing plants for the nation's agricultural products. The regime, furthermore, welcomed the opportunity to bring Jewish physicians and surgeons to work with their Dominican counterparts, and even envisioned the construction of a new hospital, funded by Jewish capital.[34]

Where better to begin the committee's search for such investors than with Trujillo's friends at the JDC. López-Penha came to New York in the winter of 1946, met with Joseph Hyman, the JDC president, and floated his idea of "an enormous Jewish bank to be capitalized and set up by Jewish financiers for investment in railroads and hydroelectric plants." He came prepared with a list of potential investment opportunities. But what struck Hyman was that "he is not so much interested in the colony [Sosúa] as he is in developing a financial base for the exploitation of Dominican resources."[35]

This represented a seismic shift in Trujillo's thinking; his earlier offer had emphasized colonization, partly because he wanted to preclude competition with native merchants and manufacturers. What warranted such a change? By 1945, Trujillo, his family members, and his cronies held monopolies on virtually every key sector of the economy. What was needed was additional capital to develop their businesses, industries, and agricultural concerns. To the extent that promoting foreign investment benefited the nation, it would be a boon to their enterprises. As historian Frank Moya Pons has noted, "In his zeal to increase his personal fortune, Trujillo faced the enormous task of developing the national wealth, because his own was necessarily contingent on it."[36]

Not only would this plan to encourage Jewish investment prove lucrative for Trujillo's expanding economic empire, welcoming displaced persons might help restore his reputation in Washington. Whereas colonization and improving the race had been the underlying motives for Évian, righting matters with policymakers and growing his businesses at home were the principal factors at work now. Indeed, Trujillo's industrialization program actually did "soar" after the Second World War as new factories—which benefited from tax exemptions, sweetheart deals, labor peace, and protectionist tariffs—were opened for a host of manufactured goods.[37]

Persuading the Joint to invest was another matter, however. Killing two birds with one stone may have been appealing to Trujillo, but David Stern knew that the JDC had its hands full resettling refugees around the world and would not commit to this initiative. In an unusually frank letter, he warned Dominican authorities, "Nobody is going to sell you Jews. Nobody is going to give you money in order to build harbors or hospitals for Jewish immigrants. It is on your own responsibility that you are bringing the people in. We will try to do our best for Sosúa, but the absorptive capacity is limited, as conditions now stand, to not more than 200 families."[38] Stern's admonition made clear that authorities were on their own and could expect little assistance from DORSA and the JDC.

Edward Warburg delivered exactly the same message to López-Penha when they met in New York late in 1945. As it was, the JDC faced the prospect of increasing its funding for Sosúa by $250,000 in the coming year. Some of that amount was earmarked for "relatives in Europe of Sosúa settlers," some for the expected arrival of refugees from Shanghai to replace the America-Leavers.

Large-scale immigration was out of the question, however. Only those refugees who could make a difference to Sosúa and the nation were under consideration, Warburg diplomatically informed López-Penha. "It is our belief that it would be advisable only for those refugees who have a fair chance of establishing themselves in the Dominican Republic to come to your country; those people who are qualified to live and work at Sosúa; those who command capital and the ability to use it fruitfully and those whose particular skills will ensure their ability to earn their livelihood. Others we fear would not be able to contribute to the program of industrial and agricultural development which your country has fostered."[39]

Never one to take no for an answer, let alone pay for immigration from state coffers, Trujillo cranked up the pressure on the philanthropists. At the same time that the Joint was debating its future commitment to Sosúa, Rosenberg learned from Stern that the Dominican government was issuing large numbers of visas in Europe to displaced Jews without consulting either DORSA or the JDC. "Once they get there," an alarmed Rosenberg wrote Warburg and Hexter, "the JDC must foresee that they will be expected to help."[40] Rosenberg, who had gone through this before, in 1938 and 1939, when Austrian and German Jews were beating down his door trying to get to the island, warned his colleagues of what to expect next. "The little Dominican Republic is the only country in the world which is opening its doors and ready to receive a substantial number of Jewish refugees. The Palestine situation is involved in deep conflict. The JDC must face the inescapable fact that Jews will be wanting to come to the Dominican Republic. How many we cannot begin to foresee. López-Penha showed Stern the files of several thousand applications. What is the JDC going to do?"[41]

For Moses Leavitt, the JDC's secretary, the prospect of hundreds, if not thousands, of refugees streaming toward Sosúa was a disaster waiting to happen. The JDC had been subsidizing El Batey's nonsettlers for years, and now, just as this group was ready to move to the United States, the Joint might be forced to step in at a potentially staggering cost because of Trujillo's pre-emptive actions. Rosenberg's superiors told him that DORSA must inform Trujillo that this was a problem of his own making and the JDC was not prepared to bail him out.[42] For the first time, the JDC was determined to say no to Trujillo. It was simply not in a position to invest in either Sosúa's or the Dominican Republic's economic future.

Mindful of Trujillo's goodwill to DORSA and Sosúa, Rosenberg urged his colleagues to inform the general of their decision as tactfully as possible. Rather than "dictating" to the dictator, the Joint should get its message across more diplomatically, saying that it was concerned about a "mighty stream of immigrants."[43]

Rosenberg may have known the best way to approach his good friend, but the JDC's determination to dig in its heels also illustrates just how far Sosúa had fallen on its list of priorities. If Rosenberg had a soft spot for Sosúa and had spent his whole life pushing territorial dreams and fighting a rearguard action against Zionism, his pragmatic colleagues at the JDC understood that 1946 was not 1938. The calculus had changed, and Palestine was the future. The 74-year-old Rosenberg recognized as much when he submitted his poignant valedictory report, stepping down as DORSA's honorary chairman two years later: "The creation of the State of Israel appears to mean that all, or most of the overseas young Jewish men and women, desirous of working on the soil, will wish to go to the State of Israel. Hence, we cannot foresee any large scale increase of DORSA work. It may well be therefore we should plan to gradually conclude this effort as one which came into being at a dark hour and which, by acting upon the humanitarianism of President Trujillo, has saved many lives with the continued cooperation of the Dominican authorities."[44]

It is hard not to read genuine disappointment in Rosenberg's carefully worded remarks. Sosúa would get sufficient funds to tide it over during this transitional phase while the JDC imported some replacements to partly compensate for the exodus of America-Leavers. Then the colony would be left on its own to sink or swim.

Funds were shifting to Palestine as the JDC spent more than $350 million in the first seven years after the war to repatriate and resettle more than 616,000 refugees; 503,350 of those DPs would go to Israel.[45] If DORSA needed more proof that Sosúa was not a priority, the JDC's bottom line spoke volumes. The JDC appropriated only $195,000 in 1946 to all Central and South American countries, a drop in the bucket when compared to an overall operating budget of more than $58 million.[46]

The general was disappointed with the JDC's decision. An interview titled "Trujillo is Gloomy on Refugee Colony" in the *New York Times* in May 1947, conveyed his frustration. "The door is wide open, but the number has decreased, rather than increased," he complained. "Four hundred fifty of the original 750 have left the colony. And only 90 new immigrants have taken their place."[47]

Seeking to soften the blow, Maurice Hexter went out of his way to show DORSA's gratitude to Trujillo by inscribing the general's name in the Book of Gold of *Karen Kayemeth le' Israel* (the Foundation for the Redemption of Israel). At a public ceremony, DORSA presented Trujillo with a handsome album containing a diploma lithographed in black and gold and inscribed in Hebrew and English, "To His Excellency, the President of the Dominican Republic, Dr. Rafael Leonidas Trujillo Molina, in recognition of gratitude for his leadership in championing the cause of the Jewish People at the Conference of Évian, France." Whether or not Hexter realized it, such recognition from *Karen Kayemeth*, an entity established in 1902 to provide seed money for agricultural settlement projects in the Holy Land, must have been a bitter pill for Trujillo to swallow. He probably interpreted it as further evidence of the philanthropy's progressive disengagement from the Dominican Republic and its growing affinity for Palestine.[48]

Trujillo's plans for American Jews to invest in his nation may not have panned out, but he still had contingency plans to restore his image in Washington. His nation's improved financial situation after the war enabled it to pay off on July 21, 1947, the remaining $9.2 million owed to *yanqui* creditors, the same debt that had been renegotiated as part of the Trujillo-Hull Treaty. Just as panegyrists six years earlier had proclaimed him "The Restorer of the Financial Independence of the Republic," he was now praised as "The Father of National Financial Independence." The government began issuing Dominican currency in lieu of U.S. dollars for the first time since before the U.S. occupation. Playing the sovereignty card also sent a message to Washington that Trujillo, no matter how his enemies perceived him, was a responsible ruler who, unlike many Latin American dictators, paid his nation's debts in full.

As the Cold War intensified, Trujillo also reinvented himself as a staunch enemy of communism. The ruler who had become an overnight foe of fascism on the eve of the Second World War now seized on anticommunism as a cause to recapture the support of U.S. hardliners. He became a master at red-baiting his opponents. Trujillo crushed leftist labor unions and increased the number of U.S. lawyers, lobbyists, and public relations agents on the payroll who flaunted his hawkish credentials in Washington.

In addition to casting himself as an anticommunist, Trujillo continued to promote his humanitarianism. Romanian diplomat Henry Helfant wrote a book, intended for American audiences, that congratulated the dictator for welcoming Spanish republican exiles and Central European Jews and suggested that such benevolent acts should become part of the fabric of the newly emerging world order. *The Trujillo Doctrine of the Humanitarian Diplomatic Asylum*, published in 1947, was probably commissioned and paid for by the regime's public relations operation; it made the tyrant appear to be a cross between Mahatma Gandhi and Woodrow Wilson.[49]

Trujillo also announced plans to take in between five thousand and ten thousand Yugoslav nationals fleeing the Iron Curtain. The refugees were to be settled on the Haitian border, just as the Spanish republicans had been a decade before. "A government spokesman said these refugees would be screened to prevent the entrance of Communists," to better reassure Washington.[50] No Yugoslavs ever made it to the Dominican Republic.

Butler, who saw through Trujillo's ploy and reported no credible evidence of "Communist activities in the country," believed that it was pure political expediency that motivated the dictator.[51] His objective was to use the growing red scare in the United States to bring about a "fairly close rapprochement with the United States Government; without, however, his having to yield an inch in his arbitrary manner of ruling the Dominican Republic."[52] The ambassador gave the cunning Trujillo his due, admiring his facility in manipulating "prominent Americans" and foreigners to bolster his image.[53] Of course, DORSA was at the very top of that short list.

While Trujillo launched his anticommunist offensive, plotting by exiles exacerbated tensions between Trujillo and his neighbors and intensified his search for arms. A planned expedition by exiles from Cuba, the Cayo Confites Rebellion, was quashed by Cuban authorities, but not before Trujillo once again implored the U.S. government to lift the ban on the sale of arms so that he could defend himself against his enemies. Trujillo's timing was better now, because Spruille Braden's influence in the State Department was on the wane.

In a twist of delicious irony, Trujillo received unexpected assistance from none other than Welles, who published a stinging critique of Braden's policies in *Foreign Affairs* in the fall of 1947. "Intervention and Interventions" argued that the foundation of FDR's Good Neighbor policy was nonintervention and that Braden's criticism of Perón and against dictators more generally throughout the hemisphere were guaranteed to diminish "the moral standing and the great prestige which this country had derived from Roosevelt's policy." U.S. intervention in the past, according to Welles, had only engendered "hatred and suspicion" for America.[54]

Welles's broadside helped undercut Braden, but it was the onset of the Cold War and the resulting changes in the geopolitical landscape that sealed his fate as the assistant secretary of state. When George C. Marshall replaced James Byrnes as secretary of state, Braden, realizing that his human rights initiative was now out of step with the administration's position, tendered his own resignation in June 1947.[55]

Concerned about Trujillo's aggressive pursuit of arms from other nations and cognizant of the Caribbean Legion's destabilizing effects on the region, Marshall announced that the United States would not permit revolutionary groups to prepare expeditionary forces from U.S. soil and agreed to lift the ban on the sale of armaments to the Dominican Republic in the summer of 1947.[56] This policy reversal coincided with the signing of the Inter-American Treaty of Reciprocal Assistance (the Rio Treaty) in the same year, which laid the basis for greater hemispheric military cooperation between the United States and regional leaders, whether they were dictators or democrats. Administration officials and U.S. defense contractors hoped that this mutual defense pact would make it possible for Latin American nations to rely exclusively on U.S. weapons.[57] A year later at the Ninth International Conference of American States in Bogotá, the United States pushed through a resolution ensuring that the hemisphere would be more vigilant in rooting out leftist subversion. Support for civilian democracies took a back seat.

By the time the Berlin crisis erupted in 1948, "containment" of communism was the central concern in Washington, and Trujillo's noisy anticommunism found greater resonance. The brief moment of U.S. hostility to the dictator was over. Key positions in the State Department were no longer manned by those opposed to Trujillo. Just as he had survived Welles's machinations, Trujillo had outlasted Braden.[58]

Once again, Rosenberg was there to validate Trujillo's anticommunist credentials, shamelessly portraying him as a defender of freedom against the forces of repression. To commemorate the tenth anniversary of the signing of the Sosúa contract in February 1950, Rosenberg praised Trujillo in a letter to the *New York Times* for having bestowed a "Magna Carta of human liberty . . . for our colonists." He wrote that letter not only to bring attention to the anniversary but to respond to a *Times* editorial, which had argued, "Haiti rather than the Dominican Republic deserves sympathy and encouragement from the U.S." In a letter that could have been penned by Trujillo's publicists, Rosenberg noted, "With horror we learn of the present persecution of Jews behind the Iron Curtain. In the Dominican Republic anti-Semitism is not tolerated. . . . I suggest that this record entitles the Dominican Government to commendation rather than criticism."[59]

Washington's postwar about-face on Trujillo complicated matters for DORSA, which nevertheless stood fast in support of its patron. In his valedictory to the DORSA board, Rosenberg noted, "There have always been mutual understanding and a frank interchange of ideas. DORSA, on its part, has always cooperated in every possible way with the Dominican Republic."[60] That was certainly no exaggeration.

While these political contretemps played out between Ciudad Trujillo, Washington, and New York, DORSA's administrators at the colony had to address the critical shortfall of workers resulting from the America-Leavers' exodus. Although the Joint had ruled out a major investment in the settlement, some patch-and-fill funds were appropriated. The number one priority was to bring in some capable replacements. They came from an unlikely place. Several years earlier, Hyman had asked Laura Margolis in Shanghai to send Jewish women to Sosúa, and she could not recruit any. This time the Joint had better luck with Jews who had survived the war in the Far East.

FOURTEEN

Golden Years

> The streets are clean, new houses have been built, the barrack life
> extinguished, the free kitchen closed, work relief ended. In other
> words, a miracle. . . . I found peasants who had become so peasant-
> like that they were clamoring, and indeed, contesting for more
> land. . . . Our settlers are upright, self-reliant and happy.
>
> MAURICE HEXTER TO MOSES LEAVITT, 1949

David Stern implored the home office to find replacements for the America-Leavers in the summer of 1946. "We need trained artisans and experts; in Sosúa we have now mostly dilettantes who are inefficient . . . I cannot see any development of Sosúa in the absence of such an important element of the population."[1] His appeal came on the heels of a more specific request from his assistant a few months earlier. "There are openings for auto mechanic, doctor, and a kindergarten teacher, a few accountants and bookkeepers, stenographer, sausage maker."[2]

The America-Leaver exodus did not happen overnight. The time lag between the filing of papers and securing visas was often significant enough that Stern and his staff were able to make adjustments and ask in advance for substitutes with specific skills. But some of the defections were difficult to overcome. As late as 1948, a census listed fifty-seven El Batey residents awaiting their visas, among them the agricultural extension expert Douglas Blackwood; Doctor Herbert Kohn; the veterinarian Hans Rosenberg; Karl Weiss, the turtle shell artisan; sausage maker Hermann Meyerstein, baker Issac Kuj, and the cabinetmaker Otto Papernick.[3] Even though the JDC's chairman, Paul Baerwald, knew it was fiscally impossible to replace all the America-Leavers, he was convinced that it was important to show good faith to "counteract the fear that people seem to have" by having a "modest number of settlers come in to fill up these gaps."[4]

Coincidentally, the JDC was responding to pleas for resettlement from Shanghai, where more than eighteen thousand Central European Jews had resided and now were anxious to leave. The JDC had been assisting refugees in Shanghai's Hongkou quarter since 1941 at a cost of roughly one hundred thousand dollars a month. The city had long been a haven for stateless exiles because it required no visa or sponsoring affidavit to enter. When the Japanese seized control of the city in 1937, they chose not to alter that open-ended visa policy; and because so few nations were willing to accept Jewish refugees, it became a very desirable location. Although a total of only 1,500 German and Austrian Jews immigrated to the Dominican Republic during the Second World War, several thousand a month came to the Chinese port, first via an extended "sort of 'ferry service' between Italy and Shanghai" in 1938 and 1939 and then, after Italy closed its borders to exiles in March 1940, via Lisbon or Marseilles, or overland through Siberia and then by ship from North China.[5] Although conditions in Shanghai were difficult, the refugees were relatively secure during the war.

That changed in 1946, when a civil war between Nationalists and Communists threatened to overrun the city. Both sides in the conflict blamed the severe economic difficulties on foreigners, especially Jews. Banners that read "The Japs and the Jews are our enemies" were hung throughout the city, and street demonstrators carried "anti-Jewish slogans and caricatures of bearded and hook-nosed Jews."[6]

The Joint's director in Shanghai, Charles Jordan, wrote to headquarters about the deteriorating situation: "We are now convinced that there is absolutely no place for the large majority of our people in either Shanghai or the rest of China . . . the solution to the problem is emigration, and we are convinced furthermore that it requires speed."[7] To determine where the exiles wanted to emigrate, the JDC conducted a survey; 40 percent listed the United States as their first choice, 26 percent asked to be repatriated to Germany or Austria, and 21 percent chose Palestine, even though at that moment it was still closed to them. Latin America and Australia were at the bottom of the list.[8]

The JDC applied to the IGC's reparations fund for $472,000 to relocate one hundred families from Shanghai to Sosúa, in the hope that Jordan could persuade that number to start a new life there. He was the perfect person to sell

Jews on the settlement because before his stint in the Far East, he had worked for the JDC in the Caribbean and had spent time at Sosúa.[9]

Both Stern and the Settlers' Council were concerned about the selection process. Remembering the problems the colony faced because of the inexperienced pioneers that Solomon Trone and other recruiters selected, the council begged the Joint to send Stern to Shanghai to identify suitable candidates. Jordan, who had firsthand knowledge of the past mistakes, was bemused at the Rat's request. "I fully understand their apprehensions, knowing from my own experience what kind of people have been selected previously from Sosúa by so-called experts abroad. On the other hand, the very settlers who are now doubting other people's ability to make a selection, have also been selected by others." He warned DORSA that it would be "pretty difficult for us to take this responsibility on if the people in Sosúa start off with a chip on their shoulder and do not have the proper perspective." It would be better if the settlers focused on how they could help the newcomers acclimate to their new surroundings. "When I was there it was simply a matter of swim or sink," Jordan recalled.[10] The JDC turned down the council's request to send Stern, and Jordan was entrusted with locating replacements.

Jordan believed that even though Shanghai's refugees were inexperienced, they had much to offer. "These . . . people, still have dignity, as well as a good sense of humor. And the youth is through and through sterling quality."[11] His principal difficulty was convincing refugees that Sosúa and farming were in their enlightened self-interest. Even though they had become acclimated to the steamy climate in Shanghai, their urban upbringing, unfamiliarity with agriculture, and the lure of other more developed and temperate sites of refuge made Sosúa appear less inviting. The only push factors that aided Jordan's sales pitch were the worsening political climate, the bureaucratic delays that kept many refugees in limbo, and negative reports they received from friends and relatives who had returned to Germany and Austria. Those returning exiles concluded that it was just too painful, after all that had transpired, to begin life anew in their place of birth. The best Jordan could do was to persuade twelve extended families, ninety men, women, and children in all, to immigrate to Sosúa in 1947.[12]

The paltry number certainly was a disappointment to DORSA officials and a blow to the settlement, which had huge skill gaps to fill. But those who came had a very favorable impact. By all accounts, they were energetic and entrepreneurial. They also possessed notable advantages that earlier pioneers had lacked. Unlike most of the first pioneers, the new arrivals came as families. Weary of being transients, they yearned to put down roots and raise their children. Although the move was not entirely voluntary and the Dominican Republic probably was not their first choice, the way they threw themselves into their work suggests that they were content with the choice they had made. The same could not be said for many who came earlier.

In part, this was because the settlement was a very different place in 1947 than it was seven years earlier. Experimentation had given way to a more secure reliance on dairying. The bickering clusters had been replaced by homesteads, and the settlers had a stake in the colony's future and no longer depended on DORSA's largesse. Moreover, the colony finally had a director who literally and figuratively spoke the homesteaders' language and who, by disposition, was collaborative and flexible.

Those arriving in 1947, furthermore, were embraced by a core group of more than 250 men, women, and children with a clear vision of how they wanted the colony to develop, who were not simply biding time and awaiting passage to the United States. The new immigrants were welcomed because their skills and ingenuity were in short supply. Numbers aside, the Shanghai cohort soon assumed a significant role in the colony's development. Several families gravitated to leadership positions in the CILCA and GANADERA cooperatives. The Strauss and Benjamin families became key figures in the colony. Erich Benjamin believed that those who came from China were "more dedicated and determined" than Sosúa's first colonists.[13] They were precisely what Stern had ordered, even if they were fewer than he wanted.

The Shanghai infusion and the America-Leavers' ongoing departure ushered in Sosúa's golden age, fifteen years of steady growth. Stern and Hexter gambled that encouraging those who had little interest in farming to leave would make for a more cohesive settlement. Those who remained accepted Stern's challenge to take responsibility for their own settlement and were rewarded for their efforts, but prosperity could not offset the colony's contraction.

SETTLING IN

New York Times correspondent Herbert Matthews, who would later gain notoriety for interviewing Fidel Castro in the Sierra Maestra mountains during Castro's early revolutionary career, visited Sosúa in March 1953 and noted that the colony was "virtually self-supporting, with assets of about one million [dollars] and no liabilities to speak of." He was impressed that the settlement's lifeline, livestock, was generating prodigious quantities of butter, cheese, sausage, ham, bacon, and eggs that were marketed to Ciudad Trujillo and other cities and towns across the island.[14]

Yet the glass was only partly full for Matthews. "Sosúa was never a utopia and there were heartbreaks and grim pioneering work before it could reach its present state of solvency," he related. The project, on some level, had to be considered a disappointment because it failed to provide "a haven for a great many refugees"; and despite its notable improvement, the prospects for the future were not promising. Roughly fifty homesteaders had left over the last three years, and thirty-five more were awaiting immigration papers. Nor had the colony generated many ripple effects; it still was an isolated enclave that had failed to benefit even nearby Charamico, which Matthews characterized as a "group of native hovels." Was it really worth the three million dollars the JDC had lavished on the small settlement? he wondered.

Despite Sosúa's obvious limitations, it had provided the refugees with an opportunity to rebuild their lives: "it is a fine project, well run, well treated by the Dominican Government and capable of providing a contented and creative if arduous life in a magnificent climate." Besides, Sosúa, he believed, should be held to a different standard. "The measure of its success or failure can be debated according to the norms and expectations applied, but no one who spends a day in this beautiful and busy spot can deny that the men and women who colonized and stuck with it have made a fine life for themselves and have contributed something valuable to the Dominican Republic."[15]

Compared to the fluff served up about Sosúa in glossy magazines put out by public relations firms hired by Trujillo or the "overcoming adversity" puff pieces that DORSA and the Joint regularly whipped up for donors, Matthews's sober appraisal is refreshing. Meanwhile, despite the modest influx from Shanghai and significant gains in productivity, Sosúa's population continued to decline after the war. An internal memorandum indicated that 757 persons had lived or passed through Sosúa at one time or another since the colony's inception, but by late 1947 only 386 remained. Among those who had departed, 320 had left for the United States, Ciudad Trujillo, or other destinations, and 23 had died. Over the next few years, approximately 200 more settlers would leave. Table 10 illustrates how the colony's size steadily diminished as it reached middle age.

Even as Stern's homesteader model ushered in an era of unprecedented affluence, Sosuaner families continued to weigh the relative merits of building a future there with testing the waters elsewhere. During the war, U.S. immigration policy and Trujillo's insistence that DORSA contain the refugees at Sosúa conspired to inhibit mobility. But now it was possible to relocate, and the colonists had options.

TABLE 10
Sosúa's Population, 1947–61

Year	Colonists
1947	386
1948	275
1949	274
1951	193
1953	181
1954	192
1955	204
1956	193
1957	187
1958	184
1959	174
1960	164
1961	155

Source: File 47, DP, JDC Archives

Letters from America-Leavers, now comfortably ensconced in New York City brownstones or the mushrooming suburbs in Westchester, New Jersey, and Long Island, painted a beautiful, if exaggerated, portrait of their new lives. They wrote their relatives and friends back at the settlement that the prospects for success were unlimited, the schools superb, the Jewish community vibrant, and New York City's cultural scene spectacular. For many former Viennese and Berliners, the vibrant atmosphere of New York (and Miami and Los Angeles) proved irresistible. Another inducement that drew colonists north was the chance to reconnect with loved ones who had survived the Holocaust and who had taken advantage of the relaxation of visa restrictions to move to America. But the factor that probably outweighed all the others was the unshakeable conviction that America offered better educational and economic prospects for their children.

Miami's proximity to the island made it almost as enticing as New York. A number of Sosuaners soon found that they could have the best of both worlds, splitting their time between South Florida and the colony, checking on their investments and catching up with their friends for part of the year, then spending the rest of their time in a more culturally inviting ambience that also offered commercial opportunities. A sure sign that absenteeism was on the rise was Hexter's refusal to extend leaves of absence to homesteaders who petitioned to stay away from Sosúa for more than the six months allowed in their contracts.[16]

Even during its golden age, an "air of impermanence" hung over the settlement, according to JDC staffer Philip Skorneck, who visited the colony in October 1948. "Practically everyone I met had made an application for visa to the United States or to some other country. No one said that he intended to remain permanently. . . . Even those who have no immediate plans for leaving, look ahead to leaving in five or ten years."[17]

The allure of the States was only part of the explanation of why settlers took leave. Many believed that an economic ceiling existed on what could be achieved. The perception was that markets for the settlement's goods would always be constrained by the "Racketera" Trujillo and the limited market afforded by the island's small, if growing, middle class.

As the size of the settlers' herds increased, moreover, and milk production soared from nine thousand to twenty-five thousand pounds a month between 1948 and 1951, land became an increasingly scarce resource at Sosúa. Pasture, by one estimate, supported one cow per hectare (two-and-a-half acres), so settlers had to lease or purchase additional properties once their herds surpassed thirty head. "To make an adequate living," settlers required "the maintenance of a herd of fifty or more cattle of which twenty-five to thirty will be producing at any one time." Stern had recognized this and sought to correct it by opening up Choco, the hilly expanse south of El Batey. Some homesteaders thought that was mistake, given the considerable cost of clearing the rocky lands, piping in water, running power lines, and putting up fences. Few wanted to live that far from El Batey, Skorneck reported.[18]

To thrive, homesteaders juggled their farms with complementary business interests as they turned over the day-to-day running of their herds to hired help. "They all have Dominican employees and although new settlers do some of the work, such as milking of cattle, many of the older settlers do not even live on their homesteads, and simply visit once a week or once in two weeks to see that the Dominicans are doing their work properly. . . . Those who have made considerable sums of money have made it through dealing in cattle, both through breeding and through buying and selling." Skorneck was struck by the drive and ingenuity of the more successful colonists, and it was apparent that their efforts were rewarded. At least two were worth fifty thousand dollars, seven had recently purchased automobiles, and a couple had purchased property from Dominicans on Sosúa's outskirts.[19]

Uncertain about the prospects for long-term success on the farm, some homesteaders bounced from one job to another to supplement their farm income. In addition to his homestead, Elie Topf, at one time or another, managed the Oasis restaurant and the hotel, opened a small general store fifteen kilometers away from Sosúa with his brother-in-law and a friend, learned how to cure hams and stuff sausage at the GANADERA, and eventually took over his brother-in-law's general store and apparel shop in El Batey after his brother-in-law left for the United States. When asked, in retrospect, if he ever felt intimidated at the prospect of learning so many new occupations and juggling such an array of responsibilities, Topf shrugged, "Every time I started something, the first year was twice as hard." But he quickly added, "You can learn to do anything if you put your mind to it." That motto applied to more than a few of Sosúa's doughty pioneers.[20]

The settlement's attrition between the end of the war and Trujillo's assassination in 1961 was a byproduct of individual decisions by homesteader families, who assessed the limitations of their present situation against the risks and potential rewards of a move. Given the circumstances, it is not surprising that a third of the colonists opted to leave during the 1950s. But those who did leave did not go empty-handed, Hexter noted. "There is one factor, however, that ought to cause us some glow of satisfaction. When these people leave for the States, they usually take enough capital with them so that they readily adjust themselves in America without appealing to anybody."[21]

DORSA staff continued to ask for replacements, but reinforcements were not forthcoming.[22] An occasional family from Europe or Israel joined the settlement during the 1950s, but the ninety immigrants from Shanghai were the last significant infusion of new settlers. Between 1952 and 1961, a total of forty settlers arrived and ninety-eight departed, while the colony recorded twenty-nine births and nine deaths. None of the forty who came could be classified as refugees, however. Some were relatives of settlers, and the eighteen who came from Israel either had failed to adapt to the demands of kibbutz life but still had an interest in farming, or were unhappy in Israel and came to Sosúa temporarily until they could move to the United States.[23] The usually optimistic Hexter offered a dreary assessment in a confidential note to Leavitt: "The number of colonists is far too small to make it psychologically and biologically self-sustaining. This forces leakage out of the colony, which complicates, of course, the very problem. It is a process which grows by feeding on its own appetites."[24]

This persistent attrition, however, did not prove as disruptive as the America-Leavers' earlier, more concerted exodus, because Sosúa was better positioned to handle the egress. Stern's innovations helped lay the groundwork for a more secure settlement, but demographics better explain its newfound stability. By 1950 the colony's 128 married couples outnumbered its 30 single men and 17 single women, a dramatic change from just five years earlier.

Stern had permitted eleven homesteaders and their families to live in El Batey, but that number would rise over the next decade, since many settlers preferred what the "town" had to offer. The school, medical clinics, public library, and synagogue were magnets. By the mid-1950s, many homesteaders had paid off their farms and "were sufficiently affluent to build a house in town."[25]

Another healthy sign was rising competition. A general store and a sausage maker now competed with El Colmado and the GANADERA, respectively, and some small cheese makers had opened up alongside CILCA. Hexter proudly reported to his superiors in New York that settlers were feeling flush enough that the colony raised four thousand dollars for the Haganah, the Jewish paramilitary force that fought for Israeli independence.[26]

The Settlers' Council was renamed the Sosúa Council, and it gradually assumed responsibility for most communal services, including the medical and dental clinics, sanitation and mosquito control, electricity, the elementary school, veterinary services, the slaughterhouse, the library, and the movie theater. DORSA gave the Rat just under eight thousand dollars in subsidies in 1949 to take the sting out of assuming those services. Only the water supply system, the police station, and fire services remained under DORSA management. But Hexter put the Rat on notice that it would have to take over these services sooner rather than later.[27]

From management's perspective, the settlement was moving in the right direction. Homestead loans were being repaid on time, and those funds were plowed back into the association's operating budget, so that the subsidies Hexter had to ask from the JDC grew progressively smaller. When Hexter returned to Sosúa in January 1949, his first visit in three years, he was stunned by how much change had occurred. Sosúa was "now a thriving community," he reported to Leavitt, and he gave the credit to Stern. "You will recollect the serious relief problem we had three years ago in Batey . . . the demoralization and pauperism which was rife. Instead, I found peasants and artisans making a living, and a good living."[28] Hexter may have mischaracterized the settlers as peasants, because they did manage to get away from actually working on the land; but he had it exactly right when he labeled these self-styled entrepreneurs "upright, self-reliant and happy."

Each week, four-and-a-half tons of the settlement's products were shipped to the capital. "Our colony has literally captured the market in Ciudad Trujillo," Hexter boasted. The capital's exclusive Hotel Jaragua purchased $800

a month of Sosúa's butter, eggs, cheeses, and meats. By 1956, the dairy cooperative was grossing $463,000 annually, and GANADERA about half that
amount.[29]

As the colony aged, it lost several valued friends. In 1948, James Rosenberg
announced that he was retiring from his law practice and stepping down as
DORSA's honorary chair to devote himself full-time to painting. Hexter, who
had, for all intents and purposes, directed operations from New York since
1943, now replaced Rosenberg as chairman of the board. Hexter personally
would continue to rely on the elder statesman for advice until Rosenberg
passed away, at the age of ninety-six, in 1970.[30]

A year after Rosenberg retired, Joseph Rosen died in New York. The colony's beloved first director had never really recovered from his illnesses and
had been relegated to assisting the colony from afar in New York since 1941.
Sosúa had never evolved the way he had drawn it up, but the homesteaders,
reflecting on his lifetime of experience in colonization work and his humane
qualities, mourned his passing.[31]

Rosenberg's retirement and Rosen's death were not entirely unexpected,
but the colony received shocking news in 1948 when it learned that Stern's
wife had been killed in an accident in Israel. Stern left Sosúa immediately and
flew to Israel to be with his daughters. Although his contract as director was
set to expire in 1949 and he had made known his intention to turn the settlement over to the colonists at that time, his sudden departure left an enormous
vacuum. It is unclear whether he would have even allowed Hexter to twist his
arm to serve a second five-year contract, but the tragedy of his wife's death
apparently precluded that possibility. In June 1949, Stern returned from Israel
and took a position with the Israeli government's purchasing mission in New
York, a job he held until his retirement. He then went back to Israel, never to
revisit Sosúa. The reason for that remains one of Sosúa's secrets.[32]

This collective passing of the old guard had significant ramifications. Hexter had to find a new director. He chose a settler, albeit one who had worked
for the administration, another sure indicator that the colony was becoming
more self-sufficient. Alfred Rosenzweig, a native of Vienna, had worked in a
textile factory in Graz before the war and had fled to England via Czechosla-
vakia before coming to Sosúa. As a farmer, the industrious Rosenzweig built
up his herd, cultivated vegetables, and worked in his spare time in DORSA's
administrative offices. He oversaw renovations to the smokehouse and sausage factory so that they met government specifications; he supervised the
clearing of new pasturelands, the construction of a fire station and twenty-

eight new homestead sites in Choco, and the laying of water pipes to those new homesteads.[33]

Hexter's subsequent visit in 1950 to celebrate Sosúa's tenth anniversary was again upbeat, but he admitted that although the bulk of the services had been turned over to the settlers, a modest subsidy was needed for the foreseeable future. The association's slow but sure withdrawal was, in Hexter's mind, akin to the protracted end of a military occupation: "I believe that . . . as we originally contemplated we would pull out with grace, dignity and honor." He permitted himself some measure of satisfaction as he assessed the state of the colony. "Such adventures cannot be phrased in dollars and cents," he wrote to Leavitt. "I could not help, while I was in Sosúa, but think of Dr. Joseph Rosen, who started the colony, and of his tasks in getting it underway. It was literally at that time (and, in some ways, it is even now) terra incognita. His energy and enthusiasm are written in many areas in Sosúa. . . . I think the time is ripe to button up what we have started."[34]

"Buttoning up" Sosúa, meaning DORSA's gradual disengagement, was a more protracted process than even Hexter could have imagined. Each phase of the withdrawal was subject to stiff negotiations with the Rat, which sought concessions for each new responsibility it assumed. For instance, in May 1953, in return for a thirty-thousand-dollar loan from DORSA at very reasonable terms, the homesteaders agreed to take over the clinic and hospital, school, library, mosquito and sanitation control, and road and bridge repairs, and to provide material assistance to children attending secondary schools outside Sosúa.[35] Two years later, in exchange for the colonists' taking over the water system, DORSA had to extend another low-interest mortgage and swallow its substantial initial investment in a costly irrigation project it had undertaken some years before.[36]

The shrewd homesteaders were able to negotiate such tough deals because they were more accustomed to cutting business deals than to clearing land. More important, they knew they had DORSA over a barrel. The philanthropy had too much invested in the colony, fiscally and morally, to let the settlement flounder, yet it was eager to diminish its exposure. Hexter's consuming workload at the Federation of Jewish Philanthropies also meant that he was more reactive than proactive when dealing with problems, and that arrangement invariably resulted in concessions.

As the settlers took more initiative, local politics took on a life of its own and often proved contentious. The settlement's decision-making bodies were the Rat, the cooperatives' boards of directors (especially the successful dairy and meat cooperatives), and, of course, DORSA. The Rat and the boards were elected positions. By giving each homesteader one vote in the cooperatives, no matter how many shares they accumulated, the colonists had hoped to forestall individuals or small cliques from imposing their views on the majority. But cliques inevitably surfaced, as some settlers were more engaged in oversight while others were more reserved. Given the settlement's small size, there was considerable overlap on these increasingly politicized committees, which meant that a few homesteaders had more say over the agenda than others. Topf, who served on the Rat and on several of the cooperatives' boards over the years, recalled that rumors, gossip, infighting, and backroom politicking were the norm.[37]

One would have also expected that as DORSA turned over responsibilities for day-to-day management, the Rat and the cooperatives would become the pillars of local government and DORSA's role would diminish. Although that shift eventually occurred, DORSA continued to exercise considerable influence throughout these years. This happened in large part because Rosenzweig proved to be a heavy-handed administrator and because he wore a number of hats: he was one of the more successful homesteaders, DORSA's head, and a key player in one of the cliques. Some settlers were quick to point out the obvious conflicts of interest. As a result, policy debates were often acrimonious, even though, as Topf related, once a vote was taken, everyone abided by the will of the majority.[38]

A persistent problem that the settlement never really solved was educating its own. While the colony's elementary school did an outstanding job of educating Sosúa's youngsters, the choices once they graduated were less than satisfactory.[39] The school offered a high-quality education for the children of the settlers and their Dominican employees during the Trujillo era, its principal, Luis Hess, recalled. Teachers were relatively well paid and prepared, and they took pedagogical and curricular workshops with an inspector from the State Department of Education who visited once a week from Puerto Plata.[40] The students, however, had to continue their education in Puerto Plata, Santiago, or the capital, and that proved an unsatisfactory and increasingly costly option for most parents. In 1948, families of the settlement's seven adolescents between the ages of fourteen and eighteen petitioned DORSA to subsidize lodging, transportation, meals, and expenses for secondary school students wherever they pursued their studies. When DORSA turned down the request, the parents were left to their own devices.[41] Four of those children did not receive any secondary schooling, one apprenticed at CILCA, another worked as a nurse at the colony's clinic, and one attended elementary school in Santiago because she had missed so many years of schooling in Shanghai during the war.[42]

Nor was there any provision for vocational training on site. Even though artisans were part of the colony, DORSA did not consider them suitable teachers. Parents interested in having "their children learn something valuable and profitable for their futures, were and are forced to emigrate with the children to the U.S. or other countries, or they send the children to Israel where they hope the State will take care of them."[43] Because Sosuaners put such a high premium on education, the inability to solve this problem was a major factor in the settlement's steady attrition.

What attracted most colonists to El Batey was not its social services and cultural attractions but the opportunities to supplement their farming income. Although homesteaders were still building their herds, the great majority had little choice but to take on additional responsibilities. Paul Cohnen and Arthur Kircheimer were cattle dealers; Harry Deutsch, a CILCA driver; Leo Goldstein the GANADERA's manager; Rudy Herzberg the credit union's administrator; Walter Bloch a plumber; Heinrich Atles an electrician; Richard Wolf ran the café and restaurant; and Heinz Lesser operated the sawmill.[44] Given the reduced number of colonists, the cooperatives and businesses remained relatively compact. CILCA was the largest employer, with a staff of ten homesteaders, three El Batey residents, and sixteen Dominicans. The GANADERA was the next largest with two homesteaders, two El Batey residents, and ten natives.

The colony, however, remained cut off from its neighbors. Only the handful of Dominican women who married settlers had meaningful social interaction with the colony. "Dominicans thought of Jews as hard workers and 'people who watch their money,'" geographers Richard Symanski and Nancy Burley reported some years later. The homesteaders' views of Dominicans continued to reflect their class and racial prejudices. They thought Dominicans were "lazy, had little sense of investment or hard work and multiplied much too quickly."[45] That bias helps to explain the colony's persistent endogamy.

Homesteaders disagreed about how to treat the hired help. Some, Topf remembered, treated (and paid) Dominican workers well and forged long-standing friendships. Others were patronizing and imposed strict discipline. Topf, observing Rosenzweig's homestead before moving onto his own, was appalled at the way he treated his staff, and asked Rosenzweig about it. "You have to treat them this way, otherwise they will take over," was the response he received. This was not the first time Topf had heard such pronouncements.

Thankfully, that kind of boorish behavior began to dissipate, he noted, as the second generation of settlers grew up (and attended school) along with local Dominicans.[46]

By 1957, the colony was, as far as DORSA was concerned, self-sufficient. Hexter no longer had to ask the JDC for additional funds to supplement the revenues from the repayments of settler mortgages. He was excited to report that new highway construction had diminished the travel time between Sosúa and the capital to four-and-a-half hours, almost one-third of the twelve hours it had taken when Hexter and Rosenberg first traveled to Sosúa from Ciudad Trujillo in the early 1940s. That had a beneficial impact on transaction costs and helped mitigate the colonists' sense of isolation. In addition, a "fabulous 22-foot-wide," all-weather asphalt road along the north coast connecting Sosúa to Samaná was, according to Hexter, "truly revolutionary in its impact." Imagine, he enthusiastically wrote Rosenberg, one could now "speed some 40 miles an hour" through the settlement. Hexter was stunned and pleased when he met with CILCA's board members to discuss their plans for modernizing their plant and they did not even "seek dollars or philanthropy."[47]

The colony's coming of age was recognized on January 1, 1959 by authorities who approved the settlement's request to make Sosúa a municipality in Puerto Plata Province. The state would now be responsible for providing services that DORSA had subsidized since the colony's inception.[48] Hexter was pleased with the association's excellent working relationship with government officials. He described to Rosenberg Trujillo's ambitious road-building program, the construction of new schools, and the rehabilitation of churches across the island. "In other words, our friend is continuing his improvement in the basic items of a civilized society, and he is doing it intelligently and consequentially."[49]

Hexter graciously acknowledged the symbolic passing of the torch in his correspondence with Rosenberg, referring to the settlement as "one of your finest paintings" and your "living opus." He added, "You were a lucky man to have seen your dreams realized and to see people . . . who failing your efforts would long ago have perished from the earth."[50]

These golden years, of course, were not without their share of disputation. Whereas Stern had unified the settlers with a coherent vision and his moshav-like combination of privatization and collaboration, his successor's methods failed to inspire the same confidence. Relations between DORSA and the settlers, which had been on the mend, again took a turn for the worse during Rosenzweig's tenure as director.

The new director's aggressive nature and arrogance put off some colonists; he also had a disturbing obsession with firearms. Other settlers thought he played favorites and rewarded friends and cronies with additional lands, not the first time that a director had been accused of preferential treatment. In Austria Rosenzweig had been a member of the conservative nationalist *Heimwehr,* or Home Guard. Similar to the German *Freikorps,* the Heimwehr opposed parliamentary democracy and Marxism, and its paramilitary forces roughed up trade unionists and leftists. Those reactionary political views put Rosenzweig at odds with some of the more progressive-minded colonists.

Given his background and political philosophy, it was not surprising that Rosenzweig, unlike his predecessors, went out of his way to cultivate relationships with the Dominican elite and the dictator himself. He became a member of the most exclusive social club in nearby Puerto Plata, a move that Trujillo offered up as proof that discrimination against Jews did not exist.[51]

In a surprising step, which indicated that Rosenzweig's ingratiating tactics were paying off, Trujillo made him a deputy in the legislature from Barahona, a district halfway across the island. It was the first time a Jew had served in the national congress. Rosenzweig's "DIPUTADO" license plates on his car annoyed his fellow settlers. Behind his back, they referred to their haughty director as the little Trujillo.

If Rosenzweig did not modify DORSA's longstanding policy of unconditional support for the dictatorship; he did make it demonstrably more public. His unique status as a national politician, settler, and DORSA administrator showered unwanted attention on the settlement and made colonists nervous. Having DORSA demonstrate its allegiance from the relative safety of New York had enabled the settlers to distance themselves from the association's actions while they went through the motions required of all citizens under the dictatorship. Rosenzweig's notoriety made it impossible to maintain that charade.

Diputado Rosenzweig spent considerable time away from Sosúa, which also did not sit well with his peers. There were unsubstantiated rumors that Trujillo had appointed him deputy in the first place because they shared a common fascination with guns and that the director was using his contacts in the States to procure guns for the dictator.[52]

As director, Rosenzweig also went out of his way to organize ostentatious celebrations of the dictator's rule. He was instrumental in staging a retrospective of Rosenberg's artwork at the Galeria Nacional de Bellas Artes in Ciudad

Trujillo in June 1951, in the dictator's honor. The fifty-piece exhibition, which included lithographs, pastels, oils, and watercolors, was pompously titled "Exposition of the Works of Dr. James N. Rosenberg, dedicated to General, Dr. Rafael L. Trujillo Molina, in recognition of our admiration and affection." Rosenzweig substituted for Rosenberg, who could not attend the opening, and presented Trujillo with two of the paintings, while two more were gifted to prominent cabinet members. Rosenzweig also arranged a subsequent reception for the exhibition at Sosúa, where the paintings were displayed at the Casa Grande.[53]

Anniversary celebrations of the contract signing were elaborate on the island and in New York. DORSA's thirteenth anniversary was one such affair at New York's Lotos Club in the summer of 1953. At a dinner in Trujillo's honor, DORSA executives presented him with a scroll of gratitude. Four settlers, including Rosenzweig, were brought up from Sosúa for the occasion; Rosenberg recounted their personal biographies before the assembled dignitaries. The theme was a familiar one—escape from persecution—carefully chosen to accentuate Trujillo's assertive anticommunism at the moment when McCarthyism was peaking in the United States. Guests learned, for instance, of Erich Benjamin's escape from Buchenwald and his subsequent odyssey to Sosúa via Shanghai. Just as he had helped Jews during their hour of need, Trujillo told the audience, he was ready to extend a helping hand to those unfortunates behind the Iron Curtain who were not permitted to worship their God because of godless, atheistic regimes.[54]

Trujillo was so pleased with what had transpired in New York that he took Rosenzweig aside and asked how he might repay the settlers' loyalty. Sosúa's director asked that the colonists be granted Dominican citizenship so that they could demonstrate their allegiance to their new homeland. Evidently, the dictator liked Rosenzweig's request. Citizenship for the settlers, so long promised and so often delayed, would now be granted.[55]

But Rosenzweig had not broached the subject with the settlers. After he returned from New York, when he informed the Rat of the "good news" and asked for its blessing, the council erupted, according to Elie Topf. In one of the most contentious meetings Topf attended during his eighteen years at the settlement, the leaders upbraided the officious Rosenzweig for taking it upon himself to ask for citizenship without consulting them beforehand and for presenting it to the Rat as a fait accompli. Some council members, such as Felix Koch, voted against the measure because "he was an Austrian citizen and had no intention of becoming a Dominican citizen," Topf remembered. Others were concerned that their children would be drafted into the army and might have to serve abroad. Still others expressed reservations about the symbolic nature of naturalization, fearing that it would be read as an unqualified statement of support and might cause political fallout at some point. Some reiterated their discomfort with Rosenzweig's affinity for the *melech* (Hebrew for king), the settlers' nickname for the dictator. Yet even though Topf was angry with Rosenzweig, he and the majority of the council reluctantly agreed to support the initiative; they worried that to reject it might make the settlers look like ingrates and it was better not to risk incurring the melech's wrath.[56]

The acrimonious debate revealed the settlers' ambivalence about their relationship with Trujillo. They did what every Dominican had to do to survive in Trujillo's world: participate in civic demonstrations when required, teach the prescribed curriculum in their school, and never utter a discouraging word publicly. But beyond that they tried to remain invisible. As Topf put it with more than a hint of ambiguity, "we were not supporters of the melech, but we were not deniers, either." He wryly noted, "we could criticize the regime any time we wanted, so long as we did it in German." Spanish republican exiles had been equally critical of Trujillo, but their complaints, voiced in the vernacular, attracted the attention of the security apparatus and led many of them to decide it was in their best interest to leave the island.[57] The Jewish colonists, on the other hand, had made the Dominican Republic their home, and were reluctant to tinker with strategies that had served them so well in the past. That is why they were so upset with Rosenzweig.

In the end the *diputado* got what he wanted—the council's blessing—and on June 21, 1953, seventy-seven settlers became naturalized Dominican citizens, Topf included. Soon thereafter, two additional "gifts" were bestowed on DORSA leaders by Trujillo. Rosenberg was awarded the Order of Duarte, the nation's highest honor; and in 1955, Hexter, like Rosenberg before him, was given an honorary degree from the Universidad de Santo Domingo, "given with almost medieval splendor."[58]

It had become *de rigueur* to include DORSA in key ceremonial functions, so it was no surprise when Trujillo's representatives asked management to celebrate his silver anniversary in power in 1955. To flaunt his civic improvements, encourage tourism, and remind Washington that he was an ally in the struggle against communism, Trujillo staged a lavish world's fair on a 125-acre tract on the outskirts of Ciudad Trujillo, an event he pompously called The International Fair for Peace and Brotherhood of the Free World. An estimated forty million dollars was spent, almost one-third the nation's annual budget.

DORSA was approached about making a contribution to the fair. Hexter and Rosenberg announced the commissioning of an Open Door Monument

FIGURE 23 DORSA contributes the Open Door Monument to Trujillo's International Peace Fair, Ciudad Trujillo, 1956. JDC ARCHIVES.

at the fairgrounds. Two bronze tablets, made in the United States, displayed bilingual text taken from the Sosúa contract's first article, guaranteeing the settlers freedom of religion. The tablets were mounted on two nine-foot-tall gray pillars carved in native marble from the Samaná quarries. Rosenberg put up the funds, and Rosenzweig and Hexter represented DORSA and the colony at the unveiling, where Hexter told the assembled dignitaries that "Trujillo had erected an indelible monument in the hearts of the settlers." The settlers who had taken the oath of citizenship two years before also were congratulated at the unveiling.[59] (See figure 23, above.)

Rosenberg was too ill to attend the fair's opening ceremonies, but he was heartened to learn of the settlement's expression of gratitude and the colony's improving condition. After he received a report of what had transpired, he wrote Hexter's wife, overcome with emotion: "Here in this world of tension, trouble, war and hate, Maurice and I are entitled to feel that we have done something useful and creative. . . . [The Open Door Monument] will never be as good, neither will my paintings, as our human life sculpture work at Sosúa."[60]

In figurative terms, however, Rosenberg, Hexter, and DORSA had stayed too long at the international fair and had been too demonstrative in their support for the melech. Trujillo's rule, the one constant in Sosúa's and, for that matter, Dominicans' lives, was about to come apart at the seams.

FIFTEEN

"The Beginning of the End"

> The Galíndez case was the most resounding international scandal
> of our time. It ensnared Trujillo in its own whirlpool, making him
> the final victim of a wave of bloodshed that he himself had un-
> leashed with that pointless crime. It initiated the destructive path
> that eventually undermined the Era of Trujillo.
>
> JOAQUÍN BALAGUER, 1975

DORSA's support for the dictator became increasingly untenable when his brutal methods extended all the way to the association's home base, New York City. On March 12, 1956, after teaching an evening graduate seminar on Latin American politics at Columbia University, Jesús de Galíndez Suárez was driven by one of his graduate students from the Morningside campus to the entrance of the subway station at Fifty-Seventh Street and Eighth Avenue. The forty-year-old part-time lecturer in government and Spanish descended the stairs of the station, intent on returning to his apartment on Fifth Avenue near Washington Square in Greenwich Village. Whether he ever reached his apartment is unclear, but soon thereafter Galíndez was forced into a vehicle at gunpoint, drugged, and then whisked away by Trujillo's henchmen to a private airport in Amityville, on Long Island. Galíndez was flown from that small airport—in a rented twin-engine Beechcraft plane outfitted with auxiliary gas tanks—to Monte Cristi on the northwest coast of the Dominican Republic. From there he disappeared. His body was never recovered. Local police and FBI investigations of the abduction proved inconclusive, and in the absence of a body, the case was never solved. Seven years later Galíndez was declared legally dead, but the enormous weight of circumstantial evidence led directly to Ciudad Trujillo.[1]

It soon became apparent why Galíndez "prompted" such heinous treatment. The Basque-born intellectual just had defended his dissertation at Columbia, a searing indictment of Trujillo's dictatorship. The thesis, which Galíndez sent to a Chilean publisher just three days before his disappearance, became an instant bestseller throughout Latin America, fueled by the sensational circumstances of his disappearance.[2]

This was not the first time Trujillo's security apparatus had pursued political opponents abroad—it was not even the first time the dictator had eliminated dissidents in New York City.[3] What distinguished the Galíndez case from past assassinations was Trujillo's insistence that Galíndez be retrieved from New York, presumably for questioning and punishment. This required advance planning, additional manpower, and a way to make sure that those who participated in the abduction kept silent. Covering up the original crime is where the Galíndez case took several macabre twists and turns, capturing the imagination of American public opinion and the attention of the U.S. Congress, the State Department, the FBI, and the CIA.

"Where is the Professor?" screamed the headline in the June 11 issue of *Newsweek*. The *New York Times* wondered how a "prominent foreigner with many influential friends could vanish from our city."[4] With each new revelation, DORSA's administrators found themselves entangled in the cover-up's web. As regime insider Joaquín Balaguer aptly put it two decades later, the crime and its cover-up were "the beginning of the end" for the dictatorship.[5]

Who was Galíndez? One of several thousand Spanish Civil War émigrés whom Trujillo had welcomed in 1939, he was a staunch advocate of Basque autonomy, a prominent member of the Basque Nationalist Party, and a sworn enemy of General Francisco Franco. Thanks to Trujillo's benevolence, the twenty-four-year-old soon was teaching law at the Foreign Ministry's diplomatic school and later served as a legal adviser for the Labor Ministry. Galíndez ran afoul of the regime in January 1946 when, as legal adviser to a minimum wage commission, he sought to settle a general strike by proposing wage increases that Trujillo deemed too favorable to the workers. After the regime cracked down on the striking workers and forced their union leader to flee to Havana, Galíndez realized that his days in the Dominican Republic were numbered, and departed for New York City in February 1946. He was singled out in the Dominican press, and a year later his name appeared on a Trujillo blacklist.[6]

In New York Galíndez found work as a registered representative of the Basque government-in-exile and appeared before the United Nations as an official observer, where he fought against Franco's Spain's inclusion in the world body.[7] Galíndez was angered by Trujillo's support for that inclusion as well as his toadying to Franco during a state visit to Madrid in June 1954. Galíndez also befriended exiles in New York's Hispanic community who opposed dictatorships on the right and the left. He traveled throughout Latin America, where he hobnobbed publicly with democrats like Rómulo Betancourt of Venezuela, José Figueres of Costa Rica, and Salvador Allende of Chile and wrote extensively for Spanish-language newspapers, magazines, and scholarly journals.[8]

Complicating matters was that Galíndez, an avowed anticommunist with excellent contacts among plotters in the exile community, moonlighted as an informant for both the FBI and the CIA, although apparently neither agency was aware that he worked for the other.[9] Assisting Washington during the height of McCarthyism was not unusual for exiles like Galíndez. For some it was a way of demonstrating their ideological opposition to totalitarianism or, apparently for Galíndez, a measure of gratitude for the State Department's moral and financial support for Basque nationalism; for still others, it was a means to supplement their income or obtain or renew residency. To be sure, Galíndez's compromising position as an informant with these agencies complicated in no small way federal and local investigations of his kidnapping and murder.[10]

Whatever Galíndez's motivations for providing information, he became consumed with his doctoral research on Trujillo's regime. As his mentor at Columbia, the historian Frank Tannenbaum, related, "Galíndez came to resemble nothing so much as a walking one-man intelligence bureau. He knew more about Trujillo than anyone else in the whole wide world."[11]

It also led him to question the costs and benefits of U.S. support for dictators like Trujillo. The CIA-assisted overthrow of the democratically elected Jacobo Arbenz in Guatemala in 1954 and the subsequent imposition of a brutal military dictatorship had stunned many Latin Americans. In an article in Columbia's *Journal of International Affairs* published less than a year before his disappearance, Galíndez drew a bright line between his principled opposition to all forms of dictatorship and North American anticommunism, which was so consumed by fear that it was predisposed to support strongarm rulers who crushed democratic elements. Washington "prefers the apparent safety of a dictator who calls himself an ally and an anti-Communist to the uncertainty of revolutions and governments of popular origin," he wrote. McCarthyism at home only undermined the legitimacy of America's foreign policy abroad. Such a "negative policy" ensured that Washington aligned itself with the forces of repression instead of democracy, thereby fanning anti-American sentiment.[12]

As far as Washington's Cold Warriors were concerned, political instability was to be avoided at all costs. As a result, in 1952 the United States had signed military pacts with several dictatorships, including the Dominican Republic. According to Galíndez, these militaries were more akin to police forces "occupying their own countries" than armies defending their nation from external attack. Even though he only alluded to Trujillo once in the piece and then in the third person, it was obvious that he thought Washington's relationship with the dictator was counterproductive. Not content to be an armchair intellectual, Galíndez was a fixture at exile-led demonstrations against Trujillo in New York.[13]

The essay that no doubt struck a raw nerve in Ciudad Trujillo was a sarcastic, muckraking piece that Galíndez published in 1955 in *Cuadernos Americanos*, a scholarly and literary journal that enjoyed wide dissemination throughout Latin America. "Un reportaje sobre Santo Domingo" was, in some respects, a précis of the dissertation, sans scholarly analysis and citations. "For the Dominicans that suffer," Galíndez began, "the Trujillist regime is a daily drama that silences lips and oppresses hearts. For foreigners with open eyes, the Benefactor and his megalomanias are a treasure trove of incredible surprises, worthy of being divulged."[14] But the similarity ends there. The dissertation allowed that Trujillo was not "as bloody as the exiles assert."[15] It credited the general with enhancing security, sustaining the arts, eliminating the national debt, creating new industries, building schools and hospitals, and addressing illiteracy, hunger, and disease. The *Cuadernos* article, in contrast, reads like a polemic. Galíndez aired the regime's dirty laundry, including its pervasive nepotism, and mocked the general's endless accumulation of laudatory titles and military promotions even though Trujillo had never set foot on a battlefield. Galíndez also documented how ridiculed and marginalized the dictator was throughout the Caribbean. Last but not least, he indiscreetly discussed the paternity of Trujillo's son, Ramfis. The dictator's likely heir apparent, the professor revealed, actually was not Trujillo's offspring but the product of his third wife's prior marriage to a Cuban.[16]

It is not surprising that Trujillo's agents tried to buy out Galíndez before his doctoral defense, allegedly offering fifty thousand dollars for his thesis.[17] Trujillo had invested tens of millions of dollars in his grandiose international fair to promote tourism and foreign investment, and the negative publicity from Galíndez's book had the potential to cripple the dictator's plans.[18]

Galíndez was well aware of the risks. "I know perfectly well that I'm playing with dynamite," he wrote to a friend.[19] A fellow journalist and Dominican dissident, Andrés Requena, had been shot in an apartment hallway in Manhattan by the general's hit men in October 1952. So it was not entirely surprising when the New York City police found a copy of Galíndez's will and an accompanying letter addressed to them in his apartment after his disappearance, dated three years earlier, just after Requena's death. It advised that should anything happen to Galíndez, the police should question the Dominican consul in New York City, a man under suspicion for Requena's murder.[20]

Galíndez successfully defended the dissertation less than two weeks before his abduction. Posthumously published as *La era de Trujillo*, it provided a wealth of detail about the dictatorship, but it was the negative publicity surrounding his disappearance that set off a firestorm and put Trujillo supporters on Capitol Hill and at DORSA on the defensive.

A few months after the furor subsided, Trujillo again inflamed U.S. public opinion. In early December 1956, a car owned by twenty-three-year-old American pilot Gerald Murphy, who worked for a Dominican airline, was found abandoned near a slaughterhouse in Ciudad Trujillo. Just as in the Galíndez case, the pilot's body was never found. It soon became apparent that the disappearances were linked; the FBI revealed that Murphy had rented the Beechcraft for eight hundred dollars in cash and then had piloted the plane that took Galíndez back to the island.

A month later, Murphy's friend and fellow pilot Octavio "Tavito" de la Maza, who the FBI believed then flew Galíndez from Monte Cristi to the capital, was appointed the fall guy for Murphy's disappearance.[21] Authorities announced that Tavito had hung himself in his prison cell, an apparent suicide, but not before leaving a suicide note that implausibly sought to explain why he took his own life.[22]

Nor were De la Maza, Murphy, and Galíndez the only ones killed, pronounced dead, or who disappeared in the cover-up. The night watchman on duty at the Amityville airport and a mechanic at the West Palm Beach airport, where the Beechcraft refueled, also died under mysterious circumstances.[23]

It was one matter to murder opponents of the regime either at home or abroad. But Trujillo had unleashed a public relations nightmare by eliminating Murphy, a U.S. citizen who, by some reports, "knew too much."[24] His family sued the Dominican government and persuaded their congressional representatives from Oregon, Representative Charles Porter and Senator

Wayne Morse, to investigate their son's disappearance. The *Washington Post*, the *New York Times*, and a riveting hour-long CBS radio broadcast on May 20, 1957, produced and narrated by Edward R. Murrow, called "The Galíndez-Murphy Case: A Chronicle of Terror," gave the story fresh "legs." The legislators called on the administration of Dwight D. Eisenhower to repudiate its support for Trujillo.

Morse used his position as chair of the Senate subcommittee on Latin American affairs as a bully pulpit, and Porter also spoke out, comparing Trujillo's methods to those of Prohibition-era gangsters and demanding a complete investigation into Murphy's murder. The congressman had his sights set on more than just securing justice for his constituents, however. Declaring that the U.S. policy of coddling dictators abroad "was partially responsible for the death of Murphy," Porter insisted that the administration reconsider its policies. He also took on those in the U.S. Congress who benefited from Trujillo's largesse and who had been quick to laud the dictator's anticommunist credentials. Then Porter called for an end to the Dominican sugar quota and the termination of all Export-Import Bank loans and military assistance to the country.[25]

After his blistering attack, Porter was sure he was a target of the regime. Taking no chances, he "armed himself to the teeth." CBS News wisely took similar precautions when it taped the Murrow broadcast, going to unusual lengths to protect the identity of its informants—using pseudonyms, distorting their voices, and filming the interviews in secret locations. Murrow later recalled that the broadcast was the most disquieting of his career, owing to the informants' palpable fear.[26]

As public opinion throughout Latin America turned against Trujillo, Porter became an overnight celebrity, accepting invitations to speak around the Caribbean. Betancourt asked Porter to come to Caracas, where he attracted a crowd of twenty thousand enthusiastic supporters just two months after Vice President Richard Nixon was spit on and pelted with rocks in the same city. The congressman also was the guest of Governor Luis Muñoz Marín of Puerto Rico in June 1957. There Porter roused a partisan audience of Dominicans and Puerto Ricans at the University of Puerto Rico, where he threw down the gauntlet, proclaiming, "If I were a Dominican, I would be a revolutionary."[27]

Realizing that he had to counteract the bad press, a grim Trujillo spared no expense. By one estimate, he spent $6 million to "soften the impact of the Galíndez case."[28] The expenses included a $750,000 payment to the Mutual Broadcasting System to air 425 minutes per month for 18 months of "news favorable to the government."[29] Porter reported that the general even paid a

$50,000 indemnity to Gerald Murphy's parents in "a rather clumsy attempt to buy [their] silence."[30]

Trujillo's supporters in the U.S. Congress circled the wagons. Louisiana Senator George Long argued that Trujillo's government might not be a dictatorship, because "after all, it held elections."[31] Senator Richard Russell of Georgia, normally a critic of U.S. support for dictatorships, allowed, "if we must have a dictatorship, Trujillo has been about as liberal a dictator as a country could have."[32]

The Galíndez-Murphy affair put the administration in a bind. The State Department had been appalled by Trujillo's repressive methods for quite some time. But now the administration was feeling the heat from congressional watchdogs, and it appeared to policymakers that the general was intent on pushing the limits of acceptable behavior.[33] How Washington should respond would be the subject of months of intense internal debate that involved intelligence agencies, the State Department, and the Department of Defense. The administration and Trujillo did share one priority: both moved quickly to counteract the negative press. Just a year before Galíndez's disappearance, Vice President Nixon had toured the region and publicly embraced and praised Trujillo before the cameras. Now the dictator's actions forced the administration to re-evaluate its "unabashed embrace of anti-Communist military dictatorships and its unwillingness to criticize, however mutedly, rampant political and civil repression in Latin America."[34]

DISTANCING ITSELF FROM THE DICTATOR

The administration had additional reasons to reconsider its support. It was unhappy with Trujillo's adventurism in the Caribbean, especially his continuing harassment of Betancourt, Figueres, and Fulgencio Batista in Cuba. Moreover, it was concerned that Trujillo's insatiable economic appetite was crowding out U.S. investment on the island, especially his desire to expand his share of the sugar sector at the expense of U.S. companies.[35]

Even so, official (and public) confirmation by Washington that the Dominican government was responsible for the murders of Galíndez, Murphy, and de la Maza was categorically ruled out. That kind of public dressing down might have unforeseen consequences, Richard Stephens, the chargé d'affaires in Ciudad Trujillo, wrote, there was no accounting for how a cornered Trujillo might respond: "Twenty-six years of absolute power, during which time any manifestation of opposition has been suppressed by the most direct methods, have produced in the Generalíssimo a state of mind that is perhaps best characterized as utter ruthlessness combined with a sense of personal righteousness. In Trujillo's eye, after a quarter century of slavish obedience and enforced adulation, he probably appears to himself as some kind of a God-like man who is above and beyond the normal restraints of human society, all of his acts being justified to himself on the basis of what he has done for his country."[36] Roy Rubottom, assistant secretary of state for interamerican affairs, warned that Trujillo "might retaliate against . . . our investors in the Dominican Republic whose holdings total nearly $100 million." In addition, the United States had "guided missile testing facilities there which the Defense Department considers 'vital.'"[37] Better to handle this discreetly, Stephens wrote, with a stern warning of future consequences if such actions reoccurred.[38]

Instead, that summer the United States withheld materiel assistance promised to the Dominican navy, turned down a Dominican request to have its squadron of F-47 fighter planes modernized, and postponed the sale of thirteen F-80C jets.[39] A more general reappraisal about how best to deal with dictators was under way. Even Nixon came to the realization that there was a price to pay for business as usual. No more *abrazos* for dictators, no need to demonstrate unnecessary or exaggerated friendliness, he concluded. That should be reserved for budding democracies. Henceforth the Trujillos of the region were due only a formal handshake.[40]

Latin America's democracies were understandably wary of U.S. rhetoric and demanded greater consistency. They urged the United States to make clear that it did not welcome and certainly would not materially assist dictatorships that paid lip service to democracy.[41]

Thanks to the public airing of the lurid details of the murders, the partial ban on arms sales, and the administration's more restrained posture toward dictators, Trujillo remained on the defensive. His fifty-four consulates (more numerous than those of any other nation) cranked out propaganda to overcome the negative press. Just as he did after the Haitian massacre some twenty years before, Trujillo began his public relations blitz by taking out a full-page advertisement in the *New York Times*, titled "The Other Side of the Galíndez Story." A widely distributed pamphlet with the same title appeared soon thereafter. But his publicists' claim that Galíndez was a card-carrying Communist rang hollow. So did the unfounded assertion that Galíndez was a confidence man who had embezzled funds the State Department had given to the Basque government-in-exile and then had engineered his own disappearance to abscond with the lucre.[42]

To repair his tattered image, Trujillo again played the all-too-familiar religious tolerance and humanitarian cards. After the Soviet invasion of Hungary in 1956, he invited twenty thousand Hungarians to resettle on the island, a move he knew would play well with American Cold Warriors.[43] Only two hundred immigrants were taken in and sent to agricultural colonies. Like the Spanish republicans before them, this most recent batch of exiles had no farming experience, and they had little desire to learn.[44]

SHILLS

Then, at a ceremony in Ciudad Trujillo in April 1957, in the presence of four Jewish members of Congress from New York, Pennsylvania, and Maryland who had been shuttled down expressly for an elaborate show-and-tell, Trujillo announced that he was prepared to admit up to five thousand Egyptian Jews.[45] (None ever actually immigrated.) At the same time, he staged a photo opportunity with the representatives when Rosenzweig officially was sworn in as *diputado*. The ceremony had its intended effect; upon his return to the United States, Representative Herbert Zelenko of New York cited the "election" of Sosúa's director as evidence of "the freedom of opportunity, freedom of worship and absence of any kind of racial or religious discrimination" in the Dominican Republic. As one critic mocked, however, "unfortunately, the visiting Congressmen did not consider it worthwhile to ask the brand-new deputy, whose taking of oath they witnessed, either how long he had campaigned or by what plurality he had been elected."[46]

Calling upon old reliable DORSA, the dictator asked Hexter to deflect the continuing criticism from the media. Hexter wrote to Louis Loeb, the president of the New York City Bar, asking him to establish a commission of inquiry to look into Galíndez's disappearance. "It is . . . utterly inconceivable that Generalíssimo Trujillo can have anything to do, directly or indirectly, with the unfortunate disappearance of Dr. Galíndez. Innuendoes have appeared in a number of places suggesting that the disappearance (and the hints of murder) [are] due to directives given by the Generalíssimo. No one who has looked him in the eye as I have on numerous occasions can have the slightest hesitation in saying that it just could not be so."[47]

Hexter also helped the Dominican government contract the services of a prominent New York civil liberties attorney, Morris L. Ernst, to investigate the disappearances. Trujillo gave Ernst and his team of investigators a one-hundred-thousand-dollar advance and an equal amount for operating expenses to conduct an "independent" inquiry. Murphy's family and Porter immediately denounced the investigation, asserting that the eventual report would have greater legitimacy if Ernst and his associates donated their exorbitant fee to charity. Not surprisingly, Ernst's subsequent report could not find "a scintilla of evidence that Galíndez had any relation of any kind to Murphy," and the "entire story in our judgment was a canard trumped up by political enemies of the Dominican Republic or . . . as a cloak to cover up the real operations of Galíndez and his so-called Basque fund of more than a million dollars."[48] Six months later, Hexter happily reported to Rosenberg that Trujillo had thanked him "for my démarche . . . which had visibly paid off."[49]

No good deed went unrewarded. The dictator announced the gift of sixty thousand dollars toward the construction of a community center for the capital's Jewish community in an upscale neighborhood near where the dictator's mother and daughter lived. Although the community center did not benefit the colony per se, a number of transplanted Sosuaners lived in Ciudad Trujillo, and the cooperatives had an office and warehouse there.[50]

Given the publicity surrounding the Galíndez-Murphy cause célèbre, it is hard to imagine that Rosenzweig, and Hexter for that matter, did not realize that they were being used as shills. But if they did, they did not give the impression that they objected, nor did they try to keep a low profile. To add insult to injury, in the summer of 1958 Rosenzweig announced plans to build a monument to the general, which would be placed "in front of the little park near the DORSA office in El Batey in time for his upcoming birthday in late October."[51]

The problem for DORSA was that Trujillo now was so badly discredited that its own reputation and the settlement's would be tarnished as well. Moreover, loyalty proved fleeting; like so many of Trujillo's underlings, Rosenzweig was discarded as soon as he was no longer needed. His "term" as deputy lasted but eighteen months.[52]

DORSA's unconditional loyalty finally backfired when Trujillo's opponents organized to overthrow him. In June 1959, just six months after Fidel Castro ousted Batista, two small expeditionary forces of dissidents left Cuba for the Dominican Republic. Cuban airplanes attempted to provide cover for the invasion, strafing the beach at Sosúa. Sonja Burian, then twelve years old, still has vivid memories of "the low-flying planes and the sound of shooting in Sosúa and surroundings . . . at one point it looked like the planes were headed straight toward me." She remembered that parents rounded up their children and moved them from El Batey to Laguna, out of harm's way. "Fortunately no one was hurt," Hexter wrote to Rosenberg. "Some slight damage done to the [William] Bein house. . . . Likewise there was a hit on one of the buildings of the hotel."[53] The rebels were not so fortunate; they were easily hunted down, tortured, and killed by the military.

Pressure continued to mount. In 1959 Betancourt asked the Organization of American States to recognize only "regimes born of free elections and respecting human rights," and called for the Dominican Republic's immediate ouster from the mutual security organization.[54] His resolution raised concerns in Washington and throughout the hemisphere, however, because it flew in the face of the OAS charter's nonintervention doctrine.[55]

Increasingly isolated by the fall of ten regional strongmen between 1956 and 1960, Trujillo went on the offensive once again, plotting to overthrow Betancourt. He first tried to assist a military coup against the Venezuelan president, and when that failed, ordered Betancourt's assassination. On June 24, 1960, an explosive device placed in a parked car on a Caracas street was detonated just as Betancourt's automobile passed by. The president's aide was killed and his driver seriously injured, but Betancourt escaped with severe burns to his hands.

Trujillo had finally gone too far. Two months later the OAS, for the first time in its history, broke off diplomatic relations with one of its member states and imposed partial economic sanctions against the Dominican Republic.[56] Even the United States agreed, closing the doors of its embassy and leaving only a skeletal consular staff in Ciudad Trujillo.

The United States, however, initially undermined the economic sanctions agreed to by the OAS, when it permitted the Dominican Republic to fill Cuba's recently suspended sugar quota. This quadrupled the Dominican share of the quota, a windfall for Trujillo and his associates, who owned upwards of 60 percent of the island's sugar industry. When negative publicity about the windfall surfaced, the Eisenhower administration, not wanting to appear to undermine the OAS sanctions, asked Congress to suspend the Dominican quota, just as it had the Cuban quota after Castro came to power in 1959. But Trujillo still had allies in Congress, and the Senate and House Agricultural Committees balked. President Eisenhower was convinced that Trujillo had bribed several key legislators. The administration then circumvented Congress by placing a special tax on Dominican sugar imports to offset the profits earned by raising the quota.[57]

Effectively consigned to pariah status, a beleaguered Trujillo now behaved in ways that seemed out of character for a ruler who heretofore had governed so adroitly. To maintain control and crush unrest, the regime always had relied on censorship, wiretaps, extensive surveillance of foreign journalists and diplomats, and selective assassination at home and abroad.[58] Now it chose new enemies, turning its sights on two traditional bulwarks of the regime, the Catholic Church and the middle and upper classes. Repression against suspected dissidents grew daily as prominent businessmen and professionals were jailed for plotting against the regime. Adolf Berle painted a bleak picture of events in his personal diary: "The Dominican Republic is blowing up. The plots against the dictator are serious and he has responded in classic fashion—with unlimited terror and torture. . . . Each day a family discovers that some member of it has vanished, and the torture chambers of the old fortress are said to be full. The . . . dictatorship has eliminated practically all of the capable people and the terrible prospect is one of increasing anarchy."[59]

Stung by Washington's "betrayal," Trujillo now sealed his fate by flirting with the Soviet Union and Castro. The dictator, who had built a reputation as an implacable foe of Marxism, now did an about-face and legalized the Communist Party in June 1960.[60]

An economic crisis mirrored the political uncertainties as virtually every significant economic indicator declined precipitously between 1959 and 1961. Public and private investment were sharply curtailed, international reserves were drawn down to bolster the military, and investment capital took flight. All these were demonstrable signs of a lack of confidence in the regime's capacity to defuse the crisis.[61]

Concerned about the Cuban Revolution's ripple effects, the State Department began to think about how best to avoid another Castro next door. Better to remove Trujillo from power before a leftist *fait accompli*. Eisenhower told his aides, "until Trujillo is eliminated we cannot get our Latin American friends to reach a proper level of indignation in dealing with Castro."[62]

Efforts by the administration to persuade Trujillo to step down and enjoy a comfortable retirement elsewhere proved fruitless. In March 1960 Trujillo turned down an offer of asylum in the United States "with his fortune [to be] deposited in a foundation headed by U.S. and Latin American leaders."[63] Eight months later, Trujillo rebuffed a similar offer to retire to either Morocco or Portugal.[64] Even Washington's subsequent decision to cut off arms sales and pull its military missions off the island did not have the desired effect.

Meanwhile, State Department officials did their best to stitch together pro-American business, professional, and academic groups on the island into a unified opposition. After three decades of largely unqualified support, Washington's withdrawal of military assistance and its conversations with domestic leaders were read locally as an unambiguous message that the United States would no longer stand in the way of "moderate" elements. The State Department and the CIA initiated conversations with domestic coup plotters, and by May 1960, Eisenhower had authorized a contingency plan to assist in an overthrow.[65] As one State Department official put, "it's no longer a question of if Trujillo will fall, but when."[66]

DORSA's board began to express concern for Rosenzweig's safety because of his complicity with the dictatorship. "It was suggested to Hexter that it might be desirable to get Mr. Rosenzweig out of San Domingo because if the present regime should fall, he might find himself in a difficult situation. He is naturally tied up with the regime, since the entire project is under the protection and aegis of the Generalíssimo."[67] Even Hexter admitted he "was getting uneasy" and persuaded Rosenzweig to come to New York in the fall of 1960.[68]

Rosenzweig and Hexter still proved to be miserable prognosticators, insisting until the end that Trujillo would ride out the storm. Rosenzweig repeatedly assured Hexter, "everything is quiet."[69] As late as three months before Trujillo's assassination, Hexter, on a visit to the settlement, wrote to Leavitt in New York, "Politically things are calmer and easier than a year ago. The Generalíssimo is more strongly entrenched than ever. . . . I noticed less military tension this time than during the preceding years." But perhaps because the topic of regime change was on everyone's lips, he quickly added, "but, of course, no one knows what will happen in case of his death, which I don't estimate will be a violent one."[70]

How could they have misread the situation so badly? Perhaps a Dominican Republic without Trujillo was unimaginable to DORSA's leadership. It certainly was unthinkable to many Dominicans. Yet at a time when the dictator's allies were deserting him in droves and Washington had distanced itself from the regime, DORSA stayed the course, never once questioning whether it would be more politic to refrain from its obsequious backing of a discredited ruler squarely in the crosshairs of North American and Latin American public opinion. Hexter and Rosenberg each wrote Trujillo as late as the fall of 1960 that they felt bad that the OAS and the United States had turned their backs on him.[71] Hexter then asked Rosenberg whether DORSA should do more to help the aging Trujillo through the tough days ahead. "I wonder if you and I ought not to be doing something. After all, the man was helpful to our people and has always been personally friendly to you and me." Not sure what to do, he suggested that he and Rosenberg write letters of "sympathy and understanding and prepare it for eventual publication by him in case he saw fit."[72] Not only did DORSA's leadership seem oblivious to Trujillo's inevitable fall, but through their precipitous actions, they appeared to welcome reprisals from opponents.

Washington had no such illusions. Aware that an assassination attempt was imminent, administration officials remained fixated on ensuring that the Dominican Republic did not become another Cuba. In the wake of the Bay of Pigs fiasco in April 1961, however, the Kennedy administration, uneasy about who might fill the power vacuum left by Trujillo's ouster, did an about-face and actively discouraged the dissidents. On May 25, 1961, President Kennedy approved a contingency plan to deal with a post-Trujillo regime, but instructed the director of the CIA to avoid "the risk of U.S. association with political assassination." Pro-U.S. groups could count on U.S. military support, the contingency plan noted, but if "unfriendly elements" seized power, the CIA was to urge our friends to "declare themselves the provisional government" and request immediate military assistance from Washington.[73]

Five days later, fourteen conspirators with varying motives, a number of them prominent Trujillistas, took matters into their own hands. Led by Tavito de la Maza's brother, Antonio, eight of the plotters, all of whom held personal grudges against the general, intercepted the dictator's Chevrolet late in the evening and riddled his body with twenty-seven rounds of ammunition.[74]

News of the gangland-style slaying rocked the settlement and DORSA headquarters in New York. Cecil Hess, then an impressionable twelve-year-old Sosuaner, recalled how he felt the day he learned about the assassination: "It was devastating. I grew up thinking that Trujillo was the best thing that ever happened to Sosúa. I never had heard anything bad about him. It was as if the world had stopped. It wasn't until years later that I started to become aware of the real problems of the dictatorship."[75]

Hexter immediately sent telegrams of condolence to Trujillo's widow and to Joaquín Balaguer, his successor, which avowed that "the world is poorer for the loss of your illustrious *jefe*" and praised the dictator for helping "my co-religionists escape persecution and secure another chance at freedom." When the interim government held a nationwide day of mourning for Trujillo in early June, Sosúa's synagogue followed suit and held its own memorial service. Rosenzweig, who attended the service, wrote Hexter, "You could see the grief in all the faces. He will be missed for many, many years to come."[76]

In December 1961, DORSA, fearing for its director's safety, removed Rosenzweig and his family from its employ, moved them to Jacksonville, Florida, and gave him a generous severance package.[77] A month later, Hexter asked the JDC's assistant treasurer to remove Trujillo's name from the Board of Directors on DORSA stationery.[78]

Bereft of their longtime patron and protector, DORSA and Sosúa were vulnerable. Clientelistic relationships would have to be forged with new political actors, and quickly. Fortunately, the settlement knew a key politico who, over the next two decades, would help the colony steer through turbulent waters. As with Trujillo, however, there would be a price to pay for his services.

SIXTEEN

Ravages of Aging

> I was terribly distressed that you still had no word from the
> appropriate authorities with respect to the intruders at Sosúa.
> I had hoped that in the light of our full cooperation that we
> manifested to the Government . . . they would long ago have
> regularized the situation.
>
> MAURICE HEXTER TO BRUNO PHILIPP, 1962

Nation and settlement held their collective breath after Trujillo's
assassination. The plotters had eliminated their prey but failed
to dislodge the dictator's family or his feared security apparatus from
power. A week after the assassination, writing in his personal diary,
Adolf Berle Jr. accurately predicted that matters would get much
worse before they improved. Trujillo's son, Ramfis, and the head of the
secret police, Johnny Abbes, "are pretty nearly the lowest form of life . . .
there will be another period of dictatorship by the most cut-throat
elements going."[1] Berle proved prophetic; over the next seven months,
the two of them took revenge on those suspected of involvement in
the plot, brutally torturing and killing all but two, Tony Imbert and
coconspirator Luis Amiama Tió, who went into hiding to avoid retri-
bution. In the interim, a provisional government was put in place with
Joaquín Balaguer as its titular head, but Ramfis held sway. The dictator
was dead, but for a tense interval, the regime lived on.

Even bucolic Sosúa could not escape the reign of terror. Alejandro
Martínez, a respected doctor who worked at Sosúa's clinic, and Pedro
Clisante, a young man employed by a local business establishment,
made the deadly mistake of imprudently shouting anti-Trujillo slogans in front of police headquarters. Neither was a leftist firebrand,

but in that tense political climate, when the secret police was conducting nationwide sweeps for possible suspects, anti-Trujillista criticism was dealt with severely. Authorities surrounded Martínez's house, the police called for him to come out, and he was machine-gunned down in cold blood. Clisante became a casualty soon thereafter. For the first time in the settlement's brief history, repression had made its presence felt, and the settlers, who must have felt especially vulnerable given past displays of support for Trujillo, kept their counsel.[2]

Not until massive popular demonstrations and old-fashioned U.S. gunboat diplomacy combined to drive the Trujillo clan into exile in late November 1961 did the nation take its first halting steps toward forging a new political destiny. Five tumultuous years followed, during which Dominicans witnessed fourteen different governments (six of which lasted sixteen days or less), a series of coups and abortive takeovers, and a U.S. military intervention. In July 1966, Balaguer assumed the presidency, a post he then occupied for twenty-two of the next thirty years. The nation appeared to have come full circle.

Twenty-six Dominican political parties, along with the Kennedy and Johnson administrations, bickered and sought unsuccessfully to fill the vacuum left by the assassination and usher in a democracy. Meanwhile, Dominican peasants, no longer fearful of reprisals, took matters into their own hands. Agrarian reform initiatives, encouraged by Kennedy's Alliance for Progress and Dominican politicians currying favor with rural constituents, promised meaningful change and raised expectations. But the ephemeral governments disagreed on the methods and scope of the reform and lacked the political will and resources to respond quickly to the pent-up demand.[3] As a result, land-hungry campesinos invaded unoccupied privately held lands. Attorney General Antonio García Vásquez admitted to *El Caribe* that during the summer of 1962, eight thousand peasants had occupied lands illegally. It was up to the landowners, he added, to solve this problem, a startling admission of the once impregnable state's inability to protect private property.[4]

Lands owned by the Trujillos and their associates were especially inviting targets, and DORSA's property proved no exception. Choco, the settlement's hilly, largely undeveloped southern flank, was overrun by "several thousand" peasants in the months after the ouster of the Trujillo clan. To be sure, dozens of peasants, working on dairy fincas or at the cooperatives, had squatted on the colony's lands for years, but the timing and magnitude of these invasions unnerved administrators and settlers.[5] A powerless Hexter, frustrated with the attorney general for not responding to his call for help, wrote in September

1962, "What I find uniquely disturbing is that the person in charge acts as though this is our problem."[6]

The U.S. ambassador, John Bartlow Martin, who visited Sosúa soon thereafter, painted an unsettling picture. "Dominican campesinos resented the colonists as Trujillo collaborators, moved in, overran their grazing lands, built squatters' shacks, cut down splendid timber, and planted corn on hillsides so steep that after a single season rain washed the topsoil away. Then they abandoned the land they ruined and moved deeper into the colony's lands." The colonists had appealed to the police and the local army commander, but to no avail. This was not the least bit surprising to Martin. "Authority had nearly broken down even in the capital; it could hardly be expected to operate here." Even though Sosuaners informed him that they were taking no chances and packing guns for their own safety, they believed that they deserved the U.S. government's protection. Martin gently informed the settlers that as much as the embassy would like to help, there was little it could do. What was left unsaid, but which he later admitted in his memoirs, was that the residents were German, Austrian, or Dominican nationals, not Americans, and would have been better served if they had turned elsewhere for assistance.[7]

Martin's reasoning would have puzzled DORSA administrators and the settlers. The association was an American nonprofit, headquartered in New York and established with FDR's blessing. It still owned property at the settlement, and administrators felt, with some justification, that it deserved their government's protection. But the settlement was anomalous. It was now a municipality, and much of the land was, as Martin noted, not owned by U.S. citizens. Even if he had wanted to help, given the unstable situation, there was little he could have done to rectify the problem. The Sosuaners and DORSA were left wondering whom they could turn to and whether Sosúa's ambiguous character and its past affiliation with the dictatorship would expose it to attacks from Trujillo's enemies.

The land invasions, Trujillo's death, and the forced exile of Alfred Rosenzweig, left the settlement without political cover in the capital or leadership on site. To complicate matters, a new agrarian reform law passed in 1962 mandated that properties held by Trujillo and his inner circle were to be confiscated by the state and redistributed. Sosúa, of course, originally had been the dictator's property, and ever since the contract was signed, he had been an *ex officio* member of DORSA's board and a minor shareholder. The caretaker Council of State that replaced Balaguer's provisional government in early 1962 contemplated expropriating the Sosúa tract.[8] Fortunately for the colony, the council decided not to do so and instead requested and received from the association the one hundred shares of DORSA stock that its board had given Trujillo in 1940 as symbolic compensation for his original donation.[9]

Given the unsettled climate, Hexter knew he needed assistance from someone with good contacts in the capital, now renamed Santo Domingo. He asked Bruno Philipp, a successful businessman residing in the capital who moonlighted as Israel's honorary consul, to represent the colony. Philipp's initial pleas to officials for assistance about the squatters fell on deaf ears, however. When the usually upbeat Hexter learned of the Council of State's intransigence, he was upset that authorities did not respond. "In light of our full cooperation," he expected no less.[10]

Hexter ordered Philipp to sell off some of DORSA's disposable assets, including $64,000 worth of cattle; its warehouse inventories at Sosúa and in Santo Domingo, worth approximately $25,000 to $30,000; and its automobiles and tractors.[11] He also asked him to dispose of several properties in El Batey. Hexter also took steps to reduce subsidies. He had written to Rosenzweig two months before Trujillo's death that the subsidy would be cut from $500 to $300 a month after July 1, 1961. By January 1, 1962, the subvention was reduced to $200 a month; and by the end of that year, the settlement was entirely on its own. These transactions foreshadowed more significant divestments that DORSA would make in the 1970s.[12]

Why didn't Hexter sell off all of DORSA's assets, including some valuable beachfront land it still possessed, and cut its ties with Sosúa for good? After all, he had promised JDC executives he would do so once the settlement was self-sustaining. Yet even though the settlement was now a municipality and the colonists had assumed responsibility for most services, it still depended on DORSA's generosity. Pulling out was easier said than done.

Deserting the colonists at that difficult moment was probably unthinkable, but what legally tied DORSA's hands was David Stern's 1945 pact with the homesteaders. At that time, a forward-looking Rat had been concerned about the very same questions. Could authorities ever seize their properties? What rights would they have under the law when DORSA was no longer present to protect their interests? Although Trujillo had taken very little interest in Sosúa and had left the association on its own, the wary refugees, most of whom had lost their own possessions when they left their homeland, insisted on writing safeguards into the homesteader agreements. As a result, the Rat and DORSA had agreed that the homesteaders' "basic colonization debts" could not be sold off without their consent. As of January 1, 1963, forty-five settlers still owed DORSA more than $165,000. Those debts would not be paid off for some time; and that meant that despite Hexter's best efforts to close down operations, DORSA and the settlement remained tied to each other for the foreseeable future.[13]

The "continuance of intrusion and assaults" by squatters, however, persuaded a number of homesteaders to move to the relative safety of El Batey. This pattern of affluent families moving off their fincas and constructing homes in the community center had begun in the 1950s, but increased significantly after the land invasions. Sosuaners also prudently safeguarded their funds, preferring, at least for the moment, capital flight over reinvestment in their fincas and businesses.[14]

Administrators and settlers had to confront a new political reality with no way of predicting where it would lead. But a nation's political culture cannot change overnight, and three decades of authoritarian rule had left a legacy of patron-client ties, corruption, political manipulation, and a cowed citizenry. Moreover, the bloated thirty-thousand-troop military and the national police force, once firmly under the dictator's control, now operated with little restraint during the political free-for-all after 1961. Periodic bouts of repression reminded civilians that Trujillista methods had not been eradicated. Another unfortunate carryover from the past was *yanqui* meddling, as Ambassador Martin, on the prowl for communists, kept company with former Trujillistas. With civilian governments coming and going so regularly, it was critical that individuals, families, and businesses forge new alliances with influential powerbrokers who could provide the protection that was no longer forthcoming from the central government.[15]

SOSÚA'S PATRÓN

Fortunately, Philipp and Hexter were acquainted with a well-connected politician who knew Sosúa like the back of his hand. Antonio Imbert Barrera, former governor of Puerto Plata, was one of the two surviving hit men who had ambushed the dictator. Tony Imbert's stepfather had been manager of the United Fruit Company's Sosúa property, and the young boy had grown up near the beachfront. Of German and Spanish descent, the Imberts were one of the leading families on the north coast. Tony was the great-grandson of General José María Imbert, a war hero who led a military campaign against the Haitians during the struggle for independence; and his grandfather had been vice president of the nation. A town in the province bore the family name.[16]

Tony and his brother Segundo had served with the rural guard at the settlement.[17] Segundo developed a reputation for cruelty as military commander of the Eighth Company stationed in Puerto Plata Province in the late 1940s.

Tony was named governor of Puerto Plata in 1949; and though his tenure lasted only ten months, it was not uneventful. When exiles landed at nearby Luperón intent on overthrowing Trujillo, five of the rebellion's ringleaders were captured and the invasion was quashed. Governor Imbert's treatment of the prisoners was "distinguished . . . by . . . severity." But he made the mistake of telegraphing Trujillo that one of the exiles wanted to meet with him, and the dictator was furious that Imbert had left a paper trail. "You've saved these bastards by sending me that damn telegram," he screamed at the soon-to-be ex-governor.[18]

When Segundo was discharged from the army, he declared himself an enemy of the regime and fled to Puerto Rico. As a result, Tony and his family were deemed untrustworthy. He was imprisoned twice and kept under surveillance while Segundo remained in exile. But in Trujillo's world, even those who had violated his trust could win their way back into his good graces. Tony did just that over time, and was rewarded with a succession of government posts.[19]

His brother was less fortunate. Segundo returned to the island in 1955 to attend Trujillo's international fair, professing allegiance to the regime. He was promptly arrested and sentenced to thirty years' hard labor for the murder of a union leader eight years before. Tony, who visited his brother once a week in La Victoria prison, was one of the first to join the plot to assassinate the general. Although years later he professed patriotic motivations for his participation, it was obvious that for Tony and a number of collaborators, hatred of Trujillo was personal and familial, nurtured by years of humiliation and resentment.[20]

History's judgment of Tony Imbert has not been kind. As one of only two to survive Ramfis's bloody settling of scores (and the only one who actually participated in the shooting and lived to tell the tale), he felt, with some justification, that he deserved to be recognized as a national hero. For "services to the Fatherland," Imbert and Amiama Tió actually were both named brigadier generals and given round-the-clock personal bodyguards, modest monthly pensions, and an undisclosed cash bonus. Both were appointed members of the initial Council of State and remained influential interlocutors. But the newly formed political parties distrusted them.[21] "So, too, did some officials in the U.S. Embassy and Washington," Martin averred. "Most people seemed to fear they would become a new two-headed Trujillo."[22]

In reality, Imbert's Machiavellian politicking undermined his legacy. He may have been partly responsible for eliminating the dictator, but he never shook off his Trujillista roots. Imbert worked behind the scenes to resist calls to purge the military, but elements within the leadership never reciprocated his *abrazo*; they considered him an outsider who had never paid his dues. He enjoyed more success building a power base in the national police.

Initially established as a paramilitary force in the 1930s, the national police had devolved by 1961 into "the most oppressive, most corrupt, and most Trujillista of all the Armed Forces."[23] During his tenure on the Council of State, Imbert increased the size of the force from three thousand to ten thousand and brought in American police officers to train Dominicans in "public safety" methods.[24] In addition, he and Amiama Tió "kept pushing their relatives and friends deeper and deeper into the Government's power centers," Martin recalled, as they came to control the secret police, the immigration service, and "the machinery of criminal justice."[25]

Imbert also knew how to tar political opponents as communists whenever he needed to score points with Washington, and when to court left-wing groups like the 14th of June Movement, just as the dictator had. Whether cutting deals with the left, the right, or the Americans, Imbert was in the midst of the political horse trading that went on during those anarchic first five years after Trujillo's ouster. He played a key role in the coup that deposed the democratically elected Juan Bosch in 1963 and was a signatory of the communiqué issued by the Dominican armed forces that announced Bosch's ouster to the nation. Lyndon Johnson, who knew something about political maneuvering, thought Imbert was the second coming of Trujillo.[26]

Imbert was shrewd enough to know that he needed to cultivate the U.S. ambassador. The State Department considered the Dominican Republic a high priority in the wake of the Cuban Revolution, and Martin wanted to shepherd the transition from dictatorship to democracy and make the island a showcase for economic development, constitutional rule, and agrarian and social reform. Although copious assistance was poured in to accomplish those goals, and the United States did succeed in forestalling another communist beachhead in the Caribbean—always its primary objective—altering the praetorian political culture proved much more difficult.

Martin and the State Department did all they could and perhaps more than they should have to bring about democratic rule and to prop up the political carousel.[27] As U.S. assistance saturated the island, Martin and Imbert used each other to advance their own agendas. The ambassador needed Imbert to promote his reform project and to identify and root out leftist opposition; Imbert wanted Martin's imprimatur to bolster his legitimacy domestically.

Imbert also emulated Trujillo's methods when he attempted to build a power base among the underclass. He presented himself to "the poor as a feudal lord might have. . . . He carried large rolls of ten-dollar bills and distributed them to crowds, often he would give fifty or a hundred dollars to men who came to him at the Palace or at home; often, too he gave them jobs on the police force. . . . He believed that anyone could be bought. It was Trujillo's way."[28]

Scholars have characterized Imbert as ambitious and unsavory, a political operator who consistently obstructed efforts to democratize the nation.[29] Martin, however, offers a more complex portrayal. Yes, Martin's protégé "was an intelligent man, shrewd and devious," but he was much more than a "blunt power-grabber."[30]

His involvement in Trujillo's execution had left figurative and literal scars. A stocky forty year old with a receding hairline, Imbert looked old beyond his years. The gunshot wounds he received the night of Trujillo's assassination may have healed, and the ten-thousand-dollar bounty (dead or alive) Ramfis had placed on his head was said to have been lifted after the Trujillos fled, but Imbert had reason to believe that he was living on borrowed time. Convinced that the Trujillo clan would take their revenge even from abroad, he wore a "heavy-buckled belt and a gold-plated .45-caliber Colt automatic with the hammer back" wherever he went.[31] The journalist Bernard Diederich interviewed Imbert at home thirteen years after the assassination and was shown a closet "lined with automatic rifles and shotguns and one of the M-1s, supplied by the CIA [for the assassination]." Imbert actually survived several attempts on his life, including one eerily reminiscent of Trujillo's execution. On March 21, 1967, he was badly wounded and narrowly escaped death in a drive-by shooting that left twenty-four bullet holes in his car. At a press conference held in the hospital two days later, a bandaged Imbert accused Trujillistas of the assassination attempt. It was rumored that Ramfis Trujillo had paid gunmen one hundred thousand dollars to avenge his father's death.[32]

"Without power," Martin remarked, Imbert "could not protect himself from Trujillo's vengeance."[33] The incessant wheeling and dealing, leading the national police, currying favor with a factionalized military establishment, forging a close working relationship with the U.S. embassy, creating a loyal clientele through patronage and kickbacks, and his unsuccessful efforts to become president, plus the around-the-clock security detachment that turned his home into an armed fortress all reflected his determination to insulate himself from his enemies.

It is therefore ironic that Tony Imbert today has lived to a ripe old age and outlasted many of those enemies, all the while lurking in and around the corridors of power. But the scheming finally caught up with him in 1978 when President Balaguer, an even craftier political operator, forced Imbert out of his cabinet within days of his appointment—for allegedly masterminding a coup.[34]

It is unclear whether Hexter and the settlement turned to Imbert after the government ignored their pleas for assistance with the land invasions or whether Imbert, responding to a request from Ambassador Martin after his 1962 visit to the colony, offered his services. No matter; from that point on, he became, in Luis Hess's phrase, "Sosúa's *patrón*." His nationwide stature, his clout as head of the national police, and his name recognition throughout the province certainly made him a valuable insurance policy in the eyes of DORSA's leadership and the settlers.

Martin recalled that Sosúa's "troubles eased" after Imbert intervened. DORSA considered this relationship significant enough that it opened a running account for Imbert at El Colmado and gave him what turned out to be an exceedingly valuable piece of beachfront property, known locally as *el campamento*, or the encampment.[35] Imbert constructed a lavish home on the 150,000-square-meter parcel and had helicopter pads built to facilitate his comings and goings. It still remains in the family. But his and his family's security was never far from his mind. Cecil Hess remembered that Imbert's children were always surrounded by bodyguards at el campamento.[36] There is more than a hint of irony in that the settlement, to ensure its survival, handed over a piece of what Trujillo originally had given it to the person who had played a key role in the general's assassination.

Since that time, Imbert has been brought back to the community on occasion to inaugurate openings of new businesses. Settlers stated in interviews more than once (but never for attribution) that he always has been accommodating with their requests to make the wheels of government run more smoothly.

Although no new land incursions occurred after Imbert had made his presence felt, as late as 1968, three thousand squatters were still ensconced on the colony's lands.[37] DORSA kept trying without success to get authorities to help. Five years after the initial complaint to the Agrarian Reform Institute, Philipp was still petitioning officials that an "urgent solution" was required in Choco, because campesinos were cutting down forests, disrupting the flow of aqueducts that carried water to homesteads, tapping into water pipes, and washing clothes in cattle troughs. If the government agreed to move the squatters out of Choco, Philipp added, the campesinos were welcome to rent out lands that DORSA owned in Espaillat Province. When that request fell on deaf ears, Philipp wrote to Balaguer in 1968 and offered the Espaillat parcel to the government outright, if it intervened. But the president declined the offer, and the squatters stayed put.[38]

Philipp and Hexter had to come up with creative solutions. But before they tackled that problem, the political unrest that had percolated during the early 1960s finally erupted into full-scale civil war in April 1965. Even though the violence was, for the most part, localized in the capital and other urban centers, its effects reverberated throughout the country.[39]

Persuaded that a communist takeover was imminent, President Johnson ordered a massive military intervention to restore order. DORSA's sales office and warehouse near the central market in Santo Domingo caught fire and went up in flames during the fighting. This was no minor matter, since at that time, the capital and its environs represented 80 percent of Sosúa's market. It did not set the determined colonists back for long, however. Just a few weeks later, a beaming president of the GANADERA cooperative, Walter Blum, told the *New York Times* correspondent, "We drove a truck into Santo Domingo's international security zone and sold sausages from the steps of the Fine Arts Palace."[40]

The civil war, which cost more than three thousand lives, left the settlers pondering their future. "We were all shaken up when the shooting started in Santo Domingo," Arthur Kirchheimer told the *New York Times*. The successful cattle dealer seriously contemplated leaving the island, but was "immensely relieved when the United States troops landed."[41] A few, like Yoshi Milz's and Paul Cohnen's families, decided to move to South Florida, but they were the exceptions. Several factors appeared to have calmed the settlers' nerves. They saw U.S. marines on furlough in Sosúa; their protector, Imbert, became provisional president of the nation for three short months during the summer of 1965; and Balaguer won the presidential election a year later.

In retrospect, DORSA's and the settlement's fidelity to Trujillo had not exacted too steep a price. Despite the tumult, many of the same operating principles that had worked so well under the ancien régime were still in play, and democracy had not altered the political landscape enough so that Hexter and Philipp could not work the system to its minimum disadvantage.

Unlike past administrators, Bruno Philipp and his son, Tommy, lived in the capital, tending to their business interests and visiting the settlement occasionally. This was part and parcel of DORSA's strategy of gradual disengagement. Philipp never received a salary like that of his predecessor, Rosenzweig.

Instead, DORSA gave him a percentage of "the collected sums of leases and sales" and covered his expenses, provided that he kept overhead to a minimum. To this end, the Philipps hired two elderly colonists as bookkeepers to collect settler debts, lease and sell off parcels, and handle office matters, while Hexter continued to visit the settlement every February.[42]

The anticipated backlash against Trujillo loyalists failed to scare off the remaining settlers. They had lived through far worse. By the mid-1960s, the settlement's size had diminished to approximately 35 families and 150 residents, most of that decline attributable to attrition and aging, not fear of reprisals. Most of them protected themselves and their investments and waited things out. Choco's squatters were disconcerting, but since that land was relatively undeveloped and located at a distance from settler properties, the situation had little impact on the settlers' financial balances. Thanks to Imbert's patronage, they focused on their fincas, businesses, and cooperatives. That degree of commitment, however, was not shared by their children.

WITHERING AWAY

By the mid-1960s, the settlement was static and aging. Hexter and Stern had warned years before of the hazards of freezing the settlement, but the last sizable influx of refugees had arrived in the late 1940s. Of even greater concern was that Sosúa's youth were moving away. Encouraged by their parents to pursue educational and economic opportunities abroad, most had little interest in returning to take over the family farms and businesses.

A case in point was Harry Floersheim, who had worked from an early age on his parents' homestead before moving to El Batey and taking a job as a mechanic for the municipal waterworks. All of his peers, Harry recalled, talked about leaving Sosúa when the opportunity first presented itself. Other than the occasional Saturday night dance at the Oasis, watching old French or English movies, or lying on the beach, there was little to offer the young and restless. As soon as he turned eighteen, Harry left for Chicago and never looked back. Although he inherited his parents' farm, he eventually decided to sell it off (although not without some regret).[43]

Cecil Hess was another of the second generation who moved away, but he had much more ambivalent feelings about his childhood years than did Floersheim. The product of the settlement's first mixed marriage, Cecil and his older brother, Franklin, learned Dominican customs at an early age. His German father and Dominican mother always spoke Spanish at home, and siestas were mandatory as the boys were growing up.[44]

An honest day's work was a crucial value in the Hess household. Cecil watched his father get up at the crack of dawn and head out to his finca in La Bombita, some eight kilometers away, where he put in several hours before heading back to El Batey to work for the rest of the day at the elementary school. When school was out of session, Cecil did the same, riding his bicycle or hopping on a horse to work on the finca early in the morning. Later on, Cecil would make extra spending money at the CILCA and GANADERA cooperatives during his summer vacations.

Although neither of Cecil's parents was particularly religious, he decided to receive religious instruction from Hebrew teachers who had been sent to Sosúa from New York. He was circumcised at the age of thirteen, and received his bar mitzvah the following year. His ecumenical education continued when his parents sent him to a Christian private high school in Santiago. But his parents' reason for sending him to boarding school had little to do with religion and everything to do with the quality of education. His father, an advocate of public education during the Trujillo years, was convinced that the quality of public schools had declined sharply after 1961.

Cecil's high school years were a defining period, a time when he was forced to come to terms with his unique identity. For the first time in his life, he was regarded not just as an outsider but as a foreigner. "I looked Dominican, I spoke Dominican, but I couldn't get used to the way things were in Santiago," Hess recalled. What stunned the teenager was that he could not date a girl in Santiago without being accompanied by a chaperone. In Sosúa, "boys and girls were always together all the time without chaperones; the concept simply did not exist. Boys and girls went to the beach together, we partied together." At boarding school, his classmates viewed their world through the prism of social class. Conversely, at Sosúa, little attention was paid to such matters: "everybody was a worker, a farmer, we didn't think in terms of class, there was not as pronounced a hierarchy." In Santiago, the elite thought itself superior, and many of Hess's classmates were part and parcel of that entrenched oligarchy. "They invited me to join them at private social clubs and although I was happy to go and make friends, after awhile I couldn't stomach it. I was appalled at the way they treated other Dominicans. Of course, we [Sosuan kids] were not free of prejudice, we could tell the difference between the kids who lived in Charamico and those from Sosúa. Those were two different worlds, but we went to [primary] school together, they were part of our group, and we played together."

Cecil also received valuable lessons about the intersection of race and class during his high school years. When he went to the park one day in Santiago, the shoeshine boy cried out, "*Rubio*, do you want your shoes shined?" Cecil wondered, "why did he call me blondie when I had black hair?" Of course, Cecil realized that he had a lighter complexion than the shoeshine boy, but for the first time, away from home, he had to come to grips with his identity as a light-skinned Dominican who had more in common with his prep school peers than he cared to consider. He had grown up playing baseball and marbles with shoeshine boys at the settlement, but in Santiago, the way he dressed, the amount of money he had in his pocket, and his skin tone dictated who he was expected to associate with and how his peers thought of and treated him.

There were half a dozen Jewish students at his boarding school, including a few from Sosúa. Cecil recalled that virtually all the Jewish boys excelled in the classroom and their academic success prompted a backlash from jealous peers about "egghead Jews." He remembered, with a wink, that he was very pragmatic about asserting his "Jewishness" when it suited him, especially if it meant getting time off from classes or extensions for papers during the High Holidays. Although there was no overt anti-Semitism, Cecil understood that he was different from the great majority of his classmates, and not just when it came to questions of faith.

After graduation, Cecil enrolled at a recently opened private university in Santiago, La Universidad Católica Madre y Maestra, in large measure because the public universities were dysfunctional during the mid-1960s. Student and faculty strikes, episodes of rioting, and insufficient funding had disrupted the learning process at the Universidad Autónoma de Santo Domingo and other public institutions of higher learning. After Hess received a degree in engineering in 1971, he and his new bride, Josefina, had to make a decision about whether to return to Sosúa or move elsewhere. He actually was interviewed for a position at La Corporación, the settlement's eventual holding company in Sosúa, but was offered so little money that he decided instead to pursue his master's and doctoral degrees in mechanical engineering at the University of California, Berkeley. Although he returned at one point to Santiago to teach at Madre y Maestra for two years, he and Josefina decided to make their home in Southern California, where he founded a successful business that today fills defense contracts for laser-guided equipment.

When asked why he chose to leave Sosúa and a start a new life in the United States, he admitted that the opportunities for someone with a Ph.D. in engineering were limited on the island. Just as significant was that America offered a "better education for my kids and better opportunities in general." In contrast to Floersheim, Cecil has revisited Sosúa periodically, although not as much as he would like to. He is emblematic of the second generation of Sosuaners who had mixed feelings about leaving their home, who genuinely enjoyed their childhood, and who appreciated what the settlement had to offer, but nevertheless chose to relocate.

Unlike Cecil, Sonja (Topf) Burian, who was born in Sosúa in 1947 and spent her first twelve years there, was heartbroken when her family moved away. Today a psychotherapist who has lived and worked in Vienna for the last three decades, Sonja as a child sensed that she was relatively well off. "We led a somewhat 'spoiled' life; everyone had at least one maid, and yet we were not at all wealthy." She was struck by the ambivalent character of day-to-day life for Sosúa's younger generation: "Living in Sosúa . . . was like in a big family. . . . Even though it was quite clear that we did not belong to the general population it felt like having your feet in two worlds; the one we lived in day to day, and the one we heard fragments of, over there in Europe. We all spoke two languages, and probably felt more at home in Spanish than German and, as a result, ended up speaking something of a mixed salad to our parents. We knew no discrimination but could feel a certain apprehension coming from some of our parents. The Europeans, we were led to believe, were 'educated,' the Dominicans were not."[45]

The Topfs and others felt strongly that their daughters should be well educated and have a career, surely progressive thinking in the 1950s and 1960s. They also recognized Sosúa's limitations and isolation. Sonja's parents had her tutored by Luis Hess and Judith Kibel after school, and periodically took their children to Europe and the United States. But they never considered sending their daughters off to Santiago or Ciudad Trujillo to attend high school or college, as Cecil Hess's parents did. So when the decision became unavoidable, leaving as a family unit was, in their minds, the only viable alternative. The Topfs both had come from broken homes and were determined not to separate. "This is a peculiarity of my family . . . having to do with diverse reasons to be found in their personal family histories before the war, but certainly also with the Holocaust," Sonja explained.[46]

The Topfs' decision to leave was shaped partly by the simple fact that they had two daughters and no sons. Her parents and, one suspects, other parents who had young girls did not want their daughters to marry Dominicans. From what Sonja's family observed, Dominicans formed loose common-law marriages and appeared to practice a kind of serial monogamy; a man would live with a woman for a time, have a child or two, and then leave and begin another relationship. That simply was not acceptable for their daughters. Or for other Sosuans, for that matter; when Sonja's friend got pregnant by a

Dominican and had the child out of wedlock in the mid-1960s, the community was scandalized.

Some families led a divided existence, splitting time between the United States and Sosúa, and they offer a fascinating counterpoint to the prevailing view that the adolescents were anxious to leave and unlikely to return. Eva Cohnen-Brown moved with her family to the United States after the political unrest of the 1960s; she spent school years in South Florida and summers in Sosúa. Even though she grew up and was educated in the United States and has lived away for much of her adult life, she declared that Sosúa always has felt like home. It was where "all the pieces fit together, where there was a sense of community and people respected each other." Growing up in Miami, she felt as if she were looking in from the outside, whereas in Sosúa she felt centered.[47]

Reflecting on how Sosúa shaped who she is today, Cohnen-Brown recalled, "Appreciation of nature's beauty, a love of the ocean, a sense of wanting to be part of a community of people who care about each other, and encouraging those who are going through difficult trials . . . and my first exposure to what it means to be Jewish are all owed to my upbringing there."[48] Her spirituality is rooted in an appreciation for what her parents' generation had to overcome. "To know that most of those around me were willing to suffer, and maybe even die, for something so precious has led me to love the G-d of Abraham, Isaac and Jacob . . . and to understand more fully why we are called the 'People of the Book.' " In an interview, she declared, "This is where I belong," even though today she lives thousands of miles away in Alaska and is less than sanguine about what has happened to Sosúa over the last few decades.

Her reflections on tacking back and forth between her two worlds are revealing. "When I was growing up there in the 1960s and 1970s, it was a lovely paradise, a place of refuge. . . . People all knew who you were, and cared about you. You couldn't walk around El Batey quickly, as there'd be too many folks to say hi to along the way. I used to think that was a problem. . . . Now I know better and long for those days. The natural beauty of my beloved Sosúa was always breathtaking, a tonic for my city-frazzled mind. . . . I still remember seeing the (comparatively) dirty water of Miami's beaches fade into the background, and a few hours later the clear aquamarine of the island's beaches came into view. It was always a homecoming I looked forward to, and it felt cleansing and healing."[49]

Another example that goes against the grain and illustrates that Sosúa had sunk a taproot in the younger generation is Joe Benjamin's personal odyssey. Like many of his peers, Joe went away to school, receiving an electrical engineering degree at Carnegie Institute of Technology, and then worked for thirteen years in Pittsburgh. But he returned in 1976 because Sosúa was "in his blood," and assumed a management position in La Corporación.[50]

Still, the overwhelming tide was in the other direction.[51] Most of Joe's peers left and returned only on occasion, if at all. The exodus was also felt in Luis Hess's elementary school. By the early 1970s, nine out of ten students were Dominican, "and there was no longer demand or pressure for foreign language teaching."[52]

Adolescents were not the only ones to leave; so did people with marketable skills. At one time the settlement boasted six doctors, but by 1972 not one remained, and the town relied on the services of a Dominican physician. Absentee ownership also increased as more families split their time between Miami and Sosúa. A handful of entrepreneurial residents defied the general trend, purchasing lands outside the original settlement, buying out their less committed neighbors, investing in costly irrigation equipment, and improving their herds.

The exodus of the skilled and the young left aging Sosuaners fatalistic about the future. The geographers Richard Symanski and Nancy Burley, who visited in the early 1970s while researching the development of the tourist industry on the north coast, reported, "They talk about their age and oncoming death, their children who have gone abroad and will not return and their Dominican wives and children who will inherit their properties in Sosúa."[53] Journalists were even less kind; they were writing Sosúa's epitaph prematurely in the late 1960s. Robert Crassweller waxed philosophical: Sosúa would survive but "only as a small memorial to old sacrifices and hopes."[54]

No individual emerged to lead the colony after Rosenzweig left the country. The aging Sosuaners were now consummate free agents, tending to their businesses and coming together only as shareholders to set policy for the cooperatives and to address matters affecting the municipality. Residents rightfully took pride in what they had accomplished. Although some had achieved greater success than others, the *New York Times* reported in 1965, the settlers owned more than 10,000 head of livestock, and their farms and factories employed 110 Dominican workers.[55]

For quite some time, however, Sosúa had not functioned as an agricultural colony. Privatization, autonomy, and independence were the paths chosen in 1945; even the impulse to establish cooperatives was driven by rational choice, not by a collaborative zeitgeist. By and large, the settlers were not close friends; and as they became more financially secure, as some achieved a degree of success that others envied, as still others retired and distanced themselves from day-to-day operations, whatever loose ties had bound them together frayed. A series of caustic oral histories collected by German sociologists in the late 1960s revealed scant evidence of solidarity.[56]

How well the cooperatives performed depended on the source of information. Ever the promoter, Hexter boasted after his seventeen-day visit in 1961 that sales were at an all-time high, new Edam and Gouda cheeses had been developed with the assistance of a German consultant and were well received by the public, all the milk processed was now pasteurized, and the dairy factory had been tiled and enlarged to include additional cool room space. The meat cooperative had undergone a similar expansion, adding freezing rooms and smoke cabinets.[57]

While sales were on the uptick, management also met criticism for being too set in its ways and for failing to introduce greater efficiencies. Two German dairy technicians brought in to streamline production characterized plant administrators as amateurs dead-set against change, content to "do everything the way they did it 25 years ago." Four German workers, they exaggerated, could perform the work done by the dairy plant's staff of forty, and the coordination of tasks was conspicuously lacking, resulting in "huge amounts of cheese . . . spoiled." Echoing earlier complaints of CILCA shareholders, the dairy specialists noted that most settlers shortsightedly insisted on receiving their dividends rather than reinvesting, which left insufficient funds to modernize the plant. Worse yet, a recent audit had found a ninety-thousand-dollar shortfall, raising questions about corruption or mismanagement, or both.[58]

Even though Dominican ranchers now supplied as much milk as their Jewish counterparts, they were not allowed to become co-op members, and as a result, they had to settle for lower prices for their milk. When a discussion was initiated about attracting Dominican capital to expand the dairy and meat plants, a majority of the shareholders balked, preferring to keep the business in-house.[59]

Steps were taken to increase capitalization, enhance efficiency, and bolster production. A new holding company, La Corporación Sosúa C. por A., brought the previously separate dairy and meat operations together. Efforts to integrate the two co-ops were only partly successful, however. Each continued to maintain its own bylaws and boards of directors, and they paid their taxes separately as they had in the past. The settlers continued to place a greater value on autonomy than on cooperation.[60]

The former CILCA did shift to a more corporate model, in which votes were apportioned on the basis of the number of shares held, but the GANADERA doggedly maintained the principle of one shareholder, one vote. Those who had chosen to reinvest their shares, which once were thought to be worth less than toilet paper, came to play a more prominent role in the new company. Considerable overlap on the two boards continued, but over time, four families dominated decision making and acquired more than 80 percent of the company's shares: the Strausses, the Benjamins, the Milzes, and the Cohnens. Just as important for the future, second-generation Sosuaners, such as César Estrella and Joe Benjamin, began to assume a larger role in daily operations during the 1960s and 1970s.[61]

All of La Corporación's products now carried the brand name "Productos de Sosúa," but partnerships with regional distributors were revised as La Corporación took a more active role in marketing and distribution than it had previously, and profits (and risk) were now shared equally with distributors. Management continued to focus on the domestic market, because neighboring countries had stiffer requirements for meat importers that would have necessitated a costly upgrade of the slaughterhouse.[62]

El Batey in the mid-1960s had the look and feel of a tiny Midwestern town rather than a Dominican pueblo. The original barracks had been transformed into municipal offices, a movie theater, a synagogue, apartments, and other businesses. The downtown now boasted a supermarket and a convenience store, "relatively large residential lots . . . well-kept and sizable wooden and concrete homes," and a fair number of automobiles and pickup trucks.[63]

As the Jewish presence waned during the late 1960s and early 1970s, Dominicans moved into what was now an attractive beachfront community. Sosúa was no longer a foreign enclave, as wealthy Dominicans from as far away as the capital and as close as Puerto Plata purchased and built luxurious homes in the hills overlooking the bay, fueling real estate speculation. For example, the Brugal and Bermudez families, who owned the two largest rum distilleries on the island, bought seasonal waterfront properties in El Batey and Charamico, respectively. Middle-class residents of Santiago, some two hours away, bought or leased small apartments to use on weekends; and when a 1968 flood in nearby Sabaneta nearly destroyed the town, a number of its residents relocated to Sosúa. Moreover, retiring Sosuaners sold off farms to Dominicans.[64]

The sum total of all these changes altered Sosúa for good. Census figures show that between 1960 and 1970, the municipality's population effectively doubled, to 4,204 inhabitants; fewer than 200 of them were Jews.[65] Symanski and Burley explain that the changes went well beyond numbers. "Ten years ago the Jewish-owned restaurant offered such dishes as gefilte fish, stuffed derma, matzoball soup, and *Fridattensuppe*, but today the restaurants are Dominican-owned and a good Jewish dinner is only to be had by private invitation. Even synagogue services, which were a natural and regular event in Sosúa until recently, are now held irregularly."[66]

The changes were by no means uniform. El Batey's growing prosperity and its middle-class character continued to contrast sharply with Charamico. The latter's streets were unpaved, the palm-thatched huts with dirt floors were makeshift and poorly constructed, and "population and small business densities . . . very high as compared to its bayside neighbor."[67] Although some Dominicans found work in the factories or on local farms, unemployment and underemployment were endemic. Moreover, Jews rarely ventured over to Charamico; its only Jewish establishment was a movie house. Many of Charamico's residents were squatters. But given the burgeoning real estate bubble, it would not be long before wealthier Dominicans moved in and bought out the squatters.

Significant further change was on the way. Authorities and developers touted tourism as the magic elixir that would transform the community and generate prosperity. The geographers were uncannily accurate in their prognosis: "We forecast the eventual disappearance of the original Jewish colony, increasing Dominicanization of the farm lands and El Batey, additional consolidation of the farm lands, and significant tourist development around El Batey."[68] By 1980 Sosúa was no longer an agricultural settlement; tourism was its new economic motor.

For quite some time, Sosuaners had toyed with the idea of complementing their incomes by luring tourists to the handsome beach, but they had lacked investment funds, and the long and arduous drive from the capital, where the only international airport in the country was located until 1980, limited the flow of tourist revenues. Improvements to the highway between Santo Domingo and Puerto Plata in the mid-1950s cut travel time in half, but tourism did not become a priority until the authorities, realizing that they were lagging far behind other Caribbean countries, decided to conduct feasibility studies in the early 1970s. The area in and around Puerto Plata was one of five "development poles" identified by planners. Authorities predicted that by the mid-to-late 1980s, the north coast would receive more than a third of the country's tourist dollars.

Planners were well aware that the north coast could not compete with more developed Caribbean tourist destinations, which had a well-established clientele, four- and five-star hotels, and better infrastructure. They pegged their hopes instead on drawing blue collar workers from the United States and Canada.[69] When plans were unveiled to build the nation's second international airport ten kilometers west of Sosúa, and cruise ships began calling at Puerto Plata in March 1972, local residents realized that change was in the offing.[70]

A few enterprising residents rented out rooms and built bungalows to accommodate the growing numbers of vacationers. A pioneer in Sosúa's tourist trade, Felix Koch, joked years later that he threw five hundred chickens out of his shed and transformed it into his first bungalow for rent. "That single chicken coop evolved into eight attractive bungalows that are perched along a bluff overlooking Sosúa's spectacular curve of a beach," a travel writer gushed in 1995.[71] Even Otto Papernik, who had left for New York in 1951, returned in the early 1980s, bought a house, and turned it into a small hotel, the Hotel Tropix, which he presented to his daughter Sylvie. One of the original Sosúa babies, Sylvie suspected that his reason had less to do with cashing in on the burgeoning tourist trade and more with keeping her connected to Sosúa.[72] It would be one of Otto's last gifts to his daughter; he died in 1983. Sylvie managed the hotel for more than two decades. Other Sosuaners, like Edith Meyerstein, who opened an amber jewelry shop in El Batey, also catered to the tourist trade. But Sosúa's tourist sector would soon be dominated by Dominican and foreign entrepreneurs.

Although funding and construction delays pushed back the opening of La Unión International Airport, located between Puerto Plata and Sosúa, until 1980, the national tourist development plan sparked a land boom along the north coast. The Philipps and Hexter knew that there was money to be made by selling off DORSA's lands, especially along the nine-kilometer beachfront. Bruno and Tommy Philipp were eager to make the most of the spike in real estate prices, while Hexter's motivation was to finish with the settlement once and for all.

Instead of selling DORSA lands outright to the Philipps, however, which would attract unwanted government attention, DORSA gave the father and son two broad powers of attorney so that they could sell its lands for whatever the market would bear, while the properties remained in DORSA's name. Alexander Dothan, the Israeli Ambassador to the Dominican Republic, got wind of the arrangement and sent a blistering memo to the Joint, titled "The Joint's Dealings with Land in SOSUA-Santo Domingo and the Danger of a Scandal."[73]

Dothan argued that the Joint had a legal and ethical obligation to notify authorities about the sell-off because the government was a minority shareholder, and added, "There is, therefore, justification for a judicial inquiry. The corruption is so obvious that it is simply a miracle it has not caught the public attention yet, but it is a question of time before it will."

He acknowledged that the DORSA properties varied in quality. A fifth of the lands were located in Choco, which were "bad for agriculture and tourism" and still occupied by squatters. The Philipps, who had tried for some time to have authorities evict the squatters, now had "decided on a more efficient and less expensive method: a small compensation in cash to the poor who hold the land illegally." They simply paid the squatters to vacate out of funds generated from the sale of the beachfront properties. Dothan contended that the squatters should keep those lands "to create goodwill for the Jewish community."[74]

Hexter, Bruno Philipp, and Joint executives and their legal counsel huddled at JDC headquarters in New York in January 1972, where Philipp and Hexter defended themselves against the allegations. Hexter related that he first had asked Philipp if he was interested in buying up DORSA lands after Trujillo was killed, but the businessman had not been in a position to acquire the properties then. When they revisited the proposition years later, it was not because he wanted to repay Philipp for all his good work for DORSA, but that the "JDC considered itself fortunate to be able to sell off the land and if Mr. Philipp saw a way of making a profit, he was welcome to it."

Hexter understood why this arrangement had raised concerns, but insisted that the JDC and DORSA had done nothing wrong. The JDC was using funds generated from the sales to "reimburse itself for the substantial outlay it had made in behalf of the settlers; the monies so recovered would again be spent for relief in Israel and elsewhere and thereby used for the original purpose." With beachfront property values escalating, when word of the land sales leaked out in Sosúa, Hexter admitted that "a number of people" were suspicious, and "some of the settlers must have concluded that Mr. Philipp was vulnerable on a number of issues."

Inadequate documentation concerning the land transactions, along with DORSA's and the Philipps' efforts to evade detection by the Dominican government, make it difficult to assess the motives of the principals and the consequences of their actions. In the end, the Joint vouched for the Philipps, and they weathered the storm.[75] The properties were sold—although documentation is lacking on the amount of money the sales generated—and the partnership between DORSA and the Philipps continued. But snippets of documentation suggest that Dothan had reason to suspect that the JDC and the Philipps had something to hide. In a cryptic 1975 memo, the JDC's legal counsel recommended that DORSA not sell its remaining shares to Philipp.

Since Bruno was "close to the authorities in Santo Domingo, at some point, as the major shareholder, [he] would have to tell the other . . . stockholders, including the Government of Santo Domingo, much concerning DORSA which now is being dealt with '*en famille*.'"[76]

As late as 1978, the Philipps were still collecting settler debts for DORSA. The JDC agreed to keep DORSA "alive until Mr. Philipp has succeeded in cashing in the accounts receivable he purchased from DORSA." Unless DORSA continued to exist as a legal entity, Philipp could not take action against those who failed to pay their debts. If DORSA decided to go out of existence, Philipp first "would have to sell the accounts back to DORSA and it would be stuck with them. This Dr. Hexter wants to avoid," an internal memo concluded.[77]

Shutting down DORSA proved harder than Hexter ever thought imaginable. But once the association had divested itself of its properties during the early 1970s, the Philipps were relegated to the status of glorified debt collectors, and DORSA's ties to the settlers gave new meaning to the term *tenuous*. By 1978, only the "diehards," as Bruno Philipp referred to them, remained at the settlement: twenty-three families and nine individuals (four of them widows). Of that number, two were listed as living in Miami and one had moved to the capital, although Philipp indicated that a number of other families and individuals were on the list who "come only from time to time to Sosúa."[78]

These "diehards" were at once proud and defensive about what they had accomplished, and increasingly ambivalent about the future as the settlement approached its fortieth anniversary. They now found themselves in a peculiar situation. Sosúa had been their world, but by 1980 they were a distinct minority in their own community. The municipality boasted more than seventeen thousand inhabitants, and the once-tiny enclave was now home to a host of business establishments, most of them linked to the mushrooming tourist industry. The upcoming anniversary celebration would give old-timers and members of the second generation an opportunity to pause, take stock, and reflect.

"WE WERE BORN HERE FOR SOMETHING"

The president of the republic, Antonio Guzmán, and his wife attended the weekend-long festivities in early May, which were broadcast live on television. In addition to an ecumenical service, a dance was held at the Oasis Restaurant, where Rene Kirchheimer, son of Arthur, sang a merengue about Sosúa that he had composed especially for the occasion. Copies of a recently published memoir written by Josef Eichen, one of the original pioneers, were sold, and funds were raised to renovate the synagogue, which was badly riddled with termites.[79]

Capturing the anniversary celebration for posterity were two American documentary filmmakers, Harriet Taub and Harry Kafka, who had arrived a few weeks earlier to tape the annual Passover seder. Lauding the settlers' accomplishments, the film recounted how the dairy plant had meant prosperity for Sosúa's Jewish residents and well-paying jobs for Dominicans. The absence of anti-Semitism was noted, and Dominican-Jewish relations generally were portrayed in a favorable light. But Taub and Kafka also highlighted the community's fragility in the face of change, and their questions pushed residents to reflect on their identity as Jews in this unique setting.[80]

The filmmakers deftly captured endearing moments of interaction between Dominican and Jewish residents. Whether they were working alongside each other in the kitchen before the seder, preparing trays of matzoh balls and cooking vats of chicken to be served to guests, or participating in the seder itself, when a resident retold the age-old story of Passover in Spanish and two girls sang the ritual four questions in Hebrew, it was clear that this small community was at ease with its eclectic character.

That same sense of community was evident during the anniversary celebrations a few weeks later. Filming of the ecumenical service captured images of a Catholic priest and a Jewish rabbi intoning prayers in Spanish and Hebrew, respectively, while elderly Jewish residents wearing skull caps and Dominican guests intently listened in the audience. During the evening a merengue band performed, while the 72-year-old Luis Hess danced with unbridled enthusiasm not too far from some giggling girls performing a makeshift hora to the pulsating beat. Taub and Kafka earlier had caught on tape a memorial service for a settler at the family's home. Both Catholic and Jewish prayers were offered up, and refreshments were served to family members and friends, who comforted the widow and each other.

Stitched together from the documentary's mosaic of narration and images is a picture of a community no longer set apart from its neighbors. After forty years, a small group of Jews, some but not all of whom had intermarried and had children, had forged a hybrid culture, part Dominican and part Jewish. Otto Kibel expressed as much to a *Los Angeles Times* reporter during the anniversary festivities. "For me and the others who remained, we are Dominicans now . . . [our] bloodlines are well established on the island now." Jewish settlers were fully bilingual, speaking "with each other, their children and grandchildren in German, and Spanish to their neighbors."[81]

Several years later a *New York Times* reporter, who had just attended the annual seder, chided Sosúa's Jews for falling away from their faith and customs. "Although the wives and children proudly wear the Star of David around their necks, they know little of Jewish culture. It is easy here to hold a seder for a hundred people; it is more difficult to find a minyan of ten for the twice monthly services."[82] In truth, Sosúa had never been a religious community; attendance at *shabbat* services had been sparse at best since the colony's inception. But Sosuaners, no matter whether they were born in Europe or on the island, continued to identify as Jews, celebrate their traditions, and openly welcome their neighbors to learn about their customs.

Given Sosúa's growing Dominicanization, the dying off of the original settlers, and its evolving hybridity, Taub and Kafka asked residents what they thought would happen to the community. Not surprisingly, that question elicited a range of responses, more or less split along generational lines. Community elders were pessimistic. Judith Kibel lamented that the younger generation knew little Jewish history. An insightful Erich Benjamin noted that Dominicans had been so welcoming that settlers had not felt compelled to assert their ethnic identity. Luis Hess mused that the community's Jewish character was ebbing and its future lay in tourism: "Sooner or later, Sosúa will disappear as a Jewish community." A few years later, he drove home the point more poignantly in an interview with a *New York Times* reporter: "There will always be traces of Jewish culture, but it has become rather lonesome for us here. There are now more settlers in our Jewish cemetery than there are living here."[83]

Frances Henry, an anthropologist who visited in the early 1980s, pronounced Sosúa's Jews a dying community in a 1985 article. She thought Sosúa's Jewish children were ethnically confused "in terms of their identity and values" and that the "few original settlers and very few of the children [who] hang on" had been increasingly marginalized, "unable to become part of the strange country in which they unwittingly found themselves."[84]

But the younger generation, though few in number, was decidedly more optimistic than either Henry or their parents, reveling in Sosúa's special character and openly embracing their generation's responsibility to preserve it. As Juli Wellisch put it: "Being a daughter of a refugee makes me feel like that I was—that we were—born here for something. This is special place that we should try by all means to preserve." Joe Benjamin said he returned to Sosúa because he missed the ocean, the serenity, and because he and his wife had adopted two biracial children in Pittsburgh and believed they would experience less discrimination than in the States. His American-born wife sounded almost defensive when she encouraged the filmmakers to look beyond facile stereotypes of a moribund community. "Life feels positive and optimistic here. . . . You might see this as an old Jewish community," but in contrast to the United States, "here everything is alive and wide open." Others would have taken exception to her sentiments, but it was evident that the handful who decided to stay were committed to preserving the community's unique character, even if it was an uphill battle. Manfred Neumann acted on just these tenets when he established a Beneficent Fund for Sosúa Patrimony, whereby donors contributed "to preserve the synagogue and the cemetery to remind future generations" of Sosúa's legacy.[85]

A large number of America-Leavers and their families from New York, Miami, and Los Angeles came back for the fortieth anniversary. For more than a few, it was their first return visit. A formative part of their childhood had been spent at the colony, and they had mixed emotions about all the changes the community had undergone. Sonja Burian, who came with her two young children and parents and then returned again in 1981 and 1984, was appalled at what had happened to her home. The new airport had prompted "a locust-like invasion of tourists, but also a new population of Germans, Canadians and Americans who had begun settling . . . buying up land and building houses, hotels, etc. Sosúa's old face had begun to change drastically and I felt disenchanted and alienated."[86] Her memories, admittedly tinged by the "rose-colored glasses" of nostalgia for a simpler past, would have to suffice.

We have rightfully focused attention on settlers who made Sosúa their home. But those who left also carried the settlement with them. If the colony had not been a tropical paradise for everyone who took leave, it did shape their lives long after they left, and it had an impact on their children.

Epilogue

> Sosúa served its purpose. It saved lives.
>
> JOE BENJAMIN, 2006

In October 1947 my father, Heinrich Wasservogel, left Sosúa for New York with his personal belongings and a piece of native hardwood, which he later fashioned into a beautiful acoustic guitar. He had wrestled with the decision to leave, because he had enjoyed farming when he worked in Otto Wohlmuth's cluster. Years later, he still spoke enthusiastically about milking cows, tending chickens and pigs, and caring for his mare. Thanks to Otto Papernik's mentoring in his woodworking shop, Sosúa also provided the former typesetter with invaluable skills that stood him in good stead when he came to the States. One of his most prized possessions was designed in that El Batey workshop: a beautiful chess set with hand-carved pieces, which he kept in a handsome inlaid cedar box. The reader may recall that when the musically inclined Wasservogel fled his native Austria in the summer of 1938, he pretended to be a tourist and carried only a lute and a rucksack on his back. Nine years later, as he boarded a flight from Ciudad Trujillo to Miami, the rucksack was replaced by a suitcase and the lute had been exchanged for what would become his future calling card, his acoustic guitar.

My dad taught himself to play guitar at the settlement when he and Papernik formed a small ensemble that played folk songs on weekends. At one point, he had a steady relationship with a Dominican from a prominent family, and gave serious thought to marrying and settling down. David Stern even tempted him at the last minute by offering him an opportunity to manage DORSA's sawmill. Wasservogel was pushing thirty by war's end and it was time to get married and settle down. But not there; America's lure was irresistible.

Unlike other America-Leavers, he had no relatives waiting to assist him when he reached New York. With no one to sponsor him, the best he could obtain was a six-month transit visa. He booked a ticket back to his native Austria with a stopover in Miami. He never had any intention to return to Vienna, not after what had happened to his parents and twin brothers during the Holocaust. He had six months to find an American bride; failing that, he was prepared to cross into Canada and try his luck there. After all, he had crossed a border illegally once before when he escaped to Switzerland after the Anschluss. As he always told his family with his characteristic bravado, "I made my way."

His early years in America were a typical immigrant story. He fell in with former Sosuaners in New York City, and within six months he found a wife—a refugee who had left Czechoslovakia just as Hitler was invading the Sudetenland. He apprenticed himself to a succession of woodworking shops, lived in a fifth-floor walk-up on the Upper East Side, and attended night school to learn English. Three years later, he and his bride started a family. Heinrich, now Henry Wells—no longer Wasservogel because his wife refused to sign "that ridiculous name" on every check—became a citizen and moved his family out of the city to Long Island. Henry and his wife were proud owners of a new home. For the next two decades, he was self-employed as a cabinetmaker, producing high-end, custom-built furniture for upwardly mobile suburbanites. Like so many America-Leavers, Henry was living the American dream.

Still, Sosúa continued to mark him in often unexpected ways. The backyard became his natural sanctuary, where apple, peach, plum, and pear trees blossomed and bore fruit and his vegetable garden overflowed with produce. That passion for gardening persisted even after he semiretired to Florida, with papayas, bananas, grapefruits, oranges, lemons, and limes substituting for the more temperate fruits in what my mother playfully called "the jungle." The Dominican Republic had prepared him well for the suffocating heat of a South Florida summer. Evenings, weekends, whatever slender slivers of time he took off from cabinetry invariably found him outside, puttering away. Even the one fruit that bedeviled this master gardener in his golden years was a tropical infatuation. It aggravated him no end that no matter how he pampered and tried to protect his beloved mangoes from the vagaries of weather and disease, they never prospered in his South Florida backyard.

His seven years in Sosúa also impressed upon him the importance of the Spanish language. My dad never lost an opportunity to speak in his adopted tongue, and a number of apprentices and hired hands in his woodworking shop were Latin American immigrants. He insisted that I take Spanish in elementary and secondary school; German was the language of the old country, he groused, Spanish was the idiom of the future. Perhaps it is not a surprise that my sister became a Spanish teacher and that language has come in handy in my line of work. Despite his admonitions, he and my mother spoke a combination of German and English in the home and did the same when they visited ex-Sosuaners.

As with all his peers, educating his children was paramount. Even though he had only finished trade school in Vienna, it was a given that his children would go to college. There was never any room for negotiation on such matters; when we were growing up, our household was not a democracy. He never wanted his children to work as hard as he did, and heaven forbid they should work with their hands. This despite the creativity and artistic flair that was evident in all his cabinet work and furniture refinishing and the pride he took in his craft.

Just as he had been in Sosúa, he was the life of every party; his friends begged him to bring along his guitar, and he helped them relive the old days by singing Russian, German, Italian, Spanish, French, and Argentine songs at their get-togethers. His voice, at once resonant and haunting, not infrequently brought tears to the eyes of his nostalgic friends. No matter; they never stopped asking him to bring his guitar.

He owed his livelihood and, in large part, his work ethic to Sosúa. Solomon Trone had told the then–twenty year old in Switzerland that he would select those willing to work hard in the tropics, and Heini never disappointed, at the settlement or later in life. He was driven to succeed in America, toiling six to seven days a week and evenings when necessary to establish his business.

He was a perfectionist in his craft, industrious, and stubborn; these attributes were in no small measure a legacy of his time spent in the tropics. He drove himself in everything he did, and he had nothing but contempt for those who did not do the same. Those very character traits made him difficult to work with, whether as an employee or a boss. It was an understatement to say that he was never the trusting sort; but given what he and his fellow refugees had been through, it would have been surprising if he had been otherwise.

Sosúa remained a part of him even after he stopped revisiting the settlement or attending reunions in New York. He regaled anyone who would listen with stories about his years there. And when his eyes betrayed him later in life, he somehow took up painting, an unintended homage to his father, who had been a painter and a restorer of Old Masters in Vienna. Macular degeneration left Henry in a shadowy world in his last years, but it did not prevent him from imagining and painting Sosuan landscapes on canvas.

Henry never looked at failures as such; they were just part of life's learning curve. He just picked himself up and started over. The only failure he would acknowledge was one that tormented him to his grave: his inability to get his family out of Europe. All his pleas to DORSA administrators went for naught, and he never forgave them or himself for not doing enough. Sosúa and Trujillo may have saved his life, but in his mind, there was an unacceptably high price to pay for that privilege.

Like Henry, Otto Papernik and his wife, Irene, also wrestled with the emotional baggage they brought with them. On the final page of his two-hundred-page memoir, Papernik fixated on the guilt they carried with them about not getting family and friends out. But Papernik was more of an optimist than his erstwhile apprentice, and despite pangs of regret, he managed to come to terms with what had transpired. "We tried to forget all the bad things that had happened to . . . our family and friends, only sadness remained that we were unable to help more, save their lives and get them out, when there was still time. Reluctantly, we survivors had to accept . . . that we . . . could not have done more for our loved ones."[1]

Generalizing about such rugged individualists is hazardous, but by and large, the children of Sosuaners who left and those who stayed behind describe their parents in similar terms. Many shared the drive to succeed, an indefatigable work ethic, an innate belief in their abilities, and a characteristic toughness and resilience. All emphasized the importance of educating their children. Such traits, of course, were typical of many immigrants seeking a fresh start in America.

None of the former settlers with whom I conversed admitted to regretting their decision to leave. Nor was a return to Sosúa ever considered. They looked forward rather than dwelling on the past. For those who survived the Holocaust, classicist Daniel Mendelsohn writes, " the great danger is the tears, the unstoppable weeping that the [ancient] Greeks . . . knew was not only a pain but a narcotic pleasure too; a mournful contemplation so flawless, so crystalline, that it can, in the end, immobilize you." But as Mendelsohn readily admits, and as Sosúa's interlocutors have emphasized in interviews and in their memoirs, it is impossible to entirely separate the understandable urge to focus on the here and now from the "searing regret for the pasts we must abandon, [the] tragic longing for what must be left behind."[2]

In one key respect, however, ex-Sosuaners did differ from their peers who stayed on. Whereas those committed to making their permanent homes at the settlement gradually acculturated to Dominican society, America-Leavers as a rule showed less interest in their neighbors and surroundings. They rarely thought of themselves as immigrants, but as exiles or visitors. Most felt that the island was, in Sylvie Papernik's words, "an alien environment."[3] As a result, they did not attempt to learn the language, put down roots, or retain material possessions that might tie them down. Instead, they walled themselves off from "the natives." They were pleasantly surprised by the absence of anti-Semitism and grateful for the hospitable welcome, but they never thought of Sosúa as their home. One suspects that they felt the way that the young Leo Spitzer did when he left Bolivia in 1950: "I was going to live in the United States. That would be my future. . . . Already I seemed to think of Bolivia as a concluded chapter. Time to turn the page."[4]

That reluctance to acculturate vanished overnight in America. They were intent on "not sticking out" and becoming Americans, thick accents notwithstanding. They relied on their children, the mass media, and night school to learn the new language and speed the acclimation process. Papernik proved to be a quick study. When he bragged to a Sosuan friend that he had bargained well for his 1947 Mercury and paid the salesman in cash, he was taken aback when the ex-settler called him crazy and asked how he ever thought he was going to establish his creditworthiness. Realizing the "error" of his ways, Papernik reconsidered: "I was still doing business the way my parents taught me; save up the money and then buy whatever you want. I had to learn how it was done in the United States." It did not take him long to become a dyed-in-the-wool American consumer.

> Seeing for the first time the new invention, "television," we could not resist having one too. I did not want to spend our saved money, for the first time we bought a set the "American way," on time. . . . When it came to pay I told the salesman that I wanted to pay in installments with a substantial down payment. With no references and not owning an automobile or credit card it became a larger problem than we thought. I showed the salesman my pay envelope, our passports and green cards. . . . The next day the set was delivered and we started to use it all day and half the night. For me, it became a pleasant way of learning English, much better than the radio, because seeing the lip movement when people spoke made it much easier to understand what they were saying.[5]

An experienced cabinetmaker, Papernik was gainfully employed and financially on his feet in no time at all. Within six months, he had opened a woodworking shop and moved out of Manhattan to a more affordable one-bedroom apartment in Elmhurst, Queens. Similar success stories were achieved by Hellie Goldman and Lola Bryan (neé Brienholter). They had learned their trade as seamstresses in Vienna, earned additional cash making dresses in Zurich and in the refugee camps, and worked side by side in Sosúa's barracks, and then continued to collaborate on stylish dresses for wealthy New Yorkers. Hellie joked that whenever acquaintances learned that the Goldmans were from Vienna, they said to her husband, Hans, "Your wife must be such a good cook and baker." Hans always responded that his wife was an exceptional dressmaker. For Hellie, that was Hans's sweet way of letting others know that perhaps cooking was not her greatest attribute.[6]

Not all former Sosuaners had readily transferable skills or as much good fortune as Goldman, Papernik, or Wasservogel. Some gravitated back to vocations acquired in the old country, like Lola's husband, Franz, who had gone to trade school in Vienna and learned to be a tool and dye maker. He took up shoemaking in Sosúa, but eventually came full circle by working in a machine shop in Long Island City. Others had to start from scratch and take whatever they could find. A forward-looking Elie Topf, who owned three farms and a combined apparel shop and general store in El Batey, prepared for his new life in America by taking a correspondence course in accounting in Sosúa before departing for Los Angeles in 1960. After working in a warehouse, he soon began a career as an accountant for a local tax firm, while his wife, who had worked in Sosúa's kindergarten, opened a nursery school.[7]

More than a few of the transplants were well educated and now were forced to take menial positions. Papernik remembered running into a Sosuan friend outside of a Manhattan shoe store and "very reluctantly he greeted us. One of the first things he said was, 'please, don't tell anybody that I am working here as a salesman, it is only temporary.'" Papernik, who "was always told that nobody should be ashamed whatever the job was, as long as it is honest," thought the prideful refugee's response foolish, "but knowing him, we shouldn't have been surprised."[8]

Even as we search for patterns, each idiosyncratic life story offers fresh insights into the reasons for leaving Sosúa and the rigors of adaptation. The longer one stayed in Sosúa, the more complicated the decision to leave became. Although the Topfs almost moved to New York in 1951, problems with Elie's paperwork and the unexpected arrival of his brother's family from Switzerland forced them to shelve their plans at the eleventh hour. They decided to make Sosúa their home, and their second child, Lesley, was born in 1954. "We never would have had Lesley if we were still thinking of moving," Elie related years later. By 1960, Elie and Susi were well established and living a comfortable life. Their farms and store were doing well enough that they could employ two maids to help out at home and with the children. They were fluent in Spanish, and enjoyed an easy banter with their staff at the store and on the farms.

"We lived without bars on the windows" was Elie's way of saying that they felt safe and secure at Sosúa. More than most of the colonists, Topf was aware of what was happening during the dictatorship's final years. He listened to the radio and read between the lines of the government-controlled newspapers, keeping abreast of the unfolding turmoil. But the unrest seemed a million miles away. Nor was he worried about reprisals should something happen to Trujillo. "Sosúa was a happy island on an island"; political factors would not influence the Topfs' decision to leave.[9]

It was not until Elie made a trip to Los Angeles in 1958 to visit his sister and brother-in-law that America emerged as a realistic alternative. He came away impressed with the many neighborhoods dotted with small, well-kept homes and manicured lawns. "Not just rich people owned homes," he excitedly told Susi upon his return, "but whites, blacks and Hispanics." He liked it that Los Angeles was a melting pot where there would be ample opportunity to utilize their Spanish. There was prejudice in America, he noted, but not the kind of anti-Semitism he had encountered (and heard about) when he had visited his sister in Austria a few years before. He also relished the prospect of living in a democracy after living under dictatorships in Europe and the Dominican Republic. More important, he envisioned a better future for his family in America.

Pros and cons had to be carefully weighed. Unlike Wasservogel, who was single and, in his words, "living into the day" at Sosúa, the Topfs had a family and two decades' worth of sweat equity invested there. Moving, it was true, would mean better schooling for their daughters, an opportunity to reconnect with siblings living in Los Angeles, and a better chance to keep the family unit intact. But Sosúa had its virtues, too; their fincas and store were finally turning a profit, they owned their own home, and enjoyed their friends and the familiar surroundings. At forty-one and thirty-six, respectively, Elie and Susi were not the youngest to be starting all over again, and they had only small savings they had scrimped together. Moreover, employment prospects were uncertain at best. Given the circumstances, they made a prudent decision. They went to Los Angeles for a year to test the waters. Hedging their bets, they asked a friend to manage their farms, leaving open the possibility of return.

"The first one-and-a-half years were hell for all of us," their daughter Sonja recalled.[10] As Elie and Susi searched for employment and the children struggled to find social acceptance, the Topfs began to question their decision. Particularly difficult was the switch from their sunny, open home in Sosúa to a small, dreary apartment in Southern California. Susi and Sonja were homesick and wanted to return, but Elie was determined to stick it out. Like their peers, he and Susi worked long hours to get established. The turning point was when the Topfs purchased their first home. Still, they held onto their Sosúa fincas until the mid-1970s and even built a small house near Papernik's Hotel Tropix in the 1980s as a way of keeping their family connected to the past. But they never contemplated returning permanently or even retiring to Sosúa.

What helped the Topfs and others to ease their adjustment anxieties in New York, Los Angeles, and Miami was small networks of fellow Sosuaners. These informal support groups became their extended family, greeting new arrivals at the docks or airports, helping them find lodging, and instructing them on how to survive in America. Papernik fondly remembered weekly get-togethers with friends at Bickford's Cafeteria on Broadway in Manhattan. Unlike the settlement, where "people did not get along too well . . . because one had a few cows more or for some other motive," in New York, keeping up with your friends was an acceptable part of the American way of life: "with everybody being more or less settled and comfortable . . . one could hear and see the effort everybody made to impress the other, showing new clothes or dresses or even a new automobile, but it was a harmless competition everybody accepted."[11]

The refugees gravitated toward communities composed largely of immigrant Jews. For those who had experienced persecution, it was better to share confidences among family and friends and, if necessary, with others who came from similar backgrounds and had comparable aspirations. In certain respects, this practice retarded the acclimation process and bred embarrassment for youngsters who Americanized faster than their elders. Keeping to a tight circle of immigrant friends also reinforced the prevalent idea that "only Jews could be trusted." Burian noted that her parents stayed in touch with former Sosuaners and, in turn, those friends introduced them to their relatives and friends. "In effect their circle of friends grew, but did not entail Americans, unless they were married to one of the old group. . . . Of course, my family came in touch with many Americans . . . [but] they did not cultivate friendships, take on American customs fully. . . . Old customs and traditions, including European food, continue until this day to define home life and friendships."[12]

Former Sosuaners attended annual reunions at restaurants and celebrated rites of passage, such as bar mitzvahs, weddings, and, as the years went by, too many funerals. Jeannette (Kahane) Izenberg and Edith (Brienholter) Horowitz remembered spending several summers at Camp Solidarity, run by the Workmen's Circle, in upstate New York with a number of Sosúa children who lived in the New York metropolitan area.[13]

Adjustment was never smooth, especially for teenage Sosúa "kids" now removed from the settlement's secure cocoon. Burian left in 1960 at the prickly age of thirteen, and transitioning from an isolated, "insignificant" rural community in the Dominican Republic to the bustling metropolis of Los Angeles was a huge jolt. "You knew everyone and everyone knew you, in Sosúa . . . it was a place where you could fall prey to your illusions." Southern California, on the other hand, represented the unknown, at once "alluring and promising" but "very threatening." Sonja despised her unusual Dominican-German accent and was embarrassed not to know what other California teenagers seemed to take for granted.

The parents' propensity for looking forward and their children's magnetic attraction to American culture meant that family conversations about Sosúa were limited at best. Only a handful of the second generation interviewed had more than a rudimentary knowledge of what the colony entailed. A few had an understanding of Trujillo's racist designs; fewer still knew what their parents did there. With some exceptions, the former settlers had been reluctant to share their past with their children. Franz and Lola Bryan never took the family back to Sosúa; and Edi, even though she was born there in 1942, grew up with virtually no knowledge of its history. She was shocked to "rediscover" Sosúa when her parents shared a copy of the 1981 video documentary, which included a still photograph of them stepping off the boat at Santo Domingo.[14]

Several of the second generation who live in the States have returned to the island out of curiosity, but for most, Sosúa remains a distant part of who they are. As they age, of course, comes an understandable desire to know more. An email distribution list of Sosúa kids keeps them abreast of the birth of children and grandchildren and notifies them about weddings and funerals, but the ties among them are attenuated at best, and reunions are infrequent.

Even those "children" who have gone back recently to reconnect with their roots are appalled at how tourism, crime, and the influx of Dominican migrants and foreign expatriates have transformed this quiet seaside community. On this they are in complete agreement with those who stayed behind.

FIGURE 24 Hotels crowd the beach, 2006. PHOTO BY THE AUTHOR.

THE HIGH COST OF GLOBALIZATION

Since the early 1970s, Dominican planners have pigeonholed Sosúa as a relatively low-end resort, and it has never transcended that niche. Its short stretch of beach, limited infrastructure, and lack of major hotel chains ensure that the town will maintain its place in the national tourist hierarchy for the foreseeable future (see figure 24). Regular transatlantic service to La Unión Airport, however, and lodging at a reasonable cost have attracted droves of working- and middle-class tourists in search of affordable vacations.

If its market has remained unchanged, the town has grown appreciably since the mid-1980s to accommodate the influx of seasonal tourists and a budding foreign expatriate community. Some expats have opened business establishments in El Batey, while others have retired in and around the area. The population of Sosúa's twin communities (El Batey and Los Charamicos) has nearly tripled over the last three decades. The local school, fittingly re-named Colegio Luis Hess, has expanded apace, and now serves more than six hundred students.[15] Like most resorts, the town's density ebbs and flows with the seasons; it is much more congested from December to March than in the summertime.[16] It has also fueled an ongoing real estate boom, and a number of Sosuaners have cashed in by selling off their fincas and their holdings in El Batey.

Sosúa today has an international look and feel. Billboards and signs in English, French, and German are ubiquitous; European newspapers are for sale; supermarkets are filled with imported foods; and ethnic restaurants make it clear that this once remote agricultural settlement is now part and parcel of the global age. About three-quarters of all business establishments are foreign-owned, including the larger hotels along the beach and the better restaurants.

Sosúa is also a more heterogeneous community than it ever was. German nationals, French Canadian sun worshippers, American retirees, Dominican and Haitian migrants seeking employment, and a dwindling number of settlers and their descendants intermingle amid a swirl of night clubs, beer gardens, cafés, juice stands, souvenir shops, guest houses, and art galleries.[17] It has become ground zero for Germans, its single largest foreign contingent, an irony not lost on the remaining Jewish Sosuaners. Competitive pricing appears to be the determining factor for many visitors, and some enjoy it so much they decide to stay. Germans have opened bars, T-shirt shops, delicatessens, bakeries, and Internet cafés in El Batey, and as anthropologist Denise Brennan notes, they "transform themselves from workers far from retirement with heavy tax burdens to privileged neocolonials in a state of quasi-early retirement." A German-language newspaper and radio and television stations testify to their sizable presence along the north coast.[18]

There is also a considerable Dominican informal sector that hawks tourist goods, although the municipality has made efforts to contain it and keep it at a distance from the beach. Some grumble that the town has lost its Dominican identity, that there is "no place to buy a plate of Dominican rice, red beans and chicken" in the downtown, and that "here instead of going to Church like other Dominicans, people go to the disco."[19] In reality, the agricultural colony altered El Batey's Dominican character long before the more recent wave of foreign tourists overran Sosúa.

Despite Sosúa's cosmopolitan character, its two communities remain unabashedly segregated. While most foreigners live in El Batey or east of the downtown in subdivisions and condominium complexes along the road to Cabarete, Dominicans, as they have since the colony's heyday, still predominate southwest of the beach. Just as in the past, when Charamico's residents made the trek to the town center and the neighboring fincas to find work, today's residents of Los Charamicos, many of them recently arrived from other parts of the country, walk along the beach or hop onto motorbikes to work in the tourist sector. Deep-rooted inequalities still remain.[20]

What is different about this latest phase of Sosúa's development is the extent of sex tourism. Its consumption, and the growing commodification between Afro-Dominicans and Afro-Haitians and white foreigners has brought Sosúa unwelcome notoriety and has spawned a host of related ills. To be sure, prostitution, which is legal in the Dominican Republic, was a concern to residents well before the recent spike in tourism, but the explosion of the sex trade during the 1980s and 1990s was unlike anything residents had witnessed before. It has fueled an "anything goes," violent environment, which has attracted criminal elements who traffic in drugs and stolen or laundered money. Safety and security have been sex tourism's most notable casualties.[21]

Sosúa has become synonymous with AIDS and HIV transmission as the number of tourists and Dominican nationals engaging in unsafe sex has proliferated. "Sex workers" who flock to tourist bars and nightclubs in the evenings, Brennan reports, have come to "embody Sosúa's transformation . . . into a dangerous, decadent hybrid space."[22] Sex workers are, by definition, vulnerable, and are preyed on by hotel personnel, taxi drivers, and especially the police. Until recently, authorities either have looked the other way or actually profited from the trade.[23]

Local business owners, concerned about the perception of Sosúa as the north coast center of vice, pressed authorities to crack down in the mid-1990s. Periodic arrests of sex workers, curfews at establishments that sold alcoholic beverages, and bar closures by authorities led to the perception that the trade had diminished, but as Brennan learned when she returned in 2003, sex workers and their pimps are now just more circumspect about where to ply their trade.

The entire tourist sector was hit hard by the decline in international travel since September 11, 2001. More than twenty hotels closed down in Sosúa alone. An online publication reported that the closures were "attributed to high operational costs, lack of money to renovate, competition from newer all-inclusive resorts in the area, competition from newer resorts in other areas of the North Coast and the Dominican Republic, [and the] vendor-packed Sosúa beach."[24]

All-inclusive resorts, where visitors are encouraged to stay on site, grew up as a response by resort owners to the island's "dysfunctional power grid and dubious water system." They are a particular source of concern for smaller "mom and pop" hotels and pensions. Whether this is temporary or a harbinger of a generalized decline in local tourism is difficult to predict, but it suggests that Sosúa's market segment carries significant constraints. The

Dominican Republic may rank third in tourist dollars to Mexico and Brazil, and high-end tourism is booming at pricey resorts like Punta Cana, but Sosúa's tourist sector is stagnant at best.[25]

NO HEIRS

Understandably, residents—former settlers and Dominicans alike—are dismayed at what has happened to "their" community even as property values have increased. All pine for the time when Sosúa was a much quieter, more secure place. One of the most outspoken critics is the ninety-eight-year-old Luis Hess, who rattles off tourism's ills—"drugs, crime, noise, pollution, corruption, commercialization, prostitution, traffic, vendors, and litter"—and concludes, "If I were a tourist, I wouldn't go to Sosúa." Even so, Hess continues to live downtown, right next to a number of nightclubs, despite the blaring music and the motorbikes' infernal racket until the wee hours of the morning. When asked why, he says with resignation, "you can't transplant an old tree."[26] A few old-timers have become so upset with how tourism has altered their community that they have moved away to pursue commercial opportunities in the capital or to join their children in the United States.

Eva Cohnen-Brown, who returns periodically, is more charitable. "Now that 'progress' has caught up," she says, "I no longer see so much beauty. There's been unbridled, thoughtless development that is a visual cancer on the beach and in the town. People are desperate for opportunities, and some try to find it in the easiest way possible, even allowing for the corruption of their own bodies and souls. Why should Sosúa, my beloved home, be exempt? I had hoped that it would not be, but people are people, and they have many needs."[27]

The core group of families has continued to decline, partly from defections but more from the march of time. Only about ten families remain; a handful of those are aging settlers in their eighties and nineties. With a few exceptions, all who stayed intermarried with Dominicans. They retain investments in Sosúa's tourist sector and elsewhere throughout the country.

Signs of the original settlement are disappearing (see figure 25). The colony's signature success, "Productos Sosúa," was sold in 2004. Even though sales had reached forty million dollars annually, profits were stagnating. High property values along the beachfront persuaded the board of directors to sell the valuable property where the CILCA plant stood to an all-inclusive hotel, La Casa Marina Reef, and a new factory was opened off the main highway to Cabarete in 2001. But building a new plant did not correct La Corporación's

FIGURE 25 Productos Sosúa factory before it was sold to a Mexican firm. PHOTO BY THE AUTHOR.

old bugaboo, inefficiency. Some board members remained resistant to modernizing operations. Most were long separated from their livelihood. Hermann Strauss was the only settler to continue to sell milk to the factory; the rest of the company's supply came from Dominican ranchers.[28]

When the Mexican conglomerate Sigma Alimentos, which had with operations in Mexico, Central America, and the Caribbean exceeding a billion dollars a year, established a foothold in the country, the board knew the time had come to make a decision.[29] It sold the brand name "Productos Sosúa" and the factory to Sigma.

The public reason given for the sale—no heirs—might be an epitaph for the settlement itself. La Corporación survived the sale, more as a landlord than anything else; although the GANADERA portion of the holding company does not have many assets, Joe Benjamin said in an interview, CILCA still owns quite a bit of real estate in Sosúa.

Steps are being taken to preserve the settlement's legacy and its modest religious character. The remaining families maintain the wood-frame synagogue with its beautiful stained glass windows, take pride in the recently opened museum, and oversee communal celebrations. Services conducted by a lay religious leader are held once or twice a month, drawing anywhere "from a handful of locals to a full house of curious vacationers." The Passover seder is held at a local restaurant and is still open to the community. A

FIGURE 26 Sosúa's synagogue. PHOTO BY THE AUTHOR.

Colombian-born rabbi who works in the capital comes to Sosúa once a month, but because he cannot leave his own congregation to conduct services on the High Holidays, substitute rabbis are flown in from abroad.[30] In the fall of 2006, High Holiday services were presided over by a rabbi imported from Toronto, who refused to count women in the minyan. While we waited for additional male congregants to arrive, I asked the woman sitting nearby if this was usually a problem. She quipped, "No, we usually count furniture." (See figure 26, above.)

The Museo Judío, which was dedicated in 1990, was renovated for the settlement's sixtieth anniversary, thanks in large part to the indefatigable efforts of Ivonne Milz, a second-generation Sosuaner. Opened to the public on February 3, 2003, the small, circular museum, which stands beside the synagogue, chronicles the colony's history and includes the text of the original agreement between Trujillo and DORSA, photographs, faded news clippings, the original, rusted telephone switchboard, farm implements, and videos of snatches of interviews with the original settlers. Artwork by photographer Kurt Schnitzer and painter Ernesto Loher, both children of original settlers, adorns the museum's walls. Each settler's name, the date they arrived in Sosúa, and their country of origin are printed on a chart that extends from the ceiling to the floor.[31] A small archive, consisting primarily of DORSA papers left in the Casa Grande, has been organized and is now open to researchers. Milz is exploring partnerships with U.S. museums and archives because funding is limited.

Guidebooks and old newspaper and magazine articles about the Jewish settlement bring in curiosity seekers. Some tourists inquire about the synagogue and the museum, but most are surprised to learn that the town itself once was a Jewish agricultural colony. A number of original settlers complain that they are "interviewed out" and have decidedly mixed feelings about the attention. Most are skittish when the issue of the community's support for Trujillo is raised.

It is reasonable to assume that the settlement's unusual history will continue to draw attention, especially since so many tourists visit each year. As the old-timers pass away and the second and third generations have ever fewer reasons to stay, this chapter of Sosúa's history will be preserved for posterity in the memories of those who remain and at its small museum. Joe Benjamin predicts that Sosúa's Jewish community will die out within ten to fifteen years because, even though there are a handful of Jews who recently have moved to Sosúa, the younger generation of former settlers is just not very interested in maintaining the customs and traditions. He is at peace with that. "Sosúa served its purpose," he explains matter-of-factly. "It saved lives."[32]

Acknowledgments

I first began to think about Sosúa as a research topic in 1999, during a short visit with my parents, when I sat down and interviewed my dad about his time spent at the colony between 1940 and 1947. Growing up in Sosúa always had seemed like a fairytale, replete with heroes and villains, told by a father who seldom tired of relating his experiences. But I always had resisted investigating the topic, perhaps because it was too close to home. Safer was my rationalization that the subject was undoable; the materials, I reasoned, would be in German, a language I never mastered. After all, whenever our family vacationed in Sosúa or visited with transplanted Sosuaners in the New York metropolitan area, German, not Spanish, had been the lingua franca. To my pleasant surprise, much of what I found in the archives about Sosúa was in Spanish and English.

What happened next followed a peculiar logic familiar to authors. In *The Human Stain*, Philip Roth's alter ego, writer Nathan Zuckerman, describes what occurs when authors lose all sense of perspective and become consumed by their subject: "When I realized where I was headed . . . the course of events seemed logical enough. This is what happens when you write books. There's not just something that drives you to find out everything—something begins putting everything in your path. There is suddenly no such thing as a back road that doesn't lead headlong into your obsession." As I traveled those back roads, no matter how far they took me from the settlement, the tantalizing threads of the Sosúa story drew me in, and I came to share my dad's fixation.

I am grateful to a number of institutions that provided support for this project. A seed grant from Bowdoin College's Fletcher Family

Fund in 2001 made it possible to locate archival sources and conduct a first round of interviews in the Dominican Republic. Fellowships from the John Simon Guggenheim Foundation and the American Council of Learned Societies (with supporting funds from the Social Science Research Council and the National Endowment for the Humanities) and a timely sabbatical from Bowdoin College enabled me to complete the research and provided the gift of time necessary to write this up. Ann Ostwald and Craig McEwen in our dean's office deserve special thanks for seeing to it that all the pieces of an extended leave came together.

Archivists and librarians in Cambridge, Massachusetts; Hyde Park, New York; New York City; Washington; Santo Domingo; Sosúa; and Brunswick, Maine, were most helpful in locating materials. The unfailing courtesy and assistance of Misha Mitsel and Sherry Hyman at the JDC Archives and Edward Jaquéz Díaz of the Archivo General de la Nación merit special acknowledgment. Thanks to Ivonne Milz and Jason Steinhauer for organizing the holdings of the recently opened Archivo del Museo Judío Sosúa. Guy Saldanha and his superb interlibrary loan staff at Bowdoin's Hawthorne-Longfellow Library were relentless in tracking down obscure materials, enjoying the search for rare ephemera as much as I relished reading what they found. Just as *Tropical Zion* went into production (and unfortunately too late for me to profit from), Marion Kaplan's first-rate study of the settlement during the war years, *Dominican Haven: The Jewish Refugee Settlement in Sosúa, 1940–1945* (New York: Museum of Jewish Heritage, 2008), appeared in print.

This book was enhanced immeasurably by dozens of informants at Sosúa and throughout the Diaspora. Their recollections are the heart of the second half of the book. Several Sosuaners—Elie Topf, Sonja Burian, Joe Benjamin, Luis Hess, Cecil Hess, Eva Cohnen-Brown, and the late Hellie Goldman—deserve a special *danke*. Thanks to Sylvie Papernik, who lent me a copy of her father's rich memoir, and Edith Meyerson de Bloch, who supplied papers that helped the war years come alive. Hank Goldman and Jeanette Isenberg Bersh spread the word about this study to the "Sosúa kids," a number of whom then came forward and offered their recollections. In addition to the interviews listed in the bibliography, other first- and second-generation Sosuaners responded to my questionnaire. Space did not permit me to include the contributions of all of the respondents, but their insights informed my understanding of the settlement's evolution.

As a professional historian, I have been trained to think critically about sources. I challenge my students to wrestle with documents, to consider motivation, to understand the context, and to be sensitive to bias. Since I have so much admiration for how Sosúa's settlers built new lives for themselves at such a difficult moment, I have struggled to maintain a critical distance. At times, evidence is cited that makes a larger point about the colony or the DORSA administration but presents individuals in a less than flattering light. My personal ties to this story have made me see, more so than with previous projects, how difficult it is to walk in others' shoes.

Tropical Zion builds on the insights of scholars of Dominican history, U.S.–Latin American relations, American Jewish history, the Holocaust, international history, and race and racism, among other fields of study. While I am responsible for any factual errors and interpretive flaws, I owe a great deal to specialists in these disparate fields. A novice in Dominican history, I am especially grateful to Roberto Cassá, Robin Derby, and Raymundo González, who warmly welcomed a stranger to their fascinating field. I also have benefited greatly from Richard Turits's probing analysis of the Trujillo regime.

All Latin Americanists who venture into the field of international history owe a great intellectual debt to Friedrich Katz. In my case, I'm especially grateful to Friedrich, who offered thoughtful reflections on the exile experience.

I had the good fortune to test my ideas at several venues. Colleagues and students at the University of California, Irvine; Binghamton University; Harvard University; the University of California, San Diego; and the University of Miami posed excellent questions that helped to refine my thinking. Jeannette Hopkins made a number of useful suggestions that helped shape an unkempt manuscript at an early stage. I am indebted to William Taylor, Peter Hayes, Matthew Klingle, and Kermit Smyth for reading and commenting on the entire manuscript. *Muito obrigado a* Steve Topik who suggested the book's title. Bill Taylor and Steve Topik embody the best of what our profession is about and are splendid critics, mentors, and friends.

I am fortunate to work at such a collegial place. Members of the faculty and staff in the History Department, the Latin American Studies program, and my students at Bowdoin acted as sounding boards, suggested sources, critiqued my work, and connected me to scholars in their fields. I'd especially like to express my gratitude to Kevin Johnson, Steve Cerf, Marianne Jordan, and Enrique Yepes for their encouragement, friendship, and assistance. Tina Michels assisted with German language translation while the late Paul Nyhus did the same with Swiss materials. Paul was a gentle and kind colleague whose wisdom and experience I tapped to get through rough patches. He is sorely missed.

Thanks to Valerie Millholland at Duke University Press, who believed in this project and did her best to convince a stubborn author that less can be more.

Miriam Angress and Mark Mastromarino patiently (and with good cheer) shepherded the manuscript to publication. I am very grateful to Eleanor Lahn who has once again worked her editing magic on one of my manuscripts.

Family and friends have been enormously supportive. Thanks especially to Vicki and Burt Laub, Alice Wells, Charlotte and Joe Heil, Pat and Jim Wagner, Ann and Mike Scalzo, Natalie and Fritz Kempner, Katharine Watson, Joel Natter, Vivian and Dan Dorman, and Miranda and Chris DeLisa.

To David, Emily, and Anna, who have given me so much joy and who have lived with this single-minded preoccupation so good-naturedly, may you share this part of our family's history with your loved ones. To Kathy, my best friend, wife, and most insightful critic, thank you for your gentle encouragement, patience, and good humor. By listening to my ideas or offering advice on drafts, you have made Sosúa almost as much a part of your life as it is of mine. Thanks for sharing the journey and for the heartfelt suggestion that I read aloud portions of the manuscript to my dad during my last visit with him.

It is sobering to realize that I have been working on this book for as long as my father lived at the settlement. In his last years, excited that I was investigating a slice of his past, he reminisced about Sosúa frequently, calling me at any hour of the day—at work, at home, it didn't matter—about some small detail he thought he had omitted, even if he had mentioned it several times before. Some of my fondest memories are of leisurely conversations about our shared interest. My one regret is that I did not finish this book in time to present it to him.

Brunswick, Maine
September 2007

Notes

PROLOGUE

Epigraph: Heinrich Hauser, in Winer, "Jews of Sosúa," 8.

1. "Typescript of interview with Burton R. Laub III of Henry Wells (nee Heinrich Was-servogel)," June 12, 1990; and Interview, Henry Wells, February 3, 1999.
2. Interview, Elie Topf, August 12, 2006.
3. See Karbach, "The Liquidation of the Jewish Community"; and Gottlieb, "Boycott, Rescue and Ransom," 235–37.
4. Tartakower and Grossman, *The Jewish Refugee*, 545–47.
5. Marrus, *The Unwanted*, 131.
6. Wischnitzer, *To Dwell in Safety*, 192–93; Rubinstein, *The Myth of Rescue*, 25; and Simpson, *The Refugee Problem*, 154.
7. Those fleeing Hitler in the mid- to late 1930s did not commonly self-identify as refugees, but rather as emigrants. Spitzer, *Hotel Bolivia*, 58. On the flight of Austrian Jewry, see Tenenbaum, "The Crucial Year, 1938"; Rosenstock, "Exodus, 1933–1939"; and Goldner, *Austrian Emigration*.
8. Rosenkranz, "The Anschluss," 490.
9. "Typescript of interview . . . of Henry Wells."
10. Ibid.
11. Jewish relief efforts in Switzerland were impressive. *Aid to Jews . . . 1939*, 37; and Wischnitzer, *To Dwell in Safety*, 229–30.
12. Tartakower and Grossman, *The Jewish Refugee*, 297, 299.
13. E.g., Rotenberg, *Emissaries*; and Lowrie, *The Hunted Children*.
14. *Aid to Jews . . . 1939*, 37; and *American Jewish Year Book 5702*, 186.
15. "Typescript of interview . . . of Henry Wells."
16. Kreis, "Swiss Refugee Policy," 119; Independent Commission, *Switzerland and the Refugees*, 159–64; Laserre, *Frontières et camps; and Pfanner*, "The Role of Switzerland," 235–48.
17. "Typescript of interview . . . of Henry Wells."
18. Felix Bauer, "Leading to and Living in the U.S.A.," Memoir, Felix Bauer Collection, LBI.

19. Oral History Interview with Felix Bauer (videocassette), April 30, 1992, RG-50, 166*02, USHMMLA.

20. Interview, Henry Wells, February 3, 1999.

21. Marrus, *The Unwanted*, 155–56; and Tenenbaum, "The Crucial Year 1938," 52–53.

22. Quoted in Marrus, *The Unwanted*, 252–53.

23. Häsler, *The Lifeboat is Full*, 316; Laserre, "Los refugiados," 278–79; *Switzerland and the Refugees*, 14; and Sassen, *Guests and Aliens*, chapter 5.

24. Kreis, "Swiss Refugee Policy," 118; and Friedlander, *When Memory Comes*, 88–90.

25. Häsler, *The Lifeboat is Full*, 30–53; and *Switzerland and the Refugees*, 75–83.

26. Marrus, *The Unwanted*, 157–58.

27. Ibid., 92–96.

28. Since many of these refugees technically were still considered German nationals yet had been deprived of the use of German passports and could not obtain identity documents or visas to travel, they were at legal risk of being returned to Germany or imprisoned and later expelled. See Holborn, "The Legal Status," 692–93.

29. Schwartz to Rosenberg, August 27, 1940, File 49, DP, JDC Archives.

30. Cables, Schwartz to Rosen, September 3 and 4, 1940, File 49, DP, JDC Archives.

31. "18 Refugees Sail for Sosua Colony," *New York Times*, September 20, 1940.

32. Interview, Henry Wells, February 3, 1999.

33. Luxner, "Moving Memorial," 5.

34. Taub and Kafka, "Sosúa," video documentary, 1981.

35. Statistical data on the colony are found in File 47, DP, JDC Archives; and Hyman Kisch, "The Golden Cage."

36. Argentina and Brazil combined to admit more than forty-five thousand Jews. Milgram, *Entre la aceptación*, 10.

37. On the suppression of dissent during his first term, see Thomson, "Dictatorship in the Dominican Republic."

38. Published estimates of the death toll vary from ten thousand to eighteen thousand. The literature on the massacre is voluminous. A good place to begin is Vega, *Trujillo y Haití, 1930–1937*. Interpretations that go against the grain are Derby and Turits, "Historias de terror"; and Turits, "A World Destroyed." For a Haitian perspective, see Price-Mars, *La República de Haití*. Also see Castor, *Migración y relaciones*; Malek, "Dominican Republic's General"; Prestol Castor, *El masacre*; Cuello, *Documentos del conflicto*; and Fiehrer, "Political Violence."

39. Moya Pons, *The Dominican Republic: A National History*. Cf. Suter, "Continuismo," which contends that Trujillo made up his mind not to seek re-election before the massacre.

40. Quoted in Sagás and Inoa, *The Dominican People*, 160.

41. On the Good Neighbor policy, see Wood, *The Making*; Gellman, *Good Neighbor Diplomacy*; Green, *The Containment*; and Gilderhus, *The Second Century*, chapter 3.

42. On U.S.-Dominican relations, see Roorda, *The Dictator Next Door*; Atkins and Wilson, *The United States and the Trujillo Regime*; and Pulley, "The U.S. and the Dominican Republic."

43. Folder 6, 37–42, SWP, FDR Library.

44. Quoted in Malek, "Dominican Republic's General," 148. See also *New York Times*, December 22, 1937, 17.

45. Dozer, *Are We Good Neighbors?*, 26.

46. Schoultz, *Beneath the United States*, 315.

47. Lieuwin, *Arms and Politics*, 62; and Haines, "Under the Eagle's Wing."

48. Beals, *The Coming Struggle for Latin America*, 302.

49. Wade, *Blackness and Race Mixture*, 11.

50. *Resumen general*, 11; and Turits, "A World Destroyed," 592, n9.

51. Cassá, "El racismo"; Cassá, "Las manifestaciones"; Baud, "Manuel Arturo Peña Batlle"; Baud, "'Un permanente guerrillero'"; González, "Peña Batlle"; and Howard, *Coloring the Nation*.

52. Derby, "Haitians, Magic and Money," 524.

53. For an overview of the historiography on the dictatorship, see Derby, "The Magic of Modernity," chapter 1. Also see Galíndez, *La era de Trujillo*; Wiarda, *Dictatorship and Development*; Cassá, *Capitalismo y dictadura*; and Crassweller, *Trujillo: The Life and Times*. In addition to Derby, among the recent works that have informed, as they have complicated, our understanding of Trujillo's rule are Turits, *Foundations of Despotism*; Mateo, *Mito y cultura*; Inoa, *Estado y campesinos*; and Sagás, *Race and Politics*.

54. Feingold, "Roosevelt and the Resettlement Question."

55. On immigration policy, see Breitman and Kraut, *American Refugee Policy*; Wyman, *Paper Walls*, and his sequel, *The Abandonment*; Friedman, *No Haven for the Oppressed*; and Feingold, *The Politics of Rescue*.

56. Despite FDR's support for dictatorial regimes, scholars continue to praise the Good Neighbor policy's emphasis on nonintervention and mutual reciprocity, especially in comparison to later Cold War interventions in the backyard. Grandin, *Empire's Workshop*, 27–33.

57. On the U.S. occupation, see Calder, *The Impact of Intervention*; Franks, "The *Gavilleros* of the East"; Knight, *The Americans in Santo Domingo*; and Goldwert, *The Constabulary*.

58. Pratt, *Imperial Eyes*, 6–7.

59. On a client's ability to maneuver within a hegemonic relationship, see Coatsworth, *Central America and the United States*, chapter 1; and Joseph et al., *Close Encounters of Empire*.

60. On Zionism in the United States, see Berman, *Nazism, the Jews*; Urofsky, *American Zionism*; Urofsky, *We Are One*; and Laqueur, *A History of Zionism*.

61. *American Jewish Year Book 5705*, 563; and Kaufman, *An Ambiguous Partnership*, 12.

62. Knee, "Jewish Non-Zionism"; and Kolsky, *Jews Against Zionism*.

63. "Discussion Concerning the Future of Agricultural Settlement at Sosua," October 1940, File 2, DP, JDC Archives.

64. Bauer, *American Jewry and the Holocaust*, 459.

65. Feingold, *Bearing Witness*, 89–90.

66. One tendency of this fractious historiography contends that American Jews "abandoned" their brethren in Europe, while others argue they did what they could but were largely powerless to influence events. The polar extremes in this debate are

Wyman, *The Abandonment*, and Medoff, *The Deafening Silence*, who view the response as tepid; and Rubinstein, *The Myth of Rescue*, who attacks critics for viewing the past through the prism of the Holocaust, a luxury that American Jews did not have until news of the Final Solution surfaced. For a thoughtful discussion that concludes that American Jewry did what it could under difficult circumstances, see Novick, *The Holocaust in American Life*, chapter 3.

67. The Joint continues to fund relief, rescue, and resettlement programs worldwide. It is the fiftieth-largest charity in the United States, with an annual income of more than $250 million. *Christian Science Monitor*, November 19, 2007, 16.

68. On the National Origins bill, the standard work is Higham, *Strangers in the Land*. On the act's restrictive character, see Lewis and Schibsby, "Status of Refugees."

69. On the perceived threat of immigrant labor and its impact on policy, see O'Rourke and Williamson, *Globalization and History*, 193–205. On quotas, see Lacquer, *Generation Exodus*, 22; and Feingold, *A Time for Searching*, 229. For a counterpoint to the prevailing interpretation of an unwelcoming America, see Rubinstein, *The Myth of Rescue*, chapter 2. The only serious effort to alter the quota was an unsuccessful campaign in 1939 to pass the Wagner-Rogers Bill in Congress, which would have permitted twenty thousand refugee children to enter the country over and above quota limits. Berman, *Nazism, the Jews*, 23.

70. Rubinstein, *The Myth of Rescue*, chapter 2.

71. Wischnitzer, "The Historical Background"; Kisch, "The Jewish Settlement"; Kisch, "Rafael Trujillo: Caribbean Cyrus"; Eichen, *Sosúa, una colonia hebrea*; Symanski and Burley, "The Jewish Colony of Sosúa"; Kätsch et al., *Sosua-Verheissenes Land*; Gardiner, *La política de inmigración*; and Moritzen, "Santo Domingo: A Haven for European Refugees."

1. "OUR ETHNIC PROBLEM"

Epigraph: Rafael Trujillo at the DORSA contract signing, Ciudad Trujillo, January 30, 1940. *Memoria . . . Relaciones Exteriores, 1940*, 84.

1. Bauer, *My Brother's Keeper*, 231; and Stewart, *United States Government Policy*, 272.

2. Adler-Rudel, "The Évian Conference."

3. Marrus, *The Unwanted*, 170.

4. Stewart, *United States Government Policy*, 297; and Kisch, "The Golden Cage," 20.

5. Stewart, *United States Government Policy*, 109.

6. Caron, *Uneasy Asylum*, 172, 184, quote 186; and Maga, *America, France*, 95–98.

7. That figure excluded Russia's Jews. Skran, *Refugees in Inter-War Europe*, 209.

8. Marrus, *The Unwanted*, 142–45.

9. Read and Fisher, *Kristallnacht*, 198.

10. Identifying them in this way was consistent with international legal definitions that emerged during the interwar period, which distinguished between refugees and migrants seeking economic opportunity. Skran, *Refugees in Inter-War Europe*, 111–12.

11. Quoted in Wischnitzer, *To Dwell in Safety*, 202.

12. Shirer, *Berlin Diary*, 120.

13. Friedman, *No Haven*, 57.

14. Estorick, "The Évian Conference and the Intergovernmental Committee," 137; and Intergovernmental Committee, *Proceedings of the Intergovernmental Committee.*

15. Stein, "Great Britain and the Évian Conference," 44.

16. On the IGC's mandate, see Weingarten, *Die Hilfeleistung*; and Sjöberg, *The Powers and the Persecuted.*

17. Intergovernmental Committee, *Proceedings of the Intergovernmental Committee*, passim; and Fields, *The Refugee in the United States*, introduction.

18. Quoted in Friedman, *No Haven*, 60.

19. Urofsky, *We are One!* 8–9; and Kaufman, *An Ambiguous Partnership*, chapter 1.

20. Quoted in Wyman, *Paper Walls*, 49.

21. Sassen, *Guests and Aliens*, chapter 5; and Skran, *Refugees in Inter-War Europe*, chapters 1–2.

22. Popper, "International Aid," 193.

23. Feingold, *Bearing Witness*, 134.

24. George Warren to Joseph Chamberlain, July 16, 1938, Joseph Chamberlain Papers, YIVO Archives.

25. *American Jewish Year Book 5699*, 338–39; Friedman, *No Haven*, 61, 62, 68; Inman, "Refugee Settlement in Latin America"; and Lesser, *Welcoming the Undesirables.*

26. Quoted in Habe, *The Mission*, 127.

27. Wistrich, *Hitler and the Holocaust*, 58.

28. Benjamin Welles, *Sumner Welles*, 224.

29. Perl, "Paradise Denied," 78; and Divine, *American Immigration Policy*, 93.

30. Quoted in Fields, *The Refugee*, 202–3.

31. On Father Coughlin and his self-described Christian Front, see *American Jewish Year Book 5700*, 209–12; Baldwin, *Henry Ford*, chapter 19; Teller, *Strangers and Natives*, 182; and White, *Remembering Ahanagran*, 227–28, 246.

32. Smith, *To Save a Nation*, 148–51.

33. Jonas, *Isolationism in America.*

34. By 1939, 83 percent were opposed to altering the quotas. See Wyman, *Paper Walls*, 47; and Breitman and Kraut, *American Refugee Policy*, 230. Cf. Rubinstein, who refutes the charge of widespread anti-Semitism. *The Myth of Rescue*, 45–50.

35. Quoted in Stiller, *George S. Messersmith*, 124.

36. Quoted in Neuringer, "American Jewry and United States Immigration Policy," 237. See also Medoff, *The Deafening Silence*, 42–43. Some Jewish groups did advocate relaxing quota restrictions. Letter, Harry Schneiderman to Morris Waldman, April 5, 1938, in *Archives of the Holocaust*, 17: 73–75.

37. Arad, *America, Its Jews*, 173.

38. Lookstein, *Were We Our Brothers' Keepers?*, 30–32; Brody, "American Jewry, the Refugees," 224–25; and Lazin, "The Response."

39. Auerbach, "Joseph Proskauer," 110.

40. For a scathing attack on the reticence of the Jewish leadership to attack Roosevelt, see Feingold, " 'Courage First and Intelligence Second.' "

41. Auerbach, *Rabbis and Lawyers*, 166; and Arad, *America, Its Jews*, 130, 155.

42. Auerbach, *Rabbis and Lawyers*, 166.

43. Intergovernmental Committee, *Proceedings of the Intergovernmental Committee*, 32.

44. Oficina Nacional de Estadística, *República Dominicana en cifras*, 5: 11.

45. Quoted in Avni, "Latin America and the Jewish Refugees," 55.

46. Quoted in Vega, *Trujillo y Haiti*, 1: 284. See also H. F. Arthur Schoenfeld to Hull, April 1, 1936, Roll 33, RG59, NA.

47. Vega, *Nazismo*, 71, 180. An additional theory advanced for Trujillo's interest in Jewish immigration is anecdotal and difficult to assess. Apparently, a Jewish teenager from Frankfurt, Lucy Mai (née Kahn), befriended—when no one else would—Flor de Oro, the dictator's daughter, at a Swiss finishing school. In 1937, when Kahn and her family were seeking to leave Germany, Trujillo provided visas for Kahn and her family and found a position for Kahn's husband in a tobacco business. Hexter, *Life Size*, 125; and Eichen, *Una colonia hebrea*, xviii.

48. Hoetink, *El pueblo dominicano*; and Lockward, *Presencia judía*.

49. Vega, "El fallido esfuerzo"; and Wischnitzer, "The Historical Background." Luperón's plan was one of many initiatives to encourage European immigration. Abad, *La República Dominicana*; *Informe que presenta al poder ejecutivo*; Clausner, *Rural Santo Domingo*, 230–31; Box and Box-Lasocki, "¿Sociedad fronteriza"; Balaguer, *La política demográfica*; and Bosch, *Composición social dominicana*.

50. Vega, *Nazismo*, 71, 180.

51. On Dominicanization, see *La frontera*, especially 80–83; Moya Pons, *The Dominican Republic*, 369; and Peguero, *The Militarization*, 109.

52. Turits argues that before the massacre, ethnic Haitians and Dominicans complemented each other economically; a porous border, an abundance of land, and the absence of class conflict combined to foster a relatively integrated frontier society. "A World Destroyed."

53. Elite racism was not only directed at Haitians. Elites were uncomfortable with nineteenth-century Dominican black political leaders like Buenaventura Báez and Ulises Heureaux, who both assumed the presidency. Turits, *Foundations of Despotism*, 48–49.

54. The Dominican elite's anti-Haitianism did not extend to French-educated Haitian mulattos, whom they admired and sought to emulate. See Castor, *Migración y relaciones*, 85–88; and Cassá, "El racismo." On elite ambivalence about the need for cheap manual labor, see Corten, "Migraciones e intereses," 65–82.

55. Moya Pons, "Dominican National Identity," 21. Manuel de Jesús Galván's novel *Enriquillo*, inspired by an indigenous uprising against colonial rule, recast the indigenous role in Dominican history. It conveniently omitted the participation of escaped African slaves, or maroons, who fought with the rebellion's indigenous leader, Enriquillo. Despradel, "Las etapas del antihaitianismo," 95. See also Cassá, "El racismo"; and Torres-Saillant, "Tribulations of Blackness," 139.

56. The 1935 census identified almost one million mestizos (68 percent), 192,000 whites (13 percent), and 287, 000 blacks (19 percent). *Resumen general*, 11. On passports, see Castor, *Migración y relaciones*, 82. Peasant archetypes were similarly transformed in Puerto Rico and Cuba. Sagás, *Race and Politics*, 3.

57. Marrero Aristy, *Over*, 114; and Sommer, *One Master for Another*, 145, translation by Sommer.

58. Turits, "A World Destroyed," 605; and Fennema, "Hispanidad y la identidad nacional."

59. As late as 1960, Trujillista census takers were instructed to list as white all Dominicans not obviously black. Moya Pons contends that most Dominicans believe that only Haitians are actually black. "Dominican National Identity," 20.

60. Cf. Gould, *To Die in This Way*; and Euraque, "The Banana Enclave."

61. Quoted in Baud, "'Un permanente guerrillero,'" 204.

62. Quoted in Fennema, "Hispanidad y la identidad nacional," 230; and Balaguer, *La política demográfica*.

63. Torres-Saillant, "Tribulations," 133.

64. Turits, *Foundations of Despotism*, 163.

65. Quoted in Baud, "Manuel Arturo Peña Batlle," 173.

66. When Trujillo traveled to the United States, criticism of the massacre dogged him. But he continued to deny his government's role, dismissing press reports of ten thousand Haitian dead as "greatly exaggerated" and comparing "those incidents" to the minor border skirmishes between the United States and Mexico that anticipated the U.S.-Mexican War in 1846. Gimbernard, *Trujillo*, 137; and Sagás, *Race and Politics*, 47.

67. Calder, *The Impact of Intervention*, 58–59.

68. Pérez Cabral, *La comunidad mulata*, 185–86; Fiehrer, "Political Violence in the Periphery," 10; and Atkins and Wilson, *The Dominican Republic and the United States*, 78–79. Among the personal effects on display at the Dominican Museum of History and Geography in Santo Domingo is a "small shiny case containing light pancake makeup which [Trujillo] used every day to smooth and lighten his complexion." Wucker, *Why the Cocks Fight*, 51.

69. *Revista de Agricultura* 30: 124 (January 1940), 11.

70. *Dominican Republic: Report of the Special Emergency Agent*, 40.

71. Vega, *Trujillo y Haití*, I: 285–86. See also Castor, *Migración y relaciones internacionales*, 84.

72. *La Opinión*, February 13, 1939.

73. Edward Anderson, "Restrictions Imposed Upon the Admission of Refugee Immigrants into the Dominican Republic," March 2, 1939, Roll 33, RG 59, NA.

74. *Informe que presenta al poder ejecutivo*; and Turits, "A World Destroyed," 600–601, 604.

75. Inoa, *Estado y campesinos*.

76. Turits, *Foundations of Despotism*, 194–95; and Peguero, *The Militarization*, 115.

77. On Spanish emigration see Gardiner, *La política de inmigración*; Vega, *La migración española*; Llorens, *Memorias de una emigración*; Sullivan, "Dominican Crossroads"; and Hicks, *Blood in the Streets*, 170–72.

78. Quoted in Levine, *Tropical Diaspora*, 134. See also Kirchwey, "Caribbean Refuge," 468.

79. Urquijo, *La tumba abierto*, 89; and Turits, *Foundations of Despotism*, 197–98.

80. Roorda documents the North American alarm over these "flirtations." *The Dictator Next Door*, 203–8.

81. Vega, *Nazismo*, 72–74.

82. Roorda, "The Dominican Republic," 77–79; Turits, *Foundations of Despotism*, 5; and Crassweller, *Trujillo: The Life and Times*, 73.

83. Galíndez, *La era de Trujillo*.

84. Quote from unnamed minister, 1940, in Vega, *Nazismo*, 141.

85. Robert McClintock, "Outline of the Eighth Year of the Government of President of the Dominican Republic," November 1, 1938, Roll 5, RG 59, NA.

86. Hinkle to Hull, September 9, 1938, Roll 5, RG59, NA.

87. Office of the Coordinator of Intelligence, "The Trujillo Regime in the Dominican Republic," in Vega, *Los Estados Unidos y Trujillo, 1946*, 2: 97–99.

88. Vega, *Nazismo*, 157–59.

89. Quoted in Roorda, *The Dictator Next Door*, 82.

90. Sumner Welles, *Naboth's Vineyard*, 2: 918–25; Dozer, *Are We Good Neighbors?*, 18–19; Benjamin Welles, *Sumner Welles*, 121; and Hanson, "Sumner Welles and the American System," 30–31.

91. Quoted in Bendiner, *The Riddle*, 155. Welles's first attempt to practice what he preached, when he was sent to Cuba in 1933 to remove the dictator Gerardo Machado from power and bring about a peaceful resolution to a political crisis, proved to be just as heavy-handed as previous U.S. interventions. See Gellman, *Roosevelt and Batista*.

92. Hanson, "Sumner Welles and the American System," 181, 207.

93. Gellman, *Secret Affairs*, chapter 8.

94. Quoted in Benjamin Welles, *Sumner Welles*, 131; and *Report of the Dominican Economic Mission*.

95. Benjamin Welles, *Sumner Welles*, 136, 150–51; and Hartlyn, "The Dominican Republic: The Legacy," 61–64.

96. Rodríguez Demorizi, *Trujillo and Cordell Hull*, 31.

97. Gellman, *Secret Affairs*, xi; and, Roorda, *The Dictator Next Door*, 59–60.

98. Benjamin Welles, *Sumner Welles*, 125.

99. Ibid., 281, 353.

100. Roorda, *The Dictator Next Door*, 78–79; and Woods, *The Roosevelt Foreign-Policy Establishment*, chapter 2.

101. Hull, *The Memoirs*, I: 176–77; and Steward, *Trade and Hemisphere*, chapter 1.

102. Bendiner, *The Riddle*, 145.

103. Langer and Gleason, *The Challenge to Isolation*, 7–9.

104. Woods, *The Roosevelt Foreign-Policy Establishment*, chapter 2, and quote, 219n; and Neustadt, *Presidential Power*.

105. Weil, *A Pretty Good Club*, 131; and Bendiner, *The Riddle*, 151.

106. Gellman, *Secret Affairs*, 68.

107. Ibid., 98.

108. Berle and Jacobs, *Navigating the Rapids*, 206.

109. Doenecke and Stoler, *Debating Franklin D. Roosevelt's Foreign Policies*, 11–12, quote, 12; and Bendiner, *The Riddle*, 150, 152. On the Welles-Hull rift, see Acheson, *Present at the Creation*, 12; Gellman, *Secret Affairs*, 110; and Weil, *A Pretty Good Club*, 129.

110. Quoted in Sagás and Inoa, *The Dominican People*, 160.

111. Thomson, "Dictatorship in the Dominican Republic," 36.

112. Quoted in Roorda, *The Dictator Next Door*, 198.

113. Crassweller, *Trujillo: The Life and Times*, 158.

114. Vega, *Trujillo y el control*, 347–50; Roorda, *The Dictator Next Door*, 76–87, 111–12, 194–97; and McClintock, "Ninth Year."

115. Trujillo to Roosevelt, July 26, 1939; Roosevelt to Trujillo, August 4, 1939; File 1, DP, JDC Archives; Papers; *New York Times*, September 23, 1939; FRUS, *1938*, 5: 491–502; FRUS, *1939*, 5: 579–95; and Balaguer, *El tratado Trujillo-Hull*, 149–53.

116. Thomson, "Dictatorship in the Dominican Republic," 39–40.

117. Turits, *Foundations of Despotism*, 181.

118. Memo of James McDonald–Sumner Welles meeting, August 23, 1939, Folder 68, Chamberlain Papers, YIVO Archives; Feingold, *Bearing Witness*, 109–10; and Kisch, "The Golden Cage," 24.

119. Stepan, "*The Hour of Eugenics*," 1.

120. Laughlin, *The Codification and Analysis*, 89–90, 96.

121. Strauss, "Jewish Emigration from Germany (II)," 349; and Tartakower and Grossman, *The Jewish Refugee*, 84–85.

122. Ngai, "The Architecture of Race."

123. Yarrington, "Populist Anxiety," 74–75.

124. Popper, "International Aid," 193.

125. Harrington to Hinkle, October 7, 1938. Roll 33, RG 59, NA; Anderson, "An Analysis of the Dominican Immigration Laws and Regulations," July 1, 1939, Roll 33, RG 59, NA. See also R. Henry Norweb to Hull, May 12, 1938.

126. Roorda, *The Dictator Next Door*, 144; and *Memoria . . . Interior y Policía . . . 1938*, 437.

127. Anderson, "Restrictions Imposed."

128. "Report of Alfred Houston's Trip to the Dominican Republic for the Refugee Economic Corporation," January 6, 1939, Roll 1, Chamberlain Papers, YIVO Archives; and Anderson, "Restrictions Imposed."

129. *Memoria . . . Interior y Policía . . . 1940*, 20.

130. *Memoria . . . Interior y Policía . . . 1939*, 533.

131. *Colección de leyes . . . 1940*, 1: 22–25. On the number of applications from German Jewish refugees, see Hinkle to Hull, January 5, 1939, RG 84, Roll 23, 840.48/Refugees, NA.

132. *Memoria . . . Interior y Policía . . . 1939*, 19–20; and "Modificaciones a la ley de inmigración," *Revista de Agricultura*, March 1940, 127.

133. Anderson, "Restrictions Imposed."

134. Vega, *Los Estados Unidos y Trujillo, 1946*, 2: 132.

2. THINK BIG

Epigraph: Roosevelt, at the IGC's opening session, the White House, Washington, D.C., October 17, 1939, quoted in press release, Tomo 264, AGN.

1. Caron, *Uneasy Asylum*, 188.

2. Read and Fisher, *Kristallnacht*; Simpson, *The Refugee Problem*, 517; Sherman, *Island Refuge*, 168–69; and Gottlieb, "Boycott, Rescue and Ransom," 237–38.

3. For example, Paul Cohnen was arrested and taken to Dachau, where he was detained for four months, while Erich Benjamin spent time in Buchenwald before fleeing to Shanghai and then to the Dominican Republic.

4. Strauss, "Jewish Emigration from Germany (II)," 367.

5. Fox, "German and European Jewish Refugees," 77; and Wistrich, *Hitler and the Holocaust*, 65.

6. Friedman, *No Haven*, 31; and Stewart, *U.S. Government Policy*, 391.

7. Kolsky, *Jews Against Zionism*, 15; Bauer, *My Brother's Keeper*, 280; and Wyman, *Paper Walls*, 36–37.

8. Knee, "Jewish Non-Zionism," 219.

9. Strauss, "Jewish Emigration from Germany (II)," 364.

10. Caron, *Uneasy Asylum*, 211.

11. Prinz, "The Role of the Gestapo," 214–16.

12. Sherman, *Island Refuge*, 133, 237.

13. Levine, *Tropical Diaspora*, chapter 4, especially 132, 166. See also Levine, "Cuba," in Wyman, ed., *The World Reacts to the Holocaust*, 789–91.

14. London, *Whitehall and the Jews*, 136–37.

15. Wyman, *Paper Walls*, 38–39; Breitman and Kraut, *American Refugee Policy*, 70–74; correspondence in *Archives of the Holocaust*, 10: 249, 250, 254–55, 261, 282; and Winik, "The Hunt for Survivors," 4–6.

16. Stewart, *U.S. Government Policy*, 346, 438–8, passim.

17. Shepardson, *The United States in World Affairs*, 367–68.

18. Quoted in Bauer, *My Brother's Keeper*, 289.

19. Thompson, *Refugees: Anarchy*, 72; and Buxton, *Economics of the Refugee Problem*.

20. Quoted in Bauer, *Nazi-Jewish Negotiations*, 36.

21. Quoted in Wistrich, *Hitler and the Holocaust*, 67.

22. Maga, *America, France*, 127.

23. Quoted in Sherman, *Island Refuge*, 170; and Stewart, "United States Government Policy," 322–23.

24. Benjamin Welles, *Sumner Welles*, 224.

25. Wise to McDonald, December 21, 1938, and McDonald to Wise, December 28, 1938, D361, 165, James G. McDonald Papers, LL, CU.

26. Sherman, *Island Refuge*, 193–202, quote, 200; Bauer, *Jews for Sale?*, 34; and Feingold, *A Time for Searching*, 230–31, 237. Rublee doubted Roosevelt's desire to find a solution. "The Reminiscences of George Rublee," 2 vols. Typescript, BL, CU Oral History Research Office, Vol. 2: 283–84.

27. Bauer, *Jews for Sale?*, 39–40; and Breitman and Kraut, *American Refugee Policy*, 105.

28. Quoted in Stewart, *U.S. Government Policy*, 455.

29. Bauer, *Jews for Sale?*, 41.

30. Friedman, *No Haven*, 81–82.

31. Smith, *American Empire*, 298.

32. Ibid., 245–47, 315.

33. Ibid., 295–96, 307.

34. Stewart, *U.S. Government Policy*, 482–84; and Feingold, *Bearing Witness*, 107–8.

35. Smith, *American Empire*, 298. On the more promising resettlement sites, see Wischnitzer, *To Dwell in Safety*, 217–21; and Feingold, *Zion in America*, 293–94. FDR also commissioned noted resettlement expert Henry Field to examine 666 possible sites over the next few years. Field later oversaw the secret "M" project, which determined where the expected millions of refugees could be resettled after the war was over. But the "M" proj-

ect was never meant to be a quick fix, nor was it designed to help those already driven out by the Reich. Field, *The Track of Man*, 339–42; and Field, *"M" Project*.

36. Minutes of the PACPR meetings for 1938–40 are found in Roll 1, Chamberlain Papers, YIVO Archives. See also Genizi, *American Apathy*, 77–79. For a detailed catalogue of resettlement efforts, see Feingold, "Roosevelt and the Resettlement Question," 123–82.

37. Warren to Hull, November 25, 1938, D357, P60, McDonald Papers, LL, CU.

38. Koelsch, "Robert De Courcy Ward," 146.

39. Quoted in Livingstone, "Human Acclimatization," 373. See also Stepan, "Biological Degeneration,"104.

40. Seltzer, "The Jew—His Racial Status," 616.

41. Quoted in Ward, "The Acclimatization," 626.

42. Price, *White Settlers*, 172; and Huntington, "The Adaptability of the White Man."

43. Not surprisingly, Ward was a nativist and an advocate of eugenics, who chaired the American Breeders Association Committee on Immigration and successfully lobbied for the passage of restrictive immigration bills in Congress. Ward, "Can the White Race," 153–54; Ward, *Climate*, 294; Livingstone, "The Moral Discourse"; and Koelsch, "Robert De Courcy Ward," 146.

44. Huntington, "The Adaptability of the White Man," 194, 198. See also the bibliography on "Acclimatization" in Bowman, *Limits of Land Settlement*, 339–40.

45. Kohlbrugge, "The Influence," 31–32; and Ward, "Can the White Race," 151–52.

46. Ward, "Can the White Race," 152.

47. Ward, "The Acclimatization"; and Stepan, "Biological Degeneration," 103.

48. Stepan, "Biological Degeneration," 103.

49. Kohlbrugge, "The Influence," 31–32.

50. *British Guiana: Problem of Large Scale Settlement of Refugees from Middle Europe to the President's Advisory Committee on Political Refugees* (no publisher, 1939), 4, Box 311, Joseph A. Rosen Papers, YIVO Archives.

51. Livingstone, "Human Acclimatization," 370.

52. Ward, "The Acclimatization," 16, quote, 43.

53. Holdridge Report, n.d., Folder 75, Chamberlain Papers, YIVO Archives. See also Inman, "Refugee Settlement," 192; Price, *White Settlers*, 235; and Bowman, *The Pioneer Fringe*.

54. The Nazis continued to propose Madagascar as a solution even after the determination had been made to exterminate the Jews. Yahil, "Madgascar," 317, quote, 322.

55. Caron, *Uneasy Asylum*, 202–3; and Popper, "The Mirage of Refugee Resettlement."

56. Popper, "The Mirage of Refugee Resettlement."

57. Ibid., 135.

58. Rosen, "Immigration Opportunities," 321; *The British Guiana Refugee Commission*; *British Guiana: Problem of Large Scale Settlement*; "Minutes of PACPR meetings," passim, Chamberlain Papers, YIVO Archives; and Newman, "The Colonial Office," 263.

59. Bowman, "Memorandum on the Report of the British Guiana Commission," in D357, P62, McDonald Papers, LL, CU.

60. Bauer, *My Brother's Keeper*, 281; Stewart, *U.S. Government Policy*, 470–71; and Sherman, *Island Refuge*, 230–31.

61. Quoted in Arad, *America, Its Jews*, 206.

62. Medoff, *The Deafening Silence*, 66.

63. Stewart, *United States Government Policy*, 475–77. The JDC initially had investigated the possibility of Alaska as a site for refugee resettlement in the fall of 1938. See *New Horizons for Alaska: A Survey of Economic Resources for Future Development of the Territory* (Washington: no publisher, 1939), 6–7, Rosen Papers, YIVO Archives; and Medoff, *Baksheesh Diplomacy*, 137.

64. Morris M. Rose to Franklin Roosevelt, November 21, 1939, Tomo 264, AGN.

65. Feingold, *Bearing Witness*, chapter 6.

66. Medoff, *Baksheesh Diplomacy*, 142; and Hull (and Roosevelt) to Taylor, January 14, 1939, *FRUS, 1939*, 2: 66–69.

67. Feingold, *Bearing Witness*, 107.

68. Welles to Van Zeeland, December 6, 1939, *FRUS, 1939*, 2: 156–57.

69. Stewart, *United States Government Policy*, 477–82.

70. Welles to Roosevelt, January 12, 1939, and Welles to Taylor, January 14, 1939, RG 84, Roll 23, 840.48/Refugees, NA; and Roosevelt to Taylor, January 16, 1939, *FRUS, 1939*, 2: 68.

71. Welles to Taylor, January 14, 1939, RG 84, Roll 23, 840.48/Refugees, NA.

72. Ibid.

73. The Refugee Economic Corporation, underwritten largely by the JDC, was a nonsectarian agency founded in 1934 by Felix Warburg and a diverse group of politicians, religious leaders, and businessmen. Its purpose was to encourage large-scale refugee resettlement from Germany, principally in Palestine. The agency also sent Rosen from Russia to Guatemala and Costa Rica in 1936 to assess their suitability for resettlement. Szajkowski, *The Mirage*, 194; and Szajkowski, "Relief for German Jewry," 126–27.

74. *Concerning Refugee Settlement.*

75. "Report of Alfred Houston's Trip"; and "Plan for the Settlement of Political Refugees in Santo Domingo," n.d., RG84, 840.48/Refugees, NA.

76. Ibid. See also "Minutes of PACPR Meeting, January 23, 1939," Roll 1, Chamberlain Papers, YIVO Archives.

77. "Report of Alfred Houston's Trip."

78. Hinkle to Welles, RG 84, Roll 23, 840.48/Refugees, January 5, 1939, NA.

79. Quoted in Stewart, *United States Government Policy*, 474.

80. Hull to Rublee, January 18, 1939, *FRUS, 1939*, 2: 70–71.

81. "Minutes of PACPR Committee meeting, December 23, 1938," Chamberlain Papers, YIVO Archives; and Isaiah Bowman to Warren, March 14, 1939, D357, P61, McDonald Papers, LL, CU.

82. "Report Covering Field Investigations of Settlement Potentialities Existent on Selected Lands in the Dominican Republic (At the Request and Under the Auspices of the President's Advisory Committee on Political Refugees)," 1939. Tomo 264, AGN.

83. Apparently, Trujillo pursued other unrelated schemes. His brother Virgilio was in contact with Czech Jews who had plans to bring three thousand refugees to the island in the summer of 1939, but Hitler's annexation of the Sudetenland put an end to those negotiations. Warren to Theodore Achilles, August 4, 1939, D357, P63, McDonald Papers, LL, CU; and McClintock, "Ninth Year Report of the Trujillo Administration in the Dominican Republic," August 16, 1939, RG 59, NA.

84. "Discussion Concerning the Future of Agricultural Settlement at Sosúa," October 1940, File 2, DP, JDC Archives.

85. "Minutes of the Joint Meeting of the Boards of Agro-Joint and DORSA," New York, June 11, 1946, File 6A, DP, JDC Archives.

3. JEWISH FARMERS

Epigraph: James N. Rosenberg, *On the Steppes*, 1927, 90.

1. Memo, Rosenberg to Agar, April 2, 1958, File 4, DP, JDC Archives.

2. Dekel-Chen, *Farming the Red Land*, 4.

3. Cassidy, *J. Robert Oppenheimer*, 23–39, quotes, 23, 24; and Schweber, *In the Shadow of the Bomb*, 51.

4. Schweber, *In the Shadow of the Bomb*, chapter 2, quote, 46.

5. Ibid., 50.

6. Quoted in Kagedan, *Soviet Zion*, 49–50.

7. Hacker and Hirsch, *Proskauer*, 26.

8. Typescript of an Interview of James N. Rosenberg by Mark Hirsch, March 25, 1964. Included in the Joseph Proskauer Typescript, BL, CU Oral History Research Office. Rosenberg's highest-profile case was the Depression-era bankruptcy of Ivar Kreuger's international match monopoly. Shaplen, *Kreuger*, 240–41.

9. Typescript of an Interview of James N. Rosenberg.

10. Hacker and Hirsch, *Proskauer*, 23. See also Proskauer, *A Segment of My Times*, chapter 4; and, Rosenberg, *Painter's Self Portrait*, 32.

11. From the *Menorah Journal* (Autumn 1915) in Rosenberg, *Unfinished Business*, 265. See also Auerbach, *Rabbis and Lawyers*, 150–51; and Arad, *America, Its Jews*, 26.

12. From the *Menorah Journal* (Autumn 1915) in Rosenberg, *Unfinished Business*, 265–70.

13. Ibid., 270. See also Arad, *America, Its Jews*, 94.

14. Moore, *At Home in America*, 149–51.

15. Yehuda Bauer has characterized Rosenberg as enthusiastic yet conservative, someone who "left an indelible mark on the JDC." A generous spirit, a conservationist, an artist and art collector, a member of the Joint's inner circle, a proponent of Jewish colonization, and a staunch opponent of Zionism, he reflected many of the values of German American Jewry's plutocracy. *My Brother's Keeper*, 21.

16. Jeffrey Gurock has challenged the uptown-downtown dichotomy, noting that a substantial number of Russian émigrés settled in Harlem, adjacent to areas where established German American Jews resided. *When Harlem was Jewish*.

17. Medoff, *Baksheesh Diplomacy*.

18. Kuznets, "Immigration of Russian Jews"; Sassen, *Guests and Aliens*, 80; Diner, *The Jews of the United States*; and Sarna, "The Myth of No Return."

19. Kolsky, *Jews against Zionism*, 15, 22, 28; and Hirschler, *Jews from Germany*. On the origins of Reform Judaism in America, see Weinryb, "German Jewish Immigrants"; Cohen, "The Ethnic Catalyst"; Rischin, "Germans versus Russians"; and Birmingham, "Our Crowd."

20. Neuringer, "American Jewry and United States Immigration Policy," 3–4, 18–31, 64–66, 83–85, 167–68. Cf. Panitz, "The Polarity of American Jewish Attitudes," 119–28;

Cohen, "The Ethnic Catalyst"; and Szajkowski, "The *Yahudi* and the Immigrant," 13–45.

21. Quoted in Brody, "American Jewry," 238. See also Medoff, *Baksheesh Diplomacy*, 6–7.

22. From 1914 to 1920, the JDC disbursed more than thirty-five million dollars in aid to Eastern European Jews. Hirschler, "Jews from Germany in the United States," 84.

23. Medoff, *Baksheesh Diplomacy*, 23.

24. Cohen, "The Ethnic Catalyst," 132; and Feingold, *Bearing Witness*, 222.

25. The pamphlet was enclosed in Rosenberg to Wise, May 26, 1936, D361, 130, McDonald Papers, LL, CU.

26. Ibid. See also Kolsky, *Jews Against Zionism*, 40–41.

27. Quoted in Werner, *Julius Rosenwald*, 249.

28. Kagedan, "American Jews and the Soviet Experiment," 156; and Bauer, *My Brother's Keeper*, 25.

29. Werner, *Julius Rosenwald*, 251.

30. Urofsky, *We Are One!*, 17; Kaufman, *An Ambiguous Partnership*, chapter 1; Cohen, *Not Free to Desist*; Knee, "Jewish Non-Zionism"; and Schachner, *The Price of Liberty*.

31. Stern, *The Court Jew*, 189, 227; Auerbach, "Joseph M. Proskauer," 109, 113; and Feingold, "Courage First."

32. Auerbach, "Joseph M. Proskauer," 113–14.

33. Ibid., 115.

34. Szajkowski, "Relief for German Jewry."

35. Werner, *Julius Rosenwald*, 91–92; and Medoff, *Baksheesh Diplomacy*, 10–11.

36. An important precursor movement, which originated in Russia and later, in the 1880s, spread to the United States, and which emphasized cooperative values and productive labor, was *Am Olam* (Eternal People). See Dekel-Chan, *Farming the Red Land*, 6; and Wischnitzer, *To Dwell in Safety*, 60–64.

37. Quoted in Goldin, *Why They Give*, 56. See also Lee, *Moses of the New World*; Grossmann, *The Soil's Calling*, 98–17; and Lesser, "Watching the Detectives," 236.

38. Neuringer, "American Jewry and United States Immigration Policy," 17; Eisenberg, *Jewish Agricultural Colonies*; and Kagedan, "American Jews and the Soviet Experiment," 158–59.

39. Joseph, *History of the Baron de Hirsch*, 69–89; and Bogen, *Born a Jew*, 63–71.

40. Kirsch, *The Jew and the Land*; and Brandes, *Immigrants to Freedom*, 40, 306.

41. Reich, "The Economic Structure," 1:161–62; and Panitz, "The Polarity of American Jewish Attitudes," 115–16.

42. Glazer, *Dispersing the Ghetto*, 33, 45; and Brandes, *Immigrants to Freedom*, passim.

43. "James Rosenberg, 90, Limits His Horizons to Two Careers," *New York Times*, December 6, 1964.

44. Some of his paintings found a home at the New York Metropolitan Museum of Art, Harvard's Fogg Museum, and other college museums. Rosenberg, *Painter's Self Portrait*, 60.

45. *New York Times*, January 12, 1930. *Dies Irae* was shown most recently at the Library of Congress as part of an exhibition, "Life of the People: Realist Prints and Drawings from the Ben and Beatrice Goldstein Collection," October 20, 1999–January 29,

2000. On Miller's career, see Smithsonian Institution, *George Miller and American Lithography.*

46. "Ironism," catalogue, June 26–July 12, 1944, Ferragil Gallery, New York, D361, 130, McDonald Papers, BL, CU. Rosenberg painted full-time after his "retirement" in 1947. A retrospective exhibition was held when he turned 90 in 1964. "Rosenberg, 90, Opens Retrospective Show," *New York Times*, December 14, 1964. He never received more than a thousand dollars for any of his paintings, and admitted, "I have given away thousands until I have denuded my home." Ibid.

47. Rosenberg, *On the Steppes*, 215.

48. Rosenberg, "The Story of Sosúa," 9; and Bauer, *My Brother's Keeper*, 64.

49. Quoted in Kagedan, *Soviet Zion*, 56.

50. In 1920 Rosen's Rye took the first twenty-two prizes at the International Grain and Hay Show in Chicago; it soon became the standard rye variety in the U.S. Midwest. Szajkowski, *The Mirage of American Jewish Aid*, 90.

51. Dalrymple, "Joseph A. Rosen," 157–60; *Universal Jewish Encyclopedia*, 9: 202; Handlin, *A Continuing Task*, 45; and Szajkowski, *The Mirage of American Jewish Aid*, 90–91.

52. Quoted in Rosenberg, *On the Steppes*, 92.

53. Ibid., 140.

54. Quoted in Handlin, *A Continuing Task*, 58. See also *Report of Dr. Joseph A. Rosen*, 15–16.

55. The Pale of Settlement, a tract of land that straddled present-day eastern Poland and western Russia, was created by Catherine the Great in 1791 as a means of confining all of Russia's Jews in one district. On the relative costs of colonization, see Feingold, *A Time for Searching*, 177. On Rosen's criticisms of Russian Zionists, see Szajkowski, *The Mirage of American Jewish Aid*, 93.

56. Rosen, "Immigration Opportunities for Jews," 317.

57. Bentwich, *Wanderer between Two Worlds*, 196.

58. Quoted in Chernow, *The Warburgs*, 292.

59. Ibid., 296.

60. Reflecting the reason for its inception, the Joint was initially called the Joint Distribution Committee of American Funds for the Relief of Jewish War Sufferers. It shortened its name in 1931. See Dobrowski, *Jewish American Voluntary Organizations*, 50–59. On the JDC's evolution, see Bauer, *My Brother's Keeper*; Handlin, *A Continuing Task*; Hyman, *Twenty-Five Years of American Aid*; Agar, *The Saving Remnant*; Leavitt, *The JDC Story*; and Nooter, "Displaced Persons from Bergen-Belsen," 331.

61. Sassen, *Guests and Aliens*, 85.

62. Baron, *The Russian Jew*, 210–13.

63. Kenez, "Pogroms and White Ideology," 293; Heifetz, *The Slaughter of the Jews*; and Trotzky, "Jewish Pogroms in the Ukraine."

64. Neuringer, "American Jewry and United States Immigration Policy," 126; Abramsky, "The Biro-Bidzhan Project," 64; and Baron, *The Russian Jew*, 221.

65. Marrus, *The Unwanted*, 85; Sassen, *Guests and Aliens*, 86; Fisher, *The Famine in Soviet Russia*, 460; and Weissman, *Herbert Hoover and Famine Relief*. On the JDC's role with the ARA and then independently, see Szajkowski, *The Mirage of American Jewish Aid*, chapters 3–10; and Gitelman, *Jewish Nationality and Soviet Politics*, 238.

66. Chernow, *The Warburgs*, 292.

67. See Filene, *Americans and the Soviet Experiment*, chapter 4; Wilson, *Ideology and Economics*; Sutton, *Western Technology and Soviet Economic Development*; and Szajkowski, *The Mirage of American Jewish Aid*, 77–80.

68. Kagedan, "American Jews and the Soviet Experiment,"154; and Szajkowski, *The Mirage of American Jewish Aid*, 83.

69. E.g., Grant, *The Passing of the Great Race*. See also Higham, *Strangers in the Land*, 270–72; Divine, *American Immigration Policy*, 11–12; and Daniels, "American Refugee Policy in Historical Perspective."

70. Arad, *America, Its Jews*, 64–65. On similar restrictions by European states, see Zolberg et al., *Escape from Violence*, 18–19.

71. See Feingold, *A Time for Searching*, 28–29; Tartakower and Grossman, *The Jewish Refugee*, 84–85; Wischnitzer, *To Dwell in Safety*, 154; and Friedman, *No Haven*, 20–21.

72. Arad, *America, Its Jews*, 65; and Chernow, *The Warburgs*, 292.

73. Quoted in Bauer, *American Jewry and the Holocaust*, 35.

74. Kagedan, *Soviet Zion*, 10–12; and Brown, "A Biography of No Place," 115.

75. Dekel-Chen, *Farming the Red Land*, 32.

76. Bauer, *My Brother's Keeper*, 62; Neuringer, "American Jewry and United States Immigration Policy," 2; and Dekel-Chan, *Farming the Red Land*, 7.

77. Quoted in Kagedan, "American Jews and the Soviet Experiment," 156. See also Baron, *The Russian Jew*, 226–27.

78. *The Activities of the Joint Distribution Committee . . . 1931*, 15.

79. Szajkowski, *The Mirage of American Jewish Aid*, 157, 174.

80. "Dr. Joseph Rosen, Agronomist, Dies," *New York Times*, April 2, 1949, 15; and "Minutes of a Joint Meeting of the Board of Directors of DORSA and Agro-Joint," New York City, November 26, 1940," File 2, DP, JDC Archives. Agro-Joint leaders, reliant on the generosity of the American Jewish community, had a vested interest in casting as bleak a picture as possible of the plight of Russian Jewry. In reality, not all Jews suffered during the first revolutionary decade. Vaksberg, *Stalin against the Jews*, 60.

81. Bogen, *Born a Jew*, 318; Bauer, *My Brother's Keeper*, 59; and Chernow, *The Warburgs*, 290.

82. Grossmann, *The Soil's Calling*, 73; and Bauer, *My Brother's Keeper*, 60.

83. Schwarz, *The Jews in the Soviet Union*, 270–72; and Schwarz, "Birobidzhan: An Experiment," 345. Dekel-Chen gives a more conservative estimate of nearly one million acres allocated. *Farming the Red Land*, 4, 16.

84. Baron, *The Russian Jew*, 262.

85. Szajkowski, *The Mirage of American Jewish Aid*, 83, 131–32, 143; Hyman, *Twenty-Five Years*, 30; and Baron, *The Russian Jew*, 227.

86. "Dr. Joseph Rosen, Agronomist, Dies," *New York Times*, April 2, 1949, 15.

87. On the importation of tractors, see Dalrymple, "The American Tractor." On the artesian wells, Agar, *The Saving Remnant*, 51.

88. Dekel-Chan, *Farming the Red Land*, 30.

89. Hyman, *Twenty-Five Years*, 28; and Agar, *The Saving Remnant*, 52.

90. Szajkowski, *The Mirage of American Jewish Aid*, 85, 144.

91. *Report of Dr. Joseph A. Rosen*, 41; *Founding a New Life*; and Embree, "Jews on the Steppes."

92. Kagedan, *Soviet Zion*, 21–23.

93. Slezkine, "The USSR as a Communal Apartment"; Suny, *The Revenge of the Past*; and Simon, *Nationalism and Policy*.

94. Szajkowski, *The Mirage of American Jewish Aid*, 133.

95. Dekel-Chan, *Farming the Red Land*, 98–99.

96. Schwarz, "Birobidzhan," quote, 354; and Weinberg, *Stalin's Forgotten Zion*.

97. The idea of a Jewish home in Birobidzhan carried tremendous resonance in the Soviet Union and Central Europe. Sosúa émigré Wasservogel, who grew up in Vienna, recalled that the idea of a Jewish homeland in Russia was a powerful elixir for socialist youths in Depression-era Austria. Interview, February 3, 1999. See also Baron, *The Russian Jew*, 152–53, 230–36; Szajkowski, *The Mirage of American Jewish Aid*, 158–59, 179; and Bauer, *My Brother's Keeper*, 92–96.

98. Kagedan, *Soviet Zion*, 98–00.

99. Bauer, *My Brother's Keeper*, 69–71, 76.

100. *Report of Dr. Joseph A. Rosen*.

101. Ibid., 102.

102. Dekel-Chen, *Farming the Red Land*, 71.

103. Feingold, *A Time for Searching*, 179.

104. Kagedan, "American Jews and the Soviet Experiment," 154.

105. Bauer, *My Brother's Keeper*, 64; Kagedan, *Soviet Zion*, 96; and Scheler, "The 'Back-to-Land' Movement," 37.

106. Wise to Mordecai Kaplan, April 6, 1928, in Wise, *Stephen S. Wise*, 154–55. Jewish members of the U.S. Communist Party also demeaned the project. Epstein, *The Jew and Communism*, 168–69.

107. Dekel-Chan, *Farming the Red Land*, 92.

108. Bauer, *My Brother's Keeper*, 87–89.

109. Bauer, "The Relations between the American Jewish Joint Distribution Committee," 276.

110. Fitzpatrick, *Stalin's Peasants*. Whether the Jewish colonies were hit as hard is a matter of scholarly dispute. Cf. Kagedan, *Soviet Zion*, 10; and Dekel-Chan, *Farming the Red Land*, 116ff.

111. Dekel-Chan, *Farming the Red Land*, 116ff.

112. Feingold, *A Time for Searching*, 182. Cf. Bauer, *My Brother's Keeper*, 66–75, passim.

113. Dekel-Chan, *Farming the Red Land*, 165.

114. Szajkowski, *The Mirage of American Jewish Aid*, 131.

115. Dekel-Chan, *Farming the Red Land*, 143, 146, 176, 177.

116. Aronson, "The Jewish Question," 182–83.

117. Szajkowski, *The Mirage of American Jewish Aid*, 92.

118. Quoted in Bauer, *My Brother's Keeper*, 99.

119. Bauer estimates that only fourteen thousand families remained on the land in 1938. Ibid., 103. On how the settlements avoided the purges, see Dekel-Chan, *Farming the Red Land*, 173ff.

120. Ehrenburg and Grossman, *The Black Book*, 61, 63; Rhodes, *Masters of Death*, 191, 248; and Goldstein, "The Fate of the Jews," 94.

121. Kagedan, "American Jews and the Soviet Experiment," 155.

122. Quoted in Levin, *The Jews in the Soviet Union*, I: 237.

123. Ibid.

124. Dekel-Chan, *Farming the Red Land*, 195. While in Israel, Rosenberg encountered a former Crimean colonist, who told him that he knew of no other survivors from the settlements. It turned out that he was wrong. Curti, *American Philanthropy Abroad*, 371; and Memo, Rosenberg to Agar, April 2, 1958, File 4, DP, JDC Archives.

125. *Concerning Refugee Settlement*.

126. Rosen, "Immigration Opportunities for Jews," 318.

4. "THE EYES OF THE WORLD ARE ON
THE DOMINICAN REPUBLIC"

Epigraph: Trujillo to Rosenberg, October 19, 1939. *Jewish Telegraphic Agency* 6:69 (October 27, 1939), Box 55, Folder 13, SWP, FDR Library.

1. Roorda, *The Dictator Next Door*, 178–82; and *Memoria . . . Relaciones Exteriores, 1939*, 127–29, 142.

2. McClintock, "Ninth Year Report of the Trujillo Administration in the Dominican Republic," August 16, 1939, RG 59, NA.

3. Quoted in Roorda, *The Dictator Next Door*, 180.

4. Rodríguez Demorizi, *Trujillo and Cordell Hull*; Roorda, *The Dictator Next Door*, 178–82; Crassweller, *Trujillo: The Life and Times*, 173–74; and Vega, *Nazismo*, 97–98, 159.

5. Higher-level meetings between Taylor and Trujillo in Paris in early August kept the momentum alive. George Warren to Theodore Achilles, August 1 and August 22, 1939, D357, P63, McDonald Papers, LL, CU.

6. Pastoriza to Arthur Lamport, July 29, 1939, RG 687, Arthur Lamport Papers, YIVO Archives.

7. "Draft Agreement," September 8, 1939, RG 687, Lamport Papers, YIVO Archives.

8. "Minutes July 19–20, 1939, IGC meeting," London, Folder 68, Chamberlain Papers, YIVO Archives.

9. Feingold, *A Time for Searching*, 230; Tartakower and Grossman, *The Jewish Refugee*, 450.

10. *Aid to Jews . . . 1939*, 8, 31.

11. "Minutes July 19–20, 1939, IGC meeting"; Stewart, *United States Government Policy*, 461; and Sherman, *Island Refuge*, 248–49.

12. McDonald to Welles, September 26, 1939, and George Warren to McDonald, Baerwald, et al., August 30, 1939, Folder 68, Chamberlain Papers, YIVO Archives.

13. Friedman, *Nazis and Good Neighbors*, introduction; Haglund, *Latin America and the Transformation*; and Roosevelt, *Roosevelt's Foreign Policy*, 169.

14. Adams, *Economic Diplomacy*, chapter 8; Frye, *Nazi Germany and the American Hemisphere*; and Friedrich Katz, "Algunos rasgos."

15. Adams, *Economic Diplomacy*, 214–19.

16. Ibid., 198–204.

17. George Warren to McDonald, August 30, 1939.

18. See also "Minutes of September 8, 1939, meeting in Arthur Lamport's home"; and George Warren to Lamport, September 20, 1939, RG 687, Lamport Papers, YIVO Archives.

19. Sjöberg, *The Powers and the Persecuted*, 62–63.

20. "Minutes of September 8, 1939," and "Minutes of September 25, 1939, meeting held at James Rosenberg's home," RG 687, Lamport Papers, YIVO Archives.

21. *Concerning Refugee Settlement.*

22. "Minutes of September 25, 1939, meeting."

23. Circular #34, Arturo Despradel, Secretary of Foreign Relations to Dominican Consuls in the United States and Pastoriza, undated, in RG 687, Lamport Papers, YIVO Archives.

24. "White House Press Release," Box 55, Folder 13, SWP, FDR Library.

25. Alfred Wagg, "Report of the Meeting of the Intergovernmental Committee at Ciudad Trujillo and the Sosúa Settlement in the Dominican Republic," February 1941, File 45b, DP, JDC Archives.

26. Rosenberg to Pastoriza, October 21, 1939, Tomo 264, AGN.

27. *Jewish Telegraphic Agency*, 6:69 (October 27, 1939), Box 55, Folder 13, SWP, FDR Library.

28. Ibid.

29. Ibid.

30. Ibid.

31. Welles to Rosenberg, October 30, 1939, Box 55, Folder 13, SWP, FDR Library.

32. Welles to Roosevelt, December 11, 1939, File 11, DP, JDC Archives.

33. *Concerning Refugee Settlement.*

34. *The Nation* 149 (November 25, 1939): 568.

35. For a list, see Rosenberg to Trujillo, February 17, 1940, Tomo 279, AGN.

36. Wise to Weizmann, January 15, 1940. in Wise, *Stephen S. Wise*, 239.

37. *American Jewish Chronicle*, March 1, 1940.

38. Quoted in Kisch, "The Golden Cage," 95.

39. Cablegram, Franco to Pell, January 17, 1940, Tomo 282, AGN.

40. Marshall to Rosenberg, November 29, 1939, File 1, DP, JDC Archives.

41. Memorandum of Conversation by the Assistant Chief of the Division of Cultural Relations (Thomson) with George Warren, January 30, 1940, *FRUS, 1940*, 2: 213–14.

42. Ross, "Sosua: A Colony," 246.

43. Rosenberg to Lamport, February 14, 1940, Lamport Papers, YIVO Archives.

44. "Meeting Held at JDC Offices on January 1972," File 45, DP, JDC Archives.

45. The company abandoned production not only in Sosúa but throughout the Dominican Republic. Moberg and Striffler, "Introduction."

46. Martínez, *De Sosúa a Matanzas*, 22–29.

47. Eichen, *Sosúa: From Refuge to Paradise*, xxvii.

48. Brookings Institution, *Refugee Settlement in the Dominican Republic*, 294.

49. "Report Covering Field Investigations of Settlement Potentialities Existent on Selected Lands in the Dominican Republic (At the Request and Under the Auspices of the President's Advisory Committee on Political Refugees)," 1939. Tomo 264, AGN.

50. Ibid.

51. Rosenberg to Pastoriza, November 22 and November 30, 1939, Tomo 264, AGN.

52. Quoted in Ross, "Sosua: A Colony," 246.

53. The journalist Freda Kirchwey visited Sosúa in early 1940 and explained why, she believed, Rosen had selected the site. Leaving aside "natural beauty and a delightful bathing beach," the only advantage Sosúa had over other tracts was existing facilities. "Caribbean Refuge," 467.

54. Brookings Institution, *Refugee Settlement in the Dominican Republic*, 23–24, 42.

55. *Concerning Refugee Settlement*.

56. "Minutes of Joint Meeting of the Agro-Joint and DORSA Board of Directors," June 11, 1946, File 6A, DP, JDC Archives.

57. "Minutes of Agro-Joint Board of Directors Meeting," December 30, 1943, File 5, DP, JDC Archives.

58. Trujillo to Rosenberg, January 20, 1940, Tomo 264, AGN. See also Rosenberg, "The Story of Sosua," 11; and Hinkle to Hull, January 18, 1940, *FRUS, 1940*, 2: 208–9.

59. Mauss, *The Gift*.

60. Paddle tennis was a scaled-down version of lawn tennis and all the rage in New York, Rosenberg informed Trujillo. Rosenberg to Trujillo, December 20, 1939, File 11, DP, JDC Archives.

61. Derby, "The Magic of Modernity," 9–10.

62. *Concerning Refugee Settlement*, 10.

63. Trujillo to Rosenberg, March 9, 1940, File 1, DP, JDC Archives.

64. Rosenberg to Pastoriza, December 18, 1939, Tomo 264, AGN. Rosenberg's art collection is described in *Painter's Self Portrait*.

65. *Análisis de la era*, 38–39.

66. On patron-client relations (or clientelism), see Schmidt et al., *Friends, Followers, and Factions*; Scott, "Patron-Client Politics"; Powell, "Peasant Society and Clientelistic Politics"; and Wolf, "Kinship, Friendship, and Patron-Client Relations."

67. Derby, "The Magic of Modernity," 278.

68. Mateo, *Mito y cultura*, 97.

69. Derby brilliantly analyzes the variegated character of the regime's "choreography of consent." "The Magic of Modernity," chapter 6.

70. The description of the contract signing and the ensuing quotations from the evening's speeches are found in *Memoria . . . Relaciones Exteriores, 1940*, 83–84.

71. "Rosenberg Lauds Sosúa Colonists," *New York Times*, March 2, 1941.

72. *Discurso del Señor James N. Rosenberg*.

73. Ibid.

74. Ibid.

75. Rosenberg diary, January 25, 1940, File 1, DP, JDC Archives.

76. Echoing Rosenberg's assessment, journalist John Gunther characterized the general as "ambitious, cool and forceful." "Hispaniola," 764–67, 771.

77. Rosenberg diary, January 25, 1940, File 1, DP, JDC Archives.

78. *Concerning Refugee Settlement*, 8.

79. Rosenberg diary, January 25, 1940, File 1, DP, JDC Archives.

80. Roorda, *The Dictator Next Door*, 145.

81. Quoted in Reyher to Rosenberg, February 1, 1940, File 40, DP, JDC Archives.

82. *Mensaje que dirige a sus compatriotas el Generalíssimo Doctor Rafael Leonidas Trujillo,* 1940.

83. Hinkle to Hull, February 5 and February 12, 1940, 839.00, Roll 1; and "Interoffice memo," January 25, 1940, 839.156, RG59, NA.

84. "Interoffice memo."

85. "A New Wave of Terrorism," Franco to State Department, January 30, 1940, 839.00, Roll #1, RG59, NA.

86. Rosenberg to Trujillo, February 17, 1940, Rosenberg to Pastoriza, March 11, 1940, and Rebecca Hourwich Reyher for Rosenberg to Pastoriza, March 13, 1940, Tomo 279, AGN.

87. Rosenberg to Taylor, February 13, 1940, Myron Taylor Papers, FDR Library.

88. *Concerning Refugee Settlement,* 12.

89. Ibid., 10.

90. Ibid., 12, 14.

91. George Warren to Chamberlain, March 8, 1940, Chamberlain Papers, YIVO Archives.

5. ONE GOOD TURN

Epigraph: James Rosenberg, at the first anniversary celebration, January 30, 1941, Ciudad Trujillo, *Memoria . . . Relaciones Exteriores . . . 1941,* 84.

1. McClintock, "Ninth Year Report of the Trujillo Administration in the Dominican Republic," August 16, 1939, RG 59, NA.

2. Trujillo gave himself wide latitude over the sugar sector, fixing each company's production quotas, overseeing exports, and examining the sugar companies' books. Hall, *Sugar and Power,* 18–20; and Vega, *Trujillo y el control,* 371.

3. Department of State to the Dominican Legation, December 13, 1938, FRUS, 1938, 5: 505–8.

4. Pastoriza debriefed Rosenberg after Rosenberg lobbied officials in the State and Treasury Departments. Pastoriza then wrote up an overview of Rosenberg's lobbying in "Confidential Memorandum for Generalíssimo Rafael L. Trujillo," undated, Tomo 279, AGN, in which Rosenberg is quoted.

5. The Dominican sugar sector produced on average less than a tenth as much as neighboring Cuba. Department of State to the Dominican Legation.

6. Pastoriza, "Confidential Memorandum for Generalíssimo Rafael L. Trujillo."

7. To generate additional revenues, in 1940 the Dominican government imposed a 20 percent windfall tax on sugar exports pegged to the commodity's world market price. Vega, *Trujillo y el control,* 450–51; and Hall, *Sugar and Power,* 19–20.

8. Quoted in Kirchwey, "Caribbean Refuge," 468.

9. Pastoriza, "Confidential Memorandum for Generalíssimo Rafael L. Trujillo."

10. Ibid.

11. Ibid.

12. Langer and Gleason, *The Challenge to Isolation,* 206.

13. Quoted in Haglund, *Latin America and the Transformation,* 102.

14. Lieuwin, *Arms and Politics*, 190–91.

15. *New York Times*, August 25, 1940. The Dominican Republic was one of the first states in Latin America to sign a mutual assistance pact with the United States. See Rout and Bratzel, *The Shadow War*, 29, 31.

16. Dallek, *Franklin D. Roosevelt and American Foreign Policy*, 234; and Peter H. Smith, *Talons of the Eagle*, 81.

17. Vega, *Trujillo y el control*, 421–22, 478–79.

18. Frye, *Nazi Germany*, 130–39; and Langer and Gleason, *The Challenge to Isolation*. On the Office of the Coordinator of Inter-American Affairs, see Colby and Dennett, *Thy Will Be Done*; Haines, "The Eagle's Wing," 380; Cobbs, *The Rich Neighbor Policy*; and Rivas, *Missionary Capitalist*.

19. Roorda, *The Dictator Next Door*, chapter 7; and McCulloch, "Latin America and the New Hemisphere Front."

20. Dallek, *Franklin D. Roosevelt and American Foreign Policy*, 175–76.

21. Meyer, *México y los Estados Unidos*; Koppes, "The Good Neighbor Policy and the Nationalization of Mexican Oil"; and Grayson, *The Politics of Mexican Oil*.

22. Rublee accepted Trujillo's invitation to meet with him in the capital in June 1940. Afterward he traveled to Sosúa. Kisch, "The Golden Cage," 39. Vega downplays Rublee's impact. *Trujillo y el control*, 421.

23. Roorda, "The Dominican Republic: The Axis," 89.

24. Dutch Surinam was of special importance to the United States because 60 percent of the U.S. supply of bauxite, the raw material used to manufacture aluminum, came from that colony. Vega, *Trujillo y el control*, 434–35.

25. Roorda, *The Dictator Next Door*, 202.

26. Quoted ibid., 201.

27. Gellman, *Secret Affairs*, 153.

28. Quoted in Gleijeses, *The Dominican Crisis*, 23.

29. "Memorandum of Conference between Representatives of the United States Government and Generalíssimo Trujillo," June 21, 1940, *FRUS, 1940*, 5: 104.

30. In return, Trujillo gave the U.S. military permission to build a naval base near Samaná Bay, to use the nation's airports and territorial waters, and to fly over its airspace. Roorda, *The Dictator Next Door*, 208–10; and Atkins and Wilson, *The Dominican Republic and the United States*, 82.

31. Wiarda, *Dictatorship and Development*, 33; and Vega, *Los Estados Unidos y Trujillo, 1946*, 2: 125.

32. *FRUS, 1940*, 5: 792–830.

33. *New York Times*, September 8, 1940, 36; Moya Pons, *The Dominican Republic*, 367; Betances, *State and Society*, 102; and Vega, *Trujillo y el control*, 424.

34. Crassweller, *Trujillo: The Life and Times*, 180.

35. Rosenberg to Trujillo, September 17, 1940, File 11, DP, JDC Archives.

36. Gimbernard, *Trujillo*, 143.

37. Vega has written an important corrective to Trujillo's claim that he liberated the nation from fiscal dependency. Vega argues that if the dictator had not extended repayment of the debt in 1931 and 1934, U.S. control of the customs houses would have ended before 1941. Furthermore, Trujillo failed to benefit from the bilateral commer-

cial agreements, deep discounts in interest rates, and debt forgiveness that the United States awarded to other Latin American states. *Trujillo y el control*, ii–iii.

38. Roorda, *The Dictator Next Door*, 213.

39. "Trujillo Borrows $3,000,000 from U.S.," *New York Times*, December 22, 1940, 25.

40. Baerwald to Rosenberg, November 28, 1940, File 2, DP, JDC Archives. Emphasis in the original.

41. Montague to Rosenberg, December 30, 1940, Tomo 279, AGN.

42. Trujillo to Rosenberg, December 26, 1940, File 40, DP, JDC Archives.

43. DORSA Press Releases, January 10 and 22, 1941, File 40, DP, JDC Archives.

44. Alfred Wagg, "Report of the Meeting."

45. Telegram, Pell to Hull, January 29, 1941, Roll 29, 840.48/Refugees, NA.

46. Trujillo to Rosenberg, December 26, 1940, and Rosenberg to Trujillo, January 21, 1941, File 40, DP, JDC Archives.

47. What follows draws on the newsreel "War Refugee Solution," February 20, 1941, Paramount Pictures Collection, Special Media Archives, NA.

48. It was so successful that a second newsreel, produced by the Hearst Company, carried much the same message. "Sosúa: Haven in the Caribbean," Hearst Metronome Newsreel, Special Media Archives, NA.

49. Roorda, *The Dictator Next Door*, 210–19; Scotten to Hull, *FRUS, 1940*, 5: 830; Balaguer, *El tratado Trujillo-Hull*; and Atkins and Wilson, *The Dominican Republic and the United States*, 70–71.

50. Trujillo to Rosenberg, August 18, 1941, and Rosenberg to Trujillo, August 27, 1941, File 11, DP, JDC Archives.

51. Ida Catlin to Rosenberg, December 4, 1940, Rosenberg to Trujillo, December 18, 1940, and Rosenberg to Flor Trujillo de Brea Messina, April 1, 1940, File 11, DP, JDC Archives.

6. LIVES IN THE BALANCE

Epigraph: Rosenberg to Rosen, May 29, 1940, File 49, DP, JDC Archives.

1. Reyher to Wagg, February 4, 1941, and Leavitt to Rosenberg, January 22, 1941, Roll 16, 839.55, Record Group 55, NA.

2. Before July 1, 1941, consular agents decided whether to issue visas to applicants; after that date, completed dossiers were sent from the Visa Division to an Interdepartmental Visa Committee, which included representatives from the Department of Justice, FBI, Navy, Army, and State Department. Even if the committee approved the application, the consul in Europe could still refuse to issue the visa "on the basis of his own information." Tartakower and Grossman, *The Jewish Refugee*, 94; and Bendiner, *The Riddle*, 100.

3. Avra Warren to Reyher, February 8, 1941, RO1116, 839.55, RG 59, NA.

4. Wagg, "Report of the Meeting."

5. Hexter to Reyher, February 17, 1943, File 50a, DP, JDC Archives.

6. "Minutes of the Agro-Joint and DORSA Joint Executive Committee Meeting," June 11, 1946, File 6A, DP, JDC Archives.

7. "DORSA Executive Committee Minutes," January 20, 1944, File 6A, DP, JDC Archives.

8. As a result, a greater number of Jewish women than men, especially elderly women, perished in the Holocaust. Kaplan, "Prologue."

9. "Confidential memo; Re: Immigration," Reyher to Hexter, June 18, 1943, File 49, DP, JDC Archives.

10. Pell to George Warren, April 20, 1940, D357, P64, McDonald Papers, LL, CU.

11. "Confidential Memo; Re: Immigration."

12. *New York Times*, April 24, 1940.

13. The term *fifth column* was first used by one of General Francisco Franco's commanders during the siege of Madrid in 1936. Four columns surrounded the Spanish capital, but a fifth column already at work in the city helped turn the tide of battle against Republican forces. Jong, *The German Fifth Column*, 3.

14. Quoted in Wyman, *Paper Walls*, 188.

15. Quoted in Jong, *The German Fifth Column*, vi. See also McKale, *The Swastika Outside Germany*, 167–71; Donovan and Mowrer, *Fifth Column Lessons for America*; and Aikman, *The All-American Front*.

16. McKale, *The Swastika Outside Germany*, 176–77; Friedman, *Nazis and Good Neighbors*, 58–59.

17. Goodwin, *No Ordinary Time*, 103; and Persico, *Roosevelt's Secret War*, 31–32.

18. Quoted in Genizi, *American Apathy*, 82.

19. Persico, *Roosevelt's Secret War*, 38–39.

20. Doenecke and Stoler, *Debating Franklin D. Roosevelt's Foreign Policies*, 35.

21. Bauer, *American Jewry*, 50.

22. Persico, *Roosevelt's Secret War*, 64.

23. Jackson, *That Man*, 68.

24. Breitman and Kraut, *American Refugee Policy*, 236–37.

25. Sjoberg, *The Powers and the Persecuted*, 65.

26. Britt, *The Fifth Column is Here*, 76.

27. Rout and Bratzel, *The Shadow War*, 18, 452–53. Before the Second World War, the Dominican Nazi Party, composed largely of German nationals, never exceeded fifty members. Roorda, "The Dominican Republic: The Axis," 85.

28. Levine, "Cuba," 793; and Bejarano, "La quinta columna."

29. Vega, *Nazismo*, 47, 54–55, 127.

30. Butler, "Intelligence Report," January 22, 1942, Roll 16, 839.55, NA.

31. Rosenberg to Rosen, May 29, 1940, File 49, DP, JDC Archives.

32. Ibid.

33. *Concerning Refugee Settlement.*

34. Rosenberg to Pell, June 4, 1940, File 1, DP, JDC Archives.

35. Quoted in Wyman, "The United States," 704.

36. Roosevelt to Rosenberg, June 28, 1940, Tomo 279, AGN.

37. "Minutes of July 18, 1940, meeting of DORSA Board of Directors," File 2, DP, JDC Archives.

38. "Confidential Memo; Re: Immigration."

39. Reyher to Falk, August 3, 1940, File 2, DP, JDC Archives. DORSA had concerns about spies in the Dominican Republic, too. Bruno Philipp, a German Jewish entrepreneur and refugee leader living in the capital, who would manage the settlement in the

1960s and 1970s, initially was believed to have ties to suspected Nazis. "Intelligence Report," July 13, 1940, Roll 28, 840.48/Refugees, NA; and Vega, *Trujillo y el control*, 450.

40. Vega, *La migración española*, 102.

41. Hinkle to Hull, June 15, 1940, 839.516. Roll 16, 839.516, NA.

42. Letters from refugees and their relatives pepper Tomo 285, AGN.

43. "Confidential memo; Re: Immigration."

44. Cable, Rosenberg to Rosen, July 2, 1940, Tomo 279, AGN.

45. Rosenberg to Rosen, July 3, 1940, File 49, DP, JDC Archives.

46. Rosenberg to Rosen, July 5, 1940, Pastoriza to Rosenberg, July 27, 1940, and Reyher to Pastoriza, August 7, 1940, Tomo 279, AGN.

47. Pastoriza to Rosenberg, July 6, 1940, Tomo 279, AGN.

48. "Confidential Memo; Re: Immigration."

49. Wagg, "Report of the Meeting"; and "1,000 More to Join Refugees' Colony," *New York Times*, January 31, 1941, p. 9.

50. "DORSA Board of Directors Meeting Minutes," April 16, 1940, File 1, DP, JDC Archives.

51. *American Jewish Year Book, 5701*, 278; and *American Jewish Year Book 5702*, 90.

52. By mid-1941, the nonsettler population on the island had reached four hundred, seventy-two of whom were receiving subsistence from the JDC. Rosenberg to Leavitt, October 2, 1940, and Leavitt to Rosenberg, October 10, 1940, File 49, DP, JDC Archives.

53. "Confidential Memo; Re: Immigration."

54. E.g., Pastoriza to Binswanger, April 5, 1940, Tomo 279, AGN.

55. Pastoriza to Vradelis, July 27, 1940, Tomo 279, AGN.

56. Vanderbilt to Pastoriza, June 1, 1940, Pastoriza to Rosenberg, June 4, 1940, and Pastoriza to Vanderbilt, June 4, 1940, Tomo 279, AGN. Steinberg would go on to have a successful and celebrated career as an artist and cartoonist for *The New Yorker*.

57. Rosenberg to Pastoriza, June 6, 1940, Tomo 279, AGN.

58. "Confidential Memo; Re: Immigration."

59. George Warren to Rosenberg, January 25, 1940, File 1, DP, JDC Archives; and Warren to Joseph Chamberlain, March 1, 1940, Roll 1, RG 278, Chamberlain Papers, YIVO Archives.

60. George Warren to Chamberlain, March 1, 1940.

61. George Warren to Chamberlain, March 8, 1940, Roll 1, RG 278, Chamberlain Papers, YIVO Archives.

62. Chamberlain to George Warren, March 22, 1940, George Warren to Chamberlain, March 22, 1940, and George Warren to Chamberlain, March 30, 1940, Roll 1, RG 278, Chamberlain Papers, YIVO Archives.

63. George Warren to Chamberlain, March 30, 1940.

64. Ibid.

65. George Warren to Chamberlain, April 9, 1940, Roll 1, RG 278, Chamberlain Papers, YIVO Archives.

66. "DORSA Contract," January 30, 1940, File 1, DP, JDC Archives.

67. George Warren to Chamberlain, April 19, 1940; "Confidential Memo; Re: Immigration"; and "Maintenance Trust Agreement in Respect of Immigration into the

Dominican Republic," File 49; and "Plan for the Admission of Temporary and Permanent Residents in the Dominican Republic," File 1, DP, JDC Archives. Authorities later tweaked the agreement so that DORSA assumed greater responsibilities for the nonsettlers once they arrived. Hinkle to Hull, May 4 and 18, 1940, *FRUS 1940*, 2: 225, 227–28.

68. Rosenberg to Rosen, May 7, 1940, File 49, DP, JDC Archives.

69. Rosenberg to Rosen, March 28, 1940, File 1, DP, JDC Archives.

70. George Warren to Chamberlain, April 19, 1940, and George Warren to Chamberlain, May 25, 1940, Roll 1, RG 278, Chamberlain Papers, YIVO Archives.

71. Rosenberg to Morris Troper, September 25, 1941, File 50, DP, JDC Archives.

72. Quoted in Vega, *La migración española*, 101.

73. Hinkle to Hull, May 18, 1940, Roll 28, 840.48/Refugees, NA.

74. "Confidential Memo; Re: Immigration."

75. Ibid. When reports of a Nazi plot to overthrow Trujillo circulated during the summer of 1940, the dictator jailed suspected Nazi sympathizers. Roorda, "The Dominican Republic: The Axis," 86–87.

76. Ibid.

77. Lamport to Rosen, May 7, 1940, RG 687, Arthur Lamport Papers, YIVO Archives.

78. "Draft Memo Re Immigration Matters in the Dominican Republic," September 25, 1940, File 49, DP, JDC Archives.

79. Ibid.

80. "Discussion Concerning the Future of Agricultural Settlement at Sosúa"; and Rosenberg to Troper, September 25, 1941, File 50, DP, JDC Archives.

81. Breitman and Kraut, *American Refugee Policy*, 237; Genizi, *American Apathy*, 81–89; and Long to Roosevelt, September 18, 1940, *FRUS, 1940*, 2: 238–40.

82. Bauer, *American Jewry*, 51.

83. Quoted in Bendiner, *The Riddle*, 102–3.

84. Avra Warren to Reyher, April 10, 1941, Roll 29, 840.48/Refugees, NA.

85. Feingold, *A Time for Searching*, 232.

86. Proudfoot, *European Refugees*, 62; and Marrus and Paxton, *Vichy France*, 114.

7. PLAYING GOD

Epigraph: Bertolt Brecht, quoted in Jackman, "Introduction," 18.

1. Rosenberg to Troper, February 16, 1940, Troper to JDC office in New York City, February 21, 1940, Cable, Rosenberg and Hyman to Rosen, February 23, 1940, File 49, DP, JDC Archives.

2. Rosen, "Selection of Settlers for the Dominican Project," File 49, DP, JDC Archives.

3. Kaplan, "Prologue: Jewish Women," 13.

4. Rosen, "Selection of Settlers."

5. "Minutes of DORSA meeting, April 11, 1940, File 1, DP, JDC Archives; and Kisch, "The Golden Cage," 77. He was just as emphatic with donors. See *Concerning Refugee Settlement*.

6. "Solicitud para la admisión de colonos en la República Dominicana." File 49, DP, JDC Archives.

7. Rosen to Mr. and Mrs. Solomon Trone, September 30, 1940, File 49, DP, JDC Archives.

8. Ibid.

9. "Minutes of Luncheon Meetings at Lawyer's Club," November 12, 1940, File 2, DP, JDC Archives.

10. Unless otherwise indicated, the following discussion of conditions in Italy and Switzerland is taken from Trone to Rosenberg, May 26, 1940, File 49, DP, JDC Archives.

11. Tartakower and Grossman, *The Jewish Refugee*, 39–40; and *American Jewish Year Book 5701*, 383.

12. Trone to Rosenberg, May 26, 1940.

13. Bauer, *My Brother's Keeper*, 271; and Tartakower and Grossman, *The Jewish Refugee*, 35.

14. *American Jewish Year Book 5701*, 383, 454.

15. Rosen to Trone, September 30, 1940, File 49, DP, JDC Archives.

16. Otto Papernik, "Memoir." Unpublished and undated mss. Sylvie Papernik Papers.

17. Interview, Helen "Hellie" Goldman, March 17, 2004.

18. Hofeller, "Timetable to Nowhere: The Sosúa Settlement," 17.

19. Jacob Sondheimer, "The Refugee Settlement 'Sosúa': A Factual Report," translated by Miriam Gerber and edited by Melvina Lipschutz. Jacob Sondheimer Collection, LBI.

20. Papernik, "Memoir."

21. Quoted in Kisch, "The Golden Cage," 60.

22. Tartakower and Grossman, *The Jewish Refugee*, 202–4; and Katz, "Mexico, Gilberto Bosques," 5.

23. Quoted in Maga, *America, France*, 183–217. In 1942 the Nazis initiated mass deportations of Jews living in France, and by war's end, more than 120,000 Jews had been apprehended and sent to concentration camps (more than half to Poland). Proudfoot, *European Refugees*, 50.

24. Kisch, "The Golden Cage," File 1, 61.

25. *American Jewish Year Book 5702*, 92, 328; and Proudfoot, *European Refugees*, 57.

26. Felix Bauer, "Leading to and Living in."

27. Interview, Goldman, March 17, 2004; and Papernik, "Memoir."

28. Elizabeth Rosenberg received her training at the University of London and practiced psychiatry and psychoanalysis. She would later become a clinical professor of psychiatry at Harvard Medical School and vice president of the International Psycho-Analytical Association. *New York Times*, November 24, 1970.

29. "Confidential Memo; Re: Immigration," Reyher to Hexter, June 18, 1943, File 49, DP, JDC Archives; and Wagg, "Report of the Meeting."

30. Mrs. Roosevelt received only veiled sympathy from the State Department, however, until she stumbled on assistance from an unlikely ally. Her husband's Republican challenger Wendell Wilkie had insisted that FDR "hear the cries of the war refugee children." Not wanting to hand such an emotional issue to his opponent, FDR agreed to make a temporary exception for the British children. Maga, *America, France*, 173–75.

31. Wyman, *Paper Walls*, chapter 6; and "Information Bulletin no. 6," National Refugee Service, April 30, 1940, File 49, DP, JDC Archives.

32. Reyher to Pastoriza, June 18, 1940, and Rosenberg to Pastoriza, June 20, 1940, Tomo 279, AGN.

33. Rosen to Trone, September 30, 1940, File 49, DP, JDC Archives.

34. Rosen to Bernhard Kahn, October 31, 1940. Reyher corroborated Rosen's critique in "Confidential Memo; Re: Immigration."

35. Adler-Rudel to Rosen, August 29, 1940, File 49, DP, JDC Archives.

36. Ibid.

37. Rosen to Adler-Rudel, November 6, 1940, File 49, DP, JDC Archives.

38. Cable, Rosen to Emerson, October 31, 1940, File 49, DP, JDC Archives.

39. Rosen to Emerson, February 6, 1941, File 3; and, for similar sentiments, Ruby Frisch to Rosenberg, November 4, 1940, File 2, DP, JDC Archives.

40. Rosen to Rosenberg, October 22, 1940, File 2, DP, JDC Archives.

41. Rosenberg to Rosen, May 7, 1940, File 49, DP, JDC Archives.

42. Rosenberg to Rosen, March 28, 1940, File 1, DP, JDC Archives.

43. Memo of Conversation, "Refugees in England," Warren and Pell, June 12, 1940, Roll 28, 840.48/Refugees, NA; and *Concerning Refugee Settlement.*

44. Rosenberg to Trujillo, March 9, 1940, File 1, DP, JDC Archives.

45. Pell to Rosenberg, October 25, 1940, File 2, DP, JDC Archives.

46. "Confidential Memo; Re: Immigration."

47. Rosenberg to Baerwald, November 7, 1940, File 2, DP, JDC Archives. Capitals in original.

48. "Confidential Memo; Re: Immigration."

49. Wagg, "Report of the Meeting."

50. Ibid.

51. Reyher to Pell, January 17, 1941, File 50, DP, JDC Archives.

52. "Notes of Telephone Conversation between Pell, Reyher and Rosen," January 18, 1941, and Pell to Reyher, January 18, 1941, File 50, DP, JDC Archives.

53. "Notes of Telephone Conversation," January 18, 1941, and Pell to Reyher, January 18, 1941, File 50, DP, JDC Archives.

54. "Confidential Memo; Re: Immigration"; and "Memorandum by the Assistant Chief of the Division of European Affairs (Pell)," February 29, 1940, *FRUS, 1940*, 2: 214–19.

55. "Confidential Memo; Re: Immigration"; and Roosevelt to Hull, March 7, 1940, *FRUS, 1940*, 2: 219.

56. Pell to Atherton, July 9, 1940, Roll 29, 840.48/Refugees, NA.

57. Pell to Atherton, February 18, 1941, Long to Welles, February 19, 1941, and Pepper to Long, March 4, 1941, Roll 29, 840.48/Refugees, NA. For biographical data on Pell, see *Register of the Department of State, October 1, 1940* (Washington, D.C.: U.S. Government Printing Office, 1940), 166–67; and *Biographic Register of the Department of State, September 1, 1944* (Washington, D.C.: U.S. Government Printing Office, 1944), 185.

58. CIV (June 30, 1941), 592–94.

59. Ibid., 594.

60. Ibid.

61. Rosen to Trone, September 30, 1940, File 49; and Cables, Löwenherz to JDC New York office, March 5, 1941, Troper to Löewenherz, March 6, 1941, DORSA New York office to Löewenherz, March 13, 1941, File 50, DP, JDC Archives.

62. *American Jewish Year Book 5701*, 449.

63. Vega, *Nazismo*, 188; and Friedman, *Nazis and Good Neighbors*.

64. Gunther, "Hispaniola," 772.

65. "Confidential Memo; Re: Immigration."

66. Rosenberg to Welles, February 27, 1941, Roll 29, 840.48/Refugees, NA.

67. Ibid.

68. Atherton to Long, March 4, 1951, Atherton to Rosenberg, March 6, 1941, Reyher to Trone, March 13, 1941, and Rosenberg to Avra Warren, March 13, 1941, Roll 29, 840.48/Refugees, NA.

69. Warren's initial response to Rosenberg was encouraging. Cf. Avra Warren to Rosenberg, March 11, 1941, and Avra Warren to Reyher, April 10, 1941, Roll 29, 840.48/Refugees, NA.

70. Letter, Rosenberg to Wasservogel, March 12, 1941, Henry Wells Papers.

71. Interview, Henry Wells, February 3, 1999.

72. "Notes of Dr. Rosen," April 10, 1941, File 3, DP, JDC Archives.

73. Dr. Harry Solomon to Rosenberg, November 17, 1941, and Dr. B. S. Oppenheimer to Rosenberg, October 21, 1941, File 11, DP, JDC Archives.

74. Rosenberg to Elizabeth Rosenberg, June 25, 1941, File 3, DP, JDC Archives.

75. "Meeting held at JDC Offices on January 19, 1972, at 11 A.M.," File 8, DP. A *New York Times* article published in 1965 posited half that amount. Kisch estimates that three thousand Dominican visas were dispensed. "The Golden Cage," 144. But evidence is lacking for any of the estimates, and documentation is lacking at the Joint or in the Dominican archives.

76. Agar, *The Saving Remnant*, 85.

8. FIRST IMPRESSIONS

Epigraph: Josef David Eichen, settler, n.d., in Eichen, *Una coloniá hebrea*, 2.

1. Felix Bauer, "Leading to and Living in the U.S.A."

2. Spitzer, *Hotel Bolivia*, 55, 57.

3. This section draws on a portion of Patterson's definition of the slave in *Slavery and Social Death*, 5. Clearly there are stark differences between the horrors slaves confronted on the middle passage and what these relatively privileged refugees faced, but their involuntary uprooting from a former way of life and consequent marginalization from family, home, and culture is something that Bauer and others shared to a certain degree with natally alienated slaves.

4. Spitzer, *Hotel Bolivia*, 59.

5. Oral History Interview with Felix Bauer.

6. Bauer, "Leading to and Living in"; Oral History Interview with Felix Bauer; Oral History Interview with Martha Bauer, April 30, 1992, RG-50, 166*03, USHMMLA; and Interview, Wasservogel, February 3, 1999.

7. Bauer, "Leading to and Living in."

8. Hofeller, "Timetable to Nowhere." Stephen S. Kalmer makes a similar point about Ellis Island's "prisonlike" atmosphere in his memoir, *Goodbye, Vienna!*, 148.

9. Gardiner, *La política de inmigración*, 114–15.

10. Papernik, "Memoir."
11. Bauer, "Leading to and Living in."
12. Ibid.
13. Interviews, Ruth and Ernie Schreiner, June 25, 2003.
14. Interview, Topf, August 14, 2006.
15. Quoted in Laura Randall, "Golden Cage," 20.
16. Kirchwey, "Caribbean Refuge," 466–67.
17. Rosen statement at press conference, New York, April 27, 1940, File 40, DP, JDC Archives.
18. Brookings Institution, *Refugee Settlement in the Dominican Republic*, 285.
19. Eichen, *Sosúa, una colonia hebrea*, 25.
20. Wagg, "Report of the Meeting," 99; and Martínez, *De Sosúa a Matanzas*, 25–27.
21. Wagg, "Report of the Meeting," 100.
22. Ibid., 102.
23. Ibid., 103–6.
24. Segal, *Other Peoples' Houses*, 196.
25. Wagg, "Report of the Meeting," 101.
26. Papernik, "Memoir," 89.
27. Frisch to Rosenberg, November 4, 1940, File 2, DP, JDC Archives.
28. *Memoria . . . Relaciones Exteriores . . . 1941*, 80.
29. Symanski and Burley, "The Jewish Colony of Sosúa," 367, 371; and "Los Charamicos," *Sosúa News*.
30. Papernik, "Memoir."
31. Schoenhals, "An Extraordinary Migration," 42.
32. Interview, Luis Hess, October 6, 2006.
33. Symanski and Burley, "The Jewish Colony of Sosúa," 371.
34. Papernik, "Memoir," 90.
35. Ibid., 96–97.
36. Cohler and Lieberman, "Ethnicity and Personal Adaptation," 35.
37. Gardiner, *La política de inmigración*, 121.
38. Papernik, "Memoir," 94.
39. Ibid.
40. Vernant, *The Refugee in the Post-War World*, 13; and Cohler and Lieberman, "Ethnicity and Personal Adaptation," 34.
41. Interview, Luis Hess, October 6, 2006.
42. Papernik, "Memoir," 90.
43. Hofeller, "Timetable to Nowhere," 235.
44. Quoted in Schoenhals, "Extraordinary Migration," 42.
45. Arons to Rosenberg, October 19, 1942, File 4, DP, JDC Archives.
46. Arons to Reyher, October 23, 1942, File 4, DP, JDC Archives.
47. Bauer, "Leading to and Living in."
48. Rosenberg to Avra Warren, December 3, 1942, 839.014, Roll 4, NA.
49. Bauer reports that several immigrants died of malaria. "Leading to and Living in."
50. The Brookings Report noted only three chronic cases. *Refugee Settlement in the Dominican Republic*, 295.

51. Wagg, "Report of the Meeting," 107.

52. *Memoria . . . Agricultura, Pecuaria y Colonización . . . 1947*, 271; and Arons to Rosenberg, October 19, 1942, File #4, DP, JDC Archives.

53. Wagg, "Report of the Meeting," 109.

54. Papernik, "Memoir," 90.

55. Eichen, *Sosúa, una colonia hebrea*, 33, 43–44, 45–46.

56. Spitzer, *Hotel Bolivia*, x.

57. Ibid., 146, 153–54.

58. Grinberg and Grinberg, *Psychoanalytic Perspectives*, 97–98.

59. Feuchtwanger's untitled essay of 1938 that appeared in the exile journal *Das Wort* is quoted in Anderson, *Hitler's Exiles*, 171.

60. Ibid.

61. Rosen, "New Neighbors in Sosúa," 476.

62. Papernik, "Memoir," 97–98.

63. Grinberg and Grinberg, *Psychoanalytic Perspectives*, 157.

64. Bar-On, "Afterword," 334, n3.

65. Kunz, "The Refugee in Flight," 137–39.

66. Grinberg and Grinberg, *Psychoanalytic Perspectives*, 158–59.

67. Quoted in Anderson, *Hitler's Exiles*, 257.

68. Papernik, "Memoir," 91.

69. *Refugee Settlement in the Dominican Republic*, 286–87.

70. "Austrian Refugees go to Sosúa Haven," *New York Times*, November 25, 1940, 14.

71. Papernik, "Memoir," 91.

72. Taub and Kafka, "Sosúa," video documentary, 1981.

73. Interview with Luis Hess, May 25, 2001.

74. Walter Sondheimer to Solomon Arons, August 8, 1943, File 5, DP, JDC Archives; and Gardiner, *La política de inmigración*, 105.

75. Papernik, "Memoir," 91.

76. Wagg, "Report of the Meeting."

77. "Sosúa Exiles Win Living from Soil," *New York Times*, December 1, 1940, p. 43.

78. *Refugee Settlement in the Dominican Republic*, 291–93.

79. Gardiner, *La política de inmigración*, 104.

80. Arons to Rosenberg, October 19, 1942, File 4, DP, JDC Archives.

81. *New York Times*, April 24, 1940; and Wagg, "Report of the Meeting," 106.

82. Papernik, "Memoir," 99.

83. *Refugee Settlement in the Dominican Republic*, 289–91; and Kisch, "The Golden Cage," 68.

84. Gardiner, *La política de inmigración*, 119.

85. Schoenhals, "An Extraordinary Migration," 42.

86. Rosen to Rosenberg, October 22, 1940, File 2, DP, JDC Archives.

87. Trone to Rosenberg and Rosen, July 28, 1941, File 3, DP, JDC Archives.

88. Quoted in Gardiner, *La política de inmigración*, 105, 116–17; and Felix Bauer, "Leading to and Living in."

89. *Concerning Refugee Settlement*.

90. Ibid.

9. FLAWED VISION

Epigraph: Joseph Rosen, "New Neighbors in Sosúa," *Survey Graphic* 30 (September 1941), 478.

1. Symanski and Burley, "The Jewish Colony," 369.
2. The Settlers' Council was later expanded in size. "Homestead Plan for Sosúa Settlers," June 1, 1941, File 37, DP, JDC Archives.
3. *Refugee Settlement*, 289–91.
4. Ibid., 294.
5. Elkin, *Jews in the Latin American Republics*, 146.
6. Eichen, *Sosúa, una colonia hebrea*, 66–67.
7. William L. Bein [Sosúa office manager] to DORSA Agriculture and Purchasing Departments, January 15, 1942, Edith Meyerstein de Bloch Papers.
8. Rosen, "New Neighbors," 478.
9. Quoted in John Hoffman Report, December 19, 1941, File 3, DP, JDC Archives.
10. Rosen to Rosenberg, November 20, 1940, File 2, DP, JDC Archives.
11. E.g., *Memoria . . . Agricultura, Industria y Trabajo . . . 1944*.
12. Quoted in Kisch, "The Golden Cage," 77.
13. Interview, Topf, August 15, 2006.
14. Symanski and Burley, "The Jewish Colony," 369.
15. Ibid., 370.
16. Settlers' Council to Solomon Arons and William Bein, August 11, 1943, File 5, DP, JDC Archives.
17. Joseph Hyman to Laura Margolis, July 16, 1941, File 50, DP, JDC Archives.
18. Hyman to Margolis, July 16, 1941, File 50, DP, JDC Archives.
19. Ibid.; and Margolis to Hyman, August 7, 1941, File 50, DP, JDC Archives.
20. Brookings Institution, *Refugee Settlement in the Dominican Republic*, 286, 293.
21. Hofeller, "Timetable to Nowhere," 238; and *The Dominican Republic*, no. 93 (November 15, 1949), 2.
22. Hofeller, "Timetable to Nowhere," 237.
23. Walker, *Journey toward the Sunlight*, 112–13, 115.
24. Hofeller, "Refugee: 1938–1946," undated typescript, Ernest B. Hofeller Collection, LBI.
25. Rosen, "New Neighbors," 478.
26. Rosen to Rosenberg, October 22, 1940, File 2, DP, JDC Archives.
27. Rosenberg to Rosen, October 29, 1940, File 2, DP, JDC Archives.
28. Ibid.
29. Ibid.
30. Trone to Rosen and Rosenberg, July 28, 1941, File 3, DP, JDC Archives.
31. Ibid.
32. Ibid.
33. Ibid.
34. Group Leaders to Rosenberg, August 10, 1941, File 3, DP, JDC Archives.
35. Rosen to Reyher, February 22, 1943, File 5, DP, JDC Archives.
36. Gardiner, "*La política de inmigración*," 146.

37. Notes of conversation between Dr. Isgur and Rosenberg, June 18, 1942, File 5, DP, JDC Archives.

38. "Reglas para el establecimiento de colonos," undated, Jack and Miriam Gerber Collection, LBI.

39. Reid Report, undated, File 5, DP, JDC Archives.

40. "Notes from private talk between Dr. Isgur and Rosenberg," June 18, 1942, File 4, DP, JDC Archives.

41. William Bein to all departments, January 5, 1942, Edith Meyerstein de Bloch Papers.

42. Arons to Homesteaders, March 3, 1943, File 5, DP, JDC Archives.

43. Baum to Rosenberg, September 16, 1944, File 6, DP, JDC Archives.

44. Eugene Rosen to Arons, July 24, 1943, File 5, DP, JDC Archives.

45. Ibid.

46. Mrs. Arons to Rosenberg, May 14, 1943, File 5, DP, JDC Archives.

47. Ibid.

48. Ibid.

49. "Minutes of Visit of Rat to Mr. Falk," January 10, 1942, Edith Bloch de Meyerstein Papers.

50. *Refugee Settlement*, 287.

51. Quoted in Memo, Bein to all departments, January 19, 1942, Edith Meyerstein de Bloch Papers.

52. Arons to Rosenberg, October 19, 1942, File 3, DP, JDC Archives.

53. Interview, Martin Katz, May 29, 2001.

54. Bauer, "Leading to and Living in."

55. "List of Settlers (Homestead) who Dropped out of Their Groups and are now in Batey, Elsewhere in the Dominican Republic or Abroad," undated, File 7, DP, JDC Archives.

56. See Oz, *A Tale of Love and Darkness*, 15–16. Thanks to Sonja Burian for bringing this elegant memoir to my attention.

57. Tartakower and Grossmann, *The Jewish Refugee*, 395.

58. Ibid.

59. Gaertner, "A Comparison of Refugee and Non-Refugee Immigrants," 106.

60. Minutes of DORSA Stockholders Meeting, May 6, 1943, File 5, DP, JDC Archives.

10. CONTAINMENT

Epigraph: Maurice Hexter to James Rosenberg, July 30, 1942, File 3, DP, JDC Archives.

1. Reyher to Hexter, July 12, 1943, File 5, DP, JDC Archives.

2. Vega, *Los Estados Unidos y Trujillo, 1946*, 2: 133.

3. Warren quoted in Reyher to Hexter, July 12, 1943.

4. Falk to David Schweitzer, October 31, 1941, and Hyman to J. B. Lightman, File 3, DP, JDC Archives.

5. Reyher to Hexter, July 9 and July 12, 1943, File 5, DP, JDC Archives.

6. Memo, DORSA meeting, September 9, 1948, File 6b, DP, JDC Archives. Passports were provisional, and citizens had to surrender them on returning from abroad. The application process was tightly controlled. Peña Rivera, *Trujillo: Historia oculta*, 112.

7. George Hourwich to Rosenberg, June 30, 1942, File 3, DP, JDC Archives.

8. Rosen to Rosenberg, April 10, 1943, File 5, DP, JDC Archives.

9. Avra Warren to George Warren, September 28, 1942, File 3, DP, JDC Archives.

10. E.g., Unger application, December 29, 1943, Secretaría de Interior y Policía, Sección de Seguridad, Legajo 3, AGN.

11. Federal Bureau of Investigation, *Totalitarian Activities, Dominican Republic Today (November 1944)* (Washington, D.C.: FBI, U.S. Department of Justice, 1944). Roll 5, 839.156, NA.

12. Vega, *Nazismo*, 186–87.

13. Ibid.

14. Vega, *Los Estados Unidos y Trujillo, 1945*, 197–200; Vega, *Los Estados Unidos y Trujillo, 1946*, 2: 126–27; Bosch, *Trujillo: causas de una tiranía*, 122, 157–58; and Crassweller, *Trujillo: The Life and Times*, 128.

15. "Minutes of Meeting held at Maurice Hexter's Office," September 20, 1944, File 6, DP, JDC Archives.

16. Bein to Falk and W. Sondheimer, January 24, 1942, Edith Meyerstein de Bloch Papers.

17. Ibid; and Quackenbos, "Sosúa: Kol Hashholeh," 133.

18. Bein to Falk and W. Sondheimer, January 24, 1942, Edith Meyerstein de Bloch Papers.

19. Gardiner, *La política de inmigración*, 161.

20. *New York Times*, September 14, 15, and 22, 1955; and Gardiner, *La política de inmigración*, 149.

21. Gardiner, *La política de inmigración*, 148.

22. *Cosmopólita* 23 (April 6, 1941).

23. Gardiner, *La política de inmigración*, 146–47.

24. Hexter, *Life Size*, 126.

25. Derby, "The Magic of Modernity," 6–11 and chapter 6.

26. Interview, Luis Hess, May 25–26, 2001.

27. Lawton to Hull, Roll 1, 839.00, NA.

28. Bein to Ruby Moses, March 4, 1944, File 41, DP, JDC Archives.

29. Papernik, "Memoir," 117–18.

30. Ibid., 127–28.

31. Ibid.

32. E.g., Sondheimer to Bein, March 5, 1945, File 6, DP, JDC Archives.

33. *Concerning Refugee Settlement*, 14.

34. Brookings Institution, *Refugee Settlement in the Dominican Republic*, vii–viii.

35. Rosenberg to Agar, April 2, 1958, File 3, DP, JDC Archives.

36. Rosenberg to Baerwald, October 8, 1942, File, 4, DP, JDC Archives.

37. Rosenberg to Agar, April 2, 1958, File 3, DP, JDC Archives.

38. Rosenberg to Baerwald, October 8, 1942, File 3, DP, JDC Archives.

39. Ibid.

40. "Minutes of Joint Meeting of the Boards of the Agro-Joint and DORSA," June 11, 1946, File 6A, DP, JDC Archives. On the state-supported irrigation projects, see Inoa, *Estado y campesinos*, 99–108.

41. Brookings Institution, *Refugee Settlement*, 341.

42. Arons to Rosenberg, October 19, 1942, File 3, DP, JDC Archives.

43. Later, in his "M" project, which studied resettlement sites, Henry Field and his team would criticize the Brookings report for underestimating the Dominican Republic's absorptive capacity. Field, "M" Project, 162–63.

44. Brookings Institution, Refugee Settlement, 46.

45. Moritzen, "Possibilities for Immigrant Settlement in the Dominican Republic," Dominican Republic 10, 5 (November–December 1942), 10–11.

46. Dominican Republic, Capacidad de la República, 15.

47. Ibid., 15–16; and Walker, Journey toward the Sunlight, 121–22.

48. Dominican Republic, Capacidad de la República, 15, 33.

49. Ibid., 24.

50. J. Schechtmann, "Failure of the Dominican Scheme: Brookings Report Writes Finis to Colonization Project," Congress Weekly, January 15, 1943, 8–9.

51. Yiddisher Kemfer, undated, File 31, DP, JDC Archives.

52. American Jewish Year Book 5705, 169–70, 207–10, 358.

53. DORSA Executive Secretary Ruby Frisch counseled Rosenberg not to respond to the Brookings study. Frisch to Rosenberg, November 6, 1942, File 3, DP, JDC Archives.

54. Falk to Rosenberg, February 12, 1942, File 3, and Rosenberg to Agar, April 2, 1958, File 4, DP, JDC Archives. Falk did not cut his ties to Sosúa entirely; he sent the settlement some excellent cattle stock and acted as an intermediary between DORSA and Trujillo.

55. Falk to Rosenberg, January 19, 1942, File 3, DP, JDC Archives.

56. "Statistical Information Regarding Refugees and Settlers in San Domingo," December 1942, File 50a, DP, JDC Archives.

57. Ibid.; and "Draft Memorandum of Sosúa Settlement," February 8, 1946, File 6, DP, JDC Archives.

58. Bein to all departments, January 26, 1942, Edith Meyerstein de Bloch Papers.

59. Hyman to Clarence Pickett, February 16, 1942, File 3, DP, JDC Archives.

60. Rosenberg to Arons, June 25, 1942, File 3, DP, JDC Archives.

61. Hexter to Rosenberg, July 30, 1942, File 3, DP, JDC Archives.

62. Walter Sondheimer and Bein to Arons, August 23, 1943, File 5, DP, JDC Archives.

11. TRIAL AND ERROR

Epigraph: James Rosenberg, "Minutes of Agro-Joint Executive Committee meeting," February 6, 1946, File 6, DP, JDC Archives.

1. Gardiner, La política de inmigración, 128.

2. Arons to Rosenberg, October 19, 1942, File 3, DP, JDC Archives.

3. Brookings Institution, Refugee Settlement in the Dominican Republic, 303.

4. Papernik, "Memoir," 129; and "Noticia en Sosúa—Productos Sosúa, the Pride of the Jewish Community," www.hotel-dominicanrepublic.com. Accessed February 28, 2006.

5. Walker, Journey toward the Sunlight, 116; Eichen, Sosúa, una colonia hebrea, 48, 70; and "Noticia en Sosúa."

6. Taub and Kafka, Sosúa, 1981. Video documentary.

7. Gardiner, La política de inmigración, 117; and Interview, Joe Benjamin, October 3, 2006.

8. *Cosmopólita* 23 (April 6, 1942).

9. Arons to Reyher, October 28, 1942, File 3, DP, JDC Archives.

10. *American Hebrew*, November 1, 1940, 12.

11. "Minutes of Agro-Joint Executive Committee meeting," February 6, 1946, File 6, DP, JDC Archives.

12. *Memoria . . . Agricultura, Pecuaria y Colonización . . .* 1947, 257.

13. "Noticia en Sosúa."

14. Harding, *The Land Columbus Loved*, 20.

15. Ibid; and "Walter Baum's Report on Batey-Administration," September 16, 1944, File 6, DP, JDC Archives.

16. "Minutes of Agro-Joint Executive Committee," February 6, 1946, File 6A, DP, JDC Archives.

17. Interview, Helen "Hellie" Goldman, March 17, 2004.

18. Ibid.

19. "Minutes of Agro-Joint Executive Committee meeting," February 4, 1946, File 6A, DP, JDC Archives.

20. Spitzer, *Hotel Bolivia*, 153.

21. Papernik, "Memoir," 108; and Kisch, "The Golden Cage," 124b.

22. Bauer, "Leading to and Living in."

23. Kisch, "Rafael Trujillo: Caribbean Cyrus," 376; and Kisch, "The Golden Cage," 124a, 126.

24. *Memoria . . . Agricultura . . .* 1947, 271.

25. Papernik, "Memoir," 104.

26. Ibid., 137.

27. Arons to Rosenberg, June 5, 1942, File 5, DP, JDC Archives.

28. Papernik, "Memoir," 97.

29. Ibid., 105.

30. *Memoria . . . Agricultura . . . 1947*, 269; "Stern Report to Directors and Officers of Agro-Joint," December 27, 1944, File 6, DP, JDC Archives; and Interview, Luis Hess, May 25–26, 2001.

31. Eichen, *Una colonia hebrea*, 78–79; Harding, *The Land Columbus Loved*, 17; Reyher to Rosenberg and Hexter, May 17, 1943, File 5, DP, JDC Archives.

32. Kisch, "The Golden Cage," 124b.

33. Sondheimer to Bein, March 5, 1945, Baum to Bein, March 14, 1945, and Sondheimer to Bein, April 2, 1945, File 6, DP, JDC Archives.

34. Arons to Reyher, October 23, 1942, File 4, DP, JDC Archives.

35. Oral History Interview with Martha Bauer, ACC, April 30, 1992, RG-50, 166*03, USHM-MLA.

36. Papernik, "Memoir," 106.

37. *Memoria . . . Agricultura . . . 1947*, 270; *Dominican Republic*, 93 (November 15, 1949), 2; and Harding, *The Land Columbus Loved*, 17.

38. Harding, *The Land Columbus Loved*, 17.

39. Hofeller, "Refugee: 1938–1946," 21; and Papernik, "Memoir," 135.

40. Hofeller, "Refugee: 1938–1946," 39.

41. Rosen to Rosenberg, April 4, 1942, File 4, DP, JDC Archives.

42. Eugene Rosen to Rosenberg, May 16, 1942, File 4, DP, JDC Archives.

43. "Notes of a Private Talk between Isgur and Rosenberg," June 11, 1942, File 4, DP, JDC Archives.

44. Rosenberg to Arons, November 25, 1942, File 4, DP. JDC Archives.

45. Ibid.

46. Arons to all Homesteaders, March 3, 1943, File 5, DP, JDC Archives.

47. Arons to Rosenberg and Reyher, October 23, 1942, File 4, DP, JDC Archives.

48. Papernik, "Memoir," 131–32.

49. Ibid.

50. Eugene Rosen to Rosenberg, July 24, 1943, File 5, DP, JDC Archives.

51. Ibid.

52. Ibid.

53. Settlers' Council to Rosenberg, August 3, 1943, File 5, DP, JDC Archives.

54. Arons to Settlers, August, 4, 1943, File 5, DP, JDC Archives.

55. Hexter to Stern, January 11, 1945, File 6, DP, JDC Archives.

56. "Minutes of Agro-Joint Board of Directors meeting," December 30, 1943, File 5, DP, JDC Archives.

57. "Minutes of DORSA Stockholders meeting," May 6, 1943, File 5, DP, JDC Archives.

58. "Minutes of DORSA Executive Committee meeting," January 20, 1944, File 5, DP, JDC Archives.

59. "Minutes of Agro-Joint Executive Committee meeting," February 4, 1946, File 6, DP, JDC Archives.

60. Bein, "Draft Memorandum"; and Research Department memo to Robert Pilpel, October 28, 1947, File 47, DP, JDC Archives.

61. Hexter to Falk, February 16, 1944, File 5, DP, JDC Archives.

62. Quoted in "Minutes of DORSA Executive Committee Meeting."

63. Hexter to Falk, January 21, 1944 and February 16, 1944, File 5, DP, JDC Archives.

64. "Minutes of DORSA Executive Committee," January 20, 1944, File 5, DP, JDC Archives.

65. Hexter to Rosenberg, February 16, 1944, File 5, DP, JDC Archives.

66. Ibid.

67. Ibid; and "Memo, Pilpel to Isaac Levy, Joseph Heyman, Moses Leavitt, et al.," October 23, 1945, File 6, DP, JDC Archives.

68. Bein, "Draft Memorandum of Sosúa Settlement," February 8, 1946, File 6, DP, JDC Archives.

69. "Ruby Moses' Minutes of Meeting at Maurice Hexter's Home," February 12 and February 14, 1945, File 6, DP, JDC Archives.

70. "Baum Report on Batey," undated, and "Moses' Minutes," File #6, DP, JDC Archives.

71. Stern to Hexter, July 14, 1944, File 5, DP, JDC Archives.

72. Stern to Hexter, July 29, 1944, File 5, DP, JDC Archives.

12. THE MAN WHO SAVED SOSÚA

Epigraph: David Stern, quoted in Harding, The Land Columbus Loved, 117–18.

1. Papernik, "Memoir," 132.

2. Stern to DORSA, May 1946, File 6A, DP, JDC Archives.

3. "Minutes of Joint Meeting of DORSA and Agro-Joint Boards," June 11, 1946, DP, JDC Archives.

4. Hexter to Baerwald, December 21, 1944, File 6, DP, JDC Archives.

5. As part of his responsibilities, Stern also was sent to Bolivia to consult on Agro-Joint operations there. Hexter to Stern, January 11, 1945, File 6, DP, JDC Archives.

6. Oral History, Maurice Hexter, typescript, William E. Wiener Oral History Library of the American Jewish Committee, New York Public Library; and *New York Times*, October 29, 1990.

7. Oral History, Maurice Hexter, typescript, 66, 77; and Hexter, *Life Size*.

8. Jacob Sondheimer, "The Refugee Settlement, 'Sosúa': A Factual Report," undated, Jacob B. Sondheimer Collection, LBI.

9. Interview, Topf, August 14, 2006.

10. Kisch, "The Golden Cage," 109.

11. Papernik, "Memoir," 132.

12. Quoted in Gardiner, *La política de inmigración*, 112.

13. Harding, *The Land Columbus Loved*, 118.

14. Stern to Hexter, August 29, 1944, File 5, DP, JDC Archives.

15. Weintraub et al., *Moshava, Kibbutz and Moshav*, chapters 1 and 4.

16. Stern, "Summary of Two Preliminary Reports of 7/31/44 and 8/7/44," File 5, and Stern to Hexter, November 26, 1945, File 6, DP, JDC Archives.

17. Sondheimer, "The Refugee Settlement, 'Sosúa.'"

18. Walter Sondheimer, "Text of Address to Joint Meeting of JDC and DORSA Boards," October 16, 1945, File 5, DP, JDC Archives.

19. Stern to Hexter, August 29, 1944, File 5, DP, JDC Archives; and *The Dominican Republic* 16, 2 (Spring 1951), 15.

20. "Minutes of Meeting at Maurice Hexter's office, September 20, 1944; "Baum Report" to Joint Meeting of JDC and DORSA, October 16, 1945, File 6; and Memo, DORSA meeting, September 9, 1948, File 6b, DP, JDC Archives.

21. Stern to Hexter, October 26, 1944, File 6, DP, JDC Archives.

22. Hexter to Baerwald, December 21, 1944; quoted in "Minutes of Meeting at Hexter's home, February 12 and 14, 1945, File 6, DP, JDC Archives.

23. "Minutes of Meeting at Hexter's home," File 6, DP, JDC Archives.

24. Interview, Topf, April 14, 2006.

25. Sondheimer to Bein, May 20, 1945, File 6; and Minutes of JDC Administrative Committee Meeting, December 20, 1946, File 6A, DP, JDC Archives.

26. "Brief Information on Sosúa Settlement," October 1952, and "Report of Sosúa Settlement for the Year, 1951," File 6c, DP, JDC Archives.

27. *Memoria . . . Agricultura . . . 1947*, 257.

28. Interview, Joe Benjamin, October 3, 2006.

29. "Stern Report to DORSA, first four months of 1946," File 6, DP, JDC Archives.

30. *Memoria . . . Agricultura . . . 1947*, 257.

31. Ibid., 261; and "Report of Sosúa Settlement . . . 1951."

32. *The Dominican Republic* 16, 2 (Spring 1951), 15.

33. Walker, *Journey toward the Sunlight*, 115–16.

34. Interview, Topf, August 14, 2006.

35. Stern to Hexter, November 26, 1945, File 6, DP, JDC Archives.

36. Stern to Hexter, August 29, 1944, and November 26, 1945, File 6, DP, JDC Archives.

37. Kätsch et al., *Sosua-Verheissenes Land*, 297–98.

38. "Stern Report to DORSA, first four months of 1946."

39. "Baum Report on Batey," October 16, 1945, File 6, DP, JDC Archives.

40. Ibid.; and *Memoria . . . Agricultura . . . 1947*, 272.

41. Bein, "Draft Memorandum of Sosúa Settlement," February 8, 1946, File 6, DP, JDC Archives.

42. "Stern Report to DORSA, first four months of 1946."

43. Ira Morris to Robert Pilpel, May 28, 1946, File 6, DP, JDC Archives. Even DORSA staffer William Baum characterized the housing in Batey as substandard. "Baum Report," File 6, DP, JDC Archives.

44. "Stern Report to DORSA, first four months of 1946."

45. Ristaino, *Port of Last Resort*, 252, 255; and Ross, *Escape to Shanghai*, 240.

46. Ristaino, *Port of Last Resort*, 255.

47. "Minutes of DORSA Executive Committee Meeting," July 5, 1945, File 6, DP, JDC Archives.

48. Papernik, "Memoir," 125–26.

49. Ibid; and Stern to Moses, July 16, 1946, File 6, DP, JDC Archives.

50. Bein, "Draft Memorandum of Sosúa Settlement."

51. Stern to Moses, July 16, 1946.

52. Homesteaders' Council to Hexter, May 8, 1946.

53. Stern to Moses, April 26, 1946, File 6, DP, JDC Archives.

54. "Stern Report to DORSA, first four months of 1946."

55. Ibid.

56. Bein, "Draft Memorandum of Sosúa Settlement."

57. Papernik, "Memoir," 155.

58. Oral History Interview with Martha Bauer, April 30, 1992, RG-50, 166*03, USHMMLA.

59. Papernik, "Memoir," 155.

60. Ibid., 157.

61. Interview, Topf, August 14, 2006.

62. Interview, Goldman, March 17, 2004.

63. Quoted in Kisch, "Rafael Trujillo," 377.

64. Bein to Hexter, September 1, 1945, File 6, DP, JDC Archives.

65. Walter Sondheimer, "Text of Address to Joint Meeting of JDC and DORSA Boards," October 16, 1945, File 5, DP, JDC Archives.

66. Ibid.

67. "Baum Report," Minutes of Joint JDC and DORSA Boards Meeting, September 1, 1945, File 6, DP, JDC Archives.

68. "Joint Meeting of the American Jewish Joint Agricultural Corporation and the Dominican Republic Settlement Association," June 11, 1946. Excerpt where indicated, the following discussion draws on this extraordinary typescript.

69. Leavitt, *The JDC Story*, 14; See also Schwarz, *The Redeemers*.

70. Hexter to Levy, March 1, 1945, File 6, DP.

13. A "SPLENDID PRESIDENT"

Epigraph: James Rosenberg to Edward Warburg and Maurice Hexter, May 23, 1946, File 6, DP, JDC Archives.

1. Roorda, *The Dictator Next Door*, 183.
2. *Memoria . . . Relaciones Exteriores . . . 1943*, 35.
3. Vega, *Los Estados Unidos y Trujillo, 1946*, 2: 91; *La Nación*, August 18, 1942; and Roorda, *The Dictator Next Door*, 182–83.
4. Roorda, *The Dictator Next Door*, 183.
5. Gellman, *Secret Affairs*, 310.
6. Doenecke and Stoler, *Debating Franklin D. Roosevelt's Foreign Policies*, 12.
7. Gellman, *Secret Affairs*, 346–47; and American Jewish Joint Distribution Committee, *So They May Live Again*, quote, 10.
8. Roorda, *The Dictator Next Door*, 185; and Briggs to Hull, July 5, 1944, 839.00/7-544, RG 59, Roll 2, NA.
9. Briggs to Hull, July 5, 1944; and Briggs to Edward Stettinius, January 3, 1945, *FRUS, 1945*, 9: 982.
10. Vega, *Los Estados Unidos y Trujillo, 1946*, 2: 150.
11. Briggs to Hull, July 5, 1944; and Briggs to Stettinius, January 3, 1945, *FRUS, 1945*, 9: 982.
12. Roorda, *The Dictator Next Door*, 185.
13. Ibid., 185–86; and Vega, *Los Estados Unidos y Trujillo, 1945*, 28.
14. Braden, *Diplomats and Demagogues*, 268–69. Briggs became director of the office of American Republic Affairs.
15. Ameringer, *The Caribbean Legion*, 31–32.
16. Quoted ibid., 13.
17. Quoted in Braden, *Diplomats and Demagogues*, 364–65.
18. Vega, *Los Estados Unidos y Trujillo, 1945*, 17–22.
19. Roorda, *The Dictator Next Door*, 305 n. 194.
20. Smith, *The Last Years of the Monroe Doctrine*, 226–27.
21. Ameringer, *The Caribbean Legion*, 19–20, quote, 14.
22. Vega, *Los Estados Unidos y Trujillo, 1945*, 28.
23. Vega, *Los Estados Unidos y Trujillo, 1946*, 2: 119.
24. Ameringer, *The Caribbean Legion*, 56, 60.
25. Ibid., 7–8.
26. Vega, *Los Estados Unidos y Trujillo, 1946*, 2: 16–17, 28.
27. George Butler to James Byrnes, November 18, 1946, *FRUS, 1946*, 11: 810; and Ameringer, *The Caribbean Legion*, 13.
28. Butler to Byrnes, October 30, 1946, *FRUS, 1946*, 11: 806.
29. *New York Times*, November 24, 1945.
30. *Memoria . . . Relaciones Exteriores . . . 1945*, 97–99; *New York Times*, December 22, 1945; and Gardiner, *La política de inmigración*, 148.
31. *New York Times*, January 29, 1946.
32. *New York Times*, January 25, 1946.

33. Dominican Republic, *Capacidad de la República*; and Gardiner, *La política de inmigración*, 129–30.

34. *Memoria . . . Relaciones Exteriores . . . 1945*, 141–43.

35. "Minutes of Joint Meeting of Agro-Joint and DORSA Boards," June 11, 1946.

36. Moya Pons, *Dominican Republic*, 361, 365.

37. Ibid., 363.

38. Quoted in "Minutes of Joint Meeting of Agro-Joint and DORSA Boards," June 11, 1946.

39. Edward Warburg to Haím López-Penha, December 17, 1945, File 6, DP, JDC Archives.

40. Rosenberg to Warburg and Hexter, May 23, 1946, File 6, DP, JDC Archives.

41. Ibid.

42. "Minutes of Joint Meeting of Agro-Joint and DORSA Boards," June 11, 1946.

43. Quoted ibid.

44. Rosenberg Report to DORSA Board of Directors, December 15, 1948, File 6B, DP, JDC Archives.

45. Leavitt, *The JDC Story*, 13.

46. JDC, *The Year of Survival*.

47. *New York Times*, May 18, 1947.

48. *The Dominican Republic* 8 (September 9, 1946).

49. Helfant, *The Trujillo Doctrine*.

50. *New York Times*, May 18, 1947.

51. Butler to Byrnes, December 24, 1946, *FRUS, 1946*, 11: 814.

52. Butler to George Marshall, June 12, 1947, *FRUS, 1947*, 8: 638.

53. Quoted in Gardiner, *La política de inmigración*, 149.

54. Sumner Welles, "Intervention and Interventions," 129.

55. Ameringer, *The Caribbean Legion*, 18.

56. *FRUS, 1947*, 8: 643–62; Vega, *Los Estados Unidos y Trujillo, 1947*, 1: 8; and Atkins and Wilson, *The Dominican Republic and the United States*, 93.

57. Smith, *The Last Years of the Monroe Doctrine*, 10–11.

58. Vega, *Los Estados Unidos y Trujillo, 1947*, I: 92.

59. *New York Times*, February 21, 1950.

60. "Report to DORSA Board of Directors," December 15, 1948, File 6B, DP, JDC Archives.

14. GOLDEN YEARS

Epigraph: Hexter to Leavitt, January 18, 1949, File 6c, DP, JDC Archives.

1. Stern to Ruby Moses, July 17, 1946, File 6A, DP, JDC Archives.

2. "Memorandum on Sosúa Settlement," February 8, 1946, File 6, DP, JDC Archives.

3. "List of Homesteaders in Sosúa and Their Outside Occupations as per November 30, 1948," File 6B, DP, JDC Archives.

4. "Minutes of Joint Meeting of Agro-Joint and DORSA Boards," June 11, 1946.

5. Margolis, "Race Against Time in Shanghai"; and Ristaino, *Port of Last Resort*, 240.

6. Quoted in Ross, *Escape to Shanghai*, 235.

7. Ibid., 236.

8. Ibid., 240.

9. Moses Leavitt to Sir Herbert Emerson, July 12, 1946, File 6, and "The Settlement of Sosúa in the Dominican Republic, 1949," File 6c, DP, JDC Archives.

10. Jordan to Pilpel, August 19, 1946; and Stern to Moses, July 17, 1946, File 6A, DP, JDC Archives.

11. Quoted in Ross, *Escape to Shanghai*, 237.

12. Morgan, "Letter from Sosúa."

13. Gardiner, *La política de inmigración*, 132–33.

14. *New York Times*, March 23, 1953.

15. Ibid.

16. "Summary of Two Meetings at Dr. Hexter's Office," November 7 and 10, 1949, File 6c, DP, JDC Archives.

17. Philip Skorneck, "Visits to Havana, Ciudad Trujillo, Sosúa and Port-au-Prince," October 6 to October 22, 1948, File 45, DP, JDC Archives.

18. Ibid; and "Report of Sosúa Settlement for the Year, 1951," File 6c, DP, JDC Archives.

19. Skorneck, "Visits to Havana."

20. Interviews, Topf, August 12–15, 2006.

21. Hexter to Leavitt, February 9, 1951, File 6c, DP, JDC Archives.

22. "Report on Sosúa Settlement for the year 1950," File 5, Lili Wronker Papers, USHMMLA.

23. Gardiner, *La política de inmigración*, 137.

24. Hexter to Leavitt, February 6, 1950, File 6c, DP, JDC Archives.

25. Ibid.; and Symanski and Burley, "The Jewish Colony of Sosúa," 372, 373.

26. Hexter to Leavitt, January 18, 1949, File 6c, DP, JDC Archives.

27. "Brief Information on Sosúa Settlement," October 1952, and "Report of Sosúa Settlement . . . 1951," File 6c, DP, JDC Archives; and "Report on Sosúa Settlement for the Year, 1949."

28. Hexter to Leavitt, January 18, 1949, File 6c, DP, JDC Archives.

29. Memo, Alfred Rosenzweig, "Sosúa Settlement," March 28, 1957, File 8, DP, JDC Archives.

30. *New York Times*, July 22, 1970, 40.

31. *New York Times*, April 2, 1949, 15.

32. Pilpel to Leavitt, January 30, 1948; and "Minutes of Annual Meeting of Board of Directors of Agro-Joint," June 9, 1949, File 6c, DP, JDC Archives.

33. Gardiner, *La política de inmigración*, 133–34, 138–39; Hexter to Leavitt, February 9, 1951, File 6c, DP, JDC Archives.

34. "Minutes of Meeting of Board of Directors of the Agro-Joint," March 23, 1951, Hexter to Leavitt, February 6, 1950, Hexter to Leavitt, January 18, 1949, and Leavitt to JDC Administration Committee, February 14, 1949, File 6c, DP, JDC Archives.

35. Contract, DORSA and The Cooperativa Sosúa C. por A., May 14, 1953, File 7, DP, JDC Archives.

36. Hexter to Rosenberg, February 10, 1955, File 7, DP, JDC Archives.

37. Interviews, Topf, August 12–15, 2006.

38. Ibid.

39. Symanski and Burley, "The Jewish Colony of Sosúa," 373.

40. Interview, Luis Hess, October 6, 2006.

41. "Report of the Sosúa Settlement . . . 1951."

42. Rosenzweig to Moses, May 13, 1949, File 6c, DP, JDC Archives.

43. Ibid.

44. "List of Homesteaders."

45. Symanski and Burley, "The Jewish Colony of Sosúa," 373. A series of interviews conducted by German sociologists in the early 1970s reiterated these biases. Kätsch et al., *Sosua-Verheissenes*, passim.

46. Interviews, Topf, August 12–15, 2006.

47. Hexter to Rosenberg, February 13, 1957, File 8, DP, JDC Archives.

48. Rosenzweig to Rosenberg, August 25, 1959, File 8, DP, JDC Archives.

49. Hexter to Rosenberg, January 25 and February 13, 1957, File 8, DP, JDC Archives.

50. Hexter to Rosenberg, January 25 and February 6, 1957, File 8, DP, JDC Archives.

51. Trujillo, *A Tribute to his Excellency*.

52. Papernik, "Memoir," 128; Interview, Harry Floerscheim, July 19, 2006; and Gardiner, *La política de inmigración*, 139–41.

53. Rosenzweig to Rosenberg, June 19, 1951, File 11, DP, JDC Archives.

54. Trujillo, *A Tribute to his Excellency*.

55. Interviews, Topf, August 12–15, 2006.

56. Ibid. See also Gigliotti, "Acapulco in the Atlantic," 42.

57. Interview, Topf, August 15, 2006.

58. *A Tribute to his Excellency*; Hexter to Warburg, February 8, 1955; and Rosenberg to Trujillo, July 8, 1953, File 7, DP, JDC Archives.

59. Hexter to Moses, November 15, 1955, File 11, DP, JDC Archives; *El Caribe*, January 30, 1956; and Gardiner, *La política de inmigración*, 135–36.

60. Rosenberg to Mrs. Maurice Hexter, File 8, DP, JDC Archives.

15. "THE BEGINNING OF THE END"

Epigraph: Joaquín Balaguer, *La palabra encadenada*, 1975, 255. Translation by Enrique Yepes.

1. A copious secondary literature has developed about the Galíndez affair. For the basics, see Russell Fitzgibbon's preface to Galíndez, *The Era of Trujillo*, xi–xviii. Three journalistic accounts fill in a number of gaps: Dios Unanue, *El caso Galíndez*; Elósegui, *El verdadero Galíndez*; and Vázquez, *Jesús de Galíndez*. The most comprehensive analysis is Urquijo, *La tumba abierta*. The fascinating plotline has been taken up by novelists and filmmakers. See Vázquez Montalbán, *Galíndez*; and *El misterio Galíndez*.

2. The Chilean publisher could not keep up with the demand as the book went through seven printings in six weeks. Soon a Buenos Aires publisher released its own edition. Bilingual excerpts also were published in a New York magazine. Galíndez apparently sent an English-language version to New York University Press but never signed a contract with the press.

3. Dios Unanue, *El caso Galíndez*, 196–97.

4. Quoted in Vázquez, *Jesús de Galíndez*, 80–81.

5. Balaguer, *La palabra*, 249.

6. Other explanations advanced for Galíndez's hasty departure include his refusal to participate in a government-sponsored rally against Rómulo Betancourt and his

unwillingness to turn in co-workers allegedly involved in subversive activities. Urquijo, *La tumba abierta*, 119–21, 24; Vázquez, *Jesús de Galíndez*, 61–63; Dios Unanue, *El caso Galíndez*, 197; and Elósegui, *El verdadero Galíndez*, 79.

7. Dios Unanue, *El caso Galíndez*, 39.

8. The United States supported the Spanish bid to join the international body after Franco agreed to permit North American military bases to be placed on Spanish soil. Vega, *Almoina, Galíndez*, 61, 64; and Ornes, *Trujillo: Little Caesar*, 279.

9. Galíndez's career as an FBI informant actually dated back to his years in the Dominican Republic. Dios Unanue, *El caso Galíndez*, 42; and Urquijo, *La tumba abierta*, 432.

10. Dios Unanue, *El caso Galíndez*, 190.

11. Quoted in Ornes, *Trujillo, Little Caesar*, 310.

12. Galíndez, "Anti-American Sentiment"; and Urquijo, *La tumba abierta*, 36.

13. Galíndez, "Anti-American Sentiment," 28–29; and Urquijo, *La tumba abierta*, 349.

14. Galíndez, "Un reportaje." A preliminary version of this essay, titled "La opereta bufa de Trujillolandia," appeared three years earlier in the Cuban magazine *Bohemia*. Galíndez continued his polemic against the regime in 1954, publishing articles in *Iberoamérica* and the *Boletín del PRD*. Vega, *Almoina, Galíndez*, 62, 79.

15. Cited in Turits, *The Foundations of Despotism*, 269, n. 26.

16. Galíndez, "Un reportaje." Vega contends that Galíndez's indiscretions about Ramfis sealed Galíndez's fate; but Ramfis's paternity was the subject of speculation well before that. Journalist John Bartlow Martin, named U.S. ambassador to the Dominican Republic in the early 1960s, mentioned it in an article published in 1938. *Overtaken by Events*, 49. José Almoina, a one-time Trujillista insider, who, like Galíndez, broke with the regime, also mentioned it in his account written under a pseudonym. Bustamante, *Una satrapía en el Caribe*, 21.

17. Apparently, Galíndez's lover, Gloria Viera, was a Trujillista spy who sought to dissuade him from publishing his thesis. The FBI did likewise, warning him about the likelihood of reprisals, refusing to guarantee his protection, and threatening to terminate his services if he became enmeshed in public controversy. Urquijo, *La tumba abierta*, 357; and Dios Unanue, *El caso Galíndez*, 64–65. Some accounts put the payoff at a more modest twenty-five thousand dollars. Diederich, *Trujillo: The Death*, 5; and Crassweller, *Trujillo: The Life and Times*, 316.

18. Urquijo, *La tumba abierta*, 472.

19. Ibid., 418.

20. Like Galíndez, Requena had served in Trujillo's foreign service and he, too, broke with the regime and went into exile. In 1949 Requena published a fictional critique of the dictatorship, *Cementerio sin cruces* (Cemetery without Crosses), dedicating it to the "thousands of Dominicans assassinated by Trujillo" and specifically referencing the young sugar workers who had heroically opposed the regime in 1946–47, the very same cane cutters Galíndez had tried to defend. Vega, *Almoina, Galíndez*, 63.

21. Telegram, Department of State to the U.S. Embassy, Ciudad Trujillo, February 19, 1957, FRUS, 1955–1957, 6: 904–5.

22. FBI handwriting experts declared the suicide note a forgery. Diederich, *Trujillo: The Death*, 19.

23. Vázquez, *Jesús de Galíndez*, 93–95, 104–5; Crassweller, *Trujillo: The Life and Times*, 317–18; and Ornes, *Trujillo: Little Caesar*, 323.

24. Gleijeses, *The Dominican Crisis*, 340–41, n. 94.

25. Elósegui, *El verdadero Galíndez*, 136; and Vázquez, *Jesús de Galíndez*, 99.

26. Elósegui, *El verdadero Galíndez*, 137–38, 155.

27. Vázquez, *Jesús de Galíndez*, 99.

28. Quoted in Crasweller, *Trujillo: The Life and Times*, 325.

29. Quoted in Cater and Pincus, "The Foreign Legion," 15; and Vázquez, *Jesús de Galíndez*, 84.

30. Charles Porter to Stanley Ross, April 2, 1958, in Morris L. Ernst, *Report and Opinion*, Exhibit, 36.

31. Atkins and Wilson, *The United States and the Trujillo Regime*, 71–72, quote, 72.

32. Quoted in Crassweller, *Trujillo: The Life and Times*, 326.

33. Smith, *The Last Years of the Monroe Doctrine*, 123; and Dispatch, Stephens to State Department, January 16, 1957, *FRUS, 1955–1957*, 6: 890.

34. Rabe, *Eisenhower and Latin America*, 40–41, 87–88.

35. Memo, Julian Fromer to Jack Neal, January 7, 1957, *FRUS, 1955–1957*, 6: 881–85.

36. Dispatch, Stephens to State Department, January 16, 1957, *FRUS, 1955–1957*, 6: 894.

37. Rubottom to the Secretary of State, February 20, 1957, *FRUS, 1955–1957*, 6: 908. The Defense Department had established the testing facilities in the Dominican Republic in 1951.

38. Dispatch, Stephens to State Department, January 16, 1957.

39. Memo, Fromer to Rubottom, June 3, 1957; Robert Barnes to William Leffingwell, July 22, 1957; and C. Allan Stewart to Fran Spalding, *FRUS, 1955–1957*, 6: 918, and 920–23.

40. Rabe, *Eisenhower and Latin America*, 104.

41. Matthews, "Diplomatic Relations," 156.

42. Vázquez, *Jesús de Galíndez*, 89–90; and Rabe, *Eisenhower and Latin America*, 157. For the Dominican government's official response, see Rafael L. Trujillo, *The Other Side*.

43. *New York Times*, January 20, 1957, 70.

44. They also showed surprisingly little respect for Trujillo's police and were soon deported. Walker, *Politics and Power Structure*, 7, 18.

45. *New York Times*, April 25, 1957, 19.

46. Quoted in Ornes, *Trujillo: Little Caesar*, 264; and Crassweller, *Trujillo: The Life and Times*, 325.

47. Hexter to Louis Loeb, May 28, 1956, File 8, DP, JDC Archives; and Trujillo, *The Other Side*, 11.

48. Vázquez, *Jesús de Galíndez*, 116–17; and Ernst, *Report and Opinion*, 45.

49. Hexter to Rosenberg, January 25, 1957, File 8, DP, JDC Archives.

50. "Minutes of Meeting of Stockholders of DORSA," December 12, 1957, File 8, DP, JDC Archives; and Papernick, "Memoir."

51. Rosenzweig to Rosenberg, August 25, 1958, File 8, DP, JDC Archives.

52. Gardiner, *La política de inmigración*, 139–40.

53. Hexter to Rosenberg, July 13, 1959, File 8, DP, JDC Archives; and Interview, Sonja Burian, August 1–2, 2006.

54. Quoted in Rabe, *Eisenhower and Latin America*, 105.

55. Quoted in Rabe, "The Caribbean Triangle," 61.

56. Atkins and Wilson, *The United States and the Trujillo Regime*, 102–4.

57. Gleijeses, *The Dominican Crisis*, 26–29; Wiarda, *Dictatorship and Development*, 160; and Rabe, *Eisenhower and Latin America*, 160.

58. *The Struggle for Democratic Politics*, 58.

59. Personal Diary Entry, February 6, 1960, *The Adolph P. Berle Diary* (Hyde Park, N.Y.: Franklin D. Roosevelt Library, 1978), Roll 7, Frame 1031.

60. For an excellent summary of the regime's last gasps, see Wiarda, *Dictatorship and Development*, chapter 8; on the legalization of the Communist Party, Hartlyn, *The Struggle for Democratic Politics*, 71. While the Soviet leader, Nikita Khrushchev, expressed only disdain for Trujillo, Castro agreed to an unofficial nonaggression pact. Vega, *Kennedy y los Trujillo*, 1991, 15.

61. Hartlyn, *The Struggle for Democratic Politics*, 72.

62. Quoted in Rabe, "The Caribbean Triangle," 67.

63. Smith, *The Last Years of the Monroe Doctrine*, 124.

64. Rabe, *Eisenhower and Latin America*, 156.

65. Turits, *Foundations of Despotism*, 259. Diederich dates CIA contact with dissidents as early as December 1958. *Trujillo: The Death*, xv.

66. Quoted in Vega, *Eisenhower y Trujillo*, 6; and Dearborn to Mann, October 27, 1960, in U.S. Senate. *Alleged Assassination Plots Involving Foreign Leaders*, 195. To facilitate the attempted assassination, the Eisenhower administration agreed to furnish the plotters with weapons. U.S. Senate. *Alleged Assassination Plots Involving Foreign Leaders*, 204–5.

67. "Minutes of the DORSA Board of Directors; re DORSA budget," March 1, 1960, File 8, DP, JDC Archives.

68. Hexter to Leavitt, May 5, 1960, File 8, DP, JDC Archives.

69. Ibid. See also Hexter to Rosenzweig, September 6, 1960, File 8, DP, JDC Archives.

70. Hexter to Leavitt, February 15, 1961, File 8, DP, JDC Archives.

71. Hexter to Trujillo, September 15, 1960, and Rosenberg to Trujillo, October 6, 1960, File 8, DP, JDC Archives.

72. Hexter to Rosenberg, July 13, 1959, File 8, DP, JDC Archives.

73. Quoted in Rabe, *The Most Dangerous Area*, 39.

74. Diederich, *Trujillo: The Death*; and Rabe, *Eisenhower and Latin America*, 161–62. Atkins and Wilson relate that there were upwards of thirty conspirators, all of them regime insiders, Trujillo associates, or members of the armed forces. *The Dominican Republic and the United States*, 119.

75. Interview, Cecil Hess, October 6, 2006.

76. Hexter to Balaguer, June 1, 1961; Hexter to Rosenzweig, July 18, 1961; and Rosenzweig to Hexter, June 8, 1961, Record Group 3, Box 68, AMJ.

77. "Minutes of the DORSA Board," December 15, 1961, File 8, DP, JDC Archives.

78. Hexter to Dorothy Speiser, January 24, 1962, File 8, DP, JDC Archives.

16. RAVAGES OF AGING

Epigraph: Maurice Hexter to Bruno Philipp, September 5, 1962, File 8, DP, JDC Archives.

1. Personal Diary Entry, June 5, 1961, Roll 8, Frames 55–56.

2. Both of the victims have streets named after them in Sosúa today. Cecil Hess, Interview, October 6, 2006; and Luis Hess, Interview, October 6, 2006.

3. Vargas-Lundius, *Peasants in Distress*, 20; Turits, *Foundations of Despotism*, 261–63; Clausner, *Rural Santo Domingo*, 232–60; and Dorner et al., *Agrarian Reform in the Dominican Republic*.

4. Hexter to Bruno Philipp, September 5, 1962, File 8, DP, JDC Archives; and quotation in Rodríguez and Fernández, "Notas sobre," 54, n. 10.

5. Symanski and Burley, "The Jewish Colony," 371; and Frank Kohn to Dorothy Speiser and Margaret Feiler, July 18, 1968, File 8, DP, JDC Archives.

6. Hexter to the Secretary of Agriculture, August 28, 1962; and Hexter to Philipp, September 5, 1962, File 8, DP, JDC Archives.

7. Martin, *Overtaken by Events*, 191.

8. Ibid.

9. "Meeting Held at JDC Offices on January 19, 1972." File 8, DP, JDC Archives.

10. Hexter to Philipp, September 5, 1962, File 8, DP, JDC Archives.

11. "Minutes of Discussion of DORSA Board," December 15, 1961, File 8, DP, JDC Archives.

12. Hexter to Rosenzweig, March 23, 1961, RG 3, Box 68, AMJ; and Hexter to Leavitt, April 11, 1963, File 8, DP, JDC Archives.

13. Hexter to Philipp, November 30, 1965, File 8, DP, JDC Archives; and Philipp to Balaguer, March 21, 1968, RG 3, Box 68, AMJ.

14. Hexter to Philipp, March 11, 1963, and Hexter to Leavitt, February 18, 1964, File 8, DP, JDC Archives.

15. Wiarda, "The Aftermath of the Trujillo Dictatorship"; and Hartlyn, *The Struggle for Democratic Politics*, 46, 60–64.

16. Diederich, *Trujillo: The Death*, 74–76.

17. Interview, Topf, August 15, 2006.

18. Diederich, *Trujillo: The Death*, 74–76.

19. Ibid.; Crassweller, *Trujillo: The Life and Times*, 436; and Gleijeses, *The Dominican Crisis*, 352, n. 216.

20. Martin, *Overtaken by Events*, 219–20.

21. Diederich, *Trujillo: The Death*, 255.

22. Martin, *Overtaken by Events*, 205.

23. Wiarda, "The Aftermath of the Trujillo Dictatorship," 99; and Peguero, *The Militarization*, 167.

24. Black, *The Dominican Republic: Politics*, 33; Lowenthal, "The United States and the Dominican Republic to 1965," 37; and Wiarda, "The Aftermath of the Trujillo Dictatorship," 119.

25. Martin, *Overtaken by Events*, 204–5, 213, and 217.

26. Slater, *Intervention and Negotiation*, 164. On Imbert's lobbying of the 14th of June Movement, see Wiarda, "The Aftermath of the Trujillo Dictatorship," 104; on his role in the Bosch coup, Draper, "The Roots of the Dominican Crisis," 16.

27. On Washington's efforts to remake the Dominican Republic into a progressive representative democracy, see Lowenthal, "The United States and the Dominican Republic to 1965," "The Limits of American Power," 87, and "Foreign Aid as a Political Instrument," 158, 159.

28. Apparently, Imbert had corruption in common with the general. When four million dollars vanished from the Haina sugar factory, Martin reluctantly pointed the finger at Imbert. Martin, *Overtaken by Events*, 203–4.

29. Rabe, *The Most Dangerous Game*, 43; Hartlyn, *The Struggle for Democratic Politics*, 75; Gleijeses, *The Dominican Crisis*, 77; Szulc, *Dominican Diary*; and Gall, "How the Agency Killed Trujillo."

30. Martin, *Overtaken by Events*, 6–7.

31. Ibid., 6–7.

32. The case was never solved. President Balaguer, who ordered an investigation, believed that Imbert was targeted by rogue elements in the military. Balaguer, *Memorias de un ex-cortesano*, 271–72. See also Bosch, *Balaguer and the Dominican Military*, 92; and Diederich, *Trujillo: The Death*, 255–57.

33. Martin, *Overtaken by Events*, 258.

34. Ibid.; Black, "Dominican Republic: The Old Man is Back"; *New York Times*, June 18, 1988; and Diederich, *Trujillo: The Death*, 255–57.

35. Hexter to Philipp, November 30, 1965, File 8, DP, JDC Archives; Interview, Luis Hess, May 26, 2001; and Martin, *Overtaken by Events*, 192.

36. Interview, Cecil Hess, October 6, 2006.

37. Frank Kohn to Dorothy Speiser and Margaret Feiler, July 8, 1968, File 8, DP, JDC Archives.

38. Philipp to Victor Garrido, February 6, 1967, RG 3, Box 68; and Philipp to Balaguer, March 21, 1968, RG 3, Box. 68, AMJ.

39. One second-generation Sosuaner, Muni Arm, an ardent Bosch supporter, was willing to fight for his convictions. When the revolution broke out he left the settlement, went to the capital, and joined the rebels. Interview, Cecil Hess, October 6, 2006.

40. *New York Times*, October 12, 1965.

41. Ibid.; and Interview, Arthur Kirchheimer, May 26, 2001.

42. Moshe Elran to Herbert Katzki, December 29, 1971, File 8, DP, JDC Archives.

43. Interview, Harry Floersheim, July 18, 2006.

44. What follows draws on an interview with Cecil Hess, October 6, 2006.

45. Interviews, Sonja Burian, July 31–August 2, 2006.

46. Ibid.

47. Interview, Eva Cohnen-Brown, January 21, 2007.

48. Ibid.

49. Eva Cohnen-Brown, response to questionnaire, December 21, 2006.

50. Taub and Kafka, "Sosúa," video documentary, 1981.49.

51. Morgan, "Letter from Sosúa."

52. Symanski and Burley, "The Jewish Colony," 373.

53. Ibid., 374–75.

54. Quoted in Kisch, "The Golden Cage," 150–51.

55. *New York Times*, October 12, 1965.

56. Kätsch et al, *Sosua-Verheissenes Land*, passim.

57. Hexter to Leavitt, February 15, 1961, File 8, DP, JDC Archives.

58. Kätsch, *Sosua-Verheissenes Land*, chapter 5.

59. Symanski and Burley, "The Jewish Colony," 374.

60. Interview, Joe Benjamin, October 3, 2006.

61. Ibid.

62. Ibid.

63. Symanski and Burley, "The Jewish Colony," 373.

64. Ibid., passim; and Brennan, *What's Love Got to Do with It?*, 62–63.

65. A 1950 census estimated Sosúa's urban population at 1,700; approximately 300 were Jews. Including the municipality's rural districts, Sosúa's total population numbered 15,710 in 1970. Symanski and Burley, "The Jewish Colony," 372, 374, 375; and Oficina Nacional de Estadística, *República Dominicana en cifras*, 5: 7.

66. Symanski and Burley, "The Jewish Colony," 373.

67. Ibid., 375.

68. Ibid., 375ff.

69. Symanski and Burley, "Tourist Development."

70. Symanski and Burley, "The Jewish Colony," 366–67.

71. Randall, "Golden Cage."

72. Papernik, "Memoir"; and Interview, Sylvie Papernik, May 26, 2001.

73. What follows, except where noted, is gleaned from Dothan's memo and the lengthy minutes of a meeting at the JDC, "Meeting Held at JDC Offices on January 19, 1972, at 11 A.M.," File 8A, DP, JDC Archives.

74. Quoted in Kisch, "The Golden Cage," 141.

75. Translation, Letter, Benno Varon to Philipp, February 22, 1972, File 8A DP, JDC Archives.

76. Herbert Katzki to Hexter, April 18, 1975, File 8A, DP, JDC Archives.

77. Katzki, "Memorandum for the Files, Re: DORSA Corporation," May 11, 1978, File 8A, DP, JDC Archives.

78. Philipp to Katzki, June 6, 1978, File 8a, DP, JDC Archives.

79. Eichen, *Sosúa, una colonia hebrea*.

80. The following draws on, unless otherwise indicated, Taub and Kafka's video documentary *Sosúa*.

81. *Sosúa Magazine* 1, 3 (June 1980); and "Jews Who Fled Hitler Prosper in Tropical Settlement," *Los Angeles Times*, April 20, 1980.

82. "Diaspora of a Dominican Jewish Town," *New York Times*, April 10, 1983.

83. Ibid.

84. Henry, "Strangers in Paradise."

85. Schoenhals, "An Extraordinary Migration."

86. Interview, Sonja Burian, August 2, 2006.

EPILOGUE

Epigraph: Joe Benjamin, Interview, October 3, 2006.

1. Papernik, "Memoir," 201.

2. Mendelsohn, *The Lost*, 447–48.

3. Interview, Sylvie Papernik, May 26, 2001.

4. Spitzer, *Hotel Bolivia*, 189.

5. Papernik, "Memoir," 165–66, 179.

6. Helen "Hellie" Goldman, Interview, March 17, 2004; and Interview, Edith Horowitz, July 18, 2006.

7. Interview, Elie Topf, August 14, 2006.

8. Papernik, "Memoir," 171, 181.

9. The following draws on interviews with Elie Topf, August 12–15, 2006.

10. Interview, Sonja Burian, July 31, 2006.

11. Papernik, "Memoir," 167, 200.

12. Interview, Sonja Burian, August 2, 2006.

13. Interview, Horowitz, July 18, 2006; and response to questionnaire, Jeannette Isenberg, July 12, 2006.

14. Interview, Edith Horowitz, July 18, 2006.

15. Morgan, "Letter from Sosúa."

16. Kermath and Thomas, "Spatial Dynamics at Resorts."

17. The following discussion draws on Brennan's excellent ethnography, *What's Love Got to Do with It?*

18. Ibid., 44.

19. Ibid., 18, 52–53.

20. Ibid., 56.

21. Ibid., 29, 52. Protestant missionaries tried to curb the oldest profession in the late 1960s and early 1970s, with only modest success. Symanski and Burley, "The Jewish Colony."

22. Brennan, *What's Love Got to Do with It?*, 52.

23. Cabezas, "Women's Work," 115.

24. "DR1—Daily News," March 8, 2001, http://dr1.com/ Accessed July 28, 2006.

25. "The Dominican Republic Offers a New Place in the Sun," *New York Times*, October 29, 2006.

26. Interview, Luis Hess, October 6, 2006.

27. Response to Questionnaire, Eva Cohnen-Brown, December 22, 2006.

28. Interview, Joe Benjamin, October 3, 2006.

29. "Noticia en Sosúa—Productos Sosúa, the Pride of the Jewish Community," July 17, 2005, http://www.hotel-dominicanrepublic.com/ (accessed July 28, 2006); and "DR1-Daily News."

30. Blumberg, "In Search of Sosúa's Synagogue"; and Randall, "Golden Cage."

31. "Moving Memorial," 5; Swerdlove, "Meet the Jewish Settlers"; and Morgan, "Letter from Sosúa."

32. Interview, Joe Benjamin, October 3, 2006.

Bibliography

PRIMARY SOURCES

UNPUBLISHED

American Jewish Joint Distribution Committee Archives, New York, New York
DORSA Papers.

Archivo del Museo Judío Sosúa, Sosúa, Dominican Republic

Archivo General de la Nación, Santo Domingo, Dominican Republic
Memoria, Secretaría de Estado de Agricultura, 1944, 1947
Memoria, Secretaría de Estado de lo Interior, 1938–1941
Memoria, Secretario de Estado de Relaciones Exteriores, 1939–1945

Columbia University Library, New York, New York
James G. McDonald Papers, Lehman Library
Oral History Research Office, Butler Library

Franklin D. Roosevelt Presidential Library, Hyde Park, New York
Myron Taylor Papers
Sumner Welles Papers
Adolph P. Berle Jr. Papers

Leo Baeck Institute, New York, New York
Felix Bauer Collection
Ernest B. Hofeller Collection
Jacob B. Sondheimer Collection
Jack and Miriam Gerber Collection

National Archives and Record Administration, Washington, D.C., and College Park, Maryland
Record Group 59 (General Records of the State Department)

Record Group 84 (Records of the Foreign Service Posts of the Department of State)
Special Media Archives

New York Public Library, New York, New York

William E. Wiener Oral History Library of the American Jewish Committee

Personal Papers

Edith Meyerstein de Bloch Papers
Sylvie Papernik Papers
Henry Wells Papers

United States Holocaust Memorial Museum Library and Archives, Washington, D.C.

Oral History Interviews
Lili Wronker Papers

YIVO Institute for Jewish Research, New York, New York

Joseph Chamberlain Papers
Arthur Lamport Papers
Joseph A. Rosen Papers

AUTHOR INTERVIEWS AND RESPONSES TO QUESTIONNAIRES

Benjamin, Joe, October 3, 2006.
Burian, Sonja, July 31–August 2, 2006.
Cohnen-Brown, Eva, January 21, 2007.
Floerscheim, Harry, July 18, 2006.
Goldman, Helen, March 17, 2004.
Hess, Cecil, October 6, 2006.
Hess, Luis, May 25–26, 2001 and October 6, 2006.
Horowitz, Edith, July 18, 2006.
Isenberg, Jeannette, July 12, 2006.
Katz, Martin, May 29, 2001.
Kirchheimer, Arthur, May 26, 2001.
Laub, Burton R. III. "Typescript of interview with Burton R. Laub III of Henry Wells (nee Heinrich Wasservogel)," June 12, 1990.
Papernik, Sylvie, May 26, 2001.
Schreiner, Ernie, June 25, 2003.
Schreiner, Ruth, June 25, 2003.
Topf, Elie, August 12–15, 2006.
Wells, Henry, February 3, 1999.

PUBLISHED

Government Documents

Colección de leyes, decretos y resoluciones de los poderes legislativos y ejecutivos de la República Dominicana. De enero a diciembre 1940. Vol. 1. Ciudad Trujillo: J. R. Vda. García Sucs., 1941.

Dominican Republic. Comisión para el Estudio del Informe de la Brookings Institution
sobre la colonización de refugiados en la República Dominicana. *Capacidad de la
República Dominicana para absorber refugiados; Dictamen de la comisión nombrada
por el poder ejecutivo.* Ciudad Trujillo: Montalvo, 1945.

Federal Bureau of Investigation. *Totalitarian Activities. Dominican Republic Today
(November 1944).* Washington, D.C.: FBI, United States Department of Justice,
1944.

Foreign Relations of the United States, Diplomatic Papers (FRUS), 1938. 5 vols. Vol. 5.
Washington, D.C.: Government Printing Office, 1956.

Foreign Relations of the United States, Diplomatic Papers, 1939. 5 vols. Vols. 2 and 5.
Washington, D.C.: Government Printing Office, 1957.

Foreign Relations of the United States, Diplomatic Papers, 1940. 5 vols. Vols. 2 and 5.
Washington, D.C.: Government Printing Office, 1961.

Foreign Relations of the United States, Diplomatic Papers, 1945. 9 vols. Vol. 9. Washington,
D.C.: Government Printing Office, 1969.

Foreign Relations of the United States, Diplomatic Papers, 1946. 11 vols. Vol. 11.
Washington, D.C.: Government Printing Office, 1969.

Foreign Relations of the United States, Diplomatic Papers, 1947. 8 vols. Vol. 8. Washington,
D.C.: Government Printing Office, 1972.

Foreign Relations of the United States, Diplomatic Papers, 1955–1957. 27 vols. Vol. 6.
Washington, D.C.: Government Printing Office, 1987.

*Informe que presenta al poder ejecutivo la comisión creada por la ley número 77 para
estudiar las tierras de la frontera y señalar los sitios en que se han de establecer las
colonias de inmigrantes.* Santo Domingo: Imprenta de la J. R. Vda. García, 1925.

*Mensaje que dirige a sus compatriotas el Generalíssimo Doctor Rafael Leonidas Trujillo
Molina, Benefactor de la patria, con motivo del décimo aniversario de haber sumido la
dirección política del pueblo domincano.* Ciudad Trujillo: Listín Diario, 1940.

Oficina Nacional de Estadística. *República Dominicana en cifras.* Vol. 5. Santo Domingo:
Oficina Nacional de Estadística, 1970.

Resumen general del tercer censo nacional de población, 1950. Ciudad Trujillo: Sección de
Estadísticas, 1953.

Trujillo, Rafael L. *The Other Side of the Galíndez Case.* New York: Dominican Republic
Cultural Society of New York, 1956.

———. *A Tribute to His Excellency Rafael Leonidas Trujillo Molina, New York City,
February 27, 1953, Dominican Republic Independence Day.* New York: Dominican
Republic Information Center, 1953.

U.S. Department of State. *Register of the Department of State, October 1, 1940.*
Washington, D.C.: Government Printing Office, 1940.

———. *Biographic Register of the Department of State. September 1, 1944.* Washington,
D.C.: Government Printing Office, 1944.

U.S. Senate. *Alleged Assassination Plots Involving Foreign Leaders: An Interim Report of
the Select Committee to Study Governmental Operations with Respect to Intelligence
Activities.* Report No. 94–465. Vols. 3–8. 94th Congress, 1st Session. Washington, D.C.:
Government Printing Office, 1975.

Newspapers and Periodicals

DOMINICAN REPUBLIC

El Caribe
Cosmopólita
La Nación
La Opinión
Listín Diario
Revista de Agricultura

UNITED STATES

American Hebrew
American Jewish Chronicle
Christian Science Monitor
Congress Weekly
The Dominican Republic
The Forward
Jewish Telegraphic Agency
Los Angeles Times
The Nation
The New Republic
New York Times
Sosúa Magazine

Books, Articles, and Pamphlets

The Activities of the Joint Distribution Committee: A Summary Report, March 22, 1931. No. 15. New York: American Jewish Joint Distribution Committee, 1931.

Aid to Jews Overseas: Report for 1939. New York: American Jewish Distribution Committee, 1939.

Aikman, Duncan. *The All-American Front*. New York: Doubleday, Moran and Company, 1940.

American Jewish Joint Distribution Committee. *So They May Live Again: 1945 Annual Report of the American Jewish Joint Distribution Committee*. New York: American Jewish Joint Distribution Committee, 1946.

———. *The Year of Survival: 1946 Annual Report of the American Jewish Joint Distribution Committee*. New York: American Jewish Joint Distribution Committee, 1947.

American Jewish Year Book 5699, September 26, 1938 to September 13, 1939. Edited by the American Jewish Committee. Vol. 40. Philadelphia: Jewish Publication Society of America, 1938.

American Jewish Year Book 5700, September 14, 1939 to October 2, 1940. Edited by the American Jewish Committee. Vol. 41. Philadelphia: Jewish Publication Society of America, 1939.

American Jewish Year Book 5701, October 3, 1940 to September 1941. Edited by the American Jewish Committee. Vol. 42. Philadelphia: Jewish Publication Society of America, 1940.

American Jewish Year Book 5702, September 22, 1941 to September 11, 1942. Edited by Harry Schneiderman for the American Jewish Committee. Vol. 43. Philadelphia: Jewish Publication Society of America, 1941.

American Jewish Year Book 5705, September 18, 1944 to September 7, 1945. Edited by Harry Schneiderman for the American Jewish Committee. Vol. 46. Philadelphia: Jewish Publication Society of America, 1944.

Balaguer, Joaquín. *El Tratado Trujillo-Hull y la liberación financiera de la República Dominicana.* Bogotá: Consorcio Editorial, 1941.

———. *La política demográfica de Trujillo.* Bogotá: Cooperativa de Artes Gráficas, 1943.

Beals, Carleton. *The Coming Struggle for Latin America.* 2nd edition. Philadelphia: Lippincott, 1938.

Bendiner, Robert. *The Riddle of the State Department.* New York: Farrar and Rinehart, 1942.

Bentwich, Norman. *Wanderer between Two Worlds.* London: Kegan Paul, Trench, Trubner and Company, 1941.

Bliven, Bruce. *The Jewish Refugee Problem.* New York: League of Industrial Democracy, 1939.

Bogen, Boris D. *Born a Jew.* New York: Macmillan, 1930.

Bowman, Isaiah. *Limits of Land Settlement: A Report on Present-Day Possibilities.* New York: Council on Foreign Relations, 1937.

———. *The Pioneer Fringe.* New York: American Geographical Society, 1931.

British Guiana: Problem of Large Scale Settlement of Refugees from Middle Europe to the President's Advisory Committee on Political Refugees. Washington, D.C.: 1939.

British Guiana Refugee Commission Report to the Advisory Committee Appointed by the President of the United States of America. London: H. M. Stationery Office, 1939.

Britt, George. *The Fifth Column Is Here.* New York: Wilfred Funk, 1940.

Brookings Institution. *Refugee Settlement in the Dominican Republic: A Survey Conducted under the Auspices of the Brookings Institution.* Washington, D.C.: Brookings Institution, 1942.

Buxton, Dorothy F. *The Economics of the Refugee Problem.* London: Focus Publishing, 1939.

Concerning Refugee Settlement in the Dominican Republic: A Meeting at the Town Hall Club, New York City, February 15, 1940. New York: Dominican Republic Settlement Association, 1940.

Discurso del Señor James N. Rosenberg, Presidente de la Dominican Republic Settlement Association, Inc., en el acto académico celebrado en la Universidad de Santo Domingo, el día 4 de febrero de 1940. Ciudad Trujillo: Listín Diario, 1940.

Dominican Republic: Report of the Special Emergency Agent for the Period October 23, 1931 to December 31, 1932. New York, 1933.

Donovan, William, Colonel, and Edgar Mowrer. *Fifth Column Lessons for America.* Washington, D.C.: American Council on Public Affairs, 1941.

Draper, Theodore. "The Roots of the Dominican Crisis." *The New Leader* 48 (May 24, 1965): 3–18.

Embree, Edwin R. "Jews on the Steppes." *Survey Graphic* 24 (January 1935): 11–15.

Ernst, Morris L. *Report and Opinion in the Matter of Galíndez.* New York: Sydney S. Baron and Company, 1958.

Fields, Harold. *The Refugee in the United States.* New York: Oxford University Press, 1938.

Fisher, Harold H. *The Famine in Soviet Russia, 1919–1923: The Operations of the American Relief Administration.* New York: Macmillan, 1927.

Founding a New Life for Suffering Thousands: Report of Dr. Joseph A. Rosen on Jewish Colonization Work in Russia. New York: United Jewish Campaign, 1925.

La frontera de la República Dominicana con Haití. [Unattributed author, José Almoina]. Ciudad Trujillo: La Nación, 1946.

Gall, Norman. "How the Agency Killed Trujillo." *New Republic* 148 (April 13, 1963): 19–20.

Grant, Madison. *The Passing of the Great Race*. New York: Scribner, 1916.

Grossmann, Vladimir. *The Soil's Calling*. Montreal: Eagle Publishing, 1938.

Gunther, John. "Hispaniola." *Foreign Affairs* 19, 4 (July 1941): 764–77.

Harding, Bertita. *The Land Columbus Loved: The Dominican Republic*. New York: Coward-McCann, 1949.

Hyman, Joseph C. *Twenty-Five Years of American Aid to Jews Overseas: A Record of the Joint Distribution Committee*. New York: Jewish Publication Society of America, 1939.

Intergovernmental Committee (Evian-les-Bains, France). *Proceedings of the Intergovernmental Committee, Evian, July 6 to 15, 1938: Verbatim Record of the Plenary Meetings of the Committee, Resolutions and Reports*. Chambéry, France: Réunies de Chambéry, 1938.

Kirchwey, Freda. "Caribbean Refuge." *Nation* 150 (1940): 466–68.

Kirsch, William. *The Jew and the Land*. Madison: American Association for Agricultural Legislation, 1920.

Laughlin, Harry H. *The Codification and Analysis of the Immigration-Control Law of Each of the Several Countries of Pan America*. Washington, D.C.: Carnegie Institution of Washington, 1936.

Margolis, Laura. "Race against Time in Shanghai." *Survey Graphic* 33 (March 1944): 168–71, 190.

Marrero Aristy, Ramón. *Over*. Ciudad Trujillo: La Opinión, 1940.

Morgan, Heather. "Letter from Sosúa: Refugees and Kin Clinging to an Island of Saved Souls." *Forward* 56, 31 (December 13, 2002): 423.

Moritzen, Julius. "Possibilities for Immigrant Settlement in the Dominican Republic." *Dominican Republic* 10, 5 (November–December 1942): 10–11.

———. "Santo Domingo: A Haven for European Refugees." *Dominican Republic* (1941): 10–13.

New Horizons for Alaska: A Survey of Economic Resources for Future Development of the Territory. Washington, D.C.: n.d.

Popper, David. "International Aid to German Refugees." *Foreign Policy Reports* 14, 16 (1938): 186–96.

———. "The Mirage of Refugee Resettlement." *Survey Graphic* 28 (January 1939): 23–25.

Report of Dr. Joseph A. Rosen on Jewish Colonization Work in Russia Delivered at the National Conference of the United Jewish Campaign, Philadelphia, September 12–13, 1925. Philadelphia, 1925.

Report of the Dominican Republic Economic Mission. Chicago: Lakeside Press, 1929.

Roosevelt, Franklin D. *Roosevelt's Foreign Policy, 1933–1941: Franklin D. Roosevelt's Unedited Speeches and Messages*. Compiled and collated by Douglas Lurton. New York: Wilfred Funk, 1942.

Rosen, Joseph A. "Immigration Opportunities for Jews." *Jewish Social Science Quarterly* 151 (1939): 317–21.

———. "New Neighbors in Sosúa." *Survey Graphic* 30 (September 1941): 474–78.

Rosenberg, James N. *On the Steppes*. New York: Alfred A. Knopf, 1927.

———. "The Story of Sosúa." *American Hebrew* (1940): 9–13, 16.

Schechtmann, J. "Failure of the Dominican Scheme: Brookings Report Writes Finis to Colonization Project." *Congress Weekly* (January 15, 1943).

Scheler, Michael. "The 'Back-to-Land' Movement of the Jews." *Reflex* 6, 1 (1930): 32–38.

Shirer, William L. *Berlin Diary: The Journal of a Foreign Correspondent, 1934–1941*. New York: Alfred A. Knopf, 1941.

Simpson, Sir John Hope. *The Refugee Problem: Report of a Survey*. London: Oxford University Press, 1939.

Tartakower, Arieh, and Kurt R. Grossman. *The Jewish Refugee*. New York: Institute of Jewish Affairs, 1944.

Thompson, Dorothy. *Refugees: Anarchy or Organization?* New York: Random House, 1938.

Thomson, Charles A. "Dictatorship in the Dominican Republic." *Foreign Policy Reports* 15, 3 (March 15, 1936): 30–40.

Wagg, Alfred. "Washington's Stepchild: The Refugee." *New Republic* 104 (June 30, 1941): 592–94.

Walker, Stanley. *Journey Toward the Sunlight: A Story of the Dominican Republic and Its People*. New York: Caribbean Library, 1947.

Welles, Sumner. "Intervention and Interventions." *Foreign Affairs* 26, 4 (October 1947): 116–33.

———. "Is America Imperialistic?" *Atlantic Monthly* 134 (1924): 412–23.

———. *The Time for Decision*. New York: Harper and Brothers, 1944.

Internet Sources

All specific website addresses and web pages on file with the author.

"The Dominican Republic Offers a New Place in the Sun." *New York Times*, October 29, 2006. http://www.nytimes.com/. Accessed November 1, 2006.

DR1-Daily News. March 8, 2001. http://dr1.com/. Accessed July 28, 2006.

"Los Charamicos." *Sosúa News*. http://www.sosuanews.com/. Accessed July 28, 2006.

"Noticia en Sosúa—Productos Sosúa, the Pride of the Jewish Community." July 17, 2005. http://www.hotel-dominicanrepulic.com/. Accessed July 28, 2006.

SECONDARY SOURCES

PUBLISHED

Abramsky, Chimen. "The Biro-Bidzhan Project, 1927–1959." In Kochan 1970. 61–75.

Acheson, Dean. *Present at the Creation: My Years in the State Department*. New York: W. W. Norton, 1969.

Adams, Frederick C. *Economic Diplomacy: The Export-Import Bank and American Foreign Policy, 1934–1939*. Columbia: University of Missouri Press, 1976.

Adler-Rudel, Solomon. "The Evian Conference on the Refugee Question." *Leo Baeck Year Book* 13 (1968): 235–76.

Agar, Herbert. *The Saving Remnant: An Account of Jewish Survival since 1914*. London: Rupert Hart-Davis, 1960.

Ameringer, Charles. *The Caribbean Legion: Patriots, Politicians, Soldiers of Fortune, 1946–1950.* University Park: Pennsylvania State University Press, 1996.

Análisis de la era de Trujillo (Informe sobre la República Dominicana, 1959), 5th edition. Santo Domingo: Editora Universitaria, UASD, 1987.

Anderson, Mark M. ed. *Hitler's Exiles: Personal Stories of the Flight from Nazi Germany to America.* New York: The New Press, 1997.

Arad, Gulie Ne'eman. *America, Its Jews, and the Rise of Nazism.* Bloomington: Indiana University Press, 2000.

Aronson, Gregor. "The Jewish Question during the Stalin Era." In Aronson et al. 1969. 171–208.

Aronson, Gregor, Jacob Frumkin, Alexis Goldenweiser, and Joseph Lewitan, eds. *Russian Jewry, 1917–1967.* New York: Thomas Yoseloff, 1969.

Atkins, G. Pope, and Larman C. Wilson. *The Dominican Republic and the United States: From Imperialism to Transnationalism.* Athens: University of Georgia Press, 1998.

———. *The United States and the Trujillo Regime.* New Brunswick: Rutgers University Press, 1972.

Auerbach, Jerold S. "Joseph M. Proskauer: American Court Jew." *American Jewish History* 49 (1979): 103–16.

———. *Rabbis and Lawyers: The Journey from Torah to Constitution.* Bloomington: Indiana University Press, 1990.

Avni, Haim. "Latin America and the Jewish Refugees: Two Encounters, 1935 and 1938." In Elkin and Merkx 1987. 45–68.

Balaguer, Joaquín. *Memorias de un ex-cortesano en la "Era de Trujillo."* Santo Domingo: Editorial Corripio, 1988.

———. *La palabra encadenada.* Mexico City: Fuentes Impresores, 1975.

Baldwin, Neil. *Henry Ford and the Jews: The Mass Production of Hate.* New York: Public Affairs, 2001.

Banton, Michael, ed. *The Social Anthropology of Complex Societies.* New York: Praeger, 1966.

Bar-On, Dan. "Afterword: Were We So Beloved? Biographical Reconstructions of German Jews." In Kirchheimer and Kirchheimer 1997. 331–50.

Baron, Salo W. *The Russian Jew under the Tsars and Soviets.* New York: Macmillan, 1964.

Baud, Michiel. "Manuel Arturo Peña Batlle y Joaquín Balaguer y la identidad nacional dominicana." In González et al. 1999. 153–79.

———. " 'Un permanente guerrillero.' El pensamiento social de Ramón Marrero Aristy (1913–1959)." In González et al. 1999. 181–212.

Bauer, Yehuda. *American Jewry and the Holocaust: The American Jewish Joint Distribution Committee, 1939–1945.* Detroit: Wayne State University Press, 1981.

———. *My Brother's Keeper: A History of the American Jewish Joint Distribution Committee, 1929–1939.* Philadelphia: Jewish Publication Society of America, 1974.

———. *Nazi-Jewish Negotiations, 1933–1945.* New Haven: Yale University Press, 1994.

———. "The Relations between the American Jewish Joint Distribution Committee and the Soviet Government, 1924–1938." In *Jews and Non-Jews in Eastern Europe, 1918–1945,* edited by Bela Vago and George L. Mosse. 271–82. Jerusalem: Israel Universities Press, Keter Publishing, 1974.

Bejarano, Margalit. "La quinta columna en Cuba (1936–1942)." *Reflejos* 3 (1994): 49–62.

Berger, David, ed. *The Legacy of Jewish Migration: 1881 and Its Impact.* New York: Brooklyn College Press, 1983.

Berle, Beatrice Bishop, and Travis Beal Jacobs, eds. *Navigating the Rapids, 1918–1971: From the Papers of Adolf A. Berle.* New York: Harcourt Brace Jovanovich, 1973.

Berman, Aaron. *Nazism, the Jews, and American Zionism, 1933–1948.* Detroit: Wayne State University Press, 1990.

Betances, Emilio. *State and Society in the Dominican Republic.* San Francisco: Westview Press, 1995.

Birmingham, Stephen. *"Our Crowd:" The Great Jewish Families of New York.* New York: Harper and Row, 1967.

Black, Jan Knippers. "Dominican Republic: The Old Man Is Back." *NACLA* (May–June 1988): 7–9.

———. *The Dominican Republic: Politics and Development in an Unsovereign State.* Boston: Allen and Unwin, 1986.

Blumberg, Debbie. "In Search of Sosúa's Synagogue." *Reform Judaism* 31, 4 (2003): 66–68.

Bokser Liwerant, Judit, and Alicia Gojman de Backal, eds. *Encuentro y alteridad: vida y cultura judía en América Latina.* Mexico City: Fondo de Cultura Económica, 1999.

Bosch, Juan. *Composición social dominicana: historia e interpretación.* Santo Domingo: Alfa y Omega, 1983.

———. *Trujillo: causas de una tiranía sin ejemplo.* Caracas: Librería Las Novedades, 1959.

Box, Loux, and Bárbara de la Rive Box-Lasocki. "¿Sociedad fronteriza o frontera social? Transformaciones sociales en la zona fronteriza de la República Dominicana (1907–1984)." *Boletin de Estudios Latinoamericanos y del Caribe* (Amsterdam) no. 46 (June 1989): 49–69.

Braden, Spruille. *Diplomats and Demagogues: The Memoirs of Spruille Braden.* New Rochelle: Arlington House, 1971.

Bramwell, Anna, ed. *Refugees in the Age of Total War.* London: Unwin Hyman, 1988.

Brandes, Joseph, in association with Martin Douglas. *Immigrants to Freedom: Jewish Communities in Rural New Jersey since 1882.* Philadelphia: Jewish Publication Society of America, 1971.

Breitman, Richard. "Roosevelt and the Holocaust." In Newton 1996. 109–27.

Breitman, Richard, and Alan M. Kraut. *American Refugee Policy and European Jewry, 1933–1945.* Bloomington: Indiana University Press, 1987.

Brennan, Denise. *What's Love Got to Do with It? Transnational Desires and Sex Tourism in the Dominican Republic.* Durham: Duke University Press, 2004.

Brody, David. "American Jewry, the Refugees and Immigration Restriction." *American Jewish Historical Society* 45 (1956): 219–47.

Bustamante, Gregorio A. (pseudonym for José Almoina). *Una satrapía en el Caribe: historia punctual de la mala vida del déspota Rafael Leonidas Trujillo.* Guatemala City: Ediciones del Caribe, 1949.

Cabezas, Amalia L. "Women's Work Is Never Done: Sex Tourism in Sosúa, the Dominican Republic." In *Sun, Sex and Gold: Tourism and Sex Work in the Caribbean,* edited by Kamala Kempadoo. 93–123. Lanham: Rowman and Littlefield, 1999.

Calder, Bruce. *The Impact of Intervention: The Dominican Republic during the U.S. Occupation of 1916–1924*. Austin: University of Texas Press, 1984.

Caron, Vicki. *Uneasy Asylum: France and the Jewish Refugee Crisis, 1933–1942*. Stanford: Stanford University Press, 1999.

Cassá, Roberto. *Capitalismo y dictadura*. Santo Domingo: Universidad Autónoma de Santo Domingo, 1982.

———. "El racismo en la ideología de la clase dominante dominicana." *Ciencia* 3, 1 (1976): 59–86.

———. "Las manifestaciones ideológicas de la dictadura Trujillista." *Cuadernos del Post-Grado UASD* 2 (1982): 57–96.

Cassidy, David C. *J. Robert Oppenheimer and the American Century*. New York: Pi Press, 2005.

Castor, Suzy. *Migración y relaciones internacionales (el caso haitiano-dominicano)*. Santo Domingo: Editora Universitaria, 1987.

Castor, Suzy, ed. *Política y sociología en Haití y la República Dominicana*. Mexico City: Universidad Autónoma de México, 1974.

Cater, Douglass, and Walter Pincus. "The Foreign Legion of U.S. Public Relations." *The Reporter* no. 30 (December 22, 1960): 15–22.

Chernow, Ron. *The Warburgs: The Twentieth-Century Odyssey of a Remarkable Jewish Family*. New York: Random House, 1993.

Clausner, Marlin D. *Rural Santo Domingo: Settled, Unsettled, and Resettled*. Philadelphia: Temple University Press, 1973.

Coatsworth, John H. *Central America and the United States: The Clients and the Colossus*. New York: Twayne, 1994.

Cobbs, Elizabeth A. *The Rich Neighbor Policy: Rockefeller and Kaiser in Brazil*. New Haven: Yale University Press, 1992.

Cohen, Naomi W. "The Ethnic Catalyst: The Impact of East European Immigration on the American Jewish Establishment." In Berger 1983. 131–48.

———. *Not Free to Desist: The American Jewish Committee, 1906–1966*. Philadelphia: Jewish Publication Society of America, 1972.

Cohler, Bertram J., and Morton Lieberman. "Ethnicity and Personal Adaptation." *International Journal of Group Tensions* 7, 3–4 (1977): 20–41.

Colby, Gerald, and Charlotte Dennett. *Thy Will Be Done: The Conquest of the Amazon*. New York: Harper Collins, 1995.

Conn, Stetson, and Byron Fairchild. *The Framework of Hemisphere Defense*. Washington, D.C.: Department of the Army, 1960.

Corten, André. "Migraciones e intereses de clases." In Castor 1974. 65–82.

Crassweller, Robert D. *Trujillo: The Life and Times of a Caribbean Dictator*. New York: Macmillan, 1966.

Cuello, José Israel, ed. *Documentos del conflicto domínico-haitiano de 1937*. Santo Domingo: Taller, 1985.

Curti, Merle. *American Philanthropy Abroad: A History*. New Brunswick: Rutgers University Press, 1963.

Dalleck, Robert. *Franklin D. Roosevelt and American Foreign Policy, 1932–1945*. New York: Oxford University Press, 1979.

Dalrymple, Dana G. "The American Tractor Comes to Soviet Agriculture." *Technology and Culture* 5, 2 (1964): 191–214.

———. "Joseph A. Rosen and Early Russian Studies of American Agriculture." *Agricultural History* 38 (1964): 157–60.

Daniels, Roger. "American Refugee Policy in Historical Perspective." In Jackman and Borden 1983. 61–77.

Dekel-Chen, Jonathan L. *Farming the Red Land: Jewish Agricultural Colonization and Local Soviet Power, 1924–1941.* New Haven: Yale University Press, 2005.

Derby, Lauren H. "Haitians, Magic and Money: *Raza* and Society in the Haitian-Dominican Borderlands, 1900–1937." *Comparative Studies in Society and History* 36, 3 (July 1994): 488–526.

Derby, Lauren H., and Richard Turits. "Historias de terror y los terrores de la historia: la masacre haitiana de 1937 en la República Dominicana." *Estudios Sociales* (Santo Domingo) 26, 92 (April–June 1993): 65–76.

Despradel, Lil. "Las etapas del antihaitianismo en la República Dominicana: el papel de los historiadores." In Castor 1974. 83–108.

Diederich, Bernard. *Trujillo: The Death of a Goat.* Boston: Little Brown, 1978.

Diner, Hasia R. *The Jews of the United States: 1654–2000.* Berkeley: University of California Press, 2004.

Dios Unanue, Manuel de. *El caso Galíndez: los vascos en los servicios de inteligencia de EEUU.* Nafarroa, Spain: Editorial Txalaparta, 1999.

Divine, Robert A. *American Immigration Policy, 1924–1952.* New Haven: Yale University Press, 1957.

Dobrowski, Michael N., ed. *Jewish American Voluntary Organizations.* New York: Greenwood Press, 1986.

Doenecke, Justus D., and Mark A. Stoler. *Debating Franklin D. Roosevelt's Foreign Policies, 1933–1945.* Lanham: Rowman and Littlefield, 2005.

Dorner, Peter, et al. *Agrarian Reform in the Dominican Republic: The Views of Four Consultants.* Madison: Land Tenure Center, 1967.

Dozer, Donald F. *Are We Good Neighbors? Three Decades of Inter-American Relations, 1930–1960.* Gainesville: University of Florida Press, 1959.

Ehrenburg, Ilya, and Vasily Grossman. *The Black Book: The Ruthless Murder of Jews by German-Fascist Invaders Throughout the Temporarily-Occupied Regions of the Soviet Union and in the Death Camps of Poland During the War of 1941–1945.* Translated by John Glad and James S. Levine. New York: Holocaust Library, 1981.

Eichen, Josef D. *Sosúa: From Refuge to Paradise.* Translated by J. Armando Bermúdez. Santiago, D.R.: Universidad Católica Madre y Maestra, 1995.

———. *Sosúa, una colonia hebrea en la República Dominicana.* Santiago, D.R.: Universidad Católica Madre y Maestra, 1980.

Eisenberg, Ellen. *Jewish Agricultural Colonies in New Jersey, 1882–1920.* Syracuse: Syracuse University Press, 1995.

Elkin, Judith Laikin. *Jews in the Latin American Republics.* Chapel Hill: University of North Carolina Press, 1980.

Elkin, Judith Laikin, and Gilbert W. Merkx, eds. *The Jewish Presence in Latin America.* Boston: Allen and Unwin, 1987.

Elósegui, Alberto. *El verdadero Galíndez*. Bilbao: Ediciones A. Saldana Ortega, 1990.

Epstein, Melech. *The Jew and Communism: The Story of Early Communist Victories and Ultimate Defeats in the Jewish Community, U.S.A., 1919–1941*. New York: Trade Union Sponsoring Committee, 1959.

Esh, Shaul, ed. *Yad Vashem Studies on the European Jewish Catastrophe and Resistance*. Vol. 2. New York: Ktav, 1975 [1958].

Estorick, Eric. "The Évian Conference and the Intergovernmental Committee." *Annals of the American Academy of Political and Social Science* 203 (1939): 136–41.

Feingold, Henry L. *Bearing Witness: How America and Its Jews Responded to the Holocaust*. Syracuse: Syracuse University Press, 1995.

———. "Courage First and Intelligence Second: The American Jewish Secular Elite, Roosevelt and the Failure to Rescue." *American Jewish History* 72 (1983): 461–76.

———. "Roosevelt and the Resettlement Question." In Gutman and Zuroff 1977. 123–82.

———. *The Politics of Rescue: The Roosevelt Administration and the Holocaust, 1938–1945*. New Brunswick: Rutgers University Press, 1970.

———. *A Time for Searching: Entering the Mainstream, 1920–1945*. Baltimore: Johns Hopkins University Press, 1992.

———. "Who Shall Bear Guilt for the Holocaust? The Human Dilemma." In Sarna 1997. 274–92.

———. *Zion in America: The Jewish Experience from Colonial Times to the Present*. New York: Twayne, 1974.

Fennema, Meindert. "Hispanidad y la identidad nacional de Santo Domingo." In González et al., 1999. 213–37.

Ferrer, Elizabeth, and Edward Sullivan, curators, and Suzanne Stratton, ed. *Modern and Contemporary Art in the Dominican Republic*. New York: Americas Society and Spanish Institute, 1996.

Fiehrer, Thomas. "Political Violence in the Periphery: The Haitian Massacre of 1937." *Race and Class* 32, 2 (October–December 1990): 1–20.

Field, Henry. *"м" Project for F.D.R.: Studies on Migration and Settlement*. Ann Arbor: Edwards Brothers, 1962.

———. *The Track of Man: Adventures of an Anthropologist*. New York: Greenwood, 1969 [1953].

Filene, Peter. *Americans and the Soviet Experiment, 1917–1933*. Cambridge, Mass.: Harvard University Press, 1967.

Finkelstein, Louis. *The Jews: Their History, Culture, and Religion*. 2 vols. New York: Harper and Brothers, 1949.

Fitzpatrick, Sheila. *Stalin's Peasants: Resistance and Survival in the Russian Village after Collectivization*. New York: Oxford University Press, 1994.

Fox, John P. "German and European Jewish Refugees, 1933–1945: Reflections on the Jewish Condition under Hitler and the Western World's Response to Their Expulsion and Flight." In Bramwell 1988. 69–85.

Fraenkel, Josef, ed. *The Jews of Austria: Essays on Their Life, History and Destruction*. London: Vallentine and Mitchell, 1967.

Franks, Julie. "The *Gavilleros* of the East: Social Banditry as a Political Practice in the Dominican Sugar Region, 1900–1924." *Journal of Historical Sociology* 8, 2 (June 1995): 158–81.

Friedlander, Henry, and Sybil Milton, eds. *Archives of the Holocaust, American Jewish Joint Distribution Committee.* 22 vols. New York: Garland, 1995.

Friedlander, Saul. *When Memory Comes.* Translated by Helen R. Lane. New York: Farrar, Straus, and Giroux, 1979 [1978].

Friedman, Max P. *Nazis and Good Neighbors: The United States Campaign against the Germans of Latin America in World War II.* New York: Cambridge University Press, 2003.

Friedman, Saul. *No Haven for the Oppressed: United States Policy toward Jewish Refugees, 1938–1945.* Detroit: Wayne State University Press, 1973.

Frye, Alton. *Nazi Germany and the American Hemisphere, 1933–1941.* New Haven: Yale University Press, 1967.

Gaertner, Miriam. "A Comparison of Refugee and Non-Refugee Immigrants to New York City." In *Flight and Resettlement,* edited by H. B. M. Murphy. 99–112. Lucerne: UNESCO, 1955.

Galíndez, Jesús de. "Anti-American Sentiment in Latin America." *Journal of International Affairs* nos. 9–10 (1955): 25–32.

———. *La era de Trujillo: un estudio casuístico de dictadura latinoamericana.* Santiago, Chile: Editorial del Pacífico, 1956.

———. "Un reportaje sobre Santo Domingo." *Cuadernos Americanos* 80, 1 (March–April 1955): 37–56.

Gardiner, C. Harvey. *La política de inmigración de Trujillo. Estudio sobre la creación de una imagen humanitaria.* Santo Domingo: Talleres de la Universidad Nacional Henríquez Ureña, 1979.

Gardner, Lloyd C. *Economic Aspects of New Deal Diplomacy.* Madison: University of Wisconsin Press, 1964.

Gay, Peter. *My German Question: Growing up in Nazi Berlin.* New Haven: Yale University Press, 1998.

Gellman, Irwin F. *Good Neighbor Diplomacy: United States Policies in Latin America, 1933–1945.* Baltimore: Johns Hopkins University Press, 1979.

———. *Roosevelt and Batista: Good Neighbor Policy in Cuba, 1933–1945.* Albuquerque: University of New Mexico Press, 1973.

———. *Secret Affairs: Franklin Roosevelt, Cordell Hull, and Sumner Welles.* Baltimore: Johns Hopkins University Press, 1995.

Genizi, Haim. *American Apathy: The Plight of Christian Refugees from Nazism.* Jerusalem: Bar-Ilan University Press, 1983.

Gigliotti, Simone. "Acapulco in the Atlantic: Revisiting Sosúa." *Immigrants and Minorities* 24, 1 (2006): 22–50.

Gilderhus, Mark T. *The Second Century: U.S.–Latin American Relations since 1889.* Wilmington: Scholarly Resources, 2000.

Gimbernard, Jacinto. *Trujillo.* 3rd edition. Santo Domingo: Editorial Corripio, 1993.

Gitelman, Zvi Y. *Jewish Nationality and Soviet Politics: The Jewish Sections of the CPSU, 1917–1930.* Princeton: Princeton University Press, 1972.

Glazer, Jack. *Dispersing the Ghetto: The Relocation of Jewish Immigrants across America.* Ithaca: Cornell University Press, 1998.

Gleijeses, Piero. *The Dominican Crisis: The 1965 Constitutionalist Revolt and American Intervention.* Baltimore: Johns Hopkins University Press, 1978.

Goldin, Milton. *Why They Give: American Jews and Their Philanthropies.* New York: Macmillan, 1976.

Goldner, Franz. *Austrian Emigration, 1938 to 1945.* New York: Frederick Ungar, 1979.

Goldstein, Anatole. "The Fate of the Jews in German-Occupied Soviet Russia." In Aronson et al. 1969. 88–122.

Goldwert, Marvin. *The Constabulary in the Dominican Republic and Nicaragua: Progeny and Legacy of United States Intervention.* Gainesville: University Press of Florida, 1962.

González, Raymundo. "Peña Batlle y su concepto histórico de la nación dominicana." *Anuario de Estudios Americanos* 48 (1991): 585–631.

González, Raymundo, Michiel Baud, Pedro L. San Miguel, and Roberto Cassá, eds. *Política, identidad y pensamiento social en la República Dominicana (Siglos XIX y XX).* Madrid: Doce Calles, Academia de Ciencias Dominicana, 1999.

Goodwin, Doris Kearns. *No Ordinary Time: Franklin and Eleanor Roosevelt: The Home Front in World War II.* New York: Simon and Schuster, 1994.

Gottlieb, Moshe. "Boycott, Rescue and Ransom: The Threefold Dilemma of American Jewry in 1938–1939." *YIVO Annual of Jewish Social Science* 15 (1974): 235–79.

Gould, Jeffrey L. *To Die in This Way: Nicaraguan Indians and the Myth of Mestizaje, 1880–1965.* Durham: Duke University Press, 1998.

Graff, Frank W. *Strategy of Involvement: A Diplomatic Biography of Sumner Welles.* New York: Garland, 1988.

Grandin, Greg. *Empire's Workshop: Latin America, the United States, and the Rise of the New Imperialism.* New York: Metropolitan Books, 2006.

Grayson, George. *The Politics of Mexican Oil.* Pittsburgh: University of Pittsburgh Press, 1980.

Green, David. *The Containment of Latin America: A History of the Myths and Realities of the Good Neighbor Policy.* Chicago: Quadrangle Books, 1971.

Grieb, Kenneth J. "Warren G. Harding and the Dominican Republic: U.S. Withdrawal, 1921–1923." *Journal of Inter-American Studies* 11, 3 (July 1969): 425–40.

Grinberg, Leon, and Rebeca Grinberg. *Psychoanalytic Perspectives on Migration and Exile.* Translated by Nancy Festinger. New Haven: Yale University Press, 1989 [1984].

Gurock, Jeffrey. *When Harlem Was Jewish, 1870–1930.* New York: Columbia University Press, 1979.

Gutman, Yisrael, and Efraim Zuroff, eds. *Rescue Attempts during the Holocaust: Proceedings of the Second Yad Vashem International Historical Conference.* Jerusalem: Yad Vashem, 1977.

Habe, Hans. *The Mission.* Translated by Michael Bullock. New York: Coward-McCann, 1966 [1965].

Hacker, Louis M., and Mark D. Hirsch. *Proskauer: His Life and Times.* Tuscaloosa: University of Alabama Press, 1978.

Haglund, David G. *Latin America and the Transformation of U.S. Strategic Thought, 1936–1940.* Albuquerque: University of New Mexico Press, 1984.

Haines, Gerald K. "Under the Eagle's Wing: The Franklin Roosevelt Administration Forges an American Hemisphere." *Diplomatic History* 1, 4 (Winter 1977): 373–88.

Hall, Michael R. *Sugar and Power in the Dominican Republic: Eisenhower, Kennedy and the Trujillos*. Westport: Greenwood Press, 2000.

Handlin, Oscar. *A Continuing Task: The American Jewish Joint Distribution Committee, 1914–1964*. New York: Random House, 1964.

Hartlyn, Jonathan. "The Dominican Republic: The Legacy of Intermittent Engagement." In Lowenthal 1991. 53–92.

———. *The Struggle for Democratic Politics in the Dominican Republic*. Chapel Hill: University of North Carolina Press, 1998.

Häsler, Alfred A. *The Lifeboat Is Full: Switzerland and the Refugees, 1933–1945*. Translated by Charles Lam Markmann. New York: Funk and Wagnalls, 1969 [1967].

Headland, Ronald. *Messages of Murder: A Study of the Reports of the Einsatzgruppen of the Security Police and the Security Service, 1941–1943*. Rutherford, N.J.: Fairleigh Dickinson University Press, 1992.

Heifetz, Elias. *The Slaughter of the Jews in the Ukraine in 1919*. New York: Seltzer, 1921.

Helfant, Henry. *The Trujillo Doctrine of the Humanitarian Diplomatic Asylum*. Mexico City: Editorial Offset Continente, 1947.

Henry, Frances. "Strangers in Paradise: The Jewish Enclave at Sosúa." *Caribbean Review* 14 (1985): 16, 39–40.

Hexter, Maurice. *Life Size: An Autobiography*. West Kennebunk, Maine: Phoenix Publishing, 1990.

Hicks, Albert C. *Blood in the Streets: The Life and Rule of Trujillo*. New York: Creative Age Press, 1946.

Higham, John. *Strangers in the Land: Patterns of American Nativism, 1860–1925*. New Brunswick: Rutgers University Press, 1985 [1955].

Hirschler, Eric E. "Jews from Germany in the United States." In Hirschler 1955. 21–100.

Hirschler, Eric E., ed. *Jews from Germany in the United States*. New York: Farrar, Straus, and Cudahy, 1955.

Hoerder, Dirk, ed. *Labor Migration in the Atlantic Economies: The European and North American Working Classes during the Period of Industrialization*. Westport: Greenwood Press, 1985.

Hoetink, Harry. *El pueblo dominicano: apuntes para su sociología histórica*. Translated by Ligia Espinal de Hoetink. 2nd edition. Santiago, D.R.: Universidad Católica Madre y Maestra and Instituto de Estudios del Caribe de la Universidad de Puerto Rico, 1972.

Hofeller, Ernest B. "Timetable to Nowhere: A Personal History of the Sosúa Settlement." *Leo Baeck Year Book* 45 (2000): 233–41.

Holborn, Louise W. "The Legal Status of Political Refugees, 1920–1938." *American Journal of International Law* 32, 4 (1938): 680–703.

Howard, David. *Coloring the Nation: Race and Ethnicity in the Dominican Republic*. Boulder: Lynne Rienner, 2001.

Hull, Cordell. *The Memoirs of Cordell Hull*. 2 vols. New York: Macmillan, 1948.

Hunt, Michael. *Ideology and U.S. Foreign Policy*. New Haven: Yale University Press, 1987.

Huntington, Ellsworth. "The Adaptability of the White Man to Tropical America." *Journal of Race Development* 5 (1914): 185–211.

Independent Commission of Experts, Switzerland—Second World War. *Switzerland and the Refugees in the Nazi Era.* Bern: BBL/EDMZ, 1999.

Inman, Samuel Guy. "Refugee Settlement in Latin America." *Annals of the American Academy of Political and Social Science* 203 (1939): 183–93.

Inoa, Orlando. *Estado y campesinos al início de la era de Trujillo.* Santo Domingo: Librería La Trinitaria, 1994.

Jackman, Jarrell C. Introduction. In Jackman and Borden 1983. 15–26.

Jackman, Jarrell C., and Carla M. Borden, eds. *The Muses Flee Hitler: Cultural Transfer and Adaptation, 1930–1945.* Washington, D.C.: Smithsonian Institution Press, 1983.

Jackson, Robert H. *That Man: An Insider's Portrait of Franklin D. Roosevelt.* Edited by John Barrett. New York: Oxford University Press, 2003.

Jonas, Manfred. *Isolationism in America, 1935–1951.* Ithaca: Cornell University Press, 1966.

Jong, Louis de. *The German Fifth Column in the Second World War.* Translated by C. M. Geyl. Chicago: University of Chicago Press, 1956.

Joseph, Gilbert M., Catherine C. LeGrand, and Ricardo D. Salvatore, eds. *Close Encounters of Empire: Writing the Cultural History of U.S.–Latin American Relations.* Durham: Duke University Press, 1998.

Joseph, Samuel. *History of the Baron de Hirsch Fund.* Philadelphia: Jewish Publication Society of America, 1935.

Juárez, Joseph R. "United States Withdrawal from Santo Domingo." *Hispanic American Historical Review* 42, 2 (Spring 1962): 152–90.

Kagedan, Allan L. "American Jews and the Soviet Experiment: The Agro-Joint Project, 1924–1937." *Jewish Social Studies* 43 (1981): 153–62.

———. *Soviet Zion: The Quest for a Russian Jewish Homeland.* London: Macmillan, 1994.

Kalmar, Stephen S. *Goodbye, Vienna!* San Francisco: Strawberry Hill Press, 1987.

Kaplan, Marion. "Prologue: Jewish Women in Nazi Germany." In *Between Sorrow and Strength: Women Refugees of the Nazi Period*, edited by Sibylle Quack. 11–48. New York: German Historical Institute and Cambridge University Press, 1995.

Karbach, Oscar. "The Liquidation of the Jewish Community in Vienna." *Jewish Social Studies* 2, 3 (1940): 255–78.

Kätsch, Siegfried, Elke-Maria Kätsch, and Henry P. David, eds. *Sosúa-Verheissenes Land: eine Dokumentation zu Adaptionsproblemen deutsch-jüdischer Siedler der Dominikanischen Republik.* Dortmund: Universität Munster, Sozialforschungsstelle, Kontaktprogramm zur Sozialwissenschaftlichen Forschung in Latein-Amerika, 1970.

Katz, Friedrich. "Algunos rasgos esenciales de la política imperialismo alemán en la América Latina de 1890 a 1941." In *Der deutsche Faschismus in Lateinamerika, 1933–1943.* 187–204. Berlin: Humboldt Universität, 1966.

———. "Mexico, Gilberto Bosques and the Refugees." *The Americas* 57, 1 (2000): 1–12.

Kaufman, Menahem. *An Ambiguous Partnership: Non-Zionists and Zionists in America, 1939–1948.* Translated by Ira Robinson. Jerusalem and Detroit: Magnes Press, Hebrew University and Wayne State University Press, 1991.

Kenez, Peter. "Pogroms and White Ideology in the Russian Civil War." In Klier and Lambroza 1992. 293–313.

Kerem, Yitzchak. "Nuevos hallazgos sobre los intentos de rescate de judíos europeos por parte de República Dominicana durante la segunda guerra mundial." In *Encuen-*

tro y alteridad: vida y cultura judía en América Latina, edited by Judit Bokser Liwerant and Alicia Gojman de Backal. 691–702. Mexico City: Fondo de Cultura Económica, 1999.

Kermath, Brian, and Robert Thomas. "Spatial Dynamics at Resorts: Sosúa, Dominican Republic." *Annals of Tourism Research* 19, 1 (1992): 173–99.

Kirchheimer, Gloria DeVidas, and Manfred Kirchheimer. *We Were So Beloved: Autobiography of a German Jewish Community*. Pittsburgh: University of Pittsburgh Press, 1997.

Kisch, Hyman J. "Rafael Trujillo: Caribbean Cyrus." *Judaism* 29, 3 (1980): 368–77.

Klier, John D., and Shlomo Lambroza, eds. *Pogroms: Anti-Jewish Violence in Modern Russian History*. New York: Cambridge University Press, 1992.

Knee, Stuart E. "Jewish Non-Zionism and Palestine Commitment, 1917–1941." *Jewish Social Studies* 39 (1977): 209–26.

Knight, Melvin M. *The Americans in Santo Domingo*. New York: Vanguard Press, 1928.

Kochan, Lionel, ed. *The Jews in Soviet Russia since 1917*. New York: Oxford University Press, 1970.

Koelsch, W. A. "Robert De Courcy Ward, 1867–1911." *Geographers: Biobibliographical Studies* 7 (1983): 145–50.

Kolsky, Thomas A. *Jews against Zionism: The American Council for Judaism, 1942–1948*. Philadelphia: Temple University Press, 1990.

Koppes, Clayton R. "The Good Neighbor Policy and the Nationalization of Mexican Oil: A Reinterpretation." *Journal of American History* 69 (1982): 62–81.

Kreis, Georg. "Swiss Refugee Policy, 1933–1945." In Kreis 2000. 103–31.

———. *Switzerland and the Second World War*. London: Frank Cass, 2000.

Kulischer, Eugene M. *Europe on the Move: War and Population Changes, 1917–1947*. New York: Columbia University Press, 1948.

Kunz, E. F. "The Refugee in Flight: Kinetic Models and Forms of Displacement." *International Migration Review* 7, 2 (1973): 125–46.

Kuznets, Simon. "Immigration of Russian Jews in the United States: Background and Structure." *Perspectives in American History* 9 (1975): 35–174.

Langer, William L., and S. Everett Gleason. *The Challenge to Isolation: The World Crisis of 1937–1940 and American Foreign Policy*. New York: Harper and Row, 1964 [1952].

Laqueur, Walter. *Generation Exodus: The Fate of Young Jewish Refugees from Nazi Germany*. Hanover, N.H.: University Press of New England, 2001.

———. *A History of Zionism*. New York: Holt, Rinehart and Winston, 1972.

Laserre, André. *Frontières et camps. Le refuge en Suisse de 1933 à 1945*. Lausanne: Payot, 1995.

———. "Los refugiados en Suiza de 1933 a 1945: Los judíos . . . y los otros." In *Discriminación y racismo en América Latina*, edited by Ignacio Klich and Mario Rapoport Klich. 273–95. Buenos Aires: Grupo Editor Latinoamericano, 1997.

Lazin, Frederick. "The Response of the American Jewish Community to the Crisis of German Jewry, 1933–1939." *American Jewish History* 68, 3 (1979): 283–304.

Leavitt, Moses. *The JDC Story, 1914–1952*. New York: American Jewish Joint Distribution Committee, 1953.

Lee, Samuel J. *Moses of the New World: The Work of Baron de Hirsch*. New York: Thomas Yoseloff, 1970.

Lesser, Jeffrey. "Watching the Detectives: Four Views of Immigrant Life in Latin America." *Latin American Research Review* 27, 1 (1992): 231–44.

———. *Welcoming the Undesirables: Brazil and the Jewish Question*. Berkeley: University of California Press, 1995.

Levin, Nora. *The Jews in the Soviet Union since 1917*. 2 vols. New York: New York University Press, 1988.

Levine, Robert M. "Cuba." In *The World Reacts to the Holocaust*, edited by David S. Wyman, project director Charles H. Rosenzveig. 782–808. Baltimore: Johns Hopkins University Press, 1996.

———. *Tropical Diaspora: The Jewish Experience in Cuba*. Gainesville: University Press of Florida, 1993.

Lewis, Read, and Marian Schibsby. "Status of Refugees under American Immigration Law." *Annals of the American Academy of Political and Social Science* 203 (1939): 74–82.

Lieuwin, Edwin. *Arms and Politics in Latin America*. New York: Praeger, 1960.

Livingstone, David N. "Human Acclimatization: Perspectives on a Contested Field of Inquiry in Science, Medicine and Geography." *History of Science* 25 (1987): 359–94.

———. "The Moral Discourse of Climate: Historical Considerations of Race, Place and Virtue." *Journal of Historical Geography* 17, 4 (1991): 413–34.

Llorens, Vincent. *Memorias de una emigración: Santo Domingo, 1939–1945*. Barcelona: Editorial Ariel, 1975.

Lockward, Alfonso, ed. *Presencia judía en Santo Domingo*. Santo Domingo: Taller, 1994.

Logan, John A. *No Transfer: An American Security Principle*. New Haven: Yale University Press, 1961.

London, Louise. *Whitehall and the Jews, 1933–1948: British Immigration Policy, Jewish Refugees and the Holocaust*. Cambridge: Cambridge University Press, 2000.

Lookstein, Haskell. *Were We Our Brother's Keepers? The Public Response of American Jews to the Holocaust, 1938–1944*. New York: Hartmore House, 1985.

Lowenthal, Abraham F. "Foreign Aid as a Political Instrument: The Case of the Dominican Republic." *Public Policy* 14 (1964): 141–60.

———. "The Limits of American Power—the Lesson of the Dominican Republic." *Harper's Magazine* (June 1964), 87–89, 94–95.

———. "The United States and the Dominican Republic to 1965: Background to Intervention." *Caribbean Studies* 10, 2 (1970): 30–55.

Lowenthal, Abraham F., ed. *Exporting Democracy: The United States and Latin America*. Baltimore: Johns Hopkins University Press, 1991.

Lowrie, Donald A. *The Hunted Children*. New York: W. W. Norton, 1967.

Luxner, Larry. "Moving Memorial to Jewish Settlers." *Américas* 56, 5 (2004): 5.

Maga, Timothy P. *America, France, and the European Refugee Problem, 1933–1947*. New York: Garland, 1985.

Malek, R, Michael. "Dominican Republic's General Rafael Trujillo and the Haitian Massacre of 1937: A Case of Subversion in Inter-Caribbean Relations." SECOLAS *Annals* 11 (March 1980): 137–55.

Marías, Luis. *El misterio Galíndez*. Edited by Gerardo Herrera. DVD. Barcelona: Telemadrid., 2003.

Marrus, Michael R. *The Unwanted: European Refugees in the Twentieth Century*. New York: Oxford University Press, 1985.

Marrus, Michael R., and Robert O. Paxton. *Vichy France and the Jews*. New York: Basic Books, 1981.

Martin, John Bartlow. *Overtaken by Events: The Dominican Crisis from the Fall of Trujillo to the Civil War*. Garden City: Doubleday, 1966.

Martínez, Rufino. *De Sosúa a Matanzas*. Santo Domingo: CETEC, 1983.

Mateo, Andres. *Mito y cultura en la era de Trujillo*. Santo Domingo: Librería La Trinitaria and Instituto del Libro, 1993.

Matthews, Herbert L. "Diplomatic Relations." In Matthews 1963. 121–75.

Matthews, Herbert L., ed. *The United States and Latin America*. 2nd edition. Englewood Cliffs: Prentice-Hall, 1963 [1959].

Mauss, Marcel. *The Gift: Forms and Function of Exchange in Archaic Societies*. Translated by Ian Cullison. Glencoe, Ill.: Free Press, 1954.

McCulloch, John I. B. "Latin America and the New Hemisphere Front." *Yale Review* 30 (1940): 291–308.

McKale, Donald M. *The Swastika Outside Germany*. Kent: Kent State University Press, 1977.

Medoff, Rafael. *Baksheesh Diplomacy: Secret Negotiations between American Jewish Leaders and Arab Officials on the Eve of World War II*. Lanham, Md.: Lexington Books, 2001.

———. *The Deafening Silence: American Jewish Leaders and the Holocaust*. New York: Shapolsky, 1987.

Melander, Göran. "The Concept of the Term 'Refugee.'" In Bramwell 1988. 7–14.

Mendelsohn, Daniel. *The Lost: A Search for Six of Six Million*. New York: HarperCollins, 2006.

Metz, Allan. "Why Sosúa? Trujillo's Motives for Jewish Refugee Settlement in the Dominican Republic." *Contemporary Jewry* 11, 1 (1990): 3–28.

Meyer, Lorenzo. *México y los Estados Unidos en el conflicto petrolero, 1917–1942*. Mexico City: El Colegio de México, 1972.

Milgram, Avraham, ed. *Entre la aceptación y el rechazo: América Latina y los refugiados judíos del nazismo*. Jerusalem: Yad Vashem, 2003.

Moberg, Mark, and Steve Striffler. Introduction. In Striffler and Moberg 2003. 1–19.

Moore, Deborah Dash. *At Home in America: Second Generation New York Jews*. New York: Columbia University Press, 1981.

Moya Pons, Frank. "Dominican National Identity: A Historical Perspective." *Punto 7 Review* 3, 1 (Fall 1996): 14–25.

———. *The Dominican Republic: A National History*. New Rochelle, N.Y.: Hispaniola Books, 1995.

Murphy, H. B. M., ed. *Flight and Resettlement*. Lucerne: UNESCO, 1955.

Neustadt, Richard E. *Presidential Power and the Modern Presidents: The Politics of Leadership from Roosevelt to Reagan*. New York: Free Press, 1990.

Newman, Joanna. "The Colonial Office and British Refugee Policy in the 1930s." In *Administering Empire: The British Colonial Service in Retrospect*, edited by John Smith. 259–67. London: University of London Press, 1999.

Newton, Verne N., ed. *FDR and the Holocaust*. New York: St. Martin's Press, 1996.

Ngai, Mae M. "The Architecture of Race in American Immigration History: A Reexamination of the Immigration Act of 1924." *Journal of American History* 86, 1 (June 1999): 67–92.

Nooter, Eric. "Displaced Persons from Bergen-Belsen: The JDC Photographic Archives." *History of Photography* 23, 4 (1999): 331–40.

Novick, Peter. *The Holocaust in American Life*. New York: Houghton Mifflin, 1999.

Ornes, Germán E. *Trujillo: Little Caesar of the Caribbean*. New York: Thomas Nelson and Sons, 1958.

O'Rourke, Kevin H., and Jeffrey G. Williamson. *Globalization and History: The Evolution of a Nineteenth-Century Atlantic Economy*. Cambridge, Mass.: MIT Press, 1999.

Oz, Amos. *A Tale of Love and Darkness*. Translated by Nicholas De Lange. Orlando: Harcourt, 2004 [2003].

Panitz, Esther L. "The Polarity of American Jewish Attitudes toward Immigration, 1870–1891." *American Jewish Historical Quarterly* 53, 2 (1963): 99–130.

Patterson, Orlando. *Slavery and Social Death: A Comparative Study*. Cambridge, Mass.: Harvard University Press, 1982.

Paz, María Emilia. *Strategy, Security, and Spies: Mexico and the U.S. as Allies in World War II*. University Park: Pennsylvania State University Press, 1997.

Peguero, Valentina. *The Militarization of Culture in the Dominican Republic: From the Captains General to General Trujillo*. Lincoln: University of Nebraska Press, 2004.

Peña Rivera, Víctor A. *Trujillo: historia oculta de un dictador*. New York: Plus Ultra, 1977.

Pérez Cabral, Pedro A. *La comunidad mulata: el caso socio-político de la República Dominicana*. Caracas: Gráfica Americana, 1967.

Perl, William R. "Paradise Denied: The State Department, the Caribbean, and the Jews of Europe." *The National Interest* no. 42 (1995): 78–85.

Persico, Joseph E. *Roosevelt's Secret War: FDR and World War II Espionage*. New York: Random House, 2001.

Pfanner, Helmut F. "The Role of Switzerland for the Refugees." In Jackman and Borden 1983. 235–49.

Powell, John W. "Peasant Society and Clientelistic Politics." *American Political Science Review* 64, 2 (1970): 411–25.

Pratt, Mary Louise. *Imperial Eyes: Travel Writing and Transculturation*. New York: Routledge, 1992.

Prestol Castor, Freddy. *El masacre se pasa a pie*. Santo Domingo: Taller, 1973.

Price, A. Grenfell. *White Settlers in the Tropics*. New York: American Geographical Society, 1939.

Price-Mars, Jean. *La República de Haití y la República Dominicana: diversos aspectos de un problema histórico, geográfico y etnológico*. Madrid: Industrias Gráficas España, 1958 [1953].

Prinz, Arthur. "The Role of the Gestapo in Obstructing and Promoting Jewish Emigration." In Esh 1975. 205–18.

Proskauer, Joseph M. *A Segment of My Times*. New York: Farrar, Straus and Company, 1950.

Proudfoot, Malcolm J. *European Refugees: 1939–1952: A Study in Forced Population Movement*. Evanston: Northwestern University Press, 1956.

Pulley, Raymond. "The U.S. and the Dominican Republic, 1933–1940: The High Price of Caribbean Stability." *Caribbean Studies* 5, 3 (October 1965): 22–31.

Rabe, Stephen G. "The Caribbean Triangle: Betancourt, Castro, and Trujillo and U.S. Foreign Policy, 1958–1963." *Diplomatic History* 20, 1 (January 1996): 55–78.

———. *Eisenhower and Latin America: The Foreign Policy of Anticommunism*. Chapel Hill: University of North Carolina Press, 1988.

———. *The Most Dangerous Area in the World: John F. Kennedy Confronts Communist Revolution in Latin America*. Chapel Hill: University of North Carolina Press, 1999.

Ramón Abad, José. *La República Dominicana. Reseña general geográfica y estadística*. Santo Domingo: Sociedad Dominicana de Bibliofilos, 1993 [1988].

Randall, Laura. "Golden Cage." *Latitudes South*, Winter (1995): 18–22.

Read, Anthony, and David Fisher. *Kristallnacht: The Unleashing of the Holocaust*. New York: Peter Bedrick, 1989.

Reich, Nathan. "The Economic Structure of Modern Jewry." In Finkelstein 1949. 123–66.

Rhodes, Richard. *Masters of Death: The SS-Einsatzgruppen and the Invention of the Holocaust*. New York: Alfred A. Knopf, 2002.

Rischin, Moses. "Germans Versus Russians." In Sarna 1997. 138–50.

Ristaino, Marcia Reynders. *Port of Last Resort: The Diaspora Communities of Shanghai*. Stanford: Stanford University Press, 2001.

Rivas, Darlene. *Missionary Capitalist: Nelson Rockefeller in Venezuela*. Chapel Hill: University of North Carolina Press, 2002.

Rodríguez, Frank, and Otto Fernández. "Notas sobre las políticas agrarias en la República Dominicana." *Ciencia* 3, 1 (1976): 43–57.

Rodríguez Demorizi, Emilio. *Trujillo and Cordell Hull*. Ciudad Trujillo: Editora del Caribe, 1956.

Roorda, Eric P. *The Dictator Next Door: The Good Neighbor Policy and the Trujillo Regime in the Dominican Republic, 1930–1945*. Durham: Duke University Press, 1998.

———. "The Dominican Republic: The Axis, the Allies, and the Trujillo Dictatorship." In *Latin America during World War II*, edited by Thomas M. Leonard and John F. Bratzel. 75–91. Lanham, Md.: Rowman and Littlefield, 2007.

Rosenberg, Emily S. *Financial Missionaries to the World: The Politics and Culture of Dollar Diplomacy, 1900–1930*. Cambridge, Mass.: Harvard University Press, 1999.

Rosenberg, James N. *Painter's Self Portrait*. New York: Crown, 1958.

———. *Unfinished Business: James N. Rosenberg Papers*. Mamaroneck, N.Y.: Vincent Marasia Press, 1967.

Rosenkranz, Herbert. "The *Anschluss* and the Tragedy of Austrian Jewry, 1938–1945." In Fraenkel 1967. 479–545.

Rosenstock, Werner. "Exodus, 1933–1939: A Survey of Jewish Immigration from Germany." *Leo Baeck Institute Yearbook* 1 (1956): 373–90.

Ross, James R. *Escape to Shanghai: A Jewish Community in China*. New York: Free Press, 1994.

Ross, Nicholas. "Sosua: A Colony of Hope." *American Jewish History* 82 (1994): 237–62.

Rotenberg, Alexander. *Emissaries: A Memoir of the Riviera, Haute-Savoie, Switzerland, and World War II.* Secaucus, N.J.: Citadel Press, 1987.

Roth, Joseph. *The Wandering Jews.* Translated by Michael Hoffman. New York: W. W. Norton, 1985 [1976].

Rout, Leslie B., Jr., and John F. Bratzel. *The Shadow War: German Espionage and United States Counterespionage in Latin America during World War II.* Frederick, Md.: University Publications of America, 1986.

Rubinstein, William D. *The Myth of Rescue: Why the Democracies Could Not Have Saved More Jews from the Nazis.* London: Routledge, 1997.

Sagás, Ernesto. *Race and Politics in the Dominican Republic.* Gainesville: University Press of Florida, 2000.

Sagás, Ernesto, and Orlando Inoa, eds. *The Dominican People: A Documentary History.* Princeton: Markus Wiener, 2003.

Sarna, Jonathan D., ed. *The American Jewish Experience.* 2nd edition. New York: Holmes and Meier, 1997 [1986].

———. "The Myth of No Return: Jewish Return Migration to Eastern Europe, 1881–1914." In Hoerder 1985. 423–34.

Sassen, Saskia. *Guests and Aliens.* New York: Free Press, 1999.

Schachner, Nathan. *The Price of Liberty: A History of the American Jewish Committee.* New York: American Jewish Committee, 1948.

Schechtman, J. B. "Soviet Russia, Zionism and Israel." In Aronson et al. 1969. 406–43.

———. "The U.S.S.R., Zionism and Israel." In *American Jewry and United States Immigration Policy, 1881–1953,* edited by Sheldon M. Neuringer. 99–124. Madison: University of Wisconsin Press, 1969.

Schmidt, Steffen W., Laura Guasti, Carl H. Landé, and James C. Scott. *Friends, Followers, and Factions: A Reader in Political Clientelism.* Berkeley: University of California Press, 1977.

Schoenhals, Kai. "An Extraordinary Migration: Jews in the Dominican Republic." *Caribbean Review* 14 (1985): 17, 41–43.

Schoultz, Lars. *Beneath the United States: A History of U.S. Policy toward Latin America.* Cambridge, Mass.: Harvard University Press, 1998.

Schwarz, Leo W. *The Redeemers: A Saga of the Years 1945–1952.* New York: Farrar, Straus and Young, 1953.

Schwarz, Solomon M. "Birobidzhan: An Experiment in Jewish Colonization." In Aronson et al. 1969. 72–87.

———. *The Jews in the Soviet Union.* Syracuse: Syracuse University Press, 1951.

Schweber, S. S. *In the Shadow of the Bomb: Bethe, Oppenheimer, and the Moral Responsibility of the Scientist.* Princeton: Princeton University Press, 2000.

Scott, James C. "Patron-Client Politics and Political Change in Southeast Asia." *American Political Science Review* 67, 1 (1973): 103–27.

Segal, Lore. *Other People's Houses.* New York: New Press, 1994 [1958].

Seltzer, Carl. "The Jew—His Racial Status." In *This is Race: An Anthology Selected from the International Literature on the Races of Man,* ed. Earl W. Count. 608–18. New York: Henry Schuman, 1950.

Shafir, Shlomo. "George S. Messersmith: An Anti-Nazi Diplomat's View of the German-Jewish Crisis." *Jewish Social Studies* 35, 1 (1973): 32–41.

Shaplen, Robert. *Kreuger: Genius and Swindler*. New York: Alfred A. Knopf, 1960.

Shepardson, Whitney H. *The United States in World Affairs: An Account of American Foreign Relations, 1939*. New York: Council on Foreign Relations and Harper and Brothers, 1940.

Sherman, A. J. *Island Refuge: Britain and Refugees from the Third Reich, 1933–1939*. Berkeley: University of California Press, 1973.

Simon, Gerhard. *Nationalism and Policy toward the Nationalities in the Soviet Union: From Totalitarian Dictatorship to Post-Stalinist Society*. Translated by Karen and Oswald Forster. Boulder: Westview Press, 1991.

Sjöberg, Tommie. *The Powers and the Persecuted: The Refugee Problem and the Intergovernmental Committee on Refugees (IGCR), 1938–1947*. Lund: Lund University Press, 1991.

Skran, Claudena. *Refugees in Inter-War Europe: The Emergence of a Regime*. New York: Oxford University Press, 1995.

Slater, Jerome. *Intervention and Negotiation: The United States and the Dominican Revolution*. New York: Harper and Row, 1970.

Slezkine, Yuri. "The USSR as a Communal Apartment, or How a Socialist State Promoted Ethnic Particularism." *Slavic Review* 53, 2 (1994): 414–52.

Smith, Gaddis. *The Last Years of the Monroe Doctrine, 1945–1993*. New York: Hill and Wang, 1994.

Smith, Geoffrey S. *To Save a Nation: American 'Extremism,' the New Deal and the Coming of World War II*. Chicago: Ivan R. Dee, 1992 [1973].

Smith, Neil. *American Empire: Roosevelt's Geographer and the Prelude to Globalization*. Berkeley: University of California Press, 2003.

Smith, Peter H. *Talons of the Eagle: Dynamics of U.S.–Latin American Relations*. New York: Oxford University Press, 1996.

Smithsonian Institution. *George Miller and American Lithography: Exhibition, February 13–April 4, 1976*. Catalogue. Washington, D.C.: Smithsonian Institution, 1976.

Sommer, Doris. *One Master for Another: Populism as Patriarchal Rhetoric in Dominican Novels*. Lanham, Md.: University Press of America, 1983.

Spitzer, Leo. *Hotel Bolivia: The Culture of Memory in a Refuge from Nazism*. New York: Hill and Wang, 1998.

Stein, Joshua B. "Great Britain and the Évian Conference of 1938." *Wiener Library Bulletin* 29, 37/38 (1976): 40–52.

Stepan, Nancy Leys. "Biological Degeneration: Races and Proper Places." In *Degeneration: The Dark Side of Progress*, edited by J. Edward Chamberlain and Sander L Gilman. 97–120. New York: Columbia University Press, 1985.

―――. *"The Hour of Eugenics": Race, Gender, and Nation in Latin America*. Ithaca: Cornell University Press, 1991.

Stern, Selma. *The Court Jew: A Contribution to the History of the Period of Absolutism in Central Europe*. Translated by Ralph Weiman. Philadelphia: Jewish Publication Society of America, 1950.

Steward, Dick. *Trade and Hemisphere: The Good Neighbor Policy and Reciprocal Trade*. Columbia: University of Missouri Press, 1975.

Stewart, Barbara McDonald. *United States Government Policy on Refugees from Nazism, 1933–1940*. New York: Garland, 1982.

Stiller, Jesse H. *George S. Messersmith: Diplomat of Democracy*. Chapel Hill: University of North Carolina Press, 1987.

Strauss, Herbert. "Jewish Emigration from Germany: Nazi Politics and Jewish Responses (II)." *Leo Baeck Year Book* 26 (1981): 343–409.

Striffler, Steve, and Mark Moberg, eds. *Banana Wars: Power, Production, and History in the Americas*. Durham: Duke University Press, 2003.

Sullivan, Edward J. "Dominican Crossroads: Notes on the Genesis of Modernity in Dominican Painting, c. 1920–1945." In Ferrer et al. 1996. 13–31.

Suny, Ronald Grigor. *The Revenge of the Past: Nationalism, Revolution, and the Collapse of the Soviet Union*. Stanford: Stanford University Press, 1993.

Suter, Jan. "Continuismo, no-reelección y estabilidad política: consolidación y crisis del Trujillismo antes de 1938." *Eme Eme* (Santo Domingo) 90–91 (1991): 43–64.

Sutton, Antony C. *Western Technology and Soviet Economic Development, 1917 to 1939*. Stanford: Hoover Institution and Stanford University Press, 1968.

Symanski, Richard, and Nancy Burley. "The Jewish Colony of Sosúa." *Annals of the Association of American Geographers* 63, 3 (1973): 366–78.

———. "Tourist Development in the Dominican Republic: An Overview and an Example." In *Geographical Analysis for Development in Latin America and the Caribbean: Selected Papers and Discussions of the Fourth General Session of the Conference of Latin Americanist Geographers*, edited by the Conference of Latin Americanist Geographers. 20–27. Chapel Hill: Conference of Latin American Geographers, 1975.

Szajkowski, Zosa. "The Attitude of American Jews to Refugees from Germany in the 1930s." *American Jewish Historical Quarterly* 61 (1971): 101–43.

———. *The Mirage of American Jewish Aid in Soviet Russia, 1917–1939*. New York: self-published, 1977.

———. "Relief for German Jewry: Problems of American Involvement." *American Jewish Historical Quarterly* 63 (1972): 111–45.

———. "The *Yahudi* and the Immigrant: A Reappraisal." *American Jewish Historical Quarterly* 63 (1973): 13–45.

Szulc, Tad. *Dominican Diary*. New York: Delacorte Press, 1965.

Taub, Harriet, and Harry Kafka. *Sosúa*. VHS. New York: Sosúa Sol Productions, 1981.

Taylor, Philip B., Jr. "Hemispheric Defense in World War II." *Current History* 56 (1969): 333–39.

Teller, Judd L. *Strangers and Natives: The Evolution of the American Jew from 1921 to the Present*. New York: Delacorte, 1968.

Tenenbaum, Joseph. "The Crucial Year 1938." In Esh 1975. 49–77.

Torres-Saillant, Silvio. "Tribulations of Blackness: Stages in Dominican Racial Identity." *Latin American Perspectives* 25, 3 (May 1998): 126–46.

Trotzky, Ilya. "Jewish Pogroms in the Ukraine and in Byelorussia (1918–1920)." In Aronson et al. 1969. 72–87.

Turits, Richard Lee. *Foundations of Despotism: Peasants, the Trujillo Regime, and Modernity in Dominican History*. Stanford: Stanford University Press, 2003.

————. "A World Destroyed, A Nation Imposed: The 1937 Haitian Massacre in the Dominican Republic." *Hispanic American Historical Review* 82, 3 (August 2002): 589–635.

Urofsky, Melvin I. *American Zionism from Herzl to the Holocaust*. Garden City: Anchor Press/Doubleday, 1975.

————. *We Are One! American Jewry and Israel*. Garden City: Anchor Press/Doubleday, 1978.

Urquijo, Iñaki Bernardo. *La tumba abierto: los vascos y los Estado Unidos*. Bilbao: Servicio Central de Publicaciones del Gobierno Vasco, 1993.

Vaksberg, Arkady. *Stalin against the Jews*. Translated by Antonina W. Bouis. New York: Alfred A. Knopf, 1994.

Vargas-Lundius, Rosemary. *Peasants in Distress: Poverty and Unemployment in the Dominican Republic*. Boulder: Westview Press, 1991.

Vázquez, Miguel A. *Jesús de Galíndez: "el vasco" que inició la decadencia de Trujillo*. Santo Domingo: Taller, 1975.

Vázquez Montalbán, Manuel. *Galíndez*. Translated by Carl Christensen and Thomas Christensen. New York: Atheneum, 1992.

Vega, Bernardo. *Almoina, Galíndez y otros crímenes en el extranjero*. Santo Domingo: Fundación Cultural Dominicana, 2001.

————. *Eisenhower y Trujillo*. Santo Domingo: Fundación Cultural Dominicana, 1991.

————. "El fallido esfuerzo de Gregorio Luperón por promover una migración judía a Santo Domingo." In Lockward 1994. 215–26.

————. *Kennedy y los Trujillo*. Santo Domingo: Fundación Cultural Dominicana, 1991.

————. *La migración española de 1939 y los inicios del Marxismo-Leninismo en la República Dominicana*. Santo Domingo: Fundación Cultural Dominicana, 1984.

————. *Los Estados Unidos y Trujillo, año 1945: colección de documentos del Departamento de Estado y de las fuerzas armadas norteamericanas*. Santo Domingo: Fundación Cultural Dominicana, 1982.

————. *Los Estados Unidos y Trujillo, año 1946: colección de documentos del Departamento de Estado y de las fuerzas armadas norteamericanas*. 2 vols. Santo Domingo: Fundación Cultural Dominicana, 1982.

————. *Los Estados Unidos y Trujillo, año 1947: colección de documentos del Departamento de Estado y de las fuerzas armadas norteamericanas*. 2 vols. Santo Domingo: Fundación Cultural Dominicana, 1984.

————. *Nazismo, fascismo y falangismo en la República Dominicana*. Santo Domingo: Fundación Cultural Dominicana, 1985.

————. *Trujillo y el control financiero norteamericano*. Santo Domingo: Fundación Cultural Dominicana, 1990.

————. *Trujillo y Haití*. 2 vols. Santo Domingo: Fundación Cultural Dominicana, 1988, 1995.

Vernant, Jacques. *The Refugee in the Post-War World*. New Haven: Yale University Press, 1953.

Wade, Peter. *Blackness and Race Mixture: The Dynamics of Racial Identity in Colombia*. Baltimore: Johns Hopkins University Press, 1993.

Walker, Malcolm T. *Politics and Power Structure: A Rural Community in the Dominican Republic*. New York: Teachers College Press, 1972.

Ward, Robert De Courcy. "The Acclimatization of the White Race in the Tropics." *New England Journal of Medicine* 201 (1929): 617–27.

———. "Can the White Race Become Acclimatized in the Tropics?" *Garlands Beltrage zur Geophysik* 32 (1931): 149–157.

———. *Climate: Considered Especially in Relation to Man*. New York: G. P. Putnam's Sons, 1908.

Weil, Martin. *A Pretty Good Club: The Founding Fathers of the U.S. Foreign Service*. New York: W. W. Norton, 1978.

Weinberg, Robert. *Stalin's Forgotten Zion: Birobidzhan and the Making of a Soviet Jewish Homeland. An Illustrated History, 1928–1936*. Berkeley: University of California Press, 1998.

Weingarten, Ralph. *Die Hilfeleistung der westlichen Welt bei der Endlösung der deutschen Judenfrage: das "Intergovernmental Committee on Political Refugees" (IGC) 1938–1939*. Bern: Peter Lang, 1981.

Weinryb, Bernard D. "German Jewish Immigrants to America." In Hirschler 1955. 103–26.

Weintraub, Dov, Moshe Lissak, and Yael Azmon. *Moshava, Kibbutz and Moshav: Patterns of Jewish Rural Settlement and Development in Palestine*. Ithaca: Cornell University Press, 1969.

Weismantel, William, ed. *Guía de Sosúa: foco del centro del barrio El Batey*. Santo Domingo: Universidad Nacional Pedro Henríquez, 1985.

Weissman, Benjamin M. *Herbert Hoover and Famine Relief in Soviet Russia: 1921–1923*. Stanford: Hoover Institution Press, 1974.

Welles, Benjamin. *Summer Welles: FDR's Global Strategist*. New York: St. Martin's Press, 1997.

Welles, Sumner. *Naboth's Vineyard: The Dominican Republic, 1844–1924*. 2 vols. New York: Payson and Clarke, 1928.

Wells, Leon Weliczker. *Who Speaks for the Vanquished? American Jewish Leaders and the Holocaust*. Edited by Michael Ryan. New York: Peter Lang, 1987.

Werner, W. R. *Julius Rosenwald: The Life of a Practical Humanitarian*. New York: Harper and Brothers, 1939.

White, Richard. *Remembering Ahanagran: Storytelling in a Family's Past*. New York: Hill and Wang, 1998.

Wiarda, Howard J. *Dictatorship and Development: The Methods of Control in Trujillo's Dominican Republic*. Gainesville: University of Florida Press, 1968.

Wilson, Joan Hoff. *Ideology and Economics: U.S. Relations with the Soviet Union, 1918–1933*. Columbia: University of Missouri Press, 1974.

Winer, Suellen, and Mark Winer. "The Jews of Sosua." *Reform Judaism* 14 (1984–85): 8.

Winik, Lyric Wallwork. "The Hunt for Survivors of a Doomed Ship." *Parade*, December 7, 2003, 4–6.

Wischnitzer, Mark. "The Historical Background of the Settlement of Jewish Refugees in Santo Domingo." *Jewish Social Studies* 4, 1 (1942): 42–58.

———. *To Dwell in Safety: The Story of Jewish Migration since 1800*. Philadelphia: Jewish Publication Society of America, 1948.

Wise, Stephen S. *Stephen S. Wise: Servant of the People, Selected Letters*. Edited by Carl Hermann Voss. Philadelphia: Jewish Publication Society of America, 1969.

Wistrich, Robert S. *Hitler and the Holocaust*. New York: Modern Library, 2003.

Wolf, Eric R. "Kinship, Friendship, and Patron-Client Relations in Complex Societies." In Banton 1966. 1–22.

Wood, Bryce. *The Making of the Good Neighbor Policy*. New York: Columbia University Press, 1961.

Woods, Randall Bennett. *The Roosevelt Foreign-Policy Establishment and the Good Neighbor: The United States and Argentina, 1941–1945*. Lawrence: Regents Press of Kansas, 1979.

Wucker, Michelle. *Why the Cocks Fight: Dominicans, Haitians, and the Struggle for Hispaniola*. New York: Hill and Wang, 1999.

Wyman, David S. *The Abandonment of the Jews: America and the Holocaust, 1941–1945*. New York: Pantheon, 1984.

———. *Paper Walls: America and the Refugee Crisis, 1938–1941*. New York: Pantheon, 1985 [1968].

———. "The United States." In *The World Reacts to the Holocaust*, edited by David S. Wyman, project director Charles H. Rosenzveig. 693–748. Baltimore: Johns Hopkins University Press, 1996.

Wyman, David S., ed. *The World Reacts to the Holocaust*, Charles H. Rosenzveig, project director. Baltimore: Johns Hopkins University Press, 1996.

Yahil, Leni. "Madagascar—Phantom of a Solution for the Jewish Question." In *Jews and Non-Jews in Eastern Europe*, edited by Bela Vago and George L. Mosse. 315–34. Jerusalem: Israel Universities Press, Keter Publishing, 1974.

Yarrington, Doug. "Populist Anxiety: Race and Social Change in the Thought of Rómulo Gallegos." *The Americas* 56, 1 (1999): 65–99.

Zolberg, Aristide R., Astri Suhrke, and Sergio Aguayo, eds. *Escape from Violence: Conflict and the Refugee Crisis in the Developing World*. New York: Oxford University Press, 1989.

UNPUBLISHED

Brown, Kathryn Lake. "A Biography of No Place: The Ukrainian Borderlands and the Making of Nation-Space." Ph.D. Dissertation, University of Washington, 2000.

Derby, Lauren. "The Magic of Modernity: Dictatorship and Civic Culture in the Dominican Republic, 1916–1962." Ph.D. Dissertation, University of Chicago, 1998.

Hanson, Gail. "Sumner Welles and the American System: The United States in the Caribbean, 1920–1940." Ph.D. Dissertation, State University of New York, Stony Brook, 1990.

Kisch, Hyman J. "The Golden Cage." Unpublished manuscript, 1970. File 1, Lili Wronker Papers, USHMMLA.

———. "The Jewish Settlement from Central Europe in the Dominican Republic." Ph.D. Dissertation, Jewish Theological Seminary, 1970.

Neuringer, Sheldon M. "American Jewry and United States Immigration Policy, 1881–1953." Ph.D. Dissertation, University of Wisconsin, 1969.

Quackenbos, Barbara. "Sosúa: Kol Haskholeh Koshoh." Senior Thesis, Princeton University, 1982.

Wiarda, Howard J. "The Aftermath of the Trujillo Dictatorship: The Emergence of a Pluralist Political System in the Dominican Republic." Ph.D. Dissertation, University of Florida, 1965.

Index

Emergency Immigration Restriction Act
(Johnson Act), 57–58. *See also* Quotas

Emerson, Sir Herbert, 71, 135, 136, 137

England. *See* Great Britain

Era de Trujillo, La, 303, 401n2

Ernst, Morris, 307–8

Escuela Cristóbal Colón (renamed Colegio
Luis Hess), 163, 195, 228, 329, 348. *See also*
Sosúa: education at

Estrella, César, 331

Ethical Culture, Society for, 45

Eugenics, xxiv, 24–25, 53–55, 369n43

Évian Conference (1938), xxiv, xxvii, xxx,
xxxi, 3–6, 9, 28, 38, 72, 75, 101, 141, 265, 272,
273, 274, 275; Dominican offer and, xxii,
9–10, 11, 85, 132

Exile opposition to Trujillo, 14–15, 77, 87, 113,
114, 271, 279, 302, 308, 318

Export-Import Bank (U.S.), 23, 69, 73; loans
to Dominican Republic, xxvii, 72, 73, 74, 95,
98, 201, 304

Falk, Leon, 81, 123, 146, 158, 195, 198, 199, 206,
216, 237, 249, 251, 266; Brookings report and,
209–10, 215, 236, 393n54

FBI (Federal Bureau of Investigation), 299,
301, 303, 402nn9, 17

Federation of Jewish Philanthropies, 245, 291

Feingold, Henry, xxix

Feuchtwanger, Lion, 167–68

Field, Henry, 368n35, 393n43

Fifth Column threat, 105, 107, 110, 112–16,
123–25, 144, 146–47, 214, 382nn13, 39. *See
also* Nazis, Nazism: espionage and

Figueres, José, 301, 304

First World War, 49

Floersheim, Harry, 324, 326

Foreign Ministry (Dominican Republic), 25,
26, 41, 74, 106, 108, 116

Fortress America. *See* United States

14th of June Movement, 320

France, xiii, 4, 9, 31, 74, 75, 100, 141; resettlement in colonies of, 34, 37–38; Vichy, and
refugees, 134, 385n283

Franco, General Francisco, xxiii, 17, 300, 301,
402n8

Franco, Persio, 77, 88

Frankfurter, Felix, 39

Frisch, Ruby, 393n53

Galíndez Suárez, Jesus de, 299–305, 307–8,
401n2, 401–2n6, 402nn9, 14, 16, 17, 20

Galván, Manuel Jesús, 364n55

GANADERA. 222, 252–53, 284, 290, 293, 330. *See
also* Corporación, C. por A.

Gardiner, C. Harvey, 202

Gellman, Irwin, 21

German American Jewry, 46–49, 51, 371n15;
tutelage of Eastern European immigrants
and, 46–49

Germany, 4, 6, 17, 74, 128, 139, 262, 370n73;
discrimination of, against Jews, xxx, 25, 26,
28–29, 85, 143, 360n28; economic inroads
of, in Latin America, 6, 72–73, 94. *See also*
Kristallnacht; Nazis, Nazism

Goebbels, Joseph, 7

Goering, Hermann, 116

Goldman, Hans, 223, 344

Goldman, Helen ("Hellie"), 133, 134, 223,
259, 344

Goldstein, Leo, 252, 293

Good Neighbor Policy, xxi–xxii, xxvii, 19–20,
86, 93, 95, 96, 98. *See also* Noninterventionism

Grau San Martin, Ramón, 272

Great Britain, xiii, 31, 72, 74, 75, 92–93, 100,
109, 112, 272; Palestine policy of, xxviii, 3, 29,
40; recruitment for Sosúa, in, 135–36, 137;
resettlement in colonial possessions of, 3–4,
34, 38–39, 74

Great Depression, 7, 16, 63, 73

Grinberg, Leon, 168, 169

Grinberg, Rebeca, 168, 169

Grynszpan, Herschel, 28

Guatemala, 271, 370n73

Haiti, 69, 95, 100, 280, 364n54; diplomatic
relations of, with Dominican Republic, xxi;
migration from, to Dominican Republic,
xxii–xxiii, 11–13, 24, 26, 213, 364nn52, 54

Haitian massacre (1937), xx–xxii, 11, 13–14, 18,
26, 78, 102–3, 271, 306, 360n28, 365n66; U.S.
response to, xxi–xxii, 21–22, 23, 70, 84, 88

Hauser, Heinrich, xi

Helfant, Henry, 278

Herzberg, Rudy, 293

Hess, Cecil, 312, 322, 324–27

Hess, Franklin, 324

Hess, Josefina, 326

Hess, Luis, 163, 164, 170, 205, 228, 292, 322, 327, 329, 336, 337, 348, 351

Hexter, Maurice, 81, 107, 109, 147, 200, 225, 244–46, 251, 266, 276, 281, 290, 314, 315–18, 322, 323, 333–35; bullishness of, on Sosúa, 286–87, 288, 289–90, 291, 294, 330; freezing of the settlement and, 198, 215–18, 324; frustration of, with nonsettlers and refugee camp, 110–11, 236–39; postwar reassessment and, 260–65; Trujillo supported by, 203, 204, 277, 294, 297, 298, 307, 311–12

Hinkle, Eugene, 18, 41–42, 88

Hirsch, Baron de, 50, 52

Hispanic heritage, xxiii, 12–13. *See also* Catholic Church

Hitler, Adolf, xx, 4, 17, 28, 38, 110, 113, 116, 153, 340, 370n83; Jewish "problem" and, 31–32. *See also* Germany; Nazis, Nazism

Hofeller, Ernest, 134. 153, 164, 187–88, 232

Holland. *See* Netherlands, The

Holocaust, xviii, 244, 262, 273, 382n8

Homesteaders, 239, 284, 287, 293; frustration of, with refugee camp, 231, 237, 258; consolidation of, 243–44, 246–51, 254–55, 260, 317

Homesteaders' Council. *See* Rat, The

Hoover, Herbert, xxi, 19, 57; American Relief Administration and, 57

Horowitz, Edith (Brienholter), 347

Hourwich, George Kennan, 103, 199

Houston, Alfred, 41–42

Hull, Cordell, xxi, xxii, 18, 42, 83, 96, 270; Trujillo and, 20, 22, 23, 24, 70; refugee crisis and, 21, 32, 134, 267–68; Welles vs., xxvi, 20–21, 267, 268

Hungary, xiii, 306–7

Hurwicz, Heinrich, 203

Hyman, Joseph, 42–43, 185–86, 217, 262–63, 274, 280

Ickes, Harold, 22–23, 96

Imbert Barrera, Antonio ("Tony"), 314, 318–24, 406nn28, 32

Imbert Barrera, Segundo, 318–19

Indians (in Dominican Republic), xxiii, 12, 13, 161, 364n55

Intergovernmental Committee on Political Refugees (IGC), 4–5, 10, 15, 38, 71, 72, 75, 136, 141, 159, 273, 282; negotiations of, with

Nazis, 32–33, 141; support of, for Sosúa initiative, 35, 74, 100

Interior Ministry (Dominican Republic), 26, 106, 217–18, 237–38

International Fair for Peace and Brotherhood of the Free World, 297–98, 302–3, 319

Isgur, Dr. Max, 191–92, 233

Isolationism, 7, 113

Italy, xiii, 25, 111, 119, 262, 282; refugee camps in, 129–31

Izenberg, Jeannette (Kahane), 347

Jewish Agency for Palestine, 245

Jewish agrarianism, xxiv, xxviii, 44, 50, 51–53

Jewish Agricultural Society, 52

Jewish Colonization Society, 51–52

Jewish relief agencies, xiv, xvi, xvii, xx, 10; in Germany and Austria, 140, 144. *See also* Switzerland: relief camps in

Jewish World Congress, 10

Jimenes Gruillón, Jaime, 114

Johns Hopkins University, 33–34

Johnson, Lyndon, 315, 323

Joint Distribution Committee. *See* American Jewish Joint Distribution Committee

Jordan, Charles, 282–83

Judaism, 45; Conservative, 48; Orthodox, 48, 49; Reform, 47, 48

Kafka, Harry, 336–37

Kahane, David, 181–82, 259

Kahane, Lisle, 181, 259

Katz, Martin, xix, 195, 220

Kennedy, John F., 312, 315

Kibbutz, 248

Kibel, Judith, xix, 155–56, 170, 327, 337

Kibel, Otto, 336

Kircheimer, Arthur, 220, 293, 323, 335

Kircheimer, Rene, 335

Kirchwey, Freda, 156, 378n53

Kirsch, William 52

Klinger, Dr. Israel, 165, 230

Klinger, Helen, 165

Koch, Felix, 296, 333

KOMZET (Committee for the Settlement of Jewish Workers on the Land), 60, 61, 63, 64

Kristallnacht, xxx, 7, 25, 28–29, 38, 130, 152

Labor Department (U.S.), 25, 112–13

Non-Zionists, 5; on quotas, xxviii, 51, 214–15, 244; response of, to Nazi boycott, xxviii, 51; Sosúa supported by, xxviii–xxix; views of, on Palestine, xxviii, 29, 49–50, 244. *See also* Court Jews

Office of the Coordinator of Inter-American Affairs (formerly Office for Coordination of Commercial and Cultural Relations between the American Republics), 95, 102

On the Steppes, 44, 53. *See also* Rosenberg, James

Organization of American States (OAS), 309

OZET (Society for the Settlement of Jewish Toilers on the Land), 60, 64

Pale of Settlement, xxiv, 55, 176, 373n55

Palestine, xxviii, 40, 49, 50, 51, 62, 65, 72, 86, 192, 197, 217, 236, 244, 248, 276, 277, 282, 370n73; desire for homeland in, 214–15, 244; idealism and, 130, 178, 245–46, 247; White Paper on, 29, 55

Panama Canal, 17, 95, 117

Pan-Americanism. *See* Good Neighbor Policy; Noninterventionism

Panic emigration, xiv–xv, xvii, xxxi; to Latin America, xx, 29–30, 40

Papernik, Irene, 131–33, 135, 168, 342

Papernik, Otto, 131–33, 135, 155, 158, 160, 161, 162, 163, 164, 168, 169–70, 186, 206–7, 222, 226, 227–28, 231, 234–35, 247, 257, 258, 259, 281, 333, 339, 342–44, 346

Papernik, Sylvie, 333, 343

Parades, 82, 204–5

Parcelation. *See* Homesteaders; Stern, David

Pastoriza, Andrés, xxi, 21–22, 92, 94, 98, 135, 136, 138, 273, 379n4; preliminary planning for Sosúa and, 70–71, 74, 76; visa matters and, 111, 117, 119. *See also* Lamport, Arthur

Pearson, Drew, 19

Pell, Robert, 42, 48, 74, 75, 83, 94, 100, 101, 106; compromised position of, at State Department, 141–42, 143; as liaison to DORSA, 111, 115, 119, 135, 138, 140–42, 145

Pelley, William Dudley, 7

Peña Batlle, Manuel, 217–18

Perlestein, Frederic, 78, 170, 171, 174, 180–81, 187, 215

Peynado, Jacinto, 41

Philipp, Bruno, 314, 317, 322–24, 333–35, 382–83n39

Philipp, Tommy, 323–24, 333–35

Pilpel, Robert, 255

Platt Amendment, 95

Porter, Charles, 303–4

President's Advisory Committee on Political Refugees (PACPR), 34–35, 37, 38, 71, 72; encouragement of, for nonsectarian settlement, 73–74, 120, 129; nonsettler visa and, 106, 107, 120–23, 125; Sosúa initiative and, 41–42, 74, 78, 100

"Productos de Sosúa." *See* CILCA; Corporación, C. por A.

Proskauer, Joseph, 46

Protocols of the Elder of Zion, 7

Puerto Plata, 79, 161, 189, 223, 227, 229, 230, 252, 263, 292, 295, 318, 332–33

Puerto Rico, 95, 155, 304, 319, 364n56

Quotas (U.S.), xxv, xxvi, xxx, 6–8, 24, 29, 32, 58, 113, 363n34. *See also* National Origins Act

Rat, The, 177, 178, 185, 194, 195, 202–3, 236, 243, 249–50, 253, 283, 289, 290, 291, 296–97

Receivership. *See* Convention of 1924

Reed-Johnson Act. *See* National Origins Act

Refugee Economic Corporation, 41, 370n73

Refugees, 359n7, 360n28, 362n10; Eastern European, 4, 29, 40–41; Fifth Column threat and, 105, 107, 112–16, 120–23, 125, 144; Jewish, from Germany and Austria, xiii–xiv; 29–30, 40, 71, 129–31, 139, 143; gender of, 109; psychological transformation of, 151–52, 167–69, 188–89, 225, 234; prohibition of, from German-occupied territory, 111, 113, 139–40, 142, 144, 145; transportation difficulties of, 131, 134, 146. *See also* Fifth Column threat; Nazis, Nazism: espionage and

Requena, Andrés, 303, 402n20

Resettlement, xxiv, 37–40, 75, 76, 368n35, 370n73; Latin American opposition to, 5–6. *See also* Roosevelt, Franklin Delano: resettlement initiatives and

Reyher, Rebecca, 105–6, 135, 136, 138, 144, 145, 180, 191, 228; visa matters and, 110–11, 115, 118, 120, 122, 124, 139–41, 146

Reynolds, Robert, 7

Rio Treaty (Inter-American Treaty of Reciprocal Assistance), 279

Rockefeller, Nelson, 95, 268, 269–70

Roorda, Eric, 98

Roosevelt, Eleanor, 21, 125, 134, 135, 138, 385n30

Roosevelt, Franklin Delano, 270, 271; immigration policy of, xxvi, 29; Évian Conference and, xxii, 3; refugee crisis and, xxx, 31, 32, 34–35, 72, 141, 142, 385n30; relations of, with Trujillo regime, xxi, xxii, xxv, 17, 22–23, 69–70; resettlement initiatives and, xxiv, 28, 33–34, 39–40, 75, 368n35; support of, for Sosúa initiative, xix, xxvi, 76, 138; *See also* American Jewish community; Fifth Column threat; Good Neighbor Policy; Hull, Cordell; Noninterventionism; Welles, Sumner

Rosen, Dr. Joseph, xxix, 37, 38, 49, 55, 57, 157, 168, 186, 191, 209, 220, 233, 239, 245, 247, 249, 254, 290, 291, 370n73; as advocate of Jewish agrarianism, 44, 52–56; assessment of settlement by, 174–75, 188; colonization program in USSR and, xxiii–xxiv, 54, 56, 59–66; critique of Trujillo by, 199–200; flawed plan for settlement and, 176–84, 188, 195–97; frustrations of, with State Department, 144, 146–47; illness of, 57, 78, 180–81, 290; innovations of, in agronomy, xxiv, 54, 59–60, 373n50; opposition of, to nonsectarian settlement, 128–29; as proponent of eugenics 54–55; selection of refugees for Sosúa and, 120–23, 127–29, 135–37; selection of Sosúa site and, 74, 78–81, 378n53; visas and, 120, 122

Rosen, Eugene, 193, 233, 235–36

Rosenberg, Elizabeth, 135, 147, 385n28

Rosenberg, Hans, 207, 281

Rosenberg, James, 31, 33, 46, 49, 76, 145–47, 188–89, 196–97, 209, 217, 233–36, 250, 261, 266, 276–77, 290, 294, 297, 298, 308, 371n15; anti-Semitism and, 46–47, 122; belief of, in eugenics, 53–54, 86; Brookings report and, 209–11, 215, 393n53; colonization program in USSR and, xxiii–xxiv, 53–54, 56, 58, 60, 64–66; education of, 45–46; FDR and, xxv, 76, 115; funding, 89, 108, 137–38, 139, 147; passion of, for art, 53, 295–96, 372n44, 373n46; planning for Sosúa and, 74, 75–76;

78, 80, 83–85; promotional strategies of, 62, 77, 87–89, 98, 100–102, 152–53; as proponent of Jewish agrarianism, 44, 51, 53; Trujillo and, xxv, 81–82, 84–87, 89–94, 98, 103, 202, 268, 277, 280, 296, 311, 379n4; Zionists criticized by, 49–50, 62. *See also* Dominican Republic Settlement Association; Fifth Column threat; Nonsettlers; "War Refugee Solution"

Rosenwald, Julius, 50, 62, 63, 89

Rosenwald, Lessing, 118, 138

Rosenzweig, Alfred, 253, 290–91, 293–94, 308, 316; as *diputado*, 295–97, 307, 311, 312, 329

Rothmund, Helmut, xvi–xvii

Rublee, George, 32–33, 42, 93–94, 141, 380n22

Rubottom, Roy, 306

Russell, Richard, 304

Russia, xxiv, 51, 56, 128, 370n73, 372n36, 373n55; anti-Semitism in, 57, 62. *See also* Union of Soviet Socialist Republics

Santiago, 16, 86, 227, 252, 292–93, 325–26, 327, 332

Santo Domingo, 317, 332. *See also* Ciudad Trujillo

Schnitzer, Kurt, 352

Schreiner, Ernie, 155

Schreiner, Ruth, 155

Schwartz, Joseph, xvii–xviii

Schweitzer, David, 174, 215, 233

Scientific racism. *See* eugenics

Scotten, Robert, 96

Second World War, 74, 108–9, 110, 112, 232, 267. *See also* Fifth Column threat

Segal, Lore, 160

Serbia. *See* Yugoslavia

Servicio de Emigración para los Refugiados Españoles (SERE), 16–17. *See also* Spanish Republican exiles

Settlers' Council. *See* Rat, The

Settlers (Sosúa), 115, 329–30; adaptation of, 161–65; citizenship of, 296–97, 298, 316; criticisms of, 174–75, 176, 178, 187–92, 194–96; cultural values of, 166–67, 225–28, 232, 331–32; debts of, 248–50, 254, 294, 317–18; diet of, 162, 164, 227, 331–32; entrepreneurialism of, 218–19, 222–25, 232, 248–49, 287–90; gendered concerns of, 109, 137, 170, 172–73, 181, 184–87, 327–28; intermarriage of,

United States Congress, xxvii, 8, 98, 102, 107, 113, 119

Universidad Autonoma de Santo Domingo, 85, 326

Universidad Católica Madre y Maestra, 326

Uruguay, 94

Váldez, Reynaldo, 15

Vanderbilt, Cornelius, Jr., 107, 119

Van Zeeland, Paul, 40, 75, 83, 138

Vázquez, Horacio, 16, 19

Vega, Bernardo, 11, 17, 380–81n37, 402n16

Venezuela, 34, 35, 271, 272, 301–4, 309

Vienna; xix, 131, 167, 170, 326, 340, 341, 344, 375n97; mistreatment of Jews in, xii, xi–xiii, xiv

Viera, Gloria, 402n17

Visas, xvi, 134; Dominican, 107, 108, 116–17, 120–23, 140, 145, 147, 276, 387n75; postwar relaxation of restrictions on, 244, 256–57, 286; U.S. transit, xviii, 105–6, 111–12, 119, 131, 141, 216, 381n2

Vodou, 12, 13, 211

Voz de Sosúa, La, 163, 228, 229

Wagg, Alfred, 105–6, 138, 140, 141; FDR's refugee policy criticized by, 142–43, 146

Wallenberg, Raoul, xiii

Warburg, Edward, 62, 261, 264, 266, 275, 276

Warburg, Felix, 51, 62, 89, 370n73

Ward, Robert De Courcey, 36, 369n43

War Refugee Board, 267–68

"War Refugee Solution" (newsreel), 100–102, 381n48

Warren, Avra: as chief of Visa Division, 106, 125, 146, 198, 216; as diplomat in Dominican Republic, 198–99, 266–67, 268, 269–70, 272

Warren, George, 35, 74, 78, 106, 120–23, 129, 136, 138, 152. *See also* President's Advisory Committee on Political Refugees; Rosen, Dr. Joseph: selection of refugees for Sosúa and

Washington, D.C., xx, xxv, 69–70, 75, 89, 141

Wasservogel, Albert, xii–xiv, 340, 341; Raoul Wallenberg and, xiii,

Wasservogel, Heinrich. *See* Henry Wells

Wasservogel, Rudolf, xii, xiii, xiv, xvii

Wasservogel, Victoria, xii, xiv, 146, 340

Weinberg, Jakob, 158, 166

Welles, Sumner, 3, 73, 97, 145; animosity of, toward Trujillo, xxvi, 18–19, 23, 41, 69, 76, 96, 280; friendship of, with FDR, 20–21; Hull vs., xxvi, 21, 267, 268; policy prescriptions of, for Latin America, 18–19, 279, 366n91; resettlement initiatives of, 33, 40, 76; response of, to Haitian massacre, xxi; tepid response of, toward Sosúa,, xxvi, 41, 72

Wellisch, Juli, 337

Wells, Henry, xxxi, 146, 152, 186, 247, 345, 375n97; flight of, from Austria, xi–xv; interview with, xviii–xix; Sosúa's impact on, 339–42; in Switzerland, xi, xii, xiv–xviii

White Paper, 29

Wilkie, Wendell, 385n30

Winterton, Lord, 39, 72, 83

Wise, Rabbi Stephen, 6, 33, 34, criticism of Non-Zionists by, 50, 51, 62; Sosúa and, 77

Wishnick, Robert, 237

Wistrich, Robert, 6

Wohlmuth, Otto, 155, 186, 339

Women (at Sosúa), 109, 137, 170–71, 172–73, 181, 184–87, 212, 327–28

World Jewish Congress, 50

World War One, 49

World War Two, 74, 108–9, 110, 112, 232, 267. *See also* Fifth Column threat

Yiddish culture, 49, 226

Yugoslavia, xiii, 278

Zionists, Zionism, xii, 5, 8, 29, 48–49, 50–51, 57, 243, 244, 245, 247, 263, 273; criticism of, toward resettlement schemes, 39, 62; negative response of, to Sosúa, xxviii, 77, 190, 209, 214–15; opposition of, to Non-Zionists, 51

ALLEN WELLS is the Roger Howell Jr. Professor of History in the Department of History at Bowdoin College. He is the author of *Yucatán's Gilded Age: Haciendas, Henequen, and International Harvester, 1860–1915* (1985), the coauthor (with Gilbert M. Joseph) of *Summer of Discontent, Seasons of Upheaval: Elite Politics and Rural Insurgency in Yucatán, 1876–1915* (1996), and the coeditor (with Steven C. Topik) of *The Second Conquest of Latin America: Coffee, Henequen, and Oil during the Export Boom, 1850–1930* (1998).

Library of Congress Cataloging-in-Publication Data
Wells, Allen, 1951–
Tropical Zion : General Trujillo, FDR, and the Jews of Sosúa / Allen Wells.
p. cm. — (American encounters/global interactions)
Includes bibliographical references and index.
ISBN 978-0-8223-4389-9 (cloth : alk. paper)
ISBN 978-0-8223-4407-0 (pbk. : alk. paper)
1. Jews—Dominican Republic—Sosúa—History. 2. Jews—Colonization—Dominican Republic—Sosúa. 3. Refugees, Jewish—Dominican Republic—Sosúa. 4. Sosúa (Dominican Republic)—Ethnic relations. 5. Trujillo Molina, Rafael Leónidas, 1891– 1961. 6. Roosevelt, Franklin D. (Franklin Delano), 1882–1945. 7. United States—Foreign relations—Dominican Republic. 8. Dominican Republic—Foreign relations—United States. 9. Dominican Republic Settlement Association, Inc. I. Title. II. Series.
F1941.J4W45 2009
305.80097293'58—dc22   2008041802